T5-DIE-564

Racial and Ethnic Relations in America

Volume II

Ethnic entrepreneurship - Political correctness

Editorial Board

Carl L. Bankston III
University of Southwestern Louisiana

SALEM PRESS, INC.
PASADENA, CALIFORNIA   HACKENSACK, NEW JERSEY

Managing Editor: Christina J. Moose   Project Editor: Rowena Wildin
Research Supervisor: Jeffry Jensen   Manuscript Editors: Rowena Wildin, Robert McClenaghan
Acquisitions Editor: Mark Rehn   Research Assistant: Jun Ohnuki
Photograph Editor: Karrie Hyatt   Production Editor: Joyce I. Buchea
Editorial Secretary: Andrea E. Miller   Design and Layout: James Hutson

Copyright © 2000, by Salem Press, Inc.

Some of the essays in this work originally appeared in the following Salem Press sets: *American Indians* (1995), *American Justice* (1996), *Ethics* (1994), *Great Events from History: North American Series* (revised edition, 1997), *Identities and Issues in Literature* (1997), *The Sixties in America* (1999), *Survey of Social Science: Psychology Series* (1993), *Survey of Social Science: Sociology Series* (1994), and *Women's Issues* (1997).

∞ The paper used in these volumes conforms to the American National Standard for Permanence of Paper for Printed Library Materials, Z39.48-1992(R1997)

Library of Congress Cataloging-in-Publication Data

Racial and ethnic relations in America / editorial board Carl L. Bankston . . . [et al.].
    p. cm.
  Includes bibliographical references (p.   ) and indexes.
  Contents: v. 1. Ability testing—Ethnic enclaves—v. 2. Ethnic entrepreneurship—Political correctness—v. 3. Politics and racial/ethnic relations in Canada—Zoot-suit riots.
  ISBN 0-89356-629-2 (set : alk. paper). — ISBN 0-89356-630-6 (vol. 1 : alk. paper). — ISBN 0-89356-634-9 (vol. 2 : alk. paper). — ISBN 0-89356-635-7 (vol. 3 : alk. paper)
  1. North America—Ethnic relations Encyclopedias.   2. North America—Race relations Encyclopedias. I. Bankston, Carl L. (Carl Leon), 1952-   .

E49.R33   2000
305.8'00973—dc21   99-29348
                                                                                                          CIP

First Printing

Racial and Ethnic Relations in America

Contents

Photo Credits in Volume II

Ethnic entrepreneurship

Significance: Ethnic entrepreneurship is self-employment by members of groups other than the dominant racial/ethnic group of a society. The attempts of subordinate group members to develop businesses can be hampered by prejudice and discrimination. Successful entrepreneurship affects the societal standing of minority groups and can lead to intergroup conflict.

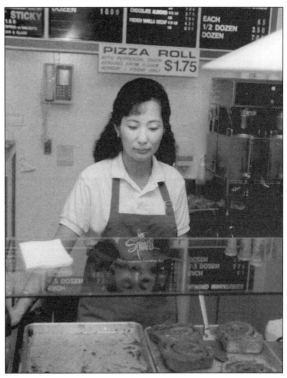

This Cambodian American (ethnic Chinese) woman owns a cinnamon roll shop in California. Many minority members become entrepreneurs rather than seeking financial success through employment with established firms.

Although members of all ethnic and racial groups own businesses, some groups have been unusually successful in creating business ventures in the United States. These groups include Jewish Americans and immigrants from China, Cuba, Greece, India, Jamaica, Japan, Korea, Pakistan, and the Arab countries. Ethnic enterprises, often stereotyped as tiny inner-city shops dealing in specialty products, range from mom-and-pop fruit stands to computer chip factories in the Silicon Valley. A particular group's chances of succeeding in business are related to the degree of hostility and discrimination directed against it. In addition, the group's entrepreneurial success both negatively and positively affects its standing in society.

Factors in Success

The reasons for the business success of certain minority groups can be categorized as assets (elements that the group brings to the situation) and mileau factors (aspects of the particular time and place). A vital asset is investment capital, a large amount of money to start or expand a business. Although some immigrant entrepreneurs bring a great deal of money with them, many begin with no personal wealth and little prospect of receiving conventional bank loans. However, investment capital can still be obtained if the minority member belongs to a cultural group that forms rotating credit associations. They are known by various names (*kye* in Korea, *pandero* in Brazil, *ko* in Japan), but rotating credit associations all consist of a circle of people who contribute at regular intervals to a money pool. The fund rotates through the group over time so that eventually each member receives a sizable sum.

A second asset is human capital, encompassing education and work experience. Education may be formal (such as a college business degree) or informal (the transmittal of trade secrets and specific knowledge about a particular industry). Some immigrants embrace values learned at the knees of merchant grandparents, including a positive view of self-employment in a trade.

Ethnic or racial solidarity is a third business advantage. Tight bonds within an ethnic or racial group mean faithful customers, loyal employees, and dependable suppliers. Ethnic entrepreneurs frequently achieve market power in the particular trade in which the group specializes. These bonds may take the form of vertical integration, close ties with purchasers and suppliers who are members of the same group, or horizontal integration, supportive alliances with members of the same minority who own similar businesses.

Milieu factors influencing success include a national government that encourages and supports minority group enterprise. This can take the form of immigration preferences for wealthy merchants, tax code loopholes, and minority set-aside programs for government contracts. Although North America and Australia have such policies, many European countries have not encouraged minority entrepreneurship, preferring that resident aliens be employees.

A second mileau factor is demand. An entrepreneur must provide goods or services that people want to buy and that are relatively scarce. Demand can come from within the group, in the form of its own consumer preferences (such as speciality ingredients used in the preparation of Asian dishes), from a new consumer

Success Factors and Consequences of Ethnic Entrepreneurship

Success Factors	Consequences
Assets	*For the Individual*
Investment capital Human capital Ethnic/racial solidarity	Income and wealth Employment
	For the Group
Mileau Elements	Employment Solidarity Group pride
National encouragement Demand conditions Reactive entrepreneurship	*For the Society*
	Economic growth Improved attitudes Negative attitudes

preference in the general population (such as the popularity of Mexican food among mainstream Americans), and from a shortage of competing suppliers because of business closures. For example, Asian and Arab American merchants found business opportunities in riot-torn urban neighborhoods from which previous vendors had fled.

A third environmental factor affecting success is reactive entrepreneurship, which refers to a group's response to an abrupt loss of status. Recent immigrants often experience an unpleasant shock when they find themselves at the bottom of their adopted country's social hierarchy. Even immigrants who enjoyed high esteem in their homelands find that in North America, they encounter verbal harassment and widespread discrimination. In reaction, many turn to entrepreneurship as a way to increase feelings of individual and group worth. They are willing to endure unpleasant living conditions and to perform difficult work, inspired by the desire to raise their status quickly.

Consequences of Ethnic Entrepreneurship

Self-employment has consequences for individuals, the ethnic group, and the society as a whole. It gives individuals the opportunity to earn a high income, accumulate wealth, and move into the middle class. Entrepreneurship provides employment opportunities for the individual and the group. Minority members, who often encounter discriminatory job practices such as employers who avoid hiring them, workplace harassment, and limited chances for promotion in the outside business world, find opportunities for job advancement and a comfortable work environment in minority-owned businesses. Self-employment also helps strengthen group solidarity—feelings of warmth, acceptance, and support—through daily contacts with members of the same minority group. In addition, the business successes of the group's members enhance the group's sense of pride and worth.

Ethnic entrepreneurship produces consequences for the host society. First, newly formed firms contribute to the growth of the national economy. The recovery of the U.S. economy in the second half of the 1990's was largely due to the job growth provided by small and middle-sized businesses, some of which were minority-owned. Second, a society's admiration of a group's work ethic and inventiveness can lead to improved attitudes toward the group. However, entrepreneurship can also cause widespread prejudices. News accounts of business successes among immigrants or minority group members can cause pervasive envy and a fear that the minority group is "taking over" the city or nation, beliefs encouraged by demagogic politicians. Business competitors often complain about monopolistic business practices. Angry inner-city customers, often themselves minority members, allege that ethnic merchants overcharge them, treat them disrespectfully, and receive undeserved government financial assistance.

Particular Ethnic Entrepreneurs

One early entrepreneurial group was the Mississippi Chinese. In the 1870's, Chinese immigrants arrived in the cotton-growing northwest corner of Mississippi. Powerful local whites welcomed the Chinese as sharecroppers, but the immigrants soon became owners of small rural general stores serving poor black customers. Certain Chinese cultural traditions, such as strong extended families and honor associated with business ownership, helped them succeed. The immigrants also filled a market niche not already occupied by either whites or blacks. The Chinese American families commonly lived frugally in a tiny room behind the store, with all family members working, and their children attended segregated public schools. By the 1970's, many of the general stores had closed. The descendants of these immigrants typically attended college and moved out of the Delta area. The Mississippi Chinese had gained social acceptance, as evidenced by their high rates of intermarriage with local whites. The Delta Chinese American population reached a peak of approximately twelve hundred in the 1960's.

Korean Americans also have a very high level of entrepreneurship. A 1990 study of foreign-born Koreans in Los Angeles estimated self-employment at 75 percent, and many of the remainder worked for Korean-owned firms. Korean Americans illustrate reactive entrepreneurship in that many immigrants have come from a high position in Korean society, and the loss in status they experience upon arrival in the United States has spurred them to better themselves. The group's business success is also attributed to high education levels, relatively high labor force participation by women, and heavy usage of rotating credit associations. Korean Americans also exemplify the way friction develops between minority groups in a vendor-customer relationship. Two thousand Korean American businesses were destroyed in the 1992 Los Angeles riots, the result of pent-up hostility on the part of Latino and African American customers. Part of the hostility was caused by cultural misunderstandings: For example, Latino and African American customers interpreted the Korean merchants' stiffness—their formal body language—as an expression of disrespect.

African American entrepreneurship presents a mixed picture. In the 1990's, African Americans owned only about 4 percent of U.S. businesses although they constituted 12 percent of the population. Black-owned businesses such as beauty shops and funeral parlors first developed to meet demand in the segregated community. Because of societal prejudice and discrimination, black entrepreneurs had difficulty luring white customers and obtaining bank financing and property insurance. Nevertheless, in areas like Chicago's South Side, African Americans owned a wide range of lucrative commercial establishments by the 1930's. As some blacks entered the middle class, they moved out of the inner-city neighborhoods and shopped elsewhere, leading to business decline in areas such as the South Side. As discrimination diminished in the 1960's and 1970's, some members of the burgeoning African American middle class became successful entrepreneurs. In the 1990's, the number of African American businesses increased because of the continued activity of the middle class and of Jamaicans and other immigrants from the West Indies.   *Nancy Conn Terjesen*

Core Resources

Sociologist Ivan Light's *Ethnic Enterprises in America* (Berkeley: University of California Press, 1972) com-

pares business development by African Americans and two Asian American groups. Light's *Immigrant Entrepreneurs: Koreans in Los Angeles* (Berkeley: University of California Press, 1988) examines resources leading to high rates of entrepreneurship and looks at relations between Korean American business owners and African American customers. Sociologist Min Zhou in *Chinatown: The Socio-Economic Potential of an Urban Enclave* (Philadelphia: Temple University Press, 1992) reports the many benefits of ethnic economies for recent immigrants. James W. Loewen's *The Mississippi Chinese: Between Black and White* (2d ed., Prospect Heights, Ill.: Waveland Press, 1988) is a participant-observer study of self-employment in the rural South, concentrating on cultural assets and mileau factors. Advertising executive Lionel Sosa wrote *The Americano Dream: How Latinos Can Achieve Success in Business and in Life* (New York: Penguin Putnam, 1998), a how-to book based on personal experience.

See also: Chinese Americans; Economics and race; Employment among African Americans; Employment among Asian Americans; Employment among Latinos; Employment in Canada; Enclave economies.

Ethnic heritage revival

Beginning in the 1960's, a resurgence of interest in ethnic identity, ancestry, and cultural heritage occurred among many Americans who were of European descent. Among the manifestations of this revival was a renewed interest in ethnic literature, music, art, folklore, and cuisine. Ethnic festivals, genealogical pursuits, and travel to ancestral homelands all signaled an increased awareness of ethnic identity. Although some people saw this as an indication of the persistence of ethnicity as a powerful element of individual self-identity, others pointed out the limitations to the revival. A minority of ethnics were actually involved in revival activities, and a revitalization of ethnic communities and institutions did not occur. Ancestral language loyalty similarly declined. People picked and chose the cultural values from their heritage to embrace, in general, selecting those that did not conflict with mainstream American values. Finally, intermarriage rates grew dramatically, complicating the ethnic identities of families. Nevertheless, for those involved in the ethnic revival, it marked an important way in which assimilated European Americans could continue to maintain a nostalgic attachment to the folkways and mores of their ancestors.   *Peter Kivisto*

See also: Ethnic studies programs; Ethnicity and ethnic groups; Euro-American; Whites.

Ethnic identities of women

Significance: The issues of ethnic identification have affected the ability of women to advance both their roles as women and their self-interest as members of particular ethnic groups. The confluence of these interests has, in turn, helped to advance interethnic understanding.

Ethnic identity is often omitted from studies of women and women's issues in the United States and Canada. History, however, shows that women have not always identified themselves as members of one particular group. Ethnicity has played a large role in women's social and political activities, in their economic activities, and in their domestic household activities. Ethnic group identification has been found to divide and bring women together depending on the issues and environment. The status of women and their activities on behalf of women can effectively be understood within the context of the general social and political history of which they are a part, especially their cultural and ethnic backgrounds. Ethnic identity for women is their individual identity; the part that is female cannot be separated from women's ethnicity.

Resurgence of Ethnicity

Ethnicity is a complex concept based roughly on common or shared cultural properties, such as language,

descent, and religion. Ethnic identity requires defining oneself according to notions of shared culture and focusing on the cultural uniqueness of a particular group. Various interpretations exist of why ethnicity persists and why it slowly diminishes. Until the ethnic violence shook Eastern Europe and Africa in the late 1980's and early 1990's, ethnicity was held by many theorists to be slowly disappearing with modernization and technological advancement. This view was held especially in modern countries such as the United States and Canada. Thus arose the problem of whether to place one's loyalty with one's ethnic group or with one's nation-state. Women faced the additional option of placing their sense of womanhood over loyalty to the ethnic group or nation-state. Since ethnicity became recognized as a factor in U.S. and Canadian societies, theorists found that it develops for self-interested reasons, such as gaining some type of economically based rewards from the political system. The basis for this position is that in competitive societies, one of the best ways to compete successfully is to organize. Organizing around ethnic groups can be effective. The tremendous increase in immigrants to the United States and Canada, many of whom were more resistant to change and assimilation than were earlier immigrants, also led to a renewed focus on ethnicity.

Ethnic vs. Gender Identity

When women organize along gender lines, it is often within the context of the cultural and political conditions in which they live. Gender, social class membership, age, and other criteria can vary from ethnic group to ethnic group. One group may fit well into modern Western society, whereas another ethnic group living in the same society will experience adjustment problems. Some ethnic groups may refuse attempts at adjustment to modernism and hold to traditionalism. This variance means that ethnicity can be a problem for women because, often, traditional cultural values of an ethnic group that define roles for women can conflict with overall societal values. In other situations, traditional values of an ethnic group can be advantageous to women dealing with real and perceived threats and roadblocks in contemporary U.S. or Canadian society. An increase in women's awareness of their ethnicity occurred alongside increased attention to women's issues. The result has been renewed recognition of an inter-

These lavishly dressed Filipino women enjoy riding on a float in a parade. Festivals give minority women a chance to celebrate their ethnicity.

woven relationship, with both positive and negative characteristics between ethnic identity and women's issues.

To place a priority on women's issues as one form of identity while minimizing another form of identity, such as ethnicity, results in incomplete analysis. Prior to the post-World War II period, ethnicity was largely associated with immigrants and any group unidentifiable as Northern European or British. The dawning of the twentieth century, for example, found women and African Americans without the right to vote, but the status of African American women was misinterpreted by white women in several of the political organizations to which they belonged. African American women were not regarded as true woman suffragists by white-dominated organizations because they practiced political action on the basis of race and gender rather than gender alone. Separation in American society of women's issues and ethnicity created gender divisions of labor and assigned particular significance regarding race and ethnicity to occupational and socioeconomic standing that was typically less favorable. For example, ethnic groups were among the lower working class, whereas members of the dominant nonethnic society occupied the upper and more desirable classes. Hence, studies of race and ethnicity often leave out issues specific to women, and studies of women deemphasize race and ethnicity. It is apparent that ethnicity and women's issues coalesce at some points. For example, it can be claimed that women and racial minorities occupy subordinate places in society; both are underrepresented in high-level occupations, and both earn lower average incomes than white men.

Inserting women's issues into the rubric of ethnic group membership is difficult in nationalistic societies such as the United States and Canada, where being American or Canadian involves a mix of several ethnic groups. There is also a tendency in these societies to be secular, while a large percentage of ethnic groups have strong religious bases. For example, an Italian American woman may encounter a conflict between Catholicism and her position on abortion. Ethnicity often infers linkages to a homeland far from U.S. and Canadian societies. In this instance, native cultural practices may persist within Western modernization through the maintenance of cultural enclaves such as Chinatown, Little Italy, and Germantown. Women who maintain close links to their respective ethnic groups often live in two different worlds. The preservation of access to membership in the group, such as knowledge of rituals and traditions, is an important function of any ethnic group, and anyone involved in these groups must know them.

Women as Culture Carriers

One of the key means of controlling ethnic group membership is through socialization of the young. One significant role for women is guiding the young into adulthood. This is especially the case in groups in which religion is a major factor in the community. As carriers of culture, women are crucial to communities. In the course of her work on the life histories of Italian American families in Northern California, Micaela di Leonardo introduced the idea of the "work of kinship," defined as the conception, maintenance, and ritual celebration of cross household kin ties, including visits, letters, telephone calls, presents, and cards to kin; the organization of holiday gatherings; the creation and maintenance of quasi-kin relations; the decision to neglect or to intensify particular ties; the mental work of reflection about all these activities; and the creation and communication of altering images of family and kin in relation to the images of others, both folk and mass media. She found that over time, women developed greater knowledge of their husbands' kin than their husbands had.

On the basis of Leonardo's review of other research, kin-work is not nearly as much an ethnic, racial, or class phenomenon as it is a gender phenomenon. She found gender-based division of labor across ethnic, racial, and class groups. To the degree that the daily behavioral expression of community membership is embedded in how one eats, dresses, and uses household space and is woven through activities that span a lifetime (for example, family-based celebrations such as family reunions), women's kin-work translates also as culture work. This critical women's role partly explains why women take on such importance in defining the ethnic community and what it stands for. Women are valuable community possessions as the principal vehicle for transmitting values from one generation to another. Many ethnic communities regard women as particularly vulnerable to defilement and exploitation by negative outside forces, and many see women as being especially susceptible to assimilation and influence by outsiders. This is one cause of the oppression ethnic women often feel. For example, an ethnic family may feel particularly threatened when a female relative leaves the house in nontraditional clothing.

Additionally, the historically symbolic role of women in the politics of cultural relations has shaped cultural expressions. As women have played important roles in the family and ethnic community through their activities as wives, mothers, and homemakers, they have also played important roles in intercultural relations through other women-based roles as teachers, missionaries, and social workers. For example, women in the Northeast region of the United States went to the Southern and Western United States to teach, civilize, Americanize, and ultimately culturally transform ethnic-based Latino, African American, American Indian, and European set-

An Asian American woman and a Muslim woman study together. Ethnic women sometimes have difficulty reconciling their ethnicity's ideal image of a woman with that found in American culture.

tler communities of the nineteenth century into culturally assimilated members of the nation.

Interpreters of women's relationships within ethnic groups have a difficult task because men tend to construct ethnic identity. Women and men come together in the family structure when competing identities, such as between male and female, could lead to disagreements. In such situations, preference usually goes to the ethnic affiliations of the male partner. Because ethnic groups often identify with physical markers, such as clothing, hairstyles, or body alterations, individuals can be identified with regard to both gender and ethnicity in the way they dress. In the area of dress and style, women and men are treated differently. For example, women are encouraged to wear traditional types of dress, whereas men can easily move from one type of dress (Western) to another (traditional).

Gender and Race

Gender and ethnic terms can influence the construction of each other. "Ethnic" does not have to mean race, and race is only a partial basis for determining ethnic identity. Race is one way in which gender and ethnicity merge when women use racial metaphors to illustrate real and perceived discrimination against women. For women, especially feminists, the gendered construction of racism serves as an excellent vehicle for faulting a male system in which women are oppressed. The experiences of European immigrant women, especially Italians and Jews, illustrate that numerous examples of discrimination can be drawn from other ethnic groups. Despite

this, race is usually treated as a secondary factor in social organization, and ethnicity is a distant third factor. Much of the feminists' perspective and activity has focused on the sexist behavior of men rather than on the positives and negatives of ethnic identification.

Part of the answer to the construction of whiteness can be traced to the cultural symbolism of European women that is rooted in a system based on good and bad, or Madonna and Magdalena symbolism. Interpretations that began to appear at the end of the eighteenth century identified particular personality traits with particular classes or races of women. Leonore Davidoff argued that the material division of household tasks in the nineteenth century caused good and bad aspects of women to be linked to socially distinct groups of women. The mistress no longer did heavy labor; all dirty, arduous physical labor was now performed by the domestic, whose stigmatizing labor accorded with her inferior character and her working-class status. Good women were wives, mothers, and spinsters, and bad women were prostitutes, laborers, and single mothers. The dual symbolism of good/bad was usually connected with race and class, but it could be used to chastise any woman moving out of her assigned place.

Women active in women's issues who are members of ethnic minorities experience conditions that are distinct from those of white feminists. The development of ethnic minority feminism and the relationships among minority feminists, white feminists, and feminists of other racial and ethnic groups are shaped by experiences in their respective communities. Unlike their white counterparts, minority women (or ethnic groups in general) face a different type of division in their construction of identity. Because of the emphasis on traditions in many ethnic groups in America, they are usually divided along lines of obedience versus independence, collective (or familial) versus individual interest, and self-control versus self-expression or spontaneity. These divisions are more complex and difficult to deal with than the good versus bad division.

African American, Asian American, and Latina female activists are aware that social inequality for women of color is two-sided. On one side, the struggle is to gain equality in male-dominated ethnic enclaves or communities; on the other side, the struggle is for equality for women in society as a whole. Among minority women, women's issues involve more than gender because, as minority women, they are affected by both ethnic identification and nationalist ideology in their everyday lives. Minority women's emphasis on ethnic pride and difficulties within a white-dominated society has provided significant political direction to the movement in addressing women's issues within ethnic communities.

Women's Movement and Ethnicity
Ethnicity creates important economic, ideological, and experiential divisions among women. These lead to differences in perception of identity and its place in society for women while at the same time, the communality of womanhood may cut across ethnic lines and provide the conditions for shared understanding. Women developed concepts around women's issues that fostered unity. One example of this is the concept of sisterhood; it has been an important unifying force in the contemporary women's movement and one with the ability to overcome ethnic differences. By stressing the similarities of women's secondary social and economic positions in all societies and in the family, the sisterhood concept is useful in the movement against sexism. Yet, sisterhood has engaged only a small segment of the female population in the United States. African American, American Indian, and Latina women are seldom involved in feminist activities. In Canada, various feminist and other women's organizations have cooperated on specific projects even though they have had different ideological perspectives. For example, an active feminist group may have interest in a child care and education project, which puts them in working contact with more moderate women's groups advancing the same issues. On the intellectual level, socialist feminist theory finds the concept of sisterhood to be apolitical and lacking in class analysis. The problem has to do with perceptions that the women's movement is an upper- and middle-class movement. Supporters of sisterhood stress the sense of being part of a collective movement toward a fairer and more equal society. Regardless of these varying positions, sisterhood has shown an ability to unify women beyond ethnic identifications.

The women's movements in the United States and Canada arose within nationalist and cultural movements. In the United States, for example, the experience white women gained from participating in the Civil Rights movement gave them the opportunity to become involved with civil rights groups in which the decision making was shared by men and women alike. During the later part of the movement (after 1965), African American men began to exercise more control in organizations, such as the Student Nonviolent Coordinating Committee (SNCC) and the Southern Christian Leadership Conferences (SCLC); they effectively isolated the women, especially the white women. Many of the original organizers of women's groups were women who gained their experience in the civil rights struggle in the South. A similar situation occurred with respect to the woman suffrage movement and other political activities for women's rights in pre-1919 United States, in which many of the politically active white women evolved out of antislavery groups. In the United States, the ethnic division appeared along racial lines.

In Canada, some ethnic tensions were clearly present in the woman suffrage movement. For example, in 1906, non-British suffragists rejected the tactics of the British suffragists as being "unwomanly." The year 1902 witnessed a conflict over ideological differences in New Brunswick between the Women's Enfranchisement Association and the Saint John Local Council of Women. Ethnic differences created a threat to cooperation among women. After 1896, substantial numbers of immigrants who were not Anglo-Saxon pushed antiethnic feelings to higher levels. The Anglo-Saxon membership of the majority of Canadian women's reform organizations did not include women of other ethnic groups. The women in these organizations identified, and consequently organized, with their own cultural or ethnic groups. For example, African Canadian women in Montreal began to meet in 1900, which constituted the first organized black women's group in that city. Canadian women's labor groups organized along Finnish, Jewish, and Ukrainian lines.

The U.S. and Canadian examples of cooperation, conflict, and exclusion illustrate the greater degree of ethnic divisions within the Canadian women's movement as compared with that in the United States. They also illustrate how women's individual identity *as* women—subjected to societal elements that affect them both as women and as members of particular religious, ethnic, or other cultural groups—can create a dilemma. It appears that when women organized from the nineteenth century to the present, they did so within the context of their contemporary cultural and political conditions.

Language is another factor affecting the acculturation and political participation of women on a nonethnic basis. Language barriers limit the extent to which women from some ethnic groups can express themselves. These barriers in turn limit their accessibility to different types of information and to women's groups that may be working on issues that positively affect them. An example of this problem can be drawn from the situation in the United States in which Chicanas often organized in isolation from mainstream feminist groups because of language differences. Language is a major problem, but cultural interpretations of womanhood also play a role in the cooperative political participation among these groups. For Europeans, the ethnic factors that brought a particular group together actually eased the task of and facilitated the process of assimilation.

Ethnicity in Canada

Because of significant differences between U.S. and Canadian experiences with women and ethnic identity, the Canadian situation merits particular attention. One of the major turning points for women in Canada occurred during World War I, with the achievement of woman suffrage. Another turning point occurred during World War II, when large numbers of married women entered the labor force. For Canadian women, ethnicity created numerous inequities. Industrial development in the late 1800's was predicated on cheap labor; thousands of immigrants, especially those from non-English-speaking countries, paid a high price for their entry into Canada by being channeled into low-paying and unsafe working conditions.

Early demographics found that Canadians of British origin decreased from 60 percent of the population in 1871 to 55 percent in 1921, and those of French origin from 31 percent to 28 percent. In terms of gender, when men began heading to the prairies and the Northwest Territories seeking economic opportunities between 1851 and 1891, women of marriageable age outnumbered men in the same age range in the original British North American provinces. Conversely, the 1881 and 1891 censuses revealed that men significantly outnumbered women in Manitoba and British Columbia. In either case, women faced a certain amount of isolation, but more so in the new settlements. Many women dealt with their isolation through maintaining links with friends and family left behind and by creating new links with women in their new communities. This proved to be much easier with those of the same ethnic origin.

In the early years of Canadian development, women supported the preservation of ethnic cultures. A negative aspect of these women's work involved certain re-

strictions they erected to prevent those who did not conform or belong to their ethnic group. Similar to particular circumstances in the United States, these women touted the superiority of their culture over other cultures. Mixed-blood women were also subjected to discrimination from English-speaking settlers in the West.

Ethnic organizing in Canada continued through the 1920's and 1930's. The organizational strategy of Jewish women, mainly of Western European origins, who worked together to form the National Council of Jewish Women, is illustrative of ethnic activity among women. Through vehicles such as fundraising and volunteer work, this council supported schools, orphanages, and summer camps and cared for senior citizens. This also illustrates that, like women in the United States, they were responsible for ethnic culture well into the future. By the 1970's, some feminists, including Jewish feminists, fought to remain within the religious community while working for change from within. Work remains for Canadian women in dealing with ethnic, cultural, and gender biases.

Organizing around ethnic identity, aboriginal women initiated social and political activities. These women redefined themselves in a way that incorporated their traditions. Iroquois women accepted that Indian women were originally active participants in policymaking decisions and should therefore assume that role in contemporary Canada. The main conflict has been between traditional means of policymaking and modern/Western methods. To take the Western route is to deny the cultural roots of the group in favor of what appears to be acceptance of white government. Without giving up their ethnic identification, Indian women formed socially and politically active groups that existed in many instances outside the cultural confines of their ethnic group and inside the Western political arena. Multiethnic cooperation also existed, as exemplified by the Ontario Native Women's Association, founded in 1972, which includes mixed-blood Indian women. Indian women also organized to deal with serious social problems, such as alcoholism and an educational system that does not include Indian traditions in its curriculum.

Ethnic Boundaries and Ethnic Identity

This discussion has illustrated both the loose and tight boundaries of ethnicity and how these boundaries can be manipulated for political purposes. Ethnic boundaries can also be manipulated for personal purposes because, unlike territorial boundaries, they are social. They do not isolate groups entirely from one another; rather, there is a continuous flow of interaction and sometimes people across them. For example, Shirlee Taylor Haizlip told how, prior to the Civil Rights movement of the

1960's, her mother, one of several children of mixed racial descent, was the only one to retain her African American identity. Since the movement, more individuals have accepted their ethnic heritage. It appears that maintaining an ethnic identity is not incompatible with simultaneous identification with a nationalist group, such as Canada and the United States.

Ethnic identity has been identified as an important part of women and women's issues. Women are found to transcend their ethnicity at critical junctures and to organize into collectives. Although some problems exist between women of different ethnic groups, there are also instances in which women cooperate strictly along gender lines. One highly visible problem is the persistence of tradition among some ethnic groups. Tradition may dictate that women are forbidden to organize or devote much time to anything other than advancing the culture by nurturing and socializing the children. It is becoming difficult, however, to remain rooted in any ethnic tradition in the United States and Canada, primarily because of communication technologies and frequent encounters among group members in the marketplace. In addition, women in these countries have historically shown that they are more likely than their male counterparts to bridge the ethnic gap and work together. This is one indication that ethnicity and women's issues are not incompatible.   *Gregory Freeland*

Core Resources

Ethnic Canada: Identities and Inequalities (Toronto: Copp, Clark and Pittman, 1987), edited by Leo Driedger, distinguishes three views of the interrelationships of class and ethnicity with a good discussion of women. *Feminism and the Politics of Difference* (Boulder, Colo.: Westview Press, 1993), edited by Sneja Gunew and Anna Yeatman, addresses ways in which women can move beyond the politics of identity. Shirlee Taylor Haizlip's *The Sweeter the Juice* (New York: Simon & Schuster, 1994) describes the choice one family made to join either white or African American culture. L. DeAne Lagerquist's *In America the Men Milk the Cows: Factors of Gender, Ethnicity, and Religion in the Americanization of Norwegian American Women* (Brooklyn, N.Y.: Carlson, 1991) is an excellent example of the problems of adjustment and development of ethnic women in the United States. Mary Waters' *Ethnic Options: Choosing Identities in America* (Berkeley: University of California Press, 1990) shows how identity definition issues are important to the transmission of ethnic culture—especially in the religious realm—from one generation to the next.

See also: African American women; American Indian women; Asian American women; Immigrant women; Latinas; Multiculturalism; Women of color.

Ethnic studies programs

> **Significance:** By exposing members of all racial and ethnic groups to the cultures of minority groups and by helping everyone understand that members of all ethnic groups have made a contribution to the history of North America, ethnic studies programs can help eliminate prejudices and racial divisions.

Ethnic studies programs are courses of study devoted to the history and culture of various ethnic groups. They are valuable for members of the ethnic group that is being studied and also for members of other ethnic or racial groups. Members of groups that are the focus of ethnic studies programs develop a sense of belonging from learning about their group's cultural history. They also develop a sense of pride and self-esteem from learning about the contributions that members of their group have made to society. When people study the achievements and histories of groups other than their own, they develop an appreciation of the contributions that all groups have made to the development of the United States and Canada. By helping students understand that every group has made its contribution to American history, ethnic studies programs can help eliminate prejudices and racial conflicts.

History

The first fully developed ethnic studies programs were black studies programs that American colleges and universities began to offer in the late 1960's and early 1970's. The first college to offer black studies courses was Merritt Junior College in Oakland, California. Courses were set up after Huey P. Newton and other members of the Black Panther Party, who were students at the college, agitated for their establishment. The first fully developed program in black studies was offered by San Francisco State University very soon after a coalition of African American students took over campus buildings in 1967 and demanded, among other things, a black studies program, dormitories for black students, and admission policies that included an affirmative action philosophy.

After the takeover of San Francisco State University, black student groups all across the United States staged demonstrations and takeovers, including a particularly hostile one at Columbia University, demanding black studies programs and other concessions that would recognize the special culture of African Americans. Larger universities such as Harvard developed black studies majors that generally included courses dealing with the history and cultures of Africa and the African American experience, including African American history, African

American literature, and sociological, psychological, and economic issues related to African Americans. Even colleges and universities that could not offer fully developed black studies programs attempted to accommodate African American students by offering courses in African American history and African American literature. Enrollment in these courses was not confined to African American students. Students of other races were very interested in finding out about the African American experience.

In the early 1970's, other ethnic groups, influenced generally by certain social trends of the 1960's, the Civil Rights movement, the women's movement, and various student uprisings, began to demand recognition of their cultural values and of their members' contributions to the American experience. Such organizations as the American Indian Movement agitated for Native American control of their children's education and for an opportunity for young Native Americans to study their culture. When federal legislation established tribal colleges on many Indian reservations in the 1970's and early 1980's, Native American studies became the topic of some of the courses taught at these colleges. All aspects of Native American culture, including history, literature, art, music, and spiritual beliefs, were part of the curriculum. In addition to the tribal colleges, other colleges and universities, particularly those situated in states with large numbers of Native Americans, began to offer courses that explored Native American history and culture.

In the 1970's, universities, particularly in California and Texas, where there are large numbers of Mexican immigrants and Mexican Americans, began to offer courses in Chicano (Mexican American) studies, usually concentrating on Mexican American history and literature. Many universities also began offering courses in Asian American history and literature.

Women's studies programs center around the issue of gender rather than ethnicity, so they cannot be truly classified as ethnic studies programs. However, some researchers have suggested that women constitute a special cultural group. Many of the women's studies programs in the 1970's were modeled on ethnic studies programs and shared similar goals of promoting understanding and increasing self-respect. Feminists believed that such programs would enhance young women's self-esteem and feelings of self-worth and that women would derive more respect from society if their contributions became well known. Women's studies programs had curriculum elements similar to those found in ethnic studies programs—history, literature, psychology, sociology, and economic issues related to women.

By the late 1980's, the number of ethnic studies courses offered by American colleges and universities had dropped since their peak in the late 1970's. Most major colleges and universities still offered many courses that related to the experiences of most major ethnic groups, particularly history and literature courses; however, these courses no longer were designed to teach members of ethnic groups about their own culture and history (the original reason given for black studies courses) but rather to acquaint the general student body with the history and culture of the ethnic group under study.

Impact on American Culture

By the early 1980's, the United States was no longer regarded as a "melting pot" in which members of various cultural groups would assimilate and adopt the values and customs of the Euro-American majority. Instead, the nation was viewed as a culture more appropriately described by terms such as "salad bowl" or "stew pot" in that members of diverse cultural groups maintained many aspects of their culture and lived for the most part in harmony with members of the majority culture. All Americans were expected to attempt to understand and respect the contributions that members of other ethnic and racial groups had made to develop, support, and sustain the nation. Ethnic studies courses contributed to these changes in the philosophical basis of American society.

Ethnic studies programs not only affected those who took these courses in colleges and universities but also changed the curriculum offered to public school students. Public schools, in the late 1970's and 1980's, began to accept the philosophical tenets of ethnic studies programs: that members of all ethnic groups should be exposed to their own history and heritage and that the history and heritage of all ethnic groups is that of the United States. Additionally, these beliefs suggested that every American needs to know and understand the history and heritage of all groups so that all citizens will have a complete understanding of the nation's culture and history.

Multiculturalism became an essential part of the curricula of public schools. By the end of the twentieth century, public school curricula all across the United States had incorporated multicultural elements. For example, literature courses used anthologies that contained writers who spoke in many different voices, not just Euro-American male writers. History courses attempted to chronicle the contributions of all of the nation's people, not just its white majority.

Advantages and Concerns

In addition to teaching ethnic and racial minorities about their cultural heritage, these programs often make minority students feel more comfortable on college and university campuses because they increase the likelihood that administrators, professors, and other students will respect their ethnic roots. The programs can serve to ease tensions on campuses as they contribute to overall understandings of various groups' contributions to society.

Some scholars express concern about ethnic studies programs because they believe these programs contribute to a fragmentation of certain disciplines. For example, some feel that the study of U.S. history is too fragmented when divided into African American, Asian American, Native American, and Chicano history. Other scholars have expressed concern that ethnic studies textbooks attempt to rewrite history, giving certain ethnic groups a predominant role in particular historical or cultural events, when, in fact, the group played only a minor role. In highlighting the contributions of all ethnic groups, these scholars argue, historical facts should not be negated or distorted.   *Annita Marie Ward*

Core Resources
Winnie Bengelsdorf took an early look at ethnic studies programs in *Ethnic Studies in Higher Education: State of the Art and Bibliography* (Washington, D.C.: American Association of State Colleges and Universities, 1972). Robert J. Cottrol discusses the value of ethnic studies and multicultural curricula in "America the Multicultural," in *American Educator* (winter, 1990). Other books on ethnic studies programs include James A. Banks's *Teaching Strategies for Ethnic Studies* (Boston: Allyn & Bacon, 1979), Johnnela E. Butler and John C. Walter's *Transforming the Curriculum: Ethnic Studies and Women's Studies* (Albany, N.Y.: State University of New York Press, 1991), and Frances Ann Day's *Multicultural Voices in Contemporary Literature* (Portsmouth, N.H.: Heinemann, 1994).

See also: Black Panther Party; Chicano movement; Multiculturalism; Prejudice: reduction; Third World strike.

Ethnicity and ethnic groups

Significance: "Ethnicity" refers to a sense of belonging and identification with a particular cultural heritage. Ethnic groups are socially defined on the basis of their cultural characteristics. Members of ethnic groups consider themselves, and are considered by others to be, part of a distinct culture or subculture. These concepts help explain the cultural diversity which can occur in a given society.

Despite the considerable amount of attention devoted to the subject, scholars have not reached a consensus on the precise meaning of ethnicity. Since ethnicity is such a complex concept, many scholars have chosen to identify ethnic groups as those groups characterized by some of the following fourteen features: common geographic origins; migratory status; race; language or dialect; religious faith or faiths; ties that transcend kinship, neighborhood, and community boundaries; shared traditions, values, and symbols; literature, folklore, and music; food preferences; settlement and employment patterns; special interests in regard to politics; institutions that specifically serve and maintain the group; an internal sense of distinctiveness; and an external perception of distinctiveness.

Sociologist Milton Yinger defines an ethnic group as one whose members are thought by themselves and others to have a common origin and who share a common culture that is transmitted through shared activities that reinforce the group's distinctiveness. The term "ethnic group" has been used by social scientists in two different ways. Some definitions of ethnic groups are broad and include both physical (racial) and cultural characteristics. Others are narrower and rely solely on cultural or nationality characteristics. Sociologist Joe R. Feagin emphasizes that ancestry, whether real or mythical, is a very important dimension of ethnic group identity.

Sociologist William Yancey and his associates argue that ethnic groups have been produced by structural conditions which are linked to the changing technology of production and transportation. Structural conditions including common occupational patterns, residential stability, concentration, and dependence on common institutions and services reinforce kinship and friendship networks. According to Yancey, common cultural heritage is not a prerequisite dimension of ethnicity. Ethnicity is a manifestation of the way populations are organized in terms of interaction patterns, institutions, values, attitudes, lifestyle, and consciousness of kind.

New Definitions
A new consciousness is emerging concerning the meaning of ethnicity. Ethnic groups are joining together into larger ethnic groupings. The adoption of a panethnic identity is common among Asian Americans, American Indians, and Hispanics. Sociologist Felix Padilla writes about the development of a Latino collective identity among Mexican Americans and Puerto Ricans. Ethnicity and one's ethnic identity are becoming matters of choice, especially for white Americans of European descent. Most people have multiple layers of ethnic identity because of generations of interethnic marriages; these layers can be added to or subtracted from one's current identity. Sociologists Richard Alba and Mary Waters acknowledge that people often know their ancestors are from a variety of ethnic groups but for one reason or

another identify with only some of them (or none of them). Often people identify with those with whom they have the least connection.

Sociologist Robert Blauner, in his influential book *Black Lives, White Lives* (1989), addresses the confusion that is often produced in the American consciousness by the concepts of race and ethnicity. Blauner argues that the imagery of race tends to be more powerful than the imagery of ethnicity and therefore often overshadows it. The reason for this is that race—although generally viewed by scientists and social scientists as a social construct rather than a scientific reality—is associated with biological and scientific imagery, whereas ethnicity is associated with cultural imagery. Other important concepts, such as class and religion, are also overwhelmed by the powerful social meanings of race. The confounding of race and ethnicity is a daily occurrence in American society. Blauner holds that African Americans represent both a racial and an ethnic group and argues that when blacks assert their ethnicity, whites perceive it instead as an assertion of racial identity. He postulates that part of the American heritage of racism has been to deny the ethnicity or cultural heritage of African Americans.

History and Interrelations of Ethnic Groups
In his book *Ethnic America* (1981), economist Thomas Sowell argues that the experiences of white ethnic groups and racial minorities have been different in degree rather than in kind. Historian Ronald Takaki, however, in his book *From Different Shores* (1987), challenges Sowell's assumption. Takaki emphasizes the facts that only blacks were enslaved, only American Indians were placed on reservations, only Japanese Americans were placed in concentration camps, and only the Chinese were excluded from naturalized citizenship. To understand fully the experiences and histories of ethnic groups one must acknowledge the role of economic and governmental contexts within which particular ethnic groups have immigrated and adjusted. The time of immigration and the resources brought by the immigrants have affected not only their economic and political success but also their social class position in the United States.

In his book *Race and Ethnic Relations* (1994), sociologist Martin N. Marger describes the American ethnic hierarchy as consisting of three parts. The top third consists primarily of white Protestants from various ethnic backgrounds. The middle third consists of Catholics from various ethnic backgrounds, Jews, and many Asians. The bottom third consists of blacks, Hispanics, American Indians, and some Asians. The most important aspect of this ethnic hierarchy is the gap between those groups in the bottom third of the hierarchy and the other two segments.

Directions
Around the time of World War II and soon thereafter, the expectation was that ethnic Americans would assimilate and their sense of ethnicity would gradually disappear. This assumption was known as the melting pot theory. During the 1950's, 1960's, and 1970's, however, sociologist Nathan Glazer and political scientist Daniel Patrick Moynihan (among others) questioned the viability of the melting pot theory. Glazer, Moynihan, and others suggested that the United States was leaning more in the direction of cultural pluralism.

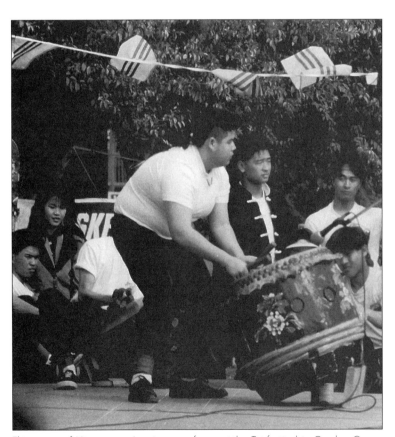

This group of Vietnamese Americans performs at the Tet festival in Garden Grove, California. Participation in groups such as this promote a sense of ethnic identity among young people.

In the 1980's and early 1990's, the debate about the melting pot versus cultural pluralism, according to Alba, no longer dominated discussions of ethnicity, especially concerning white European ethnic groups. Alba argues that ethnicity is not less embedded in the structure of American society but rather that ethnic distinctions are undergoing change. He believes that ethnic distinctions based on European ancestry are dissolving, while a new ethnic group is forming based on ancestry from anywhere on the European continent.   *William L. Smith*

Core Resources
Richard D. Alba's *Ethnic Identity* (New Haven, Conn.: Yale University Press, 1990) argues that ethnicity among non-Hispanic whites is in the midst of a fundamental transformation. Alba has also edited *Ethnicity and Race in the U.S.A.* (Boston: Routledge & Kegan Paul, 1985), a collection of studies by leading scholars of ethnicity and race. Joe R. Feagin and Clairece Booher Feagin's *Racial and Ethnic Relations* (5th ed., Englewood Cliffs, N.J.: Prentice-Hall, 1996) contains everal introductory chapters discussing key racial concepts and theoretical models relating to ethnic relations. Nathan Glazer's *Ethnic Dilemmas 1964-1982* (Cambridge, Mass.: Harvard University Press, 1983) analyzes issues of racial and ethnic conflict such as cultural pluralism, bilingualism, and the affirmative action debate. Glazer and Daniel P. Moynihan's *Beyond the Melting Pot* (2d ed., Cambridge, Mass.: MIT Press, 1970) is a classic, controversial, and often-cited book that focuses on five ethnic groups in New York City during the early 1960's, with an update for the 1970's. *From Different Shores* (New York: Oxford University Press, 1987), edited by Ronald Takaki, is a collection of essays on race and ethnicity by well-known neoconservative, liberal, and leftist scholars. *The Harvard Encyclopedia of American Ethnic Groups* (Cambridge, Mass.: The Belknap Press of Harvard University Press, 1980), edited by Stephan Thernstrom, is arguably the most important single source in print concerning ethnicity and ethnic groups.

See also: Anglo-conformity; Assimilation theories; Chinese Americans; Cultural pluralism; Ethnic identities of women; Japanese Americans; Jewish Americans; Latinos in the United States; Melting pot theory; Moynihan Report; Multiracial identity; Race as a concept; White ethnics.

Ethnocentrism

Ethnocentrism involves judging the worth of the attributes, beliefs, or customs of another people or culture by the standards of one's own culture. William G. Sumner, in his 1960 book *Folkways*, described ethnocentrism as the attitude that "one's own group is the center of everything, and all others are scaled and rated with reference to it." Ethnocentrism contrasts with relativism, which means viewing each culture on its own terms. Ethnocentrism thrives on a sense of cultural or racial superiority to more "primitive" peoples or cultures. It implies that one's customs and way of life are the correct and appropriate ones. Ethnocentrism is generally associated with a superficial knowledge of the other culture in question. When coupled with a relationship of unequal power, it may lead to persecution or subjugation of the less powerful group. Ethnocentrism is also intimately connected to moral sensibilities. For example, British colonial governors ended the traditional Indian practice of *suttee*, or the burning of a widow along with her deceased husband. To the British, the practice was barbaric. To Indians, it was the accepted way of maintaining the sanctity of the marital bond after the death of the husband. This is but one illustration of the complex moral dilemmas that often accompany ethnocentrism: The choice between tolerance of an arrangement that one finds morally offensive and denial of the right of each society to organize its affairs as it wishes.
Aristide Sechandice

See also: Afrocentrism; Eurocentrism.

Ethnocide

The prefix "ethno" commonly refers to a group of people united by common cultural characteristics, but it can also refer to the culture itself. Therefore, the term "ethnocide" means either the killing of people in an ethnic group or the destruction of the group's way of life. Many American historians use the latter definition to describe brutal attempts to destroy, for example, Native American culture. Young American Indians in the nineteenth century were sent to boarding schools (such as the famous Carlisle Indian School in Pennsylvania) far away from their parents with the goal of forced assimilation into Anglo-Protestant ways.

In other contexts, "ethnocide" signifies one ethnic group killing members of another group, often with the goal of "ethnic cleansing." In this sense, the term "ethnocide" is almost synonymous with "genocide," except that the latter usually suggests a systematic and well-organized extermination, as occurred during the Holocaust of World War II, when Nazis exterminated approximately six million Jews. In many places, diverse ethnic groups manage to coexist peacefully with one another, but ethnic rivalries frequently produce violence when two or more groups compete with each other in conditions of perceived scarcity. Fear of the "other" and a desire for revenge often create a cycle of ethnocide.

Thomas T. Lewis

See also: Carlisle Indian School; Ethnic cleansing; Ethnicity and ethnic groups; Ethnocentrism; Genocide: cultural; Genocide of American Indians; Genocide: physical.; "Other" theory.

Ethnogenesis theory

Ethnogenesis theory is a perspective used in the study of ethnic differentiation in American society. The perspective has been employed by author and researcher Andrew Greeley as an alternative to the most common considerations of ethnic differences.

Although analyses of assimilation, or the "melting pot," in American society vary, most assume that progress toward a common culture is inevitable. Pervasive throughout American society, the assimilation picture is entrenched in consciousness and established as the "official" view. The elimination of diversity, accomplished through common schools, mass media, social and political norms, and intermarriage, propels society toward a similarity in which differentiation occurs only by social class. However, this perspective contains limitations concerning the complexity of ethnicity that affect research findings and therefore frustrate the formulation of hypotheses.

Acculturation, or change in customs and beliefs resulting from living within a dominant society with different cultural traditions, also leaves unanswered questions. As a model, it fails to explain questions regarding the United States' capacity to cope with complex racial, religious, geographic, and social differentiation.

In *Ethnicity in the United States* (1974), Greeley proposes the ethnogenesis theory as an alternative and complementary perspective that focuses upon the creation of an ethnic group or the study of its genesis, free of the belief that it must eventually disappear. By stressing the complex interaction between heritage, culture, and identification, Greeley develops a model whereby American ethnic groups may be "dynamic and flexible institutions for becoming a part of society." Greeley's model indicates that in situations in which the host country and the immigrants may have common ground to begin with, immigrants and the host become more alike. Certain immigrant traits persist, and some become even become more distinctive. Challenged by American society, however, the ethnic groups develop cultural systems different from those of their immigrant predecessors and more in common with the common culture.

Although essentially an extension of the assimilation

and acculturation perspectives, the ethnogenesis model requires an enormous amount of research to collect data from the past that could facilitate the projection of trends. The natural history of ethnic groups affords an explanation of the cultural diversity that exists among them. Useful information includes knowledge of the land of origin, the strata or stratum of society from which the society migrated, under what circumstances the migration occurred, and the areas of the country in which the immigrants tended to settle. Information concerning cultural characteristics in early or late years of ethnic group history as well as family structure and childhood socialization also indicates the future social reality of an immigrant population in the United States.

Ethnogenesis theory suggests that American ethnic differentiation follows the collectivities of common origin that are tolerated and encouraged by the larger society; it also promotes the study of the genesis and history of ethnic groups as dynamic, growing mechanisms.

Mary Hurd

See also: Assimilation: cultural and structural; Assimilation theories.

Ethnoviolence

Ethnoviolence, as defined by sociologists Fred Pincus and Howard Ehrlich, has several characteristics, including motivation by prejudice and intent to impart psychological or physical damage to others *because* they are members of an ethnic group (that is, a group defined on the basis of race, nationality/national origin, sexual orientation, or religion). The forms that ethnoviolence takes include verbal abuse (such as racial slurs), harassment, property damage, and assault. Victims of ethnoviolence report greater psychological harm than do victims of similar crimes that are not ethnicity-based. Moreover, the effects of ethnoviolence may spread to other, nonvictimized group members, causing fear, distrust, or anger.

Many communities now track "hate crimes," a process hampered by greater nonreporting rates for ethnoviolence than for other, similar crimes. In the 1990's, rates of ethnoviolence in the United States were rising, however; one national organization reported a 24 percent rise in a single year, 1992. Some analysts attributed this rise to escalating prejudicial views, engendered by competition for dwindling resources, political manipulation or advances in telecommunications (such as the Internet) that allow unprecedented dissemination of prejudiced views. Others ascribe the growth to an overall increase in societal violence. Anthropologist Thomas Eriksen suggests that ethnicity need not breed ethnoviolence, but states that policies seeking unity through "color-blindness" are prone to failure—the stresses of transcending ethnic identity prove too great. However, policies that view ethnicity as difference without hierarchy show promise, allowing the benefits of ethnic identity while blunting intergroup fear, exclusion, and violence. *James B. Epps*

See also: Campus ethnoviolence; "Color-blind" society; Epithets and pejorative language; Genocide: cultural; Genocide: physical; Hate Crime Statistics Act; Hate crimes; Hate speech; Lynchings; White supremacist groups; Xenophobia, nativism, and eugenics.

Euro-American

Euro-American (or European American) is a panethnic identity that includes Americans of European ancestry (English, German, Irish, Italian, Polish, and so on), ranging from descendants of the earliest colonizers to recent immigrants. As Richard Alba observed in *Ethnic Identity: The Transformation of White America* (1990), the emergence of a Euro-American group has been shaped by the decline of individual European ethnic affiliations, the creation of a common historical narrative of immigration, struggle, and mobility, and the increasing Euro-American reaction to political challenges from peoples of color and post-1965 immigrants.

As a group label, "Euro-American" is problematic in that it is less widely used than other panethnic identities (including Asian American, Hispanic, and Native American). Dominant identities tend to be "hidden" in intergroup interactions, and the lack of awareness or use of the Euro-American label reflects the dominant status of the group in the United States. This process is compounded by the existence of competing labels for Euro-Americans: White, Caucasian, and Anglo-American—the latter term reflecting the historical dominance of British Americans within the group. The future role of Euro-American group identity will be determined by both the political and social strategies of the group itself, and the external and structural forces that mold all panethnic identities. *Ashley W. Doane, Jr.*

See also: Ethnic heritage revival; Ethnicity and ethnic groups; Race as a concept; White ethnics; Whites.

Eurocentrism

The term "Eurocentrism" most often refers to an inordinate emphasis on the cultural achievements of peoples of European ancestry. The term is used especially in reference to an educational curriculum that tends to disregard or minimize other traditions. As the United States has become more diverse, educators have increasingly attempted to promote a multicultural perspective that encompasses non-European cultures and considers the accomplishments of African Americans, Asian Americans, Latinos, and Native Americans. Some African American scholars have proposed that Eurocentrism should be replaced by an Afrocentric curriculum, at least for black students. Most educators, however, prefer to encourage pluralism rather than any one particularism.

Some Third World critics of the European tradition use the term "Eurocentrism" in a politicized way to refer to an ideology of white supremacy, as reflected in exploitative practices such as imperialism and slavery. These critics charge that the "Eurocentric paradigm" is founded on greed and racial domination. Admirers of the European tradition respond that Europeans are not more ethnocentric than other peoples and that Europeans have made worthwhile contributions such as the Scientific Revolution and the Enlightenment. Third World writer, Samir Amin, argues in *Eurocentrism* (1988) that the modernization that began in Europe during the Renaissance provides a model for all countries of the world. *Thomas T. Lewis*

See also: Afrocentrism; Ethnocentrism; Institutional racism; Muticulturalism; Pluralism vs. particularism; White "race"; Whites.

European immigration to Canada: 1867-present

> **Significance:** Canada, a largely homogeneous nation at its inception, strove to attract only "ideal" immigrants but was forced to open its doors to a wider range of immigrants to settle its western lands and work its mines and railroads. Today, Canada is an officially multicultural society.

Canada became a nation on July 1, 1867. At that time, the ethnic composition of the new country was largely homogeneous: The majority of citizens were of British (English, Scottish, Welsh, and Irish) or French origin, the latter almost entirely centered in the province of Quebec. Immigration policy in the early years of Canadian history reflected the country's British roots. The immigration policy between 1867 and 1896, however, also largely proved a failure. A depression discouraged immigrants from making the voyage to the new nation.

Many of the immigrants who did arrive (almost exclusively from the British Isles and Northern Europe) simply used Canada as a stopping-off point before moving to the United States. In several years during the 1870's and 1880's, Canada barely managed to maintain its current population, let alone increase it.

Immigration was important to Canada. Immigrants were needed in order to populate the western plains acquired in 1870. Britain was the preferred source of immigrants; many, however, came from urban areas and proved completely unsuitable for harsh rural conditions. The Canadian government had no choice but to begin to expand the definition of those deemed suitable for immigration to Canada. German-speaking Mennonites from Russia were encouraged to come to Canada; they settled in the province of Manitoba in the 1870's. Icelanders arrived in western Canada in the same decade. Even though these various groups challenged previous definitions of suitable immigrants, they were allowed in because of their competency as farmers.

The Immigration Boom, 1896-1914
The real boom in immigration to Canada, a period that reflected a changed perception of the ideal immigrant, occurred between 1896 and 1914. In 1896, Wilfrid Laurier and his Liberal Party were voted into office. Laurier's government, especially Minister of the Interior Clifford Sifton, was determined to fill western Canada with immigrants. Sifton and his ministry created an immigration policy that reflected Canada's need: European newcomers had to be farmers. For the first time, Canada began to seek immigrants from eastern Europe. Ukrainians, for example, who had experience farming in conditions much like those of Canada's west, began to arrive in large numbers.

At the same time that Sifton had in mind an ideal immigrant, he also had a vision of those who were unsuitable for Canada. This category included urban dwellers, industrial workers, southern Europeans, Asians, and African Americans. The last two groups were excluded—the Chinese formally through a head tax and then the 1923 Chinese Exclusion Act, and blacks informally through efforts by immigration agents, specifically because it was believed that they could never be assimilated into the mainstream of Canadian society. Sifton's opposition to industrial workers created tension with business interests, especially the railway, who wanted laborers to work in mines, in logging camps, and on the rail lines. These groups did everything they could to bring in such workers.

Other Canadians began to worry that too many non-British immigrants were flocking to Canada from Europe. These attitudes escalated as immigration to Canada rose in the first decade of the new century.

After Sifton resigned in 1905, his successor attempted to steer Canadian immigration policy back toward its original British emphasis. This policy failed, as record numbers of non-British immigrants arrived in Canada just before World War I. Because these European newcomers settled largely in the west, a new multiethnic society arose in that region. With the beginning of World War I in August of 1914, all immigration to Canada effectively ended.

Retraction, Expansion, and Retraction, 1919-1945
Canada's immigration policy in the immediate aftermath of World War I was strongly influenced by the war. Large numbers of immigrants had arrived from Germany and Austria-Hungary, nations that had become Canada's enemies during the war. The presence of what many called "enemy aliens" during the war caused people to openly question the continuation of the prewar immigration policy after the war ended. Immigration from "enemy alien" countries was banned into the 1920's. The policy changed again in the mid-1920's because of the lobbying effort of business interests. Companies such as the railways needed cheap labor; immigration was the best source of this. In 1925, the Railways Agreement was signed. This new policy allowed railway companies to recruit and bring immigrants to Canada specifically to work on the lines.

Despite widespread opposition, large numbers of nonpreferred European immigrants such as Ukrainians entered Canada in the last half of the 1920's. The policy changed again in the 1930's because of the Great Depression. With so many Canadians out of work, immigration and immigrants became a natural target of those affected by the economic collapse. The Railways Agreement was canceled, and once again, all immigration came to a virtual end. Many newly arrived immigrants were also deported in the 1930's. Among those prevented from entering Canada during the 1930's were Jewish immigrants from Europe attempting to escape Nazi persecution.

Postwar Immigration Boom, 1945-1968
The initial postwar years saw large numbers of European immigrants arrive in Canada. First were the "war brides," women whom Canadian soldiers had met and married while fighting overseas. "Displaced persons" were another large group of European immigrants who left the devastation of their home countries and came to Canada. Collectively, Canadian immigration between 1945 and 1955 reached record levels. Of all immigrants to Canada since 1867, 30 percent arrived during this period. Overall during this period, immigrants continued to come from traditional sources. In 1956-1957, a year with a particularly large number of immigrants, 40 per-

cent came from the United Kingdom. As Canada's economy slowed in the late 1950's, politicians began to talk about restricting immigration. Many Canadians favored such restrictions because of the increased difficulty in finding work. The economic downturn, however, slowed the growth of Canada by immigration. Between the opening years of the 1950's and the early years of the 1970's, between 25 percent and 33 percent of immigrants to Canada returned home or moved to the United States. For many immigrants, the reality of Canada did not match the perception.

Immigration Since 1968

Beginning in the 1960's and increasing in the 1970's, the ethnic and racial composition of immigrants to Canada changed dramatically. The shift in origin of immigrants began in the early 1960's, and then escalated under the Liberal governments of Lester Pearson and, after 1968, Pierre Trudeau. The government instituted a more impartial immigration system that eliminated traditional preferences given to immigrants from Europe. The Department of Manpower and Immigration was created in 1966 in an increased effort by the federal government to tie together Canada's economic and immigration policy. The numbers demonstrate a dramatic shift in the origins of immigrants to Canada. As late as 1966, 87 percent of those who came to Canada were of European origin. By 1970, fully half of newcomers came from new parts of the world including Hong Kong, the Caribbean, India, the Philippines, and Indochina. In 1968, eight of the top ten countries that supplied immigrants to Canada were European. By 1984, only two European countries, Britain and Poland remained in the top ten, and only Britain cracked the top five at fifth. Once again immigration was in the process of remaking Canada.

Steven Hewitt

Core Resources

Howard Palmer's *Patterns of Prejudice: A History of Nativism in Alberta* (Toronto: McClelland and Stewart, 1982) is a very good study of immigration and nativism on the Canadian west. Ramsay Cook and Robert Craig Brown's *Canada, 1896-1921: A Nation Transformed* (Toronto: McClelland and Stewart, 1991) details the immigration boom during the Laurier era. For a study of postwar immigration to Canada that details the experiences of a particular group, see Franca Iacovetta, *Such Hardworking People: Italian Immigrants in Postwar Toronto* (Montreal: McGill-Queen's University Press, 1992).

See also: African Canadians; Arab Canadians; Asian Indians in Canada; Chinese Canadians; French Canadians; Immigration law: Canada; Japanese Canadians; Multiculturalism in Canada; Vietnamese Canadians.

European immigration to the United States: 1790-1892

> **Significance:** Between 1790 and 1892, more than sixteen million Europeans migrated to the United States. Because they constituted nearly one-third of the total population and 53 percent of the urban residents, European immigrants had an important role in the development of American intergroup relations.

In 1790, the initial United States census was conducted and Congress passed the first uniform naturalization law. For the next 102 years, more than 90 percent of the immigrants came from Germany, Great Britain, Ireland, and Scandinavia (old immigrants). In 1892, for the first time, more arrivals were from Eastern and Southern Europe (new immigrants) than from Northern Europe. That same year, Ellis Island replaced the Castle Garden as the major receiving center for immigrants landing in New York when the federal government took control of the process. From 1821 to 1892, approximately 4.5 million German Protestants, Catholics, and Jews; 3.5 million Irish Catholics; 2.7 million British Protestants; and 1 million Scandinavian Protestants emigrated, with more than two-thirds coming to the United States. The Irish gravitated toward unskilled labor in the Eastern cities; the English, Welsh, and Scots often found work as skilled laborers in this same region. Germans tended to find positions as skilled craftspeople or in the trades in both Eastern and Midwestern cities. Many Germans, Scandinavians, and Dutch became farmers in the Midwest.

Relations with the Dominant Culture

At the onset of large-scale immigration, the descendants of the early colonists, who were mostly Protestants of English and Scotch-Irish descent, dominated the United States in numbers and control over society. They resented and discriminated against the new arrivals for a variety of reasons. As a group, they were generally satisfied with their lives in the United States and had established an "American culture" separate from that of Europe. A new wave of Europeans could disrupt this. Consequently, many Americans became nativists, hoping to prevent what they viewed as an immigrant "takeover" of the nation. The hierarchical structure of Catholicism, which they considered at odds with the tenets of democracy, negatively affected the large Irish and German Catholic population. Jews were still blamed for the death of Christ, and many people overestimated their influence in the financial world. Although American Protestants increasingly embraced temperance and

Milestones of European Immigration to the United States, 1790-1892

Year	Event
1790	First U.S. census reveals that 60.9 percent of the population is of English ancestry, 9.7 Scotch-Irish, 8.7 German, and 8.3 Scottish. This clearly indicates Euro-American dominance in the new nation. Congress passes legislation stating that any free white person who has lived in the country for two years can become a citizen.
1798	The Federalist leadership passes the Alien Act, the first attempt to impede immigrant assimilation.
1815	Napoleonic Wars end, allowing for greater emigration from Europe.
1820's	Innovations in manufacturing technology and the legalization of corporations help start the Industrial Revolution in the United States, which becomes a major draw for impoverished immigrants.
1840's	The Potato Famine drives 2 million people from Ireland.
1851-1854	First great peak in immigration occurs; 1.5 million people per year arrive in the United States.
1861-1865	Civil War curtails immigration.
1866-1873	Second immigration peak occurs; 1 million people arrive annually.
1870's	Immigration from eastern and southern Europe begins.
1881	Congress takes action to restrict immigration, ending the Open Door era.
1891	Congress establishes an agency for immigration control under the auspices of the Treasury Department, thus initiating full-scale federal control.
1892	The number of immigrants from eastern and southern Europe surpasses that of arrivals from northernwestern and central Europe. This, and the opening of the Ellis Island immigration facility, mark a new era in immigration history.

prohibition of alcoholic beverages, many Irish and German immigrants saw spirits as a part of their culture. Irish, Welsh, and English laborers often believed that organized labor was the key to better pay and working conditions; however, many native stock Americans felt that labor unions were in opposition to American individualism and free labor capitalism. Germans and Scandinavians, who desired to maintain Old World languages and traditions, were chastised for being un-American. All of these factors were responsible for divisions between colonial stock Americans and the immigrants.

Relations Among Old Immigrants

Despite commonalties of the ethnic experience, the old immigrants never viewed themselves as a unified group. Conflict between the groups was more apparent than cooperation. These differences often had European roots that combined with American circumstances.

Religious differences continued to separate people in the United States as they had in Europe. Almost all the British, Scandinavians, and Dutch were Protestants, as were half of the Germans. Like their American counterparts, the British Protestants were at odds with Irish Catholics. The religious differences in the German states were also brought to the United States. Germans viewed themselves as German Protestants, German Catholics, or German Jews rather than as a single culture.

Political issues also divided the old immigrants. Catholics and urban laborers, especially the Irish, gravitated toward the more open Democratic Party. Protestant skilled workers and midwestern farmers believed that the Whigs, and later the Republicans, reflected their interests of upward socioeconomic mobility and conservative social values. Catholics and the less conservative German Protestants objected to any laws restricting alcohol. Conversely, many English, Welsh, and German Pietist Protestant immigrants abstained from liquor and favored its prohibition. In regard to slavery, unskilled Irish laborers feared that emancipation could bring about competition with African Americans for low-paying jobs; English, Welsh, and German skilled workers and tradespeople believed that the extension of slavery would damage the free-labor, capitalist economy.

The Assimilation Process

The Americanization process for the older group of immigrants was hastened because all ethnic groups began to enjoy increased social and economic mobility by the latter part of the nineteenth century and because the arrival of the new immigrants lifted them to a higher level of social status.

The various ethnic groups achieved social and economic mobility differently. The English, Welsh, and Scots often moved from their skilled labor positions to become bosses, supervisors, and managers in corporate America. They used the school systems to educate their children, who moved into professional positions. Many descendants of the Welsh and English immigrants became teachers and administrators in elementary and secondary education systems, giving those groups a tremendous impact upon education in the United States.

Working from positions as unskilled laborers, the Irish moved through the corporate ranks. Politics was also a means of Irish mobility. Colonial stock Americans found local politics disdainful; however, the Irish recognized an opportunity to gain political power in the growing urban areas. By the late 1800's, many Eastern cities were under the control of political machines dominated by the Irish. Although colonial stock and other old immigrants criticized boss politics, the machines served the rapidly expanding urban-ethnic community at a time when official government agencies were lacking. The Irish were also able to gain mobility through their leadership in the Roman Catholic Church. The Church became a major force in American life with the arrival of numerous Catholic immigrants. The Irish Church hierarchy was instrumental in sponsoring a vast educational network that educated all Catholics from elementary school through the university.

Germans and Scandinavians were perhaps less inclined to use higher education as a means of mobility. However, as the United States rapidly expanded, the services of German tradespeople and farmers were all the more needed. This, in turn, brought about a growth in German businesses and farms, resulting in the upward mobility of ship owners and workers alike. German Jews, many of whom began as peddlers and small shopkeepers, were able to expand their businesses to meet the increasing consumer demand. This economic success combined with a strong emphasis upon education was responsible for a remarkable degree of socioeconomic mobility for German Jews.

The arrival of ten million Eastern and Southern Europeans resulted in a higher socioeconomic status for the old immigrants. The new arrivals provided a large labor pool to fill unskilled positions. The old immigrants could move into the more lucrative skilled and management jobs or expand their businesses to serve the growing population. Also, many of the values of the Northern European immigrants were more identifiable as American ideals. To both colonial stock and old immigrants, the new immigrants appeared to be considerably different. Consequently, the colonial stock found the old immigrants more acceptable.

By the mid-twentieth century, the descendants of the old immigrants were less commonly viewed as distinct ethnic groups. The British found their heritage largely assimilated into the larger American culture, and Germans' ethnic identification diminished during the two world wars. Certain groups, such as the Welsh and Scandinavians, still maintain ethnic institutions. However, these institutions are intended more to preserve the vestiges of the cultures than to help immigrants deal with challenges in the United States. To most observers, the descendants of the old immigrants are firmly entrenched in mainstream American culture.

Paul J. Zbiek

Core Resources

The Uprooted: The Epic Story of the Great Migrations That Made the American People (Boston: Little, Brown, 1951), by Oscar Handlin, one of the pioneering scholars on ethnic history, deals extensively with the old immigrant period. Marcus Lee Hansen's *The Immigrant in American History* (Cambridge, Mass.: Harvard University Press, 1940) was also an influential work on nineteenth century migration to the United States. The *Harvard Encyclopedia of American Ethnic Groups* (Cambridge, Mass.: Belknap Press of Harvard University, 1940), edited by Stephan Thernstrom, a groundbreaker in the social scientific approach to immigration studies, is an excellent reference work detailing all immigrant groups. Rowland Berthoff presents a fine overview in *British Immigrants in Industrial America, 1790-1950* (Cambridge, Mass.: Harvard University Press, 1953). Jay Dolan chronicles how the Irish and Germans established American Catholicism in *The Immigrant Church: New York's Irish and German Catholics 1815-1965* (Baltimore, Md.: The Johns Hopkins University Press, 1975). *Strangers in the Land: Patterns of American Nativism, 1860-1925* (New Brunswick, N.J.: Rutgers University Press, 1969), by John Higham, presents a clear picture of discrimination against immigrants.

See also: Anglo-Protestants; Anti-Catholicism; British as dominant group; Celtic Irish; European immigration to the United States: 1892-1943; German Americans; Immigration and emigration; Irish Americans; Irish Catholic "race"; Italian Americans; Jewish Americans; Nativism; Polish Americans; Russian Americans; Scandinavian Americans; Scotch-Irish "race."

European immigration to the United States: 1892-1943

> **Significance:** A new wave of Southern European immigrants met with nativist resentment and federal controls.

In 1808, the U.S. government purchased Ellis Island from the state of New York for ten thousand dollars. The new federal property, located in New York Harbor about one mile from the southern tip of Manhattan Island, served first as a fort and later as an arsenal. Until 1882, the state of New York had guided the influx of immigration from the old Castle Garden station at the tip of Manhattan. The opening of Ellis Island on January 1, 1892, as the first federal immigration station symbolized a new era for the United States as well as the beginning of the end of free immigration to the New World.

Congress had begun the selective process of excluding undesirable elements among those emigrating to the United States with the passage of the federal Immigration Act in 1882. That measure was designed to prevent the immigration of persons who had criminal records and those who were mentally incompetent or indigent. That same year, Congress also passed the Chinese Exclusion Act (later extended to all Asians), barring an entire nationality from entry as racially undesirable for a period of ten years. In 1904 the act's provisions were extended indefinitely, to be repealed only in 1943.

Immigration Patterns Shift

Most immigrants before the 1890's had come from northern and western Europe. In the 1880's a fundamental change occurred. In addition to the traditional immigrants, who shared common language patterns with persons already in the United States, people from

Steamships such as the S.S. *Patricia* in 1906 brought waves of immigrants from Southern and Eastern Europe to the United States.

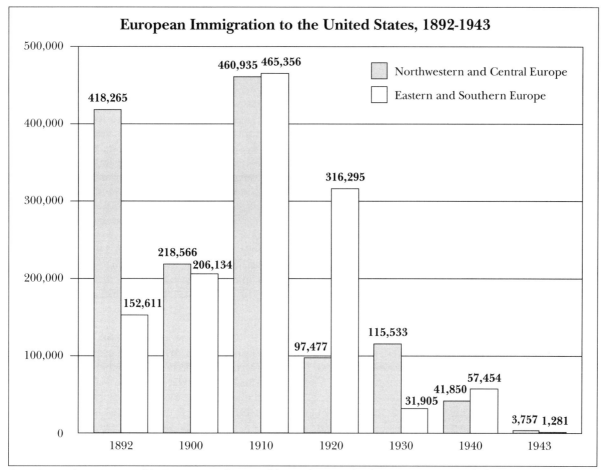

European Immigration to the United States, 1892-1943

Legend:
- Northwestern and Central Europe
- Eastern and Southern Europe

- 1892: 418,265 / 152,611
- 1900: 218,566 / 206,134
- 1910: 460,935 / 465,356
- 1920: 97,477 / 316,295
- 1930: 115,533 / 31,905
- 1940: 41,850 / 57,454
- 1943: 3,757 / 1,281

Source: Data are from U.S. Bureau of the Census, *Historical Statistics of the United States: Colonial Times to 1970, Bicentennial edition, Part 1.* Washington, D.C.: U.S. Government Printing Office, 1975.

Mediterranean and Slavic countries began to arrive in increasing numbers. One may measure the change more dramatically by comparing two peak years in U.S. immigration. In 1882, 87 percent of the 788,000 immigrants came from northern and western Europe. In 1907, only 19.3 percent were from northern and western Europe, while 80.7 percent came from southern and eastern Europe.

A great impetus to immigration was the transportation revolution engendered by the steamship. In 1856, more than 96 percent of U.S. immigrants came aboard sailing ships, on trips that took between one and three months. By 1873, the same percentage came by steamships, which took only ten days. The new steamships were specifically designed for passengers, and while still subject to overcrowding and epidemics, they were a major improvement over the sailing ships. Steamship companies competed for immigrant business and maintained offices in Europe. The Hamburg-Amerika line, for ex-

ample, had thirty-two hundred U.S. agencies throughout Europe. More than half of the immigrants in 1901 came with prepaid tickets supplied by relatives in the United States.

As the older agricultural economy of Europe was replaced by an industrial one, many former farmers moved to European cities in search of employment; often unsuccessful in that search, they were easily persuaded to try the New World, where jobs were said to be plentiful. The same railroad-building process that opened the American West to the immigrant made it easier and cheaper for the Europeans to reach their coastal areas and embark for the United States.

Most of the emigration from southern Europe was occasioned by economic distress. Southern Italy's agriculture was severely affected by competition from Florida in oranges and lemons, as well as by a French tariff against Italian wines. The Italian emigration began with 12,000 in 1880 and reached a peak of nearly 300,000 in

1914. After immigration restriction laws took full effect, Italian immigration fell to 6,203 in 1925.

From Russia and the Slavic areas, emigration was also caused by political and religious problems. Jews fled in reaction to the riots set off by the assassination of Czar Alexander II in 1882, the pogroms of 1881-1882 and 1891, and the 1905-1906 massacres of thousands of Jews. Jewish immigration to the United States began with 5,000 in 1880 and reached a peak of 258,000 in 1907. Some two million Roman Catholic Poles also arrived between 1890 and 1914. In 1925, however, the Immigration Service recorded only 5,341 entrants from Poland and 3,121 from Russia and the Baltic States.

Nativist Fears

Two issues caused the greatest concern to American nativists in the 1890's: the tendency of the new immigrants to congregate in the cities, and the fact that they spoke seemingly unassimilable languages. One of the first articulate spokesmen against unrestricted immigration, the Reverend Dr. Josiah Strong, was alarmed by the concentration of foreign peoples in cities. Strong's famous book, *Our Country*, published in 1885, clearly stated what many other U.S. citizens feared: that the new influx of immigrants would create permanent slums and perpetuate poverty.

The urban nature of the settlement was unavoidable. U.S. agriculture was suffering from the same shocks that had disrupted European agriculture, and the populist movement in the country made clear that the myth of utopia in the western United States was no longer believable. Most of the new immigrants were attracted by the pull of U.S. industry and opportunity, and they came to the United States with the express purpose of settling in a city. In addition, new industrial technology had reduced the demand for skilled labor, while the need for unskilled and cheap factory help increased. To add to the social clash between the new and old immigrants, the arrival of a new labor force in great numbers probably allowed some older laborers to move up to more important supervisory and executive positions.

Many new immigrants did not share the optimism and enthusiasm of established Americans. Some tended to be pessimistic and resigned, distrustful of change, and unfamiliar with democratic government after having lived in autocratic situations. At the height of the new immigration occurred the Panic of 1893, followed by a depression that lasted until 1897, which seemed to confirm the fears of persons already settled in the United States that the country and the system were failing. The new immigration, however, was but one of the major social, cultural, and economic changes taking place in the turbulent United States of the 1890's.

In 1907, Congress created the Dillingham Commission to investigate the problems of immigration. Many of the commission's findings reflected the fears of citizens concerning the new immigration and led to the passage of restrictive legislation in the 1920's. Unrestricted immigration ended with the passage of the National Origins Act of 1924, which restricted immigrants in any year to 154,277. Each country's quota could be no more than 2 percent of the number of its natives counted in the 1890 census, a year in which few born in southern and eastern Europe were part of the U.S. population.

When Ellis Island closed as a reception center in 1943, few immigrants still arrived by ship, and the Immigration Service could handle all arrivals at Manhattan's docks. When the Atlantic reopened after World War II, planes began to replace ships as vehicles of immigration, and there was no need for Ellis Island. By that time, much of the fear of the "new" immigration had evaporated. Italian, Slavs, and Jews had not remained in permanent slums, mired in perpetual poverty, as Strong had feared, and their descendants had fought side by side with U.S. soldiers of British and German ancestry against the Nazis and the Japanese.

In the 1940's, there was much criticism of the rigidity of the immigration restriction legislation that hampered attempts to deal with the problems of refugees. Not until 1965, however, would the rigid quota system established in 1924 be replaced with a more flexible system. When that reform opened the door to increased entry by Asians and Latin Americans, complaints about the new "new immigrants" began to echo nineteenth century uneasiness about the former "new immigrants."

Richard H. Collin, updated by Milton Berman

Core Resources

Island of Hope, Island of Tears (New York: Penguin Books, 1986), edited by David M. Brownstone, Irene M. Franck, and Douglas L. Brownstone, contains interviews with elderly people who went through Ellis Island in the early years of the twentieth century. Roger Daniels's *Coming to America: A History of Immigration and Ethnicity in American Life* (New York: HarperCollins, 1990) provides a well-written, scholarly account of U.S. immigration from the colonial period through the 1980's. Oscar Handlin's *The Uprooted* (2d. enlarged ed. Boston: Little, Brown, 1973) is a dramatic narrative focusing on the life experiences of immigrants. John Higham's *Strangers in the Land: Patterns of American Nativism, 1860-1925* (New Brunswick, N.J.: Rutgers University Press, 1955) analyzes the nativist movements that led to the passage of immigration restriction. David M. Reimers's *Still the Golden Door: The Third World Comes to America* (New York: Columbia University Press, 1985) is study of twentieth century immigration to the United States, primarily after World War II.

See also: Chinese Exclusion Act; European Immigration to the United States, 1790-1892; German Americans; Immigration Act of 1917; Immigration Act of 1924; Irish Americans; Italian Americans; Jewish Americans; Nativism; Polish Americans; Scandinavian Americans; Soviet Jewish immigrants; Yellow peril campaign; Xenophobia, nativism, and eugenics.

Ex parte Crow Dog

Crow Dog, a well-known Lakotan, killed Spotted Tail, another popular tribal leader, at the Rosebud Agency in Dakota Territory in 1883. Crow Dog was arrested, removed from the reservation, and tried in the territorial court of Dakota, where he was convicted and sentenced to death. In killing Spotted Tail, Crow Dog admitted he had broken Lakota law, but he maintained he should be punished according to Lakota customs, not by United States law. Under tribal law, Crow Dog would be shunned by his own family and would become responsible for care and protection of Spotted Tail's family.

The U.S. Supreme Court sided with Crow Dog and declared the United States had no jurisdiction over the crime of one Indian against another on Indian land. Because Congress provided no federal jurisdiction over Indian crimes on reservations, even a murderer could not be punished. Therefore, Crow Dog returned to his people.

This decision proved to be a major step in relations between Native Americans and the U.S. government, in that it encouraged Congress to enact legislation to give federal jurisdiction over Indians in certain legal matters. One key piece of legislation, the Major Crimes Act (1885), directed federal courts to assume jurisdiction over seven crimes committed on Indian land: murder, manslaughter, rape, assault with intent to kill, arson, burglary, and larceny.

Carole A. Barrett

See also: American Indians in the justice system; Tribal courts; Tribal sovereignty.

External colonialism

External colonialism is the classical form of colonialism, describing the processes that occurred during European imperialist expansion that began during the late fifteenth century and extended well into the nineteenth. External colonialism is the process of *global imperialism* that involved the political and economic control of less powerful societies by more powerful societies to acquire and exploit land, labor, and natural resources for geopolitical and economic interests. The relative power of nations reflects a disparity in levels of politico-military dominance and economic resources.

Because external colonialism was a worldwide process of empire building, it commonly involved the remote control of less powerful distant nations by powerful nations. Colonizers were typically European imperialist powers that industrialized first, while the colonized tended to be strategic territories in the path of colonial expansion. Because religious zeal commonly accompanied and justified colonization in the form of missionary expansion, the cross and the sword were typically two sides of the same colonialist coin. Five fundamental conditions were intertwined in this process of external colonialism: forced entry into a distant territory, political subjugation of the colonized people, economic exploitation of labor and natural resources, cultural alteration or annihilation of colonized peoples' ways of life, and racial ideologies justifying inferiority and colonization.

Several sociologists have studied colonialism as it relates to intergroup—particularly interracial and interethnic—relations. They include Mario Barrera (*Race and Class in the Southwest*, 1979), Robert Blauner (*Racial Oppression in America*, 1972), Albert Memmi (*The Colonizer and the Colonized*, 1965), and Christopher Bates Doob (*Racism: An American Cauldron*, 1993).

Michael P. Perez

See also: Colonial model of racism; Discrimination: racial and ethnic; Internal colonialism.

F

Fair Employment Practices Committee

In the spring of 1941, as the United States prepared to enter World War II, African American leaders pressured the administration of Franklin D. Roosevelt to eliminate segregation in the armed forces and discriminatory hiring practices in the booming war industries. A. Philip Randolph, president of the Brotherhood of Sleeping Car Porters, the largest black labor union, threatened a massive march on Washington, D.C., by a hundred thousand demonstrators under the banner Democracy Not Hypocrisy—Jobs Not Alms. Roosevelt, hoping to avoid an embarrassing racial protest that might divide the Democratic Party and his administration at a time when he needed unity for his war-preparedness program, moved to head off the March on Washington movement by meeting with Randolph and Walter White, president of the National Association for the Advancement of Colored People (NAACP). On June 25, 1941, a week before the planned march, Roosevelt issued Executive Order 8802. It prohibited discrimination by employers, unions, and government agencies involved in defense work on the basis of race, creed, color, or national origin but made no mention of desegregating the armed forces. Roosevelt established the Fair Employment Practices Committee (FEPC) to investigate complaints and redress grievances stemming from the order. Randolph and White accepted the compromise arrangement and called off the march.

Although African Americans hailed the FEPC as the greatest step forward in race relations since the Civil War, Roosevelt initially gave the agency little authority. Underfunded and understaffed, the FEPC at first could do little more than conduct investigations into complaints received and make recommendations, relying on the powers of publicity and persuasion to achieve change. In mid-1943, however, amid mounting concern that manpower shortages were hurting the war effort, Roosevelt beefed up the agency by giving it the authority to conduct hearings, make findings, issue directives to war industries, and make recommendations to the War Manpower Commission to curb discrimination.

The FEPC had a mixed record of accomplishment in eliminating racial discrimination in the war industries and government agencies. It resolved less than half of the eight thousand complaints received, and employers and unions often ignored its compliance orders with impunity. Although African American employment in the war industries increased from 3 percent in 1942 to 8 percent in 1945 and the federal government more than tripled its number of black employees, such changes had more to do with wartime labor shortages than FEPC actions. Nevertheless, the FEPC scored some significant successes. In 1944, federal troops broke up a strike by white Philadelphia transit workers and enforced an FEPC directive that blacks be upgraded to positions as streetcar operators. At war's end, despite the FEPC's shortcomings, African American leaders and white liberals hoped to transform the committee into a permanent agency. In 1946, however, southern Democrats in the Senate filibustered a bill to extend the FEPC and killed the agency. Although several northern states passed their own Fair Employment Practices acts, the Senate again blocked bills to create a permanent FEPC in 1950 and 1952. Not until the Civil Rights Act of 1964 did the federal government establish another agency devoted to eliminating racial discrimination in employment practices.

Richard V. Damms

See also: Brotherhood of Sleeping Car Porters; Civil Rights Act of 1964; Desegregation: defense; Discrimination: racial and ethnic; Employment among African Americans; Labor movement; Military desegregation; National Association for the Advancement of Colored People.

Fair Housing Act

Significance: The Fair Housing Act, which became law April 11, 1968, prohibited discrimination in housing, helping to break racial enclaves in residential neighborhoods and promoting upward mobility for minorities.

The Civil Rights Act of 1866 provided that all citizens should have the same rights "to inherit, purchase, lease, sell, hold, and convey real and personal property," but the law was never enforced. Instead, such federal agencies as the Farmers Home Administration, the Federal Housing Administration, and the Veterans Administration financially supported segregated housing until 1962, when President John F. Kennedy issued Executive Order 11063 to stop the practice.

California passed a general nondiscrimination law in 1959 and an explicit fair housing law in 1963. In 1964, voters enacted Proposition 14, an initiative to repeal the 1963 statute and the applicability of the 1959 law to housing. When a landlord in Santa Ana refused to rent to an African American in 1963, the latter sued, thus challenging Proposition 14. The California Supreme Court, which heard the case in 1966, ruled that Proposition 14 was contrary to the Fourteenth Amendment to the U.S. Constitution, because it was not neutral on the matter of housing discrimination; instead, based on the context in which it was adopted, Proposition 14 served to legitimate and promote discrimination. On appeal, the U.S. Supreme Court let the California Supreme Court decision stand in *Reitman v. Mulkey* (1967).

Johnson's Efforts

President Lyndon B. Johnson had hoped to include housing discrimination as a provision in the comprehensive Civil Rights Act of 1964, but he demurred when southern senators threatened to block the nomination of Robert Weaver as the first African American cabinet appointee. After 1964, southern members of Congress were adamantly opposed to any expansion of civil rights. Although Johnson urged passage of a federal law against housing discrimination in requests to Congress in 1966 and 1967, there was no mention of the idea during his State of the Union address in 1968. Liberal members of Congress pressed the issue regardless, and southern senators responded by threatening a filibuster. This threat emboldened Senators Edward W. Brooke and Walter F. Mondale, a moderate Republican and a liberal Democrat, respectively, to cosponsor fair housing legislation, but they needed the support of conservative midwestern Republicans to break a filibuster. Illinois Republican senator Everett Dirksen arranged a compromise whereby housing discrimination would be declared illegal, but federal enforcement power would be minimal.

In the wake of *Reitman v. Mulkey*, the assassination of Martin Luther King, Jr., on April 4, 1968, and subsequent urban riots, Congress established fair housing as a national priority on April 10 by adopting Titles VIII and IX of the Civil Rights Act of 1968, also known as the Fair Housing Act or Open Housing Act. Signed by John-

son on the following day, the law originally prohibited discrimination in housing on the basis of race, color, religion, or national origin. In 1974, an amendment expanded the coverage to include sex (gender) discrimination; in 1988, the law was extended to protect persons with disabilities and families with children younger than eighteen years of age.

Title VIII prohibits discrimination in the sale or rental of dwellings, in the financing of housing, in advertising, in the use of a multiple listing service, and in practices that "otherwise make unavailable or deny" housing, a phrase that some courts have interpreted to outlaw exclusionary zoning, mortgage redlining, and racial steering. Blockbusting, the practice of inducing a white homeowner to sell to a minority buyer in order to frighten others on the block to sell their houses at a loss, is also prohibited. It is not necessary to show intent in order to prove discrimination; policies, practices, and procedures that have the effect of excluding minorities, women, handicapped persons, and children are illegal, unless otherwise deemed reasonable. Title VIII, as amended in 1988, covers persons who believe that they are adversely affected by a discriminatory policy, practice, or procedure, even before they incur damages.

The law applies to about 80 percent of all housing in the United States. One exception to the statute is a single-family house sold or rented without the use of a broker and without discriminatory advertising, when the owner owns no more than three such houses and sells only one house in a two-year period. Neither does the statute apply to a four-unit dwelling if the owner lives in one of the units, the so-called Mrs.-Murphy's-rooming-house exception. Dwellings owned by private clubs or religious organizations that rent to their own members on a noncommercial basis are also exempt.

Enforcement

Enforcement of the statute was left to the secretary of the Department of Housing and Urban Development (HUD). Complaints originally had to be filed within 180 days of the offending act, but in 1988, this period was amended to one year. HUD has estimated that there are about two million instances of housing discrimination each year, although formal complaints have averaged only forty thousand per year. The U.S. attorney general can bring a civil suit against a flagrant violator of the law.

According to the law, HUD automatically refers complaints to local agencies that administer "substantially equivalent" fair housing laws. HUD can act if the local agencies fail to do so, but initially was expected only to use conference, conciliation, and persuasion to bring about voluntary compliance. The Fair Housing Amendments Act of 1988 authorized an administrative law tribunal to hear cases that cannot be settled by persuasion. The administrative law judges have the power to issue cease and desist orders to offending parties.

HUD has used "testers" to show discrimination. For example, a team of blacks and whites might arrange to have an African American apply for a rental; if turned down, the black tester would contact a white tester to ascertain whether the landlord were willing to rent to a white instead. That testers have standing to sue was established by the U.S. Supreme Court in *Havens v. Coleman* (1982).

Under the administrative law procedure, penalties are up to $10,000 for the first offense, $25,000 for the second offense, and $50,000 for each offense thereafter. Attorneys' fees and court costs can be recovered by the prevailing party. In 1988, civil penalties in a suit filed by the U.S. attorney general were established as up to $50,000 for the first offense and $100,000 for each offense thereafter.

Title IX of the law prohibits intimidation or attempted injury of anyone filing a housing discrimination complaint. A violator can be assessed a criminal penalty of $1,000 and/or sentenced to one year in jail. If a complainant is actually injured, the penalty can increase to $10,000 and/or ten years of imprisonment. If a complainant is killed, the penalty is life imprisonment.

Under the laws of some states, a complainant filing with a state agency must waive the right to pursue a remedy under federal law. In 1965, a couple sought to purchase a home in a St. Louis suburban housing development, only to be told by the realtor that the home was not available because one of the spouses was African American. Invoking the Civil Rights Act of 1866, the couple sued the real estate developer, and the case went to the Supreme Court. In *Jones v. Alfred H. Mayer Company* (1968), the Court decided that the Civil Rights Act of 1866 did permit a remedy against housing discrimination by private parties.

The effect of the 1968 Fair Housing Act, however, has been minimal. Without a larger supply of affordable housing, many African Americans in particular have nowhere to move in order to enjoy integrated housing. Federal subsidies for low-cost housing, under such legislation as the Housing and Urban Development Act of 1968 and the Housing and Community Development Act of 1974, have declined significantly since the 1980's. Conscientious private developers are confronted with the text of a law that aims to provide integrated housing but proscribes achieving integration by establishing quotas to ensure a mixed racial composition among those who seek to buy or rent dwelling units.   *Michael Haas*

Core Resources
James A. Kushner's *Fair Housing: Discrimination in Real Estate, Community Development, and Revitalization* (Colo-

rado Springs, Colo.: McGraw-Hill, 1983) is a compendium of legislation and litigation. George R. Metcalf's *Fair Housing Comes of Age* (New York: Greenwood Press, 1988) is a comprehensive evaluation of the precedent, purposes, and problems of enacting, implementing, and enforcing fair housing legislation. *The Fair Housing Act After Twenty Years* (New Haven, Conn.: Yale Law School, 1989), edited by Robert G. Schwemm, evaluates the political and social impediments to achieving nondiscrimination in housing.

See also: Civil Rights Act of 1964; Civil Rights Restoration Act of 1988; Housing.

Family and socialization: African Americans

Significance: In addition to facilitating the development of values, beliefs, and behaviors in children that will lead to competence as an adult, the African American family functions to buffer its members from prejudice and discrimination. Further, it must provide the skills needed to deal with the sometimes conflicting expectations of African American culture and of Euro-American society.

African American families are far from homogeneous in terms of structure, values emphasized, and the means of socialization employed. Nonetheless, several scholars have identified areas that tend to be stressed in African American families.

Kinship Bonds
In *Black Families* (1997, edited by Harriette Pipes McAdoo), Niara Sudarkasa, a scholar in African American family organization, contends that commitment to the family is the most important factor in the socialization of African American children. The existence of and reliance on the extended family for emotional, social, and financial support have been well documented and, to some extent, reflect the influences of African tribal culture and the experience of slavery on the modern African American family. The familiar saying that "It takes a village to raise a child" exemplifies this concept of shared family and community responsibility for the well-being of African American children. Sudarkasa argues that to understand household organization among African American families, one must consider the differential use of the terms "household" and "family." Although these terms are used somewhat interchangeably among Euro-Americans, African Americans employ

"household" to describe people living in the same dwelling and use "family" to designate extended family members living within and outside the home. Thus, family stability and marriage stability are not perceived to be synonymous, and family ties are maintained even after the dissolution of a marriage. Unfortunately, recent trends toward a reduction in multigenerational households may signal a decline in the availability of immediate support for single parents.

Socialization Patterns

Contrary to popular belief, African American families traditionally advocate a strong commitment to educational achievement and see higher education as the most important avenue to success in the larger American society. Evidence of this commitment can be seen in families across all economic levels who spend time talking to their children about school, college, and homework. Children, however, are more likely to model what they see rather than what they hear, making it less likely that children of non-college-educated parents will actually view college as a realistic option for advancement.

There is strong evidence that patterns of authority in two-parent African American households are more frequently equalitarian with flexible rather than traditional gender roles. Similarly, the responsibilities of children within the family have long been driven by age and birth order rather than gender. First-born and older children, regardless of gender, are expected to help around the house and provide additional care for younger household members.

A persistent stereotype concerning African Americans is that they are lazy and would rather have fun than engage in hard work. However, according to Andrew Billingsley, in *Black Families in White America* (1968), black families teach their children to work hard and to be responsible. From an early age, many of them are expected to do chores, get part-time jobs, and contribute to the financial maintenance of the family system. Inadequate training and employment opportunities and continued racial discrimination make it difficult for many African American adults to realize their potential in this area.

Respect and appreciation for elders within and outside one's family are important values among African Americans. According to Sudarkasa, it was a traditional sign of respect in the African American community to address one's elders as "Mister" and "Miss" and disrespectful for younger people to "look their elders dead in the eyes." Further, African American grandparents, especially grandmothers, often play an active role in teaching and disciplining their grandchildren. This favorable attitude toward the elderly, coupled with their continued involvement in the extended kin network, seems to give African American seniors a higher status in the family, and they report greater happiness compared with their white counterparts.

A belief common among African Americans, especially in middle-class families, is that each individual, in return for the emotional and financial support that enabled his or her success, should give something back to extended family members and to the African American community in general.

The church plays a pivotal role in the African American community and in the socialization of children. Robert Staples, in *Black Families at the Crossroads* (1993), argues that "the church is the modern-day tribe" serving to unite community and unrelated families. Being largely independent of the white authority structure, the church has served to provide moral training, feelings of self-worth, and role models to black children. In addition, black churches operate a multitude of family-related programs, including schools, recreation groups, and family welfare and adoption services.

Family Structure and Poverty

Although the percentage of children raised in two-parent households has been declining overall, U.S. government figures from 1992 indicate that the number of African American children being raised in mother-only households remains disproportionately high. The sex ratio

A boy looks on as his grandfather shows him the family album. Respect for one's elders is an important part of African American family life.

for African Americans is lower than for Euro-American groups; there are a relatively smaller number of black men in the marriage pool. This condition is due, in part, to the tenuous position of black males in the labor force and their disproportionately large numbers in the criminal justice system.

Because households in general are significantly more likely to live below the poverty line, African American children are more likely to experience poverty and to be chronically poor than are white children. Being raised in severe and persistent poverty is related to lower scores on standardized tests of verbal ability and other measures of intellectual functioning. The interpretation and meaning of these lower test scores continue to be hotly debated. What is less controversial, however, are the relatively low levels of educational attainment and constrained employment opportunities associated with African American youth and adults.

Although there continue to be a disproportionate number of households headed by single women among African Americans, 52 percent of black men and 41 percent of black women were in intact marriages in 1992. Within these households, provider and decision-making roles are more likely to be shared equally between spouses than they are in white marriages, especially among middle-class families. The father's specific position within the family and involvement in child-rearing practices are related to his ability to contribute to the economic support of his family. Clearly the role of African American fathers has not been adequately researched. One study reported by Harriette McAdoo, however, characterized the parenting style of African American fathers as nurturing, warm, and loving.

Though more extensively researched than her male counterpart, the African American mother's role has been controversial. At the heart of the debate, according to Staples, is whether mothers in female-headed households can serve as adequate role models for their male children's masculine identity. Findings suggest that mothers are able to communicate role expectations to their children and that there are male models in the extended family and community networks to supplement her teachings. Both male and female children report feeling close to their mothers and become very defensive when they believe she is not respected by others.   *Felicia F. Thomas and Gary A. Cretser*

Core Resources

For information about the African American family during slavery and the development of kin networks, see *The Black Family in Slavery and Freedom* (New York: Pantheon, 1976), by Herbert Gutman. In *Black Families in White America* (Englewood Cliffs, N.J.: Prentice-Hall, 1968), Andrew Billingsley looks at the history of the black family in the United States and its relationship with other institutions. For a discussion of interpersonal relationships in African American families, read *The Strength of Black Families* (New York: Emerson Hall, 1971), by Robert Hill. *Black Families at the Crossroads* (San Francisco: Jossey-Bass, 1993), by Robert Staples, analyzes the sociocultural variables that influence the structure and function of African American families. *Black Families* (3d ed., Thousand Oaks, Calif.: Sage, 1997), edited by Harriette Pipes McAdoo, explores a number of dimensions of black family life historically but also inclusive of current issues. See *Consequences of Growing Up Poor* (New York: Russell Sage, 1997), edited by Greg J. Duncan and Jeanne Brooks-Gunn, for an examination of the effects and correlates of poverty on children. To gain a better understanding of African American families in relation to the family characteristics of other ethnic groups read *Ethnic Families in America* (4th ed., Englewood Cliffs, N.J.: Prentice-Hall, 1998), edited by Charles H. Mindel, Robert W. Habenstein, and Roosevelt Wright, Jr.

See also: Adolescent ethnic identity; African American stereotypes; African American women; Black churches; Education and African Americans; Employment among African Americans; Poverty and race.

Family and socialization: American Indians

> **Significance:** Traditional Native American culture values harmony, balance, cyclical thinking, cooperativeness, respect for age, and interdependence, while mainstream American culture values linear thinking, time management, competition, youthfulness, and independence. These differences are sometimes a source of conflict for Native American children raised to respect traditional values.

At the end of the twentieth century, about two million Native Americans lived in the United States, about one-fourth of them on reservations. Although Native Americans are a diverse group, anthropologists have identified certain common characteristics and socialization patterns that apply generally to Native American culture, especially on reservations, where traditions are followed more closely.

Family Patterns and Characteristics

In Native American culture, the basic unit is the extended family. Mothers and fathers share the responsibility for the nurturing and care of their children; how-

Several generations of American Indians gather to dance and enjoy a powwow. In American Indian families, older people are respected for the wisdom they possess.

ever, members of the extended family are also likely to take responsibility for the care of the young. Native American children usually know the members of their extended family and often turn to them for help and advice. It is a tenet of the Native American culture that the older members of the families have wisdom; therefore, it is natural for children to look to their elders for advice.

Traditional Native Americans believe that every child should receive unconditional love and caring and that all adults are responsible for helping children develop naturally. Native American parents are often regarded as permissive by non-Indians because they do not discipline their children or punish them physically. However, Native Americans believe that, rather than telling children who or what they should be, adults should help them discover who and what they are.

Spiritual values are important within the Native American culture. Members of this culture teach their children to be respectful and generous, to live in balance, to withstand hardship, to cooperate with others, and to receive blessings appropriately. Children are also taught the proper roles for men and women because traditionally male and female roles have been highly specific and differentiated in Native American culture. When teaching cultural values, Native American parents and tribal elders use modeling, examples, and stories, training their children largely through an extensive oral tradition.

Native American Children in School

By the time they enter school, Native American children often have a world orientation that differs from that of their non-Indian peers. During the socialization process, they have developed learning styles and ways of thinking that are very different from those of white, middle-class children. In public schools, they are likely to be less competitive, more group-oriented, and quieter. Their learning style is likely to focus on relationships, and they are likely to be comfortable attending to several tasks at the same time and to be holistic thinkers. Therefore, these children may find it difficult to meet the expectations of public schools where competition, independence, and assertiveness are generally prized and where abstract problem solving, specific thinking, and performance of discrete tasks usually dominate the curriculum.

Civil rights activity during the 1960's and 1970's and the many problems experienced by Native Americans in schools run by white people caused Congress to pass laws that give Native Americans control over reservation schools and that encourage them to develop curricula that include both Indian cultural values and native language study. The process of returning control of the schools to the tribes began with the Indian Education Act of 1972 and was carried further by the Self-Determination and Assistance Act of 1975. Both the 1979 American Indian Religious Freedom Act and the 1990 Native American Languages Act encouraged self-determination and the preservation of native culture.

In order to help parents train their children to participate in the mainstream culture, many tribal colleges have Head Start programs that not only teach preschool children but also offer instruction in parenting skills. To help non-Indian educators and others understand their culture, several well-known Native Americans developed teaching programs to explain native values. Activist and singer Buffy Sainte-Marie developed the Cradleboard Project, a curriculum that introduces children to Native American ideas and values, and writer and Iroquois oral historian Paula Underwood developed Native American Learning Way, part of the Past is Prologue Educational Program. This program consists of a curriculum that brings Native American ideas into all subjects taught in elementary schools. *Annita Marie Ward*

Core Resources

Additional information on Native American cultural practices can be found in a series of books published by Courage Books of Philadelphia. These books include

Petra Press's *Indians of the Northwest: Traditions, History, Legends, and Life* (1997) and Lisa Sita's *Indians of the Great Plains: Traditions, History, Legends, and Life* (1997), *Indians of the Southwest: Traditions, History, Legends, and Life* (1997), and *Indians of the Northeast: Traditions, History, Legends, and Life* (1997). Franklin Watts of New York published a number of books on specific Indian cultures in the publisher's First Book Series.

See also: Education and American Indians; Indian Education Acts.

Family and socialization: Asian Americans

> **Significance:** Socialization and family relations in Asian American families are often different from what they are in other American families. This may create a generation gap between children, who identify with the forms of behavior and attitudes found in the larger society, and adults. Family styles may also affect the extent to which children socialize with members of other racial and ethnic groups, and they can affect mobility in American society.

The category "Asian American" includes people from a wide variety of national backgrounds, including Cambodian, Chinese, Filipino, Japanese, Korean, Laotian, Hmong, Vietnamese, and various Asian Indian Americans. Generalizations about such a diverse category are likely not to apply to many Asian American groups or individuals. Still, there are some common family traits among the major Asian American groups that can affect socialization. Families in many of the major Asian American groups are usually characterized as authoritarian, other-centered, close-knit, long-lasting, and stable. The authoritarian character of these families means that parents, especially fathers, are seen as authority figures who are to be obeyed with few, if any, questions. Researchers and theorists describe Asian American families as other-centered because family members are expected to put the needs and wishes of others in the family ahead of their own needs and wishes. These families are said to be close-knit because the cultural values of many Asian groups encourage a high degree of emotional intimacy among family members. They are long-lasting because offspring retain these intimate ties to parents and siblings throughout life. They are described as stable both because of the long-lasting nature of family ties and because most Asian groups show divorce rates substantially lower than those of other Americans.

Family Socialization and Individual Well-Being
Anthropologist Francis Hsu, an authority on the Chinese family, has argued that strong kinship ties in Asian American families enable individuals to share problems with other family members. Thus, Hsu maintains, these individuals tend to suffer less anxiety than people in more loosely organized American families. George DeVos, in studies of the Japanese family, has emphasized the importance of strongly established family roles in enabling Asian Americans to adapt to the world around them. DeVos argues that most American families have relatively weak attachments to roles, encouraging their members to be themselves rather than to act out stereotypical roles of father or mother or son or daughter. Roles, though, provide individuals with a sense of identity, so that adhering to roles can actually be a source of psychological comfort and support for individuals.

Psychologist Stanley Sue, one of the foremost experts on Asian American psychology, has argued that patterns of socialization in Asian American families can have both positive and negative consequences for individuals. He

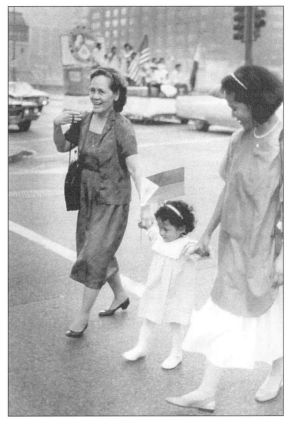

Three generations of a Filipino family take part in a parade. Many Asian American families are very close-knit and dominated by an authoritarian male figure.

maintains that, while research does support the view that relations tend to be close-knit in Asian American families, the very closeness of these families can create problems. This closeness is especially likely to create problems when it interferes with the needs of children to establish a sense of their own identities in the larger American society. Similarly, the strong roles in Asian American families, particularly the authoritarian roles of fathers, may conflict with the ideas and expectations children learn outside the family.

Family Socialization and American Society

Family socialization affects the adaptation of children to their society as well as their psychological well-being. Because children in modern times usually enter the economic and political institutions of their society by means of education, most theories and research on socialization and societal adaptation concentrate on how family socialization affects schooling. Asian cultural traditions, such as Confucianism, are often believed to be passed from parents to children through family socialization. Therefore, psychologist Nathan Caplan and his colleagues maintain that Vietnamese American families teach their children cultural values of hard work and respect for authority, enabling the children to do well in American schools and society.

Sociologists Min Zhou and Carl Bankston III have claimed that the relative success of many new Asian groups in American society is due, in part, to the close, cooperative relations in families. They have also argued that new Asian immigrants often settle in some of the nation's most disadvantaged neighborhoods, so family and community socialization must shield children from the negative influences that surround them. Shielding children from surrounding neighbors of other ethnic or racial backgrounds, however, can often hinder the development of understanding between Asian Americans and members of other groups.

A number of researchers and social workers have pointed out that ethnic gangs have emerged among young people in a number of Asian American groups. It is often argued that the gap between the culture of the parents and the culture of the children makes communication and socialization difficult, leading to inadequate socialization.   *Carl L. Bankston III*

Core Resources

The Mental Health of Asian Americans (San Francisco: Jossey-Bass, 1982), by Stanley Sue and James K. Morishima, includes a chapter on "Understanding the Asian American Family," which summarizes theoretical views on Asian American socialization. Betty Lee Sung's *The Adjustment Experience of Chinese Immigrant Children in New York City* (Staten Island, N.Y.: Center for Migration Studies, 1987) offers a picture of the challenges facing Chinese American children and of the ways in which families seek to meet those challenges. *The Boat People and Achievement in America: A Study of Family Life, Hard Work, and Cultural Values* (Ann Arbor: University of Michigan Press, 1989) presents the view that Southeast Asians help their children adapt to American society by teaching the children traditional cultural values. In *Growing Up American: How Vietnamese Children Adapt to Life in the United States* (New York: Russell Sage, 1998), Min Zhou and Carl L. Bankston III argue that cooperative social relations in Vietnamese families and communities help children adapt to life in the United States. They also look at how cultural gaps between parents and children can lead to problems in socialization.

See also: Asian Indians in the United States; Cambodian Americans; Chinese Americans; Education and Asian Americans; Filipino Americans; Hmong Americans; Japanese Americans; Korean Americans; Vietnamese Americans.

Family and socialization: Latinos

> **Significance:** Family relations and socialization patterns of Latinos affect relations between this group and non-Latinos as well as Latinos' survival and upward mobility in the United States. These patterns also influence intergenerational relations and well-being within Latino families.

The implications of family and socialization among Latinos is especially significant to racial and ethnic relations in the United States because Latinos are among the fastest-growing populations in the nation. The group known as Latinos encompasses numerous subgroups traceable to various regions of the Americas and the Caribbean and a wide range of socioeconomic, cultural, and national backgrounds. Generalizations about such a diverse group therefore will not apply to many groups and individuals who are Latinos. Nonetheless, some common family characteristics and socialization patterns exist among the major Latino groups in the United States: Mexicans, Puerto Ricans, and Cubans. These patterns of commonality are a result of similar historical experiences and colonial conditions, cultural continuity, proximity to or contact with their homelands, and exposure to discrimination. Therefore, although the first Mexicans became Americans through annexation of northern Mexico, Puerto Ricans through their

The family is a very important element in Latino life. Family events, such as this quinceañera celebration marking a girl's fifteenth birthday, sometimes become quite elaborate affairs.

Commonwealth status and political territorial relationship with the United States, and Cubans through their arrival as refugees, each group had to survive and adapt to a dramatically different social, cultural, political, and economic context in the United States. These historical conditions generated common family characteristics and socialization patterns.

Family Characteristics

Although Latino families are in flux, continuing to adapt, families in the major Latino groups can be characterized in terms of familism, extended kin structures, myths of machismo, and biculturalism. "Familism" refers to the priority placed on the family as opposed to individual interests. Family unity is believed to be central to life among many Latino families. In addition to this emphasis on family solidarity, sociologist Maxine Baca Zinn identifies other dimensions of familism among Mexican families regarding family size (demographic familism), multigenerational households (structural familism), and interaction in kinship networks (behavioral familism). These additional dimensions of familism explain the prevalence of extended kin structures among Latino families, which often provide emotional and financial support. Extended family formations also extend to nonrelatives or fictive-kin. The *compadrazgo* system, for example, establishes relations between parents and godparents or coparents, further locating the Latino family within a larger network of support and reciprocity. In addition, *respeto* (respect and support for elders) remains a viable value within the extended family structure. This is an important indicator of multigenera-

tional relations, which is central to the extended family structure.

Extended family structures are also central to generating economic resources among Cubans, in spite of blocked financial opportunities within mainstream markets of the United States. Using these extended family structures, Cuban exiles in the early 1960's generated funds for investment within ethnic enclaves. In this way, kinship relations extended to the communal level, creating ethnic communities and generating upward mobility.

Although popular notions describe Latino families as the epitome of patriarchy, authoritarianism, and machismo, more recent research suggests that Latino families are no more patriarchal than mainstream American families. In fact, Latino families continue to move toward egalitarian familial relations as Latinas continue to achieve higher familial status from their labor force participation and control of the household. Sociologist and legal scholar Alfredo Mirande dispels many myths of Latino masculinity by showing some aspects of Latino male sensitivity, emotional expression, and egalitarian family relations between Chicanos and Chicanas.

Although Latino families in the United States maintain cultural continuity, they undergo a hybridization process, incorporating new cultural forms into their traditional culture to adapt to changing social conditions. Therefore, Latino families are neither equivalent to mainstream American families nor replicas of traditional families in their homelands. For example, Puerto Rican studies professor Hector Carrasquillo describes the innovative strategy of fusing mainland U.S. values and the English language with traditional Puerto Rican culture and the Spanish language. A similar process of hybridization also seems evident among Chicanos in the Southwest.

Socialization and Psychological Well-Being

The complex history of racial and ethnic relations that shaped Latino family characteristics can affect socialization and individual well-being. Social work professors Andres G. Gil and William A. Vega noted the important role of the family in buffering stress associated with immigrant adaptation among Cuban and Nicaraguan families. They showed that low family cohesion was related to parent-child conflicts and poor adolescent self-esteem in the context of acculturation pressures.

Social scientists Kathleen Ethier and Kay Deaux explored the experiences of Hispanic students at two predominantly white Ivy League universities and analyzed the relationships between strength of cultural background, ethnic identification, self-esteem, and perceptions of threat to Hispanic identity within dominant Euro-American institutions. Based on interviews, the researchers found that the majority of Hispanic students felt their ethnic identity, derived from their family socialization, was an important dimension of the self. Strength of ethnic identification was found to buffer perceived threats and to increase collective self-esteem among Hispanic students.

Exploring extended family systems, self-esteem, and support for Hispanic elderly, social work professor Juan J. Paz showed that family support is a major source of positive self-esteem for the elderly. Hispanic elders tend to hold a collective self-identity embedded in the family, and therefore, emotional and social support from the family has positive social psychological outcomes. On the other hand, researchers Robert Strom, Lydia P. Buki, and Shirley K. Strom revealed higher levels of frustration among Spanish-speaking grandparents with the English-speaking younger generations than among bilingual grandparents. This implies that cultural and language departure create negative well-being among the Mexican American elderly. *Michael P. Perez*

Core Resources

Family Ethnicity: Strength in Diversity (Newbury Park, Calif.: Sage, 1993), edited by Harriette Pipes McAdoo, contains "Cuban Americans: From Golden Exiles to Social Undesirables," by Zulema Suarez, a good concise overview of the two major waves of Cuban immigration to the United States and subsequent family formation, and Juan J. Paz's "Support for Hispanic Elderly," which discusses research regarding the importance of family support to the social and psychological well-being of the Hispanic elderly. Alfredo Mirande's *Hombres y Machos: Masculinity and Latino Culture* (Boulder, Colo.: Westview Press, 1997) dispels the myth of machismo by revealing historical and contemporary information about Latino masculinity in terms of sensitivity and emotional expression. *Minority Families in America: A Multicultural Perspective* (2d ed., Upper Saddle River, N.J.: Prentice-Hall, 1998), edited by Ronald L. Taylor, contains Hector Carrasquillo's "The Puerto Rican Family," which addresses the concept of biculturalism in the larger context of the contemporary Puerto Rican experience in the United States; Maxine Baca Zinn's "Adaptation and Continuity in Mexican-Origin Families," a concise discussion of familism; and Lisandro Perez's "Cuban American Families," an overview of Cuban family characteristics in their historical context. Other important studies include

Kathleen Ethier and Kay Deaux's "Hispanics in Ivy: Assessing Identity and Perceived Threat," in *Sex Roles* (22, 7-8, 1990), Andres G. Gil and William A. Vega's "Two Different Worlds: Acculturation Stress and Adaptation Among Cuban and Nicaraguan Families," in *Journal of Social and Personal Relationships* (13, 3, 1996), and Robert Strom, Lydia P. Buki, and Shirley K. Strom's "Intergenerational Perceptions of English Speaking and Spanish Speaking Mexican-American Grandparents," in *International Journal of Aging and Human Development* (45, no. 1, 1997).

See also: Cuban Americans; Latinos in the United States; Puerto Rico.

Fascism in Canada

In Canada, as in several other countries in the world, fascism was largely a phenomenon of the economically destitute 1930's. Fascist organizations appeared and gained limited support, which quickly waned once World War II had begun. The main areas of fascist support in Canada during the 1930's were in the provinces of Quebec, Ontario, Manitoba, and Saskatchewan. Underlying its limited popularity was its message of anti-Semitism, anticommunism, and nationalism. Because of these sentiments, even those who did not belong to a fascist organization and would never have considered joining found fascism less of a threat to Canadian values and society than communism. Anti-Semitic feeling was widespread in Canada during the 1930's.

Fascism among French Canadians was centered in the province of Quebec and was strongly anti-Semitic in character. The leader of the Quebec movement was the charismatic Adrien Arcand. His organization, the National Social Christian Movement, was the most successful fascist movement in Canada during this period, although it still remained outside the mainstream of French Canadian society. Its anti-Semitic and anticommunist values, however, were shared by many in the province.

Fascism also had supporters among Germans and Italians who had emigrated to Canada but still remained unassimilated into Canadian society. Levels of support were never high in either the German or Italian communities, and the movements were dependent on support from Germany and Italy. In the 1920's, Italian consulates in Canada began a campaign promoting fascism. In 1934, the Deutscherbund Canada was created by German diplomats in an effort to disseminate the Nazi message among German-speaking citizens; it would eventually have two thousand members. Once the war began, however, it was suppressed, and in 1940, several hundred German and Italian fascists were arrested and interned for the duration of World War II.

In English-speaking Canada, support for fascism was centered in the cities of Toronto and Winnipeg. In the former, several small fascist organizations, motivated chiefly by anti-Semitism, formed. In 1933, an anti-Semitic display led to a violent clash between Toronto Jews and fascists. In Manitoba, a region of Canada with a history of hostility toward non-British immigrants, the Canadian Nationalist Party formed under the leadership of William Whittaker. Anti-Semitism and anticommunism were important themes in Whittaker's party, which had a swastika surrounded by the Canadian maple leaf as its symbol. Again, however, support for this organization was marginal.

In 1938, to widespread publicity, Arcand and a fascist leader from Ontario announced the merging of their parties into a single body, the National Unity Party, with the motto "Canada for Canadians" and Arcand as leader. A few days later, Nazi Germany absorbed Austria. By the end of the 1930's, with Canadians increasingly alarmed at the prospects of war with fascist Germany, support for fascism dropped. Once the war began, fascist organizations were outlawed, and in 1940, leaders such as Arcand found themselves arrested and interned by the Canadian government. *Steven Hewitt*

See also: Anti-Semitism; European immigration to Canada: 1867-present; French Canadians; Nazism; White supremacist groups.

Federal riot

A riot at Saint Mary's Church in Philadelphia on February 10, 1799, was the direct result of the passage of the Alien and Sedition Acts of 1798. These four laws—the Naturalization Act, the Alien Act, the Alien Enemies Act, and the Sedition Act—had been passed in June and July and sought collectively to limit the rights of immigrants and to silence criticism of the new U.S. government. Two main political factions dominated at the time, the conservative Federalists and the Jeffersonian Republicans. Federalists were mainly the wealthy and established, and Catholics as well as Protestants were among this group. Saint Mary's Church, considered one of the most venerable and well-respected Catholic congregations in the United States, counted many of these Federalists among its members and included both established Anglo-Americans and Irish Americans. Republicans were made up largely of immigrants, including many new Irish immigrants, and these less affluent and newer Americans felt the impact of the Alien and Sedition Acts most sharply. They circulated petitions protesting the acts and

gathered signatures throughout Philadelphia without incident. They intended to present the petitions to Congress.

Four of these immigrant Republicans—James Reynolds, Samuel Cummings, Robert Moore, and William Duane—posted fliers protesting the Alien and Sedition Acts at Saint Mary's, again requesting signatures from the Irish members of the congregation. Following the February 10, 1799, Sunday service at Saint Mary's, a violent confrontation took place between these men and members of the congregation. The four were tried on February 21, 1799, for causing the riot. Saint Mary's Father Leonard Neale, who had accused the men, strongly condemned the actions of the Republicans, while Father Matthew Carr testified that it was a long-honored tradition in Ireland to post notices and seek support for petitions following church services. The jury delivered a verdict of "not guilty" to the charge of causing a riot.

The riot signified a turning point in the early history of intergroup relations in the United States. Although the short-range effect of this conflict was to weaken the Federalist hold within Saint Mary's congregation, the "Irish riot" became a symbol of conflict between an established, dominant group and an incoming immigrant population. Such conflicts would characterize much of U.S. history. *Kathleen Schongar*

See also: Irish Americans; Irish Catholic "race"; Naturalization Act of 1790.

Federally recognized tribes

The term "federally recognized tribe" is a U.S. government designation for an American Indian tribe that has official relations with the United States. These relations have been established in various ways through the years—through treaties (treaty making ended in the late nineteenth century), executive orders, court decrees, and acts of Congress, and through meeting the requirements set forth by the Federal Acknowledgment Program. Federal recognition is both a political and economic issue, as recognized tribes are eligible for federal services that unrecognized tribes cannot receive, such as education, housing, and health benefits.

The Federal Acknowledgment Program (a Bureau of Indian Affairs program) was created in 1978. The Federal Acknowledgment Program established criteria and procedures through which unrecognized tribes could attempt to attain recognized status. The creation of a federal recognition process was hailed a victory by some American Indians, but others countered that the requirements are unnecessarily complex, even unfulfillable. Among the criteria is proof of continuous existence as a tribe; the tribe also must have a governing body, be governed by a constitution or similar document, and have membership criteria and a roll of current members.

In the 1950's a government policy known as termination successfully urged many tribes to disband. Subsequently, some terminated tribes attempted to regain recognized tribal status; the regaining of tribal status by the Menominees was the first major success. (Terminated tribes are not eligible for recognition through the Federal Acknowledgment Program.) In 1991 there were 510 federally recognized tribes; in mid-1994 the number had grown to 543. Some of these groups are very small; for example, there are some two hundred Alaskan village groups. *McCrea Adams*

See also: Indian Reorganization Act; Status Indians; Termination Resolution.

Fifteen Principles

In 1983, in the midst of federal constitutional negotiations, the province of Quebec established a legal framework to guide its relationships with the Inuit and Indian residents of Quebec. Known as the Fifteen Principles, the policy statement affirmed that the province of Quebec accepted native claims to self-determination with respect to culture, education, language, and economic development. It further acknowledged that natives are entitled to certain aboriginal rights and land claims (left to be determined by future negotiations). Finally, the Fifteen Principles recognized that those aboriginal rights applied equally to men and women.

The Fifteen Principles were adopted, in large part, to bolster the claim by the ruling Parti Québécois that Quebec is a distinct and sovereign nation either within or apart from Canada. If this was to be the case, Quebec could not argue, as it had previously, that the federal government bore sole responsibility for natives living within the borders of Quebec. In fact, it was Quebec's earlier insistence that the federal government must absorb all the costs of native administration that led to the 1939 Supreme Court decision that for legal purposes Inuit were to be regarded as Indians as specified in the British North America Act of 1867. By adopting the Fifteen Principles, Quebec attempted to place itself on equal footing with the Canadian government. *Pamela R. Stern*

See also: Indian Act of 1876; Indian Act of 1951; Indian Act of 1989; Indian-white relations: Canada; Meech Lake Accord; Proclamation of 1763; Treaties and agreements with Indians: Canada.

Fifteenth Amendment

The Fifteenth Amendment to the U.S. Constitution, adopted in 1869 and ratified in 1870, stated that the right to vote could not be denied to any citizen "on account of race, color, or previous condition of servitude." The purpose of the amendment was to extend the franchise to the African American men who had been freed from slavery as a result of the Civil War. At the time, women were not regarded as citizens and were therefore not covered by the measure. The amendment marked a continuation of the program of the Republican Party to provide political rights for black men after the defeat of the Confederacy. The Thirteenth Amendment had ended slavery, and the Fourteenth Amendment had provided civil rights to all citizens born or naturalized in the United States. These amendments, however, had not ensured that black men could vote throughout the United States. To accomplish that end, the Republicans in Congress, in a lame-duck Congress that met in early 1869, decided that ensuring the right to vote would both carry on the moral impetus of Reconstruction (1863-1877) and act to offset any political comeback of the antiblack Democratic Party.

A constitutional amendment would have the additional benefit, as the Republicans saw it, of providing a clear legal basis for enforcement of voting rights in the South. In its language, the amendment did not ensure that blacks could hold public positions nor did it rule out such barriers to voting as literacy tests or property requirements. Nonetheless, it represented a clear forward step for African Americans and offered the promise of greater participation in elections and the operations of government.

The ratification process broke down along the existing party alignments of the Reconstruction era. Republicans favored the measure and Democrats resisted it in the state legislatures that addressed ratification. It required vigorous campaigning, especially in such key states as Ohio, to achieve approval from the requisite number of states by March, 1870.

Despite its place in the U.S. Constitution, the Fifteenth Amendment did not prevent southerners from excluding African Americans from the political process at the end of the nineteenth century. With a political stalemate between Republicans and Democrats in Washington, enforcement of the amendment proved difficult. Federal courts did not encourage a broad interpretation of the amendment. In 1889-1890, the Republicans endeavored to strengthen federal legislation to ensure fair elections in the South, but Democrats defeated their efforts. When the Democrats regained control of the White House and both branches of Congress in 1893-1895, they repealed the existing legislation that gave the government authority over elections. As a result, discriminatory practices kept African Americans from voting in many parts of the South for three-quarters of a century.

In the middle of the twentieth century with the rise of the Civil Rights movement, efforts resumed to revive the Fifteenth Amendment. The Voting Rights Act of 1965 enabled blacks to enter the political process in large numbers and, in so doing, to redeem the unfulfilled promise that the framers of the Fifteenth Amendment had originally envisioned.   *Lewis L. Gould*

See also: Civil Rights movement; Fourteenth Amendment; Grandfather clauses; Jim Crow laws; Literacy tests; Poll tax; Thirteenth Amendment; Voting Rights Act of 1965.

Filipino Americans

> **Significance:** Filipino Americans are the second-largest Asian American group in the United States after the Chinese Americans, and substantial numbers of Filipino immigrants also live in a few parts of Canada such as Toronto. Although several large Filipino American communities exist, notably in California and Hawaii, members of this group can be found throughout the North American continent, often thoroughly integrated into American neighborhoods and workplaces.

The term "Filipino" refers to someone who comes from the Philippines, or whose ancestors are from the Philippines, a nation consisting of a cluster of islands located across the China Sea from mainland Southeast Asia. The Philippines has close ties to the United States because it was a U.S. possession or territory from 1898 to 1946. The United States established English as the language of instruction in high schools and colleges in the Philippines, and Filipinos have long been familiar with American movies and other media. Filipinos began settling in North America soon after the Philippines became part of the United States, and the numbers of Filipino Americans began to increase greatly in the late 1960's.

History of Filipino American Settlement
Filipino settlement in North America falls into three major periods. The first period, from 1906 to the beginning of World War II in 1941, resulted from the U.S. demand for cheap agricultural labor. Sugar plantations dominated the economy of Hawaii early in the twentieth century, and plantation owners were interested in finding hardworking field hands who would work for low

wages. The Hawaii Sugar Planters Association began recruiting in the Philippines, and by 1946, the association had brought more than a quarter of a million Filipinos to Hawaii. California, which also had a need for seasonal agricultural workers, was the home of more than thirty-one thousand of the forty-six thousand Filipinos living on the mainland in 1940. Filipino Americans continue to make up part of the migrant farm labor force of California and other western states, but the numbers of migrant Filipino workers are steadily decreasing.

The second migration period began in 1946, when the Philippines became politically independent of the United States. Large U.S. military bases had been established in the Philippines, and many of the Filipinos admitted to the United States were women married to American servicemen. At the same time, Filipinos who had become naturalized American citizens after the war were able to petition to have family members enter the United States. Because of these two factors, most immigrants in this period came as a result of marriage or family connections.

The United States maintained military bases in the Philippines until 1991, so Filipinos who married U.S. military personnel continued to arrive in the United States. Another form of migration through marriage is the phenomenon of mail-order brides, women who meet and marry American men through correspondence. In the 1990's, approximately nineteen thousand mail-order brides were leaving the Philippines each year to join husbands and fiancés abroad, with the United States as the primary destination. In 1997, social scientist Concepcion Montoya identified Filipina mail-order brides, who often establish social networks among themselves, as a rapidly emerging American community.

The third migration period began in 1965, when the United States passed a new immigration law that ended the discrimination against Asians present in all previous immigration laws. The result was a rapid growth in the Asian American population in general and in the Filipino American population in particular. The number of Filipinos living in the United States grew by roughly 100 percent in each ten-year period from 1960 to 1990: from 176,000 in the census of 1960 to 343,000 in that of 1970, to 775,000 in 1980, to more than 1,400,000 in the 1990 census.

The third period of Filipino immigration differs greatly from the earlier periods. Although immigrants before 1965 were mostly laborers from the rural Philippines, immigrants after 1965 tended to be highly educated professionals (such as doctors, nurses, teachers, and engineers), and they often came from cities. Migration to the United States became a goal for many Filipino professionals because economic opportunities were much greater in the United States. During the 1970's, one out of every five graduates of nursing schools in the Philippines left for the United States, and the majority of those nurses did not return to the Philippines. This may have created "brain drain" problems for the Philippines, because it lost many of its medical professionals, executives, and technicians to the United States, but this migration has been a benefit to the American economy. Filipino doctors and nurses are on the staffs of many U.S. hospitals, and teachers from the Philippines are employed in many U.S. schools.

Filipinos in American Society

By 1990, more than 1.4 million people in the United States identified themselves as Filipino Americans. About 740,000 of these Filipino

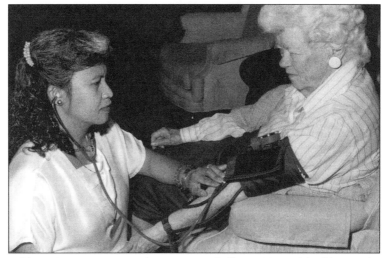

A Filipino American nurse tends a patient in California. Many of the Filipinos who immigrated to the United States after 1965 were highly trained professionals.

Americans lived in California, and 170,000 members of this group lived in Hawaii. The Chicago area is also home to a fairly large number of Filipinos.

Most Filipino Americans are immigrants. In 1990, of all Filipinos in the United States, 64 percent were foreign-born and almost one-third had arrived during the previous decade. Numbers of foreign-born Filipinos increased even more during the 1990's. From 1990 to March, 1997, according to U.S. Census Bureau estimates, the number of foreign-born Filipino Americans grew from 913,723 to 1,132,000.

Women outnumber men among foreign-born Filipinos, largely because marriage to U.S. citizens has continued to be a major source of migration from the Philippines. In 1990, women made up 57 percent of all foreign-born Filipino Americans and almost 60 percent of foreign-born Filipino Americans who had arrived during the 1980's.

The fact that professionals, especially medical profes-

sionals, have been such a large part of the third wave of immigrants has meant that many Filipino Americans hold middle-class jobs. A majority of employed Filipinos in the United States (55 percent) held white-collar jobs in 1990. Almost one out of every four employed Filipino Americans over the age of sixteen worked in health services. By contrast, fewer than one out of every ten employed Americans of all backgrounds worked in hospitals or in health-related jobs in that year.

The professional specialization of so many Filipino Americans tends to make them a relatively prosperous group. The median household income of Filipino Americans in 1990 was $43,780, compared with $30,056 among Americans in general. Further, although 10 percent of all American families lived below the poverty level in 1990, only slightly more than 5 percent of Filipino families in the United States lived in poverty.

Many Filipino Americans, especially the early agricultural laborers in California, experienced discrimination.

Year of Entry into the United States and Citizenship Status of Filipino Americans, 1990

Year of Entry	Number	Percent of all Filipino Americans	Percent who are U.S. Citizens
Born in U.S.	505,988	35.6	100.0
Arrived before 1980	465,358	32.8	80.6
Arrived 1980-1990	448,365	31.6	26.0
Total	1,419,711	100.0	71.3

Source: U.S. Bureau of the Census, *1990 Census of Population and Housing, Asians and Pacific Islanders in the United States.* Washington, D.C.: U.S. Government Printing Office.

However, contemporary Filipinos usually report relatively few problems in their relations with members of other racial and ethnic groups. Familiarity with the English language and with mainstream American culture, high levels of marriage with white and black Americans, and a concentration in skilled occupations and white-collar professions tend to help Filipino Americans in interethnic relations.

One reflection of the high degree of integration of Filipino Americans into American society is the high percentage of foreign-born Filipino Americans who take on U.S. citizenship. More than one-fourth of the Filipinos who arrived in the United States during the 1980's had been naturalized as citizens by 1990. More than 80 percent of those who had arrived before 1980 had become citizens. By contrast, fewer than 15 percent of all people who had immigrated to the United States in the 1980's had become citizens, and only 61 percent of foreign-born people who had immigrated before 1980 had become citizens.   *Carl L. Bankston III*

Core Resources
Yen Le Espiritu's *Filipino American Lives* (Philadelphia: Temple University Press, 1995) presents the narratives of thirteen Filipino Americans who tell the stories of their lives. *Filipino Americans: Transformation and Identity* (Thousand Oaks, Calif.: Sage Publications, 1997), edited by Maria P. P. Root, is a collection of essays that consider immigration from the Philippines to the United States, Filipino American communities and community institutions, mixed-heritage Filipino Americans, and Filipina mail-order brides in the United States. Luciano Mangiafico's *Contemporary American Immigrants: Patterns of Filipino, Korean, and Chinese Settlement in the United States* (New York: Praeger, 1988) describes major waves of migration, location of large communities of these three ethnic groups, and contemporary social conditions of the groups.

See also: Filipino Canadians; Filipino Veterans' movement; Immigration and Nationality Act of 1965.

Filipino Veterans' movement

In 1941, after the beginning of World War II, United States president Franklin D. Roosevelt signed an order to bring draftees and volunteers in the Philippines, then under U.S. rule, into the U.S. Army. The order promised full veterans' benefits to all Filipinos who served. In 1942, the U.S. Congress promised American citizenship to all Filipino soldiers who wanted to apply after the war. However, in 1946, when the war was over, the U.S. Congress voted to deny both veterans' benefits and citizenship to Filipino veterans of the U.S. military.

After years of lobbying by Filipinos, in 1990, Congress voted to grant U.S. citizenship to the veterans. However, they still did not have access to such normal veterans' benefits as pensions, home loan guarantees, and medical assistance. In 1997, Congress began to consider a Filipino veterans' equity bill. Of the 240,000 Filipinos who served in the U.S. military, 70,000 were still alive and about half of the survivors were living in the United States. These former soldiers organized demonstrations in cities around the United States, especially Los Angeles and Washington, D.C., during 1997 and 1998 to urge passage of the equity bill.   *Carl L. Bankston III*

See also: Filipino Americans; Military and racial/ethnic relations.

Fish-ins

During the 1960's, American Indians in the Pacific Northwest began to stage fish-ins to protest restrictions on their fishing rights, especially within the states of Washington, Oregon, and Idaho. In turn, sports fishers' groups, commercial fishing operations, and canneries pressured the state governments to get American Indians off the rivers. Controversies over fishing rights stemmed from treaties negotiated with various Pacific Northwest tribes in 1854 and 1855. In those treaties, tribes gave up claim to vast areas of land but specifically preserved fishing rights along waterways ceded to the federal government. Those treaties guaranteed to Indians "the right of taking fish, at all usual and accustomed grounds and stations . . . in common with all citizens of the Territory."

Almost from the start, the states ignored the treaty provisions, and by the 1930's, the states openly restricted Indian subsistence and commercial fishing. Some tribes challenged the states; however, they had no legal success. During the next two decades, state restrictions increased, particularly in the state of Washington, and although some cases went to court, restrictions on Indian fishing were upheld.

Finally, in the 1960's, Indian nations began to push for economic development, and tribes began to demand their treaty rights. In the Pacific Northwest, the tribes openly challenged the states' ability to exert regulatory authority over matters negotiated in treaties between the federal government and tribal nations. The state of Washington responded by issuing a series of orders forbidding Indian fishing, and in 1964, Washington set aside the treaty guarantees.

Indians from various affected tribes attempted to channel their energies in a unified front and formed the

Survival of American Indians Association in 1964. This organization began a series of actions designed to assert their rights. One important strategy was to engage in night fishing in restricted areas. Washington aggressively policed night fishing, and it confiscated boats, nets, and motors, rammed fishing boats, and prosecuted lawbreakers.

The most dramatic and effective protests sponsored by the Indian association were fish-ins. These were highly publicized events, well attended by media, in which Indian people, including many women and children, would assert their treaty rights and fish, despite state restrictions. The state response was aggressive: Often large numbers of game wardens and police swarmed over the protesters and made many arrests. The media documented these incidents, and the fish-ins attracted national attention and even celebrity participants, including actors and entertainers such as Marlon Brando, Jane Fonda, and Dick Gregory. As more Indians were arrested, various church organizations, the American Civil Liberties Union, and prominent lawyers began to provide legal assistance, and this, in turn, increased media coverage.

In 1970, the federal government brought suit to ensure that the states honored the treaties and allowed American Indians a fair harvest of fish. U.S. District Court judge George Boldt sent shockwaves through the Pacific Northwest when he ruled in favor of Indian fishing rights in *United States v. Washington* (1974) and

determined that the treaties entitled the Indians to half the fish passing through the waters.

This decision was challenged but remained in force and ultimately allowed many tribes to develop successful economic ventures such as canneries, fish hatcheries, and aquaculture programs. The fish-ins also produced a number of Indian activists who went on to participate in the early years of the American Indian Movement, including Dino Butler, Sid Mills, Janet McCloud, Joseph Stuntz Killsright, and Leonard Peltier.   *Carole A. Barrett*

See also: American Indian activism; American Indian Movement; American Indians in the justice system; Peltier killings; Treaties and agreements with Indians: United States; Water rights.

Foreign professionals

Since the beginning of the twentieth century, U.S. immigration legislation has been largely influenced by the nation's need for labor. Although earlier laws typically involved unskilled workers, legislation in the 1990's began to focus on the admittance of foreign professionals. Those who advocate increasing the number of specialty visas are primarily in, but not limited to, the health care and high-tech fields. They argue that not enough qualified people are available in the United States. To support their position, they cite the shortage in medical personnel, claiming that many rural and inner-city health care delivery systems would have collapsed if it had not been for foreign medical professionals who filled these positions. Proponents also say that U.S.-born professionals do not work as hard and are much more expensive than foreign professionals. Opponents counter that many qualified individuals are available, but companies prefer to terminate middle-aged, more expensive employees and hire foreign professionals. In addition, opponents say that these companies are creating sweatshops by not providing foreign professionals with the proper wages and benefits.

Proponents argue that by hiring foreign professionals, businesses become more competitive, have greater flexibility in reducing or augmenting the size of the workforce, and benefit from the best foreign talent; this increased competitiveness results in ad-

Three Yakima Indians prepare to defend their right to fish in the Columbia River against the state of Washington, which wanted them to buy licenses. In the 1960's, many Indians staged fish-ins to protect their treaty rights to fish in Pacific Northwestern waters.

ditional jobs and a stronger U.S. economy. For example, at Sun Microsystems, more than half of its twenty thousand employees are working on technology developed by foreign professionals who first entered on temporary visas.

To hire a foreign professional, organizations are required to demonstrate to the U.S. Department of Labor that the foreigner being hired is not taking a job that could be filled by an American citizen. Managers are highly critical of this procedure because it not only decreases organizational efficiency but also makes the U.S. Department of Labor the personnel manager of an organization. Another option that has been suggested is to tax organizations that use foreign professionals; however, organizations have been critical of this idea because it negatively affects efficiency and profits.

Two other issues—education and the phenomenon called brain drain—also come to the forefront in discussions concerning foreign professionals. As long as U.S. companies and facilities are able to hire foreign professionals cheaply, the American educational system will not develop adequate training facilities in those areas, making the United States dependent on overseas talent. In addition, the recruiting of highly educated or skilled

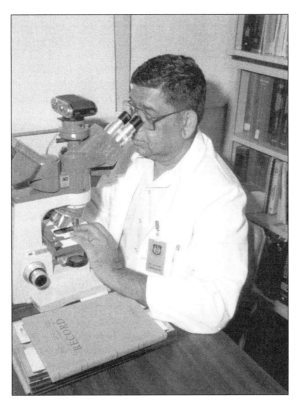

Foreign professionals such as this Asian Indian doctor have provided valuable services to the United States.

professionals from other countries by U.S. companies produces a phenomenon called brain drain—a situation in which a country loses its best and brightest to another country that can offer these people better economic opportunities. No country can afford such a loss of educated talent, and many are setting up barriers to leaving. This may result in a diminished ability to recruit foreign professionals.   *Arthur W. Helweg*

See also: Brain drain; Immigration and emigration.

Fourteenth Amendment

> **Significance:** A definition of citizenship designed for former slaves, the Fourteenth Amendment provides protection against state violations of civil rights that has become crucial to all citizens of the United States.

The Fourteenth Amendment to the U.S. Constitution, ratified by Congress in 1868, was part of the plan for Reconstruction following the Civil War (1861-1865) and was formulated by the Republican majority in the Thirty-ninth Congress. Before Congress met in December, 1865, President Andrew Johnson had authorized the restoration of white self-government in the former Confederate states, and the congressmen and senators from those states waited in Washington to be seated in Congress. The abolition of slavery had destroyed the old compromise under which five slaves counted as three free persons in apportioning representation in the House and the electoral college, and the Republicans wanted to make sure that the South did not add to its numbers in the House and thus profit from rebellion.

Between December, 1865, and May, 1866, the Republicans attempted to hammer out a program that would accomplish their purposes in the South, unite members of their party in Congress, and appeal to northern voters. Given the diversity of opinion within the party, this undertaking proved to be difficult. Radical Republicans wanted African American suffrage, permanent political proscription, and confiscation of the property of ex-Confederates. Some maintained they were authorized in these actions by the Thirteenth Amendment, which, they believed, gave Congress the power to abolish the "vestiges of slavery." Moderate Republicans, on the other hand, feared political repercussions from African American suffrage, as such a requirement would result in beginning the Reconstruction process over again. Many moderates also believed that an additional amendment to the Constitution was needed to provide precise authority for Congress to enact civil rights legislation.

From deliberations of the joint committee and debate on the floor of the House came the Fourteenth Amendment. Many Republicans believed that the proposal was in the nature of a peace treaty, although this view was not explicitly stated. If the South accepted the amendment, the southern states were to be readmitted and their senators and representatives seated in Congress; in other words, Reconstruction would end. Republicans presented a united front during the final vote as a matter of party policy. Because the amendment was an obvious compromise between radicals and moderates, it was too strong for some and too weak for others.

The Amendment

The Fourteenth Amendment became the most important addition to the Constitution since the Bill of Rights had been adopted in 1791. It contains five sections:

Section 1, the first constitutional definition of citizenship, states that all persons born or naturalized in the United States are citizens of the United States and of the state in which they reside. It includes limits on the power of states, by providing that no state may abridge the privileges and immunities of citizens, deprive any person of life, liberty, or property without due process of law, or deny to any person within its jurisdiction the equal protection of law. This section was intended to guarantee African Americans the rights of citizenship, although the amendment's framers did not define exactly which rights were included. Nor did they define "state action" to specify whether the term meant only official acts of state government or the actions of individuals functioning privately with state approval.

The courts later interpreted the due process clause to extend the rights of the accused listed in the Bill of Rights, which had applied only to the federal government, to the states. They expanded the notion of equal protection to include other categories, such as sex and disability, as well as race. They also interpreted the word "person" to include corporations as legal persons; under this interpretation, corporations found protection from much state regulation.

Section 2 gives a new formula of representation in place of the old three-fifths compromise of the Constitution, under which five slaves were counted as equal to three free persons in determining a state's representation in the House of Representatives and the electoral college. All persons in a state were to be counted for representation, but if a state should disfranchise any of its adult male citizens, except for participation in rebellion or any other crime, the basis of its representation would be reduced proportionately. While not guaranteeing suffrage to African Americans, this provision threatened the South with a loss of representation should black males be denied the vote.

Section 3 declares that no person who has ever taken an oath to support the Constitution (which included all who had been in the military service or held state or national office before 1860) and has then participated in the rebellion can be a senator or representative or hold any civil or military office, national or state. This disability could be removed only by a two-thirds vote of both houses of Congress. This section took away the pardoning power of the president, which congressional Republicans believed Andrew Johnson used too generously.

Section 4 validates the debt of the United States, voids all debts incurred to support rebellion, and invalidates all claims for compensation for emancipated slaves.

Section 5 gives Congress authority to pass legislation to enforce the provisions of the Fourteenth Amendment.

The correspondence and speeches of those who framed the Fourteenth Amendment do not support any theories of economic conspiracy or ulterior motives. The framers desired to protect the former slaves and boost Republicanism in the South by barring old Confederates from returning to Congress and the electoral college with increased voting strength. They hoped to do this without threatening the federal system or unduly upsetting the relationship between the central government and the states. At the same time, Republicans wanted to unify their party and project a popular issue for the approaching electoral contest against Andrew Johnson.

William J. Cooper, Jr., updated by Mary Welek Atwell

Core Resources

Michael Les Benedict's *A Compromise of Principle: Congressional Republicans and Reconstruction, 1863-1869* (New York: W. W. Norton, 1974) emphasizes the Republicans' concern that the Fourteenth Amendment maintain the role of the states in the federal system. LaWanda Cox and John H. Cox's *Politics, Principle, and Prejudice: Dilemma of Reconstruction America, 1865-1866* (New York: Free Press, 1963) posits that civil rights, rather than merely partisan politics, was the central issue during Reconstruction. Harold M. Hyman and William Wiecek's *Equal Justice Under Law: Constitutional Development, 1835-1875* (New York: Harper & Row, 1982) includes a thorough discussion of the Fourteenth Amendment as a logical and necessary extension of the Thirteenth Amendment. Donald E. Lively's *The Constitution and Race* (New York: Praeger, 1992) focuses on the association of attitudes toward race and constitutional interpretation.

See also: Civil Rights Acts of 1866-1875; Emancipation Proclamation; Freedmen's Bureau; Reconstruction; Thirteenth Amendment.

Francophone

The term "francophone" is of relatively recent coinage. Its first attested use was in 1949 in French. Its literal meaning is "one who speaks French." In this original use, francophone referred both to native speakers of French and to others who had learned to speak French fluently. Canada has officially been a bilingual country since the British North America Act of 1867 created Canada as an independent country, and more than 90 percent of Canadians consider either English or French to be their native language. By the 1960's, both native speakers of French and English in Canada began to use the terms "francophone" and "anglophone" to identify respectively native speakers of French and English. This modern usage of these words was important because it demonstrated to Canadians that their commitment to Canada was perfectly compatible with their love of their ethnic and linguistic heritages in a multicultural and bilingual country. Federal laws that recognized French and English as the official languages of Canada both in theory and in daily practice helped to preserve and protect linguistic diversity and equality in such a diverse country as Canada.   *Edmund J. Campion*

See also: Anglophone; Bilingualism in Canada; French Canadians; Official Languages Act.

Frank, Leo, lynching

In 1913, Leo Frank, a Jew born in Texas in 1884, was the superintendent of a pencil factory in Atlanta, Georgia. When one of his employees, a thirteen-year-old gentile girl named Mary Phagan, was murdered, Frank was accused of the crime. Credible evidence pointed to an African American janitor, Jim Conley, as the likely killer, but anti-Semitic passions outweighed the racial tensions of the time. Frank was tried, convicted, and given the death penalty. Newspapers and politicians used strident anti-Jewish stereotyping and bigotry to arouse public opinion against Frank. When Georgia governor John M. Slaton became doubtful about the verdict, he commuted Frank's sentence to life in prison. Outraged at Slaton's action, a group of armed men attacked the executive mansion. On August 16, 1915, a mob stormed the prison where Frank was being held and rushed him away to exact their own vengeance. A few hours later, on August 17, 1915, Frank was lynched. In 1984, Frank received a posthumous pardon from the state of Georgia. His well-publicized lynching was one of the most sensational and controversial examples of mob lawlessness and anti-Semitism during the early years of the twentieth century.
Lewis L. Gould

See also: Anti-Defamation League; Anti-Semitism; Jewish Americans; Lynchings.

Free African Society

> **Significance:** The Free African Society was the first major secular institution with a mission to aid African Americans.

Both the origins of the Free African Society and the long-term repercussions of its founding form an essential part of the religious history of African Americans. The original organization itself was of short duration: About seven years after it was organized in 1787, it disappeared as a formal body. In its immediate wake, however, closely related institutions emerged that tried to take over its proclaimed mission.

Generally speaking, prior to the 1790's people of African slave origins who managed to obtain their individual freedom had only one option if they wished to practice Christianity: association, as subordinate parishioners, in an existing white-run church. Several churches in the American colonies before independence, including the Quakers and Methodists, had tried to identify their religious cause with that of the black victims of slavery.

Richard Allen

Richard Allen, born in 1760 as a slave whose family belonged to Pennsylvania's then attorney general, Benjamin Chew, was destined to become one of the earliest religious leaders of the black segment of the American Methodist Church. As a youth, Allen gained extensive experience with Methodist teachings after his family was separated on the auction block in Dover, Delaware. Allen was encouraged by his second owner, Master Stokeley, to espouse the religious teachings of the itinerant American Methodist preacher Freeborn Garrettson. Allen's conversion to Methodism was rewarded when Stokeley freed him at age twenty to follow the calling of religion. His freedom came just as the Revolutionary War ended.

For six years, Allen worked under the influence of Methodist evangelist Benjamin Abbott and the Reverend (later Bishop) Richard Whatcoat, with whom he traveled on an extensive preaching circuit. Allen's writings refer to Whatcoat as his "father in Israel." With Whatcoat's encouragement, Allen accepted an invitation from the Methodist elder in Philadelphia to return to his birthplace to become a preacher. At that time, Philadelphia's religious environment seemed to be dominated by the Episcopal Church. This church had been active since 1758 in extending its ministry to African Americans. It was St. George's Methodist Episcopal Church, however, that, in the 1780's, had drawn the largest number of former slaves to its rolls. Once the circumstances of blacks' second-class status became clear to Allen, he decided that his leadership mission should be specifically dedicated to the needs of his people. Within a short time, he joined another African American, Absalom Jones, in founding what was originally intended to be more of a secular movement than a formal denominational movement: the Free African Society.

Absalom Jones
Absalom Jones was older than Allen and had a different set of life experiences. Born a slave in Delaware in 1746, Jones served for more than twenty years in his master's store in Philadelphia. He earned enough money to purchase his wife's freedom, to build his own home, and finally, in 1784, to purchase his own freedom. He continued to work for his former master for wages and bought and managed two houses for additional income. His success earned for him great respect among other free blacks and opened the way for him to serve as lay leader representing the African American membership of St. George's Methodist Episcopal Church.

Traditional accounts of Jones's role in the founding of the Free African Society assert that, when Jones refused to comply with the announcement of St. George's sexton that African American parishioners should give up their usual seats among the white congregation and move to the upper gallery, he was supported by Richard Allen, in particular. The two then agreed that the only way African Americans could worship in an environment that responded to their social, as well as religious, needs would be to be found an all-black congregation. Some sources suggest that Jones's reaction to the reseating order was the crowning blow, and that Allen previously had tried to organize several fellow black parishioners, including Doras Giddings, William White, and Jones, to support his idea of a separate congregation, only to have the idea rejected by the church elders.

Organization Goals
Whatever the specific stimulus for Allen's and Jones's actions in 1787, they announced publicly that their newly declared movement would not only serve the black community's religious needs as a nondenominational congregation but also function as a benevolent mutual aid organization. The latter goal involved plans to collect funds (through membership fees) to assist the sick, orphans, and widows in the African American community. Other secular social assistance aims included enforcement of a code of temperance, propriety, and fidelity in marriage. It is significant that a number of the early members of the Free African Society came to it from the

rolls of other Protestant churches, not only St. George's Methodist Episcopal congregation.

The dual nature of the organization's goals soon led to divisions in the politics of leadership. Apparently, it was Allen who wanted to use the breakaway from St. George's as a first step in founding a specifically black Methodist church. Others wished to emphasize the Free African Society's nondenominational character and pursue mainly social and moral aid services. Within two years, therefore, Allen resigned his membership, going on to found, in July, 1794, the Bethel African Methodist Episcopal Church. Although this move clearly marked the beginnings of a specifically African American church with a defined denominational status, Allen's efforts for many years continued to be directed at social and economic self-help projects for African Americans, irrespective of their formal religious orientation.

By 1804, Allen was involved in founding a group whose name reflected its basic social reform goals: the Society of Free People of Color for Promoting the Instruction and School Education of Children of African Descent. Another of Allen's efforts came in 1830, when Allen, then seventy years of age, involved his church in the Free Produce Society in Philadelphia. This group raised money to buy goods grown only by nonslave labor to redistribute to poor African Americans. It also tried to organize active boycotts against the marketing and purchase of goods produced by slave-owning farmers, thus providing an early model for the grassroots organizations aimed at social and political goals that would become familiar to African Americans in the mid-twentieth century.

The Free African Society passed through several short but key stages both before and after Richard Allen's decision to remove himself from active membership. One focal point was the group's early association with the prominent medical doctor and philanthropist Benjamin Rush. Rush helped the Free African Society to draft a document involving articles of faith that were meant to be general enough to include the essential religious principles of any Christian church. When the organization adopted these tenets, in 1791, its status as a religious congregation generally was recognized by members and outsiders alike. More and more, its close relationship with the Episcopal Church (first demonstrated by its "friendly adoption" by the Reverend Joseph Pilmore and the white membership of St. Paul's Church in Philadelphia) determined its future denominational status. After 1795, the Free African Society per se had been superseded by a new church built by a committee sparked by Absalom Jones: the African Methodist Episcopal Church. This fact did not, however, prevent those who had been associated with the Free African Society's origins from integrating its strong social and moral reform program with the religious principles that marked the emergence of the first all-black Christian congregations in the United States by the end of the 1790's.

Byron D. Cannon

Core Resources
Carol V. R. George's *Segregated Sabbaths: Richard Allen and the Emergence of Independent Black Churches, 1760-1840* (New York: Oxford University Press, 1973) includes discussion of the African American churches' eventual abolitionist activities. Mwalimi I. Mwadilitu's *Richard Allen: The First Exemplar of African American Education* (New York: ECA Associates, 1985) focuses on the career of Richard Allen, including his functions after 1816 as the first bishop of the African Methodist Episcopal Church.

See also: African American Baptist Church; AME Church; AME Zion Churches; American Anti-Slavery Society; Black church; Black codes; *Liberator, The*; Pennsylvania Society for the Abolition of Slavery.

Free blacks

In 1860, an estimated 500,000 free people of African ancestry resided in the United States; of these, approximately half lived in the slaveholding South. Most of these free blacks were former slaves who had purchased their freedom or were freed in their masters' wills, but a significant minority were freeborn. Their experiences varied by region; those in the northern states, although limited in economic opportunity, enjoyed greater political and social freedom than their counterparts in the South, where demand for black labor was greater but free blacks were regarded with suspicion. The majority of free blacks lived in extreme poverty; however, a small but significant number achieved modest prosperity and a few attained substantial wealth, in some instances purchasing plantations and becoming slaveholders.

Free African Americans of the antebellum period exerted profound influence upon black society in the post-slavery United States. The abolitionist rhetoric of former slaves such as Frederick Douglass and Samuel Ringgold Ward influenced later generations of black activists, and the activities of free southern blacks set precedents for race relations and relations among African Americans after emancipation. The political and legal restrictions placed on free blacks by fearful southern whites in the antebellum period provided a blueprint for racial oppression in the South during the era of segregation.

Michael H. Burchett

See also: African Americans in the Civil War; Slavery: history.

Free-Soil Party

As the Whig Party disintegrated, the Free-Soil Party was one of the factions that filled the political vacuum; in time Free-Soil Party members helped to form the Republican Party. In 1846, Representative David Wilmot introduced a measure to prohibit slavery in territories obtained as a result of the Mexican-American War, and almost immediately the political parties divided on the matter. Uniting with the Liberty Party and antislavery Whigs, the antislavery "barnburners" formed the Free-Soil Party, which nominated Martin Van Buren for the presidency in 1848. He did not obtain a single electoral vote, but he won 291,000 popular votes in the North and Midwest. The election was won by Zachary Taylor, a hero of the Mexican-American War, who refused to state his political positions.

The Free-Soilers next formed the "Free Democracy of the United States," which held a convention in 1852 during which it nominated John Hale for the presidency on the platform of "Free Soil, Free Speech, Free Labor, and Free Men." The Democratic nominee, Franklin Pierce, who favored the Compromise of 1850, won the election.

The nation seemed to want compromise and avoidance of war. This time the Free-Soil candidate received only 156,000 presidential votes, and the party seemed to have lost influence.

Even so, the antislavery forces recovered, as antagonisms between the sections intensified. War actually erupted in Kansas, as the two groups contested for control of the territory. In July, 1854, antislavery elements came together to form the Republican Party. Free-Soilers filtered into the Republican ranks and were very much in evidence at the party's 1856 convention, which nominated John C. Frémont for the presidency. With this, the Free-Soil Party dissolved.   *Robert Sobel*

See also: Abolition; Compromise of 1850; Slavery: history.

Freedmen's Bureau

> **Significance:** The Freedmen's Bureau was established by the federal government to assist newly freed African Americans in making the transition from slavery to freedom.

On March 3, 1865, Congress created the Freedmen's Bureau, a temporary agency within the War Department. The bureau, also known as the United States Bureau of Refugees, Freedmen, and Abandoned Lands, was administered by General Oliver Otis Howard from 1865 until it was dismantled by Congress in 1872. The primary objective of the Freedmen's Bureau was to help newly freed African Americans to function as free men, women, and children. In order to achieve this goal, the bureau was expected to assume responsibility for all matters related to the newly freed slaves in the southern states.

The bureau's mission was an enormous undertaking because of limited resources, political conflicts over Reconstruction policies, and a hostile environment. The work of the bureau was performed by General Howard and a network of assistant commissioners in various states, largely in the South. The Freedmen's Bureau attempted to address many of the needs of the newly freed African Americans, including labor relations, education, landownership, medical care, food distribution, family reunification, legal protection, and legal services within the African American community.

Labor and Education

In the area of labor relations, the Freedmen's Bureau dealt with labor-related issues such as transporting and relocating refugees and the newly freed persons for employment, contract and wage disputes, and harsh legislation enacted by some states. Concerning the last issue, many southern states had passed laws, called black codes, that required adult freed men and women to have lawful employment or a business. Otherwise, they would be fined and jailed for vagrancy, and sheriffs would hire them out to anyone who would pay their fine. Given the scarcity of jobs, this policy resulted in former slave owners maintaining rigid control over newly freed African Americans. Another discriminatory law gave the former owners of orphaned African Americans the right to hire them as apprentices rather than placing them with their relatives. Again, this law resulted in the continuation of free labor for many southerners. The Freedmen's Bureau has been criticized for the failure of its agents to negotiate labor contracts in the interest of the newly freed. The bureau was frequently accused of protecting the rights of the southern planters instead.

Obtaining an education was extremely important to the newly freed African Americans. They knew that learning to read and write would enable them to enter into contracts and establish businesses, and would aid them in legal matters. The Freedmen's Bureau provided some support, by providing teachers, schools, and books and by coordinating volunteers. The bureau also made a contribution to the founding of African American colleges and universities. Southern opposition to educating African Americans was a result of the southerners' fear that education would make African Americans too independent and unwilling to work under the terms established by their former owners. Therefore, southerners instituted control over the educational administration and classrooms and the entire system. Southern planters used various methods to exert control: frequent changes in administrative personnel, the use of racial stereotypes regarding the intellectual inferiority of African Americans, and educational policy decision making based on paternalism and self-interest. Consequently, educational opportunities were significantly restricted for African American youth.

Property and Other Rights

The newly freed African Americans were eager to acquire property. They demonstrated their interest in owning their own land as individuals and formed associations to purchase large tracts of land. Their sense of family and community was the basis for their strong desire to own land. The Freedmen's Bureau was initially authorized to distribute land that had been confiscated from southern plantation owners during the Civil War. The Freedmen's Bureau also attempted to provide for

In 1866, a Pennsylvania candidate for Congress made his opponent's support for the Freedmen's Bureau a campaign issue.

the social welfare of the freed persons. The agency was noted for rationing food to refugees and former slaves; it assisted families in reuniting with members who had been sold or separated in other ways during slavery.

Protecting the rights of the former slaves was a major task of the Freedmen's Bureau. Republicans believed that African Americans should have the same rights as whites. However, many southern states enacted black codes that severely restricted the civil rights of the freed men, women, and children. These laws, exacting social and economic control over African Americans, represented a new form of slavery. When state legislation prohibited African Americans' equal rights, the bureau attempted to invoke the 1866 Civil Rights Act, which offered African Americans the same legal protections and rights as whites to testify in courts, to own property, to enforce legal contracts, and to sue. The bureau found it extremely difficult to enforce the Civil Rights Act and to prosecute state officials who enforced laws that were discriminatory against African Americans. A shortage of agents and a reluctance among bureau commissioners to challenge local officials contributed to the agency's limited success in enforcing the Civil Rights Act. Finally, the Freedmen's Bureau also established tribunals to address minor legal disputes of African Americans within their own communities. In many instances, freed slaves were able to resolve their own problems. When they could not, they presented their legal concerns to bureau agents.

The task assigned to the Freedmen's Bureau was monumental. The responsibilities of the bureau significantly exceeded the resources and authority granted to it by Congress. The bureau's ability to perform its varied tasks also was impeded by personnel shortages. President Andrew Johnson's Reconstruction policies represented another major challenge to the bureau, as they were not always supportive of the bureau's mandate and objectives. Myriad problems associated with the bureau meant that the newly freed men, women, and children were not able to receive the goods and services necessary to gain economic independence. Consequently, they developed extensive self-help networks to address their needs.

K. Sue Jewell

Core Resources

Barry A. Crouch's *The Freedmen's Bureau and Black Texans* (Austin: University of Texas Press, 1982) discusses the Reconstruction era and the Freedmen's Bureau in the state of Texas. *The Freedmen's Bureau and Black Freedom* (New York: Garland, 1994), edited by Donald G. Nieman, explores the various problems that affected the bureau. Edward Magdol's *A Right to the Land: Essays on the Freedmen's Community* (Westport, Conn.: Greenwood Press, 1977) emphasizes the efforts that African Ameri-

cans pursued to acquire land and their relentless quest for self-determination.

See also: Black codes; Civil Rights Acts of 1866-1875; Fourteenth Amendment; Reconstruction; Thirteenth Amendment.

Freedom Riders

Freedom Riders were civil rights activists who traveled on interstate bus lines in 1961 in order to promote enforcement of a 1960 Supreme Court ruling that prohibited racial segregation in facilities that served interstate travelers. James Farmer, the national director of the Congress of Racial Equality (CORE), modeled the protest after a similar effort that the organization had undertaken in 1947. Like their predecessors in 1947, the Freedom Riders were both African Americans and whites committed to a nonviolent approach to achieving the goal of a racially integrated United States.

The first group of Freedom Riders, seven African Americans and six whites, met in Washington, D.C., for training sessions on May 1, 1961. They left the nation's capital three days later, traveling south on two different bus lines. The Freedom Riders met with little resistance until they arrived in Rock Hill, South Carolina. When John Lewis, an African American seminary student, and Albert Bigelow, a white retired naval officer, attempted to enter the white waiting room in the bus station, a group of white youths beat them. This incident foreshadowed the violence that the Freedom Riders would meet later on their journey through the American South. Outside Anniston, Alabama, on May 14, a mob firebombed the bus on which the Freedom Riders were traveling and attacked the passengers as they hurried off the burning wreckage. That same day, another contingent of Freedom Riders suffered beatings at the bus station in Birmingham, Alabama. Because of the violence, the bus drivers refused to carry the Freedom Riders any farther, and the protest ended with a plane flight to New Orleans, Louisiana.

The premature end of the first Freedom Ride did not mark the end of the effort, which had captured the attention of the nation and placed pressure on the administration of President John F. Kennedy to enforce the Supreme Court ruling. A second group of Freedom Riders, eight African Americans and two whites, set forth from Nashville, Tennessee, just days after the first ride had ended. After a great deal of difficulty, most of this group reached Montgomery, Alabama, where they met with a second group of eleven activists who had arrived to join the protest. Angry white segregationists confronted the Freedom Riders, and the scene at Montgom-

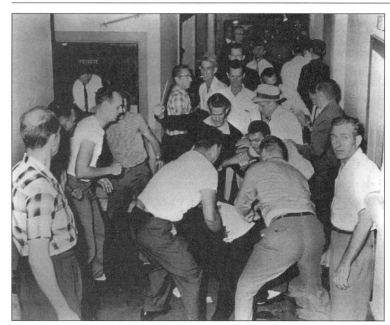

Members of the Ku Klux Klan attack a Freedom Rider at the Trailways bus station in Birmingham, Alabama, on May 14, 1961.

ery degenerated into a riot during which several Freedom Riders were badly injured. Despite this incident, supporters of civil rights throughout the nation volunteered to continue the protests. Biracial Freedom Rides continued throughout the summer of 1961, with hundreds of riders jailed in southern states for violating local ordinances. The continuing crisis prompted the Interstate Commerce Commission to issue regulations, in September, 1961, enforcing the Supreme Court ruling regarding segregation in interstate travel facilities.

The biracial nature of the Freedom Rides revealed that Americans from diverse backgrounds were willing to risk their safety, even their lives, to secure the civil rights of African Americans. The violence surrounding the Freedom Rides also proved that southerners committed to perpetuating racial segregation would attack white civil rights activists with as much abandon as they did the African American protesters.   *Thomas Clarkin*

See also: Children in the Civil Rights movement; Civil Rights movement; Congress of Racial Equality; Nonviolent resistance.

Freedom Summer

In 1964, the Council of Federated Organizations (COFO), comprising mostly volunteers from the Student Nonviolent Coordinating Committee (SNCC),

launched a black voter registration campaign in Mississippi. Leaders sought to expose the ways that whites denied blacks the right to vote and to prod the federal government into enforcing the voting rights of black Americans. The struggle would also encourage the emergence of black community leaders.

In June, the first of nearly nine hundred white student volunteers, mainly from northeastern schools, arrived in Mississippi. White and black volunteers operated about fifty Freedom Schools and about the same number of community centers.

Local white reaction was swift and violent. Even before the project started, three civil rights workers were murdered. Throughout the summer, white segregationists burned churches, shot at volunteers, and bombed homes and civil rights headquarters. The violence had the opposite effect of what whites had intended; it galvanized national opinion that the racial situation in Mississippi and the South had to change. At the same time, continued violence contributed to growing rifts within the Civil Rights movement. The Freedom Summer convinced many black SNCC workers that nonviolence and cooperation with whites were not succeeding and that more radical measures were necessary.

Robert E. McFarland

See also: Civil Rights movement; Council of Federated Organizations; Student Nonviolent Coordinating Committee.

French Canadian women

French Canadians, also known as Québécois, reside mostly in the Canadian province of Quebec and in the northeastern United States. French is their primary language and Catholicism their dominant religion. The Québécois represent about 25 percent of Canada's population. Québécois feminists are concerned with such women's issues as rape, physical harassment, abortion rights, gender equity, political representation, family issues, and women's health.

While Québécois feminists and other feminists share much in common, national concerns also help shape Québécois feminist views, particularly the struggle for autonomy for the French-speaking people of Canada.

The Quebec Act of 1774 allowed French Canadians to retain their own language, religion, and civil law, but the Meech Lake Accord that would have provided constitutional protection for French language and culture was defeated in 1990. This defeat led to the Charlottetown Accord in 1992, which would have extended constitutional recognition of Quebec's "distinct society" but which was also defeated. A resolution granting Quebec full independence was narrowly defeated in 1995.

Several prominent feminist organizations have formed in French Canada, such as the Fédération des Femmes du Québec (FFQ). The FFQ withdrew from the National Action Committee on the Status of Women (NAC), the principal Canadian women's umbrella organization, in the early 1980's but reaffiliated with NAC in the mid-1980's after a constitutional controversy had subsided. The FFQ withdrew from the NAC again in 1989, triggered by opposition from the Front de Libération des Femmes (FLF). The FLF is a vehicle for the radical Front de Libération du Québec (FLQ), which was established in 1963. Both groups share a basic commitment to an independent socialist Quebec and remain separate from groups that do not support the same objectives. Thus, the FLF has organized its own protests against Canada's abortion policies, deliberately excluding anglophone feminists in Quebec and elsewhere in Canada.

Although Franco-American groups in the United States are decidedly less separatist than their Canadian counterparts, they nevertheless promote Franco-American interests based on the belief that Franco-Americans are a distinct minority group. Like their sister organizations in Canada, Franco-American women's groups in the United States have sought solidarity with American Indian groups. Other Franco-Americans compare their struggle to that of African American women and display political characteristics not unlike those found among black separatists in the United States. *Samory Rashid*

See also: Distinct society concept; Ethnic identities of women; French Canadians; Meech Lake Accord; Separatist movement in Quebec.

French Canadians

> **Significance:** Canadians of French descent, who have formed an integral part of Canadian society since the colonial period, have often felt that their cultural beliefs and language were not sufficiently respected by English-speaking Canadians, who constitute a majority in Canada.

The very motto of Quebec, "Je me souviens" ("I remember"), clearly indicates that the distant past continues to have a profound influence on current events in the province. French Canadians refer to the British victory over French forces in 1759 as the Conquest of Canada, whereas English Canadians speak of the Seven Years' War. The decisive battle in this war took place on the Fields (or Plains) of Abraham in Quebec City in 1759, and this area has been preserved by the Quebec government as a reminder of English efforts to destroy French culture in Canada. French Canadians firmly believe that England strove to impose an alien culture on them, and they have not forgotten this perceived lack of respect for their cultural values.

Early Conflicts
In the years immediately after Canada became an English colony, successive English governments attempted to reduce French influence in Canada. Thousands of French-speaking Acadians were forced to leave Nova Scotia. English-speaking Canadians came to dominate economic and political life in Quebec. French-speaking Canadians were largely restricted to manual labor and farming. Although the French Rebellion of 1837 against the English government of Canada failed, it did create cultural unity among Catholic French Canadians against Protestant English Canadians. While Canada remained under the direct rule of England, social peace in Canada was impossible because of the extreme antagonism between the two major ethnic groups of Canada. During the American Civil War, the English government aided the Confederacy and President Abraham Lincoln had to use considerable diplomatic skill in order to prevent a declaration of war against England. As the American Civil War ended, the English government concluded that it was in England's self-interest to transform Canada from a colony into a new form of government. Quebec, Ontario, New Brunswick, and Nova Scotia agreed to join together, and the British North America Act of 1867 created the Dominion of Canada. When John A. Macdonald became the first prime minister of Canada on July 1, 1867, English and French Canadians hoped that this political unity would unite the new country socially.

From the Confederation of 1867 to World War I
With the creation of the Canadian Confederation in 1867, French Canadians were optimistic because the British North America Act of 1867 guaranteed linguistic and religious rights for all Canadians. The new Canadian government included Catholics and Protestants and English Canadians and French Canadians. The first Canadian prime minister, Macdonald, was a Protestant from Ontario, and his chief political adviser was George Étienne Cartier, a Catholic French Canadian from Que-

bec. Macdonald's sensitivity to the aspirations of French Canadians boded well for the unity of this new country, but after Cartier's death in 1873 the influence of French Canadian Catholics diminished in Canadian national politics. With the exception of the fifteen years between 1896 and 1911 when Wilfrid Laurier was prime minister, between 1867 and the election of Louis St. Laurent in 1948, all Canadian prime ministers were English-speaking Protestants. French Canadian Catholics felt excluded from high political offices. Laurier and his supporters in Quebec wanted to create an independent Canada with no interference from Britain, but Robert Borden, who served as the Conservative prime minister from 1911 to 1920, and English-speaking Cana-

dians affirmed that it was Canada's duty to fight in World War I because the British government had asked Canada and other members of the British Empire to do so. French Canadians and their leader Laurier argued that this war did not concern Canada. Borden alienated French Canadians when he questioned their patriotism because they opposed military conscription during World War I. The imposition of conscription provoked anticonscription riots in Quebec City between March 29 and April 2, 1918. Calm was restored only when Catholic bishops in Quebec and Laurier persuaded French Canadians to return to their homes because they could do nothing to change the attitudes of antagonistic English Canadians, who did not respect their culture and reli-

Milestones in French Canadian History

Year	Event	Impact
1759	Battle of Quebec	The British victory over French forces in the battle in Quebec City ends French control of Canada.
1837	French Rebellion	The brutal suppression of this French Canadian rebellion against English Canada demonstrates to French Canadians that the English will not respect their social values.
1867	British North America Act	This English law creates Canada as an independent country within the British Empire and establishes French and English as the official languages of Canada.
1896	Election of Wilfrid Laurier as prime minister of Canada	Laurier becomes the first French Canadian to serve as prime minister of Canada.
1918	Anti-conscription riots in Quebec City	Five days of rioting by French Canadians enraged by the imposition of conscription for a war that in the minds of French Candians concerns European and not Canadian interests.
1948	Election of Louis St. Laurent as prime minister of Canada	This election indicates to French Canadians that the legendary Laurier is not the only one of them who can lead Canada.
1965	Canadian Maple Leaf flag instated	Removes British symbolism from the Canadian flag.
1976	The Parti Québécois takes power in Quebec	This separatist party wins political control in Quebec under René Lévesque.
1980	Defeat of the first separatist referendum in Quebec	The defeat of this referendum in Quebec permits the continued unity of Canada.
1982	Canadian Charter of Rights and Freedoms	Reaffirms the equality between English and French as the official languages of Canada.
1995	Defeat of the second separatist referendum in Quebec	The defeat of this referendum in Quebec permits the continued unity of Canada.

gion. At that time, the profound influence of the Catholic Church in Quebec served to discourage the desire for separatism in that province.

From World War I to the 1960's
Borden's insensitivity and the comment by his minister of justice, Arthur Meighen, that French Canadians were "a backward people" because of their opposition to military conscription transformed Quebec from a province that had elected both Conservative and Liberal members of parliament into a province that sent almost exclusively Liberal members of parliament to Ottawa for the next four decades.

In the 1921 general election, for example, the Liberals won all sixty-five seats in Quebec. William Lyon Mackenzie King, who served as prime minister from 1921 to 1930 and then from 1935 to 1948, and his successor Louis St. Laurent made a determined effort to include French Canadians at the highest levels of the Canadian government, but when the Conservative leader John Diefenbaker became prime minister in 1957, he appointed almost no French Canadians to important government positions. Once again, French Canadians had been snubbed by their national leaders and made to feel like second-class citizens. By the 1960's, the social and political influence of the Catholic Church in Quebec began to wane, although most French Canadians remained practicing Catholics. Catholic bishops in Quebec no longer had the ability to dissuade French Canadians from expressing both their profound alienation from the rest of Canada and their desire to separate from Canada.

The 1960's and Subsequent Decades
Diefenbaker was succeeded as prime minister in 1963 by Lester Pearson, a distinguished Canadian diplomat and Nobel Prize laureate. Pearson understood the profound alienation of French Canadians. He undertook two specific measures to reestablish social unity in Canada. Until 1965, the Canadian flag had contained a British Union Jack, a symbol that French Canadians associated with the Conquest of Canada and efforts by English Canadians to suppress French culture in Canada. In late 1964, Parliament approved Pearson's proposal for a new red-and-white maple leaf flag. Red and white have traditionally been the colors of Canada; the maple trees grow in many regions of Canada; and the maple leaf symbolizes Canada.

This new flag was psychologically very important for Canadian unity because it contained purely Canadian images and included no reference to the earlier French and British domination of Canada. Pearson also appointed a Royal Commission on Bilingualism and Biculturalism, which affirmed in its 1967 report both the

equality between French and English as the official languages of Canada and the need for mutual respect and understanding between the two major cultural groups of Canada. His efforts to unify Canada were continued by Pierre Trudeau, who served as prime minister from 1968 to 1979 and then from 1980 to 1984.

The kidnapping in October, 1970, in Montreal of a British trade commissioner named James Cross and the kidnapping and murder soon thereafter of Quebec minister of labor Pierre Laporte provoked a major political crisis. Daniel Johnson, who was then the premier of Quebec, felt that he had no choice but to ask Prime Minister Trudeau to invoke the War Measures Act to restore peace to Quebec. Trudeau sent Canadian soldiers to Quebec to assist local police officers in their search for the hostages. Cross was released unharmed, but the terrorists murdered Laporte. The decision of Prime Minister Trudeau to send soldiers to Quebec to restore order reminded separatists that English Canadians had used military force on several occasions since the Conquest of Canada to impose their will on Quebec.

In 1976, a separatist party then called the Parti Québécois won the Quebec provincial elections and René Lévesque became the premier of Quebec. He wanted Quebec to separate from Canada. In a provincial referendum held in 1980, Quebecers soundly rejected by 59 percent to 41 percent the proposal for Quebec to separate from Canada. Fifteen years later, a similar referendum was held in Quebec and it also was defeated, although by a much closer margin than in 1980. Although the separatist movement remains strong in Quebec, it is not clear what the future holds for the multicultural and bilingual country named Canada.

Edmund J. Campion

Core Resources
Two very accessible and well-written general histories of Canada are George Woodcock's *The Canadians* (Cambridge, Mass.: Harvard University Press, 1979) and J. Bartlet Brebner's *Canada: A Modern History*, revised by Donald C. Masters (Ann Arbor: University of Michigan Press, 1970). Religious, political, and social conflicts among different ethnic groups in Canada are examined in great depth in two excellent volumes of essays: *Canadian Dualism: Studies of English-French Relations*, edited by Mason Ward and Jean Falardeau (Toronto: University of Toronto Press, 1960), and *Ethnicity and Culture in Canada: The Research Landscape*, edited by J. W. Berry and J. A. Laponce (Toronto: University of Toronto Press, 1994). Very reliable overviews of the evolving nature of the relationships between English Canadians and French Canadians during the twentieth century can be found in two complementary books: Robert Bothwell, Ian Drummond, and John English's *Canada: 1900-1945* (Toronto:

University of Toronto Press, 1987) and Robert Bothwell, Ian Drummond, and John English's *Canada Since 1945: Power, Politics, and Provincialism* (rev. ed., Toronto: University of Toronto Press, 1989).

See also: October crisis; Separatist movement in Quebec.

Friends of the Indian

Friends of the Indian organizations were formed in the last two decades of the nineteenth century by mainly eastern Christian humanitarians who were determined to influence federal Indian policy. Members of these organizations were convinced of the superiority of Christian civilization and were determined to do away with Indianness and tribal traditions; their goal was to turn individual Indians into patriotic American citizens.

The Friends of the Indian groups supported allotment in order to break up tribal land ownership and force individual ownership; they sought to end tribal jurisdiction and to bring Indians as individual citizens before the law. They supported vocational education for Indian children, particularly boarding schools, and they were generally intolerant of Indian culture or spiritual expression and worked to outlaw Sun Dances, vision questing, giveaways, plural marriages, and so on. These well-intentioned Christian men and women sought to influence and direct Indian policy by engaging in intense lobbying efforts with federal officials and by educating the general public through newsletters, pamphlets, and speakers. These reformers and their supporters were convinced of the righteousness of their cause and greatly affected federal Indian policy well into the twentieth century.

Beginning in 1883 these groups came together annually for the Lake Mohonk Conference of the Friends of the Indian in New Paltz, New York, to coordinate their efforts. General harmony and a good working relationship existed among the various groups because they shared a common religious outlook that they were doing God's will by guiding Indians from savagery to civilization. The most significant and far-reaching areas affected by these organizations were the federal Indian education system and the General Allotment Act (Dawes Severalty Act) of 1887. One of the most prominent groups, the Indian Rights Association, continues to exist; however, it now supports tribalism and tribal self-determination.   *Carole A. Barrett*

See also: General Allotment Act; Indian Citizenship Act; Indian Rights Association; Indian-white relations: United States.

Friendships, interracial/interethnic

> **Significance:** Interracial and interethnic friendships involve persons from dissimilar racial, ethnic, linguistic, or national groups. These friendships are significant for intergroup relations because they are a sign of structural assimilation or integration for the minority group. According to sociologist Milton Gordon, integration into the primary sector of society for minorities includes having acquaintances, close friends, and neighbors from the dominant group.

Since the 1950's, legislation such as the Civil Rights Act of 1964 and the Voting Rights Act of 1965 has helped to reduce discrimination against racial and ethnic groups. Similarly, the U.S. Supreme Court's 1954 decision in *Brown v. Board of Education* began the movement to desegregate public schools and, as a result, did much to break down personal barriers between blacks, whites, Latinos, Asian Americans, and other groups. As a result of such factors, contact across group lines in American schools, colleges, workplaces, neighborhoods, and social gatherings has increased, but these situations do not often lead to increased acceptance and the growth of friendships across racial and ethnic boundaries. According to numerous sources, including S. Dale McLemore's *Racial and Ethnic Relations in America* (1994) and Joseph F. Healey's *Race, Ethnicity, Gender, and Class* (1998), interracial and interethnic friendships remain relatively infrequent. This is not surprising given the centuries of racism and prejudice, as well as the differences in socioeconomic status, places of residence, and levels of education, that continue to exist between groups. Moreover, the slowly changing norms concerning issues of race and ethnicity also discourage the growth of interracial and interethnic friendships. Despite significant legal and political efforts to control them, racial stereotyping and prejudice remain powerful social forces. Whereas interactions with members of the same racial or ethnic group promote social stability, interactions with members of different racial or ethnic groups mark social change and instability, which can be seen as threatening to a group's sense of security.

Intergroup Contact

Though statistics regarding the incidence of interracial and interethnic friendships are substantially harder to find than are corresponding statistics regarding intermarriage, there is a body of research within the social sciences that addresses the issue of interracial/

interethnic friendships. Sociologist Gordon Allport's contact hypothesis is applicable to the study of these friendships. The contact hypothesis proposes that when social, political, and economic barriers to integration and equality disappear, the social distance between racial groups should also decrease. Social distance can be defined as the degree of intimacy to which an individual is willing to admit persons of other groups, ranging from intermarriage to complete segregation.

A variety of social settings in which interracial and interethnic contact leads to friendships have been studied, but the majority of research has focused on desegregated schools. Since *Brown v. Board of Education*, the desegregation of schools has facilitated the interaction of students, teachers, and parents from different racial and ethnic groups. Yet when it comes to friendship, or social interaction outside the school context, the majority of the research has found that students prefer members of their

Sociologists believe that interracial friendships such as those in the group pictured here provide evidence of a minority group's assimilation into the mainstream culture.

own racial and ethnic group as friends, although the frequency of these friendships differs depending on what racial and ethnic groups are involved. For example, studies such as Nathan Glazer and Daniel P. Moynihan's *Beyond the Melting Pot* (1970) and Richard Alba's *Ethnicity and Race in the U.S.A.* (1988) have found that social distance between white ethnic groups is being reduced by interethnic friendships and intermarriage. Similarity in attitudes, values, behaviors, and socioeconomic status are often the basis of interpersonal attraction, with race an important factor in the choice of friends. Therefore, it is understandable why interethnic friendships, especially between white European Americans, would be more common than interracial friendships.

Racial stereotypes and societal norms act as barriers to the formation of interracial friendships. One study has found that students often cite the tendency of members of other groups to segregate themselves and the perception that they lack common ground upon which to build a friendship as reasons why they do not have friends from other racial or ethnic groups. Other studies have also found that some school practices, such as tracking, contribute to the low number of interracial friendships; tracking, for example, may tend to segregate African Americans and other minorities into classrooms devoted to lower academic tracks. Another bar-

rier to the formation of interracial and interethnic friendships is the perception of negative family attitudes toward these friendships.

Among adults, research has tended to focus on the effects of residential desegregation on interracial contact and friendships. Douglas Massey and Nancy Denton's *American Apartheid* (1993) explored the issue of residential segregation and found that racial groups remain virtually segregated, even when they are of the same social class. Among adults, therefore, interracial friendships remain infrequent, both because of a lack of opportunities to interact and because of prejudices and stereotypes. One study by James E. Rosenbaum et al. found that when low-income blacks moved to middle-class white suburbs as part of a housing voucher program, considerable racial integration was achieved, including a substantial number of individual friendships.

Asian Americans, Hispanic Americans, and African Americans

Rates of interracial and interethnic friendships vary depending on the groups involved. According to sources such as S. Dale McLemore's *Racial and Ethnic Relations in America* (1994) and Joseph F. Healey's *Race, Ethnicity, Gender, and Class* (1998), Asian Americans have experienced considerable assimilation in the areas of primary relations such as friendships and marriage, especially with white European Americans. Overall the extent of intimate contact between Hispanic Americans and whites is higher than for African Americans, yet lower than for Asian Americans and whites, according to Healey. For example, according to McLemore, Mexican Americans decreasingly have only Mexican friends over the passage of time. This generational trend is more pronounced among those living in desegregated neighborhoods and among those of higher income, suggesting that if Mexican Americans continue to live, work, and send their children to school in desegregated areas, the number of friendships with non-Hispanics will continue to increase. Similarly, Clara Rodriguez's *Puerto Ricans: Born in the USA* (1989) found that rates of interracial contact increase for Hispanic Americans of the more affluent social classes who live in the cities and for the presumably more Americanized younger generations.

According to the majority of research, including McLemore's *Racial and Ethnic Relations in America* and Healey's *Race, Ethnicity, Gender, and Class,* friendships between African Americans and whites are the least frequent. These two groups remain virtually separated in their personal relationships everywhere but in the schools. Even in school, the proportion of African American/white friendships remains low. According to research, it is common for black students to remain virtually segregated within primary and secondary school systems, and black college students are increasingly forming their own sororities, fraternities, and student organizations. The low level of interracial contact between African Americans and whites is further evidenced in the low rates of intermarriage between the two groups. Therefore, McLemore, for example, concludes that the level of primary assimilation of African Americans, as evidenced in the low number of interracial friendships and marriage, is low compared to that of other racial and ethnic groups.

Improving Intergroup Friendships

One of the most commonly proposed methods of improving intergroup relations is for people to establish communication, get to know one another, and participate in group activities together. This process enables individuals to judge members of a different race or ethnicity on the basis of their individual characteristics rather than their group membership. It is often maintained that such transformations are most likely to occur if the individuals involved are of equal socioeconomic status, if they are given the chance to work cooperatively together, if their interaction is supported by those in authority, and if there is a high level of intimacy. Often, intergroup contacts that occur under different circumstances do not alter prejudices and rarely result in the formation of friendships, because they simply mirror the power differentials and inequalities of the larger society. Other factors that have been shown to influence the outcome of contacts between members of different racial and ethnic groups include minimal competition, voluntary interaction, and similarities in beliefs and values.

Schools can encourage intergroup contact by offering noncompetitive, supportive environments where different racial and ethnic groups can interact and work cooperatively. Proposed methods of accomplishing this include the implementation of small-group learning teams and interracial extracurricular activities. Moreover, positive effects on the development of interracial friendships have been observed when school officials and teachers have implemented programs that reduce status differences between students of different racial and ethnic groups. *Erica Childs*

Core Resources
Gordon Allport's *The Nature of Prejudice* (Garden City, N.Y.: Doubleday, 1958) explores the contact hypothesis, which is generally used in examining intergroup relations. Milton Gordon, in *Assimilation in American Life* (New York: Oxford University Press, 1964), identifies three subprocesses of assimilation, with one of the main stages, primary structural assimilation, being the formation of interracial and interethnic friendships. For a general summary of intergroup relations and the formation of intergroup friendships, S. Dale McLemore's *Racial and Ethnic Relations in America* (Boston: Allyn & Bacon, 1994) and Joseph F. Healey's *Race, Ethnicity, Gender, and Class: The Sociology of Group Conflict and Change* (Thousand Oaks, Calif.: Pine Forge Press, 1998) are good sources. A few of the most comprehensive scholarly articles that deal with student friendships include Maureen T. Hallinan and Ruy A. Teixeira's "Opportunities and Constraints: Black-White Differences in the Formation of Interracial Friendships" (*Child Development* 58, 1987); Maureen T. Hallinan and Richard A. Williams's "Interracial Friendship Choices in Secondary Schools" (*American Sociological Review* 54, 1989); and Maureen T. Hallinan and Richard A. Williams's "The Stability of Students' Interracial Friendships" (*American Sociological Review* 52, 1987). For an in-depth look at residential segregation and how it affects intergroup contact, Douglas Massey and Nancy Denton's *American Apartheid* (Cambridge, Mass.: Harvard University Press, 1993) is an excellent source.

See also: Assimilation: cultural and structural; Assimilation theories; Contact hypothesis; Desegregation: public schools; Diversity training programs; Interracial and interethnic marriage; Segmented assimilation theory.

Frustration-aggression theory

> **Significance:** The frustration-aggression theory, introduced in the late 1930's, attempts to explain the cause of hostile aggressive behavior. It proposes that many people will turn to intentionally hurtful behavior if they are blocked (frustrated) in pursuing their goals. If the actual blocking agents cannot be identified or attacked, aggression may be displaced onto innocent, relatively powerless groups.

From the beginning of recorded history, one can trace the theme that people often become aggressive when prevented from reaching some very basic goals—having food, feeling a reasonable degree of personal safety, having the chance to better themselves, and so on. Many people have been hurt because they were responsible for blocking the goals of others, thereby creating frustration. They have been victims of "instrumental aggression"—aggression that is primarily directed at attaining a goal rather than hurting another. Even more people, however, have been hurt as innocent victims of frustrated individuals purposely venting their rage on whatever nearby group or individual was easy to identify and was relatively powerless. This is known as "hostile aggression," and it is carried out to make the aggressor feel better.

Freud's Ideas
The seeds of a modern frustration-aggression theory can be found in the writings of Sigmund Freud, the father of psychoanalysis. He stated that aggression is an inherent characteristic of people and that they often use "displacement," an ego defense mechanism, to redirect aggression from its appropriate target to a more easily available and safer one. Freud stated that much of what people do is motivated by "unconscious" forces. By unconscious, he meant forces of which people are largely unaware but that are nevertheless active in their minds. This concept of unconscious motivation is key to the process of scapegoating. If people realized consciously that they were blaming innocent individuals for their problems, rational thought would stop them from doing so. Unconscious direction of behavior, however, bypasses such rationality.

American theorists expanded on Freud's ideas about frustration and aggression. John Dollard and his colleagues authored the now classic *Frustration and Aggression* (1939), which proposed that frustration always leads to aggression and that aggression is always preceded by frustration. The basic proposal was ultimately too simplistic, but the book motivated many researchers to examine and challenge parts of it. Leonard Berkowitz,

for example, provided support for the commonsense notions that aggression may be generated by circumstances other than frustration and that frustration may produce responses other than aggression. He also documented what he termed the "trigger effect," the ability of something in the environment to set off aggression under conditions of high frustration.

Scapegoating and Racism
When the cause of frustration is something that cannot be attacked, such as poor economic conditions, or when the cause is too dangerous to attack (for example, a powerful dictator), innocent victims often become scapegoats of hostile "displaced aggression." For the displacement of aggression to be comforting to a frustrated individual, several conditions must be satisfied. First, since displacement is carried out as a substitute for aggression against the causes of frustration that cannot directly be attacked, a good scapegoat must be a manageable target. Attacking a person, or a few people, is far more manageable than attacking the government or an environmental condition such as a drought.

Second, a satisfying scapegoat must be relatively harmless compared with other possible targets and with the real cause of the frustration. Third, a scapegoat must be readily identifiable and easy to locate. Often a group (such as an ethnic or religious group) is an easy source of such individual scapegoats. A group contains many victims, some of whom are almost always present when needed, and the fact that it may also be easily identified and used by others gives social support for displacing aggression. Others may target the scapegoat for different reasons, but such differences are immaterial. That people can agree on their hatred is sufficient. This fact illuminates the connections between frustration, aggression, and racial prejudice.

Formation of Prejudice
Historical precedent can greatly enhance the utility of a group used as a scapegoat. African Americans were the first institutionalized victims of racial prejudice in the United States. Very early in the nation's history, they became an ideal scapegoat group; because they were slaves, they were helpless to defend themselves against unjust blame, and because of their appearance, most were subject to easy identification.

Prejudice against many peoples can be explained by many of the factors that still contribute to prejudice against blacks. Immigrants have often been the targets of displaced aggression. Even those who speak English are, for a time, easily identifiable by accented speech, differences in preferred dress, and different customs. Those immigrants speaking different languages are easier to spot, and those with different features and skin color easier still. Identifiability as a factor leading to scapegoating was used in a malicious, yet clever, way by Adolf Hitler in the 1930's and 1940's. Jewish citizens were no more identifiable in pre-World War II Germany than Jewish citizens are in the United States today, so Hitler demanded that they identify themselves and their businesses by symbols (for example, a yellow star) worn on clothing or the word "Jew" displayed on properties. Hitler and his advisers well understood scapegoating, and they used it to deflect aggression away from themselves and toward a common "enemy." Historically, many politicians in the United States have done the same in an equally vile way, using Chinese, African Americans, or Hispanics, for example, as easily identified targets for hatred. Communists, intellectuals, and homosexuals have also been targets, but they have had to be somehow specially identified. Such scapegoating still occurs, but it generally takes more subtle and covert forms than it did in the past.

The long-honored view that racism can be caused by the formation of negative attitudes (prejudices) that lead to limiting behavior (discrimination) is also compatible with the frustration-aggression theory. "Aggression," as the theory uses it, can be at any level—intellectual, emotional, or behavioral. A frustrated individual who uses blacks as a scapegoat may believe that they are inferior people, may hate them, and may discriminate against them at every opportunity. Such a person holds the prejudice that is often hypothesized to underlie racism and to facilitate scapegoating.

Stereotyping
The view that stereotypes encourage racism and scapegoating is also compatible with the frustration-aggression theory. Often a group chosen as a scapegoat is far more variable than the frustrated individual recognizes. By accurate perception, a person would recognize that only some (if any) of the group members "deserve" the hostility directed at them. Widely held stereotypes simplify the process of scapegoating. If all blacks are lazy, for example, and all Jews are money-hungry, the frustrated individual can simply hate them all without giving the matter further thought.

The Authoritarian Personality
Even the most individualistic theory about scapegoating and racism, that of the authoritarian personality, meshes well with the frustration-aggression theory. An authoritarian personality, as first characterized in the 1950's, is a personality type characterized by a number of qualities that fall only a bit short of ones needed for classification as mentally ill. The person designated "high authoritarian" by a score on the F-scale devised by Theodor Adorno and the other authors of *The Authoritarian Personality*

(1950) displays several qualities—conventionalism, authoritarian aggression, superstition and stereotypy, and projectivity—that directly predispose him or her to scapegoating as well as most of the behaviors inherent in the several other theories of racism. High authoritarians have developed their personalities over a lifetime and are not likely to change spontaneously or to be changed by others' efforts. Because of their typically rigid behaviors, they face many frustrations and are especially likely to find reasons other than their own shortcomings for their problems. High authoritarians' aggressiveness under frustrating conditions is a prototype for the frustration-aggression hypothesis.

Harry A. Tiemann, Jr.

Core Resources
The Authoritarian Personality (New York: Harper, 1950), by T. W. Adorno, is the original source of the concept of the authoritarian personality and of the F-scale devised to measure it. *Roots of Aggression: A Re-examination of the Frustration-Aggression Hypothesis* (New York: Atherton, 1969), edited by Leonard Berkowitz, presents papers written to challenge and to refine the original formulation of the theory. *Frustration and Aggression* (New Haven, Conn.: Yale University Press, 1939), by John Dollard et al., is a classic source that proposed an extreme, inevitable relationship between frustration and aggression that many later researchers have questioned. Konrad Lorenz's *On Aggression*, translated by Marjorie Kerr Wilson (reprint, New York: Harcourt Brace Jovanovich, 1974), is an excellent presentation of the argument that inherent aggression must be recognized as real and that society must provide ways for it to be released with as little harm as possible. Ashley Montagu's *The Nature of Human Aggression* (New York: Oxford University Press, 1976) argues that people are capable of behaving in many ways, not only those that seem an extension of their animal ancestry. Montagu sees no merit in arguments that aggression is unavoidable and basically beyond human control; modern social science finds this hopeful view considerably more likely than its biologically based opposite.

See also: Authoritarian personality theory; Psychological theories of intergroup relations; Racism: history of the concept.

Fugitive slave laws

Although the U.S. Constitution provided for the return of fugitive slaves across state borders, it did not specify the mechanism by which this would be accomplished. Congress therefore enacted the Fugitive Slave Law of

The Oberlin Rescuers, a group of abolitionists in Oberlin, Ohio, pictured in 1859, refused to comply with fugitive slave laws.

1793, by which slaves could be seized by masters or agents crossing state lines. State officials were made responsible for the enforcement of the federal law. For the slaves, the law embodied no protection of *habeas corpus*, trial by jury, or right to testify in their own behalf. In response, many northern states passed laws granting slaves personal liberties.

The Fugitive Slave Law of 1850 made the federal government responsible for returning slaves to their owners. Interference with the law became a felony. Again, the alleged fugitive was denied personal rights. Furthermore, since commissioners received a higher fee for delivering a slave than for rejecting a claim, the law resulted in the confiscation of free people. The law's constitutionality was upheld in 1859 in *Ableman v. Booth*. Northern furor over the law and increasing abolitionist sentiment helped bring the country closer to the brink of war.   *Mary E. Virginia*

See also: Abolition; Compromise of 1850; Missouri Compromise; *Scott v. Sandford*; Slave codes; Slavery.

Fullilove v. Klutznick

In *Fullilove v. Klutznick*, the Supreme Court on July 2, 1980, ruled that setting aside a percentage of federal contracts for minority business enterprises was constitutional as long as it was intended to remedy demonstrated discrimination. In passing the Public Works Employment Act of 1977, Congress required 10 percent of local public works contracts to be "set aside" for minority businesses—businesses with at least 50 percent ownership or 51 percent stockholding by African Americans, Spanish-speaking people, Asian Americans, American Indians, Eskimos, or Aleuts. Nonminority prime contractors were

required, in subcontracting to minority businesses, to provide guidance and technical assistance in making bids, to lower or waive bonding requirements, and to assist minority businesses in obtaining working capital from financial institutions and government agencies.

Shortly after Juanita Krebs, U.S. secretary of commerce, issued administrative guidelines for bidding under the new law, several potential project grantees (H. Earl Fullilove and trustees of the New York Building and Construction Industry Board of Urban Affairs Fund, two general contractor associations, and a firm engaged in heating, ventilation, and air conditioning work) filed suit against Krebs, the city and state of New York, the New York Board of Higher Education, and the Health and Hospitals Corporation for a temporary restraining order to block implementation of the law. After they lost the case in the district court (in December, 1977) and on appeal (in 1978), they took the case to the Supreme Court. When the case was decided, Philip Klutznick was U.S. secretary of commerce. Chief Justice Warren Burger wrote the majority opinion; three justices provided concurring majority opinions, and two wrote dissents.

The Court answered the argument that government should act in a color-blind manner by noting that Congress had the power to spend money for the general welfare and thus to design a remedy for minority businesses. The argument that nonminority businesses were deprived of equal access to contracts was rejected: a 10 percent set-aside rate was considered light in view of the larger percentage of minorities. The Court responded to the argument that the definition of "minority" was underinclusive and should have added other groups by noting that such a definition was entirely up to Congress. The argument that the "minority" definition was overinclusive and might favor minority businesses unqualified to do the technical work was refuted by a reference to the statutory provisions that only bona fide minorities were covered by the law and that a waiver from the set-aside could be issued if no minority business was able to do the work.

The Supreme Court thus held that a numerical goal could be designed as a remedy for a statistically demonstrated inequality for minorities, with provisions tailored to removing specific, documented barriers to the success of minorities. Plans failing these tests have been consistently rejected by the Court, as in *Richmond v. J. A. Croson Company* (1989).   *Michael Haas*

See also: *Adarand Constructors v. Peña;* Affirmative action; Civil Rights Act of 1964; Discrimination: racial and ethnic; Quotas; *Richmond v. J. A. Croson Company;* Set-asides.

Fusion movement

Beginning in 1890, leaders of the Populist, or People's, Party courted black votes in an effort to vote Democratic "redeemers" (southern whites who had regained control of local governments after Reconstruction had ended in the 1870's) out of office in the southern states. The appeal was based on the mutual interest of all downtrodden farmers, whatever their race. Fusionists argued that black farmers shared the same economic problems as whites and that the Republican Party only wanted to help the white business community. State organizations elected black delegates to their councils and gave them a voice in the party organization. Party rallies and speeches were attended by both races, although seating was segregated. Black Populist clubs served to indoctrinate members in party principles and to encourage speakers and leaders. Sometimes deals were made with Republican bosses to deliver black votes.

Fusion was never accepted by all white Populists. In the 1894 election, the party was divided between fusionists and antifusionists led by Tom Watson of Georgia. Watson believed that fusion would taint the party by association with the party of Lincoln (the Republicans). In any case, fusion was never a formal platform but a series of local agreements that led to success at the polls across the South. The demise of fusion and the Populist Party came in the presidential election of 1896.

Robert E. McFarland

See also: Compromise of 1877; Reconstruction.

G

Gadsden Purchase

James Gadsden was a South Carolina railroad promoter turned diplomat. On behalf of President James Buchanan, he negotiated America's purchase of 45,535 square miles of territory from Mexico for the payment of fifteen million dollars (reduced later to ten million). A block of land nearly the size of New York State, the Gadsden Purchase lies south of the Gila River, forming part of present-day Arizona and New Mexico. The treaty embodying the purchase was signed on December 30, 1853, and ratified on June 29, 1854, settling boundary questions between the United States and Mexico left unresolved by the Treaty of Guadalupe Hidalgo at the end of the Mexican-American War in 1848.

The purchase was prompted by American politicians eager to build a transcontinental railroad through the Southwest. Neither the Mexican nor American government consulted with the Tohono O'odhams (Papagos) and Chiricahua Apaches who lived in the area, and these Indians subsequently ignored boundaries that were not their own. *Clifton K. Yearley*

See also: Guadalupe Hidalgo, Treaty of.

Gambling

> **Significance:** Gambling facilities have brought needed income to some native peoples, but some tribe members protest its presence on reservations.

During the late twentieth century, commercial gambling became a major source of income on Indian reservations across the United States. While many Native American cultures practiced forms of gambling (such as the Iroquois peachstone game), there was no prior large-scale experience with gambling as a commercial enterprise. The arrival of gaming has brought dividends to some native peoples, but it has brought controversy culminating in firefights and death to others.

Development of Reservation Gambling

The history of reservation gambling begins in 1979, when the Seminoles became the first Indian tribe to enter the bingo industry. By early 1985, seventy-five to eighty of the federally recognized Indian tribes in the United States were conducting some sort of organized game of chance. By the fall of 1988, the Congressional Research Service estimated that more than one hundred Indian tribes participated in some form of gambling, which grossed about $255 million a year. In October of 1988, Congress passed the Indian Gaming Regulatory Act, which officially allowed legalized gambling on reservations. The act also established the National Indian Gaming Commission to oversee gaming activities. By 1991, 150 native reservations recognized by non-Indian governmental bodies had some form of gambling. According to the U.S. Department of the Interior, gross revenue from such operations passed $1 billion that year.

Individual prizes in some reservation bingo games were reported to be as high as $100,000, while bingo stakes in surrounding areas under state jurisdiction were sometimes limited to $100. Marion Blank Horn, principal deputy solicitor of the Department of the Interior, described the fertile ground gambling enterprises had found in Indian country:

> The reasons for growth in gambling on Indian land are readily apparent. The Indian tribal governments see an opportunity for income that can make a substantial improvement in the tribe's [economic] conditions. The lack of any state regulation results in a competitive advantage over gambling regulated by the states. These advantages include no state-imposed limits on the size of pots or prizes, no restrictions by the states on days or hours of operations, no costs for licenses or compliance with state requirements, and no state taxes on gambling operations.

By the early 1990's, gambling had provided a small galaxy of material benefits for some formerly impoverished native peoples. A half-hour's drive from Minnesota's Twin Cities, blackjack players crowded forty-one tables, while 450 other players stared into video slot machines inside the tipi-shaped Little Six Casino, operated by the 103 members of the Shakopee Mdewakanton Sioux. By 1991, each member of the tribe was getting

Gamblers play at the Bay Mills Gambling Casino run by the Ojibway tribe in Michigan. Gambling has provided economic assistance to some American Indian tribes but is not without controversy.

monthly dividend checks averaging $2,000 as shareholders in the casino. In addition to monthly dividends, members became eligible for homes (if they lacked them), were guaranteed jobs (if they were unemployed), and were offered full college scholarships. The tribe had taken out health insurance policies for everyone on the reservation and established day care for children of working parents. The largest casino to open by mid-1991 was the $3 million Sycuan Gaming Center on the Sycuan Indian Reservation near El Cajon, a suburb of San Diego, California.

Death at Akwesasne
While gambling has brought benefits to some Native American communities, it brought violence to the Akwesasne Mohawks of St. Regis in upstate New York. As many as seven casinos had opened illegally along the reservation's main highway; the area became a crossroads for the illicit smuggling of drugs, including cocaine, and tax-free liquor and cigarettes.

Tension escalated after early protests against gambling in the late 1980's (including the vandalizing of one casino and the burning of another) were met by brutal attempts by gambling supporters to suppress this resistance. Residents blockaded the reservation to keep the casinos' customers out, prompting the violent destruction of the blockades by gambling supporters in late April, 1990. By that time, brutal beatings of antigambling activists, drive-by shootings, and night-long firefights had culminated in two Mohawk deaths during the early morning of May 1, 1990. Intervention of several police agencies from the United States and Canada followed the two deaths; outside police presence continued for years afterward.   *Bruce E. Johansen*

Core Resources
Rick Hornung's *One Nation Under the Gun: Inside the Mohawk Civil War* (New York: Pantheon Books, 1991), the U.S. Senate Select Committee on Indian Affairs' *Gambling on Indian Reservations and Land* (Washington, D.C.: Government Printing Office, 1985), and Roger Walke's *Gambling on Indian Reservations* (Washington, D.C.: Congressional Research Service, Library of Congress, 1989) provide information on various aspects of reservation gambling. *Indian Gaming and the Law* (2d. ed., Reno: University of Nevada, 1998), edited by Judy Cornelius and William Eadington, looks at the legal issues surrounding Indian gaming. Ambrose I. Lane, Sr.'s *Return of the Buffalo: The Story Behind America's Indian Gaming Explosion* (Westport, Conn.: Bergin & Garvey, 1995) describes the struggle of the Cabazon Indians in California for the right to operate a gambling casino on their reservation.

See also: Determined Residents United for Mohawk Sovereignty; Indian Gaming Regulatory Act; Urban Indians.

Gendered racism

Social psychologist Philomena Essed coined the term "gendered racism" to refer to the way that sexism and racism interact to subordinate minority group women. Scholars sometimes refer to minority women as a "double minority" because they are affected by cultural definitions of gender that vary by race or ethnicity. Whites historically have defined African American women, for example, as "Aunt Jemima," the overweight, subservient maid or housekeeper; or as a sexual object, to be used by men and then discarded; or as "beasts of burden." These negative images, like ones for other minority women, can be traced to the historical exploitative relationship not only between whites and minority groups but also between men and women. Gendered racism has implications for minority women by restricting their access to education, limiting their occupational options, restricting their income to minimum or below-minimum wages, and making it difficult for minority families to escape poverty. Consequently, minority women lag behind white women, and men of all racial and ethnic groups, in terms of political, economic, cultural, and social positions.   *Cheryl D. Childers*

See also: Ethnic identities of women; Women and racism; Women of color; Triple oppression.

General Allotment Act

> **Significance:** The General Allotment, or Dawes Severalty, Act, which allotted land to individual Native Americans, helped to dissolve the tribal nations.

When the General Allotment Act became law on February 8, 1887, proponents hailed it as the Indian Emancipation Act and Secretary of the Interior L. Q. C. Lamar called it "the most important measure of legislation ever enacted in this country affecting our Indian affairs."

The law dealt primarily with Native American ownership of land. It authorized the president of the United States, through the Office of Indian Affairs in the Department of the Interior, to allot the lands on reservations to individual Native Americans, so that they would hold the land in severalty instead of the tribe's owning the land communally. Each head of a household would receive a quarter-section of land (160 acres); single persons over eighteen years of age and orphans would receive 80 acres; and other persons, 40 acres. (In 1891, an amendment to the law equalized the allotments to provide 80 acres for each individual, regardless of age or family status.) The United States government would hold the allotments in trust for twenty-five years, during which time a Native American could not sell or otherwise dispose of his or her land. At the end of that period, he or she would receive full title to it. After the process of dividing up the reservation land for allotments, the federal government could sell the surplus land (often a considerable portion of the reservation) to willing purchasers (most of whom would be Euro-Americans). The money from such sales would go to a fund to benefit Native American education.

The Dawes Act also provided for Native American citizenship. Native Americans who received allotments in severalty or who took up residence apart from their tribe and adopted what Euro-Americans considered civilized ways became citizens of the United States and subject to the laws of the state or territory in which they lived. In 1924, Congress passed the Indian Citizenship Act, granting full citizenship to nearly all Native Americans who were not already citizens, and measures in the late 1940's extended such status to Arizona and New Mexico Native Americans whom the 1924 law had missed.

Support for the Act

Two groups of Euro-Americans especially welcomed the Dawes Act. Land-hungry settlers who had long cast covetous eyes on the reservation lands—which, to Euro-American thinking, were going to waste because of the lack of productive agricultural practices by Native Americans, whom they considered to be hunters and gatherers—were now able to acquire the lands left over from the allotment process. No doubt, the less scrupulous among the settlers also looked forward to the day when individual Native Americans would receive full title to their land and be able to sell, lease, or otherwise dispose of it. Then pressure, legitimate or not, would likely induce the new owner to part with the acreage.

A second group of Euro-Americans, however, was more influential in securing passage of the Dawes Act. These were the humanitarian reformers of the day, who considered private ownership of land in severalty, U.S. citizenship, education, and consistent codification of laws to be indispensable means for the acculturation of the Native Americans and their eventual assimilation into the mainstream of U.S. society. As ministers from the several Christian denominations, educators, civil servants, politicians, and even a few military personnel, these philanthropists exerted a clout beyond their numbers. Calling themselves the Friends of the Indian, these reformers had been meeting annually since 1869 at the Catskills resort of Lake Mohonk to discuss ways to bring the tribal peoples to what the conveners deemed to be civilization.

Federal politicians had long considered private ownership of land essential to the civilizing process. Thomas Jefferson and the like-minded policymakers of his time had strongly advocated it, and in 1838 the Commissioner of Indian Affairs gave voice to a widespread view when he said, "Unless some system is marked out by which there shall be a separate allotment of land to each individual . . . you will look in vain for any general casting off of savagism. Common property and civilization cannot co-exist."

Reform Efforts

It was not until the post–Civil War years, when increasing Euro-American pressures on the Native Americans created crisis after crisis, that humanitarians and philanthropists began a concerted drive for "Indian reform." Land in severalty would be the most important factor in breaking up tribalism. The reform groups that were organized—the Board of Indian Commissioners (1869), the Women's National Indian Association (1879), the Indian Rights Association (1882), the Lake Mohonk Conference of Friends of the Indian (1883), and the National Indian Defense Association (1885), to name the most important—all strongly espoused allotment in severalty. Nor were they satisfied with the piecemeal legislation that affected one tribe at a time; the panacea they sought was a general allotment law. Although supporters argued over the speed of implementing allotment, such proponents as Carl Schurz, Herbert Welsh, and the Reverend Lyman Abbott fought energetically for such legislation. They finally won to their cause Senator Henry L. Dawes, chairman of the Senate Committee on Indian Affairs, who successfully shepherded through Congress the measure that bears his name.

Only a few Euro-American voices cried out against the proposal. Congressman Russell Errett of Pennsylvania and a few others protested that the bill was a thinly disguised means of getting at the valuable tribal lands. Senator Henry M. Teller of Colorado argued that the Native Americans did not want to own land in severalty and were not prepared to assume the responsibilities that went with private property and citizenship. He denied the contention of the reformers that private ownership of land would lead to civilization. Albert Meacham, editor of *The Council Fire*, maintained that there was little enthusiasm for severalty among traditionalist Native Americans, and anthropologist Lewis Henry Morgan thought that allotment would result in massive poverty. Presbyterian missionaries apparently were disunited on the subject of allotment, and their views fell by the wayside as the juggernaut of reform forged ahead.

Native American response to allotment has largely gone unrecorded. The Cherokee, Creek, Chickasaw, Choctaw, Seminole, Sac, Fox, and a few other tribes in Indian Territory, as well as the Seneca in New York, contended that they already mostly owned land individually and won exclusion from the act's operation. By 1906, however, Congress extended allotment to them as well. Most of the complaints came after the act's passage, when Native Americans lost land and found farming difficult under its provisions.

"February 8, 1887," one optimistic spokesman of the Board of Indian Commissioners commented, "may be called the Indian emancipation day." Although much sincere Christian goodwill motivated passage of the Dawes Act, it turned out to be a disaster for Native Americans. In 1891, Congress allowed Native Americans to lease their allotments if they were not able to farm for themselves.

The allotments and the leasing moved faster and with less careful discrimination than Dawes and other promoters had intended. Instead of being a measure that turned Native Americans into self-supporting farmers, the act, through the rapid alienation of the Native Americans' lands, meant the loss of the land base on which the tribal peoples' hope for future prosperity depended. Tribal peoples held claim to about 150 million acres of land in 1887. The Dawes Act eventually diverted two-thirds of that acreage out of Native American ownership, down to about 48 million acres by 1934. Not until that year, with the passage of the Indian Reorganization Act (the Wheeler-Howard Act, also known as the Indian New Deal), did the federal government repeal the Dawes Act and encourage communal forms of ownership again, but by that time much of the former reservation land was gone as surplus sales, leases, or sales by the individual allottees. *Francis P. Prucha, updated by Thomas L. Altherr*

Core Resources
Arrell Morgan Gibson's "The Centennial Legacy of the General Allotment Act," in *Chronicles of Oklahoma* 65, no. 3 (1987), examines the long-range effects of the Dawes Act on Native Americans. Frederick E. Hoxie's *A Final Promise: The Campaign to Assimilate the Indians, 1880-1920* (Lincoln: University of Nebraska Press, 1984) interweaves the story of the Dawes Act with the larger assimilationist programs toward Native Americans. *Americanizing the American Indians: Writings of the "Friends of the Indian" 1880-1900* (Lincoln: University of Nebraska Press, 1973), edited by Francis Paul Prucha, provides a representative sampling of primary source writings about the Dawes Act. Wilcomb E. Washburn's *The Assault on Indian Tribalism: The General Allotment Law (Dawes Act) of 1887* (Philadelphia: J. B. Lippincott, 1975) is a concise summary of the attitudes that produced the act and its repercussions for Native Americans; contains the full text of the original law.

See also: Allotment system; Assimilation: cultural and structural; Friends of the Indian; Indian Reorganization Act; Indian-white relations: United States; Reservation system of the United States.

Generational acculturation

Significance: Acculturation is defined as the changes in cultural patterns of groups when two or more ethnic and racial groups interact. Generational acculturation refers to the different degree and speed of this acculturation process depending on generations. Although assimilation and acculturation are used interchangeably in sociology and anthropology, acculturation is a part of the assimilation process.

Since the colonial period, America has received immigrants from all over the world and created a mosaic of ethnic groups of various races, religions, and national origins. However, Anglo-Saxons from England had the greatest impact on American culture, particularly in the United States' language, religion, and cultural values. Many ethnic and racial groups have gone through voluntary and involuntary acculturation processes over time to conform to this Anglo-Saxon culture. Members of the second generation (children of foreign-born parents) are more acculturated than their parents, and members of the third generation (children of native-born parents) are more acculturated than theirs. The concept of generational acculturation assumes that the foreign cultures that immigrants bring with them will be attenuated over generations.

Generational Difference
The first generation of many immigrant groups established ethnic enclaves, such as Little Italies, Little Tokyos, Chinatowns, and Jewish communities, and provided new immigrants of the same national origin with elements of their old culture, including ethnic grocery stores, cafes, and restaurants, and protection from societal hostility. First-generation immigrants were able to function in their own ethnic enclaves without speaking English and without changing their religious faith or cultural values. These immigrants were structurally and culturally separated from each other and from the core society, thus creating what Horace Kallen called "structural pluralism" (in *Culture and Democracy in the United States*, 1974).

Members of the second generation (American-born children) in general, however, achieved English competence and acquired American values through the public school system and the mass media. Because of societal hostility toward immigrants who possessed cultural traits not derived from Euro-American culture, native-born children, who witnessed their parents' hardships, tended to abandon their parents' culture. The second generation's relinquishment of distinctive cultural traits frequently created a gap between them and their parents, who retained the cultural values of their nation of origin.

Linear Model
Historians often cite a theory of second-generation rejection, as if there were iron-clad laws that dictated the cultural changes undergone by immigrant children. Generational acculturation tends to assume linear assimilation of immigrants to the core culture over generations. Members of the third generation (American-born children of American-born parents) are more acculturated than their parents. According to this linear model of generational acculturation, newer generations will either eventually be absorbed into Euro-American culture or contribute to creating the American melting pot.

Since the 1960's, scholars have frequently conducted research on Chinese and Japanese Americans to study generational differences in acculturation processes. Unlike most European immigrants, the first generations of Chinese and Japanese entered the mainland of the United States during a short and distinctive span of time; then immigration was blocked. Chinese first entered the U.S. mainland as unskilled cheap labor in the 1860's,

and their immigration was blocked by the Chinese Exclusion Act in 1882. After the exclusion of Chinese, the demand for cheap labor attracted the Japanese, and their immigration continued until it was restricted by the Immigration Act of 1924. For both groups, the second generation was born during a rather distinctive span of time, and even the third generation can be fairly well defined by span of years of birth. The three generations were also rather discrete birth cohorts and experienced distinctive acculturation processes in the change of cultural and behavioral patterns, in integration with whites, and in intermarriage with other racial and ethnic groups.

Nonlinear Model
In 1952, scholar Marcus Lee Hansen described a renewed interest in ethnicity among members of the third generation: "What the second generation tries to forget, the third generation tries to remember." He argued that

An elderly Japanese American admires a bonsai. The tendency for the second generation to reject traditional values and for the third generation to pursue them has been called the Hansen effect.

there may be internal social and psychological forces rather than external social forces that explain the persistence of white ethnicity. Members of the second generation, who observed the hardships that their foreign-born parents had experienced, tended to de-emphasize their ethnicity and cultural traits to avoid prejudice and discrimination from the larger society. Hansen found that members of the third generation, who are more acculturated in terms of English skills and American values and are free from severe discrimination, try to reconnect with their grandparents and their ethnic roots.

Ethnogenesis theory, set forth by Andrew M. Greeley in *Ethnicity in the United States* (1974), also argues that ethnic identity and acculturation are situational. Although newer generations of immigrants share cultural traits with the host group, they also retain distinctive characteristics. This process of rejection and maintenance of original cultural traits is situational and contextual according to an ethnic group's nationality, mode of entrance to the United States, political and economic climate at the time of entrance, and a host of other factors. Therefore, according to Greeley, acculturation is neither linear nor accelerated over generations.

Scholars in the late twentieth century have criticized the linear acculturation model, which assumed an Anglo-conformist perspective to analyze the acculturation process of ethnic and racial minority groups. These scholars argue that acculturation of these groups was a forced and involuntary process in order for them to be accepted as members of the host society. These processes are reflected in the episodes of boarding schools for Native American children, a different taxation system for Catholics, prohibition of Spanish in public education, and so forth.

Acculturation Process for Later Immigrants

Generational acculturation of immigrants since the late 1980's is different from the patterns mentioned above. Recent immigrants tend to retain their distinctive cultural traits over generations because of the emphasis on cultural diversity in the workplace and in the educational system in American society. The motives behind cultural maintenance are also related to the social class of recent immigrants. Immigrants who lack English skills retain their own language out of necessity, but immigrants who possess English skills and high socioeconomic status retain their language and culture out of desire. These immigrant parents hope their children will become bilingual and bicultural—able to speak two languages and live in two cultures. With an increasing number of immigrants expected in the twenty-first century and a continuing appreciation of diversity, more and more immigrants are expected to retain their distinctive cultural traits.

Hisako Matsuo

Core Resources

Milton Gordon's seminal work, *Assimilation in American Life: The Role of Race, Religion, and National Origins* (New York: Oxford University Press, 1964), remains the standard reference on the assimilation process. Andrew M. Greeley's theories are described in his *Ethnicity in the United States: A Preliminary Reconnaissance* (New York: Wiley, 1974). Marcus Lee Hansen's theories on the third generation are discussed in his "The Third Generation in America," in *Commentary* (14, 1952). Horace Kallen's views on structural pluralism are described in his *Culture and Democracy in the United States* (New York: Boni and Liveright, 1924). A look at the assimilation process in Japanese Americans is presented by Hisako Matsuo in "Identificational Assimilation of Japanese Americans: A Reassessment of Primordialism and Circumstantialism," in *Sociological Perspectives* (35, 1992).

See also: Assimilation: cultural and structural; Melting pot theory; Pluralism vs. assimilation; Race relations cycle.

Genetic basis for race

> **Significance:** To most biologists and anthropologists, race is a social, not a biological, category. Though human physical diversity is complex and obvious–and is genetically based–modern genetics has shown beyond all doubt that racial classifications are arbitrary.

It is obvious that humans vary tremendously in physical appearance. Other biological features such as blood type and enzyme production are equally diverse. Many people, if asked, would probably claim that these differences are profound and consistent enough to allow for categorizing humans into various distinct racial categories. A "race" might be defined as an isolated population within a species that has little or no gene flow with other members of that species. After a substantial period of time, this subgroup may take on numerous physical characteristics that are slightly different from the others of the species.

Although there might be some human populations that could called races, the way that the term is commonly used is simply not scientifically justifiable and has little value. In short, for all practical purposes, "races" do not exist as a natural biological category in the way that "species" do. The "races" of human beings are all of the same species and, biologically, are essentially identical. To be sure, as many people can personally attest, races do exist as social categories (discrimination being just one manifestation). However, these social categories are no more real or natural than any other arbitrary cultural construct (such as having to wear ties to work in an office).

Historical Racial Typologies and Explanations

The most common way of dividing the world racially has been the tripartite "white" (Caucasian), "black" (Negroid), and "oriental" (Mongoloid), using the vernacular and pseudo-scientific terms respectively. Since the days of naturalist Charles Darwin, who developed the theory of evolution, natural selection has often been the primary explanatory device to account for the great physical diversity seen in the world's people. For example, the tall and thin East African Dinka have bodies that radiate heat, an obvious advantage in a equatorial environment. People living in the Andes or near the Arctic Circle are short and squat for the opposite reason: Their bodies have less surface area to radiate heat, a useful trait for living in the extreme cold. However, such explanations are not completely compelling, as not everyone living in a warm climate is lean and tall, nor are all peoples in cold climates fat and small. Likewise, consider skin pigmentation as an adaption to varying exposures to sunlight. Although darker skins are believed to protect against sunburn, and white skin allows for easier absorption of necessary ultraviolet light in places with long winters, some of the darkest-skinned people in the world are the Tasmanians, who lived in an area receiving only moderate sunlight. Attributes such as eye color and hair color and texture seem to have no genetic adaptive advantage whatsoever.

Racial Criteria, and Some "New" Races

If adaptive or environmental explanations of racial variation are lacking, so are the definitions of race. There are thousands of ways to define a race. In recent times in Western countries, skin color has been the primary way to classify people; however, this has not always been the case, nor is this the only characteristic that can be used to separate people. For example, if classification

The Bell Curve Debate: Race, Intelligence, and Genes

One of the most controversial books of the mid-1990's was *The Bell Curve: Intelligence and Class Structure in American Life*, by psychologist Richard Herrnstein and political scientist Charles Murry. In some eight hundred pages of dense text, charts, and graphs, Herrnstein and Murry argue that in a democracy, the more intelligent people will rise above their socioeconomic class, thus leaving the lower classes, on the average, to consist of members who are less gifted intellectually. Though couched in rather careful language, they also claim that differences in intelligence quotient (IQ) between populations are mostly due to genetics. That is, while acknowledging that any particular person from group A may or may not be more intelligent than some particular person from group B, in terms of averages, group A and group B may show striking discrepancies in IQ scores. To put it bluntly, distinct races—because of their genetic makeups—demonstrate differences in intelligence.

The two topics of *The Bell Curve*—intelligence and race—are among the most controversial in American public discourse. Murry and Herrnstein's book immediately caught the attention of the popular media (appearing, for example, on the covers of *Newsweek, The New Republic*, and *The New York Times Book Review*). In the presidential elections of 1990 and 1994, welfare reform, teen pregnancy, and chronic unemployment were some of the most widely discussed social problems brought up by the campaigns, and in many ways *The Bell Curve* focused on these concerns. However compelling the arguments in this book may appear at first glance, many technical flaws exist in the data analysis. However, more important are the two premises on which the book is based: General human intelligence can be measured by a single numerical factor such as IQ, and humans can be categorized as belonging to racial categories, forming distinct and separate genetic groupings. The first claim is doubtful, with ambiguous support at best; but the second is simply wrong.

were made by the epicanthic fold (which covers the inner edge of the eyes and is typically found among people in East Asian countries), Japanese, Chinese, Koreans, and the Kung San of Africa would fall into the same "race." The emperor of Japan and South African leader Nelson Mandela share this feature. If blood typology were used, hundreds of different races could be constructed. For instance, Scots, central Africans, and Australian aboriginals could be placed together in the same biological (racial) category, because about 75 percent of their populations have O-type blood. Using the presence or absence of the sickle-shaped red blood cell, most Africans and African Americans would be placed in the same race along with Greeks and Italians. If dentition were used, East Asians, Native Americans, and

Swedes could form a race, as they all share incisors (eyeteeth) that are "scooped out" in the back.

Problems with Definitions

Inherent in every definition of race are at least four major problems involving clines, covariation, randomness, and arbitrary or self-definitions. Although clines, or gradations, of skin color and other traits exist, people do not fall into clear-cut, distinct categories. For example, it is hard to determine whether Iraqi leader Saddam Hussein is white, black, or Asian. Even if skin color, the most common measure, is used as the primary racial criteria, no clear or natural separations exist between peoples. There are groups of light-skinned blacks and populations of swarthy whites; people exist in every skin shade from light to dark.

Traits do not covary. If races were indeed real categories, different features should vary together. For example, all members of a particular race (white, black, or Asian) should have the same hair texture, facial features, blood type, eye and hair color, and other inheritable characteristics. However, among the world's peoples are populations of blond-haired "black" Australian aboriginals, "white" people who typically have flat "oriental" noses, and "orientals" with kinky hair. The features used to classify people according to "race" do not always occur as sets, which would be the case if true biological categories existed. In addition, biological anthropologists have long known that, using measurements of almost any physical criteria, just as much random variation exists within a so-called racial category as between "races." This calls into question the notion of race as a useful, or even valid, category.

Racial designations—especially legal ones—are basically arbitrary. One Jewish grandparent was enough to make an individual a Jew in Nazi Germany. In many southern states in the United States, if a person had any black ancestors, according to the one-drop rule, that individual was black, regardless of appearance. In the 1990's, because of increasing diversity and interracial marriage in the American population, the question of racial designations became more complex. What should a person with a "white" grandfather, "black" grandmother, and "oriental" mother be called? Often, this is something that people decide for themselves. Golfing superstar Tiger Woods, for example, says that when filling out forms, he checks every racial category that applies to make certain all of his ancestries are represented. The U.S. government is also aware of the arbitrariness of the racial and ethnic categories it uses to classify people, including those used in the census. For example, in 1997, federal agencies debated whether native Hawaiians, when filling out census questionnaires, should remain grouped with Asians and Pacific

Islanders or be placed in the category with Alaskans and Native Americans. The decision was tabled, and no change regarding Hawaiians was incorporated into the year 2000 census.

Between 50,000 and 100,000 pairs of genes are required to make a human being, and perhaps 75 percent of these are the same for everyone in the world. Only a small fraction of these genes—perhaps less than a dozen pairs—might account for skin pigmentation. The genes of white and black Americans are probably about 99.9 percent alike. There is simply no way to put five million Americans into three, six, or even a hundred racial categories that makes biological sense or has any scientific validity.

James Stanlaw

Core Resources

Evolutionary biologist Stephen Jay Gould's *The Mismeasure of Man* (revised and expanded edition, New York: Norton, 1996) discusses how the grouping of people on the basis of race has led to social problems of almost every imaginable kind. It is one of the most interesting and readable indictments of biological determinism and scientific racism ever written. Physiologist Jared Diamond is a lively writer who often examines race and genetics in his monthly *Discover* magazine articles; his book *The Third Chimpanzee: The Evolution and Future of the Human Animal* (New York: Harper, 1992) is recommended for its excellent explanations of how human diversity is affected by sexual and natural selection. Mark Nathan Cohen's "Culture, Not Race, Explains Human Diversity," in *The Chronicle of Higher Education* (April 17, 1998), gives a succinct but powerful summary of why anthropologists want to purge the word "race" from the daily vernacular. Finally, the arguments for the genetic and racial basis of intelligence are presented in Richard Herrnstein and Charles Murray's *The Bell Curve* (New York: The Free Press, 1994). However, this book should be read in conjunction with one of the several refutations; Russell Jacoby and Naomi Glauberman's *The Bell Curve Debate* (New York: Random House, 1995) is one of the best.

See also: Biosocial theories; Censuses, U.S.; Color coding; One-drop rule; Race as a concept; Social Darwinism and racism; Sociobiology and race.

Genocide: cultural

Significance: Acts of cultural genocide raise various ethical questions regarding such issues as human rights, civil rights, equality, and sovereignty.

Cultural genocide is the deliberate and systematic destruction of a culture. It is not ethical to destroy the culture of another group of human beings or change it without their consent. Each culture should be judged by its own standards of excellence and morality, unless its cultural practices threaten to harm others physically or mentally.

The Canadian government outlawed many indigenous customs of the Kwakiutl Indians of the Northwest Coast of Canada in an effort to convert them to a more Euro-Canadian lifestyle. The Kwakiutl were renowned for a unique custom that they called the *potlatch*. Kwakiutl chiefs competed with one another for status and power through this custom. It involved accumulating vast wealth in the form of artistic items known as "coppers," blankets, and food. After accumulating a fortune, a chief would invite his rival and the rival's followers to a feast. During this feast, the host would wine and dine all of his guests lavishly. Dancers would entertain them. At a prearranged time, the host would conspicuously destroy the valuable coppers and other treasures to demonstrate that he could afford to do so. He would challenge his guest to top this feat or accept inferior status. Upon leaving the feast, guests were given many blankets and food to take home with them. The Canadian government viewed this practice as a wanton and savage destruction of valuable property and a waste of labor, so they outlawed the *potlatch*.

Anthropologists have argued that, in addition to serving the overt function of leveling individuals, the *potlatch* served a covert or hidden function by redistributing wealth from areas that had accumulated a surplus to areas that had experienced shortages during bad years. The destruction of this and other pivotal institutions caused the Kwakiutl culture to collapse, leaving in its wake a vacuum that was soon filled by alcoholism, dysfunctional families, and other social problems.

Another example of cultural genocide comes from Africa. In 1884, at the Berlin Conference, European powers unilaterally carved up the African continent into territories that they claimed for themselves. Africans were not invited to this meeting. These European powers pledged to support the "civilizing" of Africans by Christian missionaries, which was "calculated to educate the natives and to teach them to understand and appreciate the benefits of civilization." The missionaries immediately declared traditional religions "devil worship." They collected all indigenous statues, relics, and artifacts and destroyed them. They fought to outlaw clitoridectomy, polygyny, and other native customs that they found "repugnant." These acts led to a clash of cultures and to an identity crisis for many Africans.

The classic example of cultural genocide in North America grew out of slavery. Plantation owners feared that allowing African slaves to speak their own languages, use African names to identify themselves, or practice African culture would encourage slave revolts. Consequently, every effort was made to stamp out African culture in the United States. The people survived, but much of their culture was destroyed. Today, African Americans are culturally more like other Americans than they are like Africans, despite strong physical similarities and a common ancestry.

The assumption that one's own culture is better for others than theirs is constitutes the ultimate cultural arrogance. It assumes that one's own culture is superior and that one has the right to impose one's values on others. This imposition is unfair and unethical. Cultures, like individuals, have a right to life unless their customs threaten the lives of others. *Dallas L. Browne*

See also: Annihilation of racial and ethnic groups; Bigotry; Genocide; Genocide: physical; Prejudice: effects; Racism.

Genocide of American Indians

Significance: The impact of European colonization of North America had an immediate and devastating impact on the indigenous population.

The European discovery of the New World had devastating consequences for the native population. Within a century of Christopher Columbus's landing in 1492, the number of people living in the Americas had declined from 25 million to 1 million. Whole societies in Mexico and South America died within weeks of initial contact with Spanish explorers and adventurers. The major cause of the devastation was disease. Native Americans had lived in total isolation from the rest of the world since first arriving in the New World from Central Asia around 20,000 B.C.E.; hence, they had escaped the devastating epidemics and diseases, such as smallpox and the plague, that had afflicted the rest of humankind for generations. Such diseases normally required human carriers to pass them on to others, and such conditions did not exist in the New World until after 1492.

Deadly Contact
Columbus and his crew made four separate voyages to the New World between 1492 and 1510, and on each of those voyages sailors brought new diseases with them. Even the common flu had devastating consequences for Native American babies and children. Other people of the world had built up immunities to these killers, but

Native Americans had none, so they died in massive numbers. In the 1500's, most of the dying took place from Mexico south, since the Spanish appeared to be uninterested in colonizing North America. Only after the English settled Jamestown in 1607-1608 and Plymouth in Massachusetts in 1620 did the epidemics affect Native Americans in that region.

The first major tribe to be exterminated in North America was the Massachusetts of New England, whose population died out completely between 1619 and 1633 from a smallpox epidemic. Yet other things besides disease were killing Native Americans. Most Europeans believed that the people they came across in their explorations were not human at all, but instead savage, inferior beings who had no law and order, no cities, no wealth, and no idea of God or progress. When they died from "white man's diseases," this offered further proof of the weakness and helplessness of the population. Europeans soon turned to Africa for their supply of slave laborers; Africans, who had had a much longer history of contact with other peoples of the world, had built up immunities to the killing diseases. Native Americans were not so lucky.

Conflict over Land

As time passed, immunities were built up by native peoples, and fewer tribes were extinguished by diseases. Warfare, however, continued to take its toll. Thousands of Native Americans died defending their homelands from American settlers in the aftermath of the War for Independence. Native Americans were not made citizens by the Constitution of 1787 but were legally defined as residents of foreign nations living in the United States. Wars and conflicts over territory devastated many tribes by 1830. In that year, president Andrew Jackson and Congress adopted a program, the Indian Removal Act, that they hoped would put an end to wars with the Native Americans. Under this new act, the American government would trade land west of the Mississippi River for land owned by the tribes in the east. Land in the west, acquired from France in 1803 as part of the Louisiana Purchase, was deemed unsuitable for farming by Europeans. Native Americans, on the other hand, would be able to survive on the Great Plains, called the "Great American Desert" by most whites, by hunting buffalo and other game.

Congress authorized the president to exchange land beginning in 1831.

Three years later, a permanent Indian Country was created in the West and settlement by whites was declared illegal. By 1840, Indian Removal was complete, though it took the Black Hawk War in Illinois, the Seminole Wars in Florida, and the terrible march forcing the Cherokee from Georgia to the Indian Territory, to complete the process. At least three thousand Native American women and children died at the hands of the U.S. Army on the Cherokee Trail of Tears. Indian Removal meant death and disaster for many eastern tribes.

Conflict was reduced by the program only until whites began moving into the West in the 1860's. During the Civil War (1861-1865), several Indian Wars were fought in Minnesota and Iowa, and the infamous Chivington Massacre took place in Colorado in 1864. In this incident, 450 Native Americans were slaughtered without warning in a predawn raid by the Colorado militia. To prevent massacres in the West, Congress enacted a "reservation policy," setting aside several million acres of western lands for "permanent" Indian settlement. The Army had the job of keeping the tribes on their reservations. Frequent wars resulted as Great Plains tribes attempted to leave their reservations to hunt buffalo (bison) and the army drove them back.

Problems increased with the coming of railroads. The first transcontinental railroad began carrying passengers in 1869. Huge buffalo herds presented the railroads with a major problem, however, because they took hours and sometimes days to cross the tracks. To keep trains running on time, railroads hired hunters to kill the buffalo. By the late 1880's, they had nearly accomplished their goal of killing off all the herds. Buffalo had once numbered 100 million, but by 1888, there were fewer than

Native American Tribes That Have Been Completely Exterminated

Tribe	Region Inhabited	Years Exterminated	By Whom/ What
Calusa	Florida	1513-1530	Spanish/war
Massachusetts	New England	1617-1633	Smallpox
Pequot	New England	1637-1638	English/war
Powhatan	Virginia	1637-1705	English/war
Narraganset	Rhode Island	1675-1676	English/war
Susquehannock	New York	1675-1763	Disease/war
Chitimacha	Louisiana	1706-1717	French/war
Natchez	Mississippi	1716-1731	French/war
Chinook	Columbia River region	1782-1853	Smallpox
Yavapai	Arizona	1873-1905	Tuberculosis

1,000. With the destruction of the buffalo came the end of the Native American way of life. The final war was fought in 1890 in the Black Hills of South Dakota on the Pine Ridge Reservation. An Indian holy man claimed that the whites would disappear and the buffalo would return if Native Americans danced a Ghost Dance. Magical shirts were given to the dancers that were supposed to protect them from white men's bullets. When the white Indian agent asked Washington for help to put down the Ghost Dancers, the Army responded by killing hundreds of the Native Americans, whose magical shirts did not work.

Native Americans did not become American citizens until 1924 and were required to live on reservations. Not until 1934 was self-government granted to the tribes, and by that time the reservations had become the poorest communities in the entire United States. It is only in recent decades, with the rise in Indian activism and legislation protecting Indian civil and tribal rights, that Native Americans have begun to recover.

Leslie V. Tischauser

Core Resources

Angie Debo's *A History of the Indians of the United States* (Norman: University of Oklahoma Press, 1970), Vine Deloria, Jr.'s *Custer Died for Your Sins: An Indian Manifesto* (New York: Macmillan, 1969), Alvin M. Josephy, Jr.'s *The Indian Heritage of America* (New York: Alfred A. Knopf, 1968), and Wilcomb E. Washburn's *The Indian in America* (New York: Harper & Row, 1975) discuss the extermination of Native Americans from varying perspectives.

See also: Annihilation of racial and ethnic groups; Bigotry; Disease and intergroup contact; Genocide: cultural; Genocide: physical; Racism: history of the concept.

Genocide: physical

> **Significance:** The act of genocide, which is based on hatred, bigotry, and prejudice, is opposed to the concepts of human rights, civil rights, and basic freedoms.

Physical genocide is the deliberate and systematic attempt to annihilate an entire human population. Perpetrators of this practice direct their actions against groups that differ from their own in religious belief, race, ethnic affiliation, nationality, or sexual orientation. Often the extermination of a human group is prompted when the entire group is attributed with some presumed guilt that is associated with a small segment of that group or their ancestors.

Hitler and the Jews

Brutal massacres of entire Jewish populations were ordered by Adolf Hitler as his "final solution" to the "Jewish question" in Germany and throughout Europe. Hitler argued that many of Germany's problems stemmed from the fact that Jews formed a separate, degenerate race. To Hitler, each race inherited certain qualities through its blood and genes; the Aryans were thus a naturally superior race, while Jews were sinister and devious. Hitler accused the Jews of secretly forming an "international Jewish conspiracy" aimed at dominating the globe economically and politically by cheating everyone else. He argued that because Jews were a lower and undesirable form of life, the only real solution to the "Jewish question" was total extermination. As a result, he ordered the extermination of more than six million Jews. Hitler's Nazi Party used the Holocaust to cover up its theft of Jewish families' valuable art treasures, life savings, and property. The Nazi Party used the term *Judenrein*, meaning to clean an area of Jews, as a euphemism for genocide. Hitler applied the same flawed reasoning to Gypsies, the mentally retarded, and homosexuals. All were to be exterminated because they were considered inherently inferior and unworthy of life.

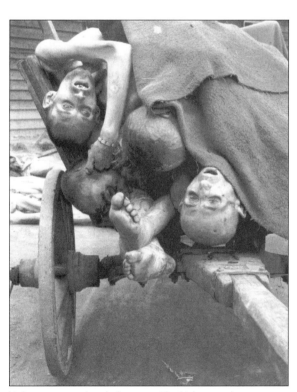

Holocaust victims lie piled in a cart. The Holocaust, the systematic killing of the Jews orchestrated by Nazi leader Adolf Hitler, is the best-known example of physical genocide.

Other Historical Examples

History provides numerous examples of genocide. When the Australian government wanted land on the island of Tasmania, the native population refused to sell it or give it away. Ultimately, the Tasmanians' water supply was poisoned. Every native Tasmanian perished, and settlers from Australia subsequently claimed the land.

Turkey offers another example of this crime against humanity. Sultan Abdul Hamid II encouraged Kurdish depredations against Armenian villages. By 1894, these actions had grown into full-scale war, and the Turkish army assisted in the massacre of Armenians. Initially, an estimated 200,000 Armenians were killed. During World War I, the Turks sided with Germany, but the Armenians sided with Russia and Britain. As a result, the Turks viewed them as subversives. To secure its border with Russia, Turkey forcibly removed millions of Armenians and forced them to march south without adequate food or shelter. Armenians claim that the result was a holocaust and that more than one million Armenians died in Turkey in 1915. The Turks took more than 90 percent of the Armenians' land. The Turkish government has never admitted guilt for these events and has claimed that Armenians killed an equal number of Turks during World War I.

The Nobel Prize-winning physicist William Shockley proposed a theory of "dysergenics" that states that African Americans are biologically inferior to whites. Shockley proposed making America more competitive globally by the forced sterilization of all African Americans living in the United States. Within one generation, there would be no race problem because the black race would die out. Shockley was barred from speaking in Britain by authorities who considered his theory outrageous. World history is replete with examples of human willingness to violate moral and ethical codes, yet genocide constitutes the gravest violation of ethical principles on record.

Dallas L. Browne

Core Resources

Zygmunt Bauman's *Modernity and the Holocaust* (Ithaca, N.Y.: Cornell University Press, 1989), Frank Chalk and Kurt Jonassohn's *The History and Sociology of Genocide: Analyses and Case Studies* (New Haven, Conn.: Yale University Press, 1990), Israel W. Cherny's *How Can We Commit the Unthinkable? Genocide: The Human Cancer* (New York: Hearst, 1982), Leo Kuper's *The Prevention of Genocide* (New Haven, Conn.: Yale University Press, 1985), and *Genocide and Human Rights* (Lanham, Md.: University Press of America, 1982), edited by Jack Nusan Porter, discuss the phenomenon of genocide from various perspectives.

See also: Annihilation of racial and ethnic groups; Anti-Semitism; Apartheid; Bigotry; Ethnic cleansing; Genocide: cultural; Genocide of American Indians; Holocaust; Racism: history of the concept.

Gentlemen's Agreement

Significance: As a consequence of this 1907 agreement between the U.S. and Japanese governments, immigration from Japan to the mainland United States was limited to nonlaborers, laborers already settled in the United States, and their families.

The first Japanese immigrants who arrived in California in 1871 were mostly middle-class young men seeking opportunities to study or improve their economic status. By 1880, there were 148 resident Japanese. Their numbers increased to 1,360 in 1891, including 281 laborers and 172 farmers. A treaty between the United States and Japan in 1894 ensured mutual free entry although allowing limitations on immigration based on domestic interests. By 1900, the number of Japanese recorded in the U.S. census had increased to 24,326. They arrived at ports on the Pacific coast and settled primarily in the Pacific states and British Columbia.

An increase in the demand for Hawaiian sugar in turn increased the demand for plantation labor, especially Japanese labor. An era of government-contract labor began in 1884, ending only with the U.S. annexation of Hawaii in 1898. Sixty thousand Japanese in the islands then became eligible to enter the United States without passports. Between 1899 and 1906, it is estimated that between forty thousand and fifty-seven thousand Japanese moved to the United States via Hawaii, Canada, and Mexico.

Tensions Develop

On the Pacific coast, tensions developed between Asians and other Californians. Although the Japanese immigrant workforce was initially welcomed, antagonism increased as it began to compete with U.S. labor. The emerging trade-union movement advocated a restriction of immigration. An earlier campaign against the Chinese had culminated in the 1882 Chinese Exclusion Act, which suspended immigration of Chinese laborers to the United States for ten years. This act constituted the first U.S. law barring immigration based on race or nationality. A similar campaign was instigated against the Japanese. On March 1, 1905, both houses of the California State legislature voted to urge California's congressional delegation in Washington, D.C., to pursue the limitation of Japanese immigrants. At a meeting in San Francisco on May 7, delegates from sixty-seven organizations launched the Japanese and Korean Exclusion League, known also as the Asiatic Exclusion League.

President Theodore Roosevelt, who was involved in the peace negotiations between Japan and Russia, observed the developing situation in California. George Kennan, who was covering the Russo-Japanese War, wrote to the president:

> It isn't the exclusion of a few emigrants that hurts here ... it's the putting of Japanese below Hungarians, Italians, Syrians, Polish Jews, and degraded nondescripts from all parts of Europe and Western Asia. No proud, high spirited and victorious people will submit to such a classification as that, especially when it is made with insulting reference to personal character and habits.

Roosevelt agreed, saying he was mortified that people in the United States should insult the Japanese. He continued to play a pivotal role in resolving the Japanese-Russian differences at the Portsmouth Peace Conference.

Anti-Japanese feeling waned until April, 1906. Following the San Francisco earthquake, an outbreak of crime occurred, including many cases of assault against Japanese. There was also an organized boycott of Japanese restaurants. The Japanese viewed these acts as especially reprehensible. Their government and Red Cross had contributed more relief for San Francisco than all other foreign nations combined.

Tension escalated. The Asiatic Exclusion League, whose membership was estimated to be 78,500 in California, together with San Francisco's mayor, pressured the San Francisco school board to segregate Japanese schoolchildren. On October 11, 1906, the board passed its resolution. A protest filed by the Japanese consul was denied. Japan protested that the act violated most-favored-nation treatment. Ambassador Luke E. Wright, in Tokyo, reported Japan's extremely negative feelings about the matter to Secretary of State Elihu Root. This crisis in Japanese American relations brought the countries to the brink of war. On October 25, Japan's ambassador, Shuzo Aoki, met with Root to seek a solution. President Roosevelt, who recognized the justification of the Japanese protest based on the 1894 treaty, on October 26 sent his secretary of commerce and labor to San Francisco to investigate the matter.

In his message to Congress on December 4, President Roosevelt paid tribute to Japan and strongly repudiated San Francisco for its anti-Japanese acts. He encouraged Congress to pass an act that would allow naturalization of the Japanese in the United States. Roosevelt's statements and request pleased Japan but aroused further resentment on the Pacific coast. During the previous twelve months, more than seventeen thousand Japanese had entered the mainland United States, two-thirds coming by way of Hawaii. Roosevelt recognized that the basic cause of the unrest in California—the increasing inflow of Japanese laborers—could be resolved only by checking immigration.

U.S. and Japan Negotiate

Negotiations with Japan to limit the entry of Japanese laborers began in late December, 1906. Three issues were involved: the rescinding of the segregation order by the San Francisco school board, the withholding of passports to the mainland United States by the Japanese government, and the closing of immigration channels through Hawaii, Canada, and Mexico by federal legislation. The Hawaiian issue, which related to an earlier Gentlemen's Agreement of 1900, was the first resolved through the diplomacy of Japan's foreign minister, Tadasu Hayashi, ambassadors Wright and Aoki, and Secretary of State Root.

Before Japan would agree to discuss immigration to the mainland, it was necessary for the segregation order to be withdrawn. In February, 1907, the president invited San Francisco's entire board of education, the mayor, and a city superintendent of schools to Washington, D.C., to confer on the segregation issue and other problems related to Japan. On February 18, a pending immigration bill was amended to prevent Japanese laborers from entering the United States via Hawaii, Mexico, or Canada. Assured that immigration of Japanese laborers would be stopped, the school board rescinded their segregation order on March 13. An executive order issued by the president on March 14 put into effect the restrictions on passports. Subsequently, the Japanese government agreed to conclude the Gentlemen's Agreement. In January, 1908, Foreign Minister Hayashi agreed to the terms of immigration discussed in December, 1907. On March 9, Secretary of State Root instructed Ambassador Wright to thank Japan, thus concluding the negotiations begun in December, 1906.

As reported by the commissioner general of immigration in 1908, the Japanese government would issue passports for travel to the continental United States only to nonlaborers, laborers who were former residents of the United States, parents, wives, or children of residents, and "settled agriculturalists." A final provision prevented secondary immigration into the United States by way of Hawaii, Mexico, or Canada.

When the Gentlemen's Agreement of 1907 cut off new supplies of Japanese labor, Filipinos were recruited to take their place, both in Hawaii and in California, as well as in the Alaskan fishing industry. As U.S. nationals, Filipinos could not be prevented from migrating to the United States.

Susan E. Hamilton

Core Resources

Raymond A. Esthus's *Theodore Roosevelt and Japan* (Seattle: University of Washington Press, 1967) provides a detailed examination of Roosevelt's relationship with Japan. Akemi Kikumura's *Issei Pioneers: Hawaii and the Mainland, 1885 to 1924* (Los Angeles: Japanese American National Museum, 1992) is a brief but well-researched text, with photographs that accompanied the premiere exhibit of the Japanese American National Museum. The U.S. Department of State's *Report of the Hon. Roland S. Morris on Japanese Immigration and Alleged Discriminatory Legislation Against Japanese Residents in the United States* (1921; reprint, New York: Arno Press, 1978) collects correspondence regarding the Gentlemen's Agreement.

See also: Alien land laws; Asian American stereotypes; Japanese Americans; Yellow peril campaign.

German Americans

Significance: German Americans constitute a major ethnic group in the United States. These early immigrants—Catholic, Protestant, Separatist, and Jewish—assimilated relatively easily and completely and dispersed throughout the country. In general, unlike the Irish, Italians, and Poles, negative characteristics were not attributed to them, although Anglo-Protestants often objected to their drinking beer on Sundays.

The first German colony was established in Germantown, Pennsylvania, in 1683 by Mennonites, an Anabaptist sect. (The Amish later separated from the Mennonites.) However, individual Germans were already present in the English colonies and in the Dutch colony of New Amsterdam. The Hutterites, another Anabaptist sect, came to America in 1874, settling in South Dakota. Although pacifists, they were subjected to conscription during World War I. Most of the community migrated to Canada, but many later returned. Two Hutterites who were sentenced for refusing conscription died from maltreatment.

Methodism developed a following among German Americans in the nineteenth century, and although the Methodist Church began phasing out the German branch in 1924, some congregations of the German Methodist Church persisted throughout the twentieth century. Germans also set up Baptist and Presbyterian churches. By 1890, nearly half of German Americans were Roman Catholic. Catholics and Lutherans did not mix much, which tended to divide German American political influence. The German and Irish wings of the

American Catholic Church experienced some conflict in the 1880's and 1890's, and before World War I, German, Irish, and Polish congregations attended separate Catholic churches. Similarly, German and Scandinavian congregations often established separate Lutheran churches, and German American and Eastern European Jews generally formed separate worship groups, although the Eastern European Jews commonly spoke Yiddish, which is more than 80 percent German. German American Jews maintained cultural ties with Germany until the Nazi period.

Relations with American Indians

The Germans seemed to have less trouble with American Indians than other settlers in the eighteenth century, and in Texas, where thriving German settlements were established in the 1830's and 1840's, the Meusenbach-Comanche Treaty of 1847, negotiated between John Meusenbach and Comanche leaders Buffalo Hump, Santana, and Old Owl, was never broken by either side.

Two German travelers and a German American made significant contributions to American Indian ethnology. Alexander Philipp Maximilian, Prince of Wied-Neuwied, visited the United States in 1832 and produced a comprehensive study of the Mandan tribe, which later became extinct. Friedrich Gerstäcker, who visited the United States from 1837 to 1843 and again in 1849 and 1867, created a detailed ethnography of American Indian culture. German American Gustavus Sohon, born in Prussia, served in the U.S. Army as a surveyor in the Northwest. There he became familiar with several American Indian tribes along the Columbia River and made numerous sketches of their lives, which are a valuable part of the anthropological record.

German Americans and Slavery

Various German American groups spoke out against slavery in the United States. The Mennonites of Germantown, Pennsylvania, made the first protest in 1688. The Salzburger Protestant colony of Ebenezer in Georgia, founded in 1734, also opposed slavery.

The failed Revolution of 1848, during which reactionary authorities in Berlin and Vienna suppressed attempts at constitutional reform, resulted in thousands of liberal intellectuals migrating to the United States. These new immigrants, who were particularly active in establishing newspapers, had a major impact on the cultural life of German American communities. The Forty-eighters, as they were known, were strongly opposed to slavery, and under their influence, a strong alliance formed between abolitionist forces and the German press in the United States.

Among the Forty-eighters was Mathilde Franziska Anneke-Giesler, an early champion of women's rights who came to the United States in 1850. Although she wrote almost exclusively in German, she was in close contact with suffragists Susan B. Anthony and Elizabeth Cady Stanton and often lectured in English. Antagonism to her feminist and antislavery attitudes caused her to go to England in 1860, where she lectured against slavery, returning to the United States in 1865.

In 1854, Germans meeting in San Antonio, Texas, declared their opposition to slavery, and German Americans fought on the North's side during the Civil War. In a battle with Confederate soldiers, one German American guard of sixty-five men lost twenty-seven people and had nine of its wounded murdered by opposition forces.

Relations with Anglo-Saxon Society

In the early nineteenth century, the German community in New York was significant enough to be courted by both political parties. A German Democratic Party organization was created in 1834, and eventually a German language newspaper was established to reflect the party's platform.

The years before the Civil War saw the rise of nativism, and anti-Catholicism was rampant. In 1855, murderous rioters in Louisville, Kentucky, attacked German Americans because many of them were Catholic and foreign-born and tended to be politically radical. The German Americans' opposition to slavery also created hostility in several regions.

Milestones in German American History

Year	Event	Impact
1671	Naturalization Act passes in Virginia (revised in 1680)	Enables the few German craftsmen and farmers then in Virginia to secure the same rights as British subjects.
1683	The first German colony is established at Germantown, Pennsylvania	Creates a community that welcomes religious dissenters and maintains German culture for two hundred years.
1710	Queen Anne sends Palatine refugees to America	Establishes a wider German population in the New World.
1735	John Peter Zenger is tried	Strengthens the concept of freedom of the press and the rights of the accused; has an important influence on the U.S. Constitution.
1775-1781	German American regiments serve in Revolutionary War	German Americans gain further acceptance as citizens and partners.
1786	Frederick the Great recognizes the United States	Provides diplomatic support and encourages migration from Germany.
1848	Revolution breaks out in Prussia, Austria, and German states	Spurs migration of liberal intellectuals committed to political reform to the United States.
1870-1871	Franco-Prussian War	Gives German Americans new pride in a united Germany and increased respect from other Americans.
1873-1887	Bismarck May laws; *Kulturkampf*	Promotes Catholic immigration.
1894	German newspapers reach their highest level in the United States	Helps maintain the German language and culture for another generation.
1901	The National German American Alliance is formed	Provides a national nonpartisan, nonsectarian organization to address issues of interest.
1917-1918	American entry into World War I creates wave of anti-German hysteria	Accelerates loss of German language and culture.
1948	German Federal Republic formed	West Germany becomes a U.S. ally.
1989	Germany reunited	With the Cold War over and most of Europe united in the European Union, Germany has less motivation to promote ties with German Americans.

German Americans experienced some friction with Anglo-Saxon Protestants of a puritanical bent, who disdained frivolity, especially on Sunday, and disliked some German customs associated with Christmas because they appeared to be pagan in origin. This immigrant group also clashed with the growing temperance movement in the nineteenth and twentieth centuries. The breweries founded by Germans in cities such as Cincinnati, Ohio; Milwaukee, Wisconsin; and St. Louis, Missouri, contributed to the economic development of these cities, and German Americans largely controlled the American brewing industry. German Americans in Texas kept that state from becoming a dry state until national Prohibition went into effect. One of the major purposes of the German American Alliance was to oppose prohibition. The German American Alliance (Deutsch-Amerikanische Nationalbund) was formed in 1901 as a national, sectarian, politically nonpartisan German American organization. It reached a membership of three million by 1916 to become the largest ethnic organization in U.S. history. Congress abrogated the organization's charter in 1918.

Germans were also active in the labor movement that began after the Civil War and in radical politics, which caused some conflict with the dominant society.

World War I

The United States' entry into World War I unleashed a tremendous irrational hostility toward anything German, including music—not just folk or popular music but classical music and opera. German Americans were harassed and subjected to physical assault, vandalism, and even murder. This hysteria existed even in areas where German Americans constituted more than one-third of the population or even a majority.

Laws in various states forbade teaching German in schools and speaking German in public, and thousands were convicted. Such laws were declared unconstitutional by the U.S. Supreme Court in 1923. Anti-German attitudes lingered for a few years after the war and accelerated Anglicization of churches, social organizations, and newspapers.

World War II

In 1936, the Deutschamerikanische Volksbund, the German American Bund, replaced an earlier organization intended to represent the Nazi Party in the United States. The membership was believed to be only sixty-five hundred, and 40 percent were not actually of German stock, but the organization's posturing, arrogance, and hostility in effect mobilized public opinion against the Nazis and complicated diplomatic relations between the United States and Germany. The Steuben Society, the most prestigious German American organization, and other German organizations felt it necessary to repudiate the Bund, and German American antifascist organizations were formed.

After World War II, German American ethnic identity became increasingly tenuous as the population moved to the suburbs, and changes in recreational tastes weakened ties to German culture. Postwar German immigrants were less inclined to take part in German cultural organizations.

In 1948, the Russian blockade of the land routes to West Berlin made that city, and by extension West Germany, a symbol of freedom and democracy, giving Americans a more positive attitude toward Germany. West Germany became a military ally, and during the second half of the century, became increasingly integrated into the Pan-European identity of the European Union. Similarly, German Americans came to identify more with the broader European American culture.

William L. Reinshagen

Core Resources

LaVern Ripley's *The German-Americans* (Boston: Twayne, 1976) is a well-written history of Germans in the United States from colonial times to the U.S. Bicentennial, explaining contemporaneous events in German Europe and mentioning prominent German Americans. Alfred Llau's *Deutschland—United States of America, 1683-1983* (Bielefeld, Germany: Univers-Verlag, 1983) covers three hundred years of immigration and German-American relations. Gerard Wilk's *Americans from Germany* (New York: German Information Center, 1976) focuses particularly on the experiences of German Americans over the years, and Irene M. Franck's *The German American Heritage* (New York: Facts on File, 1988) provides details and statistical information. *German Culture in Texas*, edited by Glen E. Lich and Dona B. Reeves (Boston: Twayne, 1980), is a collection of articles on various aspects of the German regions of Texas. The University of Wisconsin publishes *The Yearbook of German American Studies* and annotated bibliographies.

See also: Abolition; American Nazi Party; Anti-Catholicism; British as dominant group; Civil War; Indian-white relations: United States; Labor movement.

Ghost Dance religion

The Ghost Dance began in 1890 as a result of the visions of a Paiute Indian from Nevada called Wovoka. Wovoka began delivering a series of prophetic messages that described a future which would restore Native Americans to their life as it had been before contact with the European American settlers and would drive away or

Sioux Indians perform the Ghost Dance ceremony in 1893. Followers of the Ghost Dance religion envisioned the restoration of the Indian way of life.

destroy the settlers on Native American traditional lands. The Ghost Dance movement was typically hostile toward white settlers, and the movement was deeply implicated in the massacre at Wounded Knee in Pine Ridge, South Dakota.

Included among the visions of Wovoka were such basic ideas as the resurrection of tribal members who had died, the restoration of game animals, a flood which would destroy only the white settlers, the necessity and importance of the performance of a dance ritual (the Ghost Dance itself), and a coming era which would be free of suffering and disease. Of these major ideas, the primary focus seemed to be on resurrection and the restoration of important elements of the old ways, as well as the performance of the dance itself. Related developments of the Ghost Dance movement were certain ethical precepts and, at least among the Sioux, the creation and wearing of distinctive "ghost shirts," which identified adherents to the movement and were used in the performance of the ritual dancing itself.

As predicted dates for the cosmic events described by Wovoka came and passed, the initial fervor of the Ghost Dance and Wovoka's teachings in general began to dissipate. Among some tribes, however, the focus shifted from apocalyptic expectations of events to a longer-term stress on daily ethics. In short, the movement became partially institutionalized, which is not uncommon for religious groups whose roots lie in visionary experiences.

Daniel L. Smith-Christopher

See also: Genocide of American Indians; Indian-white relations: United States; Wounded Knee massacre.

Glass ceiling

After the Equal Employment Opportunity Commission (EEOC) was established in 1964 and additional legislation was passed in the 1970's by the U.S. government that made discrimination in employment illegal, more members of minority groups were hired by corporations. Although these people had good jobs, many of them soon discovered that they could rise to a certain level within the corporate structure and no further. Certain barriers, which became collectively known as the glass ceiling, prevented their further advancement, particularly in the business world. These obstacles result from bias or prejudice on the part of employers and from institutional racism and sexism; they are difficult to detect and even harder to eliminate. Tolerance of the glass ceiling often exists in companies that try to appear nondiscriminatory by opening jobs to a few token minorities and women as a means of avoiding lawsuits and criticism. Some observers have countered that standards for measuring corporate compliance with fair hiring practices fail to take into account that it takes roughly twenty-five years or more to rise to top management levels. Nevertheless, the continued existence of the glass ceiling prevents many female and minority employees from reaching top management positions even though they seem qualified for such promotions.

See also: Affirmative action; Employment among African Americans; Employment among Asian Americans; Employment among Latinos; Equal Employment Opportunity Act; Equal Employment Opportunity Commission.

Goetz, Bernhard, incident

On December 22, 1984, an unidentified white man, later dubbed the Subway Vigilante, drew a pistol and shot four black youths who surrounded him and asked him for money on a New York subway. The shooter then fled. On December 31, 1984, Bernhard Goetz, age thirty-seven, surrendered to police. Goetz was arraigned January 3, 1985, and indicted January 25.

Goetz gained support among conservative white Americans when it emerged that the young men were known offenders armed with sharpened screwdrivers, that Goetz had been a victim of a mugging in which charges were dropped, and that his request for a gun permit had been denied despite a job-related need to carry cash on the subway.

United States outside legal channels, it lowered the burden of proof to that of intermediate scrutiny. Thus a different standard of proof was made to apply in cases involving so-called illegal aliens from that which applied to those concerning lawful resident aliens. Unlike discriminatory racial classifications, which are inherently suspect, alienage has proven to be a more protean concept.

Lisa Paddock

See also: *Plyler v. Doe.*

Grandfather clauses

After the Civil War (1861-1865), the Fifteenth Amendment to the U.S. Constitution guaranteed the voting rights of people of color in southern states. It expressly stated that the right to vote could not be "denied or abridged . . . on account of race, color, or previous condition of servitude." During the period of Reconstruction (1863-1877), the military administration in charge of the former Confederate states enforced this prescription. When Reconstruction ended, and the civil authority of these states replaced the federal military administration, white southerners devised various methods of circumventing the Fifteenth Amendment. One of these methods was the grandfather clause.

Grandfather clauses based eligibility to vote on the capacity of one's grandfather to vote. Of course, the grandfathers of the vast majority of African Americans in the South had been slaves and therefore had never been allowed to vote. Seven southern states incorporated such a clause into their state constitutions. Along with poll taxes, literacy tests, and other so-called Jim Crow measures, grandfather clauses effectively prohibited African Americans from voting for several decades. In 1915, the U.S. Supreme Court declared the grandfather clause to be an unconstitutional qualification for voting.

Aristide Sechandice

See also: Fifteenth Amendment; *Guinn v. United States*; Jim Crow laws; Literacy tests; Poll tax; Reconstruction; Voting Rights Act of 1965.

Great Migration

> **Significance:** The Great Migration was the early twentieth century movement of more than a million African Americans from the rural South and Midwest to Northern cities.

The Great Migration, a demographic shift of African Americans from southern states to midwestern and northeastern states, occurred roughly between 1910 and 1930. Because migration figures are based on the U.S. census, which is conducted every tenth year, the dating of migration events is imprecise. The data indicate only that this migration took place sometime between 1910 and 1930, but other historical evidence suggests that it began sometime during World War I (between 1914 and 1918) and ended around the onset of the Great Depression in 1929.

During the Great Migration, the industrial northern and midwestern states of New York, Illinois, Pennsylvania, Ohio, and Michigan experienced the greatest net migration of African Americans. The greatest net loss of African American population was from the southern, agricultural states of Georgia, South Carolina, Virginia, Alabama, and Mississippi. As they moved from one region to another, most of the migrants also moved from rural areas to urban areas. Between 1910 and 1920, the African American population of Detroit grew from 5,000 to 40,800; that of Cleveland from 8,400 to 34,400; that of Chicago from 44,000 to 109,400; and that of New York from 91,700 to 152,400. The transition from rural to urban locales was accompanied by a transition from employment in agriculture to employment in industrial or service occupations for increasing numbers of African Americans.

Reasons for Leaving

The reasons that African Americans did not leave the South in large numbers until fifty years after the end of the Civil War have been the subject of debate among social scientists and historians. Both social and economic factors were involved. After the Civil War, owners of plantations and farms in the South imposed new ways of controlling labor that were almost as restrictive as slavery had been. As sharecroppers, former slaves and their descendants were allowed to farm land belonging to the property owner in return for part of the harvest. These arrangements usually left the sharecroppers perpetually indebted to the landowners, so that they were financially obligated to stay on the land although legally they were free to leave. In addition, many African Americans who were born during the period of slavery were accustomed or resigned to their inferior social and economic positions and were reluctant to seek change. According to W. E. B. Du Bois, a leading African American intellectual of the period, African Americans who came of age around 1910 were the first generation for whom slavery was a distant memory. Jim Crow laws that formalized segregation and discrimination and racial violence that included lynchings motivated many in this new generation of African Americans to seek better conditions in the North.

Because the vast majority of African Americans in the

South worked in agriculture, particularly in the production of cotton, several bad crop years and a boll weevil infestation in the mid-1910's contributed to the decision on the part of some to migrate when they did. The increase in out-migration was greatest in the areas that experienced the greatest crop failures.

Changing conditions in the North also played an important role in the timing of the Great Migration. Prior to World War I, immigration from Europe had supplied the labor needs of northern industry, and African Americans in northern cities usually could find work only as servants, porters, janitors, or waiters. Most industries hired African Americans only during strikes, as a way to exert pressure on Euro-American workers. Restrictions imposed during World War I reduced the number of European immigrants entering the United States by more than 90 percent, from 1.2 million in 1914 to 110,000 in 1918. This reduction in the available labor force took place just as the war increased demand for industrial production. Northern factories, mills, and workshops that previously had disdained African American workers were forced actively to recruit them, offering wages that were often twice what African Americans could earn in the South, plus inducements such as free rooms and train fare. Northward migration was encouraged by news of opportunities spread not only by personal letters home from new arrivals but also by advertisements and articles in newspapers such as the *Chicago Defender*, published by Robert Abbott, an African American editor. In some industries, managers attempted to foster racial division among their workers by encouraging segregated labor unions. The strategy was effective, and workplace competition sometimes contributed to antagonism and racial violence.

Forming of Communities

African Americans in northern cities established their own communities, including the Manhattan neighborhood of Harlem. Although it was primarily occupied by wealthy European Americans at the beginning of the twentieth century, African Americans had been in Harlem since Dutch colonial times. Philip A. Payton, Jr., was among several African American business people who saw an opportunity when a housing glut in Harlem coincided with an influx of African Americans. He leased apartment buildings and rented the apartments to African American tenants, antagonizing some of the wealthy Euro-American residents. Harlem was soon an almost exclusively African American enclave.

Harlem became not only a home for African American workers but also a center of intellectual, cultural, and political development. The Harlem Renaissance, fostered by such African American intellectuals as Du Bois and the poet Langston Hughes, was embraced by white liberals as an alternative to bourgeois American culture. Harlem also became known for African American performing arts, which attracted many white visitors seeking entertainment. Jamaican-born Marcus Garvey arrived in 1916 to establish a branch of his newly formed Universal Negro Improvement Association (UNIA), which was intended to unite all the "Negro peoples of the world." The UNIA flourished in New York and other northern cities during the 1920's. Garvey encouraged African Americans to take pride in their heritage and to establish their own businesses.

The Great Migration ended with the onset of the Great Depression. Because of poverty and the fierce competition with Euro-Americans for scarce jobs, African Americans from the South found the North to be a less desirable destination. During the 1930's, net migration of African Americans from the South was diminished by about one-half, to 347,500. The Great Migration set the stage, however, for subsequent migrations of African Americans that would be even greater in absolute numbers. By the 1940's, the trend had reversed again, with net migration growing to 1,244,700, a level that would be sustained or exceeded during subsequent decades. *James Hayes-Bohanan*

Core Resources

Nicholas Lemann's *The Promised Land: The Great Black Migration and How It Changed America* (New York: Alfred A. Knopf, 1991) describes the second Great Migration, which began in the 1940's, and includes biographical sketches of individual migrant families and a comprehensive discussion of political implications. *The Black American Reference Book* (Englewood Cliffs, N.J.: Prentice-Hall, 1976), edited by Mabel M. Smythe, provides demographic details of the migration. Ronald Takaki's "To the Promised Land: Blacks in the Urban North," in *A Different Mirror: A History of Multicultural America* (Boston: Little, Brown, 1993), uses primary sources, including music, advertisements, and letters, to detail the impacts of the migration on northern urban culture and labor relations.

See also: Employment among African Americans; Harlem Renaissance; Racial and ethnic demographics: trends; Universal Negro Improvement Association.

Green v. County School Board of New Kent County

In *Green*, the U.S. Supreme Court on May 27, 1968, determined for the first time that school boards have an affirmative duty to desegregate their schools and disallowed freedom-of-choice desegregation plans that do not result in substantial pupil mixing.

In the wake of the Supreme Court's 1954 decision in *Brown v. Board of Education* that outlawed school segregation, few southern school boards took action to integrate their schools. Finally, in the mid-1960's, under the threat of federal fund cutoffs and adverse court decisions, most southern school boards made some effort to integrate their schools. Many such school boards did so by adopting an assignment system whereby students were permitted to choose which school they wished to attend. Most such freedom-of-choice plans resulted in little racial integration. Black students typically chose to attend traditionally black schools, whereas white students chose to attend traditionally white schools. As a result, schools remained racially segregated in many southern school districts following the introduction of free-choice plans.

One school district that adopted a free-choice plan during the 1960's was the school district in New Kent County, Virginia. New Kent County is a rural county; its student population was about half black and half white, with blacks and whites scattered throughout the county. Prior to 1965, the schools in New Kent County had been completely segregated, with all the black students attending the county's one black school and all the white students attending the county's one white school. In 1965, the school board adopted a free-choice plan whereby every student was permitted to choose between the two schools. As a result of the free choice, all the white students chose to remain in the white school and 85 percent of the black students chose to remain in the black school.

A group of black parents, with the assistance of the National Association for the Advancement of Colored People (NAACP) Legal Defense and Educational Fund, filed a lawsuit challenging this free-choice plan. These parents contended that the plan was deficient because it did not effectively dismantle the old dual school system. The Supreme Court, faced with thirteen years of southern school board recalcitrance on school desegregation, agreed that the school board's free-choice plan did not satisfy constitutional standards and announced that the school board had an affirmative duty to devise a desegregation plan that actually resulted in substantial pupil mixing. This decision, the Supreme Court's most important school desegregation decision since the 1954 *Brown* decision, helped transform school desegregation law by forcing school boards to devise assignment plans that resulted in greater integration. In the wake of the *Green* decision, lower courts throughout the South required school boards to take additional action to integrate their schools.   *Davison M. Douglas*

See also: *Brown v. Board of Education*; Civil Rights movement; National Association for the Advancement of Colored People; National Association for the Advancement of Colored People Legal Defense and Educational Fund; Segregation: de facto and de jure.

Greensboro sit-ins

On February 1, 1960, four black students from the North Carolina Agricultural and Technical College sat down at the whites-only lunch counter of the Woolworth's department store in Greensboro, North Carolina, and refused to leave until served. The next day, they returned along with twenty-six more students. By the end of the week, more than three hundred black students were involved in nonviolent demonstrations in downtown Greensboro.

The white community at first refused to make any change in the status quo, but in April, white leaders offered a plan for partial desegregation. The student leadership, the Student Executive Committee for Justice, rejected this offer as a blatant attempt at tokenism.

The Greensboro sit-ins paved the way for many additional protests, including this sit-in at a restaurant counter in Jackson, Mississippi, in June, 1963.

Greensboro officials then tried arrests, sending forty-five demonstrators to jail on trespassing charges. The protesters responded with a boycott, which cut profits for retail businesspeople by one-third. Finally, six months after the protest began, the white community gave up and desegregated downtown businesses.

The sit-in at Woolworth's launched a regionwide campaign and marked the beginning of the student phase of the Civil Rights movement, led by a new organization called the Student Nonviolent Coordinating Committee (SNCC). By August of 1961, more than seventy thousand blacks and whites had taken part in similar protests and more than three thousand had been arrested.

Robert E. McFarland

See also: Civil Rights movement; Student Nonviolent Coordinating Committee.

Griffin v. Breckenridge

Griffin v. Breckenridge, decided June 7, 1971, extended federal civil rights guarantees of equal protection of the law to the protection of personal rights. On July 2, 1966, a group of African Americans who were suspected of being civil rights workers were halted on a Mississippi highway near the Alabama border by Lavon and Calvin Breckenridge, who purposely blocked the road with their car. The Breckenridges forced the African Americans from their vehicle and then subjected them to intimidation by firearms. They were clubbed about their heads, beaten with pipes and other weapons, and repeatedly threatened with death. Although terrorized and seriously injured, the African Americans (who included Griffin) survived. They subsequently filed a suit for damages, charging that they had been assaulted for the purpose of preventing them and "other Negro-Americans" from enjoying the equal rights, privileges, and immunities of citizens of the state of Mississippi and of the United States, including the rights to free speech, assembly, association, and movement and the right not to be enslaved.

A federal district court dismissed the complaint by relying on a previous U.S. Supreme Court decision, *Collins v. Hardyman* (1951), which in order to avoid difficult constitutional issues had held that federal law extended only to "conspiracies" condoned or perpetrated by states. That is, the Court tried to avoid opening questions involving congressional power or the content of state as distinct from national citizenship, or interfering in local matters such as assault and battery cases or similar illegalities that clearly fell under local jurisdiction.

The *Collins* case, however, had been decided a decade before the nationwide Civil Rights movement of the 1960's, a period marked by the enactment of a new series of federal civil rights laws as well as by attentive regard by the U.S. Supreme Court of Chief Justice Warren Burger to cases involving civil rights violations. The Burger court heard the *Griffin* case on appeal.

The Supreme Court's unanimous decision in *Griffin* was delivered by Justice Potter Stewart on June 7, 1971. The Court broadly interpreted the federal statute under which Griffin brought damages, Title 42 of the U.S. Code, section 1985. Section 1985 stipulated that if two or more persons conspired or went in disguise on public highways with the intent to deprive any person or any class of persons of equal protection of the laws or of equal privileges and immunities under the laws, a conspiracy existed and damages could be brought. The Court waived consideration of whether the *Collins* case had been correctly decided. Instead, reviewing previous civil rights legislation, starting in 1866, the justices determined that the language of the federal statute clearly indicated that state action was not required to invoke federal protection of constitutionally guaranteed personal rights from impairment by personal conspiracies. *Griffin* effectively extended federal safeguards of civil rights to reach private conspiracies under the Thirteenth Amendment as well as under congressional powers to protect the right of interstate travel.   *Clifton K. Yearley*

See also: Civil Rights movement.

Griggs v. Duke Power Company

The Supreme Court's 1971 decision in *Griggs* established the "adverse impact" test for discrimination so that an unequal statistical pattern could be used as *prima facie* evidence.

The Civil Rights Act of 1964, Title VII, prohibited workplace segregation. Shortly after the law took effect in mid-1965, Duke Power Company in North Carolina rescinded its policy of restricting blacks to its labor department, so in principle they could transfer to other departments. Nevertheless, according to a company policy, begun in 1955, all employees but those in Duke's labor department had to have a high school diploma. Therefore, all those applying for a transfer from the labor department in 1965 needed a diploma. For those lacking a high school diploma (blacks were far less likely to have completed twelve grades than whites in that part of North Carolina), an alternative was to score at the national median on two standardized aptitude tests.

Willie Griggs and coworkers in the labor department at the company's Dan River steam-generating plant filed a class-action charge with the Equal Employment Opportunity Commission (EEOC), which ruled in favor of Griggs. When the company refused to conciliate the case, Griggs and his coworkers filed suit in district court. The court held that a claim of prior inequities was beyond the scope of Title VII and that the requirements for a high school diploma or a passing score on standardized tests were not intentionally discriminatory.

The district court's decision was overruled by the Supreme Court. Chief Justice Warren Burger delivered a unanimous Supreme Court opinion (8 to 0), setting forth the adverse impact test. According to this principle, if statistics show that a job requirement screens out one race, the employer must prove that the requirement is relevant to the performance of the job. Since the percentage of black high school graduates and percentages of blacks who passed the two tests were substantially below percentages for whites, Duke Power had to prove that the jobs sought by Griggs and his coworkers required completing high school or having a level of intelligence at the national median. Since the company advanced no such evidence, the Court ruled that Title VII discrimination had occurred and decreed that "any tests used must measure the person for the job and not the person in the abstract."

The decision had an extremely broad impact: It called into question all lists of qualifications for every job in the United States. Employers were called upon to review job qualifications and to recalibrate job duties to job qualifications or risk successful discrimination suits.

In the 1980's the Supreme Court began to chip away at the *Griggs* ruling. In *Wards Cove Packing Company v. Atonio* (1989), the Court shifted the burden of proof so that those filing suit must prove that specific job requirements alone cause statistical disparities. Congress responded by passing the Civil Rights Act of 1991, codifying the original *Griggs* ruling into law.   *Michael Haas*

See also: Civil Rights Act of 1964; Civil Rights Act of 1991; Discrimination: racial and ethnic; Equality of opportunity; *Wards Cove Packing Company v. Atonio.*

Grovey v. Townsend

In *Grovey v. Townsend*, the Supreme Court ruling on April 1, 1935, upheld "whites only" primaries when approved by state party conventions without any involvement or encouragement from the state legislature.

One of the most successful devices in eliminating black voters in the South was the white primary. Since the Democratic Party dominated the solid South, whoever won the Democratic primary went on to win the general election. If blacks could not participate in the primaries, they were denied any real choice in selecting public officials.

In *Newberry v. United States* (1921), the U.S. Supreme Court held that primary elections were not constitutionally protected. Although the *Newberry* case took place in Michigan and involved the issue of vote fraud rather than racial discrimination, the South immediately took advantage of the ruling. In 1924 the Texas legislature passed a law that barred blacks from participation in that state's primary elections. Three years later, a unanimous Supreme Court struck down the Texas law in *Nixon v. Herndon* (1927), finding the actions of the Texas legislature a clear violation of the equal protection clause of the Fourteenth Amendment.

The Texas legislature then passed a law authorizing the executive committees of the political parties to determine eligibility for voting in primary elections. As expected, the executive committee of the Texas Democratic Party excluded blacks from the primary. In *Nixon v. Condon* (1932), in a 5-4 decision, the U.S. Supreme Court ruled that the executive committee had acted as the agent of the state. As such, the attempt to bar black participation in the primary still violated the equal protection clause.

Texas succeeded on its third attempt to ban black voting. Immediately after the *Condon* decision, the Texas Democratic Party convention, without any authorization from the legislature, adopted a resolution restricting party membership to whites. R. R. Grovey, a black resident of Houston, brought suit against the county clerk who refused to give him a primary ballot. On April 1, 1935, a unanimous U.S. Supreme Court upheld the actions of the state party convention. According to the Court, there was no violation of the equal protection clause because there was no state action involved. The Democratic Party was a voluntary association of individuals who acted in their private capacity to exclude blacks from primary elections.

In 1941 the U.S. Supreme Court reversed *Newberry* in *United States v. Classic* (1941). The *Classic* decision brought primary elections under constitutional protection for the first time. *Classic* also paved the way for *Smith v. Allwright* (1944), the Supreme Court case banning white primaries.   *Darryl Paulson*

See also: National Association for the Advancement of Colored People (NAACP); *Newberry v. United States*; *Nixon v. Herndon*; *Smith v. Allwright.*

Guadalupe Hidalgo, Treaty of

Signed on February 2, 1848, this treaty ended the Mexican-American War; in it, Mexico ceded to the United States about half its national territory, and the ramifications for native peoples in the ceded territory were profound.

The Mexican-American War and the treaty that

ended it were largely the result of manifest destiny, the theory used to justify American acquisition of both Indian and Mexican territory. President James K. Polk, a leading advocate of manifest destiny, was the most important figure in the Mexican-American War and the peace negotiations that followed. In Mexico, chronic instability caused by the struggle between the various political parties and leaders made waging war and negotiating peace difficult and made preserving the peace impossible.

Tension between the United States and Mexico had been increasing in the years preceding the war. Mexico was aware of, and feared, the Polk administration's desire to annex New Mexico and California. The United States was pressing claims against Mexico, and the Texas boundary dispute was becoming more critical. After fighting broke out in the disputed area along the Rio Grande, the United States declared war. Attempts to negotiate peace before and during the war were unsuccessful. Mexico saw no advantage in it, and the United States hoped to occupy more territory.

As a result of its military success, the United States was able to make acquisition of New Mexico and California a condition of peace. Polk chose Nicholas P. Trist as peace commissioner in April, 1847, and gave him a draft of a treaty which called for the cession of Alta and Baja California and New Mexico, the right of transit across the Isthmus of Tehuantepec, the Rio Grande as the Texas border, and a payment to Mexico of $15 million plus the assumption of claims of United States citizens against Mexico.

Opposition quickly developed in both Mexico and the United States to the proposed treaty. Mexico did not want an imposed peace, and the United States envisioned better terms. When Trist negotiated a peace unacceptable to Polk, the president recalled Trist. Trist remained in Mexico, however, and finally negotiated a modified treaty that Mexico accepted because of financial problems and fear of additional losses if war continued. The possibility of a successful revolution in Mexico added urgency to the peace process.

The United States dropped its demand for transit across the isthmus and agreed to stop Indian raids across the border. The treaty was signed on February 2, 1848, in Guadalupe Hidalgo, and ratification was exchanged on May 30, 1848, in Mexico City.

Although Articles IX and X guaranteed the political and property rights of Mexican citizens and Indians in the territory transferred to the United States, the Indians of California did not receive citizenship, nor were their property rights protected. As a result of violence and other factors such as disease, the Indian population declined by 100,000 within two decades. In New Mexico Territory the Indians were placed under federal protection and denied citizenship, but they did not lose their lands. Citizenship was granted to the Indians in 1869, and reservations were later created.   *Robert D. Talbott*

See also: Indian-white relations: United States; Latinos in the United States.

Guinn v. United States

The Supreme Court's June 21, 1915, decision in *Guinn v. United States* overturned Oklahoma's grandfather clause and marked a first step in the National Association for the Advancement of Colored People's campaign to use the courts to combat racial discrimination.

Though the Fifteenth Amendment supposedly prohibited racial discrimination in voting, during the late nineteenth and early twentieth centuries southern and border states found ways to prevent African Americans from voting in significant numbers. One method was the literacy test. One potential drawback to this practice, however, was that such a test would also prevent poorly educated whites from voting. A number of states solved this problem by adopting grandfather clauses, provisions that allowed anyone registered before a certain date or anyone descended from such a person to vote regardless of literacy. Since the date selected was usually set at a point when there would have been few black voters (1866 was popular), very few blacks would qualify. Thus a measure that was nonracial on the surface was decidedly discriminatory in its effects.

Many grandfather laws had only temporary application, and most southern states moved away from them in the early twentieth century. In 1910, however, Oklahoma enacted a literacy test requirement with a permanent grandfather clause. The measure threatened not only black voting rights but also the position of the state's Republican Party. Fearing the loss of several thousand black votes, the U.S. attorney brought suit under the Reconstruction-era Enforcement Acts and won a conviction against state officials who were trying to enforce the literacy test.

The state appealed the case to the U.S. Supreme Court, attracting the attention of the National Association for the Advancement of Colored People (NAACP), which was just beginning to use litigation as a strategy for combating racial discrimination. Moorfield Story of the NAACP filed a brief in support of the government. In a unanimous decision, the Court upheld the convictions and ruled that the grandfather clause was a clear attempt to thwart the Fifteenth Amendment's ban on racial discrimination in voting.

The decision had relatively little immediate impact: Only one other state still had a grandfather clause at the time, and the Court carefully avoided declaring literacy tests themselves discriminatory. Nevertheless, the decision was not without its significance. Not only did it mark a modest revival of the Fifteenth Amendment, but it also encouraged the NAACP to continue its strategy of using litigation to put the Constitution on the side of racial equality.

William C. Lowe

See also: Civil rights; Fifteenth Amendment; Grandfather clauses; Jim Crow laws; Literacy tests; National Association for the Advancement of Colored People.

Gullah

The Gullahs came to North America in the first decades of the nineteenth century as slaves, originally from Angola (hence the name). Gullah is also a creole form of English that derives from the sea islands of Georgia and South Carolina. Gullah, once similar to the language spoken on slave plantations in the South, is very different from other African American dialects of English. The Gullah dialect combines elements of English vocabulary with grammar and punctuation elements of several West African languages such as Ewe, Mandinka, Igbo, Twi, and Yoruba.

Gullah traditions, myths, and language stayed longer with the Coastal Carolina Gullahs because of the isolation and self-sufficiency they experienced on the sea islands. As with many minority languages around the world, television, education, and increased social contact have all undermined the Gullah language and culture. Many Gullah speakers use various African American English dialects in dealing with nonislanders, though Gullah remains the language of home, family, and community. Gullah has affected culture and language beyond the Carolina sea islands with words such as goober (peanuts), gumbo, and yam. The Gullah dialect and culture were spread to mainstream America through the tales of Uncle Remus and Bre'r Rabbit.

Jason Pasch

See also: Ebonics; Slavery: history.

Gypsies

The United States is home to an estimated quarter of a million to one million people of Gypsy ancestry. Nevertheless, Gypsies are one of the least assimilated and most misunderstood ethnic groups in the United States and Canada. Most scholars believe that the Gypsies are descended from a caste of entertainers in ancient India. No one knows precisely why they left their original home, but ancient historical records report that thousands of these entertainers were sent to Persia in the ninth century B.C.E. From Persia, they apparently migrated to various parts of the Middle East, North Africa, and Europe.

Some Gypsies migrated to North America and Latin America during colonial times from the British Isles and from Spain and Portugal. Napoleon Bonaparte deported hundreds of Gypsies from France to the French colony of Louisiana, which became part of the United States in 1803. During the late nineteenth and early twentieth centuries, North America received large waves of immigrants from Southern Europe, and many Gypsies arrived at this time. The fall of European communism in the early 1990's led to another wave of Gypsy migration from Eastern Europe.

Despite their long history in the United States, Gypsies have retained a distinctive ethnic identity and resisted assimilating into mainstream American culture. They frequently avoid census takers, and because of the negative stereotypes often attached to them, many Gypsies are somewhat secretive about their ethnic identity. Therefore, there is no precise count of the Gypsies in the United States, although estimates run from 250,000 to 1 million. The two largest Gypsy American groups are those who trace their ancestry to Southern and Eastern Europe and refer to themselves as the Rom and those who trace their ancestry to the British Isles and refer to themselves as Romnichals. Gypsies from Mexico, who migrated to the Americas from Spain, often call themselves Gitanos. Most Gypsy Americans speak some branch of the Romani language as well as English.

Modern Gypsies are less nomadic than their ancestors were, but Gypsies still move around much more often than most other Americans do. They tend to make their homes in large cities, where employment is available. The largest concentrations are found in Los Angeles, San Francisco, New York, Chicago, Boston, Atlanta, Dallas, Houston, Seattle, and Portland.

Relations between Gypsy Americans and other ethnic groups are often troubled by a lack of trust and understanding. Gypsy Americans do voluntarily remain separate from non-Gypsies, and traditional Gypsy belief even teaches that non-Gypsies are ritually unclean. They prefer to avoid public schooling and often educate their children within their own families, which perpetuates their distinctiveness. Popular images of Gypsies stereotype them as romantic wanderers or as career criminals preying on all outsiders. Despite the latter stereotype, though, the conviction rates of Gypsy Americans for serious crimes such as rape and murder are actually lower than the conviction rates of other Americans. Gypsy American conviction rates for theft, moreover, are no higher than those of the American population in general.

Carl L. Bankston III

See also: Assimilation: cultural and structural; Cultural citizenship; Cultural pluralism; Stereotype.

H

Haitians and Haitian refugees

> **Significance:** Haitians have immigrated to the United States, particularly New York and Florida, in significant numbers since the 1950's. In general, U.S. policy toward Haitians has been unreceptive since the 1970's, treating them as economic migrants rather than refugees.

During the 1980's and early 1990's, many Haitians seeking asylum in the United States were intercepted at sea and forced to return to Haiti. This treatment contrasts with that of Cuban asylum seekers, who have generally received a generous welcome to U.S. shores as legitimate refugees. The U.S. government's differential treatment of Cubans fleeing the Marxist-dominated Fidel Castro government and of Haitians fleeing a very poor country governed by right-wing repressive leaders caused many to question U.S. refugee policy. In addition, Haitians speak Creole and are black, leading some to suggest latent racist motivations for the U.S. government's actions.

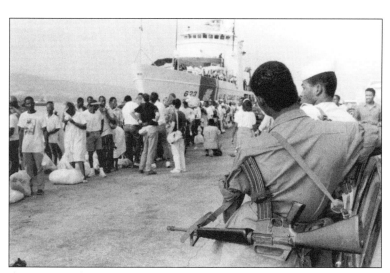

These Haitian refugees stand on the dock in Port-au-Prince, Haiti, after being sent back from the U.S. Naval Base at Guantanamo Bay, Cuba. U.S. policy resulted in many Haitian refugees being repatriated rather than allowed to immigrate.

The Haitian Immigration Experience

Haitians, like citizens of most Caribbean countries, have for many decades participated in labor-based migration throughout the Caribbean region, including the United States. Haiti's economy is among the poorest in the Western Hemisphere, providing a significant reason for migration. However, authoritarian regimes also contributed to migration, as some people fled political repression. In the 1950's and 1960's, skilled Haitian professionals legally entered the United States and Canada as permanent or temporary immigrants. Although many left Haiti in part because of political repression, they were treated as routine immigrants rather than refugees. Legal immigration continued throughout the 1970's and 1980's, but larger numbers of much poorer people also began to leave Haiti by boat.

For many years, Haiti was governed by the authoritarian regimes of François "Papa Doc" Duvalier and his son, Jean Claude "Baby Doc" Duvalier, who finally fled the country in 1986. A series of repressive regimes continued to rule the country until Haiti's first democratically elected government, that of Jean-Bertrand Aristide, was established in 1990, but this government was overthrown by a military coup in 1991 and had to be reinstalled by the international community in 1994, after three years of devastating economic sanctions imposed by the United Nations that, coupled with domestic political repression, precipitated large flows of refugees. The refugee flows subsided once the military regime gave up power, the U.N. peacekeeping forces were deployed, the Aristide government was reestablished, and the economic sanctions were removed.

Thousands of Haitians have immigrated to the United States since the early 1970's. Many thousands more were deported because they were judged to be lacking legitimate asylum claims. Those who managed to stay in the United States concentrated around already existing Haitian communities in Florida, especially in the Miami area, and in New York City, where several hundred thousand Haitians make their home. Lacking significant public assistance, the Haitians who settled in the United States during the 1970's and 1980's were obliged to rely on aid from charitable organizations and the already established local Haitian communities.

Reactions to the Immigrants

Reactions to the Haitian migration varied considerably. Generally, the earlier and more skilled migration out of Haiti was uncontroversial. As larger numbers of poorer Haitians, especially the "boat people," sought entry into the United States, however, concern about the economic implications of these undocumented migrants arose. Local politicians, especially in southern Florida, under pressure from their constituents, including elite members of the Cuban exile group, along with others concerned about the potentially disruptive Haitian flow, put pressure on Congress and successive presidents to deter the Haitian migration.

However, steps by the federal government to staunch the Haitian migratory flows eventually prompted political opposition by second-generation Cubans, voluntary agencies, human rights groups, and the Congressional Black Caucus. Many of these groups charged that the discriminatory treatment of Haitians was based at least in part on race. Efforts to detain Haitians in the United States were successfully challenged in court, and advocates for Haitians won a number of court-related victories to ensure fairer treatment for Haitian asylum seekers. The interdiction programs instituted by President Ronald Reagan, however, continued under the presidencies of George Bush and Bill Clinton. Only with the return of democracy to Haiti in 1994 did the migration pressures from Haiti to the United States ease.

Future Prospects

The return of stability to the Haitian political system and the application of considerable international economic assistance holds out hope that Haiti will benefit from economic development, thus encouraging investment at home and further reducing pressures for migration abroad. The booming economy in the United States during the 1990's and the reduction in illegal and undocumented migration from Haiti helped to reduce the controversy surrounding Haitian migration.

Robert F. Gorman

Core Resources

Alex Stepick's *Haitian Refugees in the U.S.* (London: Minority Rights Group, 1982) and Jake Miller's *The Plight of Haitian Refugees* (New York: Praeger, 1984) provide critiques of the Haitian predicament in the United

States. To set the Haitian situation into the wider immigration experience, see Alejandro Portes and Rubén G. Rumbaut's *Immigrant America: A Portrait* (Berkeley: University of California Press, 1990). For a contrast of the Cuban and Haitian refugee and resettlement experience, see Felix R. Masud-Piloto's *From Welcomed Exiles to Illegal Immigrants* (Lanham, Md.: Rowman & Littlefield, 1996). On the foreign policy implications of U.S. Haitian policy, see *Western Hemisphere Immigration and United States Foreign Policy* (University Park: Pennsylvania State University Press, 1992), edited by Christopher Mitchell.

See also: Afro-Caribbeans; Congressional Black Caucus; Cuban Americans; Refugees: U.S. policy.

Hansen effect

In *The Problem of the Third Generation Immigrants* (1937), Marcus Lee Hansen found that immigrants have more similar experiences in adjusting to life in the United States within generations than across the generations.

A Japanese American woman and her granddaughter belong to the same taiko (drum) ensemble. The Hansen effect postulates that the second generation distances itself from traditional customs and values and the third attempts to recapture them.

He reported that the first generation of immigrants, often finding it difficult to learn English and seek gainful employment, remained oriented to the home country. The first generation tended to observe customs of the home country in matters of dress, food, language spoken at home, recreation, and cultural values.

The second generation, whether born in the United States or brought to the new country at a very early age, attended school with nonimmigrant children and attempted to assimilate because of peer pressure, which often ridiculed old-fashioned habits and values. The second generation, thus, rejected an identification with the parents' home country in order to be accepted and prosper in the new country.

The third generation, in contrast, has been eager to rediscover the traditions of the root cultures from which they came. Cultural pride, in short, emerged as the third generation's reaction to the efforts of the second generation to neglect its origins and cultural heritage.

The Hansen effect was postulated primarily with reference to European Americans, however. The culture of African Americans was thoroughly suppressed, and the various generations of Asian Americans and Hispanic Americans have tended to retain the values of their ancestors.   *Michael Haas*

See also: Assimilation: cultural and structural; Generational acculturation.

Harlem Renaissance

Early in the twentieth century, hundreds of thousands of African Americans fled poverty and racial discrimination in the South to search for employment in northern cities. In their new northern homes, they gained a feeling of freedom, relieved of some of the weight of southern oppression, and some of them began to express themselves in artistic ways. During the 1920's, many of these artists were drawn to the Harlem district of New York City, which gave birth to a flurry of creativity so fresh and so productive that it became known as the Harlem Renaissance.

The Harlem Renaissance involved artists from all realms of the creative world: painters, sculptors, poets, novelists, actors, screenwriters, and musicians. Magazines such as *The Crisis*, a publication of the National Association for the Advancement of Colored People (NAACP), and *Opportunity*, the official publication of the National Urban League, were among the first to publish works by African American writers, poets, and essayists. Renaissance writers drew on common cultural experiences to create an elevated awareness and appreciation of their unique heritage. Jamaican immigrant Claude

McKay gained a large audience with *Harlem Shadows* in 1922. McKay's popularity was soon matched by other writers, including Jean Toomer (*Cane*, 1923) and James Weldon Johnson (*The Book of American Negro Poetry*, 1922). Author Langston Hughes became unofficial spokesperson for the Harlem Renaissance and its most prolific writer, publishing more than fifty books. In his works, he gave poetry a new jazz beat and spoke of African American experiences and emotions.

Renaissance sculptors and painters looked away from European masters to African art for inspiration. Painters such as Aaron Douglas, Palmer Hayden, and William H. Johnson and sculptors such as Meta Warrick Fuller, Selma Burke, and Richmond Barthe concentrated on ancestral rituals and dance, native customs and folklore, slave experiences, and themes of African American urban life.

In 1920, actor Charles Gilpin appeared in Eugene O'Neill's *The Emperor Jones*. A few years later, Paul Robeson debuted on Broadway in a revival of that play and then appeared in the title role in William Shakespeare's *Othello*. He received nationwide acclaim for his role in *Showboat* in 1927. African American musicians demonstrated why the 1920's was known as the Jazz Age. Louis Armstrong brought New Orleans jazz to popular audiences, and Duke Ellington developed big-band jazz into a new art form.

The Harlem Renaissance coincided with a highly xenophobic age in the United States. The Ku Klux Klan reached new heights of popularity, and lynchings occurred in the South at an alarming rate. However, African American artists received encouragement and financial support from many members of the white community, and audiences nationwide showed new interest in the art forms produced in a small area of Manhattan. As Hughes wrote, "The Negro was in vogue." White patrons flocked to Harlem to attend shows, readings, and exhibitions.

The economic devastation of the Great Depression in 1930 ended a significant portion of the financial support Harlem artists had received, and audiences and patrons decreased in number. Though the quantity of artistic expression diminished during the 1930's, the cultural awareness and racial pride inspired by the Harlem Renaissance continued.   *Leslie Stricker*

See also: African American literature; African American music; Great Migration.

Harlins, Latasha, murder

After a dispute over a $1.79 bottle of orange juice, fifteen-year-old Latasha Harlins was shot and killed at the Empire Liquor Market Deli in South Central Los Angeles on March 16, 1991. A security camera recorded the African American teenager being shot in the back of the head by the market owner. The merchant, Soon Ja Du, a forty-nine-year-old Korean woman, was charged with murder. Because the shooting occurred only thirteen days after African American Rodney King was beaten by Los Angeles police, it aggravated racial and ethnic tensions in Los Angeles.

At the court proceedings, Judge Joyce Karlan lectured African Americans and reportedly told Harlan's grandmother that the murder would not have occurred if her granddaughter had not gone into Ja Du's store. On March 26, 1991, Ja Du was found guilty of voluntary manslaughter, but Judge Karlan granted the defendant probation. This decision angered African Americans in Los Angeles and made Korean businesses primary targets for theft and vandalism by African Americans. In addition, the decision escalated the number of conflicts between African American and Asian youth in Los Angeles. Bitter feelings generated by the Harlins and Rodney King verdicts were unleashed during the Los Angeles riots of 1992.   *Alvin K. Benson*

See also: King, Rodney, case; Korean-African American relations; Korean Americans; Los Angeles riots of 1992.

Harper v. Virginia Board of Elections

The Supreme Court's March 24, 1966, decision in *Harper v. Virginia Board of Elections* eliminated the use of poll taxes in state and local elections.

Poll taxes, or the payment of a fee in order to vote, were widely used in southern states as a means to restrict the electorate, and in particular black voters. Because poll taxes led to corruption—as candidates and political organizations would pay the taxes of their supporters—and because there were more effective ways of eliminating black voters, many southern states started to repeal their poll taxes. Opposition to the poll tax was led by the National Committee to Abolish the Poll Tax and the National Association for the Advancement of Colored People (NAACP). On five occasions the House of Representatives passed legislation to ban the tax, but southern senators filibustered, blocking passage in the Senate. In 1964, the Twenty-fourth Amendment to the Constitution was ratified, eliminating the use of poll taxes in federal elections. Five states—Alabama, Arkansas, Mississippi, Texas, and Virginia—continued to use poll taxes in state and local elections. Arkansas dropped its poll tax in 1964 after the passage of the Twenty-fourth Amendment.

In 1965 the U.S. House of Representatives passed a poll tax ban in state elections as part of the Voting Rights Act of 1965. The Senate failed to support the ban, however, and the final version of the Voting Rights Act merely stated that the poll tax "denied or abridged" the constitutional right to vote.

Blacks in Virginia brought suit against that state's $1.50 annual poll tax as a requirement for voting in state and local elections. The U.S. district court, citing the 1937 case *Breedlove v. Suttles*, dismissed the claim. In *Breedlove*, the U.S. Supreme Court had held that, except where constrained by the Constitution, the states may impose whatever conditions on suffrage that they deem appropriate. On appeal, a 6-3 majority in the Supreme Court overruled *Breedlove* and held that the payment of a fee in order to vote violated the Constitution.

Interestingly, although the plaintiffs were black, the ruling was based on economic discrimination rather than racial discrimination. "To introduce wealth or payment of a fee as a measure of a voter's qualifications," wrote Justice William Douglas in the majority opinion, "is to introduce a capricious or irrelevant factor." In the view of the Court's majority, voter qualifications had no relationship to wealth. The three dissenters believed that a "fairly applied" poll tax could be a reasonable basis for the right to vote. The *Harper* decision actually had little direct impact. Since only four states used poll taxes as a condition for voting at the time of the *Harper* decision, the ban on poll taxes barely generated a ripple on the surface of American politics.   *Darryl Paulson*

See also: Poll tax; Voting Rights Act of 1965.

Hate Crime Statistics Act

The Hate Crime Statistics Act was passed into law on April 23, 1990, and reauthorized on September 13, 1994. It required the U.S. attorney general to collect data annually on crimes that "manifest evidence of prejudice based on race, religion, disability, sexual orientation, or ethnicity." Subsequently, the attorney general assigned the task of data collection to the Federal Bureau of Investigation (FBI).

The data enable the government and other agencies to conduct accurate research and perform statistical analysis on these types of crimes. Until passage of this law, there was no way to identify crimes that were committed as a result of hate. This was a concern both in the law enforcement community and among civil rights organizations that represented affected constituencies.

The FBI wanted to make sure that the various police agencies across the nation used sufficiently objective criteria, as described in a set of guidelines that the FBI distributed, to assess hate accurately as a motivation for a particular offense. Most jurisdictions found it necessary to create legislation to address hate crimes to facilitate the counting of these offenses. These cases were eventually litigated to the Supreme Court on First Amendment issues. The cases of *R.A.V. v. City of St. Paul* (1992) and *Wisconsin v. Mitchell* (1993) settled the constitutional questions surrounding this act and related local and state legislation.   *Michael L. Barrett*

See also: Hate crimes; Hate speech; *R.A.V. v. City of St. Paul*; *Wisconsin v. Mitchell.*

Hate crimes

> **Significance:** Hate crimes—which often occur as a result of racial or ethnic bigotry—injure the victim and society in ways that other crimes do not. It has been argued that, because of their nature, hate crimes generate more injury, distress, and suffering than do other crimes.

In 1984, Alan Berg, a Jewish talk show host on a Denver radio station, was fatally shot on his way home by several members of a neo-Nazi hate group. In 1986, three white teenagers attacked three black men in Howard Beach, New York, simply because the victims were black. Both these actions were hate crimes, defined by the Federal Bureau of Investigation as "a criminal offense committed against a person or property which is motivated, in whole or in part, by the offender's bias against a race, religion, ethnic/national origin group, or sexual orientation group." Since the mid-1980's, hate crimes have been on the rise.

Hate crimes are typically excessively brutal, and quite often they are carried out in a random fashion against strangers, as with the incidents involving the Howard Beach black men. Authors Jack Levin and Jack McDevitt have given several explanations as to why these crimes occur: the perpetrator's negative and stereotypic view of other people, the possibility that bigotry is becoming more widely tolerated, the resentment that one group feels toward another because it has been left out of the mainstream of society, a perpetrator's desire for the thrill of the action, a perpetrator's reaction to a perceived or imagined injury such as the loss of a job promotion or a benefit, and, finally, a perpetrator's wish to rid the world of evil.

Federal Laws Against Hate Crimes
There are a number of different types of laws which victims of hate crimes can use against perpetrators. In recent years, most states have enacted laws to deal specifically with these types of crimes. Several statutes also address these crimes on a federal level. There are federal laws prohibiting conspiracies against the rights of citizens, prohibiting a deprivation of rights under color of law, and prohibiting damage to religious property and obstruction of persons in the free exercise of their religious beliefs. In addition, there are federal statutes that prohibit forcible interference with civil rights and willful interference with civil rights under the fair housing laws. These federal statutes have rarely been applied to hate crimes for several reasons. First, if a president does not emphasize civil rights, the attorney general in that administration will not be likely to prosecute these crimes. Second, since most of these statutes require that the victim be engaged in an activity involving a federally protected right, such as buying a house or eating in a restaurant, they do not apply to many victims. Third, the remedies under the federal statutes are limited. Fourth, only certain groups, such as racial and religious groups, are protected under these statutes. Sexual orientation is not. Thus, the most active prosecution of hate crimes has been at the state level.

State Laws Prohibiting Expressive Conduct
On June 21, 1990, two young white men burned a cross on the property of a black family in St. Paul, Minnesota. One of the men, designated by his initials, R.A.V., because he was only seventeen at the time, was charged in accordance with a new city "bias-motivated" disorderly conduct ordinance which read, "Whoever places on public or private property, a symbol, appellation, characterization, or graffiti, including, but not limited to, a burning cross or Nazi swastika, which one knows or has reasonable grounds to know arouses anger, alarm or resentment in others on the basis of race, color, creed, religion, or gender, commits disorderly conduct and shall be guilty of a misdemeanor." R.A.V. could have been charged with simple trespass, disorderly conduct, breach of the peace, or even a more severe crime such as terroristic threats. Instead, in what was to become a test case of the statute and others similar to it, the prosecutor decided to invoke this law, which punished the expression of a viewpoint.

R.A.V.'s attorney, Edward J. Cleary, decided to challenge the constitutionality of the law under the First Amendment to the Constitution. A Minnesota district court agreed that the ordinance was unconstitutional. The prosecutor decided to appeal the decision to the Minnesota Supreme Court. This court overturned the lower court ruling. R.A.V. appealed to the Supreme Court of the United States for a review of the case. On June 22, 1992, the Court issued a unanimous opinion in *R.A.V. v. City of St. Paul* declaring that the ordinance was unconstitutional. Five of the justices held that the ordinance was unconstitutional because it prohibited the expression of subject matter protected by the First

The funeral procession of James Byrd, Jr., leaves the Greater New Bethel Baptist Church in Jasper, Texas, on June 13, 1998. Byrd died six days earlier after he was chained to the back of a pickup truck and dragged down a rural road. Three white men with ties to the Ku Klux Klan were charged in his murder.

Amendment. Four of the justices said that the ordinance was overbroad in that it included in its proscriptions expression which was protected by the First Amendment. The entire Court thought that the city had other means by which to prosecute R.A.V. Thus, the Court concluded that, offensive as the action in which R.A.V. had engaged was, the action was protected under the Constitution to the extent that it was expressive conduct.

State Hate Laws Prohibiting Conduct

In 1991, a nineteen-year-old black man, Todd Mitchell, and his friends came out of a theater showing the film *Mississippi Burning* so enraged that, upon seeing a fourteen-year-old white youth (Gregory Riddick) on the street, they assaulted him. Coming out of the theater, Mitchell said to others in his group, "Do you all feel hyped up to move on some white people?" Then, when Mitchell saw Riddick walking by, he added, "There goes a white boy—go get him." The group kicked and beat the boy for five minutes. Riddick remained in a coma for four days before he returned to consciousness with probably permanent brain damage. Mitchell was convicted of aggravated battery, normally punishable by a maximum sentence of two years. Because the jury found that the crime was motivated by racial animus, however, the sentence was increased to seven years in accordance with a state statute which read, "If a person commits the crime of aggravated battery and intentionally selects the victim 'in whole or in part because of the actor's belief or perception regarding the race, religion, color, disability, sexual orientation or ancestry of that person,' the maxi-

mum sentence may be increased by not more than five years."

Within hours after the Supreme Court announced its opinion in *R.A.V.*, the Wisconsin Supreme Court struck down this law as unconstitutional. The state appealed the decision to the Supreme Court of the United States, and on June 11, 1993, in a unanimous opinion less than half the length of *R.A.V.*, the Supreme Court reversed the decision and held that "enhancement" laws such as this which punish hate-motivated conduct are constitutional. The Court, in *Wisconsin v. Mitchell,* distinguished this case from *R.A.V.* by stating that *R.A.V.* dealt with expression and this case with conduct. The Court went on to state that with criminal acts, the more purposeful the conduct, the more severe is the punishment. Thus, when a defendant's beliefs add to a crime and motivate the defendant into action, the motive behind the conduct is relevant to the sentencing and punishment. Second, the Court stated that these enhancement laws are similar in aim to civil antidiscrimination laws and that they are justified because the conduct involved inflicts greater individual and societal harm than do other crimes. Some commentators, such as Edward J. Cleary, who argued *R.A.V.* before the Supreme Court, view *Mitchell* with alarm and sense that these enhancement statutes come dangerously close to punishing a person's thoughts and thereby infringing upon First Amendment rights. He would question why those who attack a person of another race should, because they hate that race and express it, be subject to stricter laws than those who attack in silence. By upholding the enhancement laws, Cleary suggests, the Supreme Court blurred the lines between speech and action. Others believe that, because of the Court's emphasis on the analogy between these enhancement-type laws and antidiscrimination laws, these laws are constitutional. In sum, if a statute infringes upon expression, as in *R.A.V.*, it will be held unconstitutional; if a statute prohibits conduct, it will be upheld.

By 1991, thirty-five states had adopted some form of law to deter hate crimes. These laws, if they pass constitutional scrutiny, are not without practical problems. First, in many instances (as was the case in *R.A.V.*), prosecutors may wait to find the perfect case to fit the statute. The usefulness of the statute is thereby limited. Second, if there is a successful prosecution under the statute, there may be problems in carrying out a severe punishment. Most hate crime offenders are under age twenty-one and do not have prior criminal records. Jails are overcrowded, and it seldom makes sense to jail the entire group involved in the crime. If only leaders are jailed, there is ample evidence that prison will make them worse.   *Jennifer Eastman*

Core Resources
Overviews of the subject include *Bias Crime: American Law Enforcement and Legal Responses* (Chicago: University of Illinois Press, 1991), edited by Robert J. Kelly, and Jack Levin and Jack McDevitt's *Hate Crimes: The Rising Tide of Bigotry and Bloodshed* (New York: Plenum Press, 1993), an anecdotal account. First Amendment problems raised by the hate crime statutes are addressed in *Beyond the Burning Cross: The First Amendment and the Landmark R.A.V. Case*, by Edward J. Cleary (New York: Random House, 1994), and *"Speech Acts" and the First Amendment*, by Franklyn S. Haiman (Carbondale: Southern Illinois University Press, 1993).

See also: Anti-Defamation League; Civil rights; Hate speech; Ku Klux Klan; *R.A.V. v. City of St. Paul*; *Wisconsin v. Mitchell.*

Hate speech

> **Significance:** The United States is faced with a growing divergence in its population in all aspects of life from school curriculum to religion and ever-increasing multicultural influences in art, literature, music, and entertainment. This rapid change has caught many people, both majority and minority group members, unprepared to deal with extremely divergent perspectives, encouraging some to employ what has become known as hate speech.

Generally, hate speech refers to speech that impugns an individual or group based on race, ethnicity, religion, gender, or sexual orientation. The definition of speech for this purpose includes symbols that may represent a particular viewpoint, as the Supreme Court ruled in *Tinker v. Des Moines Independent Community School District* (1969). Jokes, innuendo, playacting, street jargon or slang terminology, and nonverbal communication employed in relaying messages may also be considered hate speech. One discussion that frequently arises is the dividing line between speech and conduct. It is difficult to distinguish between speech and conduct because human activity generally contains both.

The issue is not necessarily whether the speech offends someone but rather the original intent of the speech. If the speech is presenting ideas, it can be said to be linked to thought or theory. As stated by Justice Oliver Wendell Holmes in *Abrams v. United States* in 1919, "The best test of truth is the power of the thought to get itself accepted in the competition of the market, and that truth is the only ground upon which their wishes can safely be carried out." This "marketplace of ideas" concept has remained important in the free speech debate since 1919. The core question is what counts as an idea, that is, whether ideas include emotional outbursts that have no basis in truth or sense or only speech asserting intellectual concepts.

The humanistic perspective suggests that identifiable insults should be subject to quick condemnation, that the values of social order and decency supersede or restrict the rights of free speech granted by the First Amendment. Unfortunately, it is not that easy to separate hate speech from other forms of speech; the gray areas far outnumber those that are crystal clear.

The First Amendment
Ultimately any attempt to regulate speech will lead to a legal challenge and then to a rigorous evaluation by the U.S. Supreme Court of the hate speech regulation based on First Amendment principles. For most of the twentieth century, the Court was increasingly protective of all speech regardless of the crudeness of its content. As stated by former Supreme Court justice Hugo L. Black, "Freedom of speech is indivisible; unless we protect it for all, we will have it for none."

Since its 1964 decision in *New York Times Company v. Sullivan*, the Supreme Court has upheld a legal doctrine known as affirmative First Amendment theory. This theory states that speech is protected against any restraint or sanction, and it regards any infringement on speech with intense suspicion. This theory has six provisions—neutrality, emotion, symbolism, harm, causation, and precision of speech—that govern whether speech should be controlled.

Neutrality, the heart of affirmative First Amendment theory, states that the government cannot restrict speech simply because it disagrees with the message; it must remain neutral. Also of importance is the concept that there is no such thing as a false idea, regardless of how noxious an opinion may seem. The next provision is emotion. Speech not only is intellectual in scope but also can contain passionate portions that could seem vulgar to some. The mere presence of passion or vulgarity in speech does not mean that it has to be controlled. The third provision is symbolism. Speech is not only words but also anything that is equally vivid, including objects, figures, characters, pictures, and numerous other nonverbal communication devices. The fourth provision concerns harm. Speech may be controlled if it causes physical or relational harm. The fifth provision is causation. Speech does not need to be controlled unless the harm it will cause presents a clear and present danger, that is, if the speech is directed toward inciting or producing imminent lawless action and is likely to incite or produce such action. The last provision, precision, dictates that speech, if it meets the above harm and causation tests, may only be controlled by legislation that is exactly worded so that potential speakers will know the exact boundaries of prohibited speech.

Hate Speech Laws

In the public environment, hate speech can be controlled only in limited circumstances. It can be controlled when it is presented to people in a location where they cannot escape its message. The captive audience doctrine allows speech to be restricted in certain environments: residential units, workplaces, and certain educational locales. This doctrine applies only to places where people are required to be or where they perform necessary life tasks; in the workplace, it would apply to the common office/ production areas, the lunchrooms, restrooms, and the access and egress points. It would not apply to the offices of individuals or the lockers of production workers. On a college campus, it would apply in the dormitories, bath areas, food service areas, classrooms, and public office areas. It would not apply to the auditorium, the open grounds of the campus, or a faculty office. Many colleges have tried unsuccessfully to restrict hate speech on the entire campus through conduct codes.

Hate speech can also be sanctioned when it contains "fighting words." This principle identifies as unprotected those words that originate in a face-to-face confrontation and are so inflammatory that they would be likely to produce a violent response from the average person. Legislatures must produce laws that specifically describe particular circumstances that would meet the criteria for this doctrine. The Ohio Revised Code, 2917.01, requires that a person "knowingly engage in conduct designed to urge or incite another to commit an offense of violence, under circumstances where such conduct creates a clear and present danger that an offense of violence will result, or such conduct proximately results in an offense of violence." The Supreme Court approved of this exception in the case of *Chaplinsky v. New Hampshire* in 1941. It remains part of most criminal codes as an arrestable offense.

Hate speech can be punished when it is evidence of illegal discriminatory conduct. People who are responsible under one of the many laws or provisions that regulate discriminatory activity—fair housing law, employment law, sexual harassment law, and hate crime law, to name a few—may have their speech used as evidence of discriminatory tendencies in the pursuance of civil, crimi-

nal, or administrative relief. This exception was clearly illustrated by the Supreme Court in the 1993 case of *Wisconsin v. Mitchell*. Todd Mitchell, after watching *Mississippi Burning* (the 1988 film dealing with desegregation in the South), walked out onto the street with his friends. Mitchell, an African American, was in a highly emotional state. He saw a white man walking on the sidewalk and, while shouting racial epithets at the man, urged his friends to attack him. He was convicted under a Wisconsin statute that added to the sentence for a crime when it contained a hate component. This type of sentence enhancement has become part of most states' hate-crime legislation. It was upheld by the Supreme Court because Mitchell's hate speech displayed beliefs that motivated him to action, or conduct, not mere expression. The case thus differed from statutes that punish just the speech component—for example, placing a burning cross on a lawn, as in *R.A.V. v. City of St. Paul* (1992).

Despite the rise in communication and publishing by computer, it is unlikely that any new legislative regulations will emerge regarding hate speech on the Internet. Current law covers the typical activities of the many hate groups that already have establishe Web pages. They must avoid advocating, announcing, or encouraging any acts against specific people or places and must not use e-mail to harass any person. This does not prevent private Internet providers and e-mail services from regulating their subscribers' statements or Web sites.   *Michael L. Barrett*

Core Resources

For discussion of the hate movement in the United States, see Morris Dees' *Gathering Storm* (New York: HarperCollins, 1996) and Paul Smith and Robert Allen Warrior's *Like a Hurricane* (New York: New Press, 1996). For a comprehensive discussion of the affirmative First Amendment theory, see Anthony Lewis's *Make No Law: The Sullivan Case and the First Amendment* (New York: Random House, 1991).

See also: Hate Crime Statistics Act; Hate crimes; *R.A.V. v. City of St. Paul*; *Wisconsin v. Mitchell*.

Hawaiian and Pacific Islander Americans

Significance: These ethnically diverse groups maintain relatively harmonious relationships while negotiating inclusion in the U.S. labor market and European American and Asian American institutions and exploring their rights as indigenous peoples.

Hawaiian Americans are individuals with Hawaiian ancestry who are American citizens. Pacific Islander Americans are American Samoans, Guamanians, and people of the Northern Mariana Islands and Pacific atolls who reside on their islands, in Hawaii, or on the mainland United States. Pre-1980 census publications did not differentiate Pacific Islander groups except for Hawaiians. Pacific Islanders sometimes move to the mainland United States because of the mainland's better economic prospects and educational opportunities. Generally, they adapt more easily to suburban and rural areas than to large urban areas. In the 1990's, Asian and Pacific Islander Americans were the fastest-growing minority group in the United States, with the Hawaiian group being the largest.

Guam and the Northern Mariana Islands
The territory of Guam and the U.S. commonwealth of the Northern Mariana Islands are believed to have been inhabited as early as 2,000 B.C.E. by ancient Chomorros of Mayo-Polynesian descent. Colonized by Spanish missionaries in 1668, Guam was annexed by the United States in 1898 and ceded to the United States in 1919. Guam was occupied by the Japanese during World War II and retaken by the United States in 1944. In 1950, Guam's inhabitants were given U.S. citizenship. When the 1962 Naval Clearing Act allowed other ethnic groups to make Guam their home, Filipinos, Caucasians, Japanese, Chinese, Indians, and Pacific Islanders moved there, joining the Carolinians and present-day Chomorros. The 1990 census recorded a population that was 47 percent Chomorro, 25 percent Filipino, and 10 percent Caucasian, with Chinese, Japanese, Korean, and others making up the remaining 18 percent. Ninety percent are Roman Catholics. Guam is a self-governing, organized unincorporated territory with policy relations between Guam and the United States under the jurisdiction of the U.S. Department of the Interior. A 1972 U.S. law gave Guam one nonvoting delegate to the U.S. House of Representatives. Guam remains a cosmopolitan community retaining customs and traditions from many cultures and has a flourishing tourist industry.

Saipan, Tinian, and Rota, the principal islands of the Mariana Islands, have a long history of foreign occupation, by the Spanish from 1521 to 1899, the Germans from 1899 to 1914, and the Japanese from 1914 to 1944. From 1947 to 1978, the area was recognized as a trust territory of the United Nations with the United States as the administering authority. In 1978, the islands became self-governing in political union with the United States. When the United Nations Trusteeship Council concluded that the United States had discharged its obligations to the Mariana Islands, the United States conferred citizenship upon individuals who met the necessary

qualifications. The Security Council of the United Nations voted to dissolve the trusteeship in 1990.

American Samoa
The Samoans' heritage is Polynesian. European visitors, traders, and missionaries arrived in the eighteenth century. In 1872, Pago Pago harbor was ceded to the United States as a naval station. An 1899 treaty between Britain, Germany, and the United States made Samoa neutral, but when kingship was abolished the following year, the Samoan islands east of 171 degrees were given to the United States. American Samoa remains an unincorporated territory administered by the United States Department of the Interior. The 57,366 people (as of 1995), who live mostly on Tutuila, are American nationals. Although unable to vote in federal elections, American Samoans can freely enter the United States and, after fulfilling the residency requirements, can become citizens. Their language is Samoan but many speak English. In 1995, it was estimated that 65,000 Samoans had migrated to the United States, living mainly in California, Washington, and Hawaii. In Hawaii, they have experienced "cultural discrimination" before a public housing eviction board and have been called a stigmatized ethnic group.

Hawaii
It is estimated that the final migration of Hawaiians from Polynesia occurred about 750 C.E. Hawaii's early social system consisted of the *ali'i* (nobility), who imposed hierarchical control over the *maka'ainana* (commoners), whose labor supported a population that, by the mid-1700's, had increased to at least three hundred thousand. England's Captain James Cook, who reached Kauai in 1778, named Hawaii the Sandwich Islands. King Kamehameha first unified the islands of Maui, Oahu, Hawaii, Lanai, and Molokai under a single political regime in 1795. Kauai and Niihau joined the union in 1810. The first Congregationalist missionaries arrived from New England in 1820, followed by European and American merchants and Yankee traders. With Western contact came diseases for which the Hawaiians had no immunity or treatment. By 1853, the native population had fallen to seventy-one thousand.

Chinese, Japanese, and Portuguese immigrants arrived to provide labor for the sugar plantations. Workers coming from Korea, Puerto Rico, Europe, Scandinavia, Russia, Micronesia, Polynesia, and the Philippines considered themselves temporary immigrants. By 1890, Hawaii was a multiethnic society in which non-Hawaiians made up most of the population. Hawaii's independence was recognized by the United States from 1826 until 1893, when American and European sugar plantation owners, descendants of missionaries, and fi-

A young Hawaiian couple poses wearing leis. Hawaiians organized to assert their rights and sovereignty in the 1970's.

nanciers deposed the Hawaiian monarchy, established a provisional government, and proclaimed Hawaii a protectorate of the United States. Annexed by Congress in 1898, Hawaii became a U.S. territory in 1900 and the fiftieth state in 1959.

During the 1970's, a Hawaiian rights and sovereignty movement emerged. Viewed, at first, as a radical grassroots minority, the movement gained momentum after a series of demonstrations and acts of civil disobedience. In 1977, representatives from many organizations and individual Hawaiians met in Puwalu sessions to discuss Hawaiian issues. State Supreme Court justice William Richardson advised Hawaiians to use the courts to redress grievances, challenge laws, and assert gathering, access, and water rights. A constitutional convention, primarily concerned by the state's improper use of lands ceded to the United States after annexation and transferred to the state in 1959, reviewed and revised the functions and responsibilities of Hawaii's government in 1978. The following year, the legislature created the Office of Hawaiian Affairs (OHA) to provide and coordinate programs, advocate for Hawaiians, and serve as a receptacle for reparations. Throughout the succeeding ten years, sovereignty groups strongly criticized OHA. In 1993, the U.S. Congress officially acknowledged and apologized for the actions a hundred years earlier (U.S.

Public Law 103-150). That same year, the sovereignty groups Ka Laahui and Hui Na'auao were awarded education grants, and Governor John Waihee formed the Hawaiian Sovereignty Advisory Commission, which was renamed in 1996 as Ha Hawaii. The most radical sovereignty group, the Oahana Council, declared independence from the United States in January, 1994. In 1997, a number of workshops were conducted by *kupuna* (elders) who emphasized unity among the various factions. When Governor Benjamin Cayetano resolved in his 1998 state-of-the-state address "to advance a plan for Hawaiian sovereignty," he echoed the words of former governor Waihee. Waihee had also ventured his concern that while establishing self-determination, Hawaiians would tear apart the "multicultural fabric" of contemporary Hawaiian society.

Hawaii's population, which had doubled after the islands gained statehood, fell in the 1990's, partly because of the slow growth that resulted from an economic recession and the vast reduction of the military presence on the islands. Between 1990 and 1995, the state experienced a net loss of 376,752 residents to domestic migration, partly because of the high cost of living, which in 1994 was 35 percent to 39 percent greater than the average U.S. large city, while the median income was only about 10 percent higher.

Hawaiians living on the mainland remain connected with their heritage and values through social, university, and cultural associations that promote cultural events and regularly publish newsletters. Hula halaus exist in many states, and Hawaii's music industry brings musicians to the mainland for live performances. Local Hawaiian newspapers are available on the Internet. Pacific Islanders confront various integration difficulties after moving to the United States. Because federal and state statistics combine Pacific Islanders and Asian Americans, it is impossible to obtain reliable demographics. Such statistical reporting complicates the interpretation of data on household configuration, earned income, and educational and professional attainment. The U.S. government's *Current Population Report* (1992) noted that the Asian American and Pacific Islander population was not homogeneous; a population analysis of the group as a whole masked the diversity present. Pacific Islanders do not identify with Asian Americans but with other island peoples. This issue becomes pertinent when Pacific Islanders request funding from the Administration for Native Americans. Unlike Asian Americans, Pacific Islanders qualify as Native Americans. Newly arriving Asian Americans are often placed in migrant programs. They then create businesses and quickly move out of poverty. Research at the University of Utah showed that Pacific Islanders largely work in the service sector and their family businesses mostly involve unskilled labor.

Most Pacific Islanders reside in the western states. The Pacific Islanders' Cultural Association, founded in 1995, is an umbrella organization whose aim is to meet the common needs of all Pacific Islanders living in Northern California. *Susan E. Hamilton*

Core Resources
Asians and Pacific Islanders in the United States, by demographers Herbert Barringer, Robert W. Gardner, and Michael J. Levin (New York: Russell Sage Foundation, 1995), addresses the adaptation of immigrants into American society. In his essay "The Hawaiian Alternative to the One-Drop Rule," in *American Mixed Race: The Culture of Microdiversity,* edited by Naomi Zack (Lanham, Md.: Rowman & Littlefield, 1995), F. James Davis discusses the history of the one-drop rule and the mixed-race experience on the islands. Lawrence H. Fuchs's *Hawaii Pono: An Ethnic and Political History* (Honolulu: Bess Press, 1961) is a classic study of the diverse cultural contributions to Hawaii and the impact of American settlement from 1893 to 1959. Michael Haas's *Institutional Racism: The Case of Hawaii* (Westport, Conn.: Praeger, 1992) is a well-researched inquiry into racism and ethnic relations. *From a Native Daughter: Colonialism and Sovereignty in Hawaii* (Monroe, Maine: Common Courage Press, 1993) is a collection of essays by Haunani-Kay Trask, a spokesperson for Hawaiian rights.

See also: Asian American movement; Multiculturalism; Native Americans.

Hawkins, Yusuf, murder

Yusuf Hawkins, a sixteen-year-old African American, was confronted and killed by a group of Italian American young men in the predominantly white Bensonhurst section of Brooklyn, New York, on August 23, 1989. The murder was racially motivated and served as a sign of the deep-seated animosities and racial divisions that exist in New York City.

Hawkins and three African American friends had traveled to Bensonhurst from their home in East New York to look at a used car for sale. They were confronted by a group of white youths with baseball bats led by Keith Mondello, Joseph Fama, and others. Hawkins was trapped by the group when four shots from a .32-caliber automatic pistol were fired. Hawkins was hit once in the hand and twice in the chest and died shortly after.

Police reported that the white youths mistakenly believed that Hawkins and his companions were friends of a white neighborhood girl, Gina Feliciano. Feliciano, who once dated Mondello, had reportedly begun a series of friendships with African American and Hispanic men.

The night that Hawkins was killed, Mondello was reportedly told either by Feliciano or someone else that a group of her black and Hispanic friends would arrive with bats to beat up him and his friends.

Eight men were charged in the attack. The eighteen-year-old Fama was the only one convicted of second-degree murder and sentenced to the maximum sentence on June 11, 1990. The nineteen-year-old Mondello was convicted of riot, unlawful imprisonment, discrimination, menacing, and criminal possession of a weapon and sentenced on June 11, 1990, to five and one-third to sixteen years in prison. Joseph Serrano, John Vento, and Pasquale Raucci were convicted on lesser charges. Three others were acquitted of all charges. *Erica Childs*

See also: Canarsie riots; Chin, Vincent, murder; Crown Heights conflicts; Hate crimes; Loo, Ming Hai, murder.

Head Start

Head Start is a U.S. government program established in 1965 to improve the potential for children in disadvantaged households to escape poverty and succeed later in life. The program provides early education and nutritional programs to children between the ages of three and five years old. It is targeted primarily at low-income households and children with disabilities.

In addition to the main program, the Early Head Start program targets pregnant women and infants and toddlers, and the Migrant Head Start program helps migrant workers. All the Head Start programs serve a disproportionately large number of minority children and involve federal grants to local service providers.

The programs are founded on the reasoning that early intervention is the most effective way to ensure a person's long-term success. Investment in nutrition and education during a child's early years is thought to create a solid foundation for later learning and development. Such investment would therefore reduce the need for more costly and controversial programs at later stages, such as youth counseling, welfare, drug rehabilitation, or incarceration.

Such investment is also seen as a means for increasing minority enrollment in college that is more politically acceptable than alternatives such as affirmative action. The programs are therefore highly popular with the public and politicians of both the Democratic and Republican Parties. Nevertheless, formal long-term evaluations of Head Start programs have raised serious questions about their actual effectiveness. *Steve D. Boilard*

See also: Affirmative action; Economics and race; Poverty and race; Welfare's impact on racial/ethnic relations.

Health care and racial/ethnic relations

Significance: Matters of race and ethnicity affect the provision and quality of health care in the United States. Advocates of equality in health care seek to design and implement policies that serve to erode racial inequalities and improve intergroup relations.

A series of events in the late 1990's, including Bill Clinton's Initiative on Race, the passage of various state legislation such as California's Proposition 209, and the ongoing debate regarding the rights of immigrants, have helped to highlight the challenges of living in a diverse society that is multiracial, multiethnic, and multireligious. According to W. Winborne and R. Cohen, editors of *Intergroup Relations in the United States: Research Perspectives* (1998), the attention to and understanding of issues relating to race, gender, and religion, among others, have increased exponentially in recent decades. The current social context is also marked by the dominance of race in general, and black-white relations in particular, as the dividing construct in intergroup relations in the United States.

However, intergroup relations in the United States are marked by a range of complexities and contradictions. Although considerable progress has been made since the 1950's, prejudice, discrimination, and inequality persist and are widespread. In addition, increasing ethnic, racial, and religious diversity further complicate the situation, as new conflicts emerge between the majority and new entrants and among different minority groups. In discussing the possible linkages between public policies designed to erode racial inequalities and improve intergroup relations, Winborne and Cohen observe that intergroup relations both influence and are influenced by public policy approaches to racial inequality.

Against this background, it is not surprising that issues and policies related to the health of Americans are being discussed in the context of interracial and interethnic relations. When the authors of the U.S. Department of Health and Human Services' 1990 report *Healthy People 2000* outlined its framework, they recognized that a healthier America would depend substantially on the nation's ability to improve and sustain the health promotion, disease prevention, and general health care of at-risk groups within the general population.

Minority Health Issues

The 1998 government report *One America in the Twenty-first Century: Forging a New Future* notes that gaps in longevity and health care access for minorities and people of color are well documented. The report also notes that the continuing gap in health care access undermines the vision of one America. The authors go on to proclaim that "America should not be a society where babies of different racial backgrounds have significantly different life expectancies. If our Nation is committed to the proposition that all people are created equal, our most basic indicators of life and health should reflect this principle."

In the 1998 final report of the president's Advisory Commission on Consumer Protection and Quality in the Health Care Industry, *Quality First: Better Health Care for All Americans*, the fundamental basis for developing a national policy on health care is articulated in the statement of purpose. This statement declares that the "purpose of the health care system must be to continuously reduce the impact and burden of illness, injury, and disability and to improve the health and functioning of the people of the United States."

However, statistics show that disparities in health care and delivery continue to exist and even to grow in certain areas. For example, 1998 statistics published by the U.S. Department of Health and Human Services cover a range of variables related to health risk factors, mortality, and access to health care. Analysis of these statistics reveals a number of telling facts:

(1) A higher proportion of minorities and people of color (compared to whites) were medically uninsured or lived in medically underserved areas.

(2) In the period 1983-1995, black infants remained at higher risk of dying than white infants, at every level of the mothers' education; also, as the mothers' level of education in-

Life Expectancy at Birth, Blacks and Whites, in Years

Year of Birth	Blacks		Whites	
	Man	Woman	Man	Woman
1970	60.0	68.3	68.0	75.6
1980	63.8	72.5	70.7	78.1
1990	64.5	73.6	72.7	79.4

Source: U.S. Bureau of the Census, *Statistical Abstract of the United States, 1997* (117th ed.). Washington, D.C.: U.S. Government Printing Office, 1997.

creased, white infants' mortality rates declined more rapidly than those of black infants.

(3) Hispanic adults under the age of sixty-five were substantially more likely to be uninsured than were white or black adults.

(4) Poor and near-poor adults were much more likely to be uninsured than those with high incomes regardless of race, ethnicity, or sex; poor white, black, and Hispanic men were from six to seven times as likely to be uninsured as their high-income counterparts.

(5) Black adults with health problems were less likely to have had physician care within the past year.

(6) At each level of median income area, the avoidable hospitalization rate for black persons was higher than that for whites, with the highest difference in the lowest income areas (2.7 times the rate for whites).

(7) Among poor adults, non-Hispanic white persons were more likely than black or Hispanic adults to have had a dental visit in the preceding twelve months (45 percent compared with 38 percent and 36 percent, respectively).

(8) Within each income level, non-Hispanic black women had higher mortality from heart disease than non-Hispanic white women; for adults between twenty-six and sixty-four years of age, the death rate for heart disease was higher for black men than for white men, regardless of income.

In discussing the issues of race and health, *One America in the Twenty-first Century: Forging a New Future* makes conclusions about three critical areas in health care in the context of race. The report identifies structural inequities, discrimination by providers, and the cultural competency of providers as key factors that contribute to continuing inequity in health care delivery.

Structural inequities are difficulties in accessing the health care system that stem from disparities in employment, income, and wealth. The statistics show that, on average, people of color receive medical treatment less frequently and in later stages of disease than whites. Such inequities in access affect rates of sickness, disease, suffering, life expectancy, and mortality among racial groups. Furthermore, studies indicate that racial disparities in health and health care are interrelated and sustained in various socioeconomic groups.

Racial issues may also affect relationships between health care providers and patients of color and the quality of the care delivered. The health care estab-

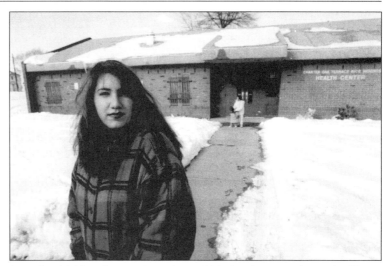

Jacqueline Maldonado, a single mother and Medicaid recipient, leaves the Charter Oak Terrace Rice Heights Health Center in Hartford, Connecticut, in 1996. Facilities such as this have improved the quality of heath care for many poor, minority patients.

lishment is disproportionately white. Health care providers, like everyone else, can be affected by racial stereotypes and may lack the language and intercultural skills to serve patients of color fully. Furthermore, providers may, intentionally or unintentionally, discriminate against patients on the basis of stereotypes. Such discrimination can result in differences in care such as inadequate, denied, or delayed medical treatment, unnecessarily prescribed treatment, or cursory care.

In addition to structural inequities and provider discrimination, racial disparities in health care access may be affected by differences in language or culture between the provider and patient. Providers need to be culturally competent in order to deliver effective medical care to people from different cultural backgrounds. Often, these cultural differences undermine the necessary cooperation between providers and clients, which in turn results in less effective medical services.

Recommendations for Change

In the late 1990's, President Bill Clinton announced efforts to eliminate long-standing racial disparities in infant mortality, cancer screening and management, heart disease, AIDS, and immunizations by the year 2010. The authors of *One America in the Twenty-first Century: Forging a New Future* outline a range of additional steps to eliminate disparities in other key areas of health care and access. These recommendations include continued advocacy for broad-based expansions in health-insurance coverage; continued advocacy of increased health care access for underserved groups; increased funding for existing programs targeted to underserved and minority populations; enhanced financial and regulatory mechanisms to promote culturally competent care; and increased emphasis on the importance of cultural competence to institutions training health care providers.

Winborne and Cohen have observed that "advocates of race consciousness in public policy believe that race functions so powerfully in American society that to ignore it is to perpetuate institutionalized inequalities and marginalization of certain groups." Furthermore, they concluded that "race-cognizant public policies may be seen as improving race relations by fostering equality and recognition of marginalized groups, despite causing backlash against groups benefitting from them." In the light of the evidence, it is clear that in order to accomplish the statement of purpose articulated in *Quality First: Better Health Care for All Americans*, it will be necessary to design and implement policies that serve to erode racial inequalities and improve intergroup relations. From a health care perspective, there is a healthy, ongoing discussion of the issues, giving reason for hope that the United States in the new millennium will provide better access to health care for a larger proportion of its population. *Yonette F. Thomas*

Core Resources

Wayne Winborne and Renae Cohen's *Intergroup Relations in the United States: Research Perspectives* (Bloomsburg, Pa.: Haddon Craftsman, 1998) provides an overview of survey research on intergroup relations in contemporary America and racial inequality and race-relations issues in selected policy areas. The U.S. Department of Health and Human Services' *Healthy People 2000* (Washington, D.C.: Government Printing Office, 1990) provides a statement of national objectives for health promotion and disease prevention. *Quality First: Better Health Care for All Americans* (Washington, D.C.: Government Printing Office, 1998), the final report of the Advisory Commission on Consumer Protection and Quality in the Health Care Industry, calls for a national effort to improve and sustain the quality of health care in the United States. *One America in the Twenty-first Century: Forging a New Future* (Washington, D.C.: Government Printing Office, 1998) is the official report of the Advisory Board to the President on issues of race. *Health: United States, 1998* (Washington, D.C.: Government Printing Office, 1998), a report on the health status of the nation, presents national trends in health statistics; it was compiled by the Centers for Disease Control and Prevention's National Center for Health Statistics. Matters of race and health are also discussed in *The Sociology of Race Relations: Reflections and Reform* (New York: The Free Press, 1980), edited by T. F. Pettigrew; Gunnar Myrdal's *An America Dilemma: The Negro Problem and Modern Democracy* (New York: Harper, 1944); and Stanford Lyman's *The Black American in Sociological Thought* (New York: Putnam, 1972).

See also: Discrimination: indirect institutionalized; Economics and race; Institutional racism; Poverty and race; Stereotype.

Heart of Atlanta Motel v. United States

The Supreme Court's December 14, 1964, decision in *Heart of Atlanta Motel v. United States* upheld the constitutionality of the public accommodations section (Title II) of the Civil Rights Act of 1964.

After the Civil War, Congress passed the Thirteenth, Fourteenth, and Fifteenth Amendments in order to establish legal and political rights for the newly freed slaves. The Fourteenth Amendment, in part, was designed to protect black citizens from discrimination by state and local governments in the South. It did not address the issue of private discrimination against blacks in hotels, restaurants, and theaters. Was discrimination by private individuals therefore legal? The U.S. Congress addressed this question when it passed the Civil Rights Act of 1875. This law made it illegal to discriminate against individuals in public accommodations. In 1883 the U.S. Supreme Court declared the Civil Rights Act of 1875 to be unconstitutional. According to the Court, the Fourteenth Amendment only protected against state discrimination and not discrimination by private individuals in their private businesses.

Almost a century later, the U.S. Congress addressed this issue again. Congressional hearings were held concerning the difficulty African Americans faced in using public accommodations. According to the hearings, blacks traveling from Washington, D.C., to New Orleans, Louisiana, in 1963 would find that the average distance between hotel and motel accommodations available to them was 174 miles. As a result of the hearings, Congress incorporated a public accommodations section as part of the Civil Rights Act of 1964. The public accommodations section prevented discrimination in hotels, motels, restaurants, theaters, sports arenas, and other public facilities. Congress based its authority to regulate public accommodations on the "commerce clause" of the Constitution, which grants Congress the authority to "regulate Commerce with foreign Nations, and among the several States."

The *Heart of Atlanta* case involves the immediate challenge to the constitutionality of the public accommodations section of the Civil Rights Act of 1964. The Heart of Atlanta Motel, a local operation, refused to serve

African Americans. As a local motel, it argued that its not serving blacks had no impact on interstate commerce. Attorneys for the U.S. government argued that interstate commerce was affected by the motel's policy because three-quarters of its clientele came from outside the state. In upholding the public accommodations section of the Civil Rights Act of 1964, a unanimous Supreme Court argued that it made no difference that the motel was a local operation. If interstate commerce is affected at all, "it does not matter how local the operation which applies the squeeze." A companion case, *Katzenbach v. McClung* (1964), involving a small, local restaurant in Birmingham, Alabama, which refused sit-down service to blacks, reached a similar conclusion. Although the Court was unanimous in upholding the public accommodations section of the Civil Rights Act of 1964, the justices did not all concur on the reasoning. A majority of the justices upheld the law on the basis of the commerce clause, but Justice William Douglas wanted to base the decision on the equal protection clause of the Fourteenth Amendment. *Darryl Paulson*

See also: Civil Rights Act of 1964; Discrimination: racial and ethnic; Fair Housing Act; Freedom Riders; Greensboro sit-ins; Housing; Segregation: de facto and de jure.

Hirabayashi v. United States

In *Hirabayashi v. United States*, the Supreme Court on June 21, 1943, ruled in favor of the military's use of a curfew in a wartime situation.

In 1942, Gordon Kiyoshi Hirabayashi, an American citizen of Japanese ancestry, was arrested for violating the curfew set by General John L. DeWitt on the West Coast and subsequently failing to report to a designated Civil Control Station for assignment to a "relocation center" (internment camp). The military acted under the authority of Executive Order 9066, issued on February 19, 1942, by President Franklin D. Roosevelt. This order authorized the secretary of war and appropriate military commanders to establish military areas from which any or all persons might be excluded. The president issued this order solely on his authority as commander in chief of the Army and Navy. After Hirabayashi was found guilty of violating the curfew and failing to report to the Civil Control Station, he appealed to the U.S. Supreme Court.

In 1943, the U.S. Supreme Court ruled 9 to 0 in favor of the United States and upheld the military's right to authorize a curfew. The majority opinion was written by Chief Justice Harlan Stone, who emphasized the grave character of the national emergency that had confronted the nation in 1942 and the possible disloyalty of

portions of the Japanese American minority. He further noted that "in time of war residents having ethnic affiliations with an invading enemy may be a greater source of danger than those of a different ancestry." The Court, he thought, ought not to challenge the conclusion of the military authorities that the federal power be interpreted as broadly as possible. While there was some question of the constitutionality of the military order under the Fifth Amendment, Justice Stone denied that the curfew was unconstitutional because the amendment contained no equal protection clause.

Interestingly, though the Court was unanimous in its holding, there were three separate concurring opinions, by Justices Frank Murphy, William O. Douglas, and Wiley Rutledge. Justice Murphy made it clear that he found restrictions upon minority rights on the basis of race odious even in wartime: "Distinctions based on color and ancestry are utterly inconsistent with our traditions and our ideals." He believed that the curfew order bore "a melancholy resemblance to the treatment accorded to members of the Jewish race in Germany and other parts of Europe." He nevertheless justified the order, constitutionally, because of the "critical military situation" on the West Coast.

While the Court upheld the act of Congress of March 21, 1942, authorizing the curfew, it seems clear that at least some of the justices were quite uncomfortable with the relocation program. Therein is the legacy of this case: Why did the justices not offer a decision on the Japanese Relocation Program? It seems evident that a majority of the justices were extremely reluctant to interfere with the program, primarily because they were unwilling to dispute the judgment of the president and military commanders as to what was necessary to win the war. Therefore, it was easier for them to determine only that the curfew order was constitutional and lay within the combined congressional and presidential powers. *Kevin F. Sims*

See also: Japanese American internment; *Korematsu v. United States*; Redress movement.

Hispanic vs. Latino

The group of United States residents who have a common connection to the Spanish language are termed Hispanics, while Americans of Latin American descent are termed Latinos. There is a great degree of overlap between the two groups, and often the terms Hispanic and Latino are used interchangeably. However, Californians, most New Yorkers, and Chicagoans favor Latino, while many Texans and almost everyone in Florida prefer Hispanic. The main distinguishing factor is that the appellation "Hispanic" is typically associated with afflu-ence, whereas "Latino" is associated with a struggle for social and economic justice. Based on this diversity, Mexican Americans, who live primarily in the Southwest, and Puerto Ricans, who live mainly in the Northeast, often call themselves Latino, while Cuban Americans, who are concentrated in Florida, tend to prefer being called Hispanic.

The U.S. Bureau of the Census uses the term "His-panic" to denote people of Spanish/Hispanic origin. According to its classification system, a person of His-panic origin may be of any race. In the 1990 census, people could self-identify as belonging to one of the Hispanic subgroups: Mexican, Puerto Rican, Cuban, or Other Spanish/Hispanic. Those in the "Other" category could write in their subgroup. For the 2000 census, respondents may select from five racial categories—African American or black, American Indian or Native Alaskan, Asian, Native Hawaiian or other Pacific Is-lander, and White—and also check "Hispanic or Latino."

Alvin K. Benson

See also: Censuses, U.S.; Latinos in the United States.

Hmong Americans

> **Significance:** Laotian mountain tribespeople from a pre-literate society experienced culture shock when they mi-grated to the United States as refugees, beginning in 1976. Their adjustment difficulties contradict the stereotype of Asian Americans as a highly educated, successful "model" minority.

The Hmong (pronounced "mong") people have a long history of escaping adversity. For centuries the Hmong were an ethnic group persecuted in China. In the early nineteenth century, they moved to Burma (Myanmar), Thailand, Vietnam, and Laos. In Laos, the Hmong set-tled in the isolated highlands. During the political tur-moil in the 1950's and 1960's, many Hmong fought for the anticommunist army under General Vang Pao. The U.S. Central Intelligence Agency (CIA) secretly ran and financed this Vietnam War effort in which Laotian men served in rescue missions and guerrilla operations. When the Communists took power in Laos in 1975 and the United States withdrew, there were reprisals against the Hmong. To escape persecution, many Hmong fled to United Nations refugee camps in Thailand. In Ban Vinai and other refugee camps, Hmong families waited to establish political refugee status so that they could emigrate to the United States.

Refugees on the Move

The first Hmong refugees arrived in the United States in 1976, assisted by world relief organizations and local organizations such as churches. Between 1976 and 1991, an estimated 100,000 Hmong came to the United States. Because of their high birthrate, the population in-creased substantially. The Hmong dispersed throughout the United States, settling wherever sponsors could be found. The Hmong later followed a secondary migration pattern within the United States, moving to concentra-tions in California, Minnesota, Montana, Wisconsin, Colorado, Washington, North Carolina, and Rhode Is-land. Areas of second settlement were selected based on climate, cheap housing, job availability, state welfare programs, and family unification. In the early 1990's, Fresno County, California, had the largest settlement, followed by the Minneapolis-St. Paul metropolitan area. The reception the Hmong received varied from hearty welcome to ethnic antagonism on the part of some Americans who were ignorant of Hmong bravery and sacrifices in the Vietnam War and who did not grasp the difficulty of Hmong adjustment to life in the United States.

Culture Shock

Three branches of the Hmong came to the United States: the Blue Hmong, the White Hmong, and the Striped Hmong. They spoke different dialects and wore distinct traditional clothing but shared many cultural traditions that made it difficult to adjust to life in a modern society. Most refugees had never experienced indoor plumbing, electricity, or automobiles. For many Hmong, their only work experience before coming to the United States was as soldiers and as farmers. The traditional crops of rice and corn were raised on fields so steep that sometimes farmers tethered themselves to a stump to keep from falling off their fields. For the Hmong who tried farming in the United States, adjust-ment was difficult. Their slash-and-burn method of clear-ing land was not permitted. They were unfamiliar with pesticides and chemical fertilizers. Refugees worked as migrant farmworkers and in many low-paid urban posi-tions that did not require English proficiency. The un-employment rate was very high for many Hmong com-munities. In 1988, 70 percent of the Fresno Hmong depended on welfare and refugee assistance.

Education was another area of difficult cultural adap-tation. In the 1990's, many Hmong children struggled in U.S. schools. Many attended English-as-a-second-language classes, and many were placed in a vocational track. Hmong children often had low scores on stan-dardized tests of vocabulary and reading comprehen-sion. When large numbers of Hmong children entered certain school systems in the late 1970's and 1980's,

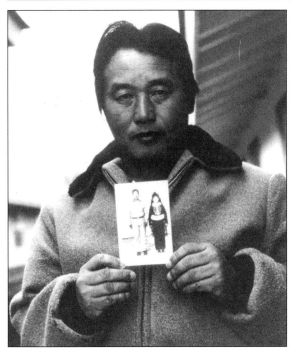

A Hmong refugee in Merced, California, in 1984 holds a photograph of his parents, who remain in Laos. Hmong refugees suffered a great deal of culture shock after their arrival in the United States.

administrators and teachers were completely unprepared. Learning English proved difficult, especially for the older Hmong who had never attended school in Laos. Special training programs first taught Hmong language literacy, then English.

Hmong beliefs about religion and medicine are very different from common attitudes in the United States. Traditional Hmong religion is a form of animism, a belief that spirits dwell in all things, including the earth, the sky, and animals. Hmong attempted to placate these spirits in religious rituals that often included animal sacrifice. In medical ceremonies, a shaman or healer tried to locate and bring back the patient's runaway soul. Many bereaved Hmong refused autopsies, believing they interfered with reincarnation.

Hmong family traditions often put them at odds with U.S. culture. The Laotian practice was to arrange marriages, usually interclan agreements in which a bride price was paid. Women married as teenagers, then derived their status from being a wife and mother of many children. Marriage by capture was part of Hmong tradition but led to U.S. criminal charges of kidnapping and rape. Divorce was discouraged but possible in Laos, and children could be kept by the husband's family. Such practices conflict with many U.S. laws and folkways.

Other conflicts arose over U.S. laws that the Hmong did not understand. Carrying concealed weapons was common in Laos but led to arrest in the United States. Zoning laws stipulating where to build a house or plant a field were unfamiliar to the Hmong. Disputes arose over Hmong poaching in wildlife refuges.

Culture shock seems to have taken a toll on the Hmong. In the 1970's and early 1980's, many apparently healthy Hmong men died in their sleep in what was labeled Sudden Unexplained Death Syndrome. Possible explanations were depression, "survivor guilt," and the stress of a new environment in which the men lacked control of their lives. The peak years for the syndrome were 1981 and 1982.

Strengths of the Hmong

Not all aspects of Hmong tradition handicapped their adjustment to life in the United States. Some members possess fine-motor skills honed in their intricate needlework. Without sewing machines or patterns, Hmong women embroider and appliqué to produce marketable products that also preserve their cultural memories. Flower cloths are square designs with symmetrical patterns. Story cloths are sewn pictures depicting past events, including war brutality and refugee camp life. Hmong developed memorization skills as part of their oral tradition of elaborate folktales. Hmong women are credited with admirable parenting skills, especially in their sensitivity to their children's needs. The Hmong typically possess a fierce independence and will to survive.

The Hmong appear to be adjusting to the new culture in which they find themselves, especially the younger generation. Hmong youth typically adopt American ways, wearing Western dress and enjoying rock music and video games. The group shows resilience in adapting traditions to changed circumstances. The Hmong have devised a custom of group support as clans form communities for mutual aid. Seamstresses have adapted their needlework patterns to satisfy Western markets. Crowded city dwellers often plant impromptu gardens in the narrow spaces between buildings.

Nancy Conn Terjesen

Core Resources

I Begin My Life All Over: The Hmong and the American Immigrant Experience, by Lillian Faderman with Ghia Xiong (Boston: Beacon, 1998), combines thirty-five narratives and emphasizes generational differences. Anne Fadiman's *The Spirit Catches You and You Fall Down: A Hmong Child, Her American Doctors, and the Collision of Two Cultures* (New York: Farrar, Straus & Giroux, 1997) looks at how cultural differences affected the treatment of a young epileptic Hmong American girl. Wendy Walker-Moffat's *The Other Side of the Asian American Success Story*

(San Francisco: Jossey-Bass, 1995) is a research report explaining negative educational experiences. Spencer Sherman's "The Hmong in America: Laotian Refugees in the Land of the Giants," in *National Geographic* (October, 1988), describes communities in North Carolina and California. Ronald Takaki's *Strangers from a Different Shore: History of Asian Americans* (Boston: Little, Brown, 1989) includes a chapter on post-1965 immigrants. Lan Cao and Himilce Novas use a question-answer format to describe seven nationalities in *Everything You Need to Know About Asian American History* (New York: Penguin, 1996).

See also: Asian American stereotypes; Cambodian Americans; "Model" minorities; Vietnamese Americans; Welfare's impact on racial/ethnic relations.

Holocaust

> **Significance:** "Holocaust" is the term used to describe the Nazi effort to exterminate Europe's Jews during the period from 1933 to 1945. Its implications for North American Jewry, and therefore for Jewish American relations with other groups, remain enormous.

The Holocaust was Nazi Germany's planned total destruction of the Jewish people and the actual murder of nearly six million of them. That genocidal campaign—the most systematic, bureaucratic, and unrelenting the world has seen—also destroyed millions of non-Jewish civilians. They included Gypsies (Roma and Sinti), Slavs, Jehovah's Witnesses, Freemasons, homosexuals, the mentally retarded, the physically handicapped, and the insane. The Nazis believed that their threat to the Third Reich approached, though it could never equal, the one posed by Jews.

In German, this unprecedented destruction process became known euphemistically as *die Endlösung*—the Final Solution. The Hebrew word *Shoah,* which means catastrophe, is also used to name it, but the term "Holocaust" most commonly signifies the event. That word has biblical roots. In the Septuagint, a Greek translation of the Hebrew Bible, the Hebrew word *olah* is translated as *holokauston.* In context, *olah* means that which is offered up. It refers to a sacrifice, often specifically to "an offering made by fire unto the Lord." Such connotations make "Holocaust" a problematic term for the devastation it names. The word's religious implications seem inappropriate, even repulsive, to many people, including many Jews. Still, Holocaust remains the term that is most widely used.

Nazi Germany's system of concentration camps, ghettos, murder squadrons, and killing centers took more than twelve million defenseless human lives. Between five million and six million of them were Jewish, including approximately one million children under fifteen. Although not every Nazi victim was Jewish, the Nazi intent was to rid Europe, if not the world, of Jews. Hitler went far in meeting that goal. Although Europe's Jews resisted the onslaught as best they could, by the end of World War II two-thirds of European Jews—and about one-third of Jews worldwide—were dead. The vast majority of the Jewish victims came from Eastern Europe. More than half of them were from Poland; there, the German annihilation effort was 90 percent successful. At Auschwitz alone—located in Poland, the largest of the Nazi killing centers—more than one million Jews were gassed.

How did the Holocaust happen and why? Those questions are both historical and ethical. Their implications are huge. As Elie Wiesel, Jewish survivor of Auschwitz and winner of the 1986 Nobel Peace Prize, has rightly said of Birkenau, the major killing area at Auschwitz: "Traditional ideas and acquired values, philosophical systems and social theories—all must be revised in the shadow of Birkenau."

History
Adolf Hitler became chancellor of Germany on January 30, 1933. He soon consolidated his power through tyranny and terror. Within six months, the Nazis stood as the only legal political power in Germany, Hitler's decrees were law, basic civil rights had been suspended, and thousands of the Third Reich's political opponents had been imprisoned.

Emphasizing the superiority of the German people, Nazi ideology was anti-Semitic and racist to the core. The Nazis affirmed that German racial purity must be maintained. Building on precedents long established by Christianity's animosity toward Jews, the Nazis went further and vilified Jews as the most dangerous threat to that goal. Jews are not, in fact, a race but a people unified by memory and history, culture, tradition, and religious observances that are widely shared. Any person of any race can become Jewish through religious conversion. Nevertheless, Nazi ideology defined Jewish identity in biological and racial terms.

German law established detailed conditions to define full and partial Jews. To cite three examples, if one had three Jewish grandparents, that condition was sufficient to make one fully Jewish. If one had only two Jewish grandparents and neither practiced Judaism nor had a Jewish spouse, however, then one was a *Mischlinge* (mongrel) first-class. A person with only a single Jewish grandparent would be a *Mischlinge* second-class. The identity of one's grandparents was determined, paradoxically, not by blood but by their membership in the Jewish religious community. Once these Nazi classifications were in effect, the identity they conferred was irreversible.

Defining Jewish identity was crucial for identifying the population targeted by the Nazis' anti-Semitic policies. Those policies focused first on segregating Jews, making their lives intolerable, and forcing them to leave Germany. Between 1933 and the outbreak of World War II in September, 1939, hundreds of decrees, such as the Nuremberg Laws of September, 1935, deprived the Third Reich's Jews of basic civil rights. When Jews tried to emigrate from German territory, however, they found few havens. In general, doors around the world, including those in the United States, were opened reluctantly, if at all, for Jewish refugees from Hitler's Germany.

World War II began with Germany's invasion of Poland on September 1, 1939. With the notable exception of its failure to subdue England by air power, the German war machine had things largely its own way until it experienced reversals at El Alamein and Stalingrad in 1942. By the end of that year, four million Jews had already been murdered.

As Hitler's forces advanced on all fronts, huge numbers of Jews, far exceeding the 600,000 who lived in Germany when Hitler took control, came under Nazi domination. For a year after the war began, Nazi planning had still aimed to enforce massive Jewish resettlement, but there were no satisfactory ways to fulfill that intention. Other tactics had to be found. The Holocaust did not result from a detailed master plan that timed and controlled every move in advance. When one step reached an impasse, however, the next was always more drastic, because the Nazis did not deviate from their basic commitment: Somehow, the Jews had to be eliminated.

The Killing Begins

In the spring of 1941, as plans were laid for the invasion of the Soviet Union, Hitler decided that special mobile killing units—*Einsatzgruppen*—would follow the German army, round up Jews, and kill them. A second prong of attack in Germany's war against the Jews became operational as well. Instead of moving killers toward their victims, it would bring victims to their killers.

Utilizing a former Austrian military barracks near the Polish town of Okwicim, the Germans made their concentration camp of Auschwitz op-

erational in June, 1940, when 728 Polish prisoners were transferred there. By the summer of 1941, the original camp (Auschwitz I) had been supplemented by a much larger camp at nearby Birkenau (Auschwitz II). Within the next year—along with five other sites in occupied Poland (Chelmno, Belzec, Sobibor, Treblinka, and Majdanek)—Auschwitz-Birkenau became a full-fledged killing center. Auschwitz "improved" killing by employing fast-working hydrogen cyanide gas, which suppliers offered in the form of a deodorized pesticide known as Zyklon B. Efficiency at Auschwitz-Birkenau was further improved in 1943 when new crematoria became available for corpse disposal. Optimum "production" in this death factory meant that thousands of Jews could be killed per day. When Schutzstaffel (SS) leader Heinrich Himmler ordered an end to the systematic killing at Auschwitz in late 1944, his reasoning was not based entirely on the fact that Russian troops were nearby. For all practical purposes, he could argue, the Final Solution had eliminated Europe's "Jewish problem."

Ethical Problems and Moral Challenges

The most crucial moral problem posed by the Holocaust is that no moral, social, religious, or political constraints were sufficient to stop Nazi Germany from unleashing the Final Solution. Only when military force crushed the Third Reich did the genocide end.

David Rousset, a French writer who endured German concentration camps, understated the case, but he was surely correct when he said simply, "The existence of the camps is a warning." Two aspects of that warning are especially challenging.

This freight car holds the bodies of emaciated prisoners who died while being transported to Dachau from another concentration camp in April, 1945. These dead men were but a few of the millions of Jews and others killed by Nazis during the Holocaust.

First, the Holocaust warns about the depth of racism's evil. It shows that racism's destructive "logic" ultimately entails genocide. If one takes seriously the idea that one race endangers the well-being of another, the only way to remove that menace completely is to do away, once and for all, with everyone and everything that embodies that race. If most forms of racism shy away from such extreme measures, Nazi Germany's anti-Semitism did not. The Nazis saw what they took to be a practical problem: the need to eliminate "racially inferior" people. Then they moved to solve it.

Consequently, the Holocaust did not result from unplanned, random violence. It was instead a state-sponsored program of population elimination made possible by modern technology and political organization. As Nazi Germany became a genocidal state, its anti-Semitic racism required a destruction process that needed and got the cooperation of every sector of German society. The killers and those who aided and abetted them directly—or indirectly as bystanders—were civilized people from a society that was scientifically advanced, technologically competent, culturally sophisticated, and efficiently organized. These people were, as Holocaust scholar Michael Berenbaum has noted, "both ordinary and extraordinary, a cross section of the men and women of Germany, its allies, and their collaborators as well as the best and the brightest."

Teachers and writers helped to till the soil in which Hitler's virulent anti-Semitism took root; their students and readers reaped the wasteful harvest. Lawyers drafted and judges enforced the laws that isolated Jews and set them up for the kill. Government and church personnel provided birth records to document who was Jewish and who was not. Other workers entered such information into state-of-the-art data-processing machines. University administrators curtailed admissions for Jewish students and dismissed Jewish faculty members. Bureaucrats in the finance ministry confiscated Jewish wealth and property. Postal officials delivered mail about definition and expropriation, denaturalization and deportation. Driven by their biomedical visions, physicians were among the first to experiment with the gassing of *lebensunwertes Leben* (lives unworthy of life). Scientists performed research and tested their racial theories on those branded subhuman or nonhuman by German science. Business executives found that Nazi concentration camps could provide cheap labor; they worked people to death, turning the Nazi motto, *Arbeit macht frei* (work makes one free), into a mocking truth. Stockholders made profits from firms that supplied Zyklon B to gas people and from companies that built crematoria to burn the corpses. Radio performers were joined by artists such as the gifted film director Leni Riefenstahl to broadcast and screen the polished propaganda that made Hitler's policies persuasive to so many. Engineers drove the trains that transported Jews to death, while other officials took charge of the billing arrangements for this service. Factory workers modified trucks so that they became deadly gas vans; city policemen became members of squadrons that made the murder of Jews their specialty. As the list went on and on, so did the racially motivated destruction of the European Jews.

Short of Germany's military defeat by the Allies, no other constraints—moral, social, religious, or political—were sufficient to stop the Final Solution. Accordingly, a second Holocaust warning is the challenge that no one should take human rights for granted. To make that warning more personal, consider Hans Maier. Born on October 31, 1912, the only child of a Catholic mother and a Jewish father, he considered himself an Austrian, not least because his father's family had lived in Austria since the seventeenth century. Hans Maier, however, lived in the twentieth century, and so it was that in the autumn of 1935 he studied a newspaper in a Viennese coffeehouse. The Nuremberg Laws had just been passed in Nazi Germany. Maier's reading made him see that, even if he did not think of himself as Jewish, the Nazis' definitions meant that in their view he was Jewish. By identifying him as a Jew, Maier would write later on, Nazi power made him "a dead man on leave, someone to be murdered, who only by chance was not yet where he properly belonged."

When Nazi Germany occupied Austria in March, 1938, Maier drew his conclusions. He fled his native land for Belgium and joined the Resistance after Belgium was swept into the Third Reich in 1940. Arrested by Nazi police in 1943, Maier was sent to Auschwitz and then to Bergen-Belsen, where he was liberated in 1945. Eventually taking the name Jean Améry, by which he is remembered, this philosopher waited twenty years before breaking his silence about the Holocaust. When Améry did decide to write, the result was a series of remarkable essays about his experience. In English, they appear in a volume entitled *At the Mind's Limits: Contemplations by a Survivor on Auschwitz and Its Realities.* "Every morning when I get up," he tells his reader, "I can read the Auschwitz number on my forearm. . . . Every day anew I lose my trust in the world. . . . Declarations of human rights, democratic constitutions, the free world and the free press, nothing," he went on to say, "can lull me into the slumber of security from which I awoke in 1935."

In *The Cunning of History: The Holocaust and the American Future,* Richard L. Rubenstein echoes Améry's understanding. "Does not the Holocaust demonstrate," he suggests, "that there are absolutely no limits to the degradation and assault the managers and technicians of violence can inflict upon men and women who lack the power of effective resistance?" Rubenstein's outlook may be debatable, but he believes that "the dreadful history of Europe's Jews had demonstrated that *rights do not belong to men by nature.*" If Rubenstein is correct, then, practically speaking, people can expect to enjoy basic rights such as those proclaimed by the Declaration of Independence—life, liberty, and the pursuit of happiness—only within a political community that honors and defends those rights successfully.

The Holocaust is forgotten at humanity's peril. Remembering it provides warnings that perhaps can make a shield for the future.   *John K. Roth*

Core Resources

Jean Améry's *At the Mind's Limits: Contemplations by a Survivor on Auschwitz and Its Realities* (Bloomington: Indiana University Press, 1980), translated by Sidney Rosenfeld and Stella P. Rosenfeld, consists of reflections by a survivor of the Holocaust that consider the status of human rights and responsibility after Auschwitz. Michael Berenbaum's *The World Must Know: The History of the Holocaust as Told in the United States Holocaust Memorial Museum* (Boston: Little, Brown, 1993) provides an excellent overview of Holocaust history and highlights effectively American responses to the destruction of the European Jews.

Christopher R. Browning's *Ordinary Men: Reserve Police Battalion 101 and the Final Solution in Poland* (New York: HarperCollins, 1992) examines how a unit of "ordinary" German men became a killing squadron. *Encyclopedia of the Holocaust* (New York: Macmillan, 1990), edited by Israel Gutman et al., concentrates on major figures, places, and particular events that are central to the ethical dilemmas posed by the Holocaust. Peter J. Haas's *Morality After Auschwitz: The Radical Challenge of the Nazi Ethic* (Philadelphia: Fortress Press, 1988) analyzes how Nazi "idealism" led many people to accept genocide as tolerable and even routine. Philip P. Hallie's *Lest Innocent Blood Be Shed: The Story of the Village of Le Chambon and How Goodness Happened There* (New York: Harper & Row, 1979) investigates how and why the people in the French village of Le Chambon risked their lives to rescue some five thousand Jews. Raul Hilberg's *The Destruction of the European Jews* (Rev. ed, New York: Holmes & Meier, 1985) is an unrivaled study of the bureaucratic process of destruction that the Nazis directed toward the Jews of Europe. Robert Jay Lifton's *The Nazi Doctors: Medical Killing and the Psychology of Genocide* (New York: Basic Books, 1986) shows how the Holocaust emerged from the Nazis' "biomedical vision" and documents how German physicians became deeply implicated in mass murder. *Different Voices: Women and the Holocaust* (New York: Paragon House, 1993), edited by Carol Carol, and John K. Roth, discusses moral dilemmas created by the Holocaust's impact on women. Richard L. Rubenstein's *The Cunning of History: The Holocaust and the American Future*

(New York: Harper & Row, 1987) analyzes how the Holocaust calls traditional moral outlooks into question, particularly the idea that human beings possess natural rights. Richard L. Rubenstein and John K. Roth's *Approaches to Auschwitz: The Holocaust and Its Legacy* (Atlanta: John Knox Press, 1987) shows how religious conflict and racism intensified the anti-Semitism that led to Auschwitz and also focuses on the roles played by the churches, industry, and the professions during the Nazi era. Gitta Sereny's *Into That Darkness: An Examination of Conscience* (New York: Vintage Books, 1983) maps the circumstances that led Franz Stangl, an Austrian policeman, to become the commandant of Nazi death camps at Sobibor and Treblinka. In Elie Wiesel's *Night* (New York: Bantam Books, 1982), translated by Stella Rodway, the winner of the 1986 Nobel Peace Prize describes his experiences in Auschwitz and Buchenwald.

See also: Anti-Semitism; Ethnic cleansing; Frustration-aggression theory; Genocide: cultural; Genocide: physical; Holocaust denial; Jewish Americans; Nazism; Segregation.

Holocaust denial

Holocaust denial is the assertion, despite documented evidence to the contrary, that the systematic Nazi extermination of an estimated five million to six million Jews between 1933 and 1945 did not occur. It was begun by Nazi commandants, who, near the end of World War II, destroyed concentration camp records and other evidence of mass destruction and carried out the orders of Reichsführer Heinrich Himmler that no prisoner should survive. After the war, many leaders of the Schutzstaffel (SS, a special Nazi military unit) fled the country and began the publication of denial materials.

The origins of Holocaust denial are in the works of European and American historical revisionists designed to absolve Germany of its role in World War I. However, one of the earliest apologists for the Nazi regime was Paul Rassinier, a French prisoner confined to Buchenwald in 1943, who claimed that there were no gas chambers in Nazi concentration camps. Despite the fact that gas chambers had been implemented in Poland and not in Buchenwald, Rassinier asserted his personal experience as proof. Rassinier's *Crossing the Line* (1948) and *The Holocaust Story and the Lie of Ulysses* (1950) maintain that the atrocities that were committed by the Germans have been greatly exaggerated and that the inmates who ran the camps, not the Germans, were the perpetrators of these atrocities.

The works of Rassinier, republished in 1977 by Noontide Press as *Debunking the Genocide Myth*, were translated by Henry Barnes of Smith College, the first American historian to pursue Holocaust denial. Barnes had denounced the United States' foreign policy during World War I, but with his discovery of Rassinier, he began to argue that the atrocity stories had been exaggerated and eventually came to insist that they had been fabricated. Barnes raised doubts about the existence of gas chambers as a means of extermination by contending that gas chambers were a postwar invention. Barnes learned of American revisionist David Leslie Hoggan, whose dissertation at Harvard University maintained that Great Britain was responsible for World War II and depicted Adolf Hitler as a victim of the Allies. Through Barnes's help, Hoggan's book *The Forced War* (1961) became a Nazi apologia.

Holocaust denial assumed a more scholarly character with the advent of Austin J. App, professor at the University of Scranton, who sought through demographic studies to prove that the estimates of Jewish victims had been inflated. App's position, that no Jews were gassed in German camps and the small number who had "disappeared" was exaggerated to victimize Germany, became a central tenet of Holocaust denial. In 1976, Arthur P. Butz, a professor at Northwestern University, published *The Hoax of the Twentieth Century*, which denies that huge numbers of gassings and cremations could have occurred given the technological limitations of the equipment used.

In 1978, the beliefs supporting Holocaust denial were incorporated in a Los Angeles-based organization, the Institute for Historical Review (IHR), funded by Willis Carto. The IHR, which makes use of Carto's periodical publication and his book publication company, Noontide Press, has also established the *Journal of Historical Review*. The following year, it initiated International Revisionist Conventions to accommodate and direct the activities of deniers around the world.   *Mary Hurd*

See also: Anti-Semitism; Holocaust; Jewish Americans.

Homelessness

Significance: "Homelessness" refers to a marginalized condition of detachment from society and to the lack of bonds that connect settled persons to a network of institutions and social orders. Although homelessness knows no racial bounds, those minorities living at or below the poverty level erroneously stand out in the minds of some white Americans as constituting the "homeless problem." Such a view arises from racist stereotypes rather than fact.

By the late 1980's, the homeless population in the United States, according to both governmental and advocacy reports, was estimated to be between 600,000 and 3 million. Included among these casualties were men, women, and children of all racial and ethnic backgrounds; urban and rural workers; displaced and deinstitutionalized persons; alcoholics, drug addicts, AIDS victims, and the mentally ill; physically abused mothers and their babies; sexually abused teenagers and preadolescents; neglected elderly people; and migrants, refugees, and veterans.

Like other social problems, the problem of homelessness has historically revolved around the way in which specific societal groups and class interests have defined the social issue in the first place. Generally, public policies in the United States regarding homelessness, the homeless, and the shortage of low-income or subsidized housing in America are influenced by and inseparable from local and national politics. Moreover, economic crises and considerations, grounded in the ideological perspectives of laissez-faire, free-market capitalism and liberal social reformism, are also at work. At the same time, while most people do not blame individual homeless people per se for their predicament, they still support a public policy ideology that essentially does nothing to alter the victimizing conditions of homelessness.

In part, this has to do with a legacy of viewing homeless people primarily as middle-aged men and elderly eccentric "shopping-bag ladies" rather than primarily as children, mothers, and families. When most people think about the homeless, rarely do images come to mind of teenage runaways, lacking marketable skills and financial resources, selling their bodies to the highest urban bidders. Typically, people do not think about homeless children, most of them abused or neglected, sleeping in abandoned buildings without heat, electricity, and running water. Most people do not think about homeless mothers who believe that it is better to exchange sexual services for shelter than to avail themselves of shelter opportunities that may entail the risk of losing their children to foster care or an adoption agency.

As a group of people, today's homeless may be thought of as a new subclass of people at the bottom of the U.S. stratification system. Although they are most obvious in urban areas, camping near downtown shelters or requesting aid at freeway offramps, there is also a less obvious group, the hidden homeless.

Far away from the more conspicuous sights of the urban homeless, on the rural roads of the corporate agrieconomy of the United States, thousands are doing their best to stay out of the way of local citizens and police, who may arrest and charge them for criminal trespassing, squatting, panhandling, or littering. In more than a few cases, these homeless persons have been arrested for merely trying to feed themselves. In the sparsely populated regions of the Midwest and the South, bankrupted and marginal farmers have been forced off their land, joining the ranks of other migrant workers in search of unskilled work. Crisscrossing the country, these members of a new migrant class, with and without their families, spend varying periods of time traveling the state highways and byways. If they are fortunate, they sleep in cars and trucks; if they are not, they sleep at rest stops, all-night truck stops, in plowed fields, or on the side of the road.

In many more communities, including medium-sized cities as well as urbanized metropolitan areas, a sizable majority of the homeless population remain, if not hidden, at least relatively invisible. That is to say, most of the urban homeless populations are warehoused out of sight in abandoned armories, terminals, or motels. In part, this situation is a result of governmental assistance and programs; it is also a result, in part, of the private efforts of concerned citizens and groups, especially of church-related assistance.

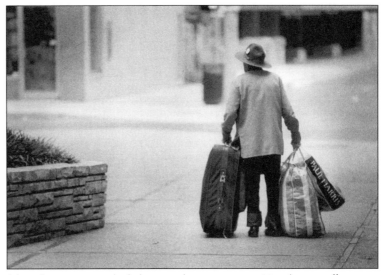

A homeless man carries his belongings down a city street. Homelessness affects men, women, and children of all races and ethnicities.

Programs and Policies

Temporary or emergency assistance is available through bureaucracies that operate at all levels of government. At the same time, public and private armories and shelters—some for whole families, some for couples only, some for single women, and some for battered women and their infants—protect these homeless groups from physical elements, at least during the night. There are also various secular and religious efforts to provide the homeless, hungry, and the nearly destitute with day shelters, soup kitchens, clothes closets, and food pantries. A few notable private nonprofit secular programs out of literally hundreds of programs nationwide are the Atlanta Day Shelter for Women, the Birmingham Partnership Assistance to the Homeless, and Cincinnati's Alcoholic Drop Inn Center Shelter-house.

Without this array of programs to regulate the behavior of the new poor and homeless, these members of society would quickly become a threatening element that would call into question established political and economic arrangements. The sheer numbers of tens of thousands of homeless people roaming the urban streets in search of food and shelter would contribute to the widespread victimization of both the homeless and oth-

ers. In turn, this would contribute to the further deterioration of the urban United States and to growing social disorder.

Despite these programs and other services, such as city policies that require the police to pick up homeless individuals and drive them to one of the nearby community shelters on cold nights when the temperatures drop below zero, hundreds of Americans still freeze to death every winter. As for the homeless of communities that do not or cannot provide forms of social welfare, most do not quickly perish. Even in the most caring and compassionate urban communities, where people do not necessarily look away as they step over or around homeless persons, after a while even those unfortunate souls who can be found sleeping in doorways, in metal trash receptacles, and in homemade cardboard shelters become invisible.

When one examines the significant increase in homelessness from some 10,000 to more than 1 million—within the context of an expanding base of poor persons in the United States—one finds that more and more people not only slipped down the socioeconomic ladder but also became part of a permanent group of have-nots. These people, many of whom had become members of the new homeless groups consisting of women and children, could therefore be regarded as marginal victims of a changing global political economy that has reduced the size of the unskilled and semiskilled industrial workforce in North America. These fundamental changes in the domestic economy must be reflected in the development of social housing for the nonaffluent. Until the United States adopts a public policy grounded in both a commitment to social and economic justice and a recognition of the need for the development of an alternative approach to homelessness and inexpensive housing, the delivery of adequate and permanent housing for all persons living in the United States will remain a utopian dream of the thousands of homeless advocates and volunteers found nationwide.   *Gregg Barak*

Core Resources
Gregg Barak's *Gimme Shelter: A Social History of Homelessness in Contemporary America* (New York: Praeger, 1991) explains not only the root causes of homelessness but also why it is not going to "go away" unless a radically different social policy is introduced. Stephanie Golden's *The Women Outside: Meanings and Myths of Homelessness* (Berkeley: University of California Press, 1992) tells the story of homeless women throughout history. Valerie Polakow's *Lives on the Edge: Single Mothers and Their Children in the Other America* (Chicago: University of Chicago Press, 1993) locates crises in U.S. social and domestic policies in the history of American institutions and the history of childhood itself. Peter H. Rossi's *Down and Out in America: The Origins of Homelessness* (Chicago: University of Chicago Press, 1989) explores the incidence of homelessness in relation to such correlates as disabilities, addictions, illnesses, lack of relatives, unemployment rates, and housing costs. David A. Snow and Leon Anderson's *Down on Their Luck: A Study of Homeless Street People* (Berkeley: University of California Press, 1993) provides the best description available of the social order of homeless society and of the varieties of resourcefulness employed by the homeless to cope with their situations.

See also: Poverty and race.

Horton, Willie, incident

Willie Horton, an African American man and convicted rapist and murderer, was the subject of an advertisement produced during the 1988 U.S. presidential election campaign in support of George Bush's bid for the presidency. The advertisement is now widely regarded as a significant example of the "politics of hate" that became prevalent in political campaigning in the late 1980's and 1990's.

The thirty-second ad, which ran for twenty-eight days on cable television, was primarily used to argue that Michael Dukakis, the governor of Massachusetts and Bush's Democratic opponent in the race for president, was soft on crime. It did so by stating that Bush "support[ed] the death penalty for first-degree murder" and that Dukakis not only opposed the death penalty but also

allowed first-degree murderers to have weekend passes from prison. As evidence, the ad showed a police photograph of a glaring Horton and announced that "Horton murdered a boy in a robbery, stabbing him nineteen times." The announcer continued by explaining that "despite the life sentence, Horton received ten weekend passes from prison. Horton fled, kidnapping a young couple, stabbing the man and repeatedly raping his girlfriend." While the announcer spoke, the words "kidnapping," "stabbing," and "raping" flashed on the screen. Over a final photo of Dukakis, the voiceover said, "Weekend prison passes. Dukakis on crime."

The advertisement, although not produced by the Bush campaign for reelection, was made by the National Security Political Action Committee (NSPAC), a political action committee that strongly supported Bush's bid for the presidency. The advertisement was widely criticized in the mass media as racist. According to one media critic, for example, the Horton advertisement was evidence of the use of the black man as a "racialized-sexualized threat to white women and white social order generally" (John Fiske's *Media Matters*, 1994). Although the script of the advertisement never mentioned race, the visual image clearly identified Horton as a menacing black man and implied, to many, that his victims were white. Despite the charges of racism in the media, Bush denied that the advertisement was racist.

Susan Mackey-Kallis

See also: African American stereotypes; Black "brute" and "buck" stereotypes; Politics of hate.

Housing

> **Significance:** The residential conditions and distribution of ethnic and racial minority groups in the United States are consequences of social and economic factors as well as of the characteristics of the localities in which these groups live. Principal processes are immigration, regional migration and distribution, acculturation and social mobility, racism, and discrimination.

African Americans, the largest U.S. ethnic or racial minority, are an overwhelmingly metropolitan-area population. About 90 percent of the African American population resides in urban areas, and two-thirds are central-city residents. In contrast, about three-quarters of the white population is metropolitan, and two-thirds of these are suburban. In part, this reflects the greater degree of home ownership by whites as compared to blacks, a majority of whom rent their homes. Furthermore, twice the proportion of whites compared to blacks live outside metropolitan areas.

The African American population has been predominantly southern; slightly more than half the African American population lives in the South. About one-fifth of American blacks live in the Midwest, slightly fewer in the Northeast, and fewer than 10 percent in the West. Whites, on the other hand, are rather evenly distributed, making up approximately 20 to 30 percent of the residents in each of the four regions. The state with the largest African American population is New York, with more than three million, followed by California, Texas, and Florida.

Hispanics, many of whom are recent immigrants, are concentrated primarily in four states. The border states of California and Texas are home to more than half the nation's Latinos, predominantly Mexican immigrants or people of Mexican ancestry. Florida's Latino population is largely Cuban American. Puerto Ricans make up the majority of Hispanics in New York State, although Spanish-speaking immigrants from other parts of the Caribbean, such as the Dominican Republic, represent a sizable contingent.

More than 90 percent of Hispanics are metropolitan area residents, primarily living in central-city neighborhoods; most rent their residences. The metropolitan area with the greatest Latino population is the Los Angeles-Anaheim-Riverside area of California, which contains one quarter of the U.S. Hispanic population. The majority of Hispanics in the New York metropolitan area are Puerto Rican.

Asian Americans are a diverse minority, consisting of descendants of earlier immigrants (primarily Japanese and Chinese) as well as newcomers from nations which, until recent decades, were not represented among the Asian American population (including Vietnamese, Asian Indians, and Southeast Asians). This minority includes Pacific Islanders (mostly Native Hawaiians) and recent Samoan and Guamanian immigrants. Ninety-four percent of Asian Americans are metropolitan-area residents, with slightly more than half being suburban. Unlike blacks and Hispanics, most are homeowners, and more than half are residents of the western states.

Causes of Residential Segregation
Waves of African American migrants have left the South since the early 1900's. Following World War II, a massive migration of blacks to the industrial centers of the Northeast, Midwest, and West resulted from the industrialization of southern agriculture, which displaced many tenant farmers and sharecroppers. Also, black veterans returning to the United States after World War II, having visited other areas of the country while in the military, were attracted to the job opportunities in northern

factories. Consequently, in several of these cities, the numbers of African Americans doubled between 1950 and 1970.

Many strategies have been employed by whites to discourage darker-skinned newcomers from moving into white residential areas, contributing to the maintenance of residential racial segregation. History records instances of violence and other acts of intimidation in order to discourage perceived intrusions into white neighborhoods. Restrictive covenants added to property deeds have been employed in order to prevent the sale of housing to minorities. In some cohesive communities, researchers have found sales and rentals of residences conducted by means of informal communications in order to avoid the use of public advertising that might result in minority applicants. Slum clearance and public housing construction in the inner city have contributed to a concentration of minority residences. Following World War II, suburbanization, stimulated by the construction of housing developments, federally guaranteed mortgages for veterans, and new highways, contributed to flight from cities by the white middle class, further segregating minorities. Court-mandated school busing and black migration to cities contributed to white flight as well. Banks in many areas adopted the practice of "redlining," which resulted in the denial of mortgage loans to prospective buyers of homes in designated areas, usually racially transitional ones. Though illegal, the practice intensified the black concentration in central city areas.

Although some have suggested that African American preferences are the root cause of residential segregation, survey evidence has repeatedly indicated a preference for racially mixed neighborhoods on the part of blacks. Similar studies among whites indicate increased tolerance by whites of black residents living in their neighborhoods so long as they represent a numerical minority.

Social scientists have offered a variety of perspectives explaining the reasons for the persistence of residential segregation. Some theorists hold that the welfare system dulls incentives for minorities and the poor in general. The supposed predictability in subsistence provided by a monthly welfare check results in laziness and a lessened ambition to improve one's lot in life. Life becomes stagnant, as do the segregated neighborhoods in which these people reside.

The "culture of poverty" view, exemplified by the writings of anthropologist Oscar Lewis, holds that poverty conditions result in a general perspective that includes psychological depression and a view of life devoid of any hope of ever extricating oneself from one's predicament. A fatalism and the feeling that any efforts to improve one's life are doomed to failure result in a cycle of poverty that continues from generation to generation.

The institutional racism perspective attributes segregation to factors inherent in the institutions serving the poor in the inner city. Deteriorating, aging schools with inexperienced teachers lacking insight into ghetto life, a political institution concerned with servicing other populations in the society that are more likely to vote, an urban economy that no longer provides a living wage as low-paying service employment has replaced manufacturing jobs, and increasing unemployment as jobs migrate to the suburbs have left the black population behind as society has changed.

Sociologist William Julius Wilson holds the view that the upward social mobility experienced by middle-class blacks as a consequence of the civil rights revolution resulted in community leaders moving out of ghetto neighborhoods. This development, coupled with changes in the economy that reduced employment opportunities in the central cities, leaves the poor who have not benefited from civil rights advances behind in increasingly deteriorating areas abandoned by many community businesses. The result is a racially homogeneous neighborhood characterized by crime, drug use, illegitimate births, and other conditions characteristic of the underclass syndrome.

Patterns of Residential Segregation
The ethnic segregation experienced by the "new" European immigrants of the late nineteenth and early twentieth centuries was a transient phenomenon. Financial limitations and the psychological comfort of familiar cultural surroundings resulted in formation of an ethnic ghetto in the central city. With cultural assimilation attained through education and upward social mobility, later generations attained "respectable" middle-class occupations.

Research by Nancy Denton and Douglas Massey on contemporary ethnic and racial minorities indicates that this scenario is not occurring for all groups. Unlike advances made by African Americans in education and the workplace, residential segregation appears to be a relatively permanent condition of life for a large majority of blacks. This is true across social class lines. Tract data from U.S. censuses are used in calculating an index of dissimilarity, a statistical indicator of the proportion of the minority population that would have to move its census tract residence in order for proportional residential "evenness" or integration to occur. The researchers used data from sixty metropolitan areas that contained the largest populations of blacks, Hispanics, and Asians.

Denton and Massey's findings indicated that for the twenty metropolitan areas containing the largest black populations, residential segregation from whites was high regardless of black social class. Social class was measured using income, education, and occupational

status, each of which was examined independently. Segregation indexes declined for blacks of higher social class but remained high. Cleveland, Detroit, and Chicago exhibited the highest degree of black/white residential segregation, Washington, D.C., and San Francisco the lowest. The authors pointed out that unlike earlier European immigrants who lived in relatively heterogeneous neighborhoods, an overwhelming majority of blacks live in racially homogeneous neighborhoods. This segregation is relatively impervious to advances in social mobility and is not transitory. Federal efforts such as the Fair Housing Act of 1968, an outgrowth of the urban disorders of the 1960's, have had little impact on this phenomenon.

Significantly smaller proportions of blacks than Hispanics and Asians live in suburbs. Data indicate that suburban blacks receive somewhat higher incomes than those residing in the inner city. The degree of residential racial segregation experienced by African Americans across class lines indicates that a high proportion of the black middle class in the suburbs lives under segregated conditions, as do their urban counterparts.

For Hispanics, in contrast to blacks, the index of dissimilarity is moderate, even for those in the lowest categories of social class. For U.S.-born Hispanics, descendants of immigrants (for research purposes, Puerto Ricans are treated as immigrants, although they are U.S. citizens), the segregation index declines with upward social mobility. For Latinos, in fact, increased education results in sharp declines in segregation, indicating a general acceptance by non-Hispanic whites of middle-class Latinos as neighbors. This decline is particularly true in Miami, where the Latino population is predominantly Cuban American and white, and in Los Angeles, where the great majority of Latinos are of Mexican ancestry. This is less the case in New York City and Newark, New Jersey, where the majority of Hispanics are of Puerto Rican descent. This Hispanic population is more segregated from whites than from blacks. Puerto Ricans are the only one of the three Hispanic populations with significant African ancestry; this may indicate that they are experiencing color prejudice, consistent with the findings for African Americans.

Federal housing studies of the residential accommodations of blacks and Latinos produce findings consistent with those groups' lower socioeconomic status. In contrast with medians for the total U.S. population, these minorities inhabit smaller living quarters, share fewer square feet per person, are less likely to have air conditioning, live in homes that are more likely to be older, and live in areas with streets or roads that are more likely to be in need of repair. Respondents from both minorities rate their neighborhoods lower as environments in which to live.

Asian Americans (including Pacific Islanders), although racially distinct from whites, experience reduced segregation with attainment of higher class status. Middle-class Asian Americans are undergoing a minority immigration experience not unlike that of the European immigrants who arrived near the beginning of the twentieth century, although they do not seem to be forming ethnic enclaves to the same extent as the European immigrants did. Most live in ethnically heterogeneous neighborhoods. In general, the dominant white population does not appear to object to sharing communities with upwardly mobile Asian Americans.

Consequences of Residential Segregation
In addition to exacerbating such urban ghetto problems as poor schools, crime, and illegal drug use, residential segregation serves to limit communication between groups and, thus, precludes cooperation between populations in solving common problems. Separation promotes distrust, feelings of hostility, and occasionally open conflict. African Americans are segregated not only from whites but also from Asian Americans and from most Hispanic Americans. For African Americans, attainment of higher education and other criteria of middle-class status do not readily translate into either acceptance as neighbors by the dominant whites or attendance at newly built, quality suburban schools by their children. Furthermore, homogeneous black neighborhoods are often perceived by political and economic powers as areas that can be sacrificed when new roads are to be built or when undesirable municipal facilities are to be erected. In addition, the ability of relatively few blacks to attain the American Dream divides the dominant whites from the largest U.S. racial or ethnic minority and breeds continual intergroup tensions.

American Indian Population
American Indians, or Native Americans, are included in a category with Eskimos and Aleuts by the U.S. Census Bureau, the two latter populations representing less than 5 percent of the total category. A little more than one third of American Indians live on reservations; however, there is substantial movement by Indians to and from reservations. Native Americans do not make up a sufficiently large population to establish enclaves equivalent to the ethnic communities of other minorities, so most urban Indians reside in heterogeneous working-class neighborhoods. Movement to the city is ordinarily for economic reasons. Returning to the reservation is often caused by loss of employment or to secure free health care from the Bureau of Indian Affairs' Indian Health Service. Poverty among Indians is two times the rate among the general population, and unemployment on some reservations may be as high as 80 percent. For many, reservation life involves overcrowded conditions, substandard housing, and lack of adequate sanitation. Government housing and mortgage programs administered by some of the individual tribes have made it easier for new home building and home improvements, and income from gaming (gambling) has promised to do more, but many Native Americans are simply too poor to consider new housing, even with the help of these agencies.

Edward V. Mednick

Core Resources
Information on housing and segregation can be found in Nancy Denton and Douglas Massey's "Residential Segregation of Blacks, Hispanics, and Asians by Socioeconomic Status and Generation" (*Social Science Quarterly* 69, 1988) and their *American Apartheid* (Cambridge, Mass.: Harvard University Press, 1993); "Stereotypes and Segregation: Neighborhoods in the Detroit Area" (*American Journal of Sociology* 100, no. 3, 1994), by Reynolds Farley et al., and William Julius Wilson's *The Truly Disadvantaged: The Inner City, the Underclass, and Public Policy* (Chicago: University of Chicago Press, 1987).

See also: Apartheid; Assimilation: cultural and structural; Banking practices; Culture of poverty; Ethnic enclaves; Fair Housing Act; Hypersegregation; Melting pot theory; Minority and majority groups; Poverty and race; Redlining; Restrictive or racial covenants; Segregation: de facto and de jure; White flight.

Human Rights Act

> **Significance:** Canada's Human Rights Act prohibits discrimination based on race, national or ethnic origin, color, religion, age, sex, marital status, or conviction for an offense for which a pardon has been granted.

Canada's Bill C-25, the Human Rights Act—first read in the House of Commons November 29, 1976, and first read in the Senate June 6, 1977—received the Royal Assent July 14, 1977, and was proclaimed to be in force August 10, 1977. The act was revised and expanded in 1985 to provide for those with physical disabilities and to clarify issues involving sexual harassment, the elderly, and women on maternity leave.

Provisions of the Act
The Canadian Human Rights Act extends the laws that proscribe discrimination and that protect the privacy of individuals. The law is premised on the notion that every

person should have an opportunity equal to that of other persons to make for himself or herself the life that he or she is able and wishes to have, consistent with his or her duties and obligations as a member of society, without being hindered in or prevented from doing so by discriminatory practices based on race, national or ethnic origin, color, religion, age, sex, marital status, or conviction for an offense for which a pardon has been granted. The privacy of individuals, and their right of access to records containing personal information concerning them for any purpose, including the purpose of ensuring accuracy and completeness, should be protected to the greatest extent consistent with the public interest.

Part 1 of the Canadian Human Rights Act defines discrimination as the denial of goods, services, facilities, or accommodations customarily available to the general public. In employment, it is discriminatory to refuse to employ, to refuse to continue to employ, or to differentiate adversely in the course of employment. Part 1, Section 11, requires that equal wages be paid to men and women for equal work value, based on skill, effort, and responsibility.

Part 2 of the act created the Canadian Human Rights Commission to administer the Canadian Human Rights Act and to ensure that the principles of equal opportunity and nondiscrimination are followed within the areas of federal jurisdiction. This commission is composed of two full-time and six part-time commissioners. The commission is authorized to investigate complaints of discrimination in employment and in the provision of services, and complaints alleging inequities in pay between men and women based on equal work. The commission monitors annual reports filed by federally regulated employers under the Employment Equity Act, and programs, policies, and legislation affecting women, aboriginal peoples, visible minorities, and persons with disabilities, to ensure that their human rights are protected. It also develops and conducts information programs to promote public understanding of the Canadian Human Rights Act and the commission's activities.

Part 3 of the Canadian Human Rights Act explains the procedures to be used when a complaint is filed with the Canadian Human Rights Commission. Upon receipt of a complaint, the commission first determines whether or not its agency is the correct one to handle the complaint. The complaint is either accepted for investigation by the commission or sent to another federal agency for appropriate action. If the commission accepts the complaint for investigation, every effort is made to reach an early settlement between the two parties. If the complaint cannot be settled, the commission prepares an investigative report requesting the appointment of a conciliator to arbitrate the dispute.

If conciliation cannot be reached, the case is returned to the commission for a decision either to dismiss the case or to refer it to a human rights tribunal. A tribunal hearing results in a written decision, binding on all parties. Tribunal decisions may be appealed to a review tribunal or to the federal courts. In some discrimination cases, Canada's Supreme Court makes the final decision. Remedies for complainants include reinstatement and/or compensation for lost wages, letters of apology, or the issuance of antiharassment policy by an employer. The Canadian Human Rights Act provides for fines of up to fifty thousand dollars for threatening, intimidating, or discriminating against an individual who has filed a complaint, or for hampering the investigation process.

Administrative Structure
The act authorized the Canadian Human Rights Commission to create an administrative structure to administer the Human Rights Act. By 1994, the Canadian Human Rights Commission had delegated to the Office of the Secretary General of the Human Rights Commission the authority to oversee staff at headquarters and regional offices that investigate discrimination complaints throughout the country, except those dealing with employment and pay equity.

The secretary general's office provides support to the Canadian Human Rights Commission and its seven specialized branch agencies: the Legal Services Branch, which represents the commission before tribunals, review tribunals, and the courts; the Anti-Discrimination Programs Branch, which handles all complaints filed with the commission, except employment and pay equity complaints; the Employment and Pay Equity Branch, which advises the Human Rights Commission on employment and pay equity matters, offers educational programs to employers and community groups, and investigates and conciliates equal pay complaints; the Policy and Planning Branch, which monitors and researches domestic and international human rights issues of interest to the commission; the Communications Branch, which explains the role and activities of the commission, discourages discriminatory practices, and fosters public understanding of the act; the Corporate Services Branch, which provides headquarters and regional operations with support services; and the Personnel Services Branch, which provides headquarters and regional operations with support services in pay, benefits, staffing, resource planning, and health and safety.

Complaints and Recommendations
Between 1985 and 1994, the Canadian Human Rights Commission received 464,535 inquiries. Actual complaints filed between 1991 and 1994 totaled 4,852, including all referrals to alternate redress. For the years 1991 to 1994, based on the number of discrimination

complaints filed, the types of complaints were ranked in the following order: disability, sex, national or ethnic origin, race or color, family or marital status, age, religion, and discrimination after being pardoned. In the same years, the ranking order of methods of disposition of complaints was dismissal, settlement approved by all parties and the commission, sent to conciliation, no further proceedings, and early resolution.

The 1995 Canadian Human Rights Commission's annual report recommended the following changes: that amendments to the Canadian Human Rights Act be adopted to prohibit discrimination based on sexual orientation, to protect the human rights of Canada's aboriginal population, and to allow anyone present in Canada, not just those lawfully present, the right to file a discrimination complaint; that the commission report directly to Parliament instead of the Department of Justice and the Treasury Board; that a permanent appeals tribunal be established to replace the existing system of ad hoc tribunals and review tribunals; that a mandatory retirement age be considered a discriminatory action; and that employers under federal jurisdiction be required to take the initiative in eliminating sex-based inequities from their compensation systems. These recommendations would enable the Canadian Human Rights Act to provide the same protection against discrimination currently institutionalized in the Canadian Charter of Rights and Freedoms, international practice, and provincial legislation.

William A. Paquette

Core Resources

Acts of the Parliament of Canada, vol. 2 (Ottawa: Queen's Printer, 1976-1977) contains the original text of the act of 1977. The Canadian Human Rights Commission's *Annual Report, 1994* (Ottawa: Minister of Supply and Service Canada, 1995) provides a detailed self-examination of Canada's record on human rights. *House of Commons Debates, Official Report*, vol. 3 (Ottawa: Queen's Printer, 1976-1977) records the parliamentary debates on the act. *Revised Statutes of Canada, 1985*, vol. 5 (Ottawa: Queen's Printer, 1985) includes the complete and revised act.

See also: Charter of Rights and Freedoms; Immigration law: Canada; Multiculturalism in Canada; Official Languages Act; Visible minority allophones in Canada.

Hymietown statement

In January of 1984, the Reverend Jesse Jackson labeled Jews as "Hymies" and referred to New York City as "Hymietown." These comments were made in the pres-

In January, 1984, Jesse Jackson created a stir by referring to New York as "Hymietown."

ence of black journalists following Jackson's presidential election campaign. One of the journalists, Milton Coleman, relayed Jackson's comments to his associates at *The Washington Post*. The remarks were printed weeks later, buried deep within a broader article discussing Jackson's attitudes on foreign policy, particularly Israeli-Palestinian conflict in the Middle East. Initially, neither the article nor Jackson's slurs garnered much attention. However, on February 18 of that year, *The Washington Post* ran an editorial denouncing Jackson's comments, thus triggering national media attention.

Jackson first denied making the remarks and claimed that Jews were conspiring to defeat his campaign. He later acknowledged making the comments and apologized, asking a group of national Jewish leaders for forgiveness in a Manchester, New Hampshire, synagogue shortly before the state's election primary. Jackson then publicly questioned whether this isolated incident should dismantle the progress made between American Jews and blacks. He argued that the remarks did not reflect his basic attitudes toward Jews or Israel, and continued to invite Jews to join his Rainbow Coalition, an organization comprising oppressed groups.

Scott A. Melzer

See also: Crown Heights conflicts; Jewish-African American relations; Rainbow Coalition.

Hypersegregation

The term "hypersegregation" refers to the excessive physical and social separation of a class, ethnic, or racial group by forcing the group, usually through institutional arrangements, to reside in a limited area or neighborhood with low-quality educational facilities and few economic opportunities.

According to sociologists Norman A. Anderson and Cheryl Armstead, many minority group members, especially African Americans and Latinos who live in large metropolitan areas in the United States, experience hypersegregation. This phenomenon creates a state of extreme isolation from resources that allow people to improve their social and economic well-being. The isolation also dimishes people's ability to obtain adequate health care and thus negatively affects their health.

Hypersegregation is the result of a number of factors, one of the most prominent being pervasive housing discrimination against low-income minority group members. Noted sociologist William J. Wilson has shown that low-income nonwhites are more likely to live in impoverished residential areas than are low-income white Americans.

Gwenelle S. O'Neal

See also: Discrimination: racial and ethnic; Health care and racial/ethnic relations; Housing; Poverty and race; Segregation; Self-segregation.

Hypodescent

The rule of hypodescent is a social mechanism that determines racial group membership of the offspring of interracial unions between European Americans and Americans of color. It defines this membership based exclusively on the background of color (including Native American, Asian American, Pacific Islander American, Latino American, and African American).

The dominant European Americans began enforcing rules of hypodescent beginning in the late 1600's in order to draw social distinctions between themselves and the subordinate groups of color. The rule of hypodescent has historically been such an accepted part of the American fabric, however, that its oppressive origins have often been obscured. The rule was implemented primarily in the area of interracial sexual relations, and more specifically, interracial marriages, in order to preserve white racial "purity." However, it has also helped maintain white racial privilege by supporting other legal and informal barriers to racial equality in most aspects of social life. These barriers have existed in public facilities and various areas of the public sphere (political, economic, educational), as well as the private sphere (residential, associational, interpersonal). At the turn of the twentieth century, these restrictions reached extreme proportions with the institutionalization of Jim Crow segregation.

The rule of hypodescent has been applied in differing degrees to the first-generation offspring of European Americans and Americans of color. In regard to later generations of individuals whose lineage has included a background of color along with European ancestry, however, the rule has been more flexible. These individuals have not invariably been designated exclusively, or even partially, as members of that group of color if the background is less than one-fourth of their lineage. Furthermore, self-identification with that background has been more a matter of choice.

This flexibility has not been extended to individuals of African American and European American descent. The first-generation offspring of interracial relationships between African Americans and European Americans, as well as later generations of individuals whose lineage has included African American and European American ancestry, have experienced the most restrictive rule of hypodescent: the one-drop rule. This mechanism designates as black everyone with any amount of African American ancestry ("one drop of blood"). It precludes any notion of choice in self-identification and ensures that all future offspring with African American ancestry are socially designated as black. Furthermore, the one-drop rule is unique to the United States and is specifically applied to Americans of African descent. It emerged in the late seventeenth and early eighteenth centuries as a means of increasing the number of slaves. The one-drop rule also exempted white landowners (particularly slaveholders) from the legal obligation of passing on inheritance and other benefits of paternity to their multiracial offspring.

American attitudes toward the offspring of unions between African Americans and other groups of color (for example, Native Americans) have varied. More often than not, these individuals have been subject to the one-drop rule. Greater ambivalence has been displayed toward offspring whose ancestry has combined other backgrounds of color (for example, Mexican American/Asian American or Native American/Mexican American), partly because these other groups of color occupy a more ambiguous position in the racial hierarchy than that of African Americans. Also, membership in these groups—except perhaps in the case of Native Americans—has been less clearly defined in U.S. law. Consequently, the racial subordination of Americans of color by European Americans, while similarly oppressive, has not been exactly the same. This makes it more difficult to assess intergroup relations among groups of color in terms of the rule of hypodescent.

In the 1960's and 1970's, the United States generally repudiated notions of racial "purity" that had supported the ideology of white supremacy. Many European Americans, nevertheless, continued to maintain notions of white racial exclusivity and privilege originating in the rule of hypodescent. Alternately, the rule of hypodescent paradoxically has had some unintended consequences. Its purpose was to draw boundaries solidifying subordinated racial identity and excluding Americans of color from having contact with European Americans as equals. However, it has also legitimated and forged group identity, which in turn has formed the basis for mass mobilization and collective action among groups of color in the struggle against racial inequality. These dynamics have thus helped reinforce, even if unintentionally, the notion that European Americans (and whiteness) and Americans of color are categories of experience that are mutually exclusive, if not hierarchical, and that have an objective and independent existence of their own.   *G. Reginald Daniel*

See also: African American-American Indian relations; Biracialism; Euro-American; Genetic basis for race; Interracial and interethnic marriage; Multiracial identity; Multiracial movement; One-drop rule; Options for ethnic identity; People of color; Race as a concept; White "race."

Hypogamy

The marriage of a woman to a man in a lower social stratum is designated "hypogamy." In an article entitled "Intermarriage and the Social Structure" (*Psychiatry*, 1941), sociologist Robert Merton described interracial marriage involving a black husband and a white wife as—given the racial hierarchy in the United States—hypogamous. Because marriages typically consist of persons within a given group (endogamy), marriage outside a given group (exogamy) calls for theoretical explanation. Hypogamy also contradicts the traditional cross-cultural patterns of homogamy (marriage consisting of persons who share similarities) and its frequent alternative, hypergamy (marriage of women upward). Anthropologists argue that hypergamy is a cultural universal because men have been the breadwinners, and women tend to seek as much prestige and financial support for themselves and their children as possible. Occupation is the route to upward mobility for men. Hypergamy, in a sexist society that deters women from entering many occupations, is one avenue to higher status.

Merton says that hypogamy occurs because white women of lower economic background trade their higher racial rank for the relatively elevated economic station of a (racially) lower-ranked African American male. Research has shown, however, that many biracial couples manifest educational and economic homogamy and marry for the same reasons that endogamous couples do.   *Gil Richard Musolf*

See also: Interracial and interethnic marriage; Marital assimilation; Miscegenation laws.

"I Have a Dream" speech

Significance: The Reverend Dr. Martin Luther King, Jr.'s "I Have a Dream" speech called for a color-blind society, identifying a new American Dream for race relations.

The spring and summer of 1963 proved to be one of the most important times of the Civil Rights movement. On June 12, NAACP leader Medgar Evers was assassinated; white supremacist Byron de la Beckwith would not be found guilty of his murder for nearly thirty years. In April, 1963, protest against discrimination in the downtown department stores of Birmingham, Alabama, culminated in protests on April 4. King's arrest during these demonstrations and the media coverage of police violence against the demonstrators catapulted both the movement and King, the leader of the Southern Christian Leadership Conference (SCLC), into the national spotlight to an even greater degree than before. The boycotts and mass marches eventually provided sufficient pressure that white leaders promised to desegregate the stores' facilities, hire African Americans to work in the stores, and establish a biracial committee for ongoing talks concerning racial problems.

These gains were achieved at a price, however: King was jailed briefly; police brutality occurred against protesters; and arrested protesters filled Birmingham's jails. Nevertheless, the filled jails negatively affected the capacity of police to arrest and hold demonstrators, which was exactly what King and other civil rights leaders had hoped; news coverage of police brutality outraged many citizens; and, while jailed, King wrote his "Letter from Birmingham Jail," a document that delineated the need for and goals of the direct action campaigns of the Civil Rights movement. The acclaim that met this document foreshadowed the reaction to his speech at the March on Washington two months later.

March on Washington

The purpose of the March on Washington (sometimes called the Poor People's March) was not merely to make an emotional plea on behalf of African Americans; its primary purpose was to expose the American public to the economic basis of racial inequality. Thus, the focus of the march was the need to increase jobs and economic opportunities for African Americans, in order for them to realize racial equality. These especially were the goals of the leaders of the March on Washington, A. Philip Randolph, labor leader and organizer of the Brotherhood of Sleeping Car Porters, and civil rights activist Bayard Rustin, one of the earliest planners of the event. In fact, the full title of the event was "The March on Washington for Jobs and Freedom." The march, therefore, had a set of important goals: more jobs, a higher minimum wage, support for President John F. Kennedy's antidiscrimination legislation, and arousing the conscience of the United States to the plight of African Americans. King's speech was especially important on this last point, for the "I Have a Dream" section of the speech was an eloquent plea for a society based on racial harmony. Nevertheless, while King's speech is best remembered for his vision of racial equality, its true import lies in the fact that the renown accorded the speech helped advance the multifaceted goals of the march, thus helping to pave the way for the Civil Rights Act of 1964.

King's Vision

The passage in which King reiterates "I have a dream" should be understood in the overall context of the talk. Although King started by reading from his prepared text, he disregarded this text about halfway through the speech and incorporated a theme he had used in some previous speeches: "I have a dream." This theme introduced into the speech two of the main tenets of the SCLC: interracial cooperation and social equality. King's eloquent vision of a future without racial divisions captured the emotions of many viewers and, later, readers of the speech. In fact, the emotional power of that section of King's remarks sometimes blurs the memory of other, equally important aspects of his speech.

King's speech has become widely known as a masterpiece of rhetoric and argumentation. One rhetorical device that King used to great effect is repetition. The most obvious example is the repetition of the phrase "I have a dream" to detail different aspects of King's vision of racial harmony, but there are other, equally important examples. In the opening section of the speech, King reiterated the phrase "one hundred years later" to emphasize that one hundred years after the Emancipation Proclamation (issued in 1863), African Americans still had not achieved equality. Immediately after the "I have a dream" section, King repeated the phrase that it is "with this faith" in his dream that he and other people could hope to transform American society. These examples demonstrate King's consciousness of the use of rhetoric to produce emotional impact.

Perhaps one of the most important rhetorical strategies of King's speech is his reference to the principles voiced by the Founding Fathers in his appeal for racial equality. This strategy was especially important in light of the fact that the government (including the Federal Bureau of Investigation and the Justice Department) was concerned that the Civil Rights movement might discredit the United States abroad. Hence, it was perceptive

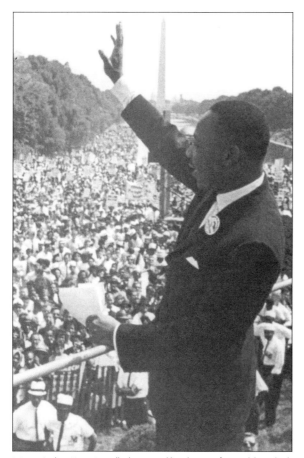

Martin Luther King, Jr., tells the crowd his dream of a world in which a person's race will not matter during the 1963 March on Washington.

of King to imply in the speech that he was not undermining the United States but asking the country to do justice to the principles that were asserted to be the bedrock of the U.S. political and societal character. King stated, for example, that his dream was "deeply rooted in the American dream," and that he dreamed of a day when Americans "will be able to sing with new meaning 'My country 'tis of thee, sweet land of liberty, of thee I sing.' " King then immediately used the words of that song to delineate the different areas of the country where he hoped the United States would soon "let freedom ring" for all its citizens. He referred to the Declaration of Independence and the Constitution as being a "promissory note" to all citizens, which those at the march now were claiming as their inheritance. The speech gained power from King's stressing that he was asking the United States to live up to its principles and thus to fulfill the greatness of its pronounced creed.

King's speech became not only one of the most publicized events of the Civil Rights movement but also one of the most highly regarded speeches in U.S. history. Although much of the acclaim rests on the emotionally powerful "I have a dream" section of the speech, the entire speech is a masterpiece of rhetoric and argument. One of the most essential aspects of the speech was at the end, when King stated that on the day "when we let freedom ring" the United States will only be speeding up the day—not arriving at it—when "all of God's children, black men and white men, Jews and Gentiles, Protestants and Catholics, will be able to join hands and sing in the words of the old Negro spiritual, 'Free at last! Free at last! Thank God Almighty, we are free at last!' " This stands as the lingering, haunting challenge of Martin Luther King's speech at the March on Washington. *Jane Davis*

Core Resources
James Baldwin's "The Dangerous Road Before Martin Luther King," in *The Price of the Ticket* (New York: St. Martin's Press, 1985) offers a detailed consideration of the difficulties facing King. David J. Garrow's *Bearing the Cross: Martin Luther King, Jr., and the Southern Christian Leadership Conference* (New York: Vintage Books, 1986) examines the strategies of civil rights protests and conflicts between various civil rights groups. Penelope McPhee and Flip Schulke's *King Remembered* (New York: Pocket Books, 1986) ia s concise introductory biography of King that focuses on his philosophy as a leader of a nonviolent movement.

See also: Civil Rights Act of 1960; Civil Rights Act of 1964; Civil Rights movement; King, Martin Luther, Jr., assaination; Little Rock school desegregation; Montgomery bus boycott; Southern Christian Leadership Conference; Watts riot.

Identification assimilation

"Identification assimilation" is the fourth of sociologist Milton Gordon's seven stages of assimilation of minority groups into a host society. At this stage, members of a minority group, usually newly arrived immigrants, develop a sense of peoplehood based exclusively on the host society, acquiring the memories, sentiments, and attitudes of people of the core culture. Assimilation of immigrants into American society provides a good example. Although racial, ethnic, and religious identity may or may not change, assimilating groups, when they reach this stage, identify themselves exclusively with the members of the host society.

The speed and number of generations required for identification assimilation vary among different racial and ethnic groups, depending upon their socioeconomic status, rate of interracial marriage with mainstream Americans, and degree of prejudice and discrimination against them. First-generation immigrants, usually foreign-born, have difficulties achieving this stage because of cultural differences, lack of integration with mainstream Americans at the primary level of socialization, and prejudice and discrimination. Most of the European Americans, descendants of immigrants between the post-colonial period and the early 1900's, have achieved identification assimilation regardless of their ethnic background. However, numerous barriers—economic, cultural, and racial, among others—have prevented some members of other racial and ethnic groups, such as African, Asian, Hispanic, and Native Americans, from achieving the same degree of identification assimilation as European Americans.

Hisako Matsuo

See also: Anglo-conformity; Assimilation: cultural and structural; Assimilation theories; Attitude-receptional assimilation; Behavior-receptional assimilation; Civic-assimilation; Marital assimilation; Structural assimilation.

Ideological racism

Ideological racism is a system of beliefs in or assertions of the genetic and/or cultural inferiority of dominated racial groups. Incorporated into eugenics theories, into social scientist Daniel Patrick Moynihan's notion of "cultural deficiency" in *The Negro Family: The Case for National Action* (1965), into appeals to the Bible by some Christian fundamentalists, and into racist stereotypes held by Americans in general, ideological racism sustains white Americans' certainty that their advantages and unequal share of resources have been achieved meritoriously, thereby legitimizing both their privileges and the depri-

vations suffered by minorities. Ideological racism functions to blame the victims for their misery and to shunt attention away from the social circumstances of both the well-off and the impoverished that reproduce their respective superior and inferior social statuses. For example, Moynihan's report counseled "benign neglect" rather than governmental action to assist African Americans. Europeans conceptualized race as an ideology to justify colonization. They conquered, enslaved, and committed genocide remorselessly, believing non-Europeans were inferiors or members of subhuman species. Almost all scientists today discredit ideological racism and affirm the equal humanity of all racial and ethnic groups.

Gil Richard Musolf

See also: Meritocracy myth; Moynihan Report; Racism as an ideology; Xenophobia, nativism, and eugenics.

Illegal aliens

The U.S. Immigration and Naturalization Service defines an alien as "any person not a citizen of the United States." An alien entering the United States or residing in the country in violation of immigration law is, therefore, typically referred to as an "illegal alien."

Aliens residing in the United States occupy a unique place in the U.S. legal system. Aliens living in the country legally enjoy most of the rights guaranteed to "the people" by the Constitution, with the most notable exception being the right to vote. Unlike citizens, however, aliens can be deported for violations of the law (deportation can be appealed to the Board of Immigration in the Department of Justice or to the courts).

Considerable debate has centered on issues such as the costs versus the benefits of the illegal alien population to American society and what the rights of illegal aliens should be. Conflicting statistics have been presented regarding whether illegal aliens are a drain on federal, state, and local governments because they use public services (such as health services) or whether the fact that many of them actually pay income taxes offsets Ssuch expenses. There are restrictions on the benefits that illegal aliens can receive from the government. Legal aliens are eligible for such things as food stamps and unemployment compensation; illegal aliens are not. The courts have held, however, that illegal aliens cannot be denied primary education and health care because of their status.

A 1982 Supreme Court case, *Plyler v. Doe*, established that states cannot refuse to finance the education of illegal alien children or exclude them from public schools. The Court used the equal protection clause of the Fourteenth Amendment to support its decision. In

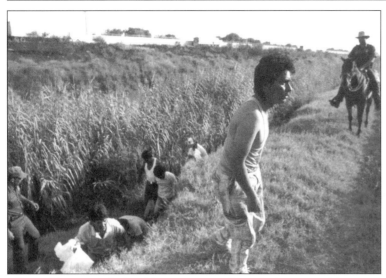

Officers of the U.S. Border Patrol discover a group of men who have entered the country illegally near Brownsville, Texas. In many border states, the provision of health care and education to illegal aliens and their children is the subject of intense debate.

that reside within a society and those peoples who immigrate to these societies voluntarily from other nations. Resident minority groups are often "marginalized," living on the fringe of society, often in poverty, lacking education, occupational skills, political power, or the means to integrate into the mainstream. These marginalized groups, like the immigrants, are frequently composed of ethnic and racial minorities.

However, compared with marginalized groups, immigrants have numerous advantages and often become successful, productive members of a society. One of the primary advantages is that immigrants *choose* to move to a new country and are therefore motivated to succeed. Another advantage is that they often have the resources needed to relocate to a new country; the immigration services work hard at keeping out low-skilled, and less educated immigrants. A third advantage is that immigrants tend to believe in the "great melting pot" ideal and want to join the mainstream society and learn the new language. To become citizens of the United States, for example, immigrants must speak, read, and write English and pass an exam on U.S. history and government. Therefore, although immigrants may start on the lowest rungs of the economic ladder, they often move up quickly, unlike marginalized resident minorities.   *Rochelle L. Dalla*

See also: Assimilation theories; Immigration and emigration; Melting pot theory.

1986, the Immigration Reform and Control Act (IRCA) addressed the issue of illegal immigration. It outlawed the hiring of illegal aliens and strengthened controls to prevent illegal entry into the country. The law mandated that employers require their employees to provide documentation that they are legally residents of the United States. IRCA also established a program through which illegal aliens who had been residing in the country since 1982 could apply for amnesty. The law apparently did little to slow illegal immigration, as aliens could easily purchase forged documents.

In the mid-1990's, the U.S. Border Patrol estimated that only about a third of aliens entering the country without proper authorization are apprehended. In most years since 1977, more than a million illegal aliens have been apprehended annually, implying that perhaps three million or more people are able to enter the country illegally each year. The majority of these individuals are Hispanic, primarily of Mexican descent, and move back and forth across the border with regularity.

Donald C. Simmons, Jr.

See also: Immigration and emigration; Immigration and Naturalization Service; Immigration Reform and Control Act; *Plyler v. Doe.*

Immigrant advantage

The term "immigrant advantage" is used by sociologists to refer to a set of distinctions between minority groups

Immigrant women

> **Significance:** Immigrant women often contend with exploitative work situations and the risk of physical abuse, including domestic violence.

Since the seventeenth century, women have journeyed alone or as members of families to North America. Coming first from England, Africa, Ireland, northern and western Europe, in the nineteenth century they immigrated from southern and eastern Europe and from China and Japan. The major source of immigration shifted in the twentieth century from Europe to Latin America and Asia.

History

In early colonial America, women arrived from England as wives or were imported as purchased wives. Many came as indentured servants who were bought and sold like slaves; they endured physical and sexual abuse. Some were transported as convicts. Female slaves were brought from Africa. Throughout the eighteenth century, although female immigrants experienced extreme job discrimination, they worked in a variety of trades.

Between 1820 and 1880, many women settled in the rural Midwest, where life on the prairies was lonely and harsh. In urban areas, the most commonly available work for young single women was domestic service, although as the century progressed they began to find employment in factories. Married women often preferred to undertake piecework at home or to take in boarders. Compared to men, there was a high proportion of destitute immigrant women. In towns and cities, women joined the developing union movement and began to speak out against intolerable working conditions. Their first strike was organized in 1825, when the United Tailoresses of New York demanded higher wages. By 1859, of the six million workers in the United States, half a million were women. They labored as domestic servants (33,000), teachers (55,000), and factory workers (181,000), half of whom were employed in textile mills. Leonora Barry, an Irish immigrant, commented on the largest problem for female workers: "Through long years of endurance they have acquired, as a sort of second nature, the habit of submission and acceptance without question of any terms offered them."

From 1880 to 1920, arrivals from Europe substantially increased. For women, positions as domestic servants continued to be most easily secured. In 1900, when white-collar jobs became available to women, Irish women worked in Canada and the United States as office workers, shop clerks, or teachers. Chinese and Japanese women immigrated to Hawaii, the continental United States, and Canada. As the number of Asian immigrants on the Pacific Coast increased, an exclusionary movement developed. The 1882 Chinese Exclusion Act abruptly curtailed Chinese immigration; it would not be repealed until 1943. The 1907 Gentlemen's Agreement strictly limited Japanese immigration. It did not exclude family members of residents, however, and therefore many Japanese women immigrated to the United States as "picture brides." In 1917, the ban on Chinese immigrants was extended to all Asian countries.

The Early Twentieth Century

In the twentieth century, many female immigrants continued to live under grim circumstances. Entering the labor force at an unprecedented rate, they faced discrimination and grueling conditions. Urban domestic service was managed by a network of unregulated and exploitative city agencies. Rents were frequently inflated. The Chicago Immigrant Protective League was founded in 1907 to help foreign-born arrivals find work, housing, and education. In New York City, new immigrants found work in sweatshops, in which conditions ranged from unhealthy to dangerous. In the winter of 1909, some women organized and voted to strike. As a result, membership increased in the International Ladies' Garment Workers' Union. Demands were won in more than three hundred shops, and some women succeeded in becoming union officials. Yet, improved factory conditions were not sufficient to prevent a number of fires, including one in 1911 at the Triangle Shirtwaist Company that killed 146 people, mostly women. That same year, social scientist Francis Kellor described immigrants as "the poorest protected of all humanity in this country . . . even worse than children."

Immigration during the first decade of the twentieth century exceeded by thirty-five million the total of any previous decade. Nativistic sentiment prompted Congress to enact new restrictions on immigration, in-

Sikh women in Toronto, Ontario, gather for a festival. Immigrant women from patriarchal cultures sometimes have difficulty reconciling their culture's gender and family roles with those of mainstream North American culture.

cluding a literacy test (1917), a quota system (1921, 1924, and 1927), and the extension of deportation criteria. The Great Depression provoked further exclusion, so that total immigration for the decade of the 1930's was lower than at any previous point since the 1820's.

Post-World War II

During World War II (1939-1945), Issei (first-generation Japanese immigrants) were interned with their families in camps by the U.S. government. Following the war, the War Brides Act (1945) allowed Chinese, Japanese, and European women to enter the United States as wives of servicemen. Similarly, in the 1960's and 1970's, such marriages were common throughout Southeast Asia. In 1962, the Migration and Refugee Assistance Act was passed to help Cubans resettle in the United States. By 1965, the major source of immigration had shifted from Europe to Latin America and Asia. The Immigration Law of 1965, which amended the Immigration and Naturalization Act of 1952, abandoned national origins quotas and introduced preference categories. After 1976, no country could send more than 20,000 people in any year to the United States, which resulted in a higher proportion of blue-collar immigration. The 1980 Refugee Act was introduced to deal with the refugees from Indochina who were admitted following the end of hostilities in Vietnam in 1975. In the 1970's, a "mail-order bride" industry developed that enabled women from the Philippines, Thailand, and Eastern Europe to immigrate to the United States.

In 1991, procedural guidelines for immigration screening were developed by the United Nations High Commissioner for Refugees. Canada developed gender-sensitive rules to make it easier for women to pass through the screening process. In 1992, in order to manage the immigration of refugees more strictly, Canada introduced new restrictive laws.

During the 1990's, women were as likely as men to immigrate to the United States. Developing nations, such as Mexico and the Philippines, became the primary source of immigration. In 1993, Mexico provided the largest number of immigrants, including numerous undocumented women. As more American women sought employment out of the home, Central American women, migrating in order to gain economic and social security, filled the need for domestic help in cities. In 1993, *The Chicago Review* addressed the exploitation of immigrant women: "To earn their living they perform the most varied jobs, many of them menial and sub-human."

Concern surfaced regarding immigrant beneficiaries of two welfare programs in the United States: Aid to Families with Dependent Children (AFDC) and Supplemental Security Income (SSI). In 1993, 6.0 percent of the immigrant population were on public assistance,

compared with 3.4 percent of all citizens. Twenty-nine percent of all legal immigrants were living below the poverty line. Since 70 percent of all Americans living below the poverty line were female, it is probable that a high percentage of them were immigrant women.

When women depart from their own cultures, they may lose their customary support systems. They have often left patriarchal and hierarchical traditions. In the United States, they enter a more egalitarian world with a more open sexuality. Gender and family roles can be thrown into disequilibrium. Domestic violence against immigrant women has increased, and there has been a higher incidence of depression and substance abuse among these women. Often eager to take advantage of opportunities, immigrant women are more willing than men to accept any job that is offered, even working in garment sweatshops. Women from different immigrant groups face many of the same issues, but how they cope with these issues varies from one culture to another.

Susan E. Hamilton

Core Resources

Roger Daniels's *Coming to America: A History of Immigration and Ethnicity in American Life* (New York: HarperCollins, 1990), Cecyle S. Neidle's *America's Immigrant Women* (Boston: Twayne, 1975), and Howard Zinn's *A People's History of the United States* (New York: Harper & Row, 1980) discuss the status and history of immigrant women.

See also: Aid to Families with Dependent Children; Asian American women; Cable Act; Ethnic identities of women; Immigration and emigration; Latinas; War Brides Act; Women and racism.

Immigration Act of 1917

> **Significance:** The Immigration Act of 1917 significantly restricted immigration into the United States by use of a literacy test, among other measures.

Public concern over immigration prompted the U.S. Congress to establish a Joint Commission on Immigration in 1907. The commission consisted of three members of the Senate, three members of the House of Representatives, and three other appointees. In 1911, the Dillingham Commission, named after the legislation's author and the commission's chairman, Senator William P. Dillingham of Vermont, issued a forty-two-volume report that advocated the restriction of immigration. It stated that recent immigrants from southern and eastern Europe were more likely to be unskilled, unsettled, and generally less desirable than the northern and western European immigrants who had arrived previously. Experts later disputed these conclusions, but the report was used to justify the new restrictions that Congress continued to write into law in the comprehensive Immigration Act of 1917.

A number of different ways to restrict immigration were suggested by the commission. They included instituting a literacy test, excluding unskilled laborers, increasing the amount of money that immigrants were required to have in their possession, and increasing the head tax. The commission also advocated the principle of racial quotas.

Major attention was directed toward the literacy test. Congress had introduced prior bills requiring literacy tests for immigrants. In 1897, such a bill was vetoed by President Grover Cleveland, who said that immigration restrictions were unnecessary. The House voted to override the president's veto on March 3, 195 to 37. The Senate referred the veto message and bill to the Committee on Immigration. When the bill resurfaced at the Sixty-second Congress, it was the Senate that voted to override President William Howard Taft's veto on February 18, 1913, while the House voted to sustain it on February 19. During the Sixty-third Congress (1914-1917), the House voted to sustain the veto of President Woodrow Wilson.

At the second session of the Sixty-fourth Congress, a bill was introduced "to regulate the immigrating of aliens to, and the residence of aliens in, the United States." Again, Wilson vetoed the bill. On February 1, 1917, the House voted to override the president's veto, 287 to 106, and the Senate voted similarly on February 5, 1917, 62 to 19. The veto was overridden, and the bill became Public Law 301. The act excluded from entry "all aliens over sixteen years of age, physically capable of reading, who can not read the English language, or some other language or dialect, including Hebrew or Yiddish." Other major recommendations made by the Dillingham Commission six years earlier were passed. The head tax was increased, and vagrants, alcoholics, advocates of violent revolutions, and "psychopathic inferiors" all were barred. A further provision created an Asiatic Barred Zone in the southwest Pacific, which succeeded in excluding most Asian immigrants who were not already excluded by the Chinese Exclusion Act and the Gentlemen's Agreement.   *Susan E. Hamilton*

A group of immigrants arrives at Ellis Island in New York. The Immigration Act of 1917 included a number of restrictive provisions designed to decrease the number of immigrants from areas other than northern Europe.

Core Resources

American Immigration Policy (Port Washington, N.Y.: Kennikat Press, 1969), edited by William S. Bernard, includes the text of the 1917 Immigration Act. Ellis Cose's *A Nation of Strangers* (New York: William Morrow, 1992) presents an overview of immigration, from colonial settlement to World War I. Part 2 of Roger Daniels's *Coming to America: A History of Immigration and Ethnicity in American Life* (New York: HarperCollins, 1990) concentrates on immigration from 1820 to 1924. Elizabeth J. Harper's *Immigration Laws of the United States* (3d ed., Indianapolis: Bobbs-Merrill, 1975) discusses immigration history and trends. Walter Nugent's *Crossings: The Great Transatlantic Migrations, 1870-1914* (Bloomington: Indiana University Press, 1992) is a thorough treatise accompanied by maps, tables, and photographs.

See also: Alien land laws; Chinese Exclusion Act; Gentlemen's Agreement; Immigration Act of 1924; Red Scare; Yellow peril campaign.

Immigration Act of 1924

Significance: The Immigration Act of 1924, also known as the National Origins Act, restricted immigration by means of a quota system.

There was no clearly defined official U.S. policy toward immigration until the late nineteenth century. The

United States was still a relatively young country, and there was a need for settlers in the West and for workers to build industry. Chinese immigrants flowed into California in 1849 and the early 1850's, searching for fortune and staying as laborers who worked the mines and helped to build the transcontinental railroad.

The earliest immigration restriction focused on Asians. In 1875, the federal government restricted the number of Chinese and Japanese coming into the country. The push for restriction of Asian immigrants was led by U.S. workers. After the depression of 1877, Denis Kearney, an Irish-born labor organizer, helped found the Workingman's Trade and Labor Union of San Francisco, an anti-Chinese and anticapitalist group. Kearney and others believed that lower-paid Chinese workers took jobs away from white workers, and they agitated for expulsion of the Chinese and legal restrictions on future immigrants. Their efforts were successful in 1882, when the Chinese Exclusion Act was passed. The act exempted teachers, students, merchants, and pleasure travelers, and remained in effect until 1943. With the act of 1882, the federal government had, for the first time, placed restrictions on the immigration of persons from a specific country. More specific policy toward European immigration began in the 1880's. In 1882, the federal government excluded convicts, paupers, and mentally impaired persons. Organized labor's efforts also were successful in 1882, with the prohibition of employers' recruiting workers in Europe and paying their passage to the United States.

Restrictive Changes

Federal law became more aggressive by the early twentieth century, with the passage of the Act of 1903, which excluded epileptics, beggars, and anarchists. In 1907, the United States Immigration Commission was formed. This group, also known as the Dillingham Commission, published a forty-two-volume survey of the impact of immigration on American life and called for a literacy test and further immigration restriction. Although several presidential vetoes had prevented a literacy requirement, in 1917, the U.S. Congress overrode President Woodrow Wilson's veto and passed a law requiring a literacy test for newcomers. The test was designed to reduce the number of immigrants, particularly those from southeastern Europe, where the literacy rate was low.

The marked change in official policy and in the view of a majority of people in the United States was caused by several factors. A strong nativist movement had begun after World War I with such groups as the American Protective Association, an organization that began in the Midwest in the 1880's and focused on prejudice against aliens and Catholics. Senator Henry Cabot Lodge organized the Immigration Restriction League in Boston,

indicating the addition of U.S. leaders and intellectuals to the restriction movement. The war had brought the United States into position as a major world power, with a resultant view that the United States should be a nation of conformity. Political and economic problems in Europe, including the war and a postwar economic depression, had led to fear of too many immigrants fleeing Europe. Changes in the U.S. economy reduced the need for manual labor, thus creating a fear of lack of job security.

The push for restriction coincided with the most intensive era of immigration in United States history. From the late 1880's until the 1920's, the nation experienced wave after wave of immigration, with millions of persons coming into the country each decade. The growth of new physical and social sciences that emphasized heredity as a factor in intelligence led many people to believe that persons such as Slavs or Italians were less intelligent than western Europeans such as the Norwegians or the English. The belief in genetic inferiority gave credence to the immigration restriction movement and helped sway the government.

At the same time that millions of newcomers were entering the United States, a spirit of reform, the Progressive Era, had grown throughout the country. Americans who saw themselves as progressive and forward-looking pushed for change in politics, society, and education, particularly in the crowded urban areas of the Northeast. Europeans had emigrated in large numbers to the cities, and newer groups, such as Italians and Poles, were seen by many progressive-minded reformers as the root of urban problems. Thus it was with the help of progressive leaders that a push was made at the federal level to restrict the number of immigrants.

Quota System

In 1921, Congress passed a temporary measure that was the first U.S. law specifically restricting European immigration. The act established a quota system that held the number of immigrants to 3 percent of each admissible nationality living in the United States in 1910. Quotas were established for persons from Europe, Asia, Africa, Australia, and New Zealand. Although only a temporary measure, the Immigration Act of 1921 marked the beginning of a permanent policy of restricting European immigration. It began a bitter three-year controversy that led to the Immigration Act of 1924.

The United States Congress amended the 1921 act with a more restrictive permanent measure in May of 1924, the Johnson-Reid Act. This act, which became known as the National Origins Act, took effect on July 1, 1924. It limited the annual immigration to the United States to 2 percent of a country's population in the U.S. as of the census of 1890. With the large numbers of northern and western Europeans who had immigrated to the country throughout the nation's history, the act effectively restricted southern and eastern European immigrants to approximately 12 percent of the total immigrant population. Asian immigration was completely prohibited, but there was no restriction on immigration from independent nations of the Western Hemisphere.

The new law also changed the processing system for aliens by moving the immigration inspection process to U.S. consulates in foreign countries and requiring immigrants to obtain visas in the native country before emigrating to the United States. The number of visas was held to 10 percent in each country per month and thus reduced the number of people arriving at Ellis Island, leading to the eventual closing of the facility.

The Immigration Act of 1924 reflects a change in the controversy that occurred in the three-year period after the act of 1921. By 1924, the major factor in immigration restriction was racial prejudice. By using the U.S. Census of 1890 as the basis for quotas, the government in effect sharply reduced the number of southern and eastern Europeans, who had not begun to arrive in large numbers until after that census year. The passage of the act codified an official policy of preventing further changes in the ethnic composition of U.S. society, and it was to remain in effect until passage of the Immigration and Nationality Act of 1965.   *Judith Boyce DeMark*

Core Resources

August C. Bolino's *The Ellis Island Source Book* (Washington, D.C.: Kensington Historical Press, 1985) includes a history of Ellis Island and immigration restriction. Thomas J. Curran's *Xenophobia and Immigration, 1820-1930* (Boston: Twayne, 1975) provides a basic overview of the reasons for immigration restriction throughout U.S. history. Robert A. Divine's *American Immigration Policy, 1924-1952* (New Haven, Conn.: Yale University Press, 1957; reprint, New York: Da Capo Press, 1972) is a comprehensive treatment of the history of immigration restriction from the 1924 act through the mid-1950's. Maxine S. Seller's "Historical Perspectives on American Immigration Policy: Case Studies and Current Implications," in *U.S. Immigration Policy* (Durham, N.C.: Duke University Press, 1984), edited by Richard R. Hofstetter, contains a chronology of the series of events leading up to the Immigration Act of 1924, with a discussion of how those events relate to recent immigration history.

See also: Alien land laws; Chinese Exclusion Act; Immigration Act of 1917; Immigration Act of 1943; Immigration and Nationality Act of 1965; Page law; Xenophobia, nativism, and eugenics; Yellow peril campaign.

Immigration Act of 1943

> **Significance:** The Immigration Act of 1943 repealed Asian exclusion laws, opening the way for further immigration reforms.

The passage by Congress of the Immigration Act of 1943, also known as the Magnuson Act, and President Franklin D. Roosevelt's signing it into law ended the era of legal exclusion of Chinese immigrants to the United States and began an era during which sizable numbers of Chinese and other Asian immigrants came to the country. It helped bring about significant changes in race relations in the United States.

The first wave of Chinese immigrants came from the Pearl River delta region in southern China. They began coming to California in 1848 during the gold rush and continued to come to the western states as miners, railroad builders, farmers, fishermen, and factory workers. Most were men. Many came as contract laborers and intended to return to China. Anti-Chinese feelings, begun during the gold rush and expressed in mob actions and local discriminatory laws, culminated in the Chinese Exclusion Act of 1882, barring the immigration of Chinese laborers for ten years. The act was renewed in 1892, applied to Hawaii when those islands were annexed by the United States in 1898, and made permanent in 1904. Another bill, passed in 1924, made Asians ineligible for U.S. citizenship and disallowed Chinese wives of U.S. citizens to immigrate to the United States. As a result, the Chinese population in the United States declined from a peak of 107,475 in 1880 to 77,504 in 1940.

The passage of the Magnuson Act of 1943, which repealed the Chinese Exclusion Act of 1882, inaugurated profound changes in the status of ethnic Chinese who were citizens or residents of the United States. It made Chinese immigrants, many of whom had lived in the United States for years, eligible for citizenship. It also allotted a minuscule quota of 105 Chinese persons per year who could enter the United States as immigrants. The 1943 bill was a result of recognition of China's growing international status after 1928 under the Nationalist government and growing U.S. sympathy for China's heroic resistance to Japanese aggression after 1937. It also was intended to counter Japanese wartime propaganda aimed at discrediting the United States among Asians by portraying it as a racist nation.

Post-World War II Changes

World War II was a turning point for Chinese-U.S. relations. After Japan's attack on Pearl Harbor in December, 1941, China and the United States became allies against the Axis powers. Madame Chiang Kai-shek, wife of China's wartime leader, won widespread respect and sympathy for China during her visit to the United States; she was the second female foreign leader to address a joint session of Congress. In 1943, the United States and Great Britain also signed new equal treaties with China that ended a century of international inequality for China. These events and the contributions of Chinese Americans in the war favorably affected the position and status of Chinese Americans. The 1943 act also opened the door for other legislation that allowed more Chinese to immigrate to the United States. In the long run, these laws had a major impact on the formation of Chinese families in the United States.

The War Brides Act of 1945, for example, permitted foreign-born wives of U.S. soldiers to enter the United States and become naturalized. Approximately six thousand Chinese women entered the United States during the next several years as wives of U.S. servicemen. An amendment to this act, passed in 1946, put the Chinese wives and children of U.S. citizens outside the quota, resulting in the reunion of many separated families and allowing ten thousand Chinese, mostly wives, and also children of U.S. citizens of Chinese ethnicity, to enter the country during the next eight years. The Displaced Persons Act of 1948 granted permanent resident status, and eventually the right of citizenship, to 3,465 Chinese students, scholars, and others stranded in the United States by the widespread civil war that erupted between the Chinese Nationalists and Communists after the end of World War II. The Refugee Relief Act of 1953 allowed an additional 2,777 refugees to remain in the United States after the civil war ended in a Communist victory and the establishment of the People's Republic of China. Some Chinese students from the Republic of China on Taiwan, who came to study in the United States after 1950 and found employment and sponsors after the end of their studies, were also permitted to remain and were eligible for naturalization.

The four immigration acts passed between 1943 and 1953 can be viewed as a result of the alliance between the United States and the Republic of China in World War II and U.S. involvement in the Chinese civil war that followed. In a wider context, they were also the result of changing views on race and race relations that World War II and related events brought about. Finally, they heralded the Immigration and Nationality Act of 1965, which revolutionized U.S. immigration policy in ending racial quotas. Its most dramatic consequence was the significant increase of Asian immigrants in general, and Chinese immigrants in particular, into the United States.

The new immigrants changed the makeup of Chinese American society and caused a change in the way the Chinese were perceived by the majority groups in the United States. Whereas most of the earlier immigrants tended to live in ghettoized Chinatowns, were poorly educated, and overwhelmingly worked in low-status jobs as laundrymen, miners, or railroad workers, the new immigrants were highly educated, cosmopolitan, and professional. They came from the middle class, traced their roots to all parts of China, had little difficulty acculturating and assimilating into the academic and professional milieu of peoples of European ethnicity in the United States, and tended not to live in Chinatowns. The latter group was mainly responsible for revolutionizing the way Chinese Americans were perceived in the United States. *Jiu-Hwa Lo Upshur*

Core Resources

Entry Denied: Exclusion and the Chinese Community in America, 1882-1943 (Philadelphia: Temple University Press, 1991), edited by Sucheng Chan, contains articles from nine scholars on different facets of the era. Fred W. Riggs's *Pressure on Congress: A Study of the Repeal of Chinese Exclusion* (1950; reprint, Westport, Conn.: Greenwood Press, 1972) gives a detailed account of the reasons for the repeal. Betty Lee Sung's *Mountain of Gold: The Story of the Chinese in America* (New York: I Company, 1967) is a good overview of Chinese immigration.

See also: Chinese American Citizens Alliance; Chinese Americans; Chinese Exclusion Act; Chinese Six Companies; Immigration Act of 1917; Immigration Act of 1924; Immigration and Nationality Act of 1965.

Immigration Act of 1990

The U.S. Immigration Act of 1990 was passed in response to a widespread belief among legislators and the general public that many of the economic and social ills of the United States were caused by large populations of poor, non-English-speaking immigrants and in response to a growing need for skilled workers in technical fields in an increasingly international marketplace. The act, one of a number of immigration laws passed since the Immigration Act of 1891, set numerical limits for immigrants to the United States and established a system of preferences to determine which of the many applicants for admission should be accepted. Under the terms of the 1990 act, only 675,000 immigrants, not including political refugees, were to be admitted to the United States each year. These immigrants were eligible for preferential admission consideration if they fell into one of three groups: immigrants who had family members already legally in the country; employment-based immigrants who were able to prove that they had exceptional ability in certain professions with a high demand; and those from designated underrepresented nations, who were labeled "diversity immigrants."

Because the new law nearly tripled the annual allotment of employment-based immigrants from 54,000 to 140,000, business and industry leaders heralded their increased opportunity to compete internationally for experienced and talented engineers, technicians, and multinational executives. Others believed that the preference for certain kinds of workers masked a preference for whites over nonwhites, and wealthier immigrants over poorer. Divisions over the law between racial and political groups intensified when successful lobbying led to refinements in the law making it easier for fashion models and musicians, especially from Europe, to gain visas, while efforts to gain admittance for more women fleeing genital mutilation in African and Arabic nations failed.

The act made it easier for certain people—contract workers, musicians and other artists, researchers and educators participating in exchange programs—to perform skilled work in the United States on a temporary basis, with no intention of seeking citizenship. At the same time, the new law made it more difficult for unskilled workers, such as domestic workers and laborers, to obtain immigrant visas.

Finally, the Immigration Act of 1990 attempted to correct criticism of the 1986 Immigration Reform and Control Act by increasing that act's antidiscrimination provisions and increasing the penalties for discrimination. In a significant change in U.S. immigration law, the act revised the reasons a person might be refused immigrant status or be deported. After 1952, for example, Communists were denied permission to enter the country on nonimmigrant work visas and were subject to deportment if identified, and potential political refugees from nations friendly to the United States were turned away as a matter of foreign policy. Under the new law, a wider range of political and ideological beliefs became acceptable.   *Cynthia A. Bily*

See also: Immigration and emigration; Immigration Reform and Control Act of 1986.

Immigration and emigration

> **Significance:** Immigration and emigration are two of the primary processes (alongside fertility and mortality) that influence a population's ethnic and racial composition and that create shifts in intergroup relations.

Migration simply consists of the movement of people from one place to another. *Migration* can be internal

(within a country) or international, and both types can have significant impacts. *Immigration* (the movement into a new country) and *emigration* (movement from a country) are forms of international migration. The term "net migration rate" refers to the difference between the rate of immigration and the rate of emigration. It is expressed as the number of people per 1,000 who enter or leave an area during one year. Migration may have a number of important effects, such as relieving population pressure in crowded areas, spreading culture from one area to another, and bringing groups into contact—and possible conflict.

Sociologists also study the experiences of immigrants in relation to prejudice, discrimination, and social stratification and mobility. They explore the differing experiences of immigrants of differing ethnicities and races; such studies have revealed much about the nature of prejudice and about the disparity between the ideology and the reality of American life. A look at various aspects of immigration to the United States allows an examination of these processes at work in the real world. Over the course of immigration to America, beginning in the sixteenth century (if one excludes the first immigration, the prehistoric migration of the ancestors of the American Indians), most immigrants have come for similar reasons: to escape persecution, to find economic opportunities, and to enjoy the freedoms available in the United States. Yet despite the traditional emphasis on the forces that pushed people out of their countries of origin and the separate forces that pulled them toward the United States, a number of studies, such as David M. Reimers's *Still the Golden Door* (1985), emphasize structural forces—economic and political—that have influenced population movements.

Immigration Patterns

Many studies of immigration to the United States identify two massive waves of immigration between 1820 and 1914. The first decades of the nineteenth century brought increasing numbers of immigrants; 151,000 arrived in the 1820's, nearly 600,000 in the 1830's, more than 1 million in the 1840's, and 2.3 million in the 1850's. Many were Irish Catholics escaping political persecution and famine and Germans fleeing political upheavals. These "old immigrants" came to cities on the East Coast; some moved inland to the farmlands of the Great Plains.

"New immigrants" were those from eastern and southern Europe who arrived between the 1880's and World War I. This second period of immigration far surpassed the earlier waves in numbers, rising from 788,000 in 1872 to 1,285,000 in 1907. By 1914 nearly 15 million immigrants had arrived in the United States, many from Austria-Hungary, Italy, Russia, Greece, Romania, and

Two Dutch children await immigration processing on Ellis Island around 1906. The United States has been called a nation of immigrants for the large number of people who migrated there.

Turkey. The federal Dillingham Commission (1907) regarded this group as poor, unskilled, and mostly male, and its report reinforced prejudices about eastern and southern Europeans. It concluded that these immigrants would be more difficult to assimilate into American society. As the children or grandchildren of immigrants became indistinguishable from other Americans, however, the concept of American society as a "melting pot" into which many nationalities merged into one, took hold.

Often invisible in early immigration studies were the numbers of Africans and Latin Americans who had not come voluntarily to the United States. Africans were forcibly brought to the United States as slaves. Many Mexicans did not technically immigrate but were absorbed into the United States when lands from Texas to California were conquered in the Mexican-American War (1846-1848). These groups needed to adapt to a new nation and a new culture, as did European immigrants, but they faced both discrimination and a lack of understanding about their circumstances. Asian immigrants formed another group that was long invisible in immigration histories. Chinese men were imported as cheap labor to build the railroads in the mid-1800's, and they

were expected to leave when their job was done. Many Japanese, Filipino, and Korean immigrants came first to Hawaii as agricultural laborers, and some moved on to California.

Reasons for Migration
Some structural reasons for emigration and immigration have not changed greatly over the last three hundred years. Many individuals have come to North America to escape religious or political persecution. Early refugees in this category included the English Pilgrims and French Huguenots. Later religious groups came from Norway, Holland, and Russia, among them Jews and Mennonites. From the early nineteenth century to the present, immigrants have come because of economic changes in their native lands and opportunities in the United States. The enclosure movement in England and Western Europe, which began in the 1700's, forced many peasants off the land. They sought new land in America. Factories brought ruin to skilled artisans, who came to the United States hoping to open workshops. Many Europeans and Asians also came to escape political turmoil. Revolutions in 1830 and 1848 in Europe, and the Taiping Rebellion in China in 1848, led refugees to seek safety in the United States. Twentieth century upheavals such as World War II, the Cuban Revolution, repression in Southeast Asia, and civil wars in Lebanon and El Salvador have continued to bring refugees to the United States.

Immigrants and U.S.-Born Americans
Immigrants and refugees have not settled equally in all regions of the United States. Large immigrant communities in California, New York, and Florida have led to the need for government services in many languages. Students in schools speak Vietnamese, Spanish, Korean, Ethiopian, Haitian, and a number of Chinese dialects. Many require courses in English as a second language. Courts need to provide translators, and social service agencies struggle to communicate with many immigrant groups.

Some Americans have responded to foreigners with resentment. Some states and localities have passed laws declaring English to be the only official language. Sociologists studying immigration, however, have found that the large number of immigrants has led to a gradual shift in the population of the United States and its culture. Television stations around the country broadcast programs in many languages. Spanish-speaking markets in particular represent many new business opportunities, and large American companies are beginning to offer advertisements in Spanish.

Americans have been proud of their heritage of immigration yet ambivalent about immigrant groups who have come to the United States. Federal legislation has expressed the varying reactions of Americans toward immigrants and immigration over time. Before 1820 there were no laws requiring lists of passengers arriving in the United States. Immigrants brought skills and talents that were needed by the new country, and they were welcomed. Non-British immigrants in the early nineteenth century, however, did experience discrimination. Irish Catholics and German immigrants, whose religion or language was different from that of the majority, faced ridicule and were stereotyped as drunkards or dullards. Asian immigrants faced racial prejudice, and Chinese people were eventually barred from immigrating to the United States.

Despite mixed reaction to foreigners, the first federal immigration law was not passed until 1875. In that year prostitutes and convicts were prohibited from entering as immigrants. Additional exclusions for lunatics and idiots were added later.

By the 1880's, increasing immigration from areas outside northern Europe, the closing of the frontier, and increasing urbanization led to attempts to control immigration. Some Americans claimed that southern and eastern Europeans were replacing American stock and that immigration produced a declining birthrate among Americans. Others were more worried about Asian immigrants. The Chinese Exclusion Act of 1882 specifically denied entry to Chinese people, while the Forant Act (1885) made it unlawful for employers to import aliens to perform labor in the United States. This law was aimed at large companies who were importing eastern Europeans to fill low-wage jobs instead of hiring American labor, and it reflected suspicion that immigration caused wages to decline. The Immigration Act of 1917 barred Asians not by nationality, but by excluding geographically any immigrants from East or South Asia.

Immigration to the United States was regulated for most of the twentieth century by the Immigration Act of 1924, which reflected the nation's desire to encourage European immigration and discourage non-Western immigrants. This law established a series of quotas for immigrants from all countries except the Western Hemisphere. Larger quotas were assigned to countries whose citizens were more traditionally identified with the American population. The Immigration and Nationality Act of 1952 tightened the quota system.

Immigration Reform

A significant change in United States policy toward immigration came with the Immigration and Nationality Act of 1965. This law removed strict quotas and Asian exclusion. Instead, it created preferences for persons with certain skills and gave priority to people with immediate family in the United States. The consequences of this legislation led to greater changes in immigration than were anticipated. By 1974, for example, foreign-born physicians made up 20 percent of all medical doctors in the United States. The "brain drain" from developing countries continued, as scientists, engineers, and scholars sought better conditions and higher salaries in the United States. The law also brought increasing non-European immigration, as family members petitioned to bring relatives from Asia, Africa, and Latin America.

The increasing number of undocumented immigrants in the United States has led to calls for policing the U.S. border with Mexico more efficiently and for penalties for employers of illegal immigrants. Illegal immigrants have been accused of stealing jobs from United States citizens, draining social services, and changing the very nature of American society. In 1986 the Immigration Reform and Control Act attempted to resolve these issues for many illegal immigrants. Those who could show permanent residency in the United States since 1982 could become legal residents. Employers who hired illegal immigrants were to be fined, and additional funds were appropriated for stronger immigration enforcement.

Immigration reforms have continued, showing the changing response of American society over time. The Kennedy-Donnelly Act of 1988 permitted a lottery to provide visas for permanent resident status, and the 1990 Immigration Act raised annual immigration ceilings and ended restrictions on homosexuals, communists, and people with acquired immune deficiency syndrome (AIDS); it also granted safe haven status for Salvadorans. This law was not without opposition from those who feared that disease or undesirable ideas would be spread by immigrants.

Refugees have become an increasingly important part of population movements. Emigration from countries experiencing conflict has increased in the twentieth century, and the United States has traditionally thought of itself as a nation receptive to the oppressed. The need to resettle large numbers of eastern European refugees after World War II was recognized by the Refugee Relief Act of 1953. In the 1980's the church-sponsored sanctuary movement broke immigration laws by providing asylum for Salvadorans who feared deportation by immigration authorities enforcing strict refugee policies. The impact of immigration on American society has continued to challenge cherished concepts and ideologies and to highlight prejudices. The idea of the United States as an open door, a place where people from all lands can find a haven, is still shared by many. Since the 1980's, however, this ideal has faced considerable challenges. The large numbers of Central Americans, Asians, and Haitians seeking asylum in the United

States has led to tighter controls at borders and interdiction on the high seas.

While some scholarship, particularly since the 1980's, has stressed structural rather than personal reasons for population movements and has challenged the concept of the melting pot, American society has continued to mold immigrants from many nations. At the same time, American society has changed as a result of this immigration.   *James A. Baer*

Core Resources
Roger Daniels's *Coming to America: A History of Immigration and Ethnicity in American Life* (New York: HarperCollins, 1990) begins with prehistoric migrations of American Indians and continues through American history. Nathan Glazer and Daniel Patrick Moynihan's *Beyond the Melting Pot* (Cambridge, Mass.: MIT Press, 1963) is a classic work that explores the experiences of African American, Italian, Irish, and Jewish groups in New York City. The authors argue against the concept of the melting pot by demonstrating continuing ethnic identity and separate communities of these groups. Maldwyn Allen Jones's *American Immigration* (2d ed., Chicago: University of Chicago Press, 1992) offers a clear history of immigration from colonists to modern refugees. David M. Reimers's *Still the Golden Door: The Third World Comes to America* (2d ed., New York: Columbia University Press, 1992) focuses on Third World immigration. *Immigration Reconsidered*, edited by Virginia Yans-McLaughlin (New York: Oxford University Press, 1990), is a collection of essays and theories of immigration, approaches to comparative research, and immigrant networks.

See also: Assimilation theories; Immigrant advantage; Immigrant women; Immigration Act of 1917; Immigration Act of 1924; Immigration Act of 1943; Immigration Act of 1990; Immigration "crisis"; Melting pot theory.

Immigration and Nationality Act of 1952

Significance: The Immigration and Nationality Act of 1952 removed a restriction on Asian immigration.

In the early 1950's, as it had periodically throughout the twentieth century, immigration again became the subject of intense national debate, and a movement arose to reform immigration law. At the time, there were more than two hundred federal laws dealing with immigration, with little coordination among them.

Reform Efforts
The movement toward immigration reform actually began in 1947, with a U.S. Senate committee investigation on immigration laws, resulting in a voluminous report in 1950 and a proposed bill. The ensuing debate was divided between a group who wanted to abandon the quota system and increase the numbers of immigrants admitted, and those who hoped to shape immigration law to enforce the status quo. Leaders of the latter camp were the architects of the Immigration and Nationality Act of 1952: Patrick McCarran, senator from Nevada, Francis Walter, congressman from Pennsylvania, and Richard Arens, staff director of the Senate Subcommittee to Investigate Immigration and Naturalization. McCarran was the author of the Internal Security Act of 1951, which provided for registration of communist organizations and the internment of communists during national emergencies; Walter was an immigration specialist who had backed legislation to admit Europeans from camps for displaced persons; Arens had been staff director for the House Committee on Un-American Activities. Each looked upon immigration control as an extension of his work to defend the United States against foreign and domestic enemies.

McCarran was most outspoken in defending the concept of restrictions on the basis of national origin, stating in the Senate that

> There are hard-core indigestible blocs who have not become integrated into the American way of life, but who, on the contrary, are its deadly enemy. . . . this Nation is the last hope of western civilization; and if this oasis of the world shall be overrun, perverted, contaminated, or destroyed, then the last flickering light of humanity will be extinguished.

Arens branded critics of the proposed act as either communists, misguided liberals enraptured by communist propaganda, apologists for specific immigrant groups, or "professional vote solicitors who fawn on nationality groups, appealing to them not as Americans but as hyphenated Americans." Among the bill's critics, however, were Harry S Truman, the U.S. president in 1952, and Hubert H. Humphrey, senator from Minnesota and future Democratic presidential nominee. One liberal senator, Herbert Lehman, attacked the national origins provisions of the existing immigration code as a racist measure that smacked of the ethnic purity policies of the recently defeated German Nazis. Truman vetoed the bill, but his veto was overridden, 278 to 113 in the House, and 57 to 26 in the Senate.

In several areas, the 1952 law made no significant changes: Quotas for European immigrants were little changed, no quotas were instituted for immigrants from

North and South American countries, and the issue of illegal immigration was given scant attention. There were significant changes in some areas, however: reversal of the ban on Asian immigration, extension of naturalization to persons regardless of race or sex, and the first provision for refugees as a special class of immigrants.

Provisions

The Asiatic Barred Zone that had been established in 1917 was eliminated by providing for twenty-five hundred entries from the area—a minuscule number for the region, but the first recognition of Asian immigration rights in decades. This small concession for Asians was offset partially by the fact that anyone whose ancestry was at least half Asian would be counted under the quota for the Asian country of ancestry, even if the person was a resident of another country. This provision, which was unlike the system of counting quotas for European countries, was specifically and openly designed to prevent Asians living in North and South American countries, which had no quota restrictions, from flooding into the United States.

The Immigration and Nationality Act of 1952, or McCarran-Walter Act, also ensured for the first time that the "right of a person to become a naturalized citizen of the United States shall not be denied or abridged because of race or sex." The provision of not denying citizenship based on sex addressed the issue of women who had lost their U.S. citizenship by marrying foreign men of certain categories; men who had married women from those categories had never lost their citizenship.

The issue of refugees was a new concern resulting from World War II. More than seven million persons had lost their homelands in the aftermath of the war, as a result of the conquering and reorganization of countries primarily in Eastern Europe. The 1952 act did not present a comprehensive solution to the problem of refugees but did give the attorney general special power, subject to congressional overview, to admit refugees into the United States under a special status. Although this was expected to be a seldom-used provision of the law, regular upheavals throughout the world later made it an important avenue of immigration into the United States.

Finally, the Immigration and Nationality Act also included stringent security procedures designed to prevent communist subversives from infiltrating the United States through immigration. Some of these harsh measures were specifically mentioned by Truman in his veto message, but the anticommunist Cold War climate made such measures hard to defeat.

Over the objections of Congress, President Truman appointed a special commission to examine immigration in September, 1952. After hearings in several cities, it issued the report *Whom Shall We Welcome?*, which was critical of the McCarran-Walter Act. Some liberal Democrats attempted to make the 1952 presidential election a forum on immigration policy, but without success. Dwight D. Eisenhower, the victorious Republican nominee for president, made few specific statements on immigration policy during the campaign. After his election, however, he proposed a special provision for allowing almost a quarter of a million refugees from communism to immigrate to the United States over a two-year period, couching his proposal in terms of humanitarianism and foreign policy. The resulting Refugee Relief Act of 1953 allowed the admission of 214,000 refugees, but only if they had assurance of jobs and housing or were close relatives of U.S. citizens and could pass extensive screening procedures designed to deter subversives. Several similar exceptions in the following years managed to undercut the McCarran-Walter Act, which its many critics had been unable to overturn outright.

Irene Struthers

Core Resources

Marius A. Dimmitt's *The Enactment of the McCarran-Walter Act of 1952* (Lawrence: University Press of Kansas, 1971) is a dissertation giving a complete discussion of the 1952 immigration bill. Michael C. LeMay *From Open Door to Dutch Door: An Analysis of U.S. Immigration Policy Since 1820* (New York: Praeger, 1987) is a comprehensive overview of the forces behind and results of changing U.S. immigration policy; chapter 5 opens with a discussion of the Immigration Act of 1952.

See also: Immigration Act of 1917; Immigration Act of 1924; Immigration Act of 1943; Immigration Act of 1990; Immigration and Nationality Act of 1965; Immigration Reform and Control Act of 1986.

Immigration and Nationality Act of 1965

Significance: The Immigration and Nationality Act of 1965 removed restrictions on non-European immigration, significantly altering the ethnic makeup of U.S. immigrants.

The Immigration and Nationality Act of 1952 codified legislation that had developed haphazardly over the past century. Although it liberalized some areas, it was discriminatory in that quotas were allotted according to national origins. This resulted in western and northern European nations receiving no less than 85 percent of the total allotment. The Immigration and Nationality

Act of 1965 allowed non-Europeans to enter the United States on an equal basis with Europeans. Before the 1965 legislation, U.S. immigration policies favored northern and western Europeans.

Reform Begins

With the election of John F. Kennedy in 1960, circumstances for meaningful immigration reform came into being: Kennedy believed that immigration was a source of national strength, the Civil Rights movement had promoted an ideology to eliminate racist policies, and the U.S. position during the Cold War necessitated that immigration policies be just. Thus, Kennedy had Abba Schwartz, an expert on refugee and immigration matters, develop a plan to revise immigration policy.

In July of 1963, Kennedy sent his proposal for immigration reform to Congress. His recommendations had three major provisions: the quota system should be phased out over a five-year period; no natives of any one country should receive more than 10 percent of the newly authorized quota numbers; and a seven-person immigration board should be set up to advise the president. Kennedy also advocated that family reunification remain a priority; the Asiatic Barred Zone be eliminated; and nonquota status be granted to residents of Jamaica and Trinidad and Tobago, as it was to other Western Hemisphere residents. Last, the preference structure was to be altered to liberalize requirements for skilled people.

After the assassination of President Kennedy, President Lyndon B. Johnson took up the cause of immigration. Although immigration was not a major issue during the 1964 campaign, both sides had courted diverse ethnic communities, whose will now had to be considered. The Democratic Party's landslide victory gave Johnson a strong mandate for his Great Society programs, of which immigration reform was a component. Secretary of State Dean Rusk argued the need for immigration reform to bolster U.S. foreign policy. Rusk, Attorney General Robert F. Kennedy, and others criticized the current system for being discriminatory and argued that the proposed changes would be economically advantageous to the United States. Senator Edward "Ted" Kennedy held hearings and concluded that "all recognized the unworkability of the national origins quota system."

Outside Congress, ethnic, voluntary, and religious organizations lobbied and provided testimony before Congress. They echoed the administration's arguments about discrimination. A few Southerners in Congress argued that the national origins concept was not discriminatory—it was a mirror reflecting the U.S. population, so those who would best assimilate into U.S. society would enter. However, the focus of the congressional debate was on how to alter the national origins system,

not on whether it should be changed. The most disputed provisions concerned whether emphasis should be on needed skills, family reunification, or limits set on Western Hemisphere immigration. Family unification prevailed.

Provisions

The new law replaced the national origins system with hemispheric caps, 170,000 from the Old World and 120,000 from the New. Spouses, unmarried minor children, and parents of U.S. citizens were exempt from numerical quotas. Preferences were granted first to unmarried adult children of U.S. citizens (20 percent); next, to spouses and unmarried adult children of permanent resident aliens (20 percent). Professionals, scientists, and artists of exceptional ability were awarded third preference (10 percent) but required certification from the U.S. Department of Labor. Married children of U.S. citizens had fourth preference (10 percent). Next were those brothers and sisters of U.S. citizens who were older than twenty-one years of age (24 percent), followed by skilled and unskilled workers in occupations for which labor was in short supply (10 percent). Refugees from communist or communist-dominated countries or the Middle East were seventh (6 percent). Nonpreference status was assigned to anyone not eligible under any of the above categories; there have been more preference applicants than can be accommodated, so nonpreference status has not been used.

The law had unexpected consequences. The framers of the legislation expected that the Old World slots would be filled by Europeans. They assumed that family reunification would favor Europeans, because they dominated the U.S. population. However, those from Europe who wanted to come were in the lower preference categories, while well-trained Asians had been coming to the United States since 1943 and were well qualified for preference positions. Once they, or anyone else, became a permanent resident, a whole group of people became eligible to enter the country under the third preference category. After a five-year wait—the residential requirement for citizenship—more persons became eligible under the second preference category. As a result, many immigrants were directly or indirectly responsible for twenty-five to fifty new immigrants.

The law set forth a global ceiling of 290,000, but actual totals ranged from 398,089 in 1977 to 904,292 in 1993. Refugees and those exempt from numerical limitations were the two major categories that caused these variations. The refugee count had varied according to situations such as that of the "boat people" from Cuba in 1981. In 1991, refugees and asylees totaled 139,079; in 1993, they totaled 127,343. Persons in nonpreference categories increased from 113,083 in 1976 to 255,059 in

1993. Total immigration for 1991 was 827,167 and for 1993 was 904,292—well above the global ceiling.

The Immigration and Nationality Act of 1965 enabled some of the most able medical, scientific, engineering, skilled, and other professional talent to enter the United States. The medical profession illustrates this trend. In the ten years after the enactment of the 1965 act, seventy-five thousand foreign physicians entered the United States. By 1974, immigrant physicians made up one-fifth of the total number of physicians and one-third of the interns and residents in the United States. Each immigrant doctor represented more than a million dollars in education costs. In addition, they often took positions in the inner-city and rural areas, which prevented the collapse of the delivery of medical services to those locations.   *Arthur W. Helweg*

Core Resources
Roger Daniels's *Coming to America: A History of Immigration and Ethnicity in American Life* (New York: HarperCollins, 1990) analyzes the causes and consequences of the Immigration and Nationality Act of 1965. *Clamor at the Gates: The New American Immigration* (San Francisco: ICS Press, 1985), edited by Nathan Glazer, contains a superb evaluation of the "new immigration" that resulted from the Immigration and Nationality Act of 1965. David M. Reimers's *Still the Golden Door: The Third World Comes to America* (2d ed., New York: Columbia University Press, 1992), provides a detailed study of the passage of the Immigration and Nationality Act of 1965.

See also: Chinese Exclusion Act; Immigration Act of 1917; Immigration Act of 1924; Immigration Act of 1943; Immigration Act of 1990; Immigration and Nationality Act of 1952; Immigration Reform and Control Act of 1986.

Immigration and Naturalization Service

The U.S. attorney general is charged with administering and enforcing all laws relating to aliens' immigration and naturalization. The attorney general delegates most such duties to the Immigration and Naturalization Service (INS). The INS has jurisdiction over aliens in the United States, handling visa petitions, adjusting people's status (as from nonimmigrant to immigrant), granting citizenship, and dealing with deportations and exclusions.

The commissioner of the INS is appointed by the president, normally on the recommendation of the attorney general, with the consent of the Senate. INS

headquarters is located in Washington, D.C. The headquarters handles administrative matters and general policy making almost exclusively. Directly under the headquarters are four INS regional offices. The basic function of the regional offices is fiscal management to assist INS field offices in their areas. Under the four regional offices are thirty-six district offices worldwide and twenty border patrol sectors throughout the United States. The district office is the basic operating unit of the INS. Each district director has authority and responsibility to grant or deny various applications or petitions submitted to the service, to initiate investigations and deportations, and to issue orders to show cause or warrants of arrest in deportation proceedings.   *Wei Luo*

See also: Illegal aliens; Immigration and emigration; Immigration Reform and Control Act of 1986.

Immigration "crisis"

Significance: Immigration to the United States increased steadily after 1965, reaching record levels in the early 1990's. Although earlier immigrants came chiefly from Europe, many of these more recent immigrants arrived from Latin America and Asia. This new trend in immigration increased ethnic diversity in the United States, and both the large numbers and the non-European origins of the immigrants created perceptions of an immigration crisis.

In 1965, the U.S. Congress passed an immigration act that did away with the European bias of the nation's immigration policy and made family reunification, rather than national origin, the primary qualification for admission. At first, it was thought that the Immigration and Nationality Act of 1965 would not greatly expand immigration. However, legal immigration increased from about 250,000 per year in the early 1960's to 1,827,167 in 1991. Illegal immigration, particularly from Mexico, also appears to have increased from the 1960's to the 1990's. A backlash against immigration began to develop among many segments of the American population.

A New Immigrant Population
According to estimates of the U.S. Bureau of the Census, the legal immigrant population in the spring of 1997 contained 25.8 million people. Immigrants, then, made up nearly one out of every ten people in the United States by the end of the 1990's. These were mostly relatively new immigrants: More than 80 percent had arrived since 1970 and more than 60 percent had arrived

Foreign-born Persons Living Legally in the United States in 1997, by Years of Entry

Years of Entry	Number	Percentage of all foreign-born
All years before 1970	4,749,000	18.4
1970-1979	4,935,000	19.2
1980-1989	8,555,000	33.2
1990-1997	7,539,000	29.2
Total	25,778,000	100.0

Source: U.S. Bureau of the Census, Current Population Reports, March, 1997. Washington, D.C.: U.S. Government Printing Office.

since 1980. In addition to these legal immigrants, approximately 300,000 to 400,000 illegal immigrants entered the United States each year. Although many of these illegal immigrants were in the United States only for seasonal or other temporary employment, the Immigration and Naturalization Service has estimated that the illegal immigrant population of the United States was about 4 million people in the 1990's.

Not only were immigrants entering the United States in large numbers; they were also coming from places that had sent relatively few immigrants to America in earlier years. Heavy immigration from Latin America and Asia, combined with comparatively large family sizes among Latin Americans and Asians, began to change the racial and ethnic makeup of the United States. For most of U.S. history, the overwhelming majority of Americans were white Europeans, with a large minority of African Americans. The new immigrants and their children, however, brought a new cultural and racial diversity to the United States. According to projections of the U.S. Bureau of the Census, the white non-Hispanic component of the population could be expected to decline from 72 percent to only 53 percent from the year 2000 to 2050. Black non-Hispanic Americans were expected to increase only slightly during this period, from 12.2 percent to 13.1 percent. Asians, who made up less than 1 percent of the U.S. population in 1970 had increased to almost 3 percent by 1990 ("Asians and Others" constituted 3.8

percent). By 2050, it was predicted that 8 percent of all Americans would be Asian. Hispanics, who were less than 5 percent of the U.S. population in 1970, had grown to 9 percent in 1990. By the year 2050, if ethnic trends in immigration and fertility continued as expected, one out of every four Americans would be Hispanic.

Although most Americans could not engage in the scientific projection of population trends, they were aware that large numbers of immigrants, both legal and illegal, were entering the country. They were also aware of the cultural changes brought about by immigration. In southern Florida, Texas, California, and other parts of the country, English-speaking Americans heard languages they could not understand and came into contact with unfamiliar cultures. Thus, both concern over the amount of immigration and reactions to cultural changes fueled the perception of an immigration crisis.

Economic Concerns over Immigration

Many of those who feel that the flow of immigrants into the United States constitutes a crisis maintain that

Projected Changes in the Ethnic and Racial Composition of the United States, 2000-2050
(Percentage of total U.S. population)

Year	White, non-Hispanic	Black, non-Hispanic	Asian & Pacific Islander	Hispanic
2000	71.8	12.2	3.9	11.4
2005	69.9	12.4	4.4	12.6
2010	68.0	12.6	4.8	13.8
2015	66.1	12.7	5.3	15.1
2020	64.3	12.9	5.7	16.3
2025	62.4	13.0	6.2	17.6
2030	60.5	13.1	6.6	18.9
2035	58.6	13.2	7.1	20.3
2040	56.7	13.3	7.5	21.7
2045	54.7	13.5	7.9	23.1
2050	52.8	13.6	8.2	24.5

Source: U.S. Bureau of the Census, Current Population Reports, Series P25-1130, "Population Projections of the United States by Age, Sex, Race, and Hispanic Origin, 1995 to 2050." March, 1997. Washington, D.C.: U.S. Government Printing Office.

immigration poses serious economic problems. Immigrants, they argue, compete for jobs with people already living in the United States. Under U.S. immigration policy, there are two primary reasons that people from other countries can receive an immigrant visa that gives them permission to settle in the United States. The first reason concerns family: People who have family members who are citizens of or residents in the United States are given priority in the granting of immigrant visas. The second reason concerns employment: People with special professional abilities or workers arriving to take jobs for which Americans are in short supply are eligible for visas.

Roy Beck, a liberal activist and an advocate of limiting immigration, argued that those who receive permission to immigrate for purposes of employment do so at the expense of employees already in the United States. He pointed out that immigration lawyers, who help people find ways to enter the United States, frequently work for businesses that wish to employ foreign labor. These lawyers, according to Beck, help employers draw up job descriptions that make it appear that no qualified American workers are available so that the employers can import cheaper foreign workers.

George Borjas, an economist specializing in immigration issues, maintained that high levels of immigration pose a problem for low-income American workers. Borjas observed that most immigrants enter the United States to join family members, and these immigrants tend to have few job skills and little educational background. Therefore, immigrants were more likely than other people to rely on public assistance, making them a financial burden, and they competed for jobs with low-skilled, low-income natives. In 1996, Borjas estimated that immigration had been the source of about one-third of a recent decline in the wages of less-educated American workers.

Cultural Concerns over Immigration

Some of those alarmed over the influx of immigrants saw it as a cultural crisis. They claimed that immigrants were arriving in such large numbers, with cultures that were so foreign to the existing culture of the United States, that they could not be assimilated readily into American culture.

Journalist Peter Brimelow maintained that immigration posed a crisis for American political culture. The arrival of masses of immigrants who did not speak English, according to Brimelow and others, threatened the position of English as a language understood everywhere around the country. Moreover, cultural critics of immigration argued that newly arrived Mexicans, Dominicans, and Chinese identified with their own cultural backgrounds rather than with mainstream American culture. Therefore, critics such as Brimelow claimed that immigration endangered national unity.

Some of those who believe that massive immigration could create a crisis for U.S. political culture argue that immigration is especially dangerous for African Americans. They point out that African Americans were likely to be replaced as the nation's largest minority and that this would decrease this group's political power. Many opponents of immigration also maintained that new immigrants would have little commitment to overcoming the racial inequality created by the United States' history of slavery and discrimination.

Responses to Claims of Crisis

Although no one denies that immigration increased greatly in the years following 1965, many political figures and scholars question whether this should be seen as an immigration "crisis." Economist Julian Simon argued that immigrants were frequently energetic and industrious and could create, not simply compete for, jobs. The economy of southern Florida, for example, boomed as a result of the activities of Cuban immigrants. Many supporters of immigration, including 1996 vice presidential candidate Jack Kemp, maintained that immigration was an economic blessing, since immigrants often performed work in areas that were experiencing labor shortages.

A number of observers believed that the influx of immigrants posed no threat to American culture. They pointed out that American culture had changed continually throughout its history. Moreover, the sociologist Alejandro Portes and other scholars cited evidence that the children of immigrants overwhelmingly became fluent in English and were often weaker in their parents' languages than they were in English.

Carl L. Bankston III

Core Resources

Roy Beck's *The Case Against Immigration* (New York: W. W. Norton, 1996) presents an economic argument for seeing immigration as a crisis. Peter Brimelow's *Alien Nation: Common Sense About America's Immigration Disaster* (New York: Random House, 1995) provides a controversial but readable argument for drastically reducing immigration to the United States. The articles in *Immigrants Out! The New Nativism and the Anti-Immigrant Impulse in the United States* (New York: New York University Press, 1997), edited by Juan F. Perea, examine the backlash against immigrants and place it in the context of U.S. history.

See also: Assimilation theories; Immigration and Nationality Act of 1965; Immigration Reform and Control Act of 1986.

Immigration law: Canada

Significance: Canadian immigration legislation delineates national responsibility for immigration.

Until the mid-twentieth century, Canada traditionally restricted immigration to northern and western Europeans. After World War II, Canada's economy boomed, and the business lobby exerted pressure to open immigration channels. Starting in the 1950's, Canada needed immigrants in order to have sufficient people to maintain its economy. On the other hand, there was a desire to maintain the predominance of northern and western Europeans in the population.

The Immigration Act of 1952 had contributed to European domination in the Canadian population by giving the minister of immigration and immigration officials wide discretionary powers to open and close off immigration to any group. However, in the 1950's, many Third World countries gained independence, and Canada had to consider their growing importance as trading partners and their influence in the United Nations. Thus, Canada started by assigning small quotas to Asian Commonwealth partners. When the expected inflow from northern and western Europe did not materialize, Canada set up offices in Italy, which started the large Italian influx that climbed into the hundreds of thousands. By the mid-1960's, Italians were the dominant laborers in Canada's construction industry.

Changing Policies

The need for laborers and the refugee issue challenged Canadian immigration policy. The change started in 1956, when Hungarian refugees, following the communist takeover in Hungary, poured into Australia. By sending teams to refugee settlements and setting aside established procedures, Canada successfully resettled thirty-seven thousand Hungarians in Canada. In the early 1960's, the Canadian market for laborers began to shrink, and active immigration work fell by 50 percent. De facto segregation existed during this period: Immigration offices were established in Europe and North America, but only two in Asia.

In the 1960's, illegal entrants became a problem. The numerous illegals caused the creation of a government commission to review all aspects of immigration. The White Paper on Immigration released in 1966 called for a complete and final overhaul of Canadian immigration policy. This policy should be free of discrimination based on race or ethnicity. The white paper also advocated the right of Canadian citizens to sponsor immediate relatives, if their educational and occupa-

tional standards met those of regular immigrants.

When the report came up for discussion in parliamentary committee, ethnic communities exhibited surprising strength. By 1970, they represented one-third of Canada's population and had become a "third force" in Canadian politics. They were confident, had economic affluence, and demanded a new deal for themselves, which included a society that demanded less conformity to the Anglo culture and a more pluralistic focus. One response to these demands, in the later 1960's, was the development and implementation of an equitable immigration system based on domestic economic requirements and on prospects for short-term and long-term integration. From 1967 to the mid-1970's, the key immigration issues for Canada were refugees (Czechoslovakian, Ugandan, Asian, and Chilean) and illegal immigration.

Report on Immigration

In 1972, Robert Andras, who was to be the chief architect of the Immigration Act of 1976, became minister of manpower and immigration. Andras not only revitalized his department but also energetically worked for immigration reform. In September, 1973, he initiated a major review of immigration and population policies, which resulted in the publication of a green paper on the subject. Because there was a lack of scholars and scholarship on the subject, the document was a disappointing, overcautious, and inadequate. Consequently, a Special Joint Committee of the Senate and House of Commons was appointed in March of 1975. The committee held fifty public hearings, heard four hundred witnesses, and received fourteen hundred briefs. The report it presented to Parliament in November, 1975, was warmly received, and sixty of its sixty-five recommendations were accepted. Its principal recommendation was that Canada continue to be a country of immigration, for demographic, economic, family, and humanitarian reasons. The report argued that a new immigration act should contain a clear and formal statement of principal objectives concerning admission, nondiscrimination, sponsorship of relatives, refugees, and classes of persons prohibited. Operational details should be specified in the regulations.

The report communicated that immigration should be a central variable in Canada's population policy to forestall the decline of Canada's population, especially of francophones. In relation to population policy, immigration should be linked to population growth and economic conditions. However, the policy and target figures should be determined and presented for parliamentary scrutiny after consulting with the provinces. Other recommendations were that the point system be retained but modified to encourage settlement in underdeveloped areas, and that more staff be hired and better enforcement procedures be instituted.

Immigration Act of 1976

These recommendations were incorporated into the immigration bill, which had its first reading on November 22, 1976 (hence that year has become linked with the name of the act), received royal assent on August 5, 1977, and became law on April 10, 1978. The act contained constructive provisions and was politically sensitive and forward-looking. It made a positive contribution to the Canadian public image in the area of immigration management. Its most significant provisions were included in a clear statement of the basic principles of Canadian immigration policy, as recommended by the Special Joint Committee—the first time that had been attempted in Canadian immigration law.

The act created a new system of planning and managing Canadian immigration. It sought to involve the provinces in immigration planning and decision making, as well as to open the process to parliamentary and public discussion. The act established three classes of immigrants: family, refugee, and others selected on the basis

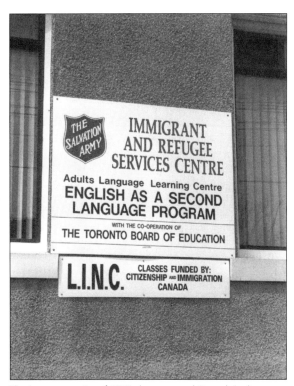

The Immigration Act of 1976 demonstrated Canada's change to a less-restrictive immigration policy. Service centers such as the one operated by the Salvation Army in Toronto help immigrants and refugees settle in Canada.

of the point system. Ministerial discretion was reduced in areas of exclusion, control, and enforcement. Other provisions dealt with refugees, revising the point system and ensuring that actual immigrant landings were consistent with announced immigration levels.

The Immigration Act of 1976 was praised as a responsible and forward-looking piece of legislation. In some respects, the act has proved worthy of that praise. In 1979, Canada's commitment to easing the distress of refugees, displaced persons, and the persecuted was seriously challenged by the "boat people" of Southeast Asia. There was a great outpouring of public concern for the situation. The government dispatched immigration officials to the refugee camps and, by the end of 1980, admitted more than sixty thousand ethnic Vietnamese, Cambodians, Laotians, and Chinese from Southeast Asia—the highest per capita "boat people" resettlement program of any nation. One group that has become highly visible is entrepreneurs, who, with an investment of $250,000, can immigrate to Canada. Hong Kong Chinese have been particularly noticeable in this category.

All has not gone as expected, however. Sympathy for those entering Canada and then claiming refugee status has waned because undocumented immigration continues to be a major problem. The law has resulted in a mounting backlog of more than twenty thousand refugee status-determining cases. The provinces, except for Quebec and Ontario, did not cooperate in setting up population guidelines. The potentially valuable Demographic Policy Steering Group and Demographic Policy Secretariat disappeared, and federal government efforts to develop a population policy were initially stalled. There has been a long-term trend of fertility falling in the industrialized world, especially in Canada, and rising in the nonindustrialized countries. Thus, by the mid-1980's, Canada had to develop a population policy for falling birth rates and emigration to the United States; it had to use immigration as a vital part of its population policy. Because western and northern European countries were no longer significant sources of immigration, Canada turned to Asia a means of maintaining a sufficient population level. The Immigration Act of 1976 nevertheless provided the framework for Canada to adapt to changing circumstances and to exhibit humanitarian behavior by providing refuge to the dispossessed in the world.   *Arthur W. Helweg*

Core Resources

Freda Hawkins's *Canada and Immigration: Public Policy and Public Concern* (2d ed., Kingston, Ont.: McGill-Queen's University Press, 1988) provides the most complete account of Canadian immigration policy. *Immigration and the Rise of Multiculturalism* (Vancouver, B.C.:

Copp Clark, 1975), edited by Howard Palmer, analyzes the relationship of immigrant communities and the development of multiculturalism in Canada. Reginald Whitaker's *Double Standard: The Secret History of Canadian Immigration* (Toronto: Lester & Orpen Dennys, 1987) discusses the unequal application of immigration policies to different ethnic groups.

See also: Multiculturalism Act; Multiculturalism in Canada; Refugees: Canadian policy.

Immigration Reform and Control Act of 1986

> **Significance:** The Immigration Reform and Control Act provided for the legalization of illegal aliens and established sanctions against employers who hire undocumented workers.

The Immigration Reform and Control Act (IRCA) was signed into law by President Ronald Reagan on November 6, 1986. The act amended the Immigration and Nationality Act of 1965 and was based in part on the findings and recommendations of the Select Commission on Immigration and Refugee Policy (1978-1981). In its 1981 report to Congress, this commission had proposed that the United States continue to accept large numbers of immigrants and enact a program of amnesty for undocumented aliens already in the United States. To deter migration of undocumented aliens to the United States, the commission also proposed to make the employment of illegal aliens a punishable offense.

Development of the Bill

These proposals were incorporated into the Simpson-Mazzoli bill, a first version of which was introduced in 1982. In the five years between its introduction and its enactment, the bill ran into opposition from a variety of quarters. Agricultural interests, especially growers of perishable commodities, were concerned that the proposed employer sanctions would jeopardize their labor supply. Mexican American advocacy groups also opposed employer sanctions, while organized labor and restrictionists who were concerned about the massive influx of foreign workers favored employer sanctions. Many liberals and humanitarians supported the notion of legalizing the status of undocumented aliens and expressed concerns over potential discrimination against them.

In the 1980's, the bill repeatedly was pronounced dead only to be revived again as various lawmakers, notably Representatives Leon Panetta, Charles Schumer, and Peter Rodino, introduced compromises and amendments to respond to their constituencies or to overcome opposition by congressional factions. Differences also developed between the House Democratic leadership and the Republican White House over funding the legalization program. On October 15, 1986, the House at last approved the bill, by a vote of 238 to 173; the Senate approved the bill on October 17, by a vote of 63 to 24.

Provisions

The major components of the Immigration Control and Reform Act provided for the control of illegal immigration (Title I), the legalization of undocumented aliens (Title II), and the reform of legal immigration (Title III). Other sections of the act provided for reports to Congress (Title IV), state assistance for the incarceration costs of illegal aliens and certain Cuban nationals (Title V), the creation of a commission for the study of international migration and cooperative economic development (Title VI), and federal responsibility for deportable and excludable aliens convicted of crimes (Title VII).

A major objective of the IRCA, the control of illegal immigration, was to be achieved by imposing sanctions on employers. The IRCA made it unlawful for any person knowingly to hire, recruit, or refer for a fee any alien not authorized to work in the United States. Before hiring new employees, employers would be required to examine certain specified documents to verify a job applicant's identity and authority to work.

The act established civil and criminal penalties, and employers could be fined up to two thousand dollars per unauthorized alien, even for a first offense. Employers who demonstrated a pattern of knowingly hiring undocumented aliens could face felony penalties of up to six months' imprisonment and/or a three-thousand-dollar fine per violation. Employers also were required to keep appropriate records. Failure to do so could result in a civil fine of up to one thousand dollars. In order to allow time for a public education campaign to become effective, penalties against employers for hiring undocumented aliens were not phased in until June, 1987.

The second major objective of the IRCA, the legalization of undocumented aliens, was to be realized by granting temporary residence status to aliens who had entered the United States illegally prior to January 1, 1982, and who had resided in the United States continuously since then. They could be granted permanent residence status after eighteen months if they could demonstrate a minimal understanding of English and some knowledge of the history and government of the United States. After a five-year period of permanent residence, they would become eligible for citizenship.

The act also permitted the attorney general to grant legal status to aliens who could show that they had entered the United States prior to January, 1972, and lived in the country since then. Newly legalized aliens were barred from most forms of public assistance for five years, although exceptions could be made for emergency medical care, aid to the blind or disabled, or other assistance deemed to be in the interest of public health.

To assure passage of the bill, support of the growers in the West and Southwest was essential. After protracted negotiations, the growers succeeded in getting the kind of legislation that assured them of a continued supply of temporary agricultural workers. The new program differed from earlier bracero programs by providing for the legalization of special agricultural workers who could work anywhere and who could become eligible for permanent resident status or for citizenship. The IRCA granted temporary residence status to aliens who had performed field labor in perishable agricultural commodities in the United States for at least ninety days during the twelve-month period ending May 1, 1986, as well as to persons who could demonstrate to the Immigration and Naturalization Service that they had performed appropriate agricultural field labor for ninety days in three successive previous years while residing in the United States for six months in each year.

The act also revised and expanded an existing temporary foreign worker program known as H-2. In case of a shortage of seasonal farmworkers, employers could apply to the secretary of labor no more than sixty days in advance of needing workers. The employer also was required to try to recruit domestic workers for the jobs. H-2 also provided that during fiscal years 1990-1993, additional special agricultural workers could be admitted to temporary residence status as "replenishment workers." Their admission was contingent upon certification of the need for such workers by the secretaries of labor and of agriculture. Replenishment workers who performed ninety days of field work in perishable agricultural commodities in each of the first three years would be eligible for permanent resident status. They were, however, disqualified from public assistance. In order to become eligible for citizenship, they would have to perform seasonal agricultural services for ninety days during five separate years.

The IRCA also provided permanent resident status for a hundred thousand specified Cubans and Haitians who entered the United States prior to January 1, 1982. The law increased quotas from former colonies and dependencies from five hundred to six thousand and provided for the admission of five thousand immigrants annually for two years, to be chosen from nationals of thirty-six countries with low rates of immigration. Alto-gether, the Immigration Reform and Control Act led to the legalization of the status of three million aliens; however, IRCA was not as successful in curbing illegal immigration as had been anticipated.

Mindful of the potential for discrimination, Congress established an Office of Special Counsel in the Department of Justice to investigate and prosecute charges of discrimination connected with unlawful immigration practices. The act also required states to verify the status of noncitizens applying for public aid and provided that states be reimbursed for the implementation costs of this provision. To reimburse states for the public assistance, health, and education costs resulting from legalizing aliens, the act provided for the appropriation of one billion dollars in each of the four fiscal years following its enactment. *Helmut J. Schmeller*

Core Resources

Frank D. Bean, Georges Vernez, and Charles B. Keely's *Opening and Closing the Doors: Evaluating Immigration Reform and Control* (Washington, D.C.: Rand Corporation and the Urban Institute, 1989) is a scholarly study of the IRCA, its implementation, and its impact on illegal immigration. Lawrence H. Fuchs's *The American Kaleidoscope: Race, Ethnicity, and the Civic Culture* (Hanover, N.H.: University Press of New England, 1990) contains a concise, well-documented discussion of the act. Aristide R. Zolberg's "Reforming the Back Door: The Immigration Reform and Control Act of 1986 in Historical Perspective," in *Immigration Reconsidered: History, Sociology, and Politics* (New York: Oxford University Press, 1990), edited by Virginia Yans-McLaughlin, is a comprehensive, well-documented account of the genesis of the IRCA.

See also: Bracero program; Immigration Act of 1917; Immigration Act of 1924; Immigration Act of 1943; Immigration Act of 1990; Immigration and Nationality Act of 1965.

Incorporation

Incorporation is the process whereby social groups, classes, and individuals are integrated into a larger social entity. This is achieved either through the extension of rights and the subsequent exacting of obligations, as in "citizenship communities," or through mechanisms such as social mobility, intermarriage, and urban desegregation. Like social closure, incorporation implies marginalized groups, elite mass relations, and co-optation. The term has been widely employed in discussions about the allegedly revolutionary role of the proletariat, whose historical mission is said to have been frustrated by the incorporation of this class through the welfare state, political representation, and home ownership. However, the term has expanded to include racial, ethnic, gender, and religious groups.

For racial and ethnic groups, incorporation can be seen as a form of assimilation. For ethnic groups to achieve rights, they not only have to acquire citizenship but also must relinquish parts of their ethnic culture to be included in mainstream society. Incorporation can also be seen as form of social and political movement, in which ethnic minority groups collectively pressure the larger society to accept and include their ethnic groups in the mainstream society.   *Mary Yu Danico*

See also: Assimilation: cultural and structural; Ethnicity and ethnic groups; Marital assimilation.

Indentured servitude

Indentured servitude is a labor relationship in which the laborer contracts to work exclusively for a single employer for a fixed period of time. Although this contract, or indenture, represents a free act of the contracting parties, it legally binds the laborer to the employer during the term fixed by the agreement. Indentured servitude initially played an important role in inducing settlement of the original American colonies. In its most common form, the employer paid the passage of a laborer to the New World, a sum that was beyond the means of ordinary laborers in Europe. In return, the laborer would agree to work for an extended period, usually seven years, in the colonies. At the end of the period of indenture, the servant would acquire land and perhaps an amount of money for fulfilling the terms of the contract, thus becoming free and independent again.

The system of indentured servitude paved the way for the establishment of slavery in North America. The first African Americans to arrive in today's mainland United States, in 1619, came as indentured servants. The expansive need for labor generated by the size of the colonies and the labor-intensive cultivation of such cash crops as tobacco was too great, however, to be met exclusively by indentured servitude. As a result, Africans were captured and imported into the colonies.   *Aristide Sechandice*

See also: Slavery: history; Slavery: North American beginnings.

Indian

In its use to refer to the native peoples of the Americas, the term "Indian" is based on historical error. In the late

fifteenth century, there was some disagreement over the size of the earth, although it had been accurately determined by the ancient Greeks many centuries earlier. Christopher Columbus and explorers who followed him believed the earth's circumference to be roughly half what we know it to be today.

The purpose of the early explorations of the Americas was to find a pathway to India by sailing west instead of east from Europe, primarily to avoid trouble with the Muslim nations that controlled the territory between Europe and India. Apparently, Columbus thought he had reached India when he landed on the island of Hispaniola (today occupied by Haiti and the Dominican Republic), named the area the West Indies, and referred to the natives as *indios* (Spanish for Indians).

While the later British and French explorers who landed in North America did not believe that Massachusetts and Quebec were India, the term was still used, translated into the appropriate languages. The term is still in wide use essentially because no better collective term has been widely accepted. Some native people find the term "Indian" deeply offensive, whereas others find it and "American Indian" acceptable and even preferable to such well-intentioned revisions as "Native American" or the less widely used "Amerind." The most accurate—and most widely accepted—way to identify a person or tradition is simply to refer to the specific tribe or group to which the person or tradition belongs.
                                        Marc Goldstein

See also: Amerind; Native American.

Indian Act of 1876

The Indian Act of 1876, the Canadian parliament's first major piece of legislation setting forth the federal government's role and responsibilities with respect to the Indians, continued nearly all of the policies established during British colonial rule. As with the British policy, the dual features of the legislation were the protection of the Indians and their eventual assimilation into Canadian society. Ironically, these goals worked at cross purposes. Paternalistic efforts to protect the Indians emphasized the distinctions between Indians and Euro-Canadians and therefore actually discouraged assimilation. This legislation first applied only to Canadians of Indian descent. It was later extended to include the Inuit as well.

The act established a series of reserved lands, which were to be laboratories for training the Indians in the ways of whites, and established elected band councils whose powers were minimal. The reserves, administered by a government agent, were exempt from taxation, and those living on a reserve had access to food and supplies in the form of disaster rations. While the reserves were intended to protect the supposedly naïve Indians from the unscrupulous practices of outsiders, they isolated Indians from most Euro-Canadians and subjected them to the sometimes unscrupulous practices of the all-powerful Indian agents. These agents had control over social, political, and economic activities on the reserves. They also had the ability to withhold rations from those who did not adhere to their dictatorial policies.

Numerous abuses occurred. For several decades Indians on the prairies were forbidden to leave their reserve without a pass from the agent. They were further prohibited from staying overnight on a reserve other than their own, and in many cases non-Indians (including non-Status Indians) were forbidden to reside on reserves. Subsequent amendments to the Indian Act banned native religious activities such as the Sun Dance and potlatch and made it illegal for Indians to solicit contributions in order to pursue land claims.

The act codified the category "Indian" as a legal rather than racial or cultural designation and gave the government the legal power to determine who qualified as an Indian. It further provided for the enfranchisement of individuals, wherein a man could surrender Indian status for himself, his wife, and his children in exchange for Canadian citizenship and a plot of land. Women who married non-Indians, including non-status Indians, lost their own Indian status and benefits. Their children were also precluded from claiming Indian status. Non-Indian women who married Status Indians became Status Indians themselves. Enfranchisement could also be imposed upon Indians who earned a college degree or entered a profession such as minister, teacher, lawyer, or doctor. Though amended many times, the Indian Act was not significantly revised until 1951.

See also: Department of Indian Affairs and Northern Development; Indian Act of 1951; Indian Act of 1989; Indian-white relations: Canada; Reserve system of Canada; Treaties and agreements with Indians: Canada; Voting rights of aboriginals: Canada.

Indian Act of 1951

Although the Indian Act of 1951 was the first comprehensive revision of Canada's 1876 Indian Act, it did little to undo the paternalism of its predecessor. Like the previous law, it gave nearly absolute control of Indian activities to the Department of Indian Affairs and Northern Development (DIAND). This included the development of Indian lands and resources as well as oversight of band councils. The new act also retained the enfran-

chisement provisions of the earlier legislation, including those that denied Indian status to women who married non-Indians. In a well-known sex discrimination suit brought by Jeannette Lavell, an Ojibwa who was denied Indian status as a result of her marriage, the Supreme Court in 1973 upheld those provisions of the act. A Maliceet woman, Sandra Lovelace, took a similar case before the United Nations in 1981. Although Canada was found to have violated international human rights covenants, the enfranchisement provisions of the Indian Act were not repealed until 1985.

The new act did, however, repeal the most blatant discrimination inherent in the Indian Act of 1876. It no longer prohibited Indian religious ceremonies, political fund-raising, or consumption of alcohol off reserve lands. Later amendments permitted the consumption of alcohol on reserves and gave Indians the right to vote in Canadian elections.

The 1951 act continued a number of benefits of the earlier legislation, including the exemption of Indian lands from property and estate taxes and exemption of income earned on reserves from taxation. Although these provisions have protected Indian property from seizure, they have also hindered economic development on the reserves. Because Indians have been unable to mortgage their lands, it has often been difficult for them to raise capital for development projects.

Despite the restrictions imposed by the 1951 Indian Act, natives have fought efforts to discard it altogether. Fearing that the federal government would abandon its responsibilities to native welfare, many natives fought the 1969 white paper proposal to repeal the Indian Act. The Indian Act was rewritten in 1985, but other than the repeal of enfranchisement provisions, it remained virtually unchanged.

See also: Department of Indian Affairs and Northern Development; Indian Act of 1876; Indian Act of 1989; Indian-white relations: Canada; Reserve system of Canada; Treaties and agreements with Indians: Canada; Voting rights of aboriginals: Canada.

Indian Act of 1989

Because of the confusion created by a diversity of local laws in different provinces under the federal government in Canada, legislators have created certain acts that cannot vary according to locality. Such is the case of the Indian Act of 1989. In effect a compendium of earlier acts (of 1927 and 1951), it also added new laws more in keeping with contemporary conditions.

The main divisions of the act provide for the designation of reserves (land vested in Her Majesty's Crown, but "reserved for Indian use"), establishment of band councils and election of band leaders, and a comprehensive Indian Register. By the act, the sole authority of the band council to assign possession of specific reserve lands to individuals is recognized for the first time. This right of possession must be recognized by the Superintendent General of Indian Affairs, who issues a Certificate of Possession. Possessors may transfer their land rights, but only to other members within their band, or back to the band council itself.

Provisions respecting the security of reserves against government expropriation ended misunderstandings that had developed over many years. With the right of security went defined areas of band responsibility (to maintain roads, bridges, and so on) which, if unfulfilled, could lead to government charges against band councils. Common responsibility between councils and government for revenues accruing to bands (through royalties or sale of Indian produced goods) is spelled out, including the government right to use such funds to assure proper sanitary facilities and disease control.

One use of government funds on reserves reflects benevolent subsidies under the 1989 act. Schools are to be provided to all bands on an equal basis, and attendance up to a minimum age is required of all Indian children. Provisions for tax-exempt status (lands, personal property, or salaries earned in reserve areas) and taxable income earned from contacts beyond the reserves are meant to protect both Indian and government interests.

The act contains brief mention of individual rights. There is a right of testamentary wills for family security. Otherwise, where individual Indian rights might be jeopardized owing to band council inaction, government intervention is allowed (mainly to aid orphans or the mentally handicapped). *Byron D. Cannon*

See also: Department of Indian Affairs and Northern Development; Indian Act of 1876; Indian Act of 1951; Indian-white relations: Canada; Reserve system of Canada; Treaties and agreements with Indians: Canada; Voting rights of aboriginals: Canada.

Indian Appropriation Act

Significance: With the 1871 passage of the Indian Appropriation Act, the U.S. Congress unilaterally determined that Native Americans no longer belonged to their own sovereign nations, ending treaty making between U.S. and tribal governments.

In 1871, Congress voted to end treaty making with Native American peoples. Since the origins of the republic, the U.S. government had dealt with tribes by recognizing each one as an independent nation living within the United States. Hence, ambassadors were sent out from Washington, D.C., to negotiate treaties, and each agreement had to be ratified by two-thirds of the Senate, as provided in the Constitution. Chief Justice John Marshall, in *Worcester v. Georgia* (1832), had determined that this process had to be followed because each tribe was self-governing and sovereign in its own territory.

The change took place because many people in the United States came to believe that the Native American nations no longer acted like sovereign states. They were too weak, post-Civil War whites believed, and many had become dependent on the federal government for their existence. Members of Congress expressed that view in a series of discussions on American Indian policy in 1870-1871. In the House of Representatives, a sense had also arisen that the House was being ignored in the development of Indian policy. The only way the House could influence Native American relations was by renouncing the treaty concept. The attack on treaty making gained strength during the debate over the money to be appropriated for the United States Board of Indian Commissioners. This agency had been created in 1869 to oversee money authorized to be spent on Indian programs.

End of Treaty Making Proposed

The commissioners' first report suggested major changes in Indian policy. It called for ending the treaty system and dealing with "uncivilized" native peoples as "wards of the government." Board chair Felix R. Brunot echoed the views of many U.S. citizens when he declared that it was absurd to treat "a few thousand savages" as if they were equal with the people and government of the United States. President Ulysses S. Grant supported that view, as did his commissioner of Indian affairs, Ely S. Parker, a member of the Seneca nation. Parker believed that it was a cruel farce to deal with the tribes as equals; in his view, most were "helpless and ignorant wards" of the federal government.

The resentment of members of the House of Representatives at their exclusion from Indian policymaking became apparent during debates over treaties negotiated in 1868 and 1869. A May, 1868, agreement with the Osage Nation in Kansas had ceded eight million acres of land to the government. The land then would be sold to a railroad company for twenty cents per acre. The House voted unanimously to recommend that the Senate not ratify the treaty because the land transfer had taken place outside the traditional methods of selling public property. The Senate responded to the House plea by rejecting the treaty. Later, however, the land was sold to the railroad company with the approval of the House.

The House took up the issue of treaty making again in 1869 during a violent debate over the Indian appropriation for 1870. It provided money for food, clothes, and education for tribe members living on reservations. The House refused to accept an increase in funds voted by the Senate. Representatives also began to question whether native peoples were capable of signing official treaties with the United States. Most members attacked the traditional system, although three congressmen spoke in favor of the treaty process. Representative William Windom of Minnesota argued that changing the process would be a breach of faith with the tribes. Revoking the process would create great confusion among Native Americans and add to their distrust of the U.S. government.

Representative John J. Logan, Republican of Illinois, responded for the majority, however, by declaring that "the idea of this Government making treaties with bands of wild and roving Indians is simply preposterous and ridiculous." Amid loud cheers and laughter, Logan attacked the character of native peoples and suggested that they were an inferior race that should not be treated as equal in status to the people of the United States. The House refused to approve the appropriation, and the Senate refused to compromise; therefore, no Indian appropriation bill passed Congress in 1869.

In the debate over the 1871 appropriation, both sides raised the same arguments. In the Senate, supporters of the treaty system argued that any change would severely injure any goodwill native peoples still held toward the U.S. government system. Senator Richard Yates reiterated the antitreaty sentiment, declaring that the tribes were not civilized and that making treaties with them had been a mistake. The Senate, however, passed an appropriation bill and sent it to the House. While the debate took place, many tribes were waiting for the money due to them under treaties negotiated in 1868 and 1869. Unless Congress agreed to an appropriation bill, they would receive nothing. In a compromise arranged between the two legislative branches, a sum of two million dollars was appropriated to pay off prior obligations. Debate over the appropriation for the next year bogged down in the House, however.

The Board of Indian Commissioners helped the House position by calling for an end to treaty making and for abrogating all existing agreements. Only Representative Eugene M. Wilson of Minnesota spoke in favor of continuing the historic policy. If Native Americans were not protected by treaties, they would be cheated out of their lands by white speculators and end up with nothing, he argued. Debate in the Senate and the House seemed far more concerned with constitutional technicalities than with the welfare of native peoples. Once

more, no bill seemed possible. On the last day of the session, President Grant urged a compromise, or, he warned, a war with the tribes was sure to break out. Under this threat, Congress agreed to put aside its differences temporarily and passed a bill.

The Act Is Created

When the new Congress opened on January 4, 1871, Representative Henry Dawes of Massachusetts led the call for change. Dawes, who in 1887 would author a major bill in the Senate drastically changing policy toward native peoples, called for a quick program of assimilation in this earlier debate. If natives were to become Americanized—a policy he supported—they should be treated as individuals rather than as members of foreign nations. Native peoples were not and never had been equal to the United States. The House passed a bill denouncing "so-called treaties."

In the Senate, an amendment to delete the words "so-called" before "treaties" led to a vigorous debate. Senator William Morris Stewart of Nevada objected to the amendment. "The whole Indian policy of feeding drunken, worthless, vagabond Indians, giving them money to squander . . . has been a growing disgrace to our country for years." Treaties with "irresponsible tribes" were no treaties at all. Only a few senators agreed with this amendment, however, and "so-called" was eliminated. This angered the House, which refused to accept the Senate version.

Many congressmen and senators were tired of the endless debate and seemed willing to compromise. A conference committee of senators and representatives agreed that past treaties would be accepted or the integrity of the United States would be compromised. It agreed that no more treaties should be negotiated with Native Americans, however. Most conferees agreed that the tribes remaining hardly seemed like legitimate nations, as they were too small, weak, and miserable. The final compromise asserted the validity of prior agreements but provided that in the future, "no Indian nation or tribe within the territory of the United States shall be acknowledged or recognized as an independent nation, tribe, or power with whom the United States may contract by treaty." Both the Senate and the House accepted the compromise, and President Grant signed it into law on March 3, 1871. Treaties would no longer be negotiated with Native American peoples. Native Americans would, instead, become "wards of the state."

Leslie V. Tischauser

Core Resources

Fay G. Cohen's *Treaties on Trial: The Continuing Controversy over Northwest Indian Fishing Rights* (Seattle: University of Washington Press, 1986) shows the continuing importance of treaties and the bitterness still evoked by pre-1871 agreements. Dorothy V. Jones's *License for Empire: Colonialism by Treaty in Early America* (Chicago: University of Chicago Press, 1982) discusses abuses of the treaty system and how native peoples failed to understand the process. Francis Paul Prucha's *American Indian Treaties: The History of a Political Anomaly* (Berkeley: University of California Press, 1994) gives the full story of the treaty-making process and its end.

See also: Apache Wars; Indian Removal Act; Indian-white relations: United States; Long Walk; Trail of Tears.

Indian Child Welfare Act

The Indian Child Welfare Act, passed into law in 1978, establishes minimum federal standards for the removal of Indian children from their families and the placement of these children in foster or adoptive homes. In essence, the act restricts the placement of Indian children in non-Indian homes and gives jurisdiction to tribal courts in deciding matters of child welfare involving adoptive or foster placement. The law removes state jurisdiction in most Indian child welfare cases, even when problems occur off the reservation.

The law affirms the continued existence and the integrity of Indian tribes and was specifically designed to end discriminatory practices of state and county welfare agencies which disregarded Indian extended family arrangements and placed large numbers of Indian children in non-Indian homes. Senate hearings conducted in 1974 documented evidence that as many as 25 percent of Indian children were being systematically removed from their natural families. This in turn was causing the breakup of the Indian family and a high degree of social disruption in Indian communities.

The law provides that when foster care or adoption is necessary, the child's extended family has first priority to assume custody. If no extended family member is available, a member of the child's tribe or an Indian from another tribe has priority over non-Indians.

Carole A. Barrett

See also: Indian-white relations: United States.

Indian Citizenship Act

The Indian Citizenship Act conferred U.S. citizenship on all American Indians born within the territorial limits of the United States, permitting dual U.S. and tribal citizenship, but did little to secure or improve Native Americans' rights.

American Indians hold a unique position in American society and law, so the acquisition of citizenship took special congressional action. Several factors made citizenship difficult to obtain. As long as Indians were members of tribes or nations which negotiated treaties with the United States government as independent political units, they could not be considered American citizens. Two significant rulings made it clear that a specific act of Congress would eventually be required to grant Indians citizenship. An 1870 Senate committee on the judiciary ruled that tribal Indians were not granted citizenship under the Fourteenth Amendment (1868), which gave citizenship to recently emancipated slaves, because Indians were not subject to the jurisdiction of the United States. In 1884, in *Elk v. Wilkins*, an Indian who had severed tribal relations and lived among whites was ruled ineligible to be a United States citizen because he had been born a tribal member.

By the 1880's many in the United States sought to end tribal sovereignty, to individualize Indians, and to make them citizens. The General Allotment Act (1887) therefore carried provisions for citizenship as a reward for adopting "the habits of civilized life." In 1901 a congressional act granted every Indian in Oklahoma Territory citizenship, and by 1917, through a variety of federal statutes, more than two-thirds of all Native Americans were United States citizens. It was World War I that reopened the debate about citizenship for all Indians.

American Indians actively supported the war effort through increased food production and contributions to the Red Cross. Most dramatically, six to ten thousand Indians, many of whom were not citizens, enlisted for military service. In return, through the act of November 6, 1919, Congress provided any Indian who received an honorable discharge from military service during World War I the right to apply for citizenship with no restriction on the right to tribal property. Still, by 1920, 125,000 Indians were not citizens, so in 1923 a citizenship bill for all Indians was introduced in Congress. Political maneuverings began at once.

Many mainstream Americans favored citizenship as a way to sever the legal relationship between Indian tribes and the federal government. Full-bloods in many tribes were fearful that citizenship would end tribal sovereignty, bring them under state jurisdiction, and ultimately destroy tribal values. These conflicting views led to a compromise. In January, 1924, Congressman Homer P. Snyder of New York introduced House Resolution 6355, authorizing the secretary of the interior to grant citizenship to all Indians yet stating that "the granting of such citizenship shall not in any manner impair or otherwise affect the right of any Indian to tribal or other property." The American Indian Citizenship Act, signed into law on June 2, 1924, by President

Calvin Coolidge, made Indians both citizens of the United States and persons with tribal relations. Ultimately citizenship changed little for Indians; the Bureau of Indian Affairs continued to treat Indians as wards of the government and to administer affairs for Indian citizens, and many Indians were denied the right to vote until the 1960's.

See also: American Indian civil rights; American Indian Civil Rights Act; American Indian Religious Freedom Act; Civil rights; Voting rights of American Indians.

Indian Claims Commission

The Indian Claims Commission was established by act of Congress in 1946. Its mandate was to review all pending territorial claims by native peoples within the forty-eight contiguous states and, where these were found to be valid, to retire them through payment of appropriate compensation.

Although the life of the commission was originally expected to be ten years, the sheer volume of the cases it encountered caused its duration to be repeatedly extended. When it was finally suspended on September 30, 1978, the ICC still had a docket of sixty-eight cases remaining to be heard (these were reassigned to the U.S. Court of Claims). In the interim, it had considered several hundred separate claims which, in aggregate, led it to reach some rather striking conclusions in its final report.

As Russel Barsh summarized the ICC's general findings, "about half a country was purchased by treaty or agreement at an average price of less than a dollar an acre; another third of a [billion] acres, mainly in the west, were confiscated without compensation; another two-thirds of a [billion] acres were claimed by the United States without presence of a unilateral action extinguishing title."

Since the ICC was specifically precluded under its authorizing legislation from effecting transfers of land title where none had previously occurred, the clear implication of the last finding was that legal ownership of the land in question remained vested in American Indians. In effect, then, the United States was engaged in the illegal occupation of approximately one-third of its claimed "domestic" territoriality. There was, however, little the ICC could do to rectify the situation, even if it had been so inclined, because its authorizing legislation also prevented it from actually restoring property to its rightful owners. *Ward Churchill*

See also: Allotment system; Indian Reorganization Act.

Indian Education Acts

The Indian Education Act of 1972, Public Law 92-318, was an attempt to remedy some of the problems in Indian education identified in the National Study of American Indian Education (carried out from 1967 to 1971) and in the hearings of the Special Senate Subcommittee on Indian Education that summarized its findings in 1969 under the title *Indian Education: A National Tragedy, a National Challenge* (also known as the Kennedy Report). Both studies found that Indian people wanted a better education for their children, wanted schools to pay more attention to Indian heritage, and wanted more to say in how their children's schools were run.

The 1972 act pertained to public schools on and off reservations and provided supplemental funding for schools with ten or more Indian students in order to meet their special needs. All public schools with Indian students could get this quasi-entitlement funding and were required to involve Indian parents and communities in designing the supplemental programs. Grant money was also provided.

Part A of the act required parental and community participation in impact-aid programs (programs that provided federal money to local school districts to make up for tax-exempt federal lands such as Indian reservations). Part B authorized a series of grant programs to stress culturally relevant and bilingual curriculum materials. Part C provided money for adult-education projects. Part D established an Office of Indian Education within the U.S. Office of Education (now the Department of Education). Part E provided funds for training teachers for Bureau of Indian Affairs (BIA) schools, with preference to be given to Indians. The act also established the National Advisory Council on Indian Education.

The Indian Education Amendments of 1978 (P.L. 95-561) established standards for BIA schools, institutionalized BIA school boards, required formula funding of BIA schools, and provided for increased Indian involvement in the spending of impact-aid funds. *Jon Reyhner*

See also: American Indian civil rights; Education and American Indians; Indian Citizenship Act; Kennedy Report.

Indian Gaming Regulatory Act

Significance: The Indian Gaming Regulatory Act regulates gaming on Indian lands by dividing it into three classes and authorizing compacts between tribes and states.

The Indian Gaming Regulatory Act of 1988 regulates and permits gaming on Indian reservations. Since its passage, many casinos, such as this one on the Morongo Indian Reservation in Cabazon, California, have opened.

The Indian Gaming Regulatory Act (IGRA), signed into law on October 17, 1988, by President George Bush, represents an amalgamation of ideas presented in various bills introduced in Congress from 1983 through 1987 and provides a system to permit and regulate gaming on American Indian lands.

The IGRA divides gaming into three classes. Class I gaming includes social games of minimal value, as well as traditional games played as a part of tribal ceremonies or celebrations. Class I gaming is exclusively regulated by the tribes. Class II gaming includes bingo, and if played within the same location, pull tabs, lotto, tip jars, instant bingo, games similar to bingo, and certain card games. A tribe may engage in Class II games if the state in which the tribe is located permits such gaming for any purpose by any person, organization, or entity. Class III gaming includes all forms of gaming other than Class I or II, for example, banking card games like blackjack, baccarat and chemin de fer, slot machines, craps, pari-mutuel horse racing, and dog racing. Class III gaming is prohibited unless authorized by a tribal-state compact.

In addition to classifying games, the IGRA established a three-member National Indian Gaming Commission within the Department of the Interior. The commission chairman is appointed by the president of the United States with Senate approval; the other two members are appointed by the secretary of the interior. At least two members must be enrolled members of an American Indian tribe. The commission has the power to approve all tribal gaming ordinances and resolutions, shut down gaming activities, levy and collect fines, and approve gaming management contracts for Class II and Class III gaming. The commission has broad power to monitor Class II gaming by inspecting gaming permits, conducting background investigations of personnel, and inspecting and auditing books and records. Regulation and jurisdiction of Class III gaming are more complicated. Class III gaming is lawful when it is authorized by a tribal ordinance, approved by the chairman of the commis-

sion, located in a state that permits such gaming (whether for charitable, commercial, or government purposes), and conducted in compliance with a tribal-state compact that is approved by the secretary of the interior.

A tribe seeking to conduct Class III gaming must request that the state in which its lands are located negotiate a tribal-state compact governing the conduct of gaming activities. The compact may include provisions concerning the application of tribal or state criminal and civil laws directly related to gaming, the allocation of jurisdiction between the state and tribe, state assessments to defray the costs of regulation, standards for operation and maintenance of the gaming facility, and other subjects related to the gaming activity. The state is not authorized to impose a tax or assessment upon a tribe unless the tribe agrees. The state cannot refuse to negotiate a compact based on its inability to impose a tax, fee, or other assessment.

The question of gaming on American Indian reservations is one that involves both sovereignty and economic issues for tribes and states alike. The IGRA grants United States district courts jurisdiction over actions by tribes. Reasons for such action include failure of a state to negotiate with a tribe seeking to enter a compact; failure of the state to negotiate in good faith; or any violation of the tribal-state compact. The IGRA provides that a federal district court may order a tribe and state to reach a compact if the state fails to meet its burden of proving that it negotiated in good faith. If no compact is forthcoming, a court may appoint a mediator to recommend a compact. In March, 1996, the United States Supreme Court ruled in *Seminole Tribe of Indians v. Florida* that Congress cannot force states into federal court to settle disputes over gambling on reservations. Federal law, through the IGRA, still permits tribes to seek help from the secretary of the interior when state officials balk at tribal plans for gaming operations.

The IGRA requires that all gaming facilities be tribally

owned and that revenue from gaming operations be directed for specific tribal programs, such as education, elderly programs, or housing. Restriction of gaming to tribal governments ensures that American Indian gaming remains a government function rather than a personal endeavor.

Controversy

The most controversial aspect of the IGRA involves the tribal-state compact required for Class III gaming. Tribal sovereignty is diminished by the IGRA, because it forces states and tribes into an agreement. Most laws recognize that tribes have a government-to-government relationship with the federal government and are not under state jurisdiction unless there is prior agreement (as Public Law 280 states). Nevertheless, the IGRA specifically requires negotiations between tribes and states.

States have objected to tribal-state compacting on the grounds that it violates their sovereignty under the Eleventh Amendment of the Constitution, which protects states from being sued in federal court against their will. In a 1996 Supreme Court decision, it was ruled that Congress cannot attempt to resolve stalled negotiations between states and tribes over on-reservation gambling by making states and their officials targets of federal lawsuits. The Eleventh Amendment rights of states were upheld.

The IGRA has been embraced by many tribes in the United States as a way to bolster reservation economies. Some of the most poverty-stricken areas in the United States are American Indian reservations, and gaming revenues give tribes income to reinvest in other business ventures. However, the compacting process can result in conflict of interest for some states that rely heavily on gaming revenues. In addition, the issue of untaxed revenues resulting from American Indian gaming operations is a factor in establishing compacts, and states in need of such revenue cannot act dispassionately with tribes when they negotiate those compacts. Gaming on American Indian reservations is fraught with issues of competing interests for both tribes and states.   *Carole A. Barrett*

Core Resources

William C. Canby's *American Indian Law in a Nutshell* (Minneapolis: West, 1981) provides simple explanations of complex legal issues in dealings between the federal government, states, and tribal nations. Allan A. MacFarlan's *Book of American Indian Games* (New York: Associated Press, 1958) discusses and describes various games, including gambling games, played by a variety of North American tribes. Roland J. Santoni's "The Indian Gaming Regulatory Act: How Did We Get Here? Where Are We Going?" (*Creighton Law Review* 26, 1993) provides a comprehensive chronology of the legislation, perti-

nent legal cases, suggested amendments, and a table of tribal-state compacts. Charles F. Wilkinson's *American Indians, Time, and the Law: Native Societies in a Modern Constitutional Democracy* (New Haven, Conn.: Yale University Press, 1987) discusses tribal sovereignty as a preconstitutional right and how this inherent right can be diminished.

See also: American Indian civil rights; American Indian Civil Rights Act; Determined Residents United for Mohawk Sovereignty; Gambling; Reservation system of the United States.

Indian New Deal

The Indian New Deal refers to John Collier's innovative years as director of the U.S. Bureau of Indian Affairs (1933-1945). Collier was an energetic and humane visionary who sought to revolutionize federal Indian policy. The keystone of New Deal Indian reform was the Indian Reorganization Act, which ended allotment, organized tribal self-government, established revolving loan programs for tribes, and provided a mechanism for tribes to buy back lost lands. Collier also targeted Indian education and health for improvement. Day schools began to replace boarding schools, and preventive health programs reduced the incidence of certain diseases. Religious freedoms also were extended to Indian people during this time, and bans on the practice of traditional ceremonies were lifted.

Possibly the most lasting achievements in the New Deal era lay in the area of economic development. Tribes were aided in developing resources, preserving the reservation land base, and participating in a variety of public programs available to other Americans. Increasingly, Collier's revolutionary ideas were attacked, in part, because they encouraged Indian traditions and respect for Indian culture rather than assimilation of Indian people into mainstream American life. Collier resigned in 1945 amid increasing criticism, but he left a definite mark on federal Indian policy.   *Carole A. Barrett*

See also: Allotment system; American Indian Defense Association; General Allotment Act; Indian Reorganization Act; Indian-white relations: United States.

Indian offenses

Courts of Indian Offenses were created by the Bureau of Indian Affairs in 1883. The judges of these courts were Indian men appointed by the federal agent on each reservation, and they heard only cases involving certain

The Ghost Dance, depicted in this 1890's watercolor by Frederic Remington, was among the traditional practices that were banned by the federal government.

cultural practices, termed "Indian offenses," which were banned on the reservations. All decisions of the court were subject to the approval of the Indian agent.

Essentially, the Indian offenses were a list of common traditional practices that the government determined were "demoralizing and barbarous" and therefore should be discontinued so that Indians could become more assimilated into mainstream American culture and values. The list of Indian offenses included prohibitions against dancing, plural marriages, feasts, giveaways, and destroying the property of the dead (a funerary custom among some tribes). Additionally, and most devastating to many Indian people, traditional religious practices including sun dances, sweat-lodge ceremonies, vision questing, and shamanism were strictly prohibited in the hope that Indian people would be more likely to convert to Christianity. In short, Indian offenses were an extensive body of religious and cultural practices that the federal government banned because they were deemed disruptive to the smooth functioning of reservations. When living within the reservation context, Indian people were not granted constitutional protections.

Carole A. Barrett

See also: American Indian civil rights; American Indian Religious Freedom Act; Indian New Deal.

Indian preference

Title VII of the United States Civil Rights Act of 1964 prohibits employment discrimination on the basis of race, sex, national origin, color, or religion. However, this provision does not apply to Indians uniformly. During the period of reforms in the John Collier era, often referred to as the Indian New Deal (1933-1945), Indian preference in employment was instituted first in the Bureau of Indian Affairs and eventually in other federal agencies, such as the Public Health Service, which work closely with Indian people. Later, tribal governments, tribal colleges, and other Indian organizations were able to invoke Indian preference in making hiring decisions.

Commonly tribes develop criteria that give first preference to members of their own tribe, next preference to an American Indian from any tribe, and last preference to a non-Indian. When Title VII provisions are dropped, there is no uniform protection against employment discrimination. Indian preference was permitted as a way to increase the numbers of Indian people working within agencies and organizations that deal primarily with American Indian populations. It was also viewed as a way to increase the number of Indian people in the workforce significantly and so address the chronic issue of Indian unemployment. *Carole A. Barrett*

See also: American Indian civil rights; Civil Rights Act of 1964; Employment among American Indians; Indian New Deal.

Indian Removal Act

The federal policy of Indian removal, formalized by the Indian Removal Act of 1830, was advocated by humanitarian reformers seeking to protect Indians from white encroachment, by white settlers who coveted Indian lands, and by state and federal officials who were challenging the vaguely defined constitutional status of Indians living within states' borders. Removal was accomplished by President Andrew Jackson, who was seeking to meliorate conflicts between states and the federal government over issues of state sovereignty.

By the 1820's, efforts to assimilate Indians through education and Christianization appeared unacceptably slow to land-hungry settlers and state officials. Because of disease, wars, treaties, illegal encroachments, and land speculations, most regions of the eastern United States already had been virtually cleared of Indians. Several tribes remained, however, including the Five Civilized Tribes—Cherokee, Creek, Choctaw, Chickasaw, and Seminole—of the South and the Iroquois of the North.

With the Louisiana Purchase of 1803 providing a vast new tract of land, President Thomas Jefferson suggested removal—the exchange of eastern for western lands—as a humanitarian measure designed to protect Indians from demoralization and corruption attending their contact with whites. After President James Monroe in 1824 recommended to Congress that all Indians be moved west of the Mississippi, some tribes and groups of individuals accepted subsequent congressional offers for relocation. Others, notably the Five Civilized Tribes, refused to vacate their ancestral lands.

When Andrew Jackson assumed the presidency in 1828, Georgia was exerting force on the federal government to meet the terms of an 1802 agreement by which Georgia had ceded claims to western lands in exchange for federal promises to extinguish Indian land claims within Georgia. The ineluctable spread of cotton agriculture and the discovery of gold on Cherokee lands in 1829 intensified Georgia's impatience. Accordingly, in 1828 and 1829, Georgia enacted laws nullifying Cherokee land claims and extended state law over the Cherokee nation. The Cherokee, in turn, lodged a congressional protest. Jackson, however, sympathized with Georgia and in 1830 secured passage of the Indian Removal Act, providing for the removal of all eastern Indians to lands west of the Mississippi. Furthermore, in 1831 and 1832, he refused to enforce Supreme Court decisions promising Cherokee federal protection.

Theoretically, removal was to have been voluntarily negotiated between the United States government and Indian tribes. Those Indians choosing to remain in the east as individuals were offered allotments of land and the right to become United States citizens. In practice, however, those who remained were victimized by land speculators and squatters, while those who rejected removal or allotment were moved westward involuntarily. The plight of the Cherokee, as they embarked on a forced march known as the Trail of Tears, symbolized the inexorable and historical dispossession of American Indians facilitated by the Indian Removal Act.   *Mary E. Virginia*

See also: Indian-white relations: United States; Trail of Tears.

Indian Reorganization Act

The Great Depression caused considerable rethinking about whether the United States was progressing toward a future of wealth and plenty. Some people, including Franklin D. Roosevelt's commissioner of Indian affairs John Collier, in their doubts looked to the close-knit, nonmaterialistic world of the American Indians for an alternative to what they saw was wrong with modern society. Through the Indian Reorganization Act (IRA) of 1934, Collier sought to preserve Indian cultures and to implement the recommendations of the 1928 Meriam Report, which was very critical of how the Bureau of Indian Affairs (BIA) had dealt with Indians.

Collier's original version of the Indian Reorganization Act (IRA) was rewritten and toned down in the legislative process, but the act was still radical for the time. The IRA ended further allotment of Indian lands and provided for Indian religious freedom, a measure of tribal self-government, a revolving loan fund for economic development, and Indian preference in hiring within the BIA. Collier hoped to revitalize Indian tribes, but many legislators, while voting in favor of the IRA in the fervor of the first years of Roosevelt's "New Deal," did not really support Collier's goal.

Through 1935, 172 tribes and communities held referendums and agreed to come under the Indian Reorganization Act; another 63 refused. Most tribes were deeply suspicious of any government efforts no matter how beneficial the government said they were. Some tribes were influenced by missionaries and Christianized Indians who saw Collier's admiration of Indian traditional religions as anti-Christian and antiprogressive.

While Collier's efforts received a setback during the termination period after World War II, the IRA continued to provide a legal framework for tribal governments, whose powers greatly expanded when the federal termination policies of the 1950's and 1960's gave way to self-determination policies in the 1970's and 1980's.

The Johnson-O'Malley (JOM, 1934) Act authorized the secretary of the interior to enter into contracts with states to pay them for providing services to Indians, including the education of Indians in public schools. Since 1891, the BIA had dealt with each school district individually. Putting Indian children in public schools was problematic. Rural teachers tended to conform to local prejudices against Indians. In addition, public schools in the 1930's were in financial crisis because of the Depression and were dropping health, physical education, shop, and other courses that Collier and others thought were basic for Indian students.

Originally, JOM funding went into the general operating fund of the school districts and could be used to support the education of non-Indian students (as pointed out by a study, *An Even Chance,* done by the National Association for the Advancement of Colored People in 1971). Such reports led to JOM funding being targeted for special programs that required Indian parent committee approval and that were only for Indian students.   *Jon Rehyner*

See also: Allotment system; Education and American Indians; General Allotment Act; Indian New Deal; Indian-white relations: United States; Oklahoma Indian Welfare Act; Termination Resolution.

Indian Rights Association

The Indian Rights Association was founded in Philadelphia in 1882 by Henry Panacoast and Herbert Welsh, and it became the most important of the humanitarian groups which formed in the last two decades of the nineteenth century to seek the assimilation of Indians into mainstream American society. Welsh and Panacoast viewed the federal reservation system as a cultural and economic failure and asserted that reservations were obstacles to the civilization of Indians.

The Indian Rights Association diligently pursued its agenda to break up tribalism and bring Christian civilization to Indians by pressing for abolition of the reservation system through allotment of tribal lands, by supporting industrial education for Indians in order to encourage self-sufficiency, and by pressing for immediate citizenship for Indians so they would come under constitutional and state laws. The organization's political goals were inextricably bound to a belief in the superiority of Christian civilization. In 1886 Welsh asserted that the organization was doing God's will by guiding Indians "from the night of barbarism into the dawn of civilization."

The Indian Rights Association was successful because it was well organized and had dedicated members who pushed its agenda. The association hired a lobbyist in order to exert constant pressure on congressional committees, legislators, and Indian affairs officials. The organization also influenced public opinion by publishing pamphlets, news articles, and speeches that advanced its views. The association got much public and congressional support for its programs because it regularly sent representatives into Indian country to gather facts that gave such programs credibility. Additionally, the organization mirrored American society of the day by combining religious sentiment with patriotism in its proposals for reforming Indian policy. The association's goal was to acculturate and assimilate Indians fully into American society, and it viewed Indian culture and traditions as being un-American and pagan.

The Indian Rights Association declined in power and influence after Welsh resigned as secretary in 1902 and as federal Indian policy gradually began to support tribalism in the 1920's. The association continues to exist, although it now supports Indian self-determination and Indian groups seeking federal recognition.

Carole A. Barrett

See also: Friends of the Indian; General Allotment Act; Indian Citizenship Act; Indian-white relations: United States.

Indian Territory

> **Significance:** Removal of eastern tribes to the lands west of the Mississippi River known as Indian Territory (centered in present-day Oklahoma) had devastating and profound effects on tribal populations and cultures.

Terms such as "Indian country" and "Indian territory" had different meanings at different times in the history of relations between the United States and various Indian nations. The concept of a defined Indian territory developed alongside the policy of removal—removing eastern tribes to lands west of the Mississippi River—created by the administration of Andrew Jackson in the late 1820's and early 1830's. It was first proposed as a large area west of the Mississippi that would include present-day Kansas and Oklahoma as well as parts of Nebraska, Colorado, and Wyoming. The land area considered Indian Territory soon shrank, however, as the government gave large parts of it away to white settlers, until it assumed the size it maintained until Oklahoma became a state in 1907. It is this area, essentially modern-day Oklahoma, that is most often meant by Indian Territory.

Indian Removal

In 1828, President Jackson recommended Indian removal legislation to Congress, and the Indian Removal Act was passed May 28, 1830. The Choctaw were the first tribe to cede their homeland and consent to removal to Indian Territory. The main body of the tribe moved between 1830 and 1833. The Creek were moved second, as a military measure. In 1836, 2,495 Creek were transported to Indian Territory and left to live or die without clothes, weapons, or cooking utensils. The Cherokee started removal around 1834, and the main tribe was forcibly removed during the bitter winter of 1838-1839. So many died that they finally agreed to manage their own removal. The Chickasaw removal proceeded without resistance during the winter of 1837-1838. They paid the Choctaw for the right to settle on Choctaw land. The Seminole resisted removal, were hunted down by the army and navy, and were taken to Indian Territory in chains. In 1856, the United States purchased land from the Creek for the Seminoles and provided school funds. The Cherokee, Choctaw, and Chickasaw established governments, school systems, and churches as quickly as possible. The Creek did also, but more slowly. The Seminole took steps to develop a government and a school system, but progress was interrupted by the Civil War.

The Osage received a large tract along the border of southern Kansas. The Quapaw were removed from Arkansas and acquired a small reservation northeast of the Cherokee. The Seneca and the Shawnee were also moved into Indian Territory. By the end of the 1830's the Indians owned land in Nebraska, a solid block of reservations along the eastern and most of the southern boundary of Kansas, and all of Oklahoma except the panhandle. This whole region was known as Indian Territory, although a territorial government was never established. Also seeking refuge in Indian Territory were bands of Shawnee, Delaware (Lenni Lenapes), and fragments of other tribes from the Old Northwest. Around 1839, more Shawnee and Delaware and some Kickapoo fled Texas and came to Indian Territory. In 1846, a peace treaty was made with the Caddo, the Tonkawa, and the Penateka (or Southern) Comanches; two reservations in Indian Territory were set aside for them in 1854. When the Kansas-Nebraska Act (1854) created Kansas and Nebraska, the Indians were moved southward and the term Indian Territory became restricted to Oklahoma.

The Civil War created great divisions among and within the tribes in Indian Territory. In 1866, the Five Civilized Tribes signed treaties, forced on them by the United States government for having allied with the Confederacy, that relinquished a large part of their western land, thus dividing Indian Territory into two parts. The eastern half belonged to the Five Civilized Tribes, and the remainder became part of the Oklahoma Territory. This western land was to be used as homes for western tribes to be settled on reservations as part of the consolidation policy. In 1907, the remaining Indian Territory, along with Oklahoma Territory, became the new state of Oklahoma.
Lynn M. Mason

See also: Indian Removal Act; Indian-white relations: United States; Trail of Tears.

Indian-white relations: Canada

> **Significance:** Historically, Indian and white relations in Canada were characterized by European Canadians' desire to dominate the aboriginal peoples, known as First Nations, and take their lands. In the late twentieth century, the Canadian government began the process of reconciliation with its aboriginal peoples.

Relations between the whites and aboriginals in Canada, or First Nations, began with exploration followed by invasion and domination by the European powers spreading into and over North America during the sixteenth and seventeenth centuries. British and French competing interests and colonialization, piqued by growing trade economies and political conflicts, decimated and divided the native nations and peoples along the Saint Lawrence waterway and the Great Lakes. Larger confederacies that were effectively destroyed include the Haudenosaunee, known as the Six Nations Iroquois Confederacy, and the Wyandot-Huron alliances. The Mohawk at Kahnesatake were particularly targeted, but they and other Iroquoian peoples, have survived as a people and a nation into modern times.

Eric Wolf in *Europe and the People Without History* (1982) describes some of these processes from the world-systems analysis perspective, including the European Canadian expansion into and incorporation of Indian lands through the fur trade and the incursion's effects on First Nations across the northern woodlands and plains and in the northern tundra and arctic regions. Small wars and internecine fighting characterized much of the Indian-white relations extending from the Great Lakes region to the western seaboard; generally peaceful negotiations were followed by large land transfers first to the incursive colonial power of England and then to the Canadian commonwealth. Major wars connected to the formation and expansion of the United States from the eastern colonies across the Great Lakes region had generally devastating effects on native peoples and their nations. Colonial powers and the Americans forced First Nation peoples into alignments with warring governments and then punished those native Canadians connected with the other side, typically not recognizing earlier treaties and agreements. The British and Americans, after forcing the French out, rarely observed treaty agreements with those First Nations who sided with them, instead whittling away at their lands and sometimes relocating them to frontier areas and usually into further conflicts.

Cultural Genocide

These wars and a series of intertribal conflicts led to the First Nation peoples involved being stereotyped as "savage" and "uncivilized." These same labels were applied to those native peoples resisting the European Canadian expansion and conquest of western and northern frontiers, pitting white settlers against Indians in struggles over land and trade. In the 1700's and 1800's, European Canadians employed coercive assimilation practices. They forced Indian children into residential boarding schools that attempted to eliminate native cultures and replace them with "civilized" white lifestyles. This attempt to destroy native families and their historical and cultural legacies exacerbated tensions between Indians and whites. Most of these practices continued well into the 1950's and 1960's. In 1867, the British North America Act established the dominion of Canada and formalized the development of "reserves" based on diminished land claims and treaty provisions. Despite the establishment of reserves and attempts to eliminate Indian culture, Canadian governance was often less harsh than that of the United States. For example, after the 1876 fight over the taking of the Black Hills in direct violation of an 1868 treaty and reservation boundaries, Sitting Bull fled to Canada, where he lived for five years with many Hunkpapa Lakota (Sioux). Also, northern Canadian native peoples such as the Inuit and Cree did not suffer the full effects of the reserve system until the twentieth century.

The policies of coercive assimilation, cultural genocide, boarding schools, relocation, land takings, and sociopolitical erosion of rights did not completely destroy the native peoples of Canada, although many of these groups have undergone intense social change. These patterns are especially evident in the development of the Metis, a mixture of French and Indian peoples, usually Ojibwa or Cree, in the provinces of Manitoba and Saskatchewan down into the Dakotas and Minnesota in the United States. In the late 1800's, Metis leader Louis Riel, Jr., led uprisings in protest of the mistreatment of Metis, the government's nonrecognition of mixed-bloods and their French language, and discriminatory practices against Cree, Ojibwa, and other native languages and cultures. The Riel-led and similar uprisings

Milestones in Indian-White Relations in Canada

Year	Event
1600's	Europeans make contact with First Nation peoples along the eastern seaboard and the St. Lawrence waterway.
1700's	British and French establish towns, colonies, and trade networks in the new land, creating multiple treaties with First Nation peoples and beginning their incursion into and taking of native peoples' land.
1763	Royal Proclamation (of Indian Country) establishes First Nation peoples as treaty-making entities with which the English crown may negotiate regarding land and trade.
1794	John Jay's Treaty (between the United States and Great Britain) completely omits mention of First Nation peoples, disregarding the Royal Proclamation of 1763.
1849	Residential boarding schools for First Nation children are established across Canada, creating a pattern of coercive assimilation and extreme discrimination against aboriginal cultures that lasts until the 1960's.
1850's	Great Lakes Ojibwa and other treaties and unilateral agreements establish physical distinctions between First Nation territories and European Canadian settlements.
1867	British North America Act (which established the Dominion of Canada) creates a singular nation without formal recognition of First Nation treaty provisions.
1880's	Attempts by the Metis to defend their rights lead to armed conflict with Canadian government forces.
1885	Louis Riel, Jr., returns to Canada after living in exile, leads a failed Metis rebellion over cultural rights and land claims, and is hanged for treason.
1900's	Series of laws, edicts, and "agreements" passed unilaterally by Canada cause erosion of cultural and sovereignty rights for First Nations and establish reserves.
1970's	James Bay and Northern Quebec Agreement, bolstered by the Meech Lake Accord, take away indigenous peoples' lands for development purposes.
1980's	Increasingly better organized indigenous peoples make claims to the United Nations about ongoing discrimination and establish the Assembly of the First Nations.
1990	In Oka, a conflict between European Canadians and Mohawks over ancient lands related to Kahnesatake leads to armed conflict with Canadian military forces and increased discrimination.
1997	Oral tradition as a basis for land claims is recognized by the Canadian Supreme Court.
1998	The Canadian government issues a Statement of Reconciliation, a formal apology to the First Nations.

were termed rebellions and put down by the federal and local military, leading to many indiscriminate killings. Riel was hanged for treason in 1885, as were four other native leaders. The Canadian government's suppression of the Metis, who represented an early mixing of European and indigenous cultures, marks the government's division of racial identities into two definite categories: white and Indian.

Further Deterioration of Relations
Indian-white relations continued to deteriorate in the first half of the twentieth century because unilateral government edicts, laws, and agreements eroded cultural and political sovereignty of native peoples. In tandem with existing negative stereotypes and active social discrimination, whites in the dominant culture ignored or repressed Indians on reserves and discriminated against urban Indians as racial minorities. These attitudinal practices, with Canadian government support, spread throughout Canada.

Boarding school policies, land-reduction strategies, and government-appointed "tribal councils" generally had negative effects and demoralized First Nation peoples, sometimes leading to friction with whites living nearby. Criminal justice systems began to target Indians more actively in the 1900's. Gradually, indigenous groups began to organize and protest against the injustices. Developments in the United States, including the Civil Rights movement of the 1960's, crossed the border into Canada, resulting in the polarization of native Canadians and European Canadians. Those sympathetic to the native peoples' causes found themselves labeled "Indian lovers" and the targets of criticism.

Conflicts and Progress
In the 1970's, provincial governments fought the First Nations in courts of law. The James Bay I and II coalitions of government and private power companies were formed to take away vast land tracts from Cree and Inuit peoples under the Northern Quebec Agreement. In the 1980's, First Nation members protested this and other governmental acts, stressing issues of sovereignty and self-determination, at meetings of the United Nations in Geneva and later in New York. Many European Canadians supported the First Nations' efforts. In response, the Assembly of First Nations was formed to provide aboriginal peoples with access to legal and constitutional resources.

Some towns made up primarily of European Canadians resented the sovereignty of First Nation peoples. In 1990, a crisis developed between the Mohawk community, descendants of the Kahnesatake, at Oka in Quebec and the neighboring European Canadians. The town wanted to build a golf course on an area called "the

Pines," but the Mohawks considered this area to be treaty land containing sacred burial sites. The Mohawk Warrior Society resisted the taking of the land, and armed forces were called in to "put down" Mohawk resistance without review of the legal grounds for either side's argument. After a long siege, the military prevailed, leading to court trials for Indian resisters. However, because of First Nations representation and public support for the Mohawks, positive dialogues grew out of this confrontation.

In December, 1997, in *Delgamuukw v. British Columbia*, the House of Delgamuukw, speaking on behalf of fifty-one hereditary First Nation chiefs, won an important court victory that recognized the oral tradition as a valid historical source for land claims and cultural authenticity. Also, in 1998, the Canada government extended a formal apology in its Statement of Reconciliation to the First Nations. This official recognition, the first of its kind in Canada, presents a potential for healing and building healthier Indian-white relations in future generations.   *James V. Fenelon*

Core Resources
Excellent sources describing interactions between First Nation peoples and European Canadians are Eric Wolf's *Europe and the People Without History* (Berkeley: University of California Press, 1982); *Justice for Natives: Search for Common Ground*, edited by Andrea Morrison (Montreal: McGill-Queen's University Press, 1997); Olive Dickason's *Canada's First Nations: A History of Founding Peoples from Earliest Times* (Norman: University of Oklahoma Press, 1992); and J. R. Miller's *Skyscrapers Hide the Heavens: A History of Indian-White Relations in Canada* (Toronto: University of Toronto Press, 1989).

See also: Aboriginal Canadians; *Delgamuukw v. British Columbia*; Indian-white relations: United States; Nisga'a Agreement in Principle; Nunavut Territory; Oka crisis; Reserve system of Canada; Riel Rebellions; Royal Commission on Aboriginal Peoples.

Indian-white relations: United States

> **Significance:** Since 1934, relations between Native Americans and the U.S. government have led from open displacement of Indian rights to self-determination policies.

The landmark Indian Reorganization Act of 1934, which remained the legislative model for relations between the U.S. government and Indian tribes until the mid-1950's, was based on a massive 1928 report entitled *The Problem of Indian Administration* (also called the Meriam Report). This report had been requested by Secretary of the Interior Hubert Work. It was intended to reexamine the effects of the General Allotment Act of 1887. Briefly stated, the 1887 act had provided for allotment to each Indian family a specific plot of land within their tribe's "traditional" holdings. Under this law, after titles had been held for twenty-five years, families would gain full property rights, including the right to sell their land. Any tribal land that was left after plot allotment to families was to be sold to the government for homesteading. It is estimated that, when the Indian Reorganization Act came into effect in 1934, Indians held legal rights to only one-third of the land they had before the General Allotment Act. This fact, coupled with a number of other critical factors pointed out in the Meriam Report (including inferior conditions in the areas of health care and education), led to the policy changes embodied in 1934's Indian Reorganization Act. Most of the responsibility for implementing these changes rested with President Franklin D. Roosevelt's appointee to the post of commissioner of Indian affairs, John Collier.

Indian Reorganization Act

In addition to slowing the loss of Indian lands, the 1934 act brought a new philosophy to the Bureau of Indian Affairs (BIA). It proclaimed a need to reverse a long-standing policy of forced assimilation of Indians into "mainstream" America and to build stronger bases for the retention of local Indian cultures. In Collier's words, it aimed at "both the economic and spiritual rehabilitation of the Indian race."

In the first domain, plans were laid to appropriate funds to buy back for the tribes Indian land that had been lost since 1887. The BIA also initiated a program to spread knowledge of land and timber conservation technology to receptive tribes and began steps to provide local development loans. Although the deepening of the Great Depression soon made special appropriations impossible, much surplus government land that had not gone to homesteading was returned. In its bid to encourage a greater sense of local tribal identity, the 1934 act also offered aid for drawing up and implementing tribal constitutions as the basis for their own local government.

World War II

In the period between 1934 and the next major redefinition of BIA policy in 1953, many domestic policy factors intervened to affect what Roosevelt's policymakers had seen as the long-term goals of the BIA. The greatest single factor affecting tens of thousands of Indian lives during the decade of the 1940's, however, was initially set in play by forces far beyond the reservations: This factor was military service in the U.S. forces during World War II. More than twenty-five thousand Indians served between 1941 and 1945. Many thousands more left reservations to work in war-related industrial factories. Indian women were also welcomed as volunteers in the army nurses' corps and the Red Cross.

Whatever their experiences in the ranks of the armed forces, still strictly segregated along racial lines, clear problems confronted thousands of returning Indian veterans at the end of the war. Part of the dilemma stemmed from continuing economic underdevelopment on the reservations they left. Equally debilitating, thousands of returning American Indian veterans felt alienated from their own people after experiencing life off the reservation.

Problems such as these impelled U.S. lawmakers to consider once again whether assimilation, rather than "protected separation," was the best policy to pursue in Indian affairs. Parties supporting the former, including outspoken conservative Republican Senator Arthur Watkins from Utah, introduced what became, in House Concurrent Resolution Number 108, the policy of "termination and relocation."

Termination Act of 1953

When HCR 108 became law in mid-1953, it pledged "to make Indians . . . subject to the same laws and entitled to the same privileges and responsibilities as . . . other citizens . . . and to end their status as wards of the United States." Even as HCR 108 was about to become law, a number of Indian spokesmen for the first tribes scheduled for termination (which meant stopping various forms of federal government "protective" intervention in their affairs) openly questioned Senator Watkins's claims that, since there were multiple sources to develop potential wealth on their reservations, the tribes should be able to "go it better alone."

Menominee leader Gordon Keshena was not alone in expressing worries that, if BIA supervision over local Indian affairs ended, the tribes' lack of experience would produce deterioration of many Indian material interests. Some congressional supporters of the general principles behind HCR 108 also admitted that the government might find itself spending large amounts of money trying to prepare the weakest and poorest Indian groups to know what forms of local autonomy might suit them best.

In fact, just as local termination bills began to appear in 1954, President Dwight D. Eisenhower seemed prepared to increase budgetary allocations to encourage the establishment of new industries in or near tribal areas. For example, by 1956, $300,000 of tribal funds formerly held in trust were earmarked to induce industrial plant owners to locate on the fringes of Navajo territory. Two companies constructed factories, one manufacturing baby furniture, the other making electronic equipment, near Flagstaff, Arizona.

In 1957 the Indian Vocational Training Act was intended to provide job skills to Indian applicants to make them attractive to potential employers, even if such jobs meant relocating off reservations. More than a hundred different occupations were included in the curriculum of free schools located in twenty-six states. This ambitious program continued to expand even as economic recession worsened in 1956 and 1957. Indian policy makers seemed convinced that the overall objectives of the 1953 termination laws would be best served if Indians who could not expect to gain employment on economically backward reservations relocated in off-reservation towns. Ideally, such a movement of families would also ease pressures on the limited economic means of their respective homelands.

Relocation
A separate budget for relocation came by the mid-1950's, to avoid negative consequences for Indians who left the reservations without adequate security. Statistics showed that, of the nearly 100,000 Indians who left reservations between 1945 to 1958, some 75,000 had relocated without federal assistance, sometimes causing familial disasters. Thus, job training and relocation funds expended in 1957 doubled in one year, reaching $3.5 million. In the same year, 7,000 Indians moved from their reservations. Controversy soon developed over shortcomings in the relocation program.

Realistic prospects for employment fell short of demands; moreover, job layoffs left many Indians "stranded" and unemployed in unsympathetic white-dominated environments. At the same time, there were very high dropout rates in BIA-sponsored vocational schools. Nurse's aide programs for women registered the lowest percentage of dropouts (21 percent), while rates for less challenging factory-type programs for men were very high (a 50 percent dropout rate for sawmill workers and a rate as high as 62 percent among furniture factory trainees).

As the 1960's approached, critics of the effects of termination and relocation, including Sophie Aberle, formerly responsible for the United Pueblos Agency, warned Indian Commissioner Glenn Emmons of trouble ahead. Emmons tried to defend his office by reiterating a philosophy that was not accepted by all—that whatever successes were occurring usually stemmed from individual initiative, whereas groups that fell back on the security of "communal lifestyle" tended to accept status quo conditions. Emmons cited gains that were not so easily measured in paychecks, such as advances in tribal health

programs and in education. The number of Indians going beyond high school by this date (the 1958-1959 school year) showed an increase of more than 65 percent in only three years.

Toward Self-Determination: 1960's and 1970's
Despite the fact that the Eisenhower administration's last BIA budget (for fiscal year 1960) was the largest ever ($115,467,000), it was during the 1960 presidential campaign that controversy over Indian policy began to come to public attention. Party platform committees actually heard testimony from tribal leaders such as Frank George, a Nez Perce who asked not for abandonment of termination but for improvement in its procedures for aiding needy tribes. Other claims, such as the Miccosukee Seminole demand for all of Florida to reconstitute their sovereignty, received less sympathy. The new tide that was coming was best expressed by La Verne Madigan of the Association on American Indian Affairs, who stated that Indians should have the right to choose freely between assimilation and "life in cultural communities of their own people."

In general, the Kennedy-Johnson Democratic years (1960-1968) witnessed a continuation of termination actions despite the views of Lyndon B. Johnson's interior secretary, Stewart Udall. It was Udall's insistence that the BIA should do more to secure better conditions of relocation that led to the replacement of Commissioner Philleo Nash by Wisconsin Oneida Indian Robert Bennett in 1966. Under Bennett's influence, the president began, in the troubled political climate of 1967, to declare the nation's need to end the termination policy. Soon thereafter, Johnson urged passage of the American Indian Civil Rights Act (1968).

The 1970's, under Presidents Richard M. Nixon, Gerald Ford, and Jimmy Carter, brought what has been described as the "self-determination" policy, emphasizing the development of tribal resources on restored reservations. Perhaps the most dramatic example of reversal of what many perceived to be the harmful effects of termination occurred in 1973, when the Menominee tribe was told that (as the tribe had requested) its twenty-year experience of termination was over and that its entire reservation was to be restored to it as "unencumbered Menominee property." Yet despite pronouncements of "better intentions" coming from Washington and the BIA, the cumulative effects of decades of misunderstanding were not to be dispelled easily. In the same year that the Menominees regained tribal control over their own destiny, a breakdown in relations between federal troops and Lakota Indians during a seventy-one-day siege on the Pine Ridge Reservation ended in an assault that the Lakotas call "Wounded Knee II." Similar confrontations with threats of violence came in different

Over the years, Indian-white relations in the United States have been marked by conflict. In 1973 during the occupation of Wounded Knee, assistant U.S. attorney general Ken Frizzell (right) meets with American Indian Movement members including Wallace Black Elk (kneeling), Russell Means, Dennis Banks, and Carter Camp (to the left of Black Elk, in that order).

regions, pressing government authorities to review its Indian policy yet again.

In May, 1977, the congressional American Indian Policy Review Commission, which included five Indian members for the first time, made more than two hundred recommendations, most of which aimed at confirming all tribes' power to enact laws within the confines of their own reservations. On the heels of this symbol of intended reform, the U.S. Congress passed the 1978 American Indian Religious Freedom Act, which guaranteed freedom for tribes to practice their own traditional religions. This act ended the mixed legacy of several centuries of insistence that missionary conversion and education following Christian principles were vital aspects of Indian-white relations in the United States.

1980's Through 1995

During the Republican presidencies of Ronald Reagan and George Bush (1980-1992), budgetary cuts seriously affected the continuity of existing programs of assistance to Indian tribes. In 1981 alone, one-half of the prior budget for health services was cut, while funding for Indian higher education was reduced from $282 million to $200 million. By the mid-1980's, the education budget had been cut further, to $169 million.

Despite alarming cutbacks in BIA funding and looming questions of Indian demands for restoration of their sovereignty, the Bush administration made one major

contribution by enacting the Native American Languages Act, which allowed tribal use of (formerly banned) traditional languages in BIA schools.

The issue of Indian land claims was prominent throughout the 1980's and early 1990's. In 1980, the U.S. Supreme Court (in *United States v. Sioux Nation*) upheld a $122 million judgment against the United States for having taken the Black Hills from the Sioux illegally. In 1986, a federal court awarded each member of the White Earth Chippewa group compensation for land lost under the 1887 General Allotment Act. A significant piece of legislation regarding land claims was the 1982 Indian Claims Limitation Act, which limited the time period during which land claims could be filed against the U.S. government.

The issue of Indian sovereignty and the related issue of gambling on Indian lands created considerable controversy among Indians and non-Indians in the early 1990's. The 1988 Indian Gaming Regulatory Act legalized certain types of gambling on reservations, and the vast amounts of income that could be generated appealed to many tribes struggling with widespread poverty. Gambling engendered protests by some non-Indians, however, and created tribal divisions that occasionally turned violent; in 1990, violence between gambling and antigambling contingents on the St. Regis Mohawk reservation caused state and federal authorities to intervene. An important court decision involving another aspect of sovereignty was handed down in 1990: The U.S. Supreme Court decided in *Duro v. Reina* that tribes do not have criminal jurisdiction over non-Indians living on reservation lands.

In 1992, a number of American Indian groups protested the celebrations planned for the five- hundredth anniversary of Christopher Columbus's arrival in the Americas. Two events in 1994 symbolized both an increasing respect for and the continuing problems of American Indians. The first facility of the National Museum of the American Indian, a new part of the Smithsonian Institution, opened in New York (funding had been approved by Congress in 1989). On the other hand, the National Congress of American Indians and the National Black Caucus announced an alliance, stating that American Indians and African Americans continued to face similar forces of political and economic oppression.

Byron D. Cannon

Core Resources

James E. Falkowski's *Indian Law/Race Law: A FiveHundred-Year History* (New York: Praeger, 1922) places the subject of U.S. government policy toward Indians in a wider context both of historical and contemporary international legal models. Donald L. Fixico's *Termination and Relocation: Federal Policy, 1945-1966* (Albuquerque: University of New Mexico Press, 1986) is a study of BIA policy from 1953 to 1960, involving presumed "self-help," including working away from home reservations. Nicholas C. Peroff's *Menominee Drums* (Norman: University of Oklahoma Press, 1982) is a case study of one of the most important examples of tribal termination actions. *Documents of United States Indian Policy* (Lincoln: University of Nebraska Press, 1975), edited by Francis Paul Prucha, discusses general policy and issues for specific tribes.

See also: Alaska Native Brotherhood and Alaska Native Claims Settlement Act; Alcatraz Island occupation; American Indian activism; American Indian Civil Rights Act; American Indian Religious Freedom Act; Declaration of First Nations; Determined Residents United for Mohawk Sovereignty; *Duro v. Reina*; Gambling; Indian Gaming Regulatory Act; Indian Reorganization Act; Indian-white relations: Canada; Oklahoma Indian Welfare Act; Relocation of American Indians; Termination Resolution; Wounded Knee occupation.

Indigenous superordination

Indigenous superordination refers to a particular type of intergroup relations whereby a "native" dominant group within a geographical area subordinates incoming immigrant groups. This process results in a particular form of stratification within the society in which the resident dominant group enjoys a disproportionate share of the resources, prestige, and power. This differential can be manifest in economic, political, or cultural realms, interactively. The power relationship is then justified by a system of beliefs that rationalizes the superiority of the indigenous group in relation to the incoming groups and that often scapegoats the immigrants by placing blame on them as the cause of various societal problems. This type of superordinate-subordinate group relationship is less overtly conflictual than migrant superordination. An example of indigenous superordination is found in the United States, where most voluntary immigrants occupy lower levels of the stratification system.

M. Bahati Kuumba

See also: Assimilation: cultural and structural; Assimilation theories; Immigration and emigration; Subordinate group.

Individual racism

Activists Stokely Carmichael and Charles V. Hamilton, in *Black Power: The Politics of Liberation in America* (1967, p.4), defined individual racism as "individual whites acting against individual blacks." Sociologist Fred L. Pincus, in an article published in *American Behavioral Scientist* (1996, p. 186), entitled "Discrimination Comes in Many Forms," renamed and expanded Carmichael and Hamilton's concept as *individual discrimination*, which he defined as "the behavior of individual members of one race/ethnic/gender group that is intended to have a differential and/or harmful effect on the members of another race/ethnic/gender group." Individual racism is distinguished from institutional racism, which is, according to Pincus, the intentional harm of minority groups by institutional practices such as the enactment of Jim Crow laws and the internment of Japanese Americans during World War II. Individual racism is here specified as actions by members of a dominant group that are intended to harm members of other racial and ethnic groups.

A range of individual racism prevails in American society, from intolerance to hate crimes. Included are incidents such as not hiring minority members in one's place of business, scapegoating minority groups for economic problems, stereotyping that leads to anti-Semitic and nativist prejudice and de facto residential segregation, and hurling racist insults and slurs. This last problem, now called hate speech, erupted on many college campuses in the late 1980's and early 1990's. Universities enacted hate-speech codes to protect minorities, but such codes were later found unconstitutional. Violent hate crimes include intimidation, harassment, assaults, beatings, church and synagogue burnings and bombings, cross burnings, destruction of personal property, lynchings, police brutality, and even an instance of white soldiers hunting African Americans as prey in 1995 at Fort Bragg, North Carolina. Police brutality, if isolated within a department, is an example of individual racism. However, if it is widespread with lax norms and *unenforced* formal sanctions against it, then, according to Pincus, it is an institutional harm. In the late 1990's, a flare-up of church burnings, reminiscent of those in the 1960's, terrorized the rural South. According to the Southern Poverty Law Center's Klanwatch Project, white supremacist hate groups—skinheads and those adhering to movements and groups such as Christian Identity, White Aryan Resistance, Aryan Nations, the Ku Klux Klan, and militias of various types—remain strong; some, such as the militias, are on the rise. Many sociologists argue that an increase in acts of individual racism stems from the growing racial diversity of American society and the intensifying competition for scarce resources, such as jobs, in a global economy. With frustration escalating from mounting class stratification, individual racism is a classic example of scapegoating, that is, displacing one's anger at the economy onto minority groups.

Social scientist Gunnar Myrdal, in *An American Dilemma* (1944), argued that a moral dilemma, or contradiction, flourishes in American society between the American creed (freedom, equality of opportunity, and justice) and discrimination. Inequality is maintained through a vicious cycle whereby dominated groups are despised, engendering discrimination. Discrimination, whether individual or institutional, perpetuates minority groups' inferior social circumstances and engenders ideologies and stereotypes that blame minority groups for their deprivation and justify dominant group advantages. Thus, individual and institutional racism are inextricably intertwined.   *Gil Richard Musolf*

See also: Discrimination: behaviors; Hate crimes; Hate speech; Institutional racism; Police brutality; White supremacist groups.

Inequality

Inequality is the unequal distribution of resources, opportunities, and rewards within society. In the United States, resources such as money, power, prestige, educational degrees, access to private clubs, political offices, and housing have been unequally distributed in a manner that has excluded racial and ethnic minorities.

Two early contributors to discussions concerning inequality were Karl Marx and Friedrich Engels. Marx and Engels, in *The Communist Manifesto* (1848), argued that the most important source of inequality relates to the control or ownership of the means of production, meaning the materials, tools, resources, and organizations by which society produces and distributes goods and services. The bourgeoisie, the owners of the means of production, are in a position to exploit and coerce the proletariat, or working class, thus enabling them to claim the greatest proportion of economic resources. Max Weber, in *Economy and Society* (1921), disagreed with Marx, arguing that stratification is multidimensional and involves economics, prestige, and power. Economic inequality is based on ownership or control of property, wealth, and income. Inequality in terms of prestige is based on the amount of esteem or respect given to an individual by others. Inequality of power is based on the differing impact individuals have on the societal decision-making process. Those with more power are better able to protect their interests and achieve their goals than the less powerful.

Kingsley Davis and Wilbert Moore, in their article "Some Principles of Stratification" (*American Sociological Review*, 1945), argued that inequality is necessary, contending that some positions are of greater importance than others to the well-being of society. If all individuals received equal shares of societal resources regardless of their position, there would be no motivation for an individual to undergo the rigorous training necessary to fill the important positions. Inequality rewards the most qualified individuals, encouraging them to take important positions in society and work to the best of their ability. Therefore, Davis and Moore assert that society would not be able to motivate people to work hard and achieve without unequal reward systems.

In the United States, the constitutional basis for many court cases challenging inequality in terms of opportunities, resources, or treatment by the government, its agents, or private citizens is the Fourteenth Amendment. This amendment, in conjunction with court rulings, declares that states cannot make laws that abridge the privileges of citizens; deprive any person of life, liberty, or property without due process of law; deny any citizen the equal protection of the laws; or deny any citizen the right to vote. As a result, by defining equal treatment, the Fourteenth Amendment and court rulings since the ratification of the amendment have defined inequality as the unequal treatment of people based on race, color, ethnic background, sexual orientation, religion, sex, or previous condition of servitude.   *Ione Y. DeOllos*

See also: Equality; Fourteenth Amendment; Marxist models; Social stratification theories.

Institutional racism

> **Significance:** Institutional racism refers to the manner in which a society's institutions operate systematically, both directly and indirectly, to favor some groups over others regarding access to opportunities and valued resources. This concept helps explain how a society can discriminate unintentionally against particular groups.

Racial discrimination, in the most general sense, is the denial of equal opportunities and rights to groups on the basis of race or ethnicity. The study of institutional racism (sometimes called institutional discrimination), rather than looking at individual attitudes as an explanation for racial inequality, focuses on the way society itself is structured or organized. Sociologist Joe R. Feagin distinguishes among four types of discrimination, and he includes two types of institutional racism in his typology: "direct institutionalized[institutional] discrimination" and "indirect institutionalized discrimination." An example of the former, which was documented by Diana Pearce in a 1976 study in Detroit, is the practice by real estate companies of "steering" African Americans away from homes in white areas. This direct form of institutional discrimination is the easiest to identify, understand, and (given the will) eradicate. Most sociologists, however, use the term "institutional racism" to refer to the second type noted by Feagin, indirect discrimination.

The term was coined in 1967 by African American civil rights activist Stokely Carmichael (Kwame Toure) and Charles V. Hamilton. Toure and Hamilton were attempting to shift attention away from individual, overt, and direct forms of racial discrimination as the principal explanation for the persistence of racial inequality.

From the perspective of sociologists studying unintentional and indirect forms of institutional racism, consequences are the most important indicator of discrimination. If the results or consequences of a policy or practice are unequal along racial lines, then indirect institutional racism is thought to exist. As sociologist Jerome Skolnick avers, "a society in which most of the good jobs are held by one race, and the dirty jobs are held by people of another color, is a society in which racism is institutionalized no matter what the beliefs of its members are."

Statistical Evidence
In the 1980's, statistical evidence of racism could be found in every institutional area. As recently as 1980, African Americans, for example, constituted nearly 12 percent of the population of the United States but only 1.5 percent of the country's elected officials. Almost 50 percent of all prison inmates in the U.S. were black. The dropout rate for blacks in education was twice that of whites. The infant mortality rate for whites in 1985 was 9.3 per 1,000 live births, but for blacks it was 18.2 per 1,000. The maternal mortality rate in 1984 for whites was 5.4 per 100,000 live births; for black women it was 19.7. Forty-three percent of black children and 16 percent of white children under the age of eighteen lived in poverty in 1986, and the median per capita wealth for blacks in 1984 was $6,837, compared to $32,667 for whites. These inequities strongly suggested the existence of institutional racism, which persists to this day.

The fact that blacks do not own businesses proportional to their percentage of the population demonstrates another important element of institutional racism: the interrelatedness of institutions. A society's institutions are interrelated in ways such that exclusion from one frequently means exclusion from all. Harold M. Baron has called this phenomenon the "web" of urban racism. Black enterprise in the United States has been stifled by discrimination in education and the job market and by discriminatory banking practices that make it difficult for African Americans to secure loans to start businesses.

Research and Remedial Efforts
The study of institutional racism also places considerable importance on the deep historical roots and lasting effects of direct racial discrimination. The effects of earlier practices, policies, and laws that were designed purposely to exclude and harm particular groups have continued to be felt even after most of them were eliminated by legislative and other measures. The cumulative effect of this discrimination left African Americans and other racial and ethnic minorities—notably Mexican Americans/Chicanos, Native Americans, and Puerto Ricans—at a competitive disadvantage with majority group members in virtually every institutional area.

Knowledge gained from the study of institutional racism is applied in a number of ways in attempts to counter institutional racism. Among the many approaches are civil rights legislation; executive orders, such as those for affirmative action; and changes in the criteria used by admissions offices in higher education.

College Admissions
Historically, college admissions officers have relied on so-called objective criteria in their decisions. The most important of these criteria have been class rank, grade point average, scores on the Scholastic Aptitude Test (SAT), participation in extracurricular activities, and the quality of the high school attended by applicants. While it was not necessarily the intent of colleges to discriminate against members of minority groups, reliance on these criteria, in effect, did so. Minority-group applicants, for example, are disproportionately poorer than majority-group applicants. As a consequence, they are more likely to have attended poorly funded schools that offer fewer extracurricular activities and that generally provide a lower-quality education. Minority students also are more likely to have to work and to care for siblings, which in turn affects their academic performance and limits their participation in extracurricular activities.

Because of studies of institutional racism, universities and colleges were able to see how their admissions policies were discriminating against members of certain groups. In the 1960's, most of these institutions adjusted their admissions processes, including the criteria used to determine admissibility and predict academic potential, to take into account the disadvantaged positions in which members of minority groups find themselves. Instead of automatically penalizing students for not participating in extracurricular activities, for example, admissions officers obtained information from applicants and high school guidance counselors on the activities available in the school and on applicants' responsibilities, including work, which may have made it difficult for them to participate in school-sponsored programs. Admissions officers also began to consider possible biases in standardized tests and accorded test scores less weight in their decision to admit or not to admit a student.

Hiring Practices

Affirmative action programs are principally intended to be remedies for institutional discrimination. Affirmative action requires race consciousness rather than "color blindness," because (as studies of institutional racism have shown) society is structured in such a way that race-neutral or color-blind policies exclude members of minority groups. In the area of employment, for example, affirmative action programs were created to increase the pool of qualified minority candidates and to eliminate discriminatory practices from the selection process. Approaches include advertising positions in places where potential candidates from minority groups can be reached more effectively.

A long-standing and common recruitment practice has been to hire new workers through personal connections. Because of prior racial discrimination, however, the people doing the hiring were disproportionately white, and their connections tended to be white as well. Hence, African Americans and members of other minority groups often were excluded. Affirmative action programs have sought to eliminate this practice, which, even if its practitioners did not intend it to be, is discriminatory. Advertising positions widely, even nationally when possible, has been one remedy prescribed.

A seemingly innocuous practice used by some police agencies provides another example of institutional racism. Many police forces maintained a minimum height requirement, which placed Latinos, Asians, and women at a disadvantage. Because members of these groups generally tend to be shorter than white or black males, this requirement reduced significantly the pool of qualified applicants from these groups. Although the height requirement seemed to be neutral, or nondiscriminatory, it in fact discriminated against particular groups; intent is not necessary for a requirement to be discriminatory. In many instances, such discriminatory job requirements have been eliminated or modified.

In yet another example, seniority systems, established to provide job security for longtime employees, discriminate against minority group members. Blacks are adversely affected in disproportionate numbers by this practice because, as a group, they were denied job opportunities on the basis of race until court decisions and legislative initiatives made it illegal to discriminate on this basis. Being the most recently hired employees, they would be the first fired when layoffs became necessary.

While seniority systems may not have been established to discriminate intentionally against members of certain groups, they did so nevertheless. As a consequence, the courts in a number of instances have ordered employers to cease the practice.

The Civil Rights Act of 1991, signed into law by President George Bush, was drafted partly in response to a number of Supreme Court decisions that, in effect, required plaintiffs in discrimination suits to prove intent on the part of the defendant, usually an employer. The bill stipulates that once the plaintiff is able to show that an employer's practice adversely affects a particular group, then the burden falls on the employer to "demonstrate that the challenged practice is job related for the position in question and consistent with business necessity." The bill is consistent with an approach designed to counter institutional discrimination. A practice is deemed discriminatory if it has a disparate impact on any group, irrespective of intent.

Between the election of President Ronald Reagan in 1980 and the passage of this bill, the tendency had been to place the burden of proof increasingly on plaintiffs in discrimination cases. In other words, a plaintiff had to prove that an employer intended to discriminate against him or her—a very difficult, often impossible, task. This approach of the 1980's was a departure from the approach that began in the 1960's, based on countering institutional discrimination. The Civil Rights Bill of 1991 returned, although in a somewhat weakened fashion, to the earlier approach intended to counter institutional racism.

Context

Prior to the 1920's, few sociologists studied race relations. When they did, beginning with the work of such sociologists as Edward Ross, Lester Ward, and William Sumner, the tendency was to view discrimination as conscious acts performed by prejudiced individuals; this view continued to dominate until the 1960's. The assumption inherent in this "prejudice causes discrimination" model, as noted by Joe Feagin and Clairece Feagin, is that the way to eradicate racial discrimination is to eliminate racial prejudice. It was believed that, with time, this would happen. Racial discrimination was seen as an aberration, inconsistent with American ideals of equality and justice. Swedish sociologist Gunnar Myrdal captured this belief well in the title of his classic and influential work on discrimination in the United States, *An American Dilemma: The Negro Problem and Modern Democracy* (1944).

Beginning with the pioneering work on immigration by American sociologist Robert Ezra Park in the first half of the twentieth century, immigration scholars as a rule predicted the eventual assimilation of various ethnic groups. While most conceded that the situation of African Americans was unique in some respects, their assimilation into American society was also predicted. Along with this, it was thought, would come the diminution and eventual elimination of racial prejudice. Milton Gordon, in the 1960's, developed a more sophisticated theory of assimilation, in which he distinguished between cultural and structural assimilation. Structural assimilation refers to the ability of members of a minority group to participate in such societal groups and institutions as businesses, government, and private clubs; Gordon pointed out that cultural assimilation does not assure equal opportunities in these areas.

In the 1950's and 1960's, the Civil Rights movement made great strides in attaining legal equality for African Americans and other minorities. Robert Blauner observed that initially the Civil Rights movement adopted the view that blacks, if guaranteed legal equality, would be able to assimilate into American society. In time, however, it became increasingly apparent to civil rights activists as well as to many scholars that racist ideologies and prejudiced attitudes were not the "essence" of racism. Rather, racism was inherent in society's institutions. This realization quickly led to a fundamental change in the study of race relations, a change spurred by the cultural climate of social unrest and protest during the 1960's. The Black Power movement of the 1960's called attention to how little the status of blacks had changed or promised to change despite progressive civil rights legislation and a reduction in racial prejudice. This relatively new way of analyzing racial stratification shifted the focus from individual expressions of racism to the manner in which society itself was structured and operated to favor some groups over others. *Héctor L. Delgado*

Core Resources

James Baldwin's *The Fire Next Time* (New York: Dell, 1963) presents a beautifully written analysis of racism and an unrivaled statement on being black in the United States. Robert Blauner's *Racial Oppression in America* (New York: Harper & Row, 1972) presents the thesis is that racial minorities in the United States are internal colonies created by the capitalist system. Stokely Carmichael and Charles V. Hamilton's *Black Power: The Politics of Liberation in America* (New York: Vintage Books, 1967) exhorts African Americans to seize the initiative in effecting social change. Joe R. Feagin's *Racial and Ethnic Relations* (Englewood Cliffs, N.J.: Prentice-Hall, 1989) discusses racial and ethnic minorities in their broader social contexts. Joe R. Feagin and Clairece Booher Feagin's *Discrimination American Style: Institutional Racism and Sexism* (Englewood Cliffs, N.J.: Prentice-Hall, 1978) remains one of the best and most accessible discussions of institutional racism and sexism. *Institutional Racism in America*

(Englewood Cliffs, N.J.: Prentice-Hall, 1969), edited by Louis L. Knowles and Kenneth Prewitt, is a collection of essays that analyze institutional racism in various institutional areas, such as the economy and education.

See also: College admissions; Discrimination: direct institutionalized; Discrimination: indirect institutionalized; Discrimination: systemic; Prejudice and discrimination: Merton's paradigm; Race relations cycle; Racism as a "system of advantage"; Racism: history of the concept.

Integration

> **Significance:** Crucial changes in U.S. public policy beginning in the 1940's helped promote the goal of racial integration. Legally, whites and nonwhites were given equal access to workplaces, schools, and neighborhoods; however, many social and economic factors acted to slow or prevent the complete intermingling of races.

A racially integrated society would be one in which African Americans and other racial or ethnic groups could participate in all aspects of national life without being handicapped by their color. In such a society, there should be no neighborhood where an African American could not reside simply because of being black; no hotel, restaurant, or other public facility that an African American could not use on equal terms with whites; no school that an African American child could not attend because of being black; no kind of vocational training, university education, or line of work from which an African American would be barred because of being black; and no public office for which an African American could not contend. In an integrated society, whites would see African Americans not as pariahs but as fellow Americans, fellow veterans, coworkers, and neighbors. This goal of a racially integrated society, despite much progress, is only half achieved; the role that public policy should play in creating a more racially integrated society remains a matter of lively debate.

Those who discuss the ethics of integration are dealing with the ethics of public policy rather than (as is the case, to some extent, with prejudice and racism) the morality of private behavior. The promotion of racial integration has been seen by its proponents as essential to the realization of an important value in public policy ethics: that of equality under the law regardless of race or color. This principle was publicly recognized in the United States by the Fourteenth Amendment to the Constitution (ratified in 1868), which mandated that every state guarantee its citizens the equal protection of the laws. Nevertheless, de facto segregation reigned for nearly three-quarters of a century before significant steps were taken to break down racial barriers.

Milestones in Integration: 1945 to 1968

Signposts of progress during these years (which witnessed the flowering of the Civil Rights movement) included the gradual desegregation of the American military, which began with President Harry S Truman's Executive Order 9981 in 1948; the Supreme Court decision of 1954, that struck down the constitutionality of segregated schools; the admission of African Americans into southern state universities; the Civil Rights Act of 1964, which established the right of equal access to public accommodations and banned discrimination in employment; the Voting Rights Act of 1965; the Supreme Court decision of 1967 that overturned state laws against black-white intermarriage; and the federal Fair Housing Act of 1968. By 1990, many of these changes had achieved general acceptance; efforts to integrate employment, schools, and housing, however, continued to arouse controversy.

The Affirmative Action Controversy

By the late 1970's, affirmative action, in which the presence or absence of a fixed percentage of African Americans in a business, government department, or university is used to determine whether that institution discriminates, had become the chief tool by which the federal government tried to open up opportunities for African Americans. In 1975, in the book *Affirmative Discrimination*, the white sociologist Nathan Glazer condemned the

application of this policy in both private businesses and government employment. Glazer argued that affirmative action undermines respect for merit and encourages ethnic and racial divisiveness; unlike many liberals, he denied that the underrepresentation of African Americans in a particular job or profession is necessarily evidence of discrimination. In the 1990's African American conservatives asserted that affirmative action stigmatizes as inferior those African Americans who do gain entrance to prestigious universities or get good jobs. Yet other thinkers—white as well as African American— argue that many employers would hire no African Americans at all if they were not prodded to do so by the existence of a numerical goal.

Racial Integration of Elementary and Secondary Schools

In *Brown v. Board of Education*, in 1954, the Supreme Court declared that officially enforced school segregation by race (then found mostly in the southern states) violated the Fourteenth Amendment to the Constitution. In a 1968 decision, the Supreme Court exerted pressure on southern school boards to end segregation more quickly; in a 1971 decision, *Swann v. Charlotte-Mecklenburg Board of Education*, the Court held that school busing—the transportation of children out of their neighborhoods for schooling—might be an appropriate tool for achieving desegregation.

In the 1960's, the question arose of what to do about the de facto racial segregation of the schools, based on neighborhood racial patterns rather than on the law, found in many northern cities. In 1973, the Supreme Court ordered, for the first time, a northern school district (Denver, Colorado) to institute a desegregation plan. In 1974, however, the Court, in a sudden shift (in the decision *Milliken v. Bradley*) banned busing for integration purposes across city-suburban boundaries. In general, the Court has ordered steps toward ending de facto segregation only when evidence exists that local authorities have deliberately rigged school district boundaries to keep the races apart.

Ever since 1954, people have argued about how necessary integration of the races in the classroom is to providing equal educational opportunities for African American children. In the 1980's, some African American thinkers, such as Thomas Sowell and Robert Woodson, had their doubts.

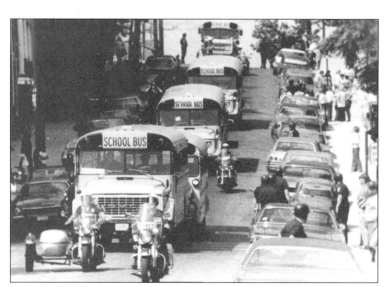

Police officers on motorcycles escort school buses leaving South Boston High School on the second day of court-ordered busing in September, 1974.

Woodson argued that a neighborhood school, even if it is exclusively African American, can become a valuable focus of neighborhood pride for low-income city dwellers; Sowell pointed nostalgically to a high-quality African American secondary school of the pre-1954 era of segregation, Dunbar High School in Washington, D.C. (Critics stress how atypical Dunbar was.)

Integrationist scholars, however, argue that forcible exclusion from the company of white schoolchildren stigmatizes and psychically wounds African American children. The African American journalist Carl Rowan thinks that such exclusion is psychically wounding even if it results from white flight to the suburbs rather than government edict. White liberal political scientist Gary Orfield suggests that racial integration of the schools is necessary if African American children are to have greater access to information about jobs and other opportunities; white liberal education writer Jonathan Kozol contends, like many African American thinkers, that all African American public schools are more likely than integrated ones to be starved of money by legislatures that are beholden to white-majority electorates.

Although the compulsory busing of children into schools predominantly of the other race may be necessary to achieve racial integration in some cases, it does severely limit the rights of parents, thereby causing some resentment. However, the rights of parents over their children are, as the African American philosopher Bernard R. Boxill points out, by no means absolute. There is a societal interest in promoting interracial harmony, Boxill suggests, that perhaps should be allowed to prevail over the wish of bigoted white parents to preserve their children from all contact with African American children, and perhaps even over the wishes of parents who simply wish to spare their children the additional time spent traveling to and from home. Rejecting the notion (found in the writings of African American conservative Glenn Loury) of an unresolvable tension between integrationist goals and individual rights, Boxill also argues that government can use inducements as well as penalties to promote integration, in education and in other areas.

To promote integration of the schools while keeping busing to a minimum, some local school authorities have instituted so-called magnet schools. By placing elementary and secondary schools with above-average endowment in facilities and curricula in the middle of African American neighborhoods, authorities have sometimes persuaded, rather than forced, white parents to accept racial integration of the schools. Yet because funds are limited, the number of magnet schools that can be established is also limited; inevitably, some African American schoolchildren have often remained in primarily minority schools.

Housing Integration

By 1990, neither the federal Fair Housing Act of 1968 nor the many state and local laws banning discrimination in the sale or rental of housing had solved the problem of racially segregated neighborhoods. One troublesome issue that arises with respect to housing integration is the tension between individual rights and the goal of keeping a neighborhood integrated over time. Many whites are reluctant to live in a neighborhood or an apartment complex when the percentage of African American residents exceeds a certain number. To prevent wholesale evacuation by whites, so-called benign quotas have been introduced limiting the African American influx in the interest of stable integration. Benign quotas have been used by real estate agents in the Chicago suburb of Oak Park and by the management of the Starrett City apartment complex in New York City; in the latter case, the constitutionality of benign quotas was challenged in the 1980's.

Another difficult question is whether poor as well as middle- or upper-income African Americans should be given the chance to live in the prosperous and mostly white suburbs. White suburbanites who might tolerate the occasional prosperous African American homeowner as a neighbor might also oppose the building of public housing projects in suburbia; yet it is the poorer African American who might benefit most from the greater employment opportunities found in the suburbs. In Chicago, the Gautreaux program attempted to circumvent the problem by settling small numbers of carefully selected poor African American families in prosperous white suburbs.

Nathan Glazer, in a 1993 magazine essay, argued that only an extremely intrusive government could make racially integrated neighborhoods remain racially integrated over time. Bernard Boxill contends, however, that not every action that is beyond the penalties of law is necessarily moral, and that government, if it cannot force whites to stay in integrated neighborhoods, can at least offer inducements for them to do so.   *Paul D. Mageli*

Core Resources

Useful studies of integration can be found in Bernard R. Boxill's *Blacks and Social Justice* (Totowa, N.J.: Rowman & Allanheld, 1984); Gertrude Ezorsky's *Racism and Justice: The Case for Affirmative Action* (Ithaca, N.Y.: Cornell University Press, 1991); Nathan Glazer's *Affirmative Discrimination: Ethnic Inequality and Public Policy* (New York: Basic Books, 1975); Andrew Hacker's *Two Nations: Black and White, Separate, Hostile, Unequal* (New York: Charles Scribner's Sons, 1992); Jonathan Kozol's *Savage Inequalities: Children in America's Schools* (New York: Crown, 1991); Glenn C. Loury's "Matters of Color—Blacks and the Constitutional Order," in *Slavery and Its Consequences: The*

Constitution, Equality, and Race, edited by Robert A. Gold-win and Art Kaufman (Washington, D.C.: American Enterprise Institute Press, 1988); Douglas S. Massey and Nancy A. Denton's *American Apartheid: Segregation and the Making of the Underclass* (Cambridge, Mass.: Harvard University Press, 1993); and Harvey Molotch's *Managed Integration: Dilemmas of Doing Good in the City* (Berkeley: University of California Press, 1972).

See also: Affirmative action; *Brown v. Board of Education*; Civil Rights Act of 1964; Civil Rights movement; Desegregation: defense; Desegregation: public schools; Housing; Military desegregation; Racism: history of the concept; Segregation; Segregation: de facto and de jure; Segregation vs. integration.

Intelligence and race

Significance: Observed differences in mean IQ levels for racial/ethnic groups have generated prolonged and intense controversy on whether intelligence is determined by environment or genetics. The fact that human DNA is nearly identical across racial and ethnic groups argues against race-based genetic differences. Consequences of the position taken on this issue are enormous for social policy, education, and overall race relations.

Contemporary debate on the relationship between intelligence and race can be traced to the nineteenth century eugenics movement initiated by Francis Galton, Charles Darwin's half-cousin. Eugenics is a science that aims to improve the hereditary characteristics of a race or breed, usually through selective mating. Galton proposed eugenics as a means of promoting the chances of "superior" races to prevail over the rapid growth of "inferior" races. In *Hereditary Genius* (1869), Galton concluded that mental traits were as inheritable as physical features. Galton's colleague, Karl Pearson, the founder of statistical correlation, shared his anxiety about a dysgenic trend, one that favored the "weaker races," which were reproducing at a higher rate than the "mentally better stock."

Galton's efforts to measure intelligence using the speed and accuracy of mental processes as criteria led to attempts to create mental tests. The term "mental test" itself was coined in 1890 by British scientist James McKeen Cattell.

Test Development
During this time, French psychologist Alfred Binet was conducting experiments on his two daughters to develop an accurate method of measuring intelligence. Binet's major concern was not eugenics but helping school-teachers distinguish the "malicious" (students who lacked motivation) from the "stupid" (students who lacked the intellectual capacity to succeed). In 1904, Binet created a scale known as the Binet-Simon Scale and advocated that all students be tested with it to separate the "malicious" from the "stupid."

At the start of the twentieth century, several U.S. psychologists including Edward L. Thorndike, Naomi Norsworthy, Henry Goddard, and Lewis Terman, all believers in eugenics, were also developing methods to test intelligence. The first version of the Stanford-Binet Intelligence Test, which improved on the Binet-Simon Scale, was produced by Terman at Stanford University in 1916. The notion of intelligence quotient, or IQ—mental age divided by chronological age of the person tested and multiplied by 100—was introduced by Wilhelm Stern, making it possible to compare people's performances. Finding that the average IQ of children from upper-class families was 107 and that of working-class children was only 93, Terman concluded that the difference was genetic, not an outcome of home environment. He questioned the utility of education to help lower-class children become "intelligent voters or capable citizens."

In the nineteenth century, Francis Galton, Charles Darwin's half-cousin, developed eugenics, a science that aims to improve the hereditary characteristics of a race or breed, usually through selective mating.

During World War I, Terman convinced the United States army to use psychological testing to assess the mental fitness of soldiers. Because many of the 1.7 million men who were tested were not proficient in English or hailed from impoverished backgrounds, their test scores were depressed, leading the researchers to conclude that immigrants from the non-English-speaking world and lower-class Americans were genetically inferior. This led to a policy of testing all immigrants who arrived at Ellis Island, spreading the view that immigrants who were not white Anglo-Saxon Protestants were of "moron grade."

In 1939, David Wechsler developed a new IQ test, the Wechsler-Bellevue test. It was very similar to the Stanford-Binet; however, it measured not only verbal skills but also performance skills. In 1955, it was renamed the Wechsler Adult Intelligence Scale (WAIS). Modifications were added later to create the Wechsler Intelligence Scale for Children (WISC-R) and the Wechsler Preschool and Primary Scale Intelligence (WPPSI). By the end of the twentieth century, hundreds of other tests, including tests designed to measure scholastic aptitude and achievement, had been created and used, revealing the United States' fascination with intelligence.

Challenges to IQ Testing

Objections to intelligence testing were first raised as early as 1913 by J. E. Wallace Wallin, a clinical psychologist from Iowa who noticed that children judged to be morons were sometimes unfairly institutionalized. Robert M. Yerks, a psychologist from Harvard University, also warned about the dangers of untrained examiners clinically diagnosing people. In response, the American Psychological Association, at its 1915 meeting, passed a resolution discouraging unqualified individuals from administering psychological testing.

Widespread criticism of psychological testing arose in the 1960's in response to two conclusions that had been reached by most psychologists: Blacks as a group consistently scored fifteen points lower than whites on standardized IQ tests, and blacks did better or at least as well as whites on test items involving simple tasks and rote memorization. These conclusions reinforced prevalent negative stereotypes of African Americans, providing justification for continued discrimination against them in education and jobs. As criticism of intelligence testing became louder, the validity of the tests was challenged in court. Civil rights activists protested against placing children in special education programs based on IQ tests. Charges of racism and examiner bias were made in professional circles as well as in the media. An avalanche of books, articles, and dissertations were produced, mostly challenging the black inferiority thesis.

Racial/Ethnic Differences and IQ

Few contest the fact that a definite difference exists in mean IQ between blacks and whites in the United States. Most people also acknowledged that regardless of race, class differences exist in mean IQ scores: Upper-class whites perform better than lower-class whites. What is contentious is the interpretation of these observed differences, that is, whether they stem from the genetic makeups of different groups or are determined by environmental factors.

The controversy was sharpened by an article published by A. R. Jensen, an educational psychologist, in the *Harvard Educational Review* in 1969. This article held that inherited factors largely accounted for individual differences in human intelligence. Jensen asserted that because of their genetic limitations, educational programs designed to raise the IQs of African American children were largely ineffective. Although he did not deny the influence of environmental factors, he claimed that they were merely "threshold variables."

Two other prominent psychologists who have for decades defended the hereditarian thesis are H. J. Eysenck, a British psychologist, and Richard Herrnstein, a psychologist from Harvard University. Eysenck supported Jensen's position and distinguished between two main types of intellectual abilities: abstract reason-

---

Average ACT and SAT Test Scores by Racial/Ethnic Group

	ACT (1998)	SAT (1997) Verbal	SAT (1997) Math
American Indian	19.0	475	475
Asian American	21.8	496	560
Black	17.1	434	423
Mexican American	18.5	451	458
Puerto Rican	—	454	447
Other Hispanic	19.6	466	468
White	21.7	526	526
Other	19.6	512	514

Note: The ACT is scored on a scale from 1 to 36; the SAT is scored on a scale from 200 to 800.

Source: Data are from *The Chronicle of Higher Education Almanac*, Vol. XLV. No. 1, August 28, 1998.

ing ability, which IQ is based on, and associative learning ability, which involves memory and rote learning. In his estimation, large racial and social class differences exist in abstract reasoning, although virtually no such differences are found in associative learning.

Herrnstein has also long maintained that genetics is a significant factor in IQ differences between racial and ethnic groups. His definitive statement, coauthored by Charles Murray, is *The Bell Curve: Intelligence and Class Structure in American Life* (1994). Herrnstein and Murray insist that race and IQ are genetically linked. Problems of the poor—unemployment, crime, poverty, and the like—are to be blamed, at least in part, on low IQ. Herrnstein and Murray are pessimistic in their assessment of programs designed to raise people's intellectual abilities. Evoking Galton's fears of a dysgenic trend, the authors believe that the United States is irrevocably turning into a caste society, stratified by IQ differences.

Critics of *The Bell Curve* question the findings of this book on several grounds: Data collected in this book are unreliable; available data do not support the thesis that intelligence is unequally distributed among various races; its authors reach conclusions that are far beyond what the data warrant; and, finally, even if genetics is a factor in intelligence, by the authors' own admission, it accounts for no more than 5 percent to 10 percent of the variance, far from what is needed to justify their fatalistic view on social stratification.

What Is Intelligence?

The difficulties in resolving the IQ controversy are many: There is no reliable method of isolating the influence of environmental variables from genetics in measuring intelligence, and the concepts used—intelligence, race, and ethnicity in particular—are not precisely definable.

Perhaps the most difficult problem is determining what constitutes intelligence. Intelligence is generally understood as a concept, rather than an objective entity, that is constructed to account for certain cognitive abilities. Intelligence tests are designed to identify and measure cognitive abilities, using quantitative methods based on some theoretical conception of intelligence. Existing intelligence tests measure such abilities as the ability to master common information (such as how many days there are in a year), verbal comprehension (such as what "serendipity" means), knowledge of culturally/legally acceptable ways to deal with problems (such as what one would do if one were the first person in a movie theater to notice smoke and fire), basic mathematical ability (such as the abilities to add, subtract, and multiply), the ability to reason abstractly, the ability to compare and contrast different objects or ideas, the ability to recall information, the ability to manipulate situations mentally, the ability to analyze and solve practical problems,

the ability to distinguish what is essential from what is merely accidental, and the ability to learn a new task.

Considerable discussion exists on whether human intelligence is a unitary idea or whether there are several kinds of intelligence. In 1904, British psychologist Charles Spearman proposed that intelligence is made up of two parts: general intelligence (g) and the specific ability measured by particular test items(s). In 1941, R. B. Cattell distinguished between fluid (Gf) and crystallized (Gc) intelligences. Going beyond Cattell, some have recognized the need to consider intelligence as comprising several types, some of which are not measured by available IQ tests. Psychologist Howard Gardner has identified many types and forms of intelligence other than cognitive. Studies also show that intelligence is not fixed but remains changeable over time, depending on new opportunities and experiences. For example, one study found that the IQs of African American college students rise significantly higher as a result of their receiving a college education.

Cultural and Other Biases

It has been pointed out that IQ tests measure, more than anything else, knowledge of white middle-class culture. Researchers have noted that subcultural differences play a decisive role in the ways in which people grasp and process information, their learning styles, and their attitudes toward test taking. Not all groups are equally familiar with the content of the test items presented to them; words are not univocal across subcultures. Researcher Janet E. Helms has suggested that socioeconomic status, culture, and race may influence a person's performance on the Wechsler Adult Intelligence Scale-Revised (WAIS-R). For example, persons from lower socioeconomic classes may not establish a trusting relationship with the examiner, and individual characteristics of the examiner and their biases in interpretation of ambiguous answers affect test scores. African Americans score lower when tested by whites than when tested by blacks, a fact that was known as early as 1936 but ignored until the 1960's. Also, people with limited vocabulary may not understand the instructions given and the explanations offered in response to their questions.

Impact on Social Policy

Intelligence testing has become an incendiary issue because of its linkages with a variety of other historically sensitive issues, including a belief in the superiority of the Anglo-Saxon race, eugenics movements, black slavery, discriminatory immigration policies, and efforts to remedy past injustices. Some observers have pointed out that the intense interest in IQ today parallels its ideological beginnings toward the end of the nineteenth century.

In the nineteenth century, when industrialization was in full swing, the pressures of the marketplace demanded greater social equality and inclusion of all social strata in the social processes. Eugenics and Social Darwinism arose as reactionary movements to oppose programs and policies designed to open up greater opportunity to the poor and the working classes.

The second half of the twentieth century saw a social revolution that in many ways paralleled the Industrial Revolution. In the United States, disadvantaged people demanded fundamental changes in social institutions and abolition of racist policies. Following the civil rights victories of the 1960's, social and educational programs were put in place to remedy the effects of past discrimination. The 1980's and 1990's witnessed the rise of a white reactionary movement that resulted in the progressive dismantling of many of these programs. Some fear that recent interest in resurrecting old arguments in support of the genetic basis of intelligence through such publications as *The Bell Curve* may well be part of a renewed attempt to reinstitute the castelike structure of racism through other means.   *Mathew J. Kanjirathinkal*

Core Resources

Those who believe that intelligence is linked to race set forth their positions in a number of books and articles, including H. J. Eysenck's *The IQ Argument* (New York: Library Press, 1971) and *The Measurement of Intelligence* (Baltimore: Williams and Wilkins Company, 1973); A. R. Jensen's "How Much Can We Boost IQ and Scholastic Achievement?" reprinted in *Environment, Heredity, and Intelligence*, a compilation of studies and commentaries (Cambridge, Mass.: Harvard Education Review, 1969); and Richard Herrnstein and Charles Murray's *The Bell Curve: Intelligence and Class Structure in American Life* (New York: Free Press, 1994).

Books and articles stating the case against a race-intelligence link include James Flyn's *Race, IQ, and Jensen* (London: Routledge, 1980); Douglas Lee Eckberg's *Intelligence and Race* (New York: Praeger, 1979); and Linda Darling-Hammond's "Cracks in the Bell Curve: How Education Matters" in *Journal of Negro Education* (64, 3, Summer, 1995).

More neutral treatments of the issue include chapters 10 and 11 in *The Legacy of Malthus: The Social Costs of the New Scientific Racism* (Urbana: University of Illinois Press, 1980), by Allan Chase; Janet E. Helms's "The Triple Quandary of Race, Culture, and Social Class in Standardized Cognitive Ability Testing" in *Contemporary Intellectual Assessment: Theories, Tests, and Issues*, edited by Dawn P. Flanagan et al. (New York: Guilford Press, 1997); Sandra Scarr's *Race, Social Class, and Individual Differences* (Hillsdale, N.J.: Lawrence Erlbaum, 1981); *The IQ Controversy: Critical Readings*, edited by N. J. Block and Gerald

Dworkin (New York: Pantheon Books, 1976); and *The Bell Curve Debate: History, Documents, Opinions* (New York: Random House, 1997), edited by Russel Jacoby and Naomi Galuberman.

See also: Ability testing; African American stereotypes; Intelligence testing; Racial/ethnic relations: race-class debate; Standardized testing and IQ testing controversies; Xenophobia, nativism, and eugenics.

Intelligence testing

Alfred Binet (1857-1911) and his colleagues first devised tests to assess the mental abilities of French children in the 1890's. A child's "mental age," divided by chronological age, gave an "intelligence quotient" (IQ). Binet thought that IQ scores could be improved through education, but many British psychologists insisted that intelligence was hereditary. Data on this issue were gathered by Cyril Burt, but some of his data were later shown to have been fabricated. American psychologists modernized Binet's tests but applied them, with considerable bias, against African Americans and immigrants. Despite early claims that the tests measure "innate intelligence," careful studies show that educational influences are strong and that most early studies were flawed.

In particular, a fifteen-point average difference between unselected whites and African Americans disappears when comparison is made between samples matched by social status, family income, and similar factors. African Americans who have attended good schools and have had similar advantages achieve higher scores than do students from disadvantaged backgrounds regardless of race.

Test bias occurs because the test is given in a particular language and because it assumes a middle-class cultural environment; the results are therefore biased against the poor and against those who speak a different language. Subtler bias includes questions about activities that are common to middle-class white males, thus discriminating against females and blacks. Bias-free exams are difficult to write.

Proponents of eugenics have advocated favorable treatment of high-IQ individuals and unfavorable treatment (including sterilization) of low-IQ subjects. Since test results can be modified by education and are subject to bias, such proposals have lost much favor since about 1940.   *Eli C. Minkoff*

See also: Ability testing; Education and racial/ethnic relations; Intelligence and race; Standardized testing and IQ testing controversies; Xenophobia, nativism, and eugenics.

Internal colonialism

Significance: An ethnic or racial group that is a victim of internal colonialism lacks the ability to guide its own destiny economically, politically, and socially because it has been singled out for exclusion from the mainstream by the dominant ethnic group.

Some observers believe that certain subordinate ethnic and racial groups are colonies within their own countries, controlled by the dominant ethnic group. The applicability of this concept is disputed by other observers, who point out difficulties in the analogy between external and internal colonialism.

External Colonialism
A nation can establish an external colony by imposing control over a territory located beyond its existing borders. To maintain control, the colonial power must send civilian and military personnel to live in the country. Military personnel are sent to keep order, that is, to suppress any opposition to the colonial power, which displaces the former indigenous power structure. Civilian personnel are sent to maintain control through economic, political, and social means.

Economic control is maintained by such methods as restricting licenses to operate local businesses, imposing heavy taxes, buying out local businesses and property, importing workers from other countries, paying lower wages to the subordinate group for the same work performed by members of the dominant ethnic group, setting up absentee landlords, turning areas into ghettos, and banning local businesses. The colonial power's objective is to dominate the market so that the colonized people will lack economic autonomy, become economically marginalized, and can be exploited in order to enrich the colonizers. Money can then flow from the dominated peoples to the rulers.

Political control is maintained by arresting independent leaders, banning opposition groups, locating pliable local leaders who will carry out the colonial agenda, and restricting civil liberties. The aim of the colonial power is to dominate the political system so that the colonized people lack any ability to influence public policy. Compliance can then result from a belief that resistance is useless.

Social control is maintained by banning the local language, controlling the educational system and the media, geographically displacing the subordinate ethnic group, moving in settlers from the home country of the colonial power, and ridiculing the supposed backwardness of the subordinate ethnic group. The aim of the colonial power is to dominate society to the extent that the colonized people believe in their own inferiority. The ruling group can then break the spirit of the subordinate population.

One example of external colonialism occurred a century ago, when the United States attempted to seize control of the Philippine islands by suppressing an armed independence struggle in 1901. U.S. military personnel arrived first, followed by bureaucrats, educators, media, traders, and others, who established themselves as colonists. This classical form of external colonialism ended in 1946, when the Philippines became an independent country and U.S. bureaucrats withdrew. U.S. armed forces, however, remained in the Philippines for more than four decades after 1946 on bases that were transferred to Philippine sovereignty.

Native Americans as Colonized People
In external colonialism, a dominant and powerful country goes overseas to take over a country that is weak and can be dominated. However, the same methods can be used inside a country: A dominant ethnic group can act as a colonial power in subordinating a weaker ethnic group inside the same country.

For many centuries, the natives of North and South America lived in isolation from the rest of the world. When Europeans set foot in the Western Hemisphere with the intent of occupying the land, conflict between the two groups was inevitable. The history of the European conquest of the Americas began as a form of external colonialism. When the countries of North and South America became independent, internal colonialism existed because the population that was of European origin continued to hold a dominant position over the indigenous population and imposed economic, political, and social control.

Today, Native Americans in the United States can live on reservations, that is, plots of land in which they alone are permitted to reside. Although tribal authorities are allowed to make some decisions on behalf of the reservation population, ultimate political authority is held by the U.S. Department of the Interior's Bureau of Indian Affairs (BIA). Native Americans can develop their own sources of income, but the BIA runs the schools in a manner quite similar to the educational systems that operate in colonies.

Many examples of internal colonialism abound outside the United States. In the seventeenth century, after suppressing an Irish rebellion, Henry VIII of England encouraged British settlers to move to Ulster, in the northern part of Ireland; the result was a colonization of Ireland. Later in the same century, Dutch settlers arrived to establish colonial enclaves amid the indigenous peoples of South Africa; however, when apartheid was adopted in 1948, it was the Africans who were forcibly relocated into enclaves. After the United States gained control of the Philippine islands from Spain in 1901, the indigenous peoples of Mindanao Island and the Sulu archipelago refused to recognize the authority of the new colonial power, so the U.S. authorities encouraged Filipinos to move to Mindanao in the role of internal colonists.

African Americans as Colonized People

Some observers claim that a form of internal colonialism involving African Americans exists in the United States. They believe that African Americans who live primarily in segregated housing and territorial enclaves have been treated as colonial subjects. For example, businesses in these enclaves tend not to be run by African Americans. As further evidence, they cite how African Americans, for more than three centuries, were denied positions of political authority, rendering them politically dependent. The dominant white population made sure that the Africans lost their own culture and, during the era of slavery, would not have an opportunity to acquire American culture.

Robert Blauner's *Racial Oppression in America* (1972) is one of the most famous statements of the thesis that African Americans have been internally colonized. Economically, African Americans have worked for white Americans in low-paying jobs. Until the 1960's, blacks rarely held executive positions in government. Indeed, the practice among whites was to deal with captive leaders in the African American community, that is, blacks who represented the interests of whites more than the needs of blacks. Moreover, blacks lost African culture and have been excluded from the mainstream of American culture. Advocates of the concept of internal colonialism argue that these facts establish the existence of a separate caste status for African Americans, who are forced to confront a split labor market in which they are the lowest-paid workers, are harassed by police, ignored by politicians, and subjected to inferior schooling so that they will not acquire the skills needed for upward mobility.

Critics of the concept of internal colonialism point out several reasons why they believe that the concept of internal colonialism does not fit the situation of African Americans. Whites and blacks can be found in all classes: Some African Americans are economically much better off than the average white American. Also, African Americans are not confined to a specific bounded territory but live in many neighborhoods. Similarly, African Americans have been elected mayors of most larger American cities, so they are hardly politically impotent. Finally, African Americans have developed their own distinctive culture within the United States, and most

Americans are well acquainted with the African American entertainers and other cultural leaders. Marxists argue that the real divisions in society are not between racial groups but rather between social classes.

Impact on Public Policy

When members of an ethnic or racial group believe that they are being colonized, at least four courses of action are open to them. One is to assimilate to the dominant culture, thereby ending discriminatory treatment. European ethnic groups in the United States, many of which initially formed enclaves such as Little Italies, have generally been successful in becoming part of the mainstream.

A second course is to leave the country to escape persecution. In the early part of the twentieth century, Turkey instituted massacres of Armenians, many of whom chose to emigrate to the United States. Chinese left Indonesia and Malaysia in the 1960's for similar reasons.

A third course is to protest unequal treatment with the aim of reversing an ethnic group's colonial status. The American Civil Rights movement of the 1960's agitated successfully for the passage of legislation to outlaw discrimination on the basis of race and sex, though enforcement of the legislation has not eliminated discrimination.

The fourth alternative is nationalism and the establishment of a separate country. However, the weaker ethnic group can expect to lose if it engages in a war of independence unless it can find an ally abroad. In 1971, for example, the peoples of East Pakistan believed that they were being exploited and badly governed by authorities in West Pakistan. After a war successfully waged with the help of India, East Pakistan was recognized as the new nation of Bangladesh. Similarly, some of the Moros of Mindanao and the Sulu archipelago have continued to agitate for an independent state consisting of the territories of the former Sultanate of Sulu. Within the United States, some members of the African American liberation movement of the 1960's, inspired by the agenda in Stokely Carmichael and Charles V. Hamilton's *Black Power* (1967), have urged the United Nations to hold plebiscites in the "black colonies of America."

Michael Haas

Core Resources

The concept of internal colonialism is developed in several publications. An excellent discussion is found in Harold Wolpe's "The Theory of Internal Colonialism," in *Beyond the Sociology of Development: Economy and Society in Latin America and Africa*, edited by Ivar Oxaal, Tony Barnett, and David Booth (London: Routledge & Kegan Paul, 1975) and Pablo Gonzales-Casanova's "Internal

Colonialism and National Development," in *Latin American Radicalism*, edited by Irving Louis Horowitz (New York: Random House, 1969). The concept is applied to Britain by Michael Hechter in *Internal Colonialism: The Celtic Fringe in British National Development* (Berkeley: University of California Press, 1975), to France by Suzanne Berger in *Peasants Against Politics: Rural Organization in Brittany, 1911-1967* (Cambridge, Mass.: Harvard University Press, 1972), and to Peru by Julio Cotler in "The Mechanism of Internal Domination and Social Change in Peru," in *Masses in Latin America*, edited by Irving Louis Horowitz (New York: Oxford University Press, 1970).

Applications to the United States were developed by Stokely Carmichael (later Kwame Toure) and Charles V. Hamilton in *Black Power: The Politics of Liberation in America* (New York: Random House, 1967) and Robert Blauner's *Racial Oppression in America* (New York: Harper & Row, 1972), Ronald Bailey and Guillermo Flores's "Internal Colonialism and Racial Minorities in the U.S.: An Overview," in *Structures of Dependency*, edited by Frank Bonilla and Robert Girling (East Palo Alto, Calif.: Nairobi Bookstore, 1973), and "The Barrio as Internal Colony," by Mario Barrera et al. in *People and Politics in Urban Society*, edited by Harlan Hahn (Beverly Hills, Calif.: Sage Publications, 1972). For critiques of the concept of internal colonialism as applied to the United States, see Michael Burawoy's "Race, Class, and Colonialism," in *Social and Economic Studies* (24, December, 1974), and Michael Omi and Howard Winant's *Racial Formation in the United States: From the 1960's to the 1980's* (New York: Routledge & Kegan Paul, 1986).

See also: Colonial model of racism; Discrimination: racial and ethnic; External colonialism; Indian-white relations: United States; Reservation system of the United States; Slavery: history.

Internalized racism

A foundational principle in sociology is that the self is socially constructed through the role-taking aspect of socialization, whereby we see ourselves from the perspectives of significant others and the general perspective of our culture. Other people and the media provide a looking glass, supplying us with reflected appraisals of the self and racial or ethnic groups. Because racist stereotypes prevail in American culture, it is possible for some minority members to internalize them and to denigrate themselves by thinking about, feeling toward, and treating themselves in the same way members of the dominant culture may. However, a caveat is warranted here, as minority members are not passive victims of oppression; if a minority individual has a favorable self-feeling through, for example, internalizing a positive racial or ethnic group identity from significant others and his or her primary groups, then the ability to resist racist evaluations is greatly enhanced. Individuals are also able to interpret situations reflectively, enabling some minority members to realize that many dominant-group representations of their groups and cultural heritages are stereotypical and ideological. Nevertheless, an individual can succumb to the enormous influence that a media-saturated culture exerts on the construction of his or her identity.

Internalized racism has been poignantly illustrated in such portraits as African American writer Jean Toomer's book *Cane* (1923) and African American novelist Toni Morrison's *The Bluest Eye* (1970). The latter novel tells the story of Pecola Breedlove, an adolescent African American girl tormented by her internalization of the white standards of beauty as symbolized by blue eyes. Social psychologist Kurt Lewin researched the phenomenon of group self-hatred. Another social psychologist, Kenneth Clark, documented the prevalence of internalized racism, providing persuasive testimony to the U.S. Supreme Court in *Brown v. Board of Education* (1954) that segregated schools taught black children that they were inferior, engendering emotional devastation and psychological harm. Along similar lines, social theorist bell hooks, in *Black Looks: Race and Representation* (1992), describes internalized racism as a "colonization of the mind."

In the United States, the Declaration of Independence declares that those who rule must have the "consent of the governed." If minority members believe that their status in society is a result of *natural* inequality in a system of fair play, meritocracy, or equality of opportunity, then their internalized racism manufactures the consent needed to be governed although oppressed. Internalizing a view of innate inferiority dissuades minorities from seeking redress for their grievances, encouraging instead accommodation, acquiescence, and resignation. Nevertheless, many minority individuals have resisted white supremacy, developing a consciousness of social injustice, igniting a movement for civil rights, and, occasionally, sparking violent protest (expressed in the slogan "No justice, no peace!"). Over the years, African Americans have forged positive self and group identities as "New Negroes" of the 1920's Harlem Renaissance and have transformed their identity from Negro to black, epitomized by the 1960's phrase, "Black is beautiful." Native Americans have acted similarly through such activities as a revival of tribal consciousness and of powwows, the rise of the American Indian Movement (AIM), and the concept of Red Power. Many Mexican Americans have responded similarly by adopting

"Chicano" as a term of group pride and Chicanismo as a counterideology and by forming the political movement of La Raza Unida.   *Gil Richard Musolf*

See also: Accommodationism; American Indian Movement; Black Is Beautiful movement; Chicano movement; Discrimination: responses to; Harlem Renaissance; Stereotyping and the self-fulfilling prophecy.

International Indian Treaty Council

The International Indian Treaty Council was founded during a conference convened on the Standing Rock Reservation (North Dakota) during July, 1974. Its initial mandate, conveyed by the Lakota elders, was to "take the 1868 Fort Laramie Treaty and place it before the community of nations." AIM leader Russell Means, asked to assume responsibility for IITC, accepted by agreeing to serve as "Permanent Trustee." Jimmie Durham, a Cherokee AIM member, became IITC's founding director.

By 1975, Means and Durham had established an office in New York and expanded the mission of the "international diplomatic arm of AIM" (American Indian Movement) to include advocacy of the rights of all indigenous peoples, worldwide. Durham then set about organizing the first major forum on indigenous rights in the history of the United States.

This resulted in the "Indian Summer in Geneva," an assembly of delegates from ninety-eight indigenous nations throughout the Western Hemisphere at the Palace of Nations in Geneva, Switzerland, during July, 1977. As the coordinating entity, IITC became the first indigenous Non-Governing Organization (NGO; Type-II, Consultative) ever recognized by the United Nations.

The assembly stimulated the United Nations to establish a formal body, the Working Group on Indigenous Populations, under its Economic and Social Council (ECOSOC) for purposes of receiving annual reports on the grievances of the world's native peoples. The Working Group's broader charge was to make the studies necessary to prepare a Draft Declaration on the Rights of Indigenous Peoples by 1992 (later extended to 1994) for ratification by the U.N. General Assembly as international law.

With this established, Durham resigned in 1981 to pursue a career as an artist. He was replaced by Russell Means's younger brother, Bill, who proved a far less appropriate director. Almost immediately, the younger Means initiated a policy of aligning IITC with a range of leftist governments, many of them oppressing indigenous peoples within their borders. The result was a steady erosion of native support for IITC.

By 1986, disputes over IITC's support of Nicaragua's Sandinista regime in its drive to subordinate the Miskito, Sumu, and Rama peoples of the country's Atlantic coast led to a purge. "Indigenists," such as Harvard-trained Shawnee attorney Glenn Morris, were summarily expelled from IITC. The Lakota elders' original mandate was negated, Russell Means displaced from his permanent trusteeship, and IITC structurally separated from AIM by its incorporation under U.S. law.

Thereafter, although Bill Means continued to speak of "representing more than a hundred indigenous nations," IITC's isolation and decline accelerated. By the early 1990's, it was increasingly encumbered by the fundraising requirements of supporting its staff. Fortunately, many of the peoples whose rights it had once championed had by then learned to represent themselves internationally.   *Ward Churchill*

See also: American Indian activism; American Indian Movement; Pan-Indianism.

Interracial and interethnic marriage

Significance: Interracial and interethnic marriages involve people from dissimilar racial, ethnic, linguistic, or national groups. These marriages are significant for intergroup relations because they are a sign of assimilation or integration for the minority group. Intermarriage can be understood as an indication of the state of race and ethnic relations, as well as an agent of assimilation. Intermarriage blurs racial and ethnic boundaries by bringing together diverse groups and producing children who can assume new multiracial and multiethnic identities.

In the United States, racial and ethnic groups have tended to marry within their own group. Throughout U.S. history, there have been laws against various types of interracial and interethnic marriage; such laws were usually directed at African Americans, Native Americans, and Asian Americans. For example, in the early twentieth century, Chinese and Japanese immigrants were denied "white" status, which meant, among other things, that they were subject to restrictions on their right to marry outside their own groups. Since the institution of slavery, interracial relations between African Americans and whites have been closely monitored and restricted. Up until 1966, seventeen states still had formal prohibitions against one or more forms of interracial marriage, and forty states at one time had laws prohibiting blacks from marrying whites. On June 12, 1967, the U.S. Supreme Court rendered a decision in *Loving v. Virginia* that overturned the sixteen existing state antimiscegenation statutes.

Intermarriage Rates

Rates of intermarriage thus differ depending on the racial or ethnic groups involved. According to numerous studies, such as Richard Alba's *Ethnicity and Race in the U.S.A.* (1988), interethnic marriages, especially between European Americans, are common. Alba has concluded that among white ethnic groups there has been a steady increase in interethnic marriage. For example, only 20 percent of Italian American men born after 1949 were married to Italian American women. Similarly, Nathan Glazer and Daniel P. Moynihan's *Beyond the Melting Pot* (1970) analyzed ethnic groups in New York City and found that distinctions between white ethnic groups were being reduced by intermarriage. Despite this increase in interethnic marriages, these two studies both found that individuals are

Richard and Mildred Loving (pictured here) married despite a Virginia law forbidding interracial marriage. Their case went before the U.S. Supreme Court and resulted in a ruling that forbade antimiscegenation laws in 1967.

still somewhat more likely to choose mates from their own ethnic group than from another.

Interethnic marriage, though, is different from interracial marriage. People are often willing to cross ethnic boundaries to marry, but there is a much greater resistance to crossing racial boundaries. In addition, there are disparities between rates of intermarriage for the various racial groups. Hispanic Americans are an interesting example, since this group can be classed as both an ethnic minority group and a racial minority group. Marriages between Hispanic Americans and whites account for only 2.6 percent of all U.S. marriages, according to 1996 U.S. Census Bureau data; however, this represents a substantial increase from 1970, when the rate was closer to 1 percent. Some studies, such as Clara Rodriguez's *Puerto Ricans: Born in the USA* (1989), have found that rates of intermarriage increase for Hispanic Americans of the more affluent social classes who live in the cities and for the presumably more Americanized younger generations.

Asian Americans have higher rates

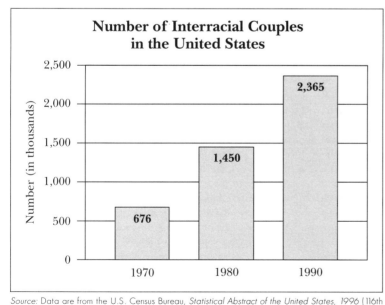

Number of Interracial Couples in the United States

Source: Data are from the U.S. Census Bureau, *Statistical Abstract of the United States, 1996* (116th ed.). Washington, D.C.: Government Printing Office, 1997.

of intermarriage than African Americans and Hispanic Americans, according to scholars Sharon Lee and Keiko Yamanaka, who found the outmarriage rate for Chinese Americans to be 15 percent and for Japanese Americans 34 percent. However, not all Asian American groups have high rates of intermarriage. Robert Jiobu's *Ethnicity and Assimilation* (1988) found that Vietnamese Americans have very low rates of intermarriage.

African Americans have the lowest rates of intermarriage among all racial groups. According to the U.S. Census Bureau, in 1995, black-white marriages accounted for less than 1 percent of all U.S. marriages. Black males have traditionally outmarried at higher rates than black women. This is consistent with a 1990 study by Tucker and Mitchell-Kernan, which found that 3.6 percent of all married black men are married to white women, while only 1.2 percent of married black women are married to white men.

Intermarriage and Prejudice

Despite the increasing occurrence of intermarriage, there is still prejudice against these unions, especially marriages between blacks and whites. This disapproval is communicated through formal channels such as social institutions as well as via informal channels such as families and friends. According to scholars Paul Rosenblatt, Terri A. Karis, and Richard D. Powell, there are various ways in which white families express their opposition to intermarriage. Not allowing black individuals in their homes is one manifestation of the rejection by whites of the possibility that blacks could become part of the family; by not allowing them in, they maintain their image as "pure" whites, thus protecting the family from losing any status or privilege with other whites. Another way that the white family demonstrates its opposition to interracial relationships is to boycott a holiday gathering that a black individual will attend, or even more directly, the interracial wedding of a family member. Refusing to attend such a wedding can be seen as a symbolic refusal to witness and endorse the public entrance of an unacceptable individual into the family. Many white families also disown a member who marries interracially, thus declaring that the offender is no longer a member of the family (and of the white community in general). Ultimately many whites choose to marginalize the white member of their family rather than accept a black individual into their primary group. According to Rosenblatt et al., the reasons given by white families for their opposition are the disapproval of others; issues of safety and well-being; the alleged clannishness of the nonwhite racial group; the problems that children of the union would have; and the likelihood of a poor economic future. By citing such reasons for their behavior, whites are able to reflect stereotypes of racial minorities and

acknowledge societal disapproval without implicating themselves personally.

Other forms of opposition that the interracial couple may face come from outside the family. According to Rosenblatt et al., the refusal to accept or acknowledge interracial marriages occurs in a variety of ways, such as not selling a house or not renting a hotel room to an interracial couple. Other typical examples are restaurant hostesses asking one member of an interracial couple if it is "one for dinner" or supermarket cashiers trying to separate their food items in line at the grocery store, which are both refusals to acknowledge that the two are a couple. Religious reasons are also widely used, with Christian groups distributing information over the Internet that "interracial marriages are not biblical" or preachers interpreting the scriptures as explicitly opposing interracial marriages. Interracial couples also cite police harassment, getting "pulled over" a disproportionate number of times when together, and being told that the white woman fits the description of a kidnap victim. Popular culture and the mass media also work against the acceptance of interracial couples by presenting negative images of interracial couples on television talk shows or by rarely casting interracial couples in television shows or films. Often, whites who intermarry are marginalized and stereotyped in much the same way as minorities, with the assumption that they have pathological problems or are "white trash." Thus, although intermarriages are often seen as representative of the improving state of race and ethnic relations, opposition to and prejudice against these marriages still exist.

Erica Childs

Core Resources

Milton Gordon, in *Assimilation in American Life* (New York: Oxford University Press, 1964), identifies seven subprocesses of assimilation, including marital assimilation, or the formation of interracial and interethnic marriages. S. Dale McLemore's *Racial and Ethnic Relations in America* (Boston: Allyn & Bacon, 1994) and Joseph F. Healey's *Race, Ethnicity, Gender, and Class: The Sociology of Group Conflict and Change* (Thousand Oaks, Calif.: Pine Forge Press, 1998) both offer a summary of interracial and interethnic marriage trends. Richard Alba's *Ethnicity and Race in the U.S.A* (New York: Routledge, 1988) and Nathan Glazer and Daniel Moynihan's *Beyond the Melting Pot* (Cambridge, Mass.: MIT Press, 1970) explore interethnic marriage. Clara Rodriguez's *Puerto Ricans: Born in the USA* (Boston: Unwin Hyman, 1989) deals with the issue of intermarriage among Hispanics, focusing primarily on Puerto Ricans. Matthew Snipp's *American Indians: The First of This Land* (New York: Russell Sage Foundation, 1989) explores interracial marriage among Native Americans. Both Sharon

Lee and Keiko Yamanaka's "Patterns of Asian American Intermarriage and Marital Assimilation" (*Journal of Comparative Family Studies* 21, 1990) and Robert Jiobu's *Ethnicity and Assimilation* (Albany: State University of New York Press, 1988) explore the issue of intermarriage among Asian Americans. There are many works that look at the issue of black-white marriage, including Belinda Tucker and Claudia Mitchell-Kernan's "New Trends in Black American Interracial Marriage: The Social Structural Context" (*The Journal of Marriage and Family* 52). Paul Spickard's *Mixed Blood: Intermarriage and Ethnic Identity in Twentieth-Century America* (Madison: University of Wisconsin Press, 1989) and Paul Rosenblatt, Terri A. Karis, and Richard D. Powell's *Multiracial Couples: Black and White Voices* (Thousand Oaks, Calif.: Sage Publications, 1995) offer a more qualitative approach that explores the actual experiences of interracial and interethnic couples. For an understanding of interethnic marriage in Canada, Clifford Jansen's "Inter-Ethnic Marriages" (*International Journal of Comparative Sociology* 23, 1982) offers a good analysis.

See also: Assimilation: cultural and structural; Assimilation theories; Discrimination: behaviors; Friendships, interracial and interethnic; Miscegenation laws; Prejudice: effects; Segmented assimilation theory.

Iranian Americans

> **Significance:** Since November 4, 1979, when Iranian student militants seized the U.S. embassy in Tehran and held sixty-six Americans hostage while demanding the return of the Shah Muhammad Reza Pahlavi from his exile in the United States, most Americans have held extremely unfavorable opinions of Iranian Americans. Iranian Americans face a constant struggle to convince other groups in the United States that they personally are not terrorists and do not support the Islamic government in Iran.

The trauma of the 1979 Iranian revolution and subsequent terror and economic deterioration, combined with the long war with Iraq, resulted in widespread dispersions of Iranians outside their homeland. It is estimated that between 1.2 million and 2 million Iranian Americans live in the United States. The majority of Iranian immigrants live in suburban areas such as Los Angeles, Washington, D.C., and Long Island, New York, and hold middle-class jobs.

Since the Iranian Revolution and the taking of the U.S. embassy, images of Iranians as unpredictable and wild anti-American fanatics and terrorists have domi-

nated the minds of the American public, according to Ali Akbar Mahdi, department of sociology/anthropology, Ohio Wesleyan University, in the February/March, 1997, issue of *The Iranian*. For example, when the federal building in Oklahoma City was bombed on April 19, 1995, at first many Americans believed that Middle East terrorists were responsible. Living in such a negative environment is a difficult but conscious choice for most first-generation Iranian immigrants. Second-generation Iranians also suffer from the negative images associated with the national origins of their parents.

Mahdi wrote that the presence of many Iranian immigrants in Western countries is partially due to the religionization of Iranian society. Most of the Iranian immigrants are secular people who do not want to mix religion with politics and education. He said that most of the Iranian immigrants in the United States consist of middle- and upper-class people who are highly educated and have a better-than-average standard of living. Many of those who came from more modest backgrounds have secured middle-class positions for themselves through education, dedication, and hard work.

Relations with Other Groups

Iranians who came to the United States before the hostage crisis received a generally positive reception. However, after that crisis and the ensuing rise of Islamic fundamentalism in the Middle East, the American perception of Iran changed from a country of peace to a country of turmoil and unpredictability. The U.S. State Department has labeled the Iranian government as a "rogue state." The unfavorable portrayal of Iranians in the U.S. media helps breed prejudice and discrimination, placing a strain on Iranian Americans. Some researchers accuse the United States of using xenophobia and ungrounded fears to motivate its citizens to follow the views of American political, religious, and cultural leaders. They say that while the United States prides itself in its sociocultural diversity, it simultaneously denounces cultures it cannot understand.

A survey of 157 Iranian Americans conducted by Laleh Khalili, a graduate student at Columbia University (*The Iranian Times*, April, 1998), showed that although 37 percent of respondents select mostly other Iranian Americans as friends, 63 percent do not. Khalili found that those who prefer friends who are not Iranian Americans associate with members of other transnational communities rather than typical white Americans. The most frequently mentioned areas of origin are Southeast Asia, the Middle East, and Latin America. "A shared knowledge of what crossing borders entails and a similarity in sociopolitical (if not always cultural) backgrounds provide a context in which the Iranian in the United States can operate comfortably," Khalili said.

A group of Iranian Americans participates in a demonstration in New York City. During the hostage crisis in the late 1970's, many Americans developed a negative image of Iranians, and by association, Iranian Americans.

Image Improvement

In an effort to focus on the achievements of Iranian Americans and not dwell on the faults of the Iranian government, some U.S. governors in states such as New York, New Jersey, Delaware, and Florida have officially declared March 21, the Iranian celebration of the new year, as the Day of Iranian Americans. In 1997, Governor Lawton Chiles of Florida said, "Individuals of Iranian heritage have earned an esteemed place in the cultural, economic, and social structure of Florida and have proved themselves an asset to the community, with many of them holding positions in the fields of medicine, research, education, law, business, the arts, and public services." He called for continued mutual understanding and friendship between established residents and those of Iranian descent. Manucher Shahidi of Long Island, New York, one of the organizers of the movement to make March 21 a special day in the United States, said that the celebration involves being recognized as an official ethnic minority group in the United States. "This gives us lobbying power in Congress, gives us the right to institute our culture and history into that of America, and most importantly, it guarantees that the United States government will protect our cultural and historical integrity," he said.

Iranian American writer Michael C. Walker said in the February 26, 1998, issue of *The Iranian*, "We must proactively teach antidiscrimination in our schools and our communities. It must explore the world's diverse cultures, religions, and ethnicities. Such educa-

tion should especially concentrate on nations like Iran where America's hatred and misunderstanding is prismed and clearly focused."

Marian Wynne Haber

Core Resources

The most current and easily accessible information about Iranian Americans is found on the Internet at www.iranian.com. Primary sources include Ali Akbar Mahdi's "The Second Generation Iranians: Questions and Concerns," *The Iranian* (February/March, 1997); Kimberly D. Martz's "To You Closet Iranians," *The Iranian* (May, 1977); Laleh Khalili's "Mixing Memory and Desire: Iranians in the United States," *The Iranian* (May 13, 1998); Michael C. Walker's "Understanding Iranians? Not a Bad Idea," *The Iranian* (February 26, 1998). For further information and a comprehensive overview of the subject, see Maboud Ansari's *The Making of the Iranian Community in America* (New York: Pardis Press, 1992).

See also: Arab Americans; Prejudice and stereotyping; Refugees: U.S. policy; Stereotype.

Irish-African American relations

Conflict has existed between Irish Americans and African Americans since the first great waves of Irish immigration in the 1840's. Before the Civil War, Irish Catholics were confronted with harsh discrimination by Anglo-Protestant Americans. When dangerous work needed to be done, many employers opted to hire cheap Irish labor instead of using slaves, preferring to risk the life of an Irishman over one of their slaves, the latter being valuable property. Struggling to survive at the bottom of the economic ladder, the Irish feared that if slaves were set free, they would face even more competition for scarce jobs. Many also believed that they should focus their energies on improving their own plight before expending any of their resources helping African Americans. Irish Americans' concern for their own survival and their view of blacks as competition worked to sour relations between the two struggling groups.

During the Civil War, Irish Americans, who were loyal to the Union generally, had no interest in fighting a war to free the slaves. During the war, when disproportionate numbers of poor Irish were drafted to serve in the Union forces, riots broke out in cities throughout the North. On July 13, 1863, antidraft rioting broke out in New York City, lasting until July 15. Irish Americans, who viewed the conflict as a rich man's war fought by the poor, took out their anger at abolitionists and African Americans by burning, looting, and beating any blacks in their path. New York militia were called out to stop the rioting.

After the Civil War, the economic struggle between African Americans and Irish Americans continued. Irish Americans and other white immigrants took jobs in the booming industrial sector, and African Americans found themselves once again relegated to southern fields. Many African Americans, seeing immigrants usurp jobs they felt rightly belonged to them, began to engage in nativist rhetoric. Many African Americans vociferously supported the anti-immigration legislation of the 1920's.

As Irish Americans gained greater political and economic power in the twentieth century, they continued to do so at the expense of African Americans. Although literacy tests and other racist laws denied the majority of African Americans the vote until the Voting Rights Act of 1965, the Irish used their access to the ballot to gain control of local political machines and city halls. As they lost their brogues and became established in the mainstream of white America, the Irish used their political influence to monopolize civil service positions while excluding blacks and new immigrants.

In the 1990's, Irish Americans exceeded the national average in education, income, and employment levels while African Americans consistently lagged behind in all three areas. Although approximately one-third of African Americans could be considered at least middle class, there were three times more poor blacks than white Americans.   *Kathleen Odell Korgen*

See also: Employment and African Americans; Irish Americans; Irish Catholic "race."

Irish American stereotypes

Between 1820 and 1920, approximately five million people emigrated from Ireland to the United States. Most of these immigrants were Irish Catholic farmers who were living in abject poverty in an Ireland dominated politically and economically by England. Until the late nineteenth century, Irish Catholics were not allowed to own farms in Ireland, and during the Potato Famine of 1845-1850, more than five hundred thousand Irish farmers were evicted from their farms. The only real choice for these displaced people was to leave Ireland

for the United States; however, they were not well received by white Protestants, who then completely controlled the nation's politics, business, and society. These Irish Catholic immigrants were viewed as a threat for several reasons. Many first-generation Irish immigrants spoke only Gaelic, and they became manual laborers who worked for low wages, creating competition for jobs. The new immigrants built their own Catholic churches and schools and made it very clear that they would not tolerate in the United States the religious discrimination that they and their ancestors had experienced in Ireland.

As early as the 1840's, extremely offensive representations of Irish immigrants began to appear in American newspapers and magazines. The magazine *Harper's Monthly* published numerous drawings in which Irish Americans were depicted as apelike creatures with whom normal Americans would not want to associate. The same magazine printed in its April 6, 1867, issue a drawing by Thomas Nast entitled "The Day We Celebrate." Nast suggested that Irish Americans celebrated St. Patrick's Day by becoming drunk and then attacking police officers. Such stereotypical images of Irish immigrants as violent drunkards appeared in numerous magazines throughout the last six decades of the nineteenth century. Frequently, racist cartoons would simultaneously criticize Irish and Jewish immigrants. The fact that overt discrimination was directed against Jews and Irish Catholics at the same time may well explain why Jewish American and Irish American immigrants came to realize that they had a great deal in common.

Other cartoons ridiculed Irish Americans because of their religious beliefs. Throughout the nineteenth century, the Bible was taught in many American public schools, but the translation used was the King James version, the official translation of Protestant churches. In the 1840's, many Catholic leaders asked school boards to allow Catholic pupils to receive religious instruction based on the Douay translation, which was the approved Catholic version. Numerous contemporary cartoons in the 1840's and 1850's suggested that Catholics were opposed to the reading of the Bible; however, nothing could be further from the truth.

Although disparaging representations of Irish Americans continued to be published in U.S. magazines, most people came to realize that these stereotypical images distorted the truth and revealed more about the prejudices of those creating the images than about Irish Americans whom they attempted to ridicule.
                                              Edmund J. Campion

See also: Anti-Catholicism; Irish Americans; Irish Catholic "race"; Jewish Americans; Religion-based ethnicities; Stereotype.

Irish Americans

> **Significance:** Irish Americans have been in the United States since the early colonial period and have played an active role in the development of industry, in labor and social reform, and in politics at all levels. They also profoundly influenced the development of many large cities and have had a lasting influence on educational practices.

The Irish have been a vital component of American life since the days of colonialism. The early Irish immigrants were mainly Presbyterian Protestants from Ulster. Although some belonged to the Church of Ireland, most came in search of financial gains. The majority of the Ulster-born Irish were tenant farmers or skilled artisans of modest means. The Irish who would follow in the famine years would be vastly different in their beliefs, their financial status, and their social standing. Each new wave of Irish immigrants would add something to the fabric of American life.

The "Famine Irish"
Whereas the earliest Irish immigrants had come to the United States to better themselves, the "famine Irish" sought simple survival in an often hostile land. The Penal Laws in Ireland had long put native Irish Catholics at a serious disadvantage in their homeland. Irish farmers were uneducated, poor, and dependent upon their rocky plots of land for subsistence. Families were large. The lifestyle was one of intense social interaction. They had little, but they shared what they had and celebrated their beliefs with tradition, song, dance, and religious ritual. They were dependent upon the potato crop as their sole food source.

When blight struck the potato crop between the years 1845 and 1854, the poor had nowhere to turn. Some had compassionate landlords. However, when Parliament passed the Poor Law Extension Act of 1847, landlords

Milestones in Irish American History

Year	Event	Impact
1776	Signing of the Declaration of Independence by Charles Carrol	Unites Irish Catholics and Anglo-Saxon Protestants in seeking freedom from Britain.
1818	Employment of three thousand Irish to dig the Erie Canal continues.	Increases trade; encourages westward expansion.
1844	Nativist riots in Philadelphia	Heighten anti-Catholic sentiment, social concerns.
1845-1849	Great Irish Famine	Sets off mass immigration of poor Irish to the United States that changes American cities.
1854	Formation of Know-Nothing Party	Advocates restrictions on immigration and seeks to protect Nativist interests.
1859	Discovery of silver in Comstock, Nevada	Creates financial boom that increases westward expansion and business.
1863	Draft riots in New York and other large cities	Impair race relations; create fear among Irish that newly freed blacks will take their jobs.
1869	Completion of the transcontinental railroad	Unites country by rail; further promotes westward expansion and land development.
1875	Elevation of Archbishop John McCloskey to cardinal	Becomes first American cardinal in the Roman Catholic Church.
1911	Triangle Factory fire in New York City	Exposes plight of the working poor; spawns labor laws and social reform.
1928	Defeat of Catholic Alfred E. Smith in presidential election	Spawns fear of possible Papal influence on American politics and anti-Catholic sentiment.
1960	Election to presidency of Catholic John F. Kennedy	Becomes first Irish Catholic president.

became responsible for the cost of care of their tenantry. Even well-meaning landowners could not cover such expense. Evictions became the rule. The poor then had the option of going to disease-infested workhouses or starving on the road in search of food and shelter. They fled their native land strictly for survival.

Between 1840 and 1860, more than 1.5 million Irish came to the shores of the United States. They settled in cities, concentrating in certain neighborhoods. A large contingent settled in New Orleans. Most of those who fled the famine stayed in eastern cities such as New York or Boston simply because they had no money and no marketable skills to move on. Some would move toward Chicago or join the movement westward in search of employment. Most of the famine Irish were poor and Catholic. They represented the first large wave of non-Anglo-Saxon immigrants in the history of the nation.

The Irish immigrants were uneducated, Catholic, and considered uncultured by the social elite in the United States. Many were unaccompanied women, a fact that set the Irish apart from previous immigrant groups. The young Irish girls took positions as domestic servants in the homes of the wealthy. They worked to save enough to rescue more relations in Ireland from starvation. These women and the unskilled Irish men who sought to make a living digging ditches or building canals or bridges were scorned by the nativists. However, from the lowest levels of society, these Irish American began to build their version of the American Dream.

Religion

The Irish Catholic poor, social by nature and custom and isolated by their religious beliefs, built their own comfortable enclaves within the cities where they settled. Irish neighborhoods in New York, Boston, Chicago, and elsewhere developed into parishes. The Catholic parishes evolved into social and educational centers within the communities. As the Irish developed a reputation for hard drinking and fighting, it was the parish priest who often served as counselor and role model. The Church cared for the immigrants' spiritual, social, educational, medical, and emotional needs. As the number of immigrants increased, parishes and religious orders built schools, hospitals, and orphanages to meet the needs of the communities.

Politics and Social Reforms

As the growing numbers of Irish immigrants began to frighten the white Anglo-Saxon Protestants already established in the cities and to threaten the status quo, the children of the famine generation began to see the possibilities that existed for them by virtue of their numbers and their ambition. Politics was a natural extension of the parish culture. Precinct by precinct, the Irish

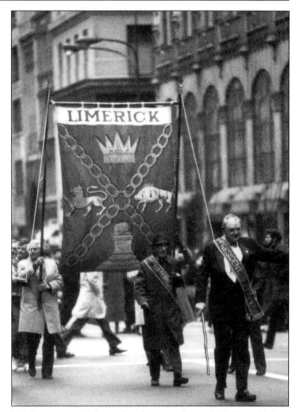

Irish Americans celebrate their heritage during the St. Patrick's Day parade in New York City. Irish Americans, particularly Catholics, were the subject of prejudice and discrimination after their arrival in the New World.

began to embrace the U.S. political system as a tool for personal advancement and a mechanism for social change.

One individual who came up from the streets of New York was young Alfred E. "Al" Smith. Raised on the streets of Brooklyn as the Brooklyn Bridge was being built, he took advantage of the political patronage in Tammany Hall to gain a foothold in politics. Under the tutelage of Charles Murphy and Jimmy Walker, Smith rose up through the political ranks in New York and eventually became the governor of New York State. Similar political machines evolved in Kansas City and Chicago, as politicians sought to serve their constituencies. Smith initiated social reforms, including child labor laws, and improved safety requirements to protect workers. Elsewhere in the nation, labor unions were gaining support.

With many successes to his credit in New York, Smith ran unsuccessfully for president in 1928. Many people still distrusted the Irish, and the nativists and many non-Catholics feared papal interference in U.S. politics should Smith be elected. The first Irish Catholic to claim the office of the president of the United States would be another descendant from Irish peasant stock, John F. Kennedy, in 1960. Kennedy would stand as a symbol of the Irish American dream brought to fruition.

Appreciation of Traditions

In the 1980's and 1990's, Irish Americans no longer bore the stigma of most negative stereotypes. The Irish generally assimilated into U.S. society, often intermarrying with other ethnic groups, yet there continued to be a lingering appreciation of Irish history and traditions, with a renewed interested in traditional Irish music and dance that became a part of American popular culture, transcending ethnic origins and religious beliefs.

Kathleen Schongar

Core Resources

Lawrence J. McCaffrey's *The Irish Diaspora in America* (Washington, D.C.: Catholic University of America Press, 1984) provides an overview of Irish immigration and explores significant religious, political, and economic factors in Ireland and in the United States that influenced ethnic relations among American immigrant groups. *A Portrait of the Irish in America*, by William D. Griffin (New York: Charles Scribner's Sons, 1981), also offers a comprehensive historical perspective on the struggles and successes of Irish assimilation into American culture. Many photographs complement the text. *The Irish in America*, edited by Michael Coffey, text by Terry Golway (New York: Disney Enterprises, 1997), offers an enlightened look at the development of Irish Americans, including personal essays by those who lived through the cultural assimilation process in the late eighteenth century and the nineteenth century. Marjorie Fallows, in *Irish Americans: Identity and Assimilation* (Englewood Cliffs, N.J.: Prentice-Hall, 1979), offers an introduction to Irish American history, cultural experiences, and expectations. Religion, labor, politics, and family dynamics are considered within the context of American life. Andrew M. Greeley, in *The Irish Americans: The Rise to Money and Power* (New York: Harper & Row, 1981), offers a sociological perspective of the Irish American experience. He examines Celtic history, family dynamics, and Irish stereotypes. He also examines the contributions of Irish politicians and writers to the American experience. Philip Bagenal offers interesting contemporary insights into the American Irish experience in *The American Irish and Their Influence on Irish Politics* (London: Kegan Paul, Trench & Company, 1882. Reprint. New York: Jerome S. Ozer, 1971). *The Irish in America: Long Journey Home* (1998) is a multivolume documentary video produced by the Public Broadcasting System (PBS).

See also: Anti-Catholicism; Celtic Irish; Irish-African American relations; Irish American stereotypes; Irish Catholic "race"; Nativism; Scotch-Irish "race."

Irish Catholic "race"

The English used notions of a "savage race" in colonialized Ireland to justify systems that dominated and oppressed the Irish long before the American colonies existed. These systems, which placed Irish Catholics on the bottom of cultural hierarchies, became codified by religion. Labels were given substance by combining religious identity with "race." The English also used immigrant groups of English and Scots for social control, according to scholar Roy Forester, in *Oxford Illustrated History of Ireland* (1989). Successive generations of English who were born in Ireland identified themselves as Irish Protestants rather than as English. Scottish people were brought to northern Ireland to serve as buffer groups against Irish kingdoms. These peoples—the Protestant Irish and Scotch-Irish—began identifying themselves as superior to the Irish Catholic "race."

These hierarchies were transferred to North America along with the waves of immigrants; however, cultural and "race" demarcations lost their sharpness in the new land. The Scotch-Irish, as they had in Ireland, acted as buffers in the American colonies until the American Revolution caused distinctions to largely disappear within southern racial slavery hierarchies. Later immigration by Irish Catholics, especially during the 1850's potato famine, in the end contributed more to the enlargement of the "white race" than to the creation of another ethnicity, according to Noel Ignatiev, in *How the Irish Became White* (1995). In the nineteenth century, Irish Catholics faced heavy discrimination, and through this process, a notion of an Irish Catholic "race" developed among other Americans. *James V. Fenelon*

See also: Celtic Irish; Irish Americans; Race as a concept; Scotch-Irish "race."

Irredentism

Irredentism is a political policy or guideline aimed at uniting irredentas—groups of people ethnically or historically related to one political system but under the control of a different polity—within ethnically or historically related territories. The word *irredenta* is Italian for "unredeemed" and was used by Italian patriots in the nineteenth and twentieth centuries who sought to liberate all Italian-speaking lands from foreign control. The hopes of these patriots, or irredentists, were basically fulfilled with the Treaty of Versailles that ended World War I.

In U.S. politics, irredentist policies have come in many forms and guises. It is possible to view programs of racial or ethnic segregation as having irredentist intents. For example, African Americans could be restricted to a particular geographic area to keep intact an Irish American neighborhood. Another way that irredentism influences U.S. politics is through the drawing of boundaries for electoral districts. Since 1812, political parties have redrawn electoral districts to favor representation of one group over another. This gerrymandering, though ruled unconstitutional by the U.S. Supreme Court in 1964, has been justified as a means of giving minority groups better political representation.   *Paul J. Chara, Jr.*

See also: Housing; Reapportionment cases; Redistricting; Representation: gerrymandering, malapportionment, and reapportionment.

Israeli Americans

> **Significance:** Israeli Americans are immigrants from the Middle Eastern state of Israel, founded in 1948. They are an ethnically and religiously diverse group. The term, "Israeli Americans," however, most often refers to Israeli Jews, both the Ashkenazim of Central and Eastern European heritage and the Sephardim of Iberian, Middle Eastern, and North African origins. As Jews, their religious observance ranges from a secular orientation to an orthodox one.

Constituting only about 1 percent of the U.S. immigrant population, Israeli immigrants often perceive themselves to be sojourners, temporary residents of the host country. They maintain social, cultural, and economic ties to their country of origin, even while living abroad. Some retain dual citizenship. With the aid of technology and the global economy, their lifestyles seem to fit the new trend of transnationalism (allegiances and orientations that go beyond the boundaries of a single nation). Rather than forsake their homelands and become completely assimilated, new immigrants actively participate in both social worlds.

Rates of Immigration

Israeli immigration rates vary depending on how the term "Israeli" is defined and whether only legal immigrants are counted. At the time of the 1990 U.S. census, approximately 90,000 Israelis lived in the United States. Most were settled in metropolitan areas, especially Los Angeles, New York City, Queens, and Brooklyn. Certain immigration trends are evident. First, the number of legal Israeli immigrants entering the United States has gradually increased since 1948. For example, data from the U.S. Immigration and Naturalization Service indicate that the numbers increased from about 1,000 to 2,000 per year between 1967 and 1976 and from 3,000 to 4,000 per year from 1976 to 1986. Second, Israeli immigration was especially pronounced during the 1970's, especially after 1975, when, as 1990 census figures reveal, rates of Israelis traveling to Los Angeles alone more than doubled from 8 percent (1970-1974) to 17 percent (1975-1979). Some have suggested the growth is due in part to increases following war, in this case, the 1973 Yom Kippur War. Third, in response to changing Israeli policy toward emigrants and economic conditions in Israel, the number of Israelis returning to Israel has risen during the 1990's. According to Israeli government estimates, the average yearly number rose from about 5,500 during 1985-1991 to nearly 10,500 during 1992-1994.

Motives for Emigration

In contrast to previous Jewish immigrants, contemporary Israelis are not "pushed" to emigrate to the United States because of persecution or extreme economic hardship. Rather, the decision to emigrate is primarily motivated by "pull" factors. Many Israelis cite personal development, particularly greater educational and economic opportunity, as most important. They seek professional advancement, as well as a higher income and standard of living. Others desire to reunite with family members already in the United States or leave to fulfill a personal need for adventure and escape from the limited confines, both geographically and socially, of Israel. Some engage in chain migration, being assisted by Israelis who have already made the trip. Travel, especially among those completing required military service, often leads to extended stays.

Certain features of Israeli society may be "push" factors: high inflation, bureaucratic red tape, burdensome taxes, housing shortages, the difficulty in developing capitalistic enterprises, and government regulations that intrude into personal life. As part of a country prone to societal violence and war, Israelis may mention the need to escape the siege mentality and the tensions permeating society, as well as reserve army duty. Interethnic tensions motivate some to flee from perceived discrimination waged by upper-class Ashkenazim against those of lower status.

Relations with the American Jewish Community

Israelis were not initially welcomed with open arms by the American Jewish community. Relations between the two groups have been strained because of historical and cultural factors. Historically, the creation of the State of Israel in 1948 realized the Zionist dream of a Jewish homeland. To emigrate to Israel, or to make *Aliyah* ("ascent"), was a firm demonstration of loyalty to the Zionist cause. To immigrate from Israel and return to the Jewish diaspora, however, has pejoratively been referred to as *Yerida* ("descent"). Hence, *Olim*, "those who go up" to Israel, are admired, in contrast to *Yordim*, "those who go down," who are disparaged for emigrating. Israeli Americans accept this stigmatized identity, often expressing guilt and shame for leaving.

In classifying Israeli immigrants as *Yordim*, American Jews were following the lead of Israelis. In 1976, Prime Minister Yitzhak Rabin himself referred to *Yordim* as "the leftovers of weaklings." Israeli emigration, coupled with rising Arab birthrates, is perceived as a threat to the future of the Jewish homeland. Israeli Americans, on the other hand, are often alienated from American Jews, who, in their minds, have offered only monetary contributions, rather than real sacrifice, for Israel. American Jews often condemn *Yordim*, yet many would never consider emigrating to Israel themselves.

Culturally, a gap exists between Israeli Americans and American Jews. They eat distinct foods and have different lifestyles, political ideologies, and entertainment preferences. Their language also differs; Israelis speak Hebrew as their primary language. Many Israeli Americans also follow the culture of their country of origin, be it Yemenite, Ethiopian, or Russian. An improved relationship between Israeli Americans and American Jews has been prompted by shifts in official Israeli policy toward *Yordim* enacted during the mid-1980's. In an effort to promote the return of Israeli Americans, the Israeli government softened its position regarding emigration and offered enticements such as employment, housing assistance, and travel loans. At the same time, a number of American Jewish organizations initiated outreach programs for Israeli Americans. Previously, such organizations provided little, if any, assistance in an effort to discourage Israelis from staying in America.

The Sojourner Mentality and Self-Identity

Stemming from the negative stereotype of *Yordim*, Israeli Americans label themselves sojourners, insisting, in the face of perhaps contrary evidence, that their stay in the United States is temporary. Lower-status Israelis frequently become settlers, integrating into the host country. Higher-status Israelis often become permanent sojourners; they intend to return to Israel but have no serious plans to do so. As permanent sojourners, they practiced what Natan Uriely, in a 1994 article in *International Society*, has termed rhetorical ethnicity. Their identity is rooted in their ethnicity, and they have a strong symbolic commitment to Israel. This is evident in their repeated desires to go home. Israelis resist identifying themselves as Americans or Israeli Americans, preferring an Israeli identity. Many never fully assimilate.

Demographic Profile

S. J. Gold and B. A. Phillips, in the *American Jewish Yearbook* (1996), have provided a demographic profile of Israeli Americans. According to their report (and at the time of their report), Israelis were young, most under age forty-five, and more likely to be male, married, and relatively well educated. They had high rates of employment and earned substantial income that was generally higher than that of the average foreign-born person. Many were employed as managers, administrators, professionals, or technical specialists. Some were engaged in sales, and a significant number (second only to Koreans in America) were self-employed in industries such as real estate, jewelry and diamonds, retail sales, and construction. Women had less labor force participation in the United States than in Israel, perhaps indicative of their rising social status in the United States.

Social Life in the United States

Israelis tend to socialize with each other, often in ethnic nightclubs, at

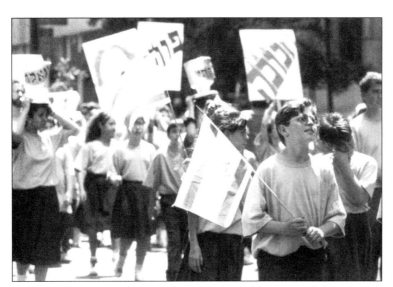

Israeli Americans participate in a Salute to Israel parade in New York City. At times, relations between Israeli and Jewish Americans have been strained.

communal singing sessions, or at ethnic celebrations such as Israeli Independence Day. A few belong to ethnic organizations such as Tzofim, an Israeli group similar to the Boy Scouts. Some form ethnic subgroups based on their country of origin. Friends frequently substitute for family and are invited to holiday observances or children's bar/bat mitzvahs. Many Israelis consider themselves to be secular Jews, linking religious observance with being Israeli rather than Jewish. However, many do participate in religious activities in the United States, by joining synagogues at a slightly higher rate than American Jews, providing their children with religious educations, and engaging in religious rituals to a greater extent in the United States than in Israel. Some of the Sephardim have found the orthodox Hasidic movement appealing. Perhaps this increased religiosity is a reaction to the transition from being a religious majority in Israel to being a religious minority in the United States.

Rosann Bar

Core Resources

Sources of information on Israel and emigration are H. Greenberg's *Israel: Social Problems* (Tel Aviv: Dekel, 1979) and D. Kass and S. M. Lipset's "Jewish Immigration to the United States from 1967 to the Present: Israelis and Others," in *Understanding American Jewry*, edited by Marshall Sklare (New Brunswick, N.J.: Transaction Books, 1982). Books and articles on the Israelis in the United States include D. Elizur's "Israelis in the U.S.: Motives, Attitudes, and Intentions," in *American Jewish Yearbook* (1979); James Feron's "The Israelis of New York," in *The New York Times* (January 16, 1977); S. J. Gold and B. A. Phillips's "Israelis in the United States," in *American Jewish Yearbook* (1996); P. Ritterbrand's "Israelis in New York," *Contemporary Jewry* (7, 1986); Moshe Shokeid's *Children of Circumstances: Israeli Immigrants in New York* (New York: Cornell University Press, 1988); Zvi Sobel's *Migrants from the Promised Land* (New Brunswick, N.J.: Transaction Books, 1986); and Natan Uriely's "Rhetorical Ethnicity of Permanent Sojourners: The Case of Israeli Immigrants in the Chicago Area," in *International Sociology* (9, 1994).

See also: Diaspora; Ethnicity and ethnic groups; Jewish Americans; Jewish ethnicity: definitions; Transnationalism and ethnonationalism.

Italian American stereotypes

The two major stereotypes regarding Italian Americans are that this group is inextricably linked to the Mafia and that Italians are fun-loving buffoons. The Mafia stereotype involves a belief that Italian Americans developed and control organized crime in the United States, which is a by-product of the Mafia, a criminal organization in Sicily, and that a significant percentage of Italian Americans are involved in organized crime. The buffoon stereotype involves the belief that Italian Americans are not achievement-oriented but simply fun-loving, easygoing individuals. Sociological investigation demonstrates that neither image of Italian Americans is accurate.

Major studies of organized crime such as *The Mythology of Crime and Criminal Justice* (1996), by Victor E. Kappeler, Mark Blumberg, and Gary W. Potter, *On the Take: From Petty Crooks to Presidents* (1978), by William Chambliss, and *Organized Crime in America* (1970), by Gus Tyler, show that organized crime in the United States was not developed by any ethnic group and that its roots lie deep within the nation's culture. These works show that the high demand for illicit drugs, sex, and gambling (and the desire for profit) are largely responsible for the creation of organized crime groups. Books such as *The City and the Syndicate: Organizing Crime in Philadelphia* (1985), by Gary W. Potter and Philip Jenkins, *The Mafia Mystique* (1975), by Dwight Smith, and *Blood of My Blood: The Dilemma of the Italian Americans* (1974), by Richard Gambino, make clear that there is no evidence supporting the belief that organized crime in the United States is an offshoot of the Mafia in Sicily. Moreover, studies, such as *Organized Crime* (1985), by Howard Abadinsky, *Disorganized Crime* (1983), by Peter Reuter, and *The Politics of Corruption: Organized Crime in an American City* (1970), by John Gardiner, found that no ethnic group exercises control over organized crime activities such as gambling and the drug trade. Furthermore, the article "America's Most Tolerated Intolerance: Bigotry Against Italian Americans," in *The Italian American Review* (Spring/Summer, 1997), by Richard Gambino, points out that only a fraction of 1 percent of all Italian Americans participate in organized crime. The research does not provide support for the Mafia stereotype of Italian Americans.

In rebuttal of the buffoon stereotype, the 1990 and 1980 U. S. census and books such as *Italian Americans into the Twilight of Ethnicity* (1985), by Richard Alba, and *Italian Americans* (1970), by Joseph Lopreato, provide data demonstrating that since the 1960's, Italian Americans have experienced high levels of occupational and educational achievements. Moreover, starting in the 1960's, the average household income of Italian Americans has been well above the U.S. average. Since the 1970's, the percentage of Italian Americans who have graduated from college has been well above the national average.

Although a very small number of Italian Americans are involved in organized crime, and a small percentage are not achievement-oriented, these represent a minority of Italian Americans. The negative images of Italian Americans created by these stereotypes have greatly distorted reality concerning this ethnic group.

Louis Gesualdi

See also: Italian Americans; Stereotype.

Italian Americans

> **Significance:** Italian Americans played an integral role in the development of the United States. Although they have been subjected to ethnic stereotypes—ranging from illiterate peasant organ grinder or shiftless vegetable peddler to unskilled laborer or violent member of an organized crime family—they have achieved distinguished success. Contributions from countless Italian Americans in entertainment, politics, and business have directly shaped and influenced the nation's social landscape.

Italy sent few immigrants to the United States before the Civil War (1861-1865). The 1850 census, the first to record ethnic group populations, listed only 3,645 Italian Americans, and these individuals were primarily skilled artisans, merchants, musicians, actors, and entrepreneurs. However, these numbers do not reflect their overall significance. Albeit sponsored by Spain, England, and France, Italian explorers helped chart the European pathway to the Americas. After Christopher Columbus navigated the Atlantic in 1492, several of his countrymen continued his pursuits. Giovanni Caboto, often referred to as John Cabot in popular history textbooks, obtained financial backing from England's King Henry VII and organized a successful expedition to the New England coast in 1497. Amerigo Vespucci helped popularize interest in America following the publication of two pamphlets highlighting the potential rewards available to new settlers on the eastern seaboard. Giovanni da Verrazano was the first European to enter New York Harbor in the early sixteenth century.

Although numerous adventurers from other countries also facilitated European migration to America, the efforts of several Italians were crucial for the success of many early colonial enterprises. Catholic missionaries helped carve out the French empire in the Mississippi Valley. Artisans developed glassware and silk industries in Jamestown, Virginia. Thomas Jefferson recruited Italian masons to help construct his home at Monticello and enlisted the aid of several musicians to form the United States Marine Corps Band. Italians also helped design and decorate the interior of the early White House, and Italian opera emerged as one of the most popular forms of entertainment among the upper classes in antebellum America. Although there were few Italian Americans in the nation, they had made a significant cultural impact.

The Great Wave
From 1880 to 1920, more than four million Italians entered the United States. Approximately 80 percent were men, and because 97 percent initially passed through New York City, the bulk of the Italian American community settled in major eastern cities such as Philadelphia, Boston, and New York; however, a large community also emerged in Chicago. Following the unification of Italy in the 1860's, southern Italians soon began to feel alienated from and experienced widespread disillusionment with northern leadership. Absentee landlords systematically exploited the peasants, and agricultural policies produced massive hunger among sharecroppers and tenant farmers. Others succumbed to outbreaks of malaria. Northern politicians enacted oppressive conscription laws forcing southerners to serve seven-year terms in the military. As Italy quickly evolved into a two-tiered system in which southerners were excluded from all facets of decision making, a large number of Italians voted with their feet and abandoned their traditional attachment to their villages, emigrating to the United States. Most Italians did not initially intend to remain in the United States. Estimates vary, but between 30 percent and 50 percent returned to the homeland. Strong familial ties and attachments to ancestral villages caused many to return despite the fact that few earned enough to reverse their impoverished status.

The majority of Italian Americans became manual laborers. Ethnic labor contractors, or *padroni*, persuaded many to emigrate from Italy by promising them unlimited economic opportunities upon arrival in North America. The *padroni* secured employment for émigrés and arranged the financing for the transatlantic voyage. Italians helped build railroads and the New York City subway system. Others toiled in dangerous and precarious conditions in factories; several became miners. Some were able to procure opportunities in agricultural communities, but the majority of Italian Americans remained locked in ethnic urban enclaves and were subjected to the outburst of nativist xenophobic practices that accompanied the great wave of migration.

Assimilation and Nativism
Racial and ethnic relations in the United States have adhered to a complex hierarchical pecking order. Generally, each wave of immigrants has encountered a number of discriminatory practices designed to eradicate all remnants of ethnic identity. Because the domi-

nant culture reflected a solid Anglo-Saxon bias following the Civil War (1861-1865), new groups from southeastern Europe were expected to embrace assimilationist policies and Americanize. Reformers demonstrated little sympathy for immigrant culture and introduced a variety of measures to diminish and weaken traditional ethnic ways.

Italian American children were extremely susceptible to Anglo-Saxon assimilationists. They were forced into a form of cultural tug-of-war. Required either to abandon their native culture or to face social ostracization and the loss of economic opportunity, the second generation began to embrace Anglo-Saxon culture. This caused considerable psychological problems. For example, Italian American children were expected to find work and contribute to the household economy. This, however, resulted in a premature departure from school. If a child decided to stay in school and pursue a profession, that child risked the wrath of his or her family. Because most Italian Americans considered the family to be sacred, young Italian Americans faced a classic dilemma. As a result, rates of socioeconomic mobility were quite low among the first few generations.

Other forms of nativism also surfaced. Public schools insisted that children speak only English, and officials often shortened and Americanized Italian family names.

Milestones in Italian American History

Year	Event	Impact
1492	Columbus travels to the Americas	Facilitates widespread European expansion in North America.
1497	Cabot explores eastern coast of Canada	Helps promote a prosperous growing British fishing industry.
1653	Italian Jesuits publish a brief history of New France	Challenges the pervasive myth surrounding the lack of civilization among Canada's Native Americans.
1770's	Political philosopher Fillipo Mazzei works with Thomas Jefferson	Italian ideas are incorporated into the U.S. Declaration of Independence.
1891	Eleven acquitted Italians are lynched in New Orleans	Reveals victimization of Italian immigrants during the great wave of immigration.
1920's	Rudolph Valentino becomes Hollywood's leading male sex symbol	Reveals the vital role of Italian Americans in the emergence of the U.S. film industry.
1921-1924	Passage of restrictive immigration quotas in the United States	Leads to the rise of vibrant Italian communities in Montreal, Toronto, and Vancouver, Canada.
1927	Anarchists Nicola Sacco and Bartolomeo Vanzetti are executed	Demonstrates how Italians were sometimes punished for radical political beliefs.
1941	New York Yankee Joe DiMaggio establishes a major league record by hitting in fifty-six consecutive games	Indicates Italian American influence on American sports.
1965	Poet John Robert Columbo publishes "Oh Canada"	Emphasizes that despite Canada's ethnic diversity, the country's culture primarily reflects a blending of English, French, and British influences.
1970	Lee Iacocca named president of Ford Motor Company	Illustrates that many Italians attained prominent positions in U.S. business and industry.
1972	Francis Ford Coppola's film, *The Godfather*, wins the Academy Award for best film	Reveals how many Americans associate Italians with organized crime.
1982	Mario Cuomo elected governor of New York	Becomes first Italian to serve as head of a state government.
1991	National Canadian census reveals that less than 3 percent of the population is Italian	Demonstrates that Italians primarily emigrated to either the United States or South America.

Some families experienced violence when they attempted to move outside the ethnic enclave. Many people were subjected to racial remarks such as *dago, wop,* and *guinea.* Although studies have shown that the rates of alcoholism and mental illness were lower compared with those of other groups, the suicide rate among Italian Americans tripled during the great wave of migration.

Perhaps the greatest example of nativist xenophobic pressure occurred in the 1920's during the trial of two Italian anarchists, Nicola Sacco and Bartolomeo Vanzetti. Nativist sentiment, spurred by fears of communism, had been growing in the United States when Sacco and Vanzetti were arrested under questionable circumstances for murder and robbery in Massachusetts. Both men were judged as violent revolutionaries and subversive ethnic agents rather than on the merits of their case. Although their guilt remains debatable, both men were executed in 1927.

Organized Crime

The average Italian American suffered from the negative impression created by a select minority of Italians who attempted to construct vast empires in organized crime. As congressional committees cracked down on criminals, some Americans concluded that all Italian Americans were associated with a nationwide crime syndicate commonly referred to as La Cosa Nostra or the Mafia. These rumors received considerable credibility in 1963 when career criminal Joseph Valachi broke a code of silence and exposed his associates. As a result, the nation became obsessed with the Mafia. References to the Mafia in *The New York Times* increased from 2 in 1962 to 359 in 1969. Mario Puzo's novel *The Godfather* (1969) was made into an Academy Award-winning film, but his violent portrayal of Italian criminals negatively affected many law-abiding Italian Americans. Other gangsters such as John Gotti acquired national fame in the 1980's, and once again Italian Americans were found guilty by association. Numerous popular authors flooded the market with books detailing how murder was used to settle disputes between Italians. Despite the fact that only a select few were involved in criminal activity, all Italian Americans were described as being sympathetic toward the Mafia.

Famous Italians

Not all Italian Americans were unskilled workers or common criminals. Many achieved considerable success in their fields. Joe DiMaggio established a major league baseball record for hitting in fifty-six consecutive games. Heavyweight boxer Rocky Marciano defeated several notable champions, including Joe Louis, Ezzard Charles, and Jersey Joe Wolcott, and retired as an undefeated champion. Frank Capra emerged as one of the nation's finest filmmakers, and his 1946 film, *It's a Wonderful Life,* is considered one of the country's classic movies. Singer Frank Sinatra, who was often unjustly accused of being in the Mafia, entertained generations of Americans with his swagger and ballads. Politician Fiorello La Guardia served as a congressman, New York City mayor, and United Nations relief official. Poet and publisher Lawrence Ferlinghetti provided much-needed support for and helped solidify the Beat generation's place in American literature. Geraldine Ferraro was the first woman to become a vice presidential candidate in 1984. Pop singer Madonna (Ciccone) evolved into a cultural icon in the 1980's. Countless others also achieved prominent status in American life, thus proving that despite being victimized by ethnic stereotyping, Italian Americans have risen to the highest pinnacles of success in the United States.   *Robert D. Ubriaco, Jr.*

Core Resources

Jerre Mangione's and Ben Morreale's *La Storia: Five Centuries of the Italian American Experience* (New York: HarperCollins, 1992) serves as the most comprehensive source on the role of Italian Americans in the United

This Italian family rides the ferry to Ellis Island in 1905. Italian immigrants faced a great deal of discrimination upon their arrival in the United States.

States since the colonial era. Roger Daniels's *Coming to America* (New York: HarperCollins, 1990) places the Italian American experience in its proper comparative framework with other ethnic groups. Gary Ross Mormino's *Immigrants on the Hill: Italian Americans in St. Louis, 1882-1982* (Urbana: University of Illinois Press, 1986) examines why this community has been able to withstand the process of assimilation that typically undermines the solidarity of ethnic urban enclaves. Virginia Yans-McLaughlin's *Family and Community—Italian Immigrants in Buffalo, 1880-1930* (Ithaca: Cornell University Press, 1971) sheds considerable light on the early immigrant ordeal in the East. *Commonwealth vs. Sacco and Vanzetti* (Englewood Cliffs, N.J.: Prentice-Hall, 1958), edited by Robert Weeks, provides key insight from court records and other primary-source documents on the trial of the reputed anarchists. Mario Puzo's *The Godfather* (New York: G. P. Putman's Sons, 1969), although a fictional account, serves as perceptive window on the life of an organized crime family.

See also: Assimilation: cultural and structural; Italian American stereotypes; Little Italies; Nativism; Sacco and Vanzetti trial; Xenophobia, nativism, and eugenics.

J

Jamaican Americans

Significance: Jamaican immigrants, to the United States, coming from a nation with different patterns of race relations, must adjust their expectations as they deal with native-born black and white Americans and often struggle with an uncertain racial and ethnic identity.

The movement of Jamaicans to the United States began in the early twentieth century and increased greatly after the 1965 relaxation of immigration restrictions. Jamaican immigrants clustered in metropolitan areas along the Eastern seaboard and in California, where many attained success as leaders in politics, religion, education, and business.

Huntley Brown, an entertainer from Jamaica, performs. Race is not important in Jamaica; consequently, many Jamaicans first experience racism after arriving in the United States.

The Caribbean island of Jamaica was colonized by Spaniards in the sixteenth century. After most of the Arawak Indians died, the Spanish brought African slaves to work their sugar plantations. The British acquired Jamaica in 1670 and continued the practice of slavery. West Indian slavery did not encourage passivity, nor did it damage slaves' self-confidence to the extent that United States slavery did. Jamaican slavery ended in 1838, a generation before slavery's demise in the southern United States. Jamaica gained national independence in 1962.

Centuries of slavery left the island with a majority black population (many of whom were very poor), a smaller mixed-race segment, and a small, prosperous white population. Jamaica, unlike the United States, never developed Jim Crow laws, rigid color castes, or a tradition of lynching. Race is not a pressing issue in Jamaica, where blacks occupy positions at all levels of society. Jamaican immigrants to the United States, most of whom are of African ancestry, often experience shock upon entering a society with a powerful white majority and a long history of blatant and rigid color prejudice and discrimination. They develop various strategies to deal with racism, such as confrontation, resignation, and development of heightened race consciousness.

Twentieth Century Immigration

Immigration from Jamaica to the United States occurred throughout the twentieth century. Many propertied and educated Jamaicans had established themselves in New York City by the 1920's. Other Jamaicans entered the country as temporary migrant farmworkers under special visas. During the World War II labor shortage, Jamaicans were encouraged to work on farms and in factories in the United States. The 1952 Immigration and Nationality Act reduced West Indian immigration; however Jamaican immigration surged following passage of the Immigration and Nationality Act of 1965, which opened admission to nonwhite immigrants from Asia, Latin America, and the Caribbean. Jamaican newcomers settled mostly in the metropolitan areas of New York City and Miami. By 1990, 435,024 Jamaicans lived in the United States, about 80 percent of whom were foreign-born. The leading states of residence were New York, Florida, California, New Jersey, and Connecticut, according to 1990 U.S. census figures. During the 1990's, Jamaican immigration averaged 18,000 people per year.

Education, Business, and Leadership

Jamaicans arriving in the first decades of the twentieth century became black community leaders in the areas of business, politics, and the arts. In New York City, many were business owners and professionals. Some, such as Marcus Garvey, became government, civil rights, or labor union leaders. Others, including Claude McKay, a prominent writer who helped found the Harlem Renaissance of the 1920's, became cultural leaders.

The 1965 immigration act established a preference for skilled migrants. Accordingly, Jamaican immigrants in the latter part of the twentieth century tended to be well educated. The departure of many technical, managerial, and professional workers badly needed for the island's economic development has produced a "brain drain" in Jamaica. The value Jamaican immigrants place on education is reflected in the school performance of Jamaican American youth. Ruben Rumbaut's 1992 survey found that the children of Jamaican immigrants tended to have high grade-point averages and to score high on standardized reading and math tests. The children reported spending a large amount of time doing homework (versus watching television) and had very high educational aspirations.

Comparisons with U.S. Blacks

Economic motivation underlies much Jamaican migration, and some transplanted islanders become business owners. Social scientists vary in their interpretations of West Indian entrepreneurship. Some, such as Thomas Sowell and Daniel Patrick Moynihan, credit West Indians with habits of thrift and hard work that cause them to be more successful economically than U.S.-born blacks. The implication is that African Americans should not blame race discrimination for their poverty. Others, including Reynolds Farley and Stephen Steinberg, argue that Jamaican immigrants constitute a select group, skilled and highly motivated before they leave the island. Farley and Steinberg also argue that the differences in economic success between immigrant and U.S.-born blacks have been exaggerated. Farley cites statistics showing that while West Indians are more often self-employed than U.S.-born blacks, the self-employment rate for whites is much larger than for either nonwhite group. Statistics for unemployment and income also place Jamaican Americans well below whites. Most Jamaican Americans are not self-employed. Many obtain advanced education and become lawyers, doctors, and teachers; others work in construction. Women have high labor force participation and many work in domestic service and nursing.

Questions of Identity

As Jamaican Americans attempt to arrive at a sense of racial or ethnic identity, they encounter opposing forces. On one hand, they tend to retain their ethnic identity, thinking of themselves as Jamaican Americans, because of the constant influx of new immigrants who revitalize distinct cultural elements of folklore, food preferences, religion, and speech. This separateness is enforced by the attitudes of African Americans, who sometimes resent the islanders because of their foreignness, their entrepreneurial success, and because some white employers apparently prefer foreign-born workers. On the other hand, Jamaican Americans may adopt an assimilated label, calling themselves black or African American, prompted by daily experiences with racism. Because of the conflicting pressures of living in the United States, second-generation islanders sometimes vacillate, at times identifying with African Americans and other times attempting to distance themselves from them.

Nancy Conn Terjesen

Core Resources

Sociologist Milton Vickerman's *Crosscurrents: West Indian Immigrants and Race* (New York: Oxford University Press, 1998) contains interviews with Jamaicans in New York City who tell of contending forces of racism and equal treatment in the United States. Reynolds Farley and Walter R. Allen include a chapter on the economic status of West Indians in their *The Color Line and the Quality of Life in America* (New York: Russell Sage Foundation, 1987). Vincent Parrillo's *Strangers to These Shores* (5th ed., Boston: Allyn & Bacon, 1997) is a general treatment of race and ethnic relations with sections on both Jamaicans and Rastafarians. Alejandro Portes edited *The New Second Generation* (New York: Russell Sage Foundation, 1996), which contains essays by many sociologists, including Ruben Rumbaut's 1992 survey of immigrant children.

See also: Afro-Caribbeans; West Indian Americans.

Japan bashing

Japan bashing, or extremely negative criticism of Japan and its people, has occurred a number of times in the nineteenth and twentieth centuries, often creating problems for Japanese Americans. In the late nineteenth and early twentieth century, dislike for the Japanese eventually led to anti-Japanese land and immigration laws on the West Coast. During World War II, the Japanese were vilified as purveyors of international destruction. This distrust, combined with other factors, resulted in Japanese Americans being confined to internment camps for most of the war. In the 1970's and 1980's, in response to higher gasoline prices, Americans began to buy fuel-efficient compact cars made in Japan, causing a decline in the demand for large American cars and a subsequent decline in the U.S. automobile industry. Many autoworkers lost their jobs, and resentment against the Japanese grew. In 1982, two Detroit men, one of whom was a laid-off autoworker, bludgeoned to death Vincent Chin, a Chinese American whom they mistakenly believed was Japanese.

In the latter part of the 1980's and early 1990's, when the Japanese economy was very strong, many U.S. politicians and journalists accused the Japanese government of being protectionist and unfairly excluding American-made goods. They suggested that the Japanese lacked creativity and had gained its economic success by producing cheap copies of American products or slight improvements on American ideas. They claimed that Japan had an unfair advantage regarding production standards because its people sacrificed their personal lives and health to keep the nation's economy strong. The Japanese school system was said to place so much pressure on children that they regularly committed suicide over their failure to succeed.

In fact, *karoshi* (death from overwork) was confirmed in only a few cases in Japan, and the suicide rate among people aged fifteen to twenty-four had been lower in Japan than in the United States since 1981. However, all of the accusations, subtle and not so subtle, hurled against the Japanese by American politicians and journalists negatively affected many Japanese Americans. Many other Americans seemed to believe that Japanese Americans shared the negative characteristics that politicians and journalists accused the Japanese of having.

Annita Marie Ward

See also: Asian American stereotypes; Chin, Vincent, murder; Japanese American internment; Orientalism; Yellow peril campaign.

Japanese American Citizens League

Significance: The Japanese American Citizens League, the largest and most influential Japanese American political organization, promotes assimilation as the most effective response to racism.

The Japanese American Citizens League (JACL) was founded in 1930 in respose to widespread anti-Asian sentiment in the United States. The JACL promoted assimilation and Americanization as the most effective way for the Nisei (second-generation Japanese Americans) to gain the approval of the general public. Initially a loose federation of loyalty leagues, the JACL's influence was minimal until 1941, when it cooperated with the federal government in carrying out President Franklin Delano Roosevelt's Executive Order 9066, which ordered the internment of Japanese Americans in restricted camps during World War II. Because of that cooperation, it lost the respect of many Japanese Americans. After World War II, the JACL achieved a positive public profile as it lobbied for civil rights legislation. However, it has remained controversial for its insistence on accommodation rather than confrontation in the political arena. Now the largest and most influential Japanese American political organization, the JACL must deal with conflicts within its own ranks regarding its basic goals.

Formation of the JACL

The roots of the JACL can be traced to 1918 in San Francisco, when Thomas Y. Yatabe and a small group of his college-educated friends met to discuss the future of the Nisei in America. Calling themselves the American Loyalty League, they were well aware of the racism blocking the economic progress of Asian immigrants and their families at that time. The Issei (first-generation Japanese Americans) hoped their children, the Nisei, would have opportunities for economic and social advancement. However, as Ronald Takaki has documented in *Strangers from a Different Shore* (1989), widespread discrimination made it very difficult for them to find employment other than manual or menial labor. Yatabe and his friends were among the fortunate few who had achieved professional success; a recent dental school graduate, Yatabe drew into his circle another dentist, a doctor, and an attorney. They realized that Nisei in general still faced an uncertain future. In their view, the best way to gain acceptance by the general public was to define themselves first and foremost as loyal Americans dedicated to advancement of democratic ideals. Individual enterprise, fair play, and respect for law and order were cornerstones of this philosophy.

In 1922, James "Jimmie" Yoshinori Sakamoto founded a similar group, the Seattle Progressive Citizens League. In 1923, Yatabe established the Fresno American Loyalty League, the first statewide league. In 1928, he and Saburo Kido founded the San Francisco New American Citizens League. All of these groups shared a commitment to being "100 percent American" in their outlook. Realizing how much more effective they would be if they joined together, Clarence Takeya Arai, who was elected president of the Seattle group in 1928, proposed a national meeting of delegates. He envisioned the formation of a national council of Japanese American citizens leagues which would present a positive public profile. This four-day meeting, called to order by Arai on August 29, 1930, in Seattle, Washington, became the founding convention of the JACL: the first national political organization of Japanese Americans.

The Nisei leadership at the convention represented a special group of college-educated professionals with economically secure, middle-class, urban backgrounds. Mostly in their late twenties and early thirties, they were strikingly unlike the majority of Nisei in America at that time, who were younger (with an average age of seventeen) and from rural, working-class backgrounds. Moreover, they were distinctly different from the Issei, who still held political, economic, and social power in local Japanese American communities through the Japanese Associations, which provided legal aid and other services for immigrants. The Issei usually chose (or were forced by racism) to remain within their own communities; their English skills often were minimal, and their direct interactions with outsiders were limited. Through Japanese Associations and other local organizations—such as prefectural associations, merchants' and farmers' mutual aid societies, vernacular newspapers, and Japanese language schools—the Issei maintained their communities as best they could within the larger American society. The Nisei leadership of the JACL, however, insisted on a completely different approach to finding a secure place for Japanese Americans in the United States. Above all, they stressed assimilation, not ethnicity, underscoring their American aspirations rather than their Japanese heritage.

Therefore, one of the first items of business at the founding convention was to remove the hyphen in "Japanese-Americans," on the basis that any Japanese aspect of Nisei identity had to be subordinated to their American destiny. More than one hundred delegates from five states (Washington, Oregon, California, Illinois, and New York) and the territory of Hawaii approved resolutions asking that Congress address two timely issues: the constitutionality of the 1922 Cable Act and the eligibility of Issei World War I veterans for citizenship. Suma Sugi became their lobbyist for amendment of the Cable Act, which stripped citizenship from any American woman who married an "alien ineligible to citizenship"; through Sugi's efforts and those of the League of Women Voters, Congress changed the law in 1931, so that citizenship could not be revoked by marriage. Tokutaro "Tokie" Nishimura Slocum became their lobbyist for veteran citizenship, which finally was secured by the Nye-Lea Bill in 1935.

JACL's Work

During its first decade of existence, however, the JACL had little direct effect on the Japanese American community. This situation changed dramatically in 1941, when President Roosevelt issued Executive Order 9066, authorizing the internment of Japanese Americans during World War II. The federal government imprisoned virtually all Issei leaders of businesses, schools, and churches on the West Coast. The JACL then took over, directing Japanese Americans not to resist relocation. In fact, the JACL cooperated with the War Relocation Authority (WRA) in identifying community members who might be subversives. Dillon S. Myer, WRA director, worked closely with Mike Masaoka, JACL official, in administering the camps—a relationship intensely resented by the majority of Japanese Americans. Attorney Wayne Mortimer Collins, who stood against popular opinion to defend Japanese American civil rights during and after World War II, went so far as to blame the JACL for much of the suffering that internees endured.

The JACL succeeded in building a positive public profile after the war by lobbying for civil rights legislation such as amendment of the Immigration and Nationality Act of 1952, thereby guaranteeing the right of all Issei to naturalized citizenship. To this day, however, it has remained a controversial organization, especially because of its conservative political stance. The JACL must deal with interfactional conflicts between its "old guard" and younger members who question its basic goals.

Mary Louise Buley-Meissner

Core Resources

Sucheng Chan's *Asian Americans: An Interpretive History* (Boston: Twayne, 1991) is a carefully researched investigation of Asian American socioeconomic, political, educational, and cultural realities that provides contexts for assessing the JACL's achievements. Richard Drinnon's *Keeper of Concentration Camps: Dillon S. Myer and American Racism* (Berkeley: University of California Press, 1987) is a painstakingly researched revisionist history of Myer's administration of War Location Authority, including his collaboration with Mike Masaoka and JACL. Bill Hosokawa's *JACL in Quest of Justice* (New York: William Morrow, 1982) was commissioned by the JACL to record its accomplishments; the book mainly covers the 1930's and 1940's, emphasizing the organization's patriotic nature. *Japanese American History: An A-to-Z Reference from 1868 to the Present* (New York: Japanese American National Museum and Facts On File, 1993), edited by Brian Niiya, is an invaluable resource including a narrative historical overview, a chronology of Japanese American history, and dictionary entries. Paul R. Spickard's "The Nisei Assume Power: The Japanese Citizens League, 1941-1942," in *Pacific Historical Review* 52, no. 2 (May, 1983), argues that early JACL leadership represented Nisei who seized the historical moment to wrest political, economic, and social power from Issei.

See also: Japan bashing; Japanese American internment; Japanese Americans; *Ozawa v. United States*; Redress movement; Yellow peril campaign.

Japanese American internment

> **Significance:** During World War II, the U.S. government's war powers were used to deny due process of law for aliens and U.S. citizens of Japanese ancestry, to the disapproval of the postwar generation.

Historically in the continental United States there were severe restrictions on Japanese immigration and naturalization, and in 1941 there were only about 40,000 foreign-born Japanese people (Issei) plus about 87,000 American-born citizens (Nisei). Many were tenant farmers under West Coast state and local restrictions on land ownership, housing, employment, and education; Japanese Americans were a semisegregated community.

Evacuation

Following the December, 1941, Japanese attack on Pearl Harbor, the Federal Bureau of Investigation arrested 2,192 Japanese security risks, followed by German and Italian counterparts. False reports of Japanese American espionage at Pearl Harbor, Japanese victories in the Pacific, and radio and press rumors combined to create unfounded fears that traitors and saboteurs might assist a Japanese invasion of the West Coast. On February 14, 1942, Lieutenant General John DeWitt, with War Department encouragement, and misrepresenting rumors as security threats, recommended removing persons of the Japanese "enemy race," including American citizens, from his West Coast command area. The Justice Department acquiesced, and on February 19, 1942, President Franklin D. Roosevelt signed Executive Order 9066, authorizing the army to create restricted zones excluding "any or all persons." On March 21, 1942, Con-gressional Law 503 provided criminal penalties for noncompliance.

Internment

DeWitt put more than 100,000 West Coast Japanese Americans under curfew, exclusion, removal, collection, and evacuation orders, which resulted in permanent job and property losses. Their ten relocation camps in the Western United States were isolated, barren, crowded, and crude, with barbed-wire fences and armed guards. Liberals and conservatives alike generally seemed to approve this mass imprisonment, conspicuously limited to the Japanese race. Internees who hoped that compliance would demonstrate their loyalty to the United States became demoralized by camp conditions and popular hostility.

In 1943, Japanese American soldiers changed the situation. Aside from their Pacific theater intelligence service, Nisei already in uniform plus volunteers from the internment camps formed the 100th Infantry Battalion and the 442d Regimental Combat Team. Their European combat and casualty records earned public respect for the Nisei soldiers and a more positive policy for the internees. By early 1944, 15,000 Nisei civilians were on restricted camp leave; finally, on December 17, 1944, the West Coast exclusion order was lifted.

Japanese Americans from near Santa Maria, California, are taken into custody by federal agents and transported to the courthouse at Santa Barbara before being sent to internment camps in 1942.

Following Japan's surrender on September 2, 1945, detention and exclusion were phased out; the last camp closed March 20, 1946. The 1948 Evacuation Claims Act offered meager compensations—about $340 per case—for those renouncing all other claims against the government.

Court Cases

Four significant wartime appeals by Nisei reached the U.S. Supreme Court. On June 21, 1943, in *Hirabayashi v. United States* and *Yasui v. United States*, the Court upheld convictions for curfew violations, ruling the curfews constitutional and the emergency real, and found that Japanese Americans "may be a greater source of danger than those of a different ancestry." The Court held that winning the war must prevail over judicial review, implicitly reversing *Ex parte Milligan* (1866). On December 18, 1944, the Court granted *habeas corpus* in *Ex parte Endo*, ruling that Congress had not authorized long-term detention for a "concededly loyal" American citizen; the Court avoided broader questions of internment. On the same day, however, in *Korematsu v. United States*, the Court upheld Korematsu's conviction, on the *Hirabayashi* precedent. Although three dissenting justices argued that the exclusion order was part of a detention process, that Korematsu's offense of being in his own home was not normally a criminal act, and that only his race made it a crime under the exclusion orders, the Court majority upheld the government's wartime powers.

Redress

America's postwar generation developed different priorities. The Civil Rights movement and Vietnam War protests emphasized racial justice and deemphasized "national security." In 1980 Congress established the Commission on Wartime Relocation and Internment of Civilians to review facts and recommend remedies. Their 1982 report, *Personal Justice Denied*, exposed General DeWitt's misrepresentations, finding that "not a single documented act of espionage, sabotage or fifth column activity was committed by an American citizen of Japanese ancestry," that Executive Order 9066 resulted from "race prejudice, war hysteria and a failure of political leadership," and that "a grave injustice was done," deserving compensation. Of the Supreme Court, the report contended that "the decision in *Korematsu* lies overruled in the court of history."

The commission's work enabled Yasui, Hirabayashi, and Korematsu to file motions to vacate their convictions in the original courts on writ of *coram nobis*, alleging prosecutorial misrepresentation and impropriety. Yasui died while his case was in progress. On April 19, 1984, U.S. district court judge Marilyn Patel granted Korematsu's petition, acknowledging the 1944 Supreme Court decision as "the law of this case" but terming it an anachronism, "now recognized as having very limited application." On this precedent, Hirabayashi's convictions were overturned in 1987.

In 1988, a congressional act signed by President Ronald Reagan accepted the findings of the 1980 commission, provided $1.2 billion in redress for 60,000 internees, and added, "for these fundamental violations of the basic civil liberties and constitutional rights of these citizens of Japanese ancestry, the Congress apologizes on behalf of the Nation." The history of Japanese American internment illustrates both the difficulty of limiting emergency powers during a popular war and the abuses caused by failing to do so.   *K. Fred Gillum*

Core Resources

Jacobus Ten Broek, Edward Barnhart, and Floyd Matson's *Prejudice, War, and the Constitution* (Berkeley: University of California Press, 1968) relates the evacuation decision. Peter Irons in *Justice at War* (New York: Oxford University Press, 1983) and *Justice Delayed* (Middletown, Conn.: Wesleyan University Press, 1989) covers the court cases. See also the Commission on Wartime Relocation and Internment of Civilians' *Personal Justice Denied* (Washington, D.C.: U.S. Government Printing Office, 1982) and Clinton Rossiter and Richard Longaker's *The Supreme Court and the Commander in Chief* (Ithaca, N.Y.: Cornell University Press, 1976).

See also: Civil Liberties Act of 1988; *Hirabayashi v. United States*; Japan bashing; *Korematsu v. United States*; Redress movement.

Japanese Americans

> **Significance:** Japanese Americans have been one of the most discriminated against groups in U.S. history. Before World War II, they were barred from becoming U.S. citizens and owning land on the West Coast. During World War II, more than 100,000 Japanese Americans were placed in internment camps in the western United States and in Canada. However, the fighting spirit of the Nisei (second-generation Japanese American) army unit during World War II contributed to a greater acceptance of Japanese Americans by other racial and ethnic groups in the postwar period. By the end of the twentieth century, Japanese Americans had received an official apology and reparations for the internment.

In the 1890's, a few of the Japanese who had moved to Hawaii in the 1880's migrated to California, but large-scale Japanese immigration did not take place until 1900. From 1900 to 1910, more than 100,000 Japanese moved to the West Coast, first and primarily to California but eventually as far north as Vancouver, British Columbia. By 1930, about 275,000 people living in the United States were of Japanese origin or descent. By the end of the twentieth century, this number had reached about 1.8 million.

Early Reaction to Japanese Immigration

In 1882, Congress passed the Chinese Exclusion Act, primarily at the insistence of Californians who claimed that the Chinese could not be assimilated into American culture. Many Californians, therefore, were outraged when after Chinese immigration was virtually stopped by the 1882 act, Japanese immigration began. These citizens simply could see no difference between Chinese and Japanese immigrants, although, in fact, the Japanese, who had been carefully screened by the Japanese

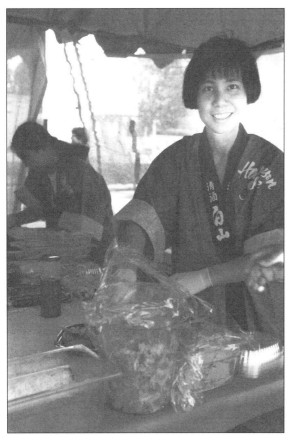

Japanese American women prepare sushi at a festival in California. During the course of U.S. history, Japanese Americans have been denied citizenship, prevented from owning land, and incarcerated in internment camps.

government, were generally better educated than the earlier Chinese immigrants.

Soon after 1900, politicians and journalists agitated to stop Japanese immigration, speaking of the "yellow peril." They maintained that the Japanese could not be assimilated into American culture and represented an outside group that would attempt to control the United States. In 1905, the public schools of San Francisco banned Japanese children from attending school with white children, causing the Japanese government to become very angry. The issue of San Francisco's school segregation was resolved in 1908 when President Theodore Roosevelt signed a Gentlemen's Agreement with the Japanese government, requiring that it not issue any more visas for workers to come to the United States. The San Francisco school board then allowed Japanese children to attend school with whites.

California and other states continued to harass Japanese immigrants. In 1913, California passed the Alien Land Act, which stipulated that Asians who were ineligible for citizenship could not own land. This meant that the Japanese immigrants, who were mostly agricultural workers, could work only as tenant farmers and could not own the land on which they worked.

Miscegenation laws, making marriages between people of different races illegal, were also enforced against the early Japanese immigrants, most of whom were men. Unable to find wives in the United States, these men turned to matchmakers in Japan. Often the immigrants would marry brides whom they had seen, before the wedding, only in a photograph. White Californians were angered by the Japanese practice of marrying "picture brides." They pointed to this behavior as further evidence that the Japanese could not be assimilated into American culture.

Japanese Americans During World War II

By the start of World War II, two generations of Japanese Americans (Issei, or first-generation Japanese Americans, and Nisei, second-generation Japanese Americans) lived in the United States and Canada. In 1942, members of the American and Canadian governments felt that the Japanese Americans posed a threat to security. Therefore, on February 19, 1942, President Franklin D. Roosevelt issued Executive Order 9066, requiring people of Japanese origin or descent living in the western part of the United States (California, Oregon, Washington, and the southern part of Arizona) to be placed in internment camps; this order affected more than 100,000 people. The Japanese Americans were given very little time to gather their property or to take care of businesses before they were interned. Property that actually belonged to Nisei (who were American citizens) was seized. Areas such as Japantown (Nihonmachi) in the Fillmore district

Milestones in Japanese American History

Year	Event
Late 1860's	Japanese agricultural workers move to Hawaii to work on plantations.
1900-1910	More than 100,000 Japanese immigrants, primarily male, come to the United States, settling mainly in California.
1905	Public schools in California require Japanese children to attend classes that are separate from those for other children.
1908	In Gentleman's Agreement between the United States and Japan, Japan agrees to restrict immigration to the United States. San Francisco schools integrate Japanese children with other children.
1912	Mayor of Tokyo gives more than 3,000 Japanese cherry trees to the United States as a gesture of friendship.
1913	California passes the Alien Land Act, which precludes most Asians, including Japanese immigrants, from owning land.
1942	Executive Order 9066 requires people of Japanese origin or descent living in the western United States to be placed in internment camps.
1943	The 42nd Regimental Combat Team, composed totally of Japanese Americans, is formed. This 30,000-soldier unit becomes the most decorated unit in U.S. military history.
1943	Supreme Court decision in *Hirabayashi v. United States* upholds the right of the United States government to place Japanese Americans in internment camps, suggests that Japanese had brought the situation on themselves by not assimilating quickly into the mainstream culture.
1943-1975	About 67,000 Japanese women enter the United States as brides of American servicemen.
1945	Japanese aliens and Japanese Americans are allowed to leave internment camps.
1952	Immigration and Nationality Act (McGarran-Walter Act) permits Japanese immigrants to become U.S. citizens.
1956	By popular vote, California repeals the Alien Land Act, making it possible for people born in Japan to own land in California.
1967	Japanese Americans living in the Fillmore District of San Francisco organize a Cherry Blossom Festival, which becomes an annual event.
1988	Congress passes the Civil Liberties Act, apologizing for internment of Japanese Americans and agreeing to pay reparations of $20,000 to each eligible person.
1990	President George Bush begins the reparations process.

of San Francisco and Little Tokyo in Los Angeles became nearly deserted. What is more, within twenty-four hours of the bombing of Pearl Harbor, the United States government detained one thousand Japanese American community leaders and teachers.

In Canada, the 1942 War Measures Act placed Japanese aliens and Japanese Canadians in camps and required them to pay for their housing. Those who objected to having to live in these camps were placed in prisoner-of-war camps along with captured German soldiers in northern Ontario. In the United States, various court cases were brought to challenge the government's treatment of Japanese Americans, but this treatment was deemed to be legal in decisions such as *Korematsu v. United States* (1944) and *Hirabayashi v. United States* (1943). In the decision handed down in *Hirabayashi*, the Court suggested that because Japanese Americans had chosen to live together as a group and had not assimilated well into the mainstream culture, the U.S. government was justified in being suspicious of them.

In January, 1945, Japanese aliens and Japanese Americans were allowed to leave the camps. Unable to live in the western United States, these people and their families settled in the East. Soon after the United States released the detainees from camps, the Canadians followed suit.

Japanese Americans After World War II

For a variety of reasons, life for Japanese Americans improved after World War II. The bravery of the Nisei soldiers during World War II had impressed upon many other Americans how loyal Japanese Americans actually were. Having seen firsthand the racial hatred practiced by the Nazis, Americans and Canadians did not want this sort of prejudice practiced in their home countries. Finally, much of the original prejudice and hatred against the Japanese and Asians as a whole stemmed from white Americans' fears of economic competition. The strength of the postwar U.S. economy lessened these fears and created advancement possibilities for many racial and ethnic groups.

In 1952, with the passage of the Immigration and Nationality Act (also known as the McCarran-Walter Act), it became possible for Japanese immigrants to become naturalized citizens. Although many Japanese citizens had entered the United States as wives of U.S. servicemen under the 1945 War Brides Act, many more entered under the 1952 act. From 1947 through 1975, 67,000 Japanese women entered as wives of U.S. servicemen, thus, becoming Japanese Americans. These new Japanese Americans encountered a very different United States from the one experienced by earlier immigrants. After 1952, it was much less likely that Japanese Americans would isolate themselves in areas where only people of Japanese heritage lived. In 1956, California, by popular vote, largely through a campaign orchestrated by Japanese American Sei Fujii, repealed its Alien Land Law, making it possible for people born in Japan to own land in California.

Japanese Americans in the Mid- and Late 1900's

In the latter part of the twentieth century, Americans became interested in all things Japanese. Japanese influences could be found in American music, fashion, architecture, philosophy, and religion. Japanese Americans were able to lead the way in introducing other ethnic and racial groups to Japanese culture and philosophy. In the 1960's, recognizing that expressions of cultural heritage were becoming popular, the Japanese Americans in the Fillmore district of San Francisco organized the first annual San Francisco Cherry Blossom Festival to share Japanese philosophy and culture associated with the cherry blossom with other Americans. Other cities such as Seattle, Washington, also organized cherry blossom festivals. One of the better-known festivals is the National Cherry Blossom Festival, held in Washington, D.C., each spring to celebrate the donation of more than three thousand Japanese cherry trees to the American people by the mayor of Tokyo in 1912.

Led by Japanese American citizens' groups, Japanese Americans for many decades attempted to obtain justice from the U.S. government for its treatment of them during World War II. Finally, in 1988, Congress passed the Civil Liberties Act. The American government acknowledged that an injustice had been done, apologized for that injustice, and agreed to pay reparations of twenty thousand dollars to each eligible Japanese American. In 1990, President George Bush began the reparations process. *Annita Marie Ward*

Core Resources

Books that provide additional information on Japanese Americans include Dorothy Hoobler, Thomas Hoobler, and George Takei's *The Japanese American Family Album* (New York: Oxford University Press, 1996) and Harry Kitano's *The Japanese Americans* (New York: Chelsea House, 1987), part of the Peoples of North America series. Robert Emmett Long edited *The Reference Shelf: Immigration* (New York: H. W. Wilson, 1996), which offers information on the state of Japanese Americans in the last decade of the twentieth century. Deborah Iida offers a fictional account of growing up in a Japanese American family in *Middle Son* (Chapel Hill, N.C.: Algonquin Books of Chapel Hill, 1996.)

See also: Alien land laws; Chinese Exclusion Act; Civil Liberties Act of 1988; Gentlemen's Agreement; *Hirabayashi v. United States*; Japan bashing; Japanese American Citizens League; Japanese American internment; Japanese Canadians; Japanese Peruvians in the United States; *Korematsu v. United States*; Yellow peril campaign.

Japanese Canadians

> **Significance:** Japanese Canadians, many of whom began as successful fishermen, were subjected to discrimination that took the form of restrictive immigration laws and incarceration in camps during World War II. In the postwar years, a new wave of immigrants with different professions and perspectives joined the older group.

The history of Japanese Canadians began in 1887, when a young pioneer, Manzo Nagano, landed in Canada full of hope for his new life. Coming from a fishing country and seeing the abundant salmon in British Columbia, he became a fisherman. According to the censuses of Canada, by 1901, of the 4,738 Japanese who emigrated to Canada, 97 percent resided in British Columbia and more than 4,000 were engaged in the fishing industry. Many were seasonal immigrants, who after the fishing season was over, returned to Japan and came back to Canada for the next fishing season.

Conflict with "White" British Columbia

Racial tension between whites and Asians had existed in British Columbia even before the Japanese arrived. However, serious racial tension between whites and Japanese started in 1899, when some Japanese fishermen broke a strike organized by the British Columbia Fishermen's Union. In addition, the rapid growth in the numbers of Japanese fishermen (by 1901, the Japanese held 1,958 fishing licenses out of a total of 4,722 issued) heightened racial tension between the two groups. As a result, in 1908, the Lemieux Agreement (called Gentlemen's Agreement in the United States) limited the annual number of Japanese immigrants to 400, and every new immigration law thereafter was more restrictive.

Picture Brides

Until 1908, Japanese immigration to Canada was exclusively limited to men. Although the Lemieux Agreement did not restrict the entry of spouses, married men, facing the possibility of further restrictions, rushed to bring their wives to Canada. Single men who wanted to build their lives in Canada arranged for marriages to "picture brides." They wrote letters to their relatives in Japan, asking them to look for women to be their wives. The relatives sought out eligible single women in their villages and arranged for an exchange of photographs and brief histories. If both parties agreed, a marriage was processed without the couple's ever actually meeting. The brides attended their wedding ceremonies without their husbands, then crossed the ocean to join their husbands in Canada. In spite of difficulties and setbacks, Japanese men and their picture brides led productive lives between the two world wars.

Detention Camp

About a week after the Japanese attack on Pearl Harbor in Hawaii in December, 1941, twelve hundred Japanese Canadian fishing boats were impounded despite the fact that all were owned or operated by Nisei, second-generation Japanese Canadians who were Canadian citizens. Moreover, by April, all Japanese Canadians were ordered to go to detention camps through notices similar to the following, issued to the Vancouver Japanese by the British Columbia Security Commission.

A Brief History of Japanese Canadians

Year	Events Involving Japanese Canadians	Germane World Events
1849		First English colonists arrive in British Columbia
1877	First Japanese immigrants arrive in Canada	
1894		Sino-Japanese War
1897	A Japanese fisherman's cooperative is established in Fraser River, British Columbia	
1905		Russo-Japanese War
1908	Leminux Agreement. "Picture brides" begin arriving in the United States	Gentleman's Agreement in North America
1913		California Alien Land Act
1924		Immigration Exclusion Act passes in the United States
1941		World War II begins
1942	Japanese Canadians are interned	Japanese Americans are interned
1944	Internees are given choice of resettlement east of the Canadian Rockies or in Japan	
1945	Deportation regardless of citizenship	Atomic bombs fall on Japan; World War II ends
1949	Japanese Canadians allowed to enter British Columbia	
1988	Compensation awarded to internees in the amount of $21,000 (CAN) per person	Compensation awarded to internees in the amount of $20,000 (US) per person in the United States

Persons of Japanese origin residing in Vancouver should terminate not later than the 30th of April, 1942, all leases or rental arrangements they may be working under. They must also be prepared to move either to Hasting Park or to work camps or to places under the Interior Housing Scheme at twenty-four hours notice. No deferments whatsoever on business grounds may be made to the above orders.

About twenty-one thousand Japanese Canadians were evacuated to camps such as Kaslo, New Denver, Slocan City, Sandon, and Greenwood. The Canadian government sold the Japanese Canadians' property while they were in the camps without any prior notice to the owners. For living quarters, the Japanese Canadians were given tents or huts that were previously used to house chickens, horses, or cattle and often lacked water and heating systems.

Oikawa Island (Don Island)

"Soon getting on the ship, I became seasick and could not eat for a week. Finally after the seventeenth day of my journey, I arrived in Victoria where my husband waited for me. On the way to the new home, I was dreaming to see a nice western-style house. What I saw was, instead, a log floating on the Fraser River. I asked my husband, not with angry voice but was a sad-surprised voice, 'What is this? Is this a house in Canada?' My life in Canada thereafter was either crying or fishing for salmon. And yet, when my husband decided to return to Japan, I was depressed to have to serve my mother-in-law in Japan again." Such was the life of a young Japanese woman living in a Japanese Canadian island fishing village in the late 1800's. Probably because she was there, her life was perhaps a little easier than that of other immigrants, but her story in many ways is quite typical.

Oikawa Island, the nickname of Don Island, is located in the south arm of the Fraser River. Jinzaburo Oikawa bought the island in 1905, and the following year, he helped smuggle eighty-three Japanese from his village in Japan to this fifteen-acre island. Unfortunately, the ship that carried the smugglers was seized by the British Columbia provincial and city police. After the smugglers paid a $2,275 (CAN) fine for illegal entry and $800 (CAN) in customs fines, the ship's passengers were free to land. From that time until the evacuation in 1942, about seventy to eighty men and some of their wives lived on Oikawa island. During the salmon season, the Oikawa residents lived in scow houseboats pulled by ships that went out on the river for fishing. During the off-season, the women farmed fields on the island and the men worked for the sawmills. Oikawa's wife and some helpers cooked every meal for the residents. On the island, they made rice, miso paste, and soy sauce. They held Japanese festivals, and strolling actors who also traveled to Hawaii and the mainland United States performed Japanese plays. On festival days, the islanders put on their own plays. The lifestyle on the island made many residents feel a little as if they were still in Japan.

Life in the camps was a daily encounter with racial discrimination and confusion of ethnic identities, especially for Nisei, who saw themselves as Canadians. The Canadian government provided educational and church services in the camps. At the same time, Japanese Canadians received New Years greeting gifts from the Japanese Red Cross, reinforcing the notion of their being "war enemies." Still, these internees made the best of their difficult circumstances. For example, by the end of the war, many camps had *furo* (Japanese-style baths) built by Japanese Canadians who followed the customs their parents practiced.

In March, 1945, just before the war ended, the Canadian government ordered Japanese Canadians to choose between "returning" to Japan or reestablishing themselves as Canadians contingent upon their living east of the Rocky Mountains. After the Japanese Canadians who had agreed to move to Japan heard about the atomic bombs dropped on Japan and the war's end, they refused to go back. Nonetheless, they were deported to Japan. Until 1949, Japanese Canadians were not allowed to return to British Columbia.

Redress Movement

In 1988, after many years of negotiating with the Canadian government to redress the internment issue, the National Association of Japanese Canadians finally received an apology and payment of twenty-one thousand Canadian dollars for each survivor who was incarcerated during World War II. Because many Issei (first-generation Japanese immigrants) are not able to read or write English, the application process was not easy. Besides the difficulty with the English language, those who were deported to Japan were not always aware of the settlement. At the same time, some Japanese Canadians donated money to develop the Japanese Canadian community. For example, $100,000 went to the *Nikkei-Voice*, a monthly newspaper published by a nonprofit organization, focusing on human rights and the development of the Japanese Canadian community and its identity.

Post-World War II

In the 1990's, approximately sixty thousand Japanese Canadians lived in Canada, about 0.2 percent of the nation's total population. This number includes post-World War II immigrants, including those who are temporary residents working for Japan-based companies. The new arrivals are called *shin-imin* by the older residents to separate them from the *kyu-imin*, the prewar immigrants. Unlike the *kyu-imin*, who immigrated as low-wage workers, the *shin-imin* immigrated as professionals, such as engineers or educators (including university professors and Japanese-language teachers); some also came as spouses of Canadians. The *shin-imin* and *kyu-imin* have separate immigrant associations and different perspectives toward the reestablishment of the Japanese social position in Canadian society. Descendants of the *kyu-imin* tend to regard redress settlement issues as the key element; however, *shin-imin* tend to believe that Japan's economic success in the 1980's and early 1990's is the major contributing factor to Japanese Canadians' social achievement and do not know very much about the redress settlement.

The New Generation

Japanese Canadians are some of the leading figures in Canadian society. For example, David Suzuki is an internationally renowned biologist, environmentalist, and broadcaster who hosts the award-winning Canadian Broadcasting Corporation television series *The Nature of Things*. He is also director of the David Suzuki Foundation, an organization dedicated to addressing worldwide environmental issues. Joy Kogawa, a novelist and poet, received the Books in Canada First Novel Award and the Canadian Authors' Association Book of the Year Award. Ken Adachi, who died in 1989, was an influential columnist for the *Toronto Star* and author of a book on Japanese Canadian history. His keen literary style was well known to most Canadians. Most Canadian sports fans recognize Paul Kariya, one of the stars of the National Hockey League, but many may not know that his father was born in a detention camp or that his grandparents were in the camps for more than five years.   *Nobuko Adachi*

Core Resources

Probably the best place to begin researching the history of Japanese Canadians is Ken Adachi's *The Enemy That Never Was: A History of the Japanese Canadians* (Toronto: McClelland & Stewart, 1991). Though he does not dismiss the war years, he also provides good coverage of the first settlers in the nineteenth century. Some firsthand stories of original immigrants can be found in Gorden Nakayama's *Issei* (Toronto: NC Press, 1984). Tomoko Makabe's *Picture Brides: Japanese Women in Canada* (Toronto: Multicultural History Society of Ontario, 1995) tells the fascinating stories of five pictures brides who came to Canada in the 1920's "determined to work hard and make a lot of money." Makabe's book *Sansei*

(Toronto: University of Toronto Press, 1997) documents the special trials and triumphs of the third generation of Japanese Canadians. The rise and fall of the Japantown in Vancouver is told in Katsuyoshi Morita's *Powell Street Monogatari* (Burnaby, B.C.: Live Canada Publishing, 1988). Of the several documentary histories of the evacuation, Robert Okazaki's *The Nisei Mass Evacuation Group and the P.O.W. Camp 101: The Japanese Canadian Community's Struggle for Justice and Human Rights During World War II* (Scarborough, Ont.: Markham, 1996) is one of the best. Cassandra Kobayashi and Roy Miki edited *Spirit of Redress: Japanese Canadians in Conference* (Vancouver, B.C.: JC Publications, 1989), which describes how the Japanese Canadian community finally forced the government to make restitution for various illegal acts during World War II. The dramatic film *The War Between Us* (Canadian Broadcasting Corporation, 1993) tells the story of the war years and how they affected both Japanese and white Canadians. Finally, the bilingual newspaper *Nikkei Voice*, published in Toronto, speaks for many in the Japanese Canadian community.

See also: Gentlemen's Agreement; Japanese American internment; Japanese Americans; Japanese Peruvians in the United States.

Japanese Peruvians in the United States

There were about thirty thousand Japanese in Peru in 1940 when an already existing anti-Japanese movement greatly expanded, and about 650 Japanese houses were targeted for assault in Lima. The following year, as soon as World War II broke out, the Peruvian government seized the property of all Japanese immigrants.

The third secretary at the U.S. embassy in Lima, John K. Emmerson, reported to the U.S. State Department that the Japanese community in Peru was led by well-organized nationalists who constituted a threat to U.S. national security. He suggested that the leaders of the Japanese Peruvian community be brought to the United States to be exchanged for American prisoners of war held in Japan. As a result, this proposal—as well as strong anti-Japanese sentiment from the Peruvian government—caused more than seventeen hundred Japanese Peruvians to be deported at gunpoint and transported to internment camps in the United States between 1942 and 1945.

When World War II was over, the Japanese Peruvians who were detained in the United States were not allowed to return to Peru or to have their belongings returned to them from the Peruvian government. In 1988, the

110,000 Japanese Americans who were placed in internment camps during the war received an official apology from the U.S. government and $20,000 per person for being incarcerated. However, those Japanese Peruvians who were also interned were denied the apology and compensation. This was because when they were deported from Peru, their passports were taken away by the Peruvian government and they were considered technically to be "illegal aliens" upon their arrival in the United States. Because they were neither U.S. citizens nor permanent residents at that time, they failed to qualify for the reparations even though a majority eventually became American citizens after the war.

Finally in June, 1998, American-interned Latin Americans received an official apology from the U.S. government; however, their compensation was only $5,000 per person. Moreover, they were allowed only two months to make their applications, the deadline being August 10.   *Nobuko Adachi*

See also: Japanese American internment; Japanese Americans; Japanese Canadians; Redress movement.

Jewish-African American relations

> **Significance:** When relations between Jews and African Americans were good, both groups dramatically advanced the cause of civil rights. Their joint efforts helped bring about the end of legal segregation.

Although the leaders of the African American and Jewish communities enjoyed undeniably good relations in the thirty years after World War II, their friendship was not the historical norm. The periods before and after these years of closeness and cooperation were marked by ambivalence. The relationship between the two communities has varied across time, depending upon economic developments, geographical proximity, and the presence of other ethnic groups.

Early U.S. History
Although both Africans and Jews came to North America early, their interaction was very limited. Most of the Africans were slaves on plantations; however, almost no Jews owned slaves or had reason to interact with them. Minimal contact began in the mid-nineteenth century in southern and border-state towns that had a population of freed slaves and a scattering of Jews from Central Europe. The Jews, many of whom opposed slavery, were

among the few merchants willing to trade with the former slaves. Both groups shared a sense of being outsiders, a strong attachment to the Hebrew Bible and its message of freedom for the slaves, and support for Abraham Lincoln and the liberal Republican Party during the Civil War (1861-1865).

Turn of the Century
Large-scale immigration of Eastern European Jews did not start until the mid-1880's. They came to the United States to escape legal discrimination, religious persecution, pogroms, and dire poverty. Very few of them had experienced any contact with blacks; however, they firmly believed in equality and the rights of the workers, the oppressed, and the poor. Therefore, they were sympathetic to the plight of the African Americans, many of whom had moved from the rural South to northern cities in which Jews lived to escape problems very similar to those from which the Jews had fled.

Depression and World War II
During the Great Depression of the 1930's, the Jewish and African American communities came into contact in large industrial cities, but relations were mixed. Both groups shared poverty and persecution and liberal Democratic affiliation. However, as some of the Jews began to prosper, conflict ensued. Many Jews went into business for themselves, partly because of prejudice against them in the workforce. Because they had limited resources, they opened small stores and later bought small apartment buildings in their urban neighborhoods. Normal shopkeeper-customer and landlord-tenant conflicts developed, intensified by the racial and ethnic differences.

During World War II, the events in Germany provided a common enemy for Jews and African Americans, but that did not eliminate problems. Nazism was not a salient issue for most African Americans. One of the serious rifts between the two groups involved a charismatic member of the Nation of Islam, Sufi Abdul Hamid, who built a reputation for himself partly by insulting Jews and their religion.

Post-World War II
World War II and its aftermath provided opportunities for both groups. African Americans, still fleeing the South, moved into the neighborhoods evacuated by Jews. A decline in public anti-Semitism, combined with higher education, allowed Jews to move from blue-collar to white-collar jobs and to escape the inner-city ghettos. Many Jews who went to college were exposed to and apparently moved by the plight of African Americans.

Early in the twentieth century, Jews had formed a number of organizations, such as the Anti-Defamation

League, to protect their rights. Several Jews worked with African American leaders to help them bolster parallel institutions to protect black people's rights, including the National Association for the Advancement of Colored People (NAACP), which had a significant Jewish presence both in funding and in legal staffing.

These civil rights organizations grew in number and in strength, especially after the sit-ins in the South during the early 1960's. The NAACP Legal Defense and Educational Fund, later headed by Jack Greenberg, took the lead in prosecuting the civil rights cases that broke down the legal support for segregation. In the most famous case, *Brown v. Board of Education* (1954), a number of Jewish defense organizations acted as supporting counsel and argued, along with Thurgood Marshall, before the U.S. Supreme Court against the segregation laws. It was this cooperation at the top that led to the golden age of Jewish-African American relations.

In the 1980's and 1990's, Louis Farrakhan, head of the Nation of Islam, expressed his hatred of the Jews and Judaism, terming it a "gutter religion."

Cooperation and support by Jews pervaded the Civil Rights movement. Jews offered much stronger support for racial equality than did other white Americans. Jews constituted more than one-third of all the northern Freedom Riders who went to the South to help organize and register African American citizens to vote. The 1964 murder of two Jewish civil rights activists, Michael Schwerner and Andrew Goodman, and of African American activist James Chaney, was one of the defining moments of the Civil Rights movement.

The Mid-1960's and Black Power
The bond between the Jews and African Americans began to unglue with the increasingly antiwhite and anti-Semitic rhetoric of young black radicals such as Stokely Carmichael (later Kwame Toure) of the Student Nonviolent Coordinating Committee. Leaders of the nascent Black Power movement wanted complete control over their destiny; they wanted to run their own organizations and to live by their own cultural standards, not those of white Europeans. The role of Jews in these movements, therefore, began to diminish.

As the Black Power movement grew, several radical African Americans started attacking Israel, hastening the departure of most Jews. Many young secular Jews grew up with a strong affinity for civil rights but were ambivalent or had weak feelings toward Israel. However, because of the shrill anti-Israel rhetoric and the threat to Israel's existence in 1967 by numerically larger Arab forces, American Jews started to become more supportive of the Israelis. As the younger generation of Jews left the Civil Rights movement in response to the rise of black power, they turned their attention to issues involving Israeli and Russian Jews, and their sense of themselves as an ethnic group increased.

Although Carmichael was critical of the Jewish people, civil rights activist Martin Luther King, Jr., had many friends among Jewish leaders. King was a hero not just to African Americans but also to Jews, in part because of his intolerance for anti-Semitism and his support for Israel. King's death accelerated the split between African Americans and Jews. In the terrible riots following his assassination, a disproportionate amount of loss was sustained by Jewish shopkeepers and landlords who had stayed in the ghetto because they could not afford to relocate. The remaining Jews left quickly.

At the end of the 1960's, a series of hostile confrontations occurred, many in New York, where unionized Jewish teachers battled local African American leaders. Disputes also arose over a proposed housing project in a middle-class Jewish neighborhood and among white-collar municipal employees over jobs and promotions. After the 1970's, many of these inner-city conflicts subsided as Jews moved to the suburbs. For example, in the Los Angeles riots of 1992, friction arose between African Americans and Koreans, not Jews. In other cities, conflicts involved African Americans and Latinos rather than Jews.

1980's and 1990's

Although friction between the two groups was more limited, it did not disappear. Black leader Jesse Jackson angered Jews during his 1984 bid for the presidency by referring to New York, which has a large Jewish population, as "Hymietown" ("hymie" is a derogatory term used to describe Jews) and courting Arab leader Yasser Arafat. On college campuses, a conflict of opinion arose over affirmative action. Jews, who had suffered from quotas that limited their enrollment in higher education, tended to oppose affirmative action, although perhaps less strongly than many white Americans. In 1991, in the racially mixed community of Crown Heights, Brooklyn, a car driven by a Hasidic Jew hit and killed an African American boy and injured his companion. In the rioting that followed, a Hasidic Jew was killed.

An ongoing source of tension in the 1980's and 1990's was Louis Farrakhan, a dynamic and media-sensitive member of the Nation of Islam with a passionate hatred of Jews and Judaism, which he called a "gutter religion." For many Jews, he was the devil incarnate; for many African Americans, he was an articulate spokesperson for black self-determinism and for self-respect and dignity.

The ties between the two groups were never completely severed, however. Both groups tended to be liberal and Democratic, so they had a common political predisposition. They typically lived in the same metropolitan areas and had a partial common history. Nonetheless, at the end of the twentieth century, their political interests diverged. African Americans were focused on the large numbers of blacks in what seemed like a permanent American underclass; Jews were worried about overseas Jews and their declining numbers due to widespread intermarriage and low birthrates. To many African Americans, Jews were just "white folks"; to many Jews, African Americans were ungrateful for the help that Jews had given in the past.   *Alan M. Fisher*

Core Resources

Murray Friedman's *What Went Wrong: The Creation and Collapse of the Black-Jewish Alliance* (New York: Free Press, 1995) provides the best single overview of relations between the two groups form a Jewish perspective. Hasia R. Diner's *In the Almost Promised Land: American Jews and Blacks, 1919-1935* (Westport, Conn.: Westview, 1977) examines the reasons behind Jewish leaders' support of African Americans. *Blacks and Jews: Alliance and Arguments*, edited by Paul Berman (New York: Delacorte Press, 1994), is a collection of stimulating essays from African Americans and Jews, many close to the New York world of race and politics. Jonathan Kaufman's *Broken Alliance: The Turbulent Times Between Blacks and Jews in America* (New York: Scribner's, 1988) brings a sensitive, human perspective on change from the 1950's to the

1980's. Mary Berry and John W. Blassingame, two revisionist African American historians, address the role of whites, especially Jews, in *Long Memory: The Black Experience* (New York: Oxford University Press, 1982).

See also: Anti-Defamation League; Anti-Semitism; Black Power movement; Civil Rights movement; Crown Heights conflicts; Eastern European Jews; Hymietown statement; Jewish Americans; Nation of Islam; National Association for the Advancement of Colored People.

Jewish American outmarriage

The striking increase in the number of marriages between Jews and non-Jews since 1960 has worried many American Jews. However, outmarriage is not a new phenomenon for Jews. In the colonial and early national period of U.S. history, the number of Jews in the population was small, immigrants were mostly men, and Jews were widely dispersed across the countryside. Jewish men therefore found it hard to find prospective brides within the Jewish population, and in 1840, when about fifteen thousand Jews were in the United States, the estimated rate of outmarriage was 28 percent.

The rate dropped significantly when the American Jewish community began to grow rapidly, as first German Jews and then Eastern European Jews arrived in substantial numbers. By 1900, approximately one million Jews lived in the United States, most in cities with extensive communal organizations, which made Jewish marriage partners easier to find. Increasing anti-Semitism from 1890 to 1940 made Jews less acceptable to Gentiles as marriage partners. In the years from 1890 to 1920, only 2 percent of Jews were involved in outmarriage; the rate increased slowly to about 6 percent in the 1950's.

A tremendous increase in outmarriage occurred during the 1960's. Although less than 10 percent of all American Jews were outmarried in 1971, a National Jewish Population Survey that year revealed that in the previous decade, more than 30 percent of new marriages were outmarriages. Jewish economic success after World War II, as well as the increasing number of young Jews who attended prestigious colleges, made it more likely that Jews would meet attractive non-Jews socially. Economic and social success, as well as the postwar decline in anti-Semitism, made Jews more attractive marriage partners.

Particularly worrying to Jews was the belief, held by most demographers, that the American Jewish birthrate had fallen below replacement level. If not enough children were born to keep the population level and one-third or more of those born left the community, a steady decline in numbers seemed inevitable. Pessimists foresaw the total disappearance of Jewish Americans. Others were more optimistic, claiming that because about one-third of non-Jewish spouses converted to Judaism and raised their children as Jews, the situation was not a disaster.

Faced with this problem, the more liberal branches of Judaism began to promote conversion to Judaism of non-Jewish marriage partners. The Reform movement established an outreach commission to support the conversion program. The Conservative movement did not engage in outreach but did urge rabbis to encourage conversion of marriage partners. Although the Orthodox rabbis accepted conversion in principle, they did not believe Reform and Conservative rabbis were competent to carry out this procedure and would not accept their converts, raising the possibility of a split within Judaism.

Rather than converts, Reform and Conservative groups began to speak of "Jews by Choice," a term that in a sense fit all Jews in the United States where religious liberty and individual freedom gave all persons the right to decide their own religious affiliation. *Milton Berman*

See also: Ashkenazic and German Jews; Eastern European Jews; Interracial and interethnic marriage; Jewish Americans; Jewish ethnicity: definitions; Judaism; Religion-based ethnicity.

Jewish Americans

> **Significance:** From their arrival in New Amsterdam in 1654, Jews were the most important non-Christian group in an overwhelmingly Christian America. Their experiences tested and helped define the meaning of religious freedom and the nature of ethnic relations in the United States.

In 1654, twenty-three Jewish refugees, who had fled Brazil when it was retaken by the Portuguese from the Dutch, arrived in New Amsterdam seeking asylum. They were not welcomed by Governor Peter Stuyvesant, who put them in jail and requested permission from the Dutch West India Company to ban all Jews from the colony. The company, which had several substantial Jewish shareholders, refused, and Stuyvesant had to permit the newcomers to remain. Despite facing prejudice, the Jews were able to worship undisturbed. The congregation grew slowly after the British conquered the colony in 1664 and renamed it New York. Other small Jewish settlements emerged in the port cities of Newport, Philadelphia, Charleston, and Savannah. Most newcomers were descendants of Spanish and Portuguese Jews who used Sephardic rituals in their synagogues and spoke a dialect of Spanish in their homes.

By 1776, the Jewish population in the British mainland colonies reached between 1,500 and 2,500. The Jews were accepted by their neighbors and could practice their religion unmolested, but they occasionally faced overt prejudice and legal disabilities. Jews could be, but were not always, barred from voting in colonial elections or holding political office because they were unable to take required oaths as a Christian. Jewish merchants and craftspeople participated fully in the commercial life of Newport, Rhode Island. However, even after the London Parliament passed a naturalization act providing special oaths for Jews in the American colonies, Rhode Island courts refused to naturalize Jews, claiming this would violate the purpose for which the colony was founded.

The state and federal constitutions established after the American Revolution shifted Jewish-Gentile relations from sometimes uneasy toleration toward civil and political equality. The U.S. Constitution and Bill of Rights provided federal protection for freedom of conscience, and the new state constitutions began to remove test oaths and disestablish religion. The movement was steady if uneven. Rhode Island did not grant Jews the right to vote or hold office until 1842; North Carolina did not do so until 1868.

German Jews
Until significant numbers of Jews from German-speaking areas of Europe arrived in the United States in the 1840's, the Jewish population remained small. In 1840, probably fewer than 15,000 Jews were in the United States; when Jewish immigration from Slavic lands began to increase in 1880, there were an estimated 250,000. Unlike their Sephardic predecessors, these Jews used Ashkenazic rituals and many spoke Yiddish. The vast majority of migrants were young men and women reacting to economic and political changes that worsened the position of Jews in their home countries.

The German Jewish immigrants flourished in the New World and greatly valued the political and economic freedoms they enjoyed in the United States. As the nation expanded, the young men moved west, some beginning as peddlers serving the scattered farmsteads, then opening mercantile establishments in the towns; a few very successful merchants established major department stores in the new cities. Their services were appreciated by their fellow townspeople; the first settlers in a town often became respected political and social leaders. In the early years of this migration, a small, thinly scattered Jewish population made finding Jewish marriage partners difficult, and a significant percentage married Gentiles. As they became economically successful, they founded families and brought young relatives to join them. Increased population meant Jews could create their own communal organizations, first a synagogue and a cemetery, then clubs that eased social isolation, and also philanthropic organizations to care for the poor and the elderly. Often unable to observe the Sabbath as commanded by orthodox Jewish law, they were particularly receptive to the relaxed requirements of the Reform movement, designed to modernize Judaism, that had already begun in Germany.

During the nineteenth century, a number of anti-Semitic incidents occurred in the United States. Civil War general Ulysses S. Grant issued an order calling for the expulsion of all Jews from his army department on December 17, 1862, after hearing that some were trading with the enemy. President Abraham Lincoln reversed the order shortly thereafter. When financially successful German Jews began to arrive in resorts that had been the preserve of the highest-ranking social groups of the United States, they experienced prejudice and discrimination. Famous resorts near New York such as Saratoga, Newport, and Long Branch began to turn away Jews, even wealthy New York City investment bankers. Lesser hotels began to use code words such as "restricted clientele" or "discriminating families only" in their advertisements.

Eastern European Jews

Between 1881 and 1924, approximately 2.5 million Jews, about one-third of the Jewish population of Eastern Europe, left their homelands; nearly 2 million came to the United States. The modernization of agriculture in Eastern Europe had eliminated many of the petty merchant and artisan occupations on which Jews depended. The major reason for the timing and scale of the migration, however, was the impact of government-sponsored anti-Semitism, especially the pogroms (anti-Jewish massacres) encouraged by the Russian government after the assassination of Czar Alexander II in 1881. Unlike the German Jews who had preceded them, these Jews concentrated in major cities, especially on the East Coast. Unlike other European groups of the period, few would return to their countries of origin. Theirs was a migration of families, with an almost even sex ratio. Lacking financial resources, they crowded into the poorest sections of the cities.

The German Jews did not welcome them. Class and cultural arrogance, anxiety that they would be burdened by masses of poor, and fear that the huge influx would exacerbate the already increasing anti-Semitism in the United States led to negative reactions toward the newcomers. Only slowly did the prosperous German Jews overcome their dislike and provide philanthropic support for those needing help. Not until the lynching of murder defendant Leo Frank in Georgia in 1913, amid violent anti-Jewish attacks, did they organize the Anti-Defamation League to combat anti-Semitism

The reaction of the non-Jewish community was even more negative. Old-line Yankees viewed the Jewish

Milestones in Jewish American History

Year	Event
1654	Arrival of twenty-three Jews, the first in North America, in New Amsterdam
1820-1880	Major years of German Jewish immigration
1880-1924	Major years of Eastern European Jewish immigration
1881-1883	Pogroms (anti-Jewish riots) in Russia after the assassination of Alexander II
1892	Foundation of American Jewish Historical Society
1906	American Jewish Committee founded to aid Jews abroad
1913	Leo Frank is lynched; raises fears of persecution in Jewish community
1913	Anti-Defamation League of B'nai B'rith founded to combat prejudice
1922	Henry Ford begins publishing anti-Semitic propaganda in his newspaper
1924	Restrictive immigration law passes, ending large-scale immigration
1933	Adolf Hitler elected chancellor of Germany
1939	United Jewish Appeal organized to coordinate relief for Hitler's victims
1939-1945	Holocaust kills about six million Jews
1948	Israel proclaims independence
1974	Anti-Semitic slurs made during Jesse Jackson's presidential campaign worry Jews
1991	Conflict erupts between Jews and blacks in Crown Heights in Brooklyn

areas of cities as a foreign intrusion corrupting the fabric of American society. Psychologists, using intelligence tests to rank ethnic groups, placed these Jews at the bottom, calling them genetically defective and ineducable. Immigration restrictionists claimed the Eastern European Jews proved the need to close the United States to new immigrants.

Anti-Jewish Prejudice and Discrimination

Dislike and fear of the newly arriving Jews helped spur the drive to restrict immigration, which took the form of legislation in 1924. It also provoked an outburst of overt prejudice and discrimination in the years from 1920 to 1940. As the children of the massive Eastern European Jewish immigration began to enter colleges and professional schools, they faced direct discrimination. Columbia College established quotas limiting admission of Jewish candidates, and other prestigious colleges and medical schools followed its example during the 1920's. Economic opportunities narrowed as few manufacturing companies, corporate law firms, major banks and insurance companies, or government bureaucracies such as the State Department were willing to employ Jews. Restrictive covenants, which barred homeowners from selling their houses to Jewish Americans or members of other "undesirable" groups, proliferated.

In 1922, Henry Ford began to publish a seven-year-long series of anti-Jewish articles in his newspaper, *The Dearborn Independent*, propagating older European stereotypes of Jews as both international bankers conspiring to control the country and communist conspirators determined to undermine capitalism. In the 1930's, the rise of Adolf Hitler inspired right-wing orators to preach ideological anti-Semitism. They defended Hitler, blaming Jews for the Great Depression and the international crises in Europe. More than one hundred anti-Semitic organizations appeared across the nation. In New York City, the Christian Front held street-corner rallies that often ended in fistfights between adherents of the movement and Jewish passersby.

The reluctance to respond effectively to the plight of German Jews in the 1930's reflected the impact of prejudice against Jews. No agency enforced immigration restriction rules more rigidly than the United States consular service in Germany, which insisted on absolute proof of the ability of prospective immigrants to be

Many Jewish Americans have become largely assimilated. Others, like these boys and their teacher, follow a more traditional Jewish lifestyle.

self-supporting. As a result, despite the desperate need of German Jews to escape, between 1933 to 1940 some 30 percent of the visas available for Germans were never issued.

Post-World War II

American revulsion at the sight of photographs of Hitler's death camps changed attitudes toward Jews. Overt anti-Semitism was no longer acceptable, and relations of Jews with other ethnic groups eased. When the courts refused to enforce restrictive covenants, the movement of Jews out of cities and into suburbs increased. Restrictions on college entry and job opportunities began to disappear. New York City home offices of major insurance companies, embarrassed by the revelation that they did not employ any Jewish stenographers in a city with a huge Jewish population, hastened to change their practices. The founding of the State of Israel and its survival under attack increased Jewish pride and improved American perceptions of Jews; they now appeared a normal ethnic group, not greatly different in its support of Old World nationalism from American Poles or Irish Americans.

Although pre-World War II anti-Semitism had surfaced predominantly among members of the Right, during the radical upheaval of the 1960's, Jews began to experience overt expressions of prejudice from members of the Left. Support of Israel when it was attacked by its Arab neighbors was a rallying point for all branches of the Jewish community. To Jewish ears, advocacy of Palestinian rights by radicals too often sounded like attacks on Jews, rather than simply criticisms of Israeli policy.

Even more disturbing was the open expression of anti-Jewish prejudices by African Americans. The long-term alliance of the two groups in the fight for civil rights seemed a thing of the past. Verbal attacks by Louis Farrakhan and his Nation of Islam followers and the slur against New York Jews uttered by Jesse Jackson in his 1984 presidential campaign were particularly worrisome because African Americans seemed the only major group believing it acceptable to express such prejudices publicly. Verbal and physical violence against Jewish shopkeepers in Harlem and the riots in Brooklyn's Crown Heights neighborhood intensified the feelings of antagonism between blacks and Jews.

Greater acceptance by other Americans helped raise the rate of outmarriage by Jews to more than 30 percent, which, combined with a birthrate that dropped below replacement level, led to fears that the American Jewish population would decline and ultimately disappear. Others were more optimistic, believing that many of the children of outmarriages would remain Jews. Immigration from Israel and the Soviet Union increased the Jewish community. Estimates in 1996 indicated that the Jewish population was stable at almost 6 million people who made up just more than 2 percent of the total American population.   *Milton Berman*

Core Resources

Jacob Marcus Rader's *The Colonial American Jew, 1492-1776* (3 vols., Detroit: Wayne State University Press, 1950, 1953, 1970) is the definitive study of those years. David and Tamara de Sola Pool's *An Old Faith in the New World: Portrait of Shearith Israel 1654-1954* (New York: Columbia University Press, 1955) describes the experience of the Sephardic Jewish community through the history of the oldest synagogue in the United States. Naomi Werner Cohen's *Encounter with Emancipation: The German Jews in the United States, 1830-1914* (Philadelphia: Jewish Publication Society of America, 1984) is a scholarly study of the reaction of this group to legal equality and citizenship. Stephen Birmingham's *"Our Crowd": The Great Jewish Families of New York* (New York: Harper & Row, 1967) is an anecdotal history of the most successful Jewish financiers and businessmen. Irving Howe's *World of Our Fathers* (New York: Harcourt Brace Jovanovich, 1976) presents a well-written description of the life of Eastern European Jews in New York City. Egon Mayer's *Love and Tradition: Marriage Between Jews and Christians* (New York: Plenum Press, 1985) provides a sociological study of this increasing phenomenon. *Anti-Semitism in American History*, edited by David Gerber (Urbana: University of Illinois Press, 1986), contains thirteen scholarly articles exploring American attitudes toward Jews.

See also: Anti-Defamation League; Anti-Semitism; Ashkenazic and German Jews; Crown Heights conflicts; Discrimination: overt/expressed vs. covert; Eastern European Jews; Frank, Leo, lynching; Housing; Hymietown statement; Immigration Act of 1924; Jewish-African American relations; Jewish American outmarriage; Jewish Americans as a middleman minority; Jewish ethnicity: definitions; Jewish stereotypes; Jewish women; Judaism; Restrictive or racial covenants; Sephardic Jewish Americans; Soviet Jewish immigrants.

Jewish Americans as a middleman minority

A middleman minority—or more simply a middle minority—is a distinctive racial or ethnic group occupying an intermediate position in the class structure between the higher and lower strata in the population (which may include other minorities). Middle minorities tend to be positioned in a special economic niche, often marginal but nonetheless of value to those in statuses above and below them. They are placed broadly within the middle class but fall into two subtypes: the small-scale shopkeepers and businesspeople who arrived poor and worked their way up and the middle-class businesspeople and professionals who were already established in their chosen lines of work before arriving in the new country.

Two Types

Small-scale shopkeepers and businesspeople and independent professionals of modest practice can be considered "middle" in a limited occupational sense. These immigrants generally arrive without much wealth and little capital; shopkeepers often rely on family members for low-cost labor. In a relatively open class structure where racial and ethnic discrimination by the majority group can be restrained, these minorities can often improve their financial status—if not in a generation, then in two or three. Basically, they serve their urban neighborhoods, which are made up of predominantly working-class and lower-middle-class populations, including their own and other minority communities.

The second type of middle minority consists of those groups who were already established in middle-class businesses and professions before leaving, as emigrants or refugees, the country of origin. Although they often start by serving their own ethnic community, after a period of transition and possibly downward mobility, they can enter horizontally into the mainstream market or state economy, and they may eventually regain their original status positions. By playing a part in the larger world of corporate business, the professions, and government, they can come to exercise a considerable degree of power within private and public institutions. Although this path of mobility is also open to the other type of middle minority, their transition is usually more difficult.

The two types of middle minorities and combined versions of them are found around the world. In the United States, middle minorities include the Chinese American community in San Francisco, the Korean Americans in Los Angeles, the Cuban Americans in Miami, and the Dominican Americans in New York. Other middle minorities include the Lebanese in certain African cities, the ethnic Chinese in Southeast Asia, and the Japanese in Brazil. Although these groups are called "middle" minorities, these communities generally contain a fair proportion of the near poor and the poverty-stricken.

Discrimination

Although one might expect that the buffer of class and in-group cultural solidarity would provide protection at least against the more extreme forms of racism, discrimination certainly affects middle minorities. In tightly knit urban neighborhoods, shopkeepers and small-business owners are vulnerable to severe outgroup hostility, especially from other minorities whose anger and frustration, far from being directed toward the dominant power structure, is diverted toward the middle minorities, whom they see and deal with every day. Economic downturns and political crises that render governments unstable can provoke severe discrimination against the second type of middle minority, their power and influence notwithstanding.

American Jews

American Jews, often described as a middle minority, fit this model, albeit with great variation. The American Jewish experience is vastly different from that of the court Jews of eighteenth century Western Europe or that of the Jewish middlemen and small traders, barred from landholding and many strategic occupations, in Eastern Europe. The 6.5 million American Jews who make up about 4 percent of the total U.S. population are highly urbanized and overwhelmingly middle-class (although some pockets of Jewish poverty exist). However, like so many other minority populations, they are quite diverse—in religion from Orthodox to Conservative to Reform to secular, in status from lower-middle-class to upper-middle-class. In addition, they are highly assimilated structurally and culturally with a high degree of outmarriage yet still strongly attached to a variously defined "Jewish cultural heritage." Nonetheless, generalization is possible.

The German Jews who arrived in the United States in the mid-nineteenth century exemplified a variation on

the theme of the middle minority: They started as itinerant peddlers and owners of small drygoods stores and moved on and up to managerial positions in large-scale retailers and mass communication and entertainment companies and became doctors and lawyers. However, as they improved their financial status, they became integrated into the economy and the urban-suburban social structure; they were no longer in a separate economic niche or necessarily in a localized community.

The millions of Eastern European Jews, many of them working-class and impoverished, who came between the 1880's and World War I to labor in the workshops of the garment industry and to establish their small shops in the heart of the cities, exemplified the first stage of the first type of middle minority. Their children pursued higher education, many entering the professions, and the Eastern European Jews, like the German Jews before them, gradually became integrated into the central economy and the urban-suburban secular culture. Despite residual anti-Semitism (for the most part confined to the societal fringe groups but still at work in some sectors of employment, housing, and social club life),

Many German Jews who arrived in the United States in the mid-nineteenth century became peddlers like these pictured in New York City in 1908.

American Jews, in their class status, their mobility patterns, and their diverse religiosity and ethnic subculture, seem distant from the conventional middleman model, particularly as expressed in Europe and Asia, because there is as much variation as commonality.

Richard Robbins

See also: Jewish Americans; Middleman minorities.

Jewish-Arab American relations

> **Significance:** Jewish Americans and Arab Americans conflict in their views of Israel, Palestinians, and the Middle East. Although some members of both groups take inflexible stances in their opposition to each other, other members are trying to bridge the gaps between the cultures.

Some scholars estimate there are between one million and three million Arab Americans, a significantly larger number than the 870,738 Arab Americans counted in the 1990 U.S. census. An accurate count is difficult to obtain because many Arab Americans are reluctant to reveal their origin for fear of discrimination or even violence from those Americans who, perhaps influenced by negative press coverage of Arabs and events in the Middle East, stereotype Arab Americans as terrorists or as anti-American.

U.S. government figures in 1994 place the number of Jewish Americans at 6 million—4 million religious and 2 million secular Jews. However, because some Jews, like Arab Americans, are reluctant to reveal their religious and ethnic identity for fear of discrimination, their actual numbers must be assumed to be greater. Of the 6 million American Jews, about 250,000 are Sephardic Jews. Of those Sephardic Jews, about 85,000 are Arab Jews, that is, Jews from Arab nations. Arab Jews in the United States are largely from Syria, Egypt, Yemen, Iraq, Saudi Arabia, Tunisia, and Morocco. If Arab Jewish Americans are included in the Arab American population, the total number of Arab Americans is significantly increased. The largest population of Arab Jews in the United States is in Brooklyn, New York. This community of Syrian Jews is stable and affluent.

Origins and Demographics

Arab Americans and Jewish Americans come from very diverse backgrounds and subcultures that sometimes seriously conflict. However, they are very much alike in terms of being better educated and more affluent than the average American.

Arab Americans trace their origins to the twenty-one countries of the Arab League (established on March 22, 1945): Algeria, Bahrain, Djibouti, Egypt, Iraq, Jordan, Kuwait, Lebanon, Libya, Mauritania, Morocco, Oman, Palestine, Qatar, Saudi Arabia, Somalia, Sudan, Syria, Tunisia, United Arab Emirates, and Yemen. The earliest Arab immigrants, who arrived between 1900 and World War II, were predominantly Christians from Syria and Lebanon. Most had little formal education and were predominantly illiterate. Their success in running small family businesses, mostly in poor neighborhoods, made it possible for their children to become well educated and enter the professions or obtain high-level, white-collar jobs. Following World War II and especially after 1965, when quota restrictions were lifted, Arab immigra-

Cities with the Largest Arab and Jewish American Populations

Arab Americans	Jewish Americans
1. Detroit, Mich. (metropolitan area)	1. New York (metropolitan area)
2. New York (metropolitan area)	2. Los Angeles, Calif.
3. Los Angeles, Calif.	3. Miami, Fla.
4. Washington, D.C.	4. Philadelphia, Pa.
5. Chicago, Ill.	5. Chicago, Ill.
6. Boston, Mass.	6. Boston, Mass.
7. Anaheim-Santa Ana, Calif.	7. San Francisco, Calif.
8. Bergen-Passaic, N.J.	8. Washington, D.C.
9. Houston, Texas	9. W. Palm Beach-Boca Raton, Fla.
10. Cleveland, Ohio	10. Baltimore, Md.

Sources: Samia El-Badry, "The Arab-American Market," *American Demographics*, Vol. 16, January, 1994, pages 22-30; David Singer, ed., *American Jewish Year Book*, 1997. New York: American Jewish Committee, 1997.

tion increased significantly. These newer immigrants were more affluent, better educated, largely Muslim professionals and businesspeople.

Arab Americans, affluent and well educated, are one of the most successful ethnic groups in the United States. About half of all Arab Americans live in large metropolitan areas, and around 20 percent in three urban areas: Detroit, Michigan, New York, and Los Angeles-Long Beach. Detroit has the largest Arab American population, which is divided roughly equally between Christians and Muslims. The 1990 U.S. census obtained the national origins of Arab Americans in the state of Michigan. Of the 77,070 people reporting Arab ancestry, 39,673 had Lebanese roots, 7,656 Syrian, 6,668 Iraqi, 2,695 Palestinian, 1,785 Egyptian, 1,441 Jordanian, 14,842 Unspecified Arab or Arabic, and 2,310 Other Arab. The census also counted 14,724 persons of Assyrian (Chaldean) ancestry. Assyrians were not included with other Arabs because most members of this group do not consider themselves Arabs.

Jews have been in North America for almost four hundred years. The earliest immigrants were Sephardic Jews in the 1600's in New York. The 1800's saw the arrival of Ashkenazic Jews from Germany and the surrounding areas. They often worked as merchants and soon became prosperous. In the late 1800's, Eastern European Jews, many of them lacking resources, migrated in great numbers to the United States, often settling in cities. These late arrivals faced prejudice from both non-Jewish Americans and the earlier German Jews. After World War II and the Holocaust, anti-Semitism diminished greatly, and all Jewish groups found greater acceptance in the United States. Most Jews came to the United States from Europe to escape religious persecution and poverty and, like Arab Americans, have prospered in their adopted country. Both groups are predominantly urban dwellers.

Arab and Jewish American Relations
Ironically, the conflicts in the Middle East have brought Arab Americans and Jewish Americans closer. Most of the efforts to improve intergroup relations have centered on events not in the United States but in the Middle East, where Israel and many members of the Arab League have been at war or in conflict since the establishment of the Arab League in 1945 and of the state of Israel in 1948.

The Arab Americans and Jewish Americans most opposed to a just and equitable settlement of the plight of the Palestinians have been the religiously orthodox and fundamentalistic members of the two groups. Those most willing to talk about peace and justice have been the more liberal Jews (Reform and secular Jews) and progressive Arabs. Most of the initiatives toward bringing Arabs and Jews together have generally originated with Jewish

Americans and been supported enthusiastically by Arab Americans. A big impediment to improving Arab-Jewish relations has been the conservative and orthodox newspapers published exclusively for Arabs and Jews. Their biases and prejudices—and sometimes blatant hatred—often stand in the way of improving intergroup relations. The politics of the Middle East and their effect on American Arabs and Jews have been the focus of social-action organizations in both communities.

Organizations Working for Togetherness
On the national level, few organizations have been as active and effective in bringing Arabs and Jews together as the New Jewish Agenda (NJA). Founded in the late 1970's, at its height it had twenty-eight chapters, most of which were in the large urban areas where Jewish Americans and Arab Americans live and work. NJA was started by Jews who felt that conservatives had dominated Jewish life in the United States and who yearned to create a strong progressive voice in the Jewish community. One of its major goals has been to have ongoing Jewish-Arab dialogues on crucial matters of mutual concern to Jews and Arabs in the United States and the Middle East, especially resolution of the Israeli-Palestinian question. Los Angeles, which has one of the largest concentrations of Jews and Arabs in the United States, has a dialogue group organized much like an NJA group. However, the Los Angeles group concentrates on Arab-Jewish issues and does not discuss issues such as racism, anti-Semitism, and nuclear disarmament, which are covered by NJA groups.

American Arab and Jewish Friends (AAJF) was founded in 1981 by George Bashara (an Arab American) and Arnold Michlin (a Jewish American) in metropolitan Detroit. It is a program of the Greater Detroit Interfaith Round Table of the National Conference for Community and Justice (formerly known as the National Conference of Christians and Jews). The AAJF's purpose is to improve mutual understanding and friendship between the Arab and Jewish communities by coming together informally through luncheons, dinners, forums, and its sponsorship of an annual essay scholarship contest for graduating seniors in area high schools. The essays, which describe innovative and meaningful approaches toward the realization of the AAJF goal, are the joint effort of two students, one Jewish and one Arab American.

In large cities such as Washington, D.C., where there are sizable Arab American and Jewish American populations, the two groups often meet at friendly gatherings held by organizations such as the Washington Area Jews for Israeli-Palestinian Peace-Friendship For several decades, this organization has regularly held dinners where Arabs and Jews can become friends, discuss the issues that divide them, and make efforts to influence policymakers who may be in a position to initiate positive changes in the bitter conflicts that separate Israelis and Palestinians.

The Seeds of Peace summer camp was started by former newspaper editor John Wallach in the early 1990's. The Otisfield, Maine, camp brings together more than 160 teenagers from the Middle East—Palestinian Arabs and Jewish Israelis as well as American Jewish and Arab youngsters—for a month of good, healthy fun as well as serious discussions. Participants are selected by their governments after writing essays on making peace. To run the camp costs about $1.2 million per year, which Wallach receives in private donations. All the campers come on scholarships, each worth around $2,000. The camp has been so successful that other such camps are being organized elsewhere in the United States.

The Middle East Friendship League was established by Professor Robert Frumkin and his colleagues at Kent State University in Kent, Ohio, following the killing of Israeli wrestlers by Arabs at the Olympic Games in Munich, Germany, in 1972. Kent State had a large number of students and faculty from Arab League nations and Israel as well as a sizable number of American Arab and Jewish students and faculty, making it an ideal setting for an experiment in improving Arab and Jewish relations. Although the main purpose of the organization was to promote friendships between Arabs and Jews, its members discussed Middle East issues and engaged in social activism aimed at enhancing the peace process and addressing issues such as Palestinian rights and terrorism. The league met monthly for several years, during which real friendships developed and remained strong even after it disbanded.

Right-Wing Organizations

No discussion of Arab-Jewish relations in the United States is complete without a mention of the Jewish Defense League (JDL) and Jewish Defense Organization (JDO), two right-wing organizations that are the antithesis of all the previously discussed organizations. The JDL and the JDO are pathologically anti-Arab. The JDL, founded by the late Meir Kahane, was not only involved in defamation of Arab Americans but also the destruction of Arab American property and even murder, including the Arab American leader Alex Odeh. Although, according to the *Encyclopedia of Associations* (published by Gale Research), the JDL is no longer functioning in the United States, its sister organization, the JDO, is. The JDO has almost four thousand members in ten states. Like the JDL, the JDO states that it will defend Jews by any means necessary and advocates the use of violence. Although the JDL frequently took credit for violent and destructive acts against Arab Americans and their property, the JDO, thus far, has not. *R. M. Frumkin*

Core Resources

Brent Ashabranner's *An Ancient Heritage: The Arab-American Minority* (New York: HarperCollins, 1991) is a well-balanced book that deals fairly with American Arab and Jewish relations. *The Development of Arab-American Identity* (Ann Arbor: University of Michigan Press, 1994), edited by Ernest McCarus (Ernest Nasseph), is an excellent anthology that covers every important aspect of the Arab American experience. On the Seeds of Peace program, see Caryle Murphy's "There's Mideast Peace in the Wilds of Maine," (*Washington Post*, August 16, 1997). For some insight into the Jewish Defense Organization, see Mordecai Levy's *By Any Means Necessary* (New York: Jewish Defense Organization, 1998). Gerald S. Stroberg's *American Jews* (Garden City, N.Y.: Doubleday, 1974) describes Jewish Americans' struggle with identity issues.

See also: Arab American intergroup relations; Arab Americans; Jewish Americans; Sephardic Jewish Americans.

Jewish Canadians

> **Significance:** Relations between Jews and other Canadians serve as a barometer of the degree to which the people and leaders of Canada practice religious toleration. The most hostile expressions of anti-Semitism occurred during the 1930's, replaced by more favorable attitudes after World War II.

Jews first arrived in Canada after the British conquest in 1763 and by 1768 had consecrated their first synagogue in Montreal. The Jewish population was small until persecution of Jews in the Russian empire during the 1880's and the early 1900's intensified, creating a surge of refugees. From approximately 2,500 in the early 1880's, the Jewish population in Canada rose to 16,000 by 1900; the census of 1921 counted 126,000. Few Jews were permitted to enter in the 1920's and 1930's.

The 1991 federal census counted 365,315 Jews, 1.3 percent of the Canadian population of 27 million. More than 95 percent of the Jewish population lived in urban areas; three-fourths were concentrated in two cities, 163,000 in Toronto and 101,000 in Montreal.

Anti-Semitism

Jews were not welcomed by either French-or English-speaking Canadians. Jews were barred from entering Canada while it was part of the French empire. The British granted Jews equal civil and political rights with other Canadian subjects in 1832. Although Canada encouraged immigration between 1880 and 1914, attempts by Jewish organizations to settle Jewish refugees on farms in the Canadian prairie provinces received little support and sometimes open opposition from government officials.

By the 1920's, young Canadian-born Jewish men and women applying for admission to colleges and universities faced both overt and covert barriers. McGill University, particularly attractive because it taught in English, secretly began to require higher grades from Jewish candidates than from other applicants, thereby successfully reducing the percentage of Jewish students from 25 percent to 12 percent. L'Université de Montréal was less successful in maintaining secrecy. French nationalists openly questioned the presence of Jews, who were less than 5 percent of the student body. The agitation spurred the 1929 undergraduate student association to petition the administration for the expulsion of all persons of Jewish origin. In the summer of 1934, interns at the university-affiliated Notre-Dame Hospital went on strike over the admission of a Jewish intern, who was consequently forced to resign.

Canada began to restrict all immigration in the 1920's, and with the coming of the Great Depression, the barriers to entry became almost impenetrable. Jewish community organizations desperately petitioned the Canadian government to grant exceptions for refugees from Nazi Germany but failed to convince any officials. The manuscripts left by the director of the immigration office reveal him as totally contemptuous of Jews, devising bureaucratic tactics to prevent any from entering Canada. Appeals to accept refugee Jewish children— whose parents were inadmissible—were rejected on the grounds that it was bad policy to break up families. The director's policies were approved by the prime minister and supported by public opinion throughout the country. The French Quebec press and political leaders were especially vigorous in opposing admission of any more Jews. Although the government claimed in 1943 that it had admitted 39,000 immigrants since 1933, most of them refugees, the total actually included 4,500 German civilians who had been interned in Great Britain and 25,000 Axis prisoners of war. Fewer than 5,000 Jews managed to enter Canada in the entire 1933-1945 period.

Post-World War II
During the first years after the war, the Canadian government policy, supported by public opinion, was no more generous than before in accepting Jewish survivors of the Holocaust. Finally, in 1948, the government reversed its position on immigration and began to accept new immigrants; it also removed the barriers to Jewish immigration. Changing attitudes, as Canadians began to celebrate their multicultural diversity, eased relations between Jews and their fellow Canadians, one consequence of which was an increase in marriages between Jews and non-Jews, which made some Jewish community leaders worry about the future survival of Jews in Canada.

Relations between Jews and the Quebec separatists have been strained. English-speaking Jews have overwhelmingly supported the federalists in the various referendums on independence from Canada, leading to open expressions of hostility on the part of the separatists. The premier of Quebec blamed the narrow defeat of the October, 1995, referendum on the "ethnic vote," which Jews understood included them, and promised that Québécois would take their revenge in their own country. Anxiety about the future led many Jews to move from Montreal to Toronto and the cities of western Canada. Montreal's Jewish population stagnated as immigrants (including a significant group of French-speaking Jews driven out of Arab lands in North Africa) barely replaced the young men and women who had left.

All signs of anti-Semitism have not disappeared. Instances of vandalism against synagogues and cemeteries occasionally occur. A constant irritant to Jewish Canadians is the presence of people who deny that the Holocaust ever happened. That assertion also includes the accusation that Jews control the media, using it to convince the public of a falsehood, thus conspiring to manipulate public opinion and use the government for group advantage. Yet most Jewish leaders view the position of Jews in Canada as eminently satisfactory.

Milton Berman

Core Resources
Stuart E. Rosenberg's *The Jewish Community in Canada— Volume I: A History* (Toronto: McClelland and Stewart, 1970) contains a well-illustrated narrative of Jewish immigration and life to 1960, focusing heavily on Montreal and Toronto. Irving Arbella and Harold Troper's *None Is Too Many. Canada and the Jews of Europe, 1933-1948* (Toronto: Lester and Orpen Dennys, 1982) is the classic, detailed revelation of the way governmental action, supported by public opinion, refused to admit Jewish refugees from Nazi Germany to Canada. The articles in *Anti-Semitism in Canada: History and Interpretation* (Waterloo, Ont.: Wilfrid Laurier University Press, 1992), edited by Alan Davies, cover the nineteenth century as well as post-World War II developments. Daniel J. Elazar and Harold M. Waller's *Maintaining Consensus: The Canadian Jewish Polity in the Postwar World* (Lanham, Md.: University Press of America, 1990) deals with ways Jewish organizations approached problems in Canada. The essays in *The Canadian Jewish Mosaic* (Toronto and New York: John Wiley & Sons, 1981), edited by J. Weinfeld, W. Shaffir, and I. Cotler, attempt to provide a comprehensive description and analysis of the Canadian Jewish community, including comparative material on Jews in the United States.

See also: Anti-Semitism; Jewish Americans; Jewish women; Judaism; Refugees: Canadian policy; Separatist movement in Quebec.

Jewish Defense League

The Jewish Defense League (JDL) was founded in 1968 by thirty young Jews who believed that the position of Jews in the United States was deteriorating and who also felt that the activities of established Jewish organizations did not meet the present needs of Jews. They argued that such organizations as B'nai B'rith, the American Jewish Committee, and the American Jewish Congress no longer served the interests of Jewish Americans because they focused too heavily on non-Jewish causes such as civil rights. The founders feared that overt expressions of black anti-Semitism and the increasing impact of street crime against Jews indicated that the United States was experiencing something similar to the Nazi street violence that had prepared the way for the Holocaust. Using the slogan "Never Again," the members of the JDL looked for ways to alert the world to what they perceived as a marked deterioration everywhere in the quality of Jewish life. Meir Kahane, an Orthodox rabbi, soon emerged as the leader of the JDL.

In 1969, the JDL attracted national attention by dramatizing the plight of Soviet Jewry in demonstrations before the Soviet mission to the United Nations and at other Soviet agencies in the New York City area. Their forceful picketing of the Soviet airline at John F. Kennedy Airport disrupted air travel between the United States and the Soviet Union. The JDL believed that agitating against American-Soviet sport and cultural exchanges and trying to disrupt trade between the two countries would embarrass the Soviet government and convince it to improve the position of Jews in the Soviet Union as well as end the ban on emigration from the country by Jews.

The JDL turned its attention to Israel in 1971 and began to urge American Jews to emigrate to Israel. Only by doing so, they argued, could American Jews recapture their religious zeal and offer effective resistance to anti-Semitism. There they could join with the Israelis in defending the land from attacks by the Palestinians. As Kahane studied the situation in Israel, he became convinced that the only solution to the problem was for Israel to expel all Arabs from the country. He explained his reasoning in his 1981 book, *They Must Go.* Shortly after publishing his book, Kahane moved to Israel with his family, founded the KACH political party, and was elected to the Knesset, the Israeli parliament, in 1984.

The high point in JDL membership was in 1972, when its membership reached fifteen thousand people. However, the shift in the JDL's focus from the United States to Israeli politics, the increasing rigidity of its ideology, and accusations that the JDL had gone beyond militancy to illegal use of force, including bombings, disillusioned many of its members. Their numbers declined markedly. Kahane remained popular, and his speeches drew crowds and press coverage, but after he was assassinated in New York City in 1990, the JDL ceased to exert much influence on Jewish life in the United States.

Milton Berman

See also: American Jewish Committee; American Jewish Congress; Anti-Defamation League; Jewish Americans.

Jewish ethnicity: definitions

Jews trace a four-thousand-year history to a common origin in the biblical characters of Abraham and Sarah of Ur (Southeastern Iraq). Eventually twelve tribes settled the land of Israel. Modern Jews are descendants of the southern tribe, Judah, which maintained Jerusalem, the temple, and the kingship of David. From their beginnings, Jews were a diverse group. They have often existed as "alien residents" among other peoples, which has made them targets for exploitation, attack, and expulsion. Their ancient language of Hebrew became their common religious language. Monotheism, circumcision of males, and concern about social justice all have ancient Jewish origins. Because of their preservation of the Torah (Bible) and their study and practice of its ethical and religious laws, Jews have been called "the people of the Book." Because both Christianity and Islam credit Judaism for their beginnings, early Jewish history continues to be known throughout the world.

The question of who is a Jew is variously answered. The traditional *halacha* (*rabbinic* religious rulings) upheld by Orthodox and Conservative branches is that a Jew is born from a Jewish mother (matrilineal descent) or has undergone a conversion that includes religious instruction, immersion in water, and, for men, circumcision. The liberal Reform movement ruled that patrilineal descent would be accepted if the child was raised as a Jew. These differences in rulings create problems for marriages between Jews. The *bar/bat mitzvah* remains an affirming religious ceremony for adolescents in all branches of Judaism.

Jews in the United States are drawn from many countries to which their ancestors were dispersed after the Romans' conquest of Israel in 70 C.E. The main subgroups are Ashkenazic (Polish, German, Russian, and other Eastern European), Sephardic (Latin American, Spanish), and Middle Eastern (Israeli, Ethiopian). Secular Jews maintain social, cultural, and national connections but not religious involvement with the Jewish community.

Like Irish, Greek, and Italian immigrants, Jews in the United States were initially defined as "nonwhite." However, by the 1950's, Jews were viewed as religious rather than racial or ethnic in their differences from the European American mainstream. Indeed, much of what distinguishes Jews has religious roots: the weekly Sabbath from sundown Friday to sundown Saturday; holidays such as Yom Kippur, Rosh Hashanah, Sukkot, Hanukkah, Purim, and Pesah (Passover); dietary restrictions against eating pork and certain seafood; keeping *kosher;* males wearing *kippah* (skullcaps); and foods such as *matzah* and *halah.* Like some other religious minority groups, Jews maintain religious day schools and advanced religious educational institutions. *Jews by Choice* (1991), by Brenda Forster and Joseph Tabachnik, contains detailed descriptions of the religious and ethnic aspects that are part of Jewish culture.

Jews share concerns that include maintaining Jewish identity, supporting the state of Israel, opposing anti-Semitism, maintaining "separation of church and state," remembering the Holocaust, and handling intermarriage or outmarriage. Jewish Federation data indicate that by 1990, half of Jews were marrying Gentiles (non-Jews). Because only an estimated 5 percent of spouses convert to Judaism and only 28 percent of children born of interfaith marriages are raised as Jews, there is serious concern about the survival of Jews and of Judaism. Additionally, religious involvement is increasingly being replaced by "symbolic" Jewish identification through consumption of "Jewish foods," collection of Jewish art and religious objects, going to Yiddish plays, listening to *klezmer* music, and following Jewish entertainers, athletes, politicians, and other influential persons.   *Brenda Forster*

See also: Ashkenazic and German Jews; Eastern European Jews; Interracial and interethnic marriage; Jewish American outmarriage; Jewish Americans; Jewish stereotypes; Jewish women; Judaism; Religion-based ethnicities; Sephardic Jewish Americans.

Jewish stereotypes

Jewish stereotypes include negative and positive images that are based on perceived physical traits and cultural patterns. In the late 1800's, cartoons depicted Jewish Americans as having big noses. Jewish Americans have also been portrayed as clannish people who have undue influence and power in politics and in the world of finance. Other stereotypes involve the image of the Jewish American Princess (JAP), a spoiled, privileged young woman, or the Jewish mother, an interfering mother who makes her children feel guilty. More favorable stereotypes portray Jewish Americans as industrious people who are good financial providers and value education for themselves and their children.

Clannishness is the outgrowth of being part of a minority, feeling left out, or not belonging and sometimes feeling inferior. According to Sidney J. Jacobs and Betty J. Jacobs's *Clues About Jews for People Who Aren't* (1985), minority members often seek a sense of belonging and comfort by forming groups with similar people. Clannishness may be the price Jews and other minority groups pay to retain distinctive cultural and religious practices. Jews may interact closely with each other partly because they have been barred from joining the greater society by restrictive housing clauses, university quotas limiting the number of Jews admitted, country clubs that refused to accept Jews, and discrimination that kept them out of top executive jobs.

Several stereotypes of Jews involve finance. Some of the earliest Jewish immigrants in the United States as well as the Eastern European Jews were peddlers and shopkeepers, and perhaps because of non-Jewish resentment of this role, Jews have been accused of being crafty, devious merchants. An old European stereotype saw Jews

This issue of *The Dearborn Independent,* automotive giant Henry Ford's Michigan newspaper, perpetuates the stereotype that Jewish bankers wield unusual power over financial markets.

as international bankers trying to control the financial world; this image was accepted by many Americans, some of whom still believe that Jews control the U.S. banking industry. To the contrary, according to the November 25, 1974, issue of *Time* magazine, "Jews view the [banking] industry as one of the last bastions of discrimination against them." In the 1920's, the old European stereotype of Jews as political radicals was revived, with Jewish people cast as communists and anticapitalists.

The Jewish American Princess (JAP) stereotype depicts a spoiled, hedonistic, self-centered young American Jewish woman who has been pampered and overindulged by her wealthy parents. This exaggerated and offensive portrayal may reflect non-Jewish jealousy of some Jewish Americans' socioeconomic success. Because the term "JAP" is part of the American vocabulary, many people who use the term may be unaware of its offensive nature.

The Jewish mother stereotype portrays a woman who invokes guilt in her children. Jewish American authors such as Philip Roth and Woody Allen have used this stereotype in their writing for dramatic or humorous effect. Such use of racial and ethnic stereotypes by members of the minority group has been criticized as promoting prejudice but also defended as the minority member's right to create an in-joke.

To promote better relations between Jews and non-Jews and to attempt to eliminate stereotypes, Jewish religious congregations sometimes hold interfaith activities and worship services. Rabbis and board members frequently serve on citywide boards and committees. Jews play an active role in such organizations as the National Conference of Christians and Jews (now known as the National Congress for Community and Justice), formed in 1927 to combat racism, bias, and bigotry in the United States. *Marian Wynne Haber*

See also: Jewish Americans; Jewish Canadians; Judaism; Prejudice and stereotyping; Stereotype; Stereotyping and the self-fulfilling prophecy.

Jewish women

Significance: In seeking an identity for themselves, many Jewish women have become involved in the women's movement.

Between 1654 and 1920, five thousand Jews migrated from Spain, Portugal, and Brazil to North America and settled in New York, Newport, Savannah, Philadelphia, Charleston, and Richmond. By the 1870's, another fifty

thousand Jews had arrived from Ireland, Austria, Bohemia, Hungary, and Germany and settled into trade and commerce activities, moving up to banking and department stores. In the late nineteenth and early twentieth centuries, a Jewish immigration of more than two million came from Russia, Galicia, Romania, and Hungary. Perhaps some of these Jews had migrated to Canada and, like other immigrants, quickly left for the United States. These Eastern European Jews were lower-middle-class, and they and their descendants made the greatest impact of all the Jews in the United States. By 1971, two-fifths of the nearly six million Jews lived in and around New York City. Some had moved to Boston, Philadelphia, Baltimore, and Chicago.

History
Jewish immigrants brought with them traditions of family and family work groups. Consequently, women made up 43.4 percent of all Jews between 1899 and 1910. They were concentrated in the clothing, metalworking, woodworking, building, textile, and tobacco industries; the majority found work in the needle trades. By 1890, 60 percent of employed Jews worked in the garment industry, and by 1939, the percentage was even higher.

Initially, working conditions were poor. Families labored in tiny shops, in factories, and in home sweatshops for long hours and low wages. Because there was no public assistance, every Jewish community helped the immigrants. In 1893, the National Council of Jewish Women was organized to serve as a bridge to a new life for the immigrants.

Many Jews became involved in the labor movement and, in 1900, helped to found the International Ladies' Garment Workers' Union (ILGWU). The union movement helped the Jews improve their labor conditions. With the availability of educational and business opportunities, Eastern European Jews made economic and social advances quickly because they wanted to "Americanize" their children by having them learn the language and customs of the new country.

Change in Lifestyle
Second in importance to learning the English language was wearing fashionable clothing. Dress was seen as a major symbol of assimilation. Jewish women embraced American lifestyles and American clothing with a high level of enthusiasm. Their dominant role in the garment industry and needle trades gave them ample exposure to the latest clothing trends and a heightened fashion-consciousness. Growing up in a religious culture that used clothing as symbolic wares to give meaning to their lives, Jewish women honored their religious holidays with new articles of dress. In America, this meant, among other things, replacing huge, out-of-style country boots

with thin-soled, high-heeled American shoes. The acculturation process also included wearing a corset to emphasize a small waist and rounded hips.

Part of the Americanizing process resulted in the establishment of the Jewish Theological Seminary of America (JTSA) in New York City to train Conservative rabbis. Conservatism provided a compromise between Reform Judaism and Jewish Orthodoxy because it preached American values while retaining most Orthodox traditions. Through their religious institutions, Jewish women began making strides. Historically, the Talmud, consisting of the Jewish laws, was studied only by men. Conservative and Reform Jews ordained male and female rabbis, but their Talmud study remained in the rabbinical schools. Orthodox Jews did not ordain women, but Talmud study for women became more available. For centuries, women were given little access to the Bible and the Jewish laws, but increased exposure excited the women and gave them greater respect for the development of Jewish laws. The Drisha Institute, a school of Jewish studies for women, was established in New York City.

This type of intellectual awakening was a reflection of women's advances in secular education. A National Jewish Population Study in the early 1990's found that two-thirds of Jewish women age twenty-five to forty-five had college degrees, as opposed to less than one-fifth of the general population. In the 1970's, they began to investigate the role of women in Jewish history and society. Holocaust survivors wrote with a feminist consciousness. Others wrote about spirituality, lesbianism, sociology, religious life, theology, history, and biblical scholarship; these subjects reflected the religious and feminist impulses of Jewish women.

Advances in secular education and in feminism reflected a revolution in the lifestyle of Jewish women. Prior to 1970, they were likely to obtain a college education first and marry slightly later than the general population. They had three or four children and remained home to raise them, returning to the labor market only after all their children were well into adolescence. This probably resulted in the even higher educational level and resourcefulness of Jewish children, which has been attributed to the fact that many Jewish mothers devote comparatively more time to playing, reading, and talking with their children than do women in the general population.

The 1990's saw a change in the Jewish family. Marriage and family formation were postponed by more Jews until they were into their thirties and forties. The Jewish family consisted of one or two children. This shrinkage in family size was a result of family planning, infertility, and the parents' placing more emphasis on careers and social lives. Studies indicate that the majority of mothers with children under six years old worked outside the home for pay. Although the divorce rate among Jews increased, it was lower than among families in general.

The revolution in the lifestyle of Jewish women reflected that of middle-class coreligionists. They were getting married later, having children later, and working throughout their offspring's preschool years. Because of the higher divorce rate, they encountered special problems, such as alcoholism and family violence, and had needs such as high-quality infant and toddler day care and after-school programs. The Jewish family became a microcosm of the general population. Its demands for communal support reflected the same calls throughout American society.

Bill Manikas

Core Resources

Useful sources on Jewish women include *A Heritage of Her Own* (New York: Simon & Schuster, 1979), edited by Nancy Cott and Elizabeth Pleck; Milton Finkelstein, Jawn A. Sandifer, and Elfreda S. Wright's *Minorities: U.S.A.* (New York: Globe Book, 1971); *Women's America: Refocusing the Past* (2d ed., New York: Oxford University Press, 1987), edited by Linda Kerber and Jane De Hart-Mathews.

See also: Ethnic identities of women; Immigrant women; Jewish Americans; Jewish Canadians; Judaism.

Jim Crow laws

Significance: Jim Crow laws were part of an organized attempt throughout the American South to keep African Americans permanently in a socially subordinate status in all walks of life and to limit possibilities for any form of contact between people of different racial backgrounds.

The precise origins of the term "Jim Crow" are unknown. It may have first appeared in 1832, in a minstrel play by Thomas D. "Big Daddy" Rice. The play contained a song about a slave titled "Jim Crow." The expression was used commonly beginning in the 1890's. In 1904, the *Dictionary of American English* listed the term "Jim Crow law" for the first time.

Jim Crow laws had predecessors in the so-called black codes, passed in many southern states after the Civil War (1861-1865) to limit the freedom of African Americans and assure a continuous labor supply for the southern plantation economy. Radical Reconstruction, which placed most parts of the South under military government, put an end to this. Even after the official end of Reconstruction in 1877, race relations in the South remained in a state of flux.

The Jim Crow Era

Jim Crow laws emerged during the 1880's and 1890's as conflict over political control in the South between different parties and between factions within parties intensified. Disfranchisement of African Americans and the segregation of whites and blacks were intended to assure the permanent subjugation of the latter and the prevention of future biracial political movements which could challenge white rule in the South. Domestic politics do not bear the sole responsibility, however: Jim Crow laws emerged at a time when the United States acquired colonies in the Pacific and the Caribbean and in the process subjugated the indigenous populations of those areas. Race theories used to justify American imperialism did not substantially differ from the white supremacy rhetoric of southern politicians.

The first Jim Crow law was passed by the state of Florida in 1887, followed by Mississippi in 1888, Texas in 1889, Louisiana in 1890, Alabama, Arkansas, Georgia, and Tennessee in 1891, and Kentucky in 1892. North Carolina passed a Jim Crow law in 1898, South Carolina in 1899, and Virginia in 1900. Statutes requiring racial segregation had been quite common in northern states before the Civil War, but only in the post-Reconstruction South did racial segregation develop into a pervasive system regulating the separation of white and black in all walks of life. Jim Crow laws segregated public carriers, restaurants, telephone booths, residential areas, workplaces, public parks, and other recreational spaces. Mobile, Alabama, passed a special curfew law for African Americans in 1909. In Florida, the law required separate textbooks, which had to be separately stored. The city of New Orleans segregated white and black prostitutes in separate districts. Many states outlawed interracial marriages. Jim Crow laws were not even limited to life: Cemeteries, undertakers, and medical school cadavers were all subjects of segregation under the laws.

These laws, however, represented only symptoms of larger and even more pervasive patterns of discrimination and racial oppression. White vigilante groups, such as the Ku Klux Klan, often enforced their own brand of racial justice through violent means, frequently with the quiet consent and even cooperation of law enforcement officers. In addition, contract labor laws and corrupt law enforcement and prison officials created a system of peonage, which kept large numbers of African Americans in the turpentine and cotton belts in debt slavery.

U.S. Supreme Court

In the process of legally entrenching racial segregation through so-called Jim Crow laws, the U.S. Supreme Court served as a willing handmaiden. In the 1883 *Civil Rights* cases, the Supreme Court ruled that segregation in privately owned railroads, theaters, hotels, restaurants, and similar places comprised private acts of discrimination and as such did not fall under the Fourteenth Amendment. In the 1896 case of *Plessy v. Ferguson*, concerning the constitutionality of a Louisiana Jim Crow law, the Supreme Court redefined segregation from a matter of private prejudice into a mandate of state law. In *Plessy v. Ferguson*, the Supreme Court approved of segregation as long as facilities were "separate but equal." In the 1930's and 1940's, the Supreme Court began to strike down segregation. Eventually, on May 17, 1954, the Supreme Court, in the landmark decision in *Brown v. Board of Education*, declared that separate facilities by their very nature were unequal, thereby reversing previous decisions.

Thomas Winter

Core Resources

An excellent starting point in understanding the Jim Crow era is C. Vann Woodward's *The Strange Career of Jim Crow* (3d rev. ed., New York: Oxford University Press, 1974). For a valuable survey of the relations between African Americans and the law, see Loren Miller's *The Petitioners: The Story of the Supreme Court of the United States and the Negro* (New York: Pantheon Books, 1966). See also Paul Finkelman, ed., *Race, Law, and American History, 1700-1900* (11 vols., New York: Garland, 1992). Of particular interest in this series is volume 4, *The Age of Jim*

This drawing depicts Thomas D. "Big Daddy" Rice in his role as Jim Crow in a minstrel show in the mid-1800's.

Crow: Segregation from the End of Reconstruction to the Great Depression. On peonage, see Pete Daniel, *The Shadow of Slavery: Peonage in the South, 1901-1969* (Urbana: University of Illinois Press, 1972).

See also: Black codes; *Brown v. Board of Education*; Civil rights; *Civil Rights* cases; Discrimination (all entries); Ku Klux Klan; Literacy tests; Lynchings; Miscegenation laws; National Association for the Advancement of Colored People; *Plessy v. Ferguson*; Poll tax; Restrictive or racial covenants; Segregation: de facto and de jure; Slavery and race relations.

Job Corps

The Job Corps is a United States government agency that provides job training, education, health care, and personal counseling for disadvantaged youth, many of whom come from racial and ethnic minority groups. The corps was established by the Economic Opportunity Act of 1964 as part of President Lyndon B. Johnson's War on Poverty program. From 1973 to 1982, the program was funded under the Comprehensive Employment and Training Act, but since then it has operated with open-ended annual funding under the Job Training Partnership Act. The Job Corps organization provides its services at 108 residential centers located across the United States and Puerto Rico.

By the mid-1990's, the Job Corps housed, educated, and trained approximately 62,000 young men and women between the ages of sixteen and twenty-two. Training lasts from six to twenty-four months, and most of the residential centers serve people from a particular state or region and design their programs to meet job needs in that locality. By training together in the Job Corps programs, youth of different races and ethnic backgrounds learn how to cooperate and work together. More than 90 percent of the young people who complete the program find a job, return to school, or join the armed forces.   *Alvin K. Benson*

See also: Culture of poverty; Employment among African Americans; Employment among Asian Americans; Employment among Latinos; Poverty and race.

John Brown's raid

> **Significance:** This attempt by a militant abolitionist to liberate and arm Virginia slaves hastened the Civil War.

John Brown's abortive raid on the federal arsenal at Harpers Ferry, Virginia (now West Virginia), on October 16-18, 1859, stands out as a critical episode in the spiraling sequence of events that led Northerners and Southerners into the Civil War in 1861. Brown, long a militant abolitionist, emigrated to Kansas Territory in 1855 with five of his sons to participate in the struggle between proslavery and Free State forces for control of the territory. Their insurrection was in the same spirit as earlier violence perpetrated by abolitionist, Free State militias such as the Border Ruffians following election of a proslavery, territorial legislature in 1854. With a small band of Free State men, Brown helped initiate civil war in Kansas by murdering five allegedly proslavery settlers along Pottawatomie Creek, in May, 1856. Historians would later dub this era "Bleeding Kansas."

Brown's Plan

Brown's experience in the Kansas civil war convinced him that a conspiracy existed to seize the national territories for slavery. Having long since lost faith in combating slavery by peaceful means, Brown vowed to strike a violent blow at the heart of slavery. An intense Calvinist, Brown had come to believe that he was God's personal instrument to eradicate the inhuman institution. As early as 1857, he had decided to seize a mountain fortress in Virginia with a small guerrilla force and incite a bloody slave rebellion that would overthrow the slave powers throughout the South.

To that end, Brown sought funds and arms from abolitionists in the North. Under the guise of seeking money to continue the Free State fight in Kansas, Brown secured the friendship and financial aid of the Massachusetts State Kansas Committee—a group dedicated to helping the Free-Soil forces in Kansas and elsewhere. The resolute and persuasive Brown won the support of six prominent antislavery figures, who agreed to form a secret Committee of Six to advise him and raise money for his still-secret mission. The Secret Six consisted of a well-educated group of dedicated abolitionists and reformers: Franklin B. Sanborn, a young Concord schoolteacher and secretary of the Massachusetts State Kansas Committee; Thomas Wentworth Higginson, a "disunion abolitionist" and outspoken Unitarian minister; Theodore Parker, a controversial theologian-preacher; Samuel Gridley Howe, a prominent physician and educator; George Luther Stearns, a prosperous merchant and chairman of the Massachusetts State Kansas Committee; and Gerrit Smith, a wealthy New York landowner and reformer.

Throughout the remainder of 1857, the indefatigable Brown trained a small group of adventurers and militant abolitionists in preparation for his mission. In May, 1858, Brown moved on to Chatham, Canada, holding a secret

Five African Americans who participated in John Brown's raid on Harpers Ferry were (left to right) Osborne Perry Anderson, Dangerfield Newby, John Anthony Copeland, Lewis Sheridan Leary, and Shields Green.

"Constitutional Convention" attended by thirty-four African Americans and twelve whites. There, he outlined his plans to invade Virginia, liberate and arm the slaves, defeat any military force brought against them, organize the African Americans into a government, and force the southern states to concede emancipation. Under Brown's leadership, the convention approved a constitution for a new state once the slaves were freed and elected Brown commander in chief with John Kagi, his chief lieutenant, as secretary of war.

Brown's proposed invasion was delayed in 1858, when a disgruntled follower partially betrayed the plans to several prominent politicians. The exposé so frightened the Secret Six that they urged Brown to return to Kansas and create a diversionary operation until rumors of the Virginia plan dissipated. Brown also agreed not to inform the Secret Six of the details of his plans, so that they could not be held responsible in case the invasion failed. In December, 1858, Brown conducted the diversion as planned, by leading a raid into Missouri, liberating eleven slaves, and escorting them to Canada. He then began final preparations for the invasion of Virginia.

The Raid

Harpers Ferry, situated at the confluence of the Potomac and Shenandoah Rivers in northern Virginia, was the initial target in Brown's plan, because he needed weapons from the federal arsenal there to arm the liberated slaves. Brown and three of his men arrived at Harpers Ferry on July 3, 1859, and set up headquarters at the Kennedy farm, seven miles east of Harpers Ferry in Maryland. The rest of Brown's twenty-one young recruits (sixteen whites and five African Americans) slowly trickled in. On the night of October 16, 1859, after several

months of refining his plans, Brown led eighteen of his followers in an assault on the arsenal and rifle works at Harpers Ferry. They quickly captured the arsenal, the armory, and a nearby rifle works, and then seized hostages from the townspeople and surrounding countryside.

Fearing a slave insurrection, the armed townspeople gathered in the streets, and church bells tolled the alarm over the countryside. Brown stood his ground, anxiously waiting for the slaves from the countryside to rally to his cause. By 11:00 A.M. the next day, Brown's men—holed up in the small fire-enginehouse of the armory—engaged in a pitched battle with the assembled townspeople, farmers, and militia. By dawn the following morning, a company of horse Marines under the command of Colonel Robert E. Lee took up positions in front of the armory. When Brown refused Lee's summons to surrender unconditionally, the Marines stormed the armory, wounded Brown, and routed his followers. Seventeen people died in the raid; ten of the dead, including two of Brown's sons, were raiders. Five raiders were captured, two were taken prisoner several days later, but five escaped without a trace.

The Consequences

Governor Henry A. Wise of Virginia decided that Brown and his coconspirators should be tried in Virginia rather than by federal authorities, even though their attack had been against federal property. Brown and the captured raiders stood trial at Charles Town, Virginia; on October 31, the jury found them guilty of inciting a slave rebellion, murder, and treason against the state of Virginia. After the trial, in a final attempt to save his life, Brown's lawyers collected affidavits from many of his friends and relatives alleging that Brown suffered from hereditary insanity and monomania. Brown rejected his defense, claiming that he was sane. He knew that he could better serve the abolitionist cause as a martyr, a sentiment shared by Northern abolitionists. Governor Wise agreed that Brown was sane, and on December 2, 1859, John Brown was hanged at Charles Town. Six of his fellow conspirators met a similar fate.

Brown's raid intensified the sectional bitterness that led to the Civil War. Although the vast majority of Northerners condemned the incident as the work of a fanatic, the outraged South, racked by rumors of a slave insurrection, suspected all Northerners of abetting Brown's crime. Republican denials of any link with Brown were of little avail. Northern abolitionists, including the Secret Six, who had been cleared of complicity, gathered by the hundreds throughout the North to honor and acclaim Brown's martyrdom. The South was in no mood to distinguish between the Northern Republicans who wanted to contain slavery and the small group of abolitionists who sought to destroy the institution. The South withdrew even further into a defense of its peculiar institution, stifled internal criticism, and intensified its hatred and suspicion of the "Black Republican" Party. In 1861, Northerners marched to war to the tune of "John Brown's Body"—fulfilling Brown's prophecy that "the crimes of this guilty land will never be purged away; but with Blood." *Terry L. Seip, updated by Richard Whitworth*

Core Resources
Richard O. Boyer's *The Legend of John Brown: A Biography and a History* (New York: Alfred A. Knopf, 1972) covers not only the events but also the temper of the era that culminated in the Civil War. Stephen B. Oates's *Our Fiery Trial: Abraham Lincoln, John Brown, and the Civil War Era* (Amherst: University of Massachusetts Press, 1979) shows how Lincoln, Brown, and Nat Turner were interconnected in the events that hurled the United States toward civil war. Oates's *To Purge This Land with Blood: A Biography of John Brown* (2d ed., Amherst: University of Massachusetts Press, 1984) is an evenhanded account of Brown and the events he precipitated. *Blacks on John Brown* (Urbana: University of Illinois Press, 1972), compiled by Benjamin Quarles, includes selections by Frederick Douglass, W. E. B. Du Bois, Countee Cullen, and Langston Hughes. Edward J. Renehan's *The Secret Six: The True Tale of the Men Who Conspired with John Brown* (New York: Crown, 1995) details the lives of the six unlikely revolutionaries—five aristocratic Bostonians and one moneyed New Yorker—who financed John Brown's bloody raid.

See also: Abolition; Bleeding Kansas; Civil War; Compromise of 1850; Kansas-Nebraska Act.

Jokes and humor

> **Significance:** Racial and ethnic jokes and humor can centralize or marginalize groups by making them the butt of mockery or satiric comment. Because much of this comedy deals with stereotypes, it offers some insights into the dynamics of intergroup relations (including their stratification and boundaries of identity) and the possibilities of a multiethnic community.

The last half of the nineteenth century in the United States saw the growth of dialect humor, particularly the Double Dutch of Charles Godfrey Leland's Hans Breitmann, which was a parody of German English, the "Dutch" being a phonetic approximation of *Deutsch*. The confused vowel sounds, extra consonants, and intermingling of German words with English made for lively vaudeville entertainment on the printed page or on stage, where actors impersonated German American characters.

American vaudeville in the 1870's was a large brotherhood of dialect comics, some in blackface, others portraying Irish, Jewish, Scottish, English, or "Dutch" characters, who mocked predominant ethnic traits. The Irish, for instance, were shown as belligerent, bewildered, comic drunks; Italians were represented as promiscuous, irresponsible, hyperemotional rascals; blacks were lazy, dishonest, promiscuous, and irresponsible; Jews were canny and manipulative; Germans were stodgily conservative. All ethnic groups shared the quality of "dumbness," that is, stupidity or naïveté. The reason is that "stupid" jokes, unlike jokes about religion or sex, are universally transferable because everybody seems to have a common view of stupidity. "Stupid" jokes export their qualities from joke tellers in one group and pin them on some other regional, ethnic, or national group. For instance, "dumb" Irish jokes can be turned into "dumb" Polish jokes by a mere change in name or accent.

The reverse of the "stupid" is the "canny," which is a label attached to groups whose members are stereotyped as urban, mobile, innovative, and entrepreneurial (such as Jews, Armenians, Scots, and Dutch) by their respective competitive opponents. For example, a Pakistani can tell a "stupid" or "canny" joke about an Indian, or a Finn about a Swede, and vice versa. Such jokes are a means of attributing human deficiencies to or making other criticisms of rival groups, and as in the days of vaudeville, they continue to propagate stereotypes.

Values of Ethnic Humor
Ethnic jokes about another group reflect joke tellers' perceptions of themselves and their own merits. Jokes told by one group about another magnify differences of

language, culture, behavior, and values, but they are told because of basic *similarities* between the groups, for the butts of these jokes (who are regarded as comic anomalies or imperfect people) tend to live on the periphery of the joke tellers' society. In the case of the Double Dutch jokes, the comedy and anti-immigrant bias were correlated; in the late 1880's, the United States was a rapidly growing nation that distrusted linguistic diversity in the fear that "foreigners" would subvert the American way of life. However, on the other side of the issue was the fact that dialects and ethnic jokes were attempts to find ways of expressing conditions of life in the New World. The comic accents represented people struggling to find a language that would help them cope as small communities within society at large.

Some jokes dealt with immigrant assimilation. In one such joke, Cohen thanks a gentile friend for a nice salmon dinner. When his host corrects him, saying it was ham, Cohen retorts: "So who asked you?" The joke works two sides of the issue: On one hand, it expresses the non-Jew's hospitality, while on the other, it marks an underlying problem in assimilation. In this case, the "ethnic" wins, for while Cohen is targeted for hypocrisy and glib manipulation, he is obviously able to eat his salmon and have his ham too.

Ethnic humor has been judged acceptable when it is not ruthlessly insulting, for, like racial joking by individuals within a homogeneous group, it serves as a safety valve to let off steam and reduce ethnic tensions, as in this multiethnic definition of foreplay:

> *Italian version:* Yo, baby, get ovah heah!
> *Irish version:* A six-pack.
> *Jewish version:* Two hours of begging.

This type of joke actually builds a sense of community among disparate groups by drawing on multiple ethnic groups in the joke context. It confirms how individuals receive their impressions of others from folkloric sources and enables one to appreciate minority idiosyncrasies and restrictions by recognizing stereotypes—as in the following case: "How do we know Jesus was Jewish? Because he lived at home with his mother until he was thirty; he went into his father's business; and he had a mother who thought he was God."

Historians of ethnic humor disagree about the value of such comedy. Joseph Boskin argues that such humor allows cruel, hostile, negative sentiments to directly or indirectly sanction and frame oppressive social control, whereas Constance Rourke, leading historian of American humor, contends that the object of ethnic humor is to create fresh bonds of fellowship in society. The most incisive view comes from Christie Davies, who maintains that the oppositional pairs that form the basis of ethnic

humor (stupid versus canny; lazy versus relentlessly ambitious; cowardly versus aggressive) allow a society to establish boundaries of approved or scorned behavior from within its own circumference. Moreover, the social and cultural factors are subordinate to their cognitive value or the ways in which they contribute to acculturation. Davies points out that the uses and scope of ethnic humor depend on a number of variables, including who says what to whom under what circumstances.

Ethnic Jokes and Stratification

Social and political factors account for the nature of some ethnic jokes. Anti-Semitism, the cyclical incompetence of Italian governments, and the ferocity of uniformed Germans are facts in themselves and serve to shape the perceptions of joke tellers. Social pecking order also determines the nature of jokes. For instance, sixteenth century and early seventeenth century jokes about the belligerent Welsh were based on a satirical English view of an impoverished small gentry in a backward rural society who cultivated excessive pride in their ancestry and martial tradition. Similarly, the earliest joke about German militarism dates back to a Prussian belief in order, discipline, obedience, and a determined use of force. Such jokes reveal which group is at the center of power and which is not. They also show that the culture of the mocked group is subordinate to or derived from that of the joke teller.

What Jokes Reveal About People

Ethnic jokes about the "stupid" are jokes told at the expense of certain groups who are seen as the antitheses of those telling the jokes. The dynamic of joke telling is competition, but ethnic jokes are not necessarily good indications of the joke teller's feelings toward the butts of the jokes. Performers do not necessarily dislike those they caricature or debunk. Ethnic jokes may indicate that it is not an individual who is ridiculous, but rather the stereotype itself—as in Phil Nee's joke about himself as a Chinese American: "It's not always fun being Chinese. My girlfriend left me last week for a guy who looks exactly like me." The self-reflexive humor has a point: Members of a stereotypical group cannot even tell themselves apart because their identity is blurred by a stereotype. This is an acknowledgment of a certain reality, and it is not a snide dismissal but a coping mechanism. It confirms the fallibility of categorizing and generalizing, even in jokes.

Keith Garebian

Core Resources

Joseph Boskin's *Humor and Social Change* (Boston: Boston Public Library, 1979) takes a jaundiced view of ethnic humor, pointing out that it allows or licenses negative sentiments about groups, thereby subjugating these ethnic classes to the control of dominant groups. Boskin's view is offset by much of the material in Christie Davies' *Ethnic Humor Around the World: A Comparative Analysis* (Bloomington: Indiana University Press, 1990), an exhaustive study of jokes from every continent, explaining with a profusion of examples how, why, and about whom people tell ethnic jokes. Davies links these jokes to relative social, economic, and political positions of the jokes' subjects and their tellers.

See also: African American stereotypes; American Indian stereotypes; Asian American stereotypes; Epithets and pejorative language; Irish American stereotypes; Italian American stereotypes; Jewish stereotypes; Latino stereotypes; Social stratification theories; Stereotype.

Jones Act of 1917

> **Significance:** The Jones Act of 1917 formed a unique relationship between the United States and Puerto Rico.

On December 10, 1898, the Treaty of Paris between Spain and the United States ended the Spanish-American War and set forth terms that became effective April 11, 1900. The agreement transferred the control of Puerto Rico to the United States, thereby legitimizing the occupation of the island and its satellites by U.S. forces. One of the provisions of the Treaty of Paris was as follows: "The civil rights and the political status of the native inhabitants of the territories hereby ceded to the United States shall be determined by the Congress." The natives of Puerto Rico, no longer subjects of the Spanish crown, now found themselves without any citizenship recognized under international law or U.S. domestic law.

The Organic Act of 1900 (known as the Foraker Act, after its sponsor) established a political entity called the People of Porto Rico (Puerto Rico), but there was no mention of U.S. citizenship for those born on the island, only that they would be "held to be citizens of Porto Rico, and as such entitled to the protection of the United States." Puerto Ricans were now stateless, essentially confined to their island because of the difficulty of traveling without a passport. The U.S. Supreme Court, in cases such as *Downes v. Bidwell* (1901), confirmed that Puerto Rico was merely a possession of the United States, not an incorporated territory, to be disposed of by the U.S. Congress.

The Citizenship Debate
The reelection of William McKinley to the U.S. presidency in 1900 favored U.S. imperial expansion. Never-

theless, the debate as to whether racially, culturally, and linguistically distinct peoples brought under U.S. control should be granted U.S. citizenship and, if so, with what rights, continued intermittently between 1900 and 1916. In that year, the Philippines, also seized by the United States from Spain in the war, was promised independence by the Organic Act of the Philippine Islands (also known as the Jones Act). The Organic Act of 1917 (the Jones Act of 1917) did not similarly grant independence to Puerto Rico, but it did confer U.S. citizenship collectively on the natives of the island. Although the Jones Act changed the status of Puerto Ricans from that of U.S. nationals—noncitizens, but owing allegiance to and subject to the protection of the United States—the granting of citizenship did not give the islanders the right to vote in U.S. federal elections because the territory fell short of statehood. In *Balzac v. Porto Rico* (1922), the Supreme Court ruled that as citizens of an unincorporated territory, the islanders enjoyed only fundamental provisions in the Bill of Rights of the U.S. Constitution, not procedural or remedial rights such as the guarantee of trial by jury.

The extent to which Puerto Ricans participated in the debate relating to their prospective status between 1900 and 1917 remains a matter of conjecture. For one thing, the spokesmen of the Puerto Rican community—such as Resident Commissioner Luís Muñoz Rivera and the Puerto Rican House of Delegates (the local legislature)—were ambivalent and contradictory on the subject. For another, much of the evidence placed before the Congress about the Puerto Ricans' preferences during the drawn-out debate was impressionistic and anecdotal rather than objective.

Accordingly, while some U.S. legislators talked of the yearnings, longings, and aspirations of Puerto Ricans to citizenship, critics claim that citizenship was pressed on the islanders. It is also charged that the expediency of acquiring additional recruits for military service only weeks before President Woodrow Wilson sought a declaration of war on Germany on April 4, 1917, was not absent from congressional thinking. Whatever the truth, making Puerto Ricans native U.S. citizens and the establishment of a seemingly permanent political link between the United States and Puerto Rico by the Jones Act of 1917 contrasted with the creation of an articulately temporary relationship between Washington, D.C., and the Philippines. In fact, the defining of the latter's status under the 1916 Jones Act catalyzed the following year's Jones Act relating to Puerto Rico. The racist comments peppering the congressional debates were infinitely harsher as they related to Filipinos, partly because of their spirited resistance to U.S. occupation, than in regard to Puerto Ricans, who were much more receptive to occupation. Some legislators even produced statistics to "prove" that a high percentage of the islanders were white in order to justify their being granted U.S. citizenship.

The Act

The final version of the Jones bill, introduced in the House on January 20, 1916, was only slightly different from Congressman Jones's earlier versions. The only noteworthy change was that Puerto Ricans residing on the island were allowed one year, instead of six months, to reject U.S. citizenship if they desired. The House passed the bill by voice vote on May 23, 1916; the Senate approved it on February 20, 1917; and the House-Senate Conference Committee followed suit on February 24, 1917. President Wilson, a Democrat, signed it into law on March 2, 1917. Only 288 Puerto Ricans legally declined to accept U.S. citizenship within the statutory period, thereby losing their right to hold or run for any public office on the island. Because the Jones Act had established five different categories in determining the status of different individuals, there was great confusion as to who qualified for citizenship. The U.S. Congress subsequently passed several additional laws in the interest of administrative simplification.

In 1952, the U.S. Territory of Puerto Rico became the Commonwealth of Puerto Rico, known in Spanish as a "free associated state." As such, Puerto Rico elected a nonvoting representative to the U.S. Congress but cast no vote in presidential, congressional, or senatorial elections. While islanders paid no federal taxes, the aid Puerto Rico received from Washington was less than it would have received had it been a state.

On November 14, 1993, a nonbinding referendum, which President Bill Clinton nevertheless pledged to respect, was held regarding the island's future status. Puerto Ricans who opted for continued commonwealth status cast 48.4 percent of the votes; statehood received 46.2 percent; and 4.4 percent of the 2.1 million ballots cast favored independence. The spread between the first two options had narrowed drastically since an earlier referendum in 1967. The issue of Puerto Rico's status— and thus the nature of the citizenship of the islanders— was far from over. It now was up to Puerto Ricans themselves, increasingly aware of their Latino roots, to decide their own political future.   *Peter B. Heller*

Core Resources

Jose A. Cabranes's *Citizenship and the American Empire: Notes on the Legislative History of the United States Citizenship of Puerto Ricans* (New Haven, Conn.: Yale University Press, 1979) is a well-annotated, objective account of how Congress decided that the people of a colonial territory should be made U.S. citizens. Kenneth L. Karst's *Belonging to America: Equal Citizenship and the Constitution* (New Haven, Conn.: Yale University Press, 1989) argues that equal citizenship for cultural minorities who have experienced exclusion, forced conformity, and subordination under the influence of U.S. nativism has become more topical over the years.

See also: Puerto Rico.

Jones v. Alfred H. Mayer Company

Reversing many precedents, the Supreme Court held in this 1968 decision that the 1866 Civil Rights Act prohibited both private and state-backed discrimination and that the Thirteenth Amendment authorized Congress to prohibit private acts of discrimination as "the badges of slavery."

Joseph Lee Jones, alleging that a real estate company had refused to sell him a house because he was African American, sought relief in a federal district court. Since the case appeared before the passage of the Civil Rights Act of 1968, Jones and his lawyer relied primarily on a provision of the 1866 Civil Rights Act that gave all citizens the same rights as white citizens in property transactions. Both the district court and the court of appeals dismissed the complaint based on the established view that the 1866 law applied only to state action and did not address private acts of discrimination. The U.S. Supreme Court, however, accepted the case for review.

All the precedents of the Supreme Court supported the conclusions of the lower courts. In the *Civil Rights* cases (1883) the Court had ruled that the Thirteenth Amendment allowed Congress to abolish "all badges and incidents of slavery," but the Court had narrowly interpreted these badges or incidents as not applying to private acts of discrimination. In *Hodges v. United States* (1906) the Court held that Congress might prohibit only private actions that marked "a state of entire subjection of one person to the will of another," and even in *Shelley v. Kraemer* (1948) the Court recognized the right of individuals to make racially restrictive covenants.

In *Jones*, however, the Court surprised observers by voting 7 to 2 to overturn its precedents. Writing for the majority, Justice Potter Stewart asserted that Congress under the Thirteenth Amendment possessed the power "to determine what are the badges and incidents of slavery, and the authority to translate that determination into effective legislation." In addition, the majority reinterpreted the 1866 law so that it proscribed both governmental and private discrimination in property transactions—an interpretation that is questioned by many authorities.

Justice John M. Harlan wrote a dissenting opinion which argued that the majority probably was wrong in its interpretation of the 1866 law. Harlan also wrote that the passage of the Fair Housing Act of 1968 eliminated the need to render this decision that relied on such questionable history.

Since the *Jones* decision was based on the Thirteenth rather than the Fourteenth Amendment, it was important in diluting the Court's traditional distinction between state and private action, and it appeared to grant Congress almost unlimited power to outlaw private racial discrimination. *Jones* became a precedent for new applications of the almost forgotten post-Civil War statutes in cases such as *Griffin v. Breckenridge* (1971) and *Runyon v. McCrary* (1976). In the quarter-century after *Jones*, however, the Congress did not pass any major legislation based upon the authority of the Thirteenth Amendment.

Thomas T. Lewis

See also: Civil rights; Civil Rights Act of 1968; Civil Rights Acts of 1866-1875; *Civil Rights* cases; *Griffin v. Breckenridge; Moose Lodge No. 107 v. Irvis; Runyon v. McCrary*; Segregation: de facto and de jure; *Shelley v. Kraemer*.

Judaism

> **Significance:** Judaism is one of the world's major religions, with origins deeply rooted in antiquity. Its chief features are monotheism, historical ethnocentrism, and a strong moral foundation.

Judaism has a complex history of development that has been traced as far back as the twentieth century B.C.E. Most scholars agree, however, that modern Judaism is rooted either in the Haskala (the Enlightenment) of the Ashkenazic Jews of eastern and central Europe in the eighteenth century C.E. or, somewhat earlier, in the acculturation of the Sephardic Jews in Italy and western Europe. These two branches of diaspora Jews, with some minor doctrinal differences, held firmly to the traditional beliefs of Judaism and the basic authority of the Talmud, the collection of rabbinical writings making up the religious and civil codes of Jewry.

While monotheism, messianism, and other fundamental tenets of their faith remained intact, adherents of Judaism gradually broke with the passivity that had marked Jewry throughout the Middle Ages, rejecting its self-perception as a people patiently awaiting redemption from their suffering in exile among the Gentiles, infidels who persecuted them for their beliefs or, worse, expelled or destroyed them in pogroms (anti-Jewish massacres).

While the insularity that marked Jewish communities in the diaspora never completely vanished, from the end of the eighteenth century on there was a greater trend toward cultural assimilation, especially in North America and industrialized Europe. By the nineteenth century, in most European nations emancipated Jews could study at universities and enter such professions as medicine and law, long prohibited to them. It was a considerable step forward: Through much of their history, in their dealings with Christians, European Jews had been limited to such activities as itinerant trading and usury (money lending). The risk for Jewry was that in adopting the culture of their host nations, Jews would abandon their faith, as did happen in some families. While most did not go to that extreme, many did begin to think of themselves as citizens of their adopted country first and as Jews only by religious conviction.

Discrimination

Discrimination against Jews in the diaspora has continued despite the fact that in most industrialized nations its legal sanctions have been removed for almost two centuries. This discrimination partly results from the fact that residual discrimination against ethnic minorities tends to outlive legalized or institutionalized discrimination, even when there are statutory safeguards against it. Anti-Jewish discrimination is compounded by the fact that it has evolved from both anti-Judaism and anti-Semitism, which are not precisely the same thing, though the distinction between them is largely moot.

Anti-Judaism first arose in antiquity, in both polytheistic paganism and Pauline Christology. According to many scholars, the earliest Christians, themselves Semites, had to compete with Jews in efforts to win new converts to their separatist faith. At the time, the Hebrews were militant and zealous proselytizers who dared to defy even the Romans, as their unyielding mass suicide at Masada in 73 C.E. testifies.

In the diaspora, at least in the medieval Christian world, the Jews carried the stigma of being "Christ killers" and a reputation for theological intractability for not accepting Jesus as the true messiah. Their ethnocentrism led to terrible suspicions—that, for example, they desecrated the host, sacrificed Christian children (the notorious "blood libel"), and brought on the Black Death (1348-1350) by poisoning wells—but the persecutions largely remained religiously based. Some Jews, notably moneylenders, were despised for other reasons, but the official sanctions against them were usually imposed on more theological than ethnic grounds. Ironically, given contemporary events in the Middle and Near East, in some Islamic areas, notably in Spain, the Sephardic Jews, considered "people of the book," were often treated much better, and some even rose to great political prominence. It was there, under the Arab sponsorship of arts and letters, that they produced the Golden Age of Hebrew Literature (c. 1000-1150 C.E.).

The persecution of Jews until the time of the Enlightenment was partly prompted by their self-imposed insularity, their insistence that they were in exile from their Promised Land. For their distinct self-identity, they were forced to pay a terrible price. By the end of the sixteenth century, in most European cities, they were required to live in their own quarter, or ghetto, under all sorts of legal restrictions and prohibitions. They were at times expelled from some countries, including England.

Judaism in the Twentieth Century

Even in the United States, with its fundamental doctrine of religious freedom, Jews did not escape a more insidious sort of persecution based on ethnic prejudices rather than strong religious convictions. Jews were often accused of being clannish, secretive, miserly, aggressive, and, at times, un-American. Among other important Americans, industrialist Henry Ford was rabidly anti-Semitic. He used the newspaper he controlled, *The Dearborn Independent,* to spread the idea that there was an international Jewish conspiracy dedicated to overthrowing legitimate governments by fostering atheism and anarchy. It was to counter such libels that the ecumenical National Conference of Christians and Jews was founded in 1928.

In Europe, particularly in post-World War I Germany, the Jews were subjected to an increasingly virulent persecution that would reach its full horror under the regime of Adolf Hitler. Many disillusioned Jews had already turned to Zionism, believing that their only hope lay in the creation of a nation of their own in Palestine, their ancestral home. Some Jews did place their hopes on radical sociopolitical change, including socialism and communism, but most rejected the atheism at the core of Marxism. Modern Zionism was actually a rekindling of beliefs that had been suppressed in the Enlightenment and Emancipation, centering on the idea that someday, under the providential guidance of Jehovah, the Jews would return from exile, restored to their rightful nation-home. It would take its vigorous secular and militant "back to Jerusalem" form after the Holocaust, resulting in the

creation of the state of Israel, but it was advocated decades earlier, even in the United States, where the new Zionism was espoused by the Reconstructionist followers of Mordecai Menahem Kaplan (1881-1983) as early as the 1920's.

Zionism in Europe was even more trenchant. By the end of the nineteenth century, liberal Jews who had sought an end to Jewish-Christian conflict had their hopes dashed in eastern Europe, especially Russia, where the Orthodox Church aided and abetted the pogroms and disseminated the spurious *Protocols of the Elders of Zion,* one source of the Jewish conspiracy theory that poisoned the minds of many non-Jews. Despairing of ever reconciling their Jewish culture to the non-Jewish religions and cultures of their host nations, Jews in eastern Europe either hunkered down in their segregated tradition, emigrated, or sought solutions in Zionism. Zionism also attracted radical antireligious Jews and socialistic Jews whose Zionism was purely secular in vision.

The plight of nonemigrating European Jews was gravely intensified with the rise of Adolf Hitler in Germany and his racist theories of Aryan supremacy. While most European Christians stood by silently and watched without protest, Hitler vilified the Jews. They were an

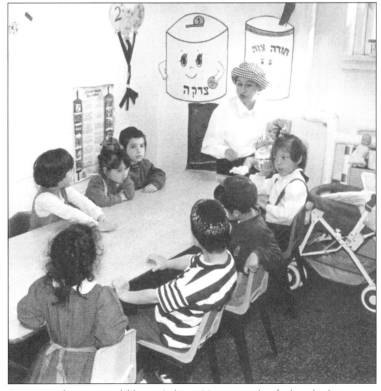

A young mother instructs children in Judaism. Maintaining their faith and culture is very important to many Jewish Americans.

easy scapegoat, especially in the romantic anti-intellec-
tualism that characterized the Nazi vision of the world.
When he came to power, Hitler began a systematic
campaign of persecution that, during World War II,
culminated in the "final solution"—the genocidal extermination of Jews. Jews were rounded up throughout the
conquered nations of Europe and North Africa and sent
to extermination camps, where more than six million
were put to death.

The Holocaust severely reduced the number of Jews
in Europe, which, until the war, had been the center of
Jewish culture and tradition in the diaspora. In effect, it
severed the ties of many emigrant Jews to their past,
obliterating such important Jewish cultural enclaves as
the Warsaw ghetto. It also resulted in a major demographic shift, moving the centers of contemporary Judaism away from Europe to the United States and Israel.

Aftermath of the Holocaust

In the Holocaust the Jews experienced the greatest single calamity in their history, surpassing even their loss of
sovereignty over Palestine with the Roman destruction
of Jerusalem in 70 C.E. The Nazi efforts to exterminate
the Jews resulted in three major changes: the destruction
of whole communities of diaspora Jews in Europe and
North Africa, the disappearance of millennial Jewish
settlements in Islamic countries in the Middle East, and
the "ingathering" of exiled Jews in the nation-state of
Israel.

Although Israel was created in 1948 as a secular democracy, it fostered pride in Jews throughout the world,
particularly in its succession of victories over the Islamic
nations that had vowed to drive the Jews out of the Holy
Land. Many liberal Jews who had neglected or even
rejected their heritage before the Holocaust made a new
commitment to it in the post-World War II years. They
also won the sympathy of many Christians, who were
shocked by the horror and dehumanizing impact of the
Nazi policy. As Stephen Sharot notes in *Judaism: A Sociology* (1976), in the postwar "Western Diaspora there was
a sharp decline of overt anti-Semitism and all forms of
discrimination." Cultural and religious insularity, where
it persists in the West, reflects choice rather than com-
pulsion. The vestiges of anti-Semitism in the West are
largely found in such settings as private clubs, where
membership may exclude religious, ethnic, or racial
minorities.   *John W. Fiero*

Core Resources

J. H. Hexter's *The Judaeo-Christian Tradition* (New York:
Harper & Row, 1966) is an excellent, concise overview
of the evolution of ancient Judaism and the Hebraic
foundations of early Christianity in the Roman era.
James Parkes's *End of an Exile: Israel, the Jews, and the*
Gentile World (Marblehead, Mass.: Micah Publications,
1982) deals with Judaism and the creation of Israel from
a sympathetic Christian perspective. Raphael Patai's *The
Vanished Worlds of Jewry* (New York: Macmillan, 1980)
offers a fine survey of Jewry in Europe, North Africa,
India, and the Near East, showing how its rich tradition
was severely damaged by the Holocaust and the expulsion of "millenial" Jews from Muslim countries in Asia
Minor. Milton Steinberg's *Basic Judaism* (New York: Harcourt, Brace, 1947) explains the fundamentals of Judaism in simple terms unencumbered by excessive historical detail. Geoffrey Wigoder's *The Encyclopedia of Judaism*
(New York: Macmillan, 1989) is an excellent companion
work for the study of Judaism.

See also: American Jewish Committee; American Jewish
Congress; Anti-Defamation League; Anti-Semitism;
Black Jews; Eastern European Jews; Holocaust; Israeli
Americans; Jewish-African American relations; Jewish
American outmarriage; Jewish Americans; Jewish Americans as a middleman minority; Jewish-Arab American
relations; Jewish Canadians; Jewish Defense League; Jewish ethnicity: definitions; Jewish stereotypes; Jewish
women; Sephardic Jewish Americans; Soviet Jewish immigrants; United Jewish Appeal; Zionism.

Jury nullification

Under the U.S. system of justice, three questions must
be answered before a person can be convicted of a crime:
What are the facts, what was the defendant's moral
intent, and what is the law? The jury decides the first two
under definitions of the law which are presented to it by
the judge. "Jury nullification" takes place when the jury
ignores (or nullifies) the law and acquits the defendant
in spite of the judge's instructions. Under the constitutional provision forbidding "double jeopardy," the defendant cannot be tried again.

Historically, before juries could exercise this power,
two great issues had to be settled. The first was whether
judges have the power to punish jurors for bringing in
the "wrong" verdict. A precedent was established in
England in 1670, in what is generally referred to as
Bushel's case. Bushel was one of twelve jurors who refused to convict William Penn (later to become governor
of the American colony of Pennsylvania) of fomenting a
riot. Penn had been preaching a Quaker sermon in
public at a time when the Quakers were being persecuted. After the jurors refused to change their verdict,
the judge fined them forty marks apiece. They refused
to pay and were committed to Newgate Prison. Eventually they were released on bail, and when England's
high court finally decided the case a year later, it was

held that no jury can be punished for its verdict.

The second issue was whether juries could return "general verdicts" or only "special verdicts." A special verdict results when the jury is only allowed to answer specific questions of fact. A general verdict determines whether the accused is guilty or innocent. To render a general verdict, juries must judge the application of the facts to the law. The move from special to general verdicts was largely the result of unpopular prosecutions brought against printers by royal governors in the eighteenth century. At the trial of John Peter Zenger for seditious libel, Zenger's attorney argued that the jury had the power to decide whether Zenger was truly guilty of seditious libel. The prosecution argued that the jury could decide only whether Zenger had published the articles at issue in the case. Zenger was acquitted when the jury brought in the general verdict of "not guilty."

It is the general verdict that allows jury nullification. Juries may decide to disobey the judge's instructions if they believe either that the law is unjust or that the defendant's act was admirable or justified in some way. Prosecutors have no recourse, because acquittal is final in the American judicial system. During the nineteenth century, there was a substantial free jury movement in the United States, led by the radical American essayist Lysander Spooner. Although the movement subsided, many still argue that judges should inform jurors that they may "nullify" the law if they think it unjust. Regardless of whether juries are formally notified of this power, there are undoubtedly cases in which nullification takes place. For example, it is sometimes suggested that African American jurors are prone to acquit African American defendants, particularly on less serious charges, because they believe that there is considerable official harassment of blacks. It is difficult to tell with any certainty how common this practice may be. *Robert Jacobs*

See also: Criminal justice system; Jury selection.

Jury selection

> **Significance:** Equal protection of the law is at the heart of ensuring that no category of people is systematically favored over any other. If any category of people is limited in its access to participation in the U.S. legal system—especially in passing judgment on a member of that category who may have been accused of a crime—justice may be imperiled. If members of different racial or ethnic groups have the perception that justice is not blind, their full participation in society is jeopardized.

Before the Civil War (1861-1865), Massachusetts was the only state that permitted nonwhites to serve on juries. After the war, most southern states enacted legislation that effectively barred African Americans and other minorities from jury service, irrespective of the protections of the Fourteenth Amendment. Northern states tended to produce largely the same outcome mostly through the use of an exclusive *venire* (jury pool) process, whereby "prominent" citizens (which effectively left out minorities) filled out the rolls.

The exclusionary laws typical in the southern states were struck down when the U.S. Congress criminalized racism in jury selection in 1875. However, Congress left the exclusionary *venire* procedures common in the North unaddressed. These procedures soon became quite prevalent in the South as well.

Twentieth Century Reforms

Although nonexclusionary *voir dire* (selection to sit on a jury) became the standard guideline by the middle of the twentieth century, major changes were not initiated until the 1960's, when the United States Fifth Circuit Court began overturning convictions and indictments within its jurisdiction (mostly southern states) on the basis of exclusionary selection. Although the U.S. Supreme Court ruled in *Swain v. Alabama* (1965) that constitutional requirements were satisfied as long as minorities were on the *venire* and part of the grand jury that brought down an indictment, it was not until the Jury Selection and Service Act (1968) that Congress outlawed "blue ribbon" juries in federal courts. Consequently, the *venire* process had to be more open. In *Taylor v. Louisiana* (1975) the Supreme Court extended this requirement to the state and local courts.

Nevertheless, exclusion persisted through use of the peremptory challenge in petit (trial) jury *voir dire*—whereby attorneys have the right to strike potential jurors without stating any reason. Such screening of potential grand jurors is less prevalent. In *Batson v. Kentucky* (1986), the Supreme Court curtailed unrestricted use of peremptory challenge in petit juries by allowing judges to inquire as to the rationale for and to limit strikes (dismissals) of potential jurors when there appeared to be a pattern of exclusion. However, it is difficult to determine motivation definitively unless the prosecutor is unusually inept or unusually honest. The fact that more minorities have had adverse contacts with the criminal justice system can be used as a rationale for exclusion.

Consequently, some experts argued that "affirmative action" is necessary to guarantee representative juries. Others criticized this idea, saying that affirmative action in jury selection would translate into imposing quotas of minorities on juries, and some local jurisdictions did impose quotas on jury selection. However, in *Holland v. Illinois* (1990), the Supreme Court held that as long as the *venire* provided an appropriate cross section of the community, *voir dire* did not have to produce representative results because the Constitution merely guarantees equality of opportunity, not necessarily representativeness.

Jury Nullification

The most potentially problematic issue in the late twentieth century involved the Fully Informed Jury Association (FIJA) and related initiatives. FIJA proponents tend to be opposed to governmental authority in that they try to encourage potential jurors—especially those who may be judging antigovernment activists—to ignore the facts and/or the law in order to acquit. This "jury nullification," about which the government has no legal appeal (unless there is evidence of something like jury tampering), may contribute to even greater use of "scientific" jury selection. This innovation uses social research and psychological studies to profile and include or exclude (through peremptory challenge) jurors who may be more or less favorable to the case presented.

The jury nullification notions of the FIJA appear to be shared by some minority activists, who argue that members of their communities on juries judging their peers have a duty to vote for acquittal in almost all instances in order to redress the social injustices visited upon their community by the majority. Although this might accomplish nothing more than "hung" (unable to decide) juries—which permit the government to retry the cases—if minority members on subsequent juries act

the same way, government efforts to convict members of the minority will be stymied. If such postures become widespread, racially based peremptory challenges might become acceptable with the rationale that these minorities have an antigovernment bias such that they cannot meet the requirement of impartiality.

Scott Magnuson-Martinson

Core Resources

Randall Kennedy's *Race, Crime, and the Law* (New York: Pantheon, 1997) offers a comprehensive history of race and criminal justice in the United States—with several chapters on how it affects the composition of juries. Hirosaki Fukarai, Edgar W. Butler, and Richard Krooth elaborate the history of discrimination in U.S. jury selection in *Race and the Jury: Racial Disenfranchisement and the Search for Justice* (New York: Plenum, 1993). In *Guilty: The Collapse of Criminal Justice* (New York: Random House, 1996), Judge Harold J. Rothwax criticizes past legal methods of excluding minority participation on juries as well as some of the more extreme modern remedies. Albert W. Alschuler makes an argument for affirmative action in jury selection in "Racial Quotas and the Jury," in *Duke Law Journal* (44, 1995), and Paul Butler proposes that certain minorities use their jury participation to protect their communities in "Racially Based Jury Nullification: Black Power in the Criminal Justice System," in *Yale Law Journal* (105, 1995).

See also: *Batson v. Kentucky;* Crime and race/ethnicity; Criminal justice system; Jury nullification.

K

Kansas-Nebraska Act

Senator Stephen A. Douglas, chairman of the Committee on Territories, introduced legislation to organize the land west of Missouri and Iowa as the Nebraska Territory. New settlements in the region and the potential for a transcontinental rail route prompted Douglas's action. It soon became apparent to Douglas that obtaining support from the South required two major revisions. First, the region was split into the Kansas and Nebraska territories. Second, the bill called for repeal of that part of the Missouri Compromise of 1820 which prohibited slavery north of 36° 30′ latitude. Rather, settlers in each territory would vote to accept or prohibit slavery.

Douglas viewed slavery from economic rather than moral grounds, reasoning that its unprofitability in northern climates would be its demise. Douglas's concessions to slave states reflected both the desire to get on with nation building and the necessity of obtaining Southern support for his presidential ambitions. The act, which became law May 30, 1854, widened the growing rift between North and South and encouraged the formation of the Republican Party.   *John A. Sondey*

See also: Abolition; Bleeding Kansas; Civil War; John Brown's raid; Lincoln-Douglas debates; Missouri Compromise; Slavery: history.

Keeler Commission

The intent of federal Indian policy from 1953 to 1962 was to dissolve government obligations and responsibilities toward Native Americans in order to bring about assimilation. This disastrous program was called "termination." It undermined tribal governments and resources, eroded ethnic identities, and impoverished groups such as the Klamath of Oregon and Menominee of Wisconsin. By the end of the decade, so much criticism had been generated by these developments that a new political consciousness concerning Indian problems began to emerge.

John F. Kennedy, elected president in 1960, affirmed that Indian land would be protected, that self-determination would be promoted, and that steps would be taken to avoid undermining the cultural heritage of any group. Secretary of the Interior Stewart Udall appointed a special task force on Indian affairs in February of 1961 with an eye toward reorganizing the Bureau of Indian Affairs (BIA) in order to carry out this mandate.

William Wayne Keeler, a top-level executive with Phillips Petroleum Company and principal chief of the Cherokee Nation, was appointed chairman of the task force. Other members included Philleo Nash, an anthropologist and former lieutenant governor of Wisconsin who had participated in the Menominee termination plans; James Officer, a University of Arizona anthropologist; William Zimmerman, Jr., assistant commissioner of the BIA from 1933 to 1950; and consultant John Crow. After hearings and field trips to western reservations, the commission filed its seventy-seven-page report on July 10, 1961. Nash also included a summary of the report in the *Annual Report of the Commissioner of Indian Affairs* for 1961.

The commission's main finding was that future BIA policy should emphasize development rather than termination. Recommendations included the attraction of industries to reservations, along with job training and placement services. Loan programs were encouraged, rapid settlement of Indian Claims Commission cases was urged, and increased efforts to educate the general public about Indian culture were promoted. The report also stressed the need for Indian participation in government programs.

In the 1960's, Congress granted authorization for Indian loans, tribal resources increased, and development of reservation resources replaced the focus on assimilating Indians through relocation to the cities. The Keeler Commission played a small but noticeable role in the shift away from the termination policy.   *Gary A. Olson*

See also: Indian Claims Commission; Relocation of American Indians; Reservation system of the United States; Termination Resolution.

Keetoowah Society

The Keetoowah Society was founded by two white clergymen in 1859 in an effort to advance the interests of full-blooded Cherokee. The men were abolitionists, and their goal, ostensibly, was to organize Cherokee opposition to slavery. Members of the order were full-bloods, and some called themselves "Pin Indians," wearing crossed pins on their left lapels. The Keetoowah Society evolved from simple support of abolition to a group whose purpose was the protection of Cherokee interests. Society goals were taken from the ancient Anti-Kutani, designed to oppose adoption of European American ways. "Pin Indians" were Christians who wished to syncretize their religion with ancient tribal rites.

The Keetoowah Society was popular and at one time had a membership of more than two thousand men. It was fiercely loyal to the Union during the Civil War (1861-1865). That fact threatened the Confederacy, which impressed society members into military service. Stories abound of men who were forced to serve the South and deserted at the first opportunity.

Following the Civil War, the Keetoowah Society remained active in Cherokee political and social life. It opposed the Dawes Commission in the 1890's, insisting on the observance of treaty obligations, a guarantee of self-government, and freedom from territorial organization. When the Cherokee delegation reached agreement with the Dawes Commission in 1900, the full-blood Keetoowah Society urged its members to boycott the agreement. In 1906, the Dawes Commission agreement prevailed. The society then functioned as a political party (the Union Party) and fraternal lodge, the only fraternal lodge in the United States whose principal emblem is the United States flag. *David N. Mielke*

See also: Abolition; General Allotment Act; Indian-white relations: United States; Slavery and race relations.

Kennedy Report

In 1967, the United States Senate created the Special Subcommittee on Indian Education. Senator Robert F. Kennedy chaired the committee, which held hearings and authorized studies of educational programs for Native Americans. His brother Edward "Ted" Kennedy was the chair when the subcommittee released its final report in November, 1969. Entitled *Indian Education: A National Tragedy, a National Challenge,* but more commonly called the Kennedy Report, the study concluded that "national policies for educating American Indians are a failure of major proportions." The report blamed efforts to force Indian children to accept cultural values other than their own as one of the major flaws in Indian education and as a leading cause of high dropout rates. The subcommittee offered sixty recommendations for improving Indian education, which included emphasizing Indian culture and history and increasing funding for existing programs. Although government officials responsible for Indian education rushed to defend their programs, the Kennedy Report raised serious questions in the minds of many Americans concerning the government's management of Indian affairs. The report's findings helped promote passage of the Indian Education Act of 1972, which implemented some of its recommendations. *Thomas Clarkin*

See also: Education and American Indians; Indian Education Acts.

Kerner Report

The Kerner Report was a formal attempt to explain one of the greatest explosions of urban racial violence in the history of the United States. The report, the product of a commission appointed by President Lyndon B. Johnson, blamed pervasive racist attitudes and practices for the riots in the nation's cities.

Beginning in 1963, the United States experienced an unprecedented number of urban racial disorders. In 1967 alone, more than one hundred U.S. cities exploded in episodes of violence and looting. In November, 1967, President Johnson appointed the Kerner Commission (formally known as the National Advisory Commission on Civil Disorders), headed by Governor Otto Kerner of Illinois, to conduct an investigation to determine exactly what had happened and why and to make recommendations to solve the problem.

The commission reported that the basic cause of the urban disorders was white racism and that white, moderate, responsible America was where the responsibility for the riots ultimately lay. It had conducted detailed case studies of cities where violence had erupted and found that the riots had not been caused by any single factor or precipitating incident and were not the result of an organized plan or conspiracy. Its report stated that "the single overriding cause of rioting in the cities was not any one thing commonly adduced—unemployment, lack of education, poverty, exploitation—but that it was all of those things and more, expressed in the insidious and pervasive white sense of the inferiority of black men." The commission emphasized that the source of the problems was the very structure of American society; it did not seek explanations in the psychology of individuals. The report pointed out, "What white Americans have never fully understood—but what the Negro can never forget—is that white society is deeply implicated in the ghetto. White institutions created it, white institutions maintain it, and white society condones it." The report concluded, "Our nation is moving toward two societies, one black, one white—separate and unequal."

According to the commission, although racism was behind the riots, the more proximate causes of the unrest were pervasive discrimination and segregation in employment, education, and housing and the concentration of impoverished blacks in the inner city, produced by black migration into and white exodus from urban areas. Other contributing factors included the frustration of African Americans with civil rights legislation that failed to deliver the greater opportunity it promised; dissatisfaction with police practices that, for many African Americans, symbolized the oppression associated with racism; and society's apparent tendency to approve of violence against civil rights activists. The commission also noted enhanced racial pride, especially among young African Americans, and a feeling of powerlessness that led some to conclude that violence was the only effective means of change.

The Kerner Commission concluded that discrimination and segregation were serious problems that presented a threat to the future of the nation and must be eliminated. It indicated that three options were open to the nation: to maintain existing, admittedly inadequate policies regarding integration and the elimination of poverty; to focus on improving life in African American ghettos and ignore the goal of integration; or to pursue integration by improving conditions in the ghetto and implementing policies that would encourage movement out of the inner city.

The commission stated that the first option, to maintain existing policies, would permanently divide the United States into two separate and unequal societies and create an irreversible, polarized, police state rather than a democracy. The second option, described as "gilding the ghetto," would enrich the inner city but would further promote a separate, segregated society. Option three, a national commitment to change that involved moving a substantial number of African Americans out of the ghettos, was viewed as the most viable. This option was designed to create a single society in which all citizens would be free to live and work according to their capabilities and desires, not their color.

The Kerner Commission made a series of recommendations related to jobs, housing, education, law enforcement agencies, and nearly every other aspect of American life. It asked Americans to tax themselves to the extent necessary to meet the vital needs of the nation. Specific goals included the elimination of barriers to job choice, education, and housing and increasing the responsiveness of public institutions to relieve feelings of powerlessness. Other goals were to increase communication across racial lines to destroy stereotypes; to halt polarization, distrust, and hostility; and to create com-

mon ground for efforts toward public order and social justice.   *Frank E. Hagan*

See also: Civil Rights movement; Detroit riot; Newark race riots; Race riots in the twentieth century; Watts riot.

Keyes v. Denver School District No. 1

Decided June 21, 1973, this ruling outlawed de facto desegregation and expanded prohibitions on segregation. *Brown v. Board of Education* (1954) invalidated laws that required or permitted segregated black and white schools. Nevertheless, many school districts remained segregated, in part because of de facto segregation (segregation "in fact" rather than de jure, or "by law"). Wilfred Keyes did not want his daughter, Christi Keyes, to attend any kind of segregated school in Denver. In 1970, when a newly elected school board rescinded a desegregation plan adopted by the previous board in 1969, he brought a class-action suit.

In 1970, the district court ordered Park Hill schools desegregated after hearing evidence that the school board deliberately segregated its schools through school site selection, excessive use of mobile classroom units, gerrymandered attendance zones, student transportation routes, a restrictive transfer policy, and segregated faculty assignment to schools. Keyes was also successful before the court in arguing that inner-city schools, with substantial black and Hispanic student populations, should also be desegregated, but Denver prevailed on appeal in 1971, arguing that the large percentages of black and Hispanic students in these schools resulted from a "neighborhood school" policy.

Justice William J. Brennan delivered the opinion of the U.S. Supreme Court. Six justices joined Brennan, one justice affirmed the decision in part and dissented in part, and the remaining justice dissented. The Supreme Court ruled that since intentional segregation was proved in one part of the city, there was a presumption of intentional discrimination in the other case. The burden of proof thus shifted to the school board to prove that the intentional segregation of one section of the district was isolated, separate, and unrelated to the pattern of pupil assignment to the "core city schools."

When the case was sent back to the district court in 1973, Denver was determined to have practiced unlawful segregation in both areas of the city, and the school board was required to desegregate. When the school board failed to design an adequate plan to desegregate by 1974, the court drew up a plan of its own.

The effect of *Keyes* was to open all northern school

districts to the possibility of desegregation lawsuits. Eventually almost every city of at least moderate size then grappled with desegregation plans, voluntary or court ordered. The lone exception is the statewide school district of Hawaii, which has never been desegregated despite the existence of schools situated to serve certain geographic areas where only persons of Hawaiian ancestry by law can reside.   *Michael Haas*

See also: *Brown v. Board of Education*; Segregation: de facto and de jure; *Sweatt v. Painter*.

King, Martin Luther, Jr., assassination

> **Significance:** The murder in 1968 of the nation's most prominent civil rights leader touched off widespread urban unrest and dealt a severe blow to the Civil Rights movement.

For more than a decade, Martin Luther King, Jr., led the Southern Christian Leadership Conference (SCLC) and was, for many people, the quintessential symbol and spokesman for nonviolence. By the spring of 1968, however, King had lost some of his mystique, as the relatively simpler issues of voting rights and access to public facilities were superseded by more costly and divisive social and economic problems, accompanied by the deepening U.S. involvement in the Vietnam War.

King had lost his close alliance with President Lyndon B. Johnson because of his opposition to the president's Vietnam policy. King also faced challenges from younger, more militant African American leaders, for whom King's philosophy of passive resistance seemed too slow.

On the evening of April 4, King walked onto the balcony of his Memphis motel and was struck down by a bullet, fired from a building across the street. He died almost instantly. Initial attempts to identify and apprehend the killer failed, and while fires and riots raged in several cities in protest of King's death, an intensive search began, spreading eventually to Canada and Great Britain. On June 8, British immigration officials arrested an escaped U.S. convict traveling under the name of Roman George Sneyd and returned him to the United States to stand trial for the murder of King. The prisoner, whose real name was James Earl Ray, pleaded guilty to the charge in March, 1969, and was sentenced to ninety-nine years in prison. Later, Ray changed his position, claimed innocence, and wrote a book entitled *Who Killed Martin Luther King?* (1992), with a foreword by the Rev-

erend Jesse Jackson that cautiously endorsed Ray's conspiracy argument.

The immediate aftermath of King's death was marked by serious urban rioting in several cities, and somewhat later, by the granting of a substantial number of the strikers' demands in Memphis. More difficult to appraise is the place that his martyrdom earned for him and for his ideas in the Civil Rights movement. At a time when his influence was threatened by men such as H. Rap Brown and Huey P. Newton, King was killed in a way that served to restore his prestige among many African Americans. Under the leadership of King's longtime assistant Ralph David Abernathy, the SCLC continued to play a leading role in the Civil Rights movement after King's death. On the other hand, some African Americans, finding in King's death a confirmation of the futility of passive resistance, turned instead to more militant tactics.

In death, King remained an inspiring symbol, even a martyr, to many people who supported his causes. The SCLC, which King helped to found and which he led for eleven years as its president, continued under presidents Ralph Abernathy and Joseph E. Lowery to keep the vision of a nonviolent society central to their organizational and personal goals.

Courtney B. Ross, updated by Thomas R. Peake

Martin Luther King, Jr., holding his wife's hand, leads the march from Selma, Alabama, to Montgomery in March, 1965. His death in 1968 spawned riots in many U.S. cities.

Core Resources

Gerold Frank's *An American Death: The True Story of the Assassination of Dr. Martin Luther King, Jr.* (Garden City, N.Y.: Doubleday, 1972) is a well-documented analysis of King's assassination that argues that Ray acted alone. William Bradford Huie's *He Slew the Dreamer: My Search for the Truth About James Earl Ray and the Murder of Martin Luther King* (New York: Delacorte Press, 1970) rejects Ray's contention that King was the victim of a conspiracy and that Ray had been framed for the murder. James Earl Ray's *Who Killed Martin Luther King? The True Story by the Alleged Assassin* (Washington, D.C.: National Press Books, 1992), an apparently self-serving account by King's convicted assassin, argues that Ray did not commit the murder but was a scapegoat set up by the Federal Bureau of Investigation and other agencies.

See also: Black Power movement; Civil Rights movement; Southern Christian Leadership Conference.

King, Rodney, case

> **Significance:** The arrest and beating by police of Rodney King, a black man, sparked a major investigation of police brutality in Los Angeles and violent race riots after a California court acquitted the officers involved.

Following a high-speed chase along a Los Angeles highway that ended just after midnight on March 3, 1991, California Highway Patrol officers Timothy and Melanie Singer stopped driver Rodney Glen King and his two passengers, Bryant Allen and Freddie Helms, for questioning. More than twenty Los Angeles Police Department (LAPD) officers soon arrived on the scene in Los Angeles' Lake View Terrace neighborhood. Police sergeant Stacey Koon, assisted by officers Theodore Briseno, Laurence Powell, and Timothy Wind, took over the investigation. The police quickly subdued and handcuffed Allen and Helms without incident. Their encounter with King, however, caused a controversy with far-reaching legal and social consequences.

King's Arrest

According to the four white police officers who arrested King, a black man, King refused at first to leave the car and then resisted arrest with such vigor that the officers considered it necessary to apply two jolts from a Taser electric stun gun, fifty-six blows from aluminum batons, and six kicks (primarily from Briseno) to subdue King before they successfully handcuffed and cordcuffed King to restrain his arms and legs. The event probably

would have gone unnoticed had not George Holliday, an amateur cameraman who witnessed the incident, videotaped the arrest and sold the tape to a local television station news program. The videotape became the crucial piece of evidence that the state of California used to charge the four LAPD arresting officers with criminal assault and that a federal grand jury subsequently used to charge the officers with civil rights violations.

Broadcast of Holliday's tape on national news programs elicited several responses from the LAPD. On March 6, 1991, the LAPD released King from custody and admitted that officers failed to prove that King had resisted arrest. On March 7, Los Angeles Police Chief Daryl Gates announced that he would investigate King's arrest and, if the investigation warranted it, would pursue criminal assault charges against the arresting officers. On March 14, a Los Angeles County grand jury indicted Sergeant Koon and officers Briseno, Powell, and Wind for criminal assault, and they subsequently pleaded not guilty.

Investigation of Police Brutality

Overwhelming public sympathy for King following the national broadcast of Holliday's videotape prompted Los Angeles Mayor Thomas Bradley to investigate charges that instances of police brutality motivated by racism were commonplace during LAPD arrest operations. On April 1, 1991, Mayor Bradley appointed a nonpartisan commission, headed by Warren Christopher (who had formerly served as President Jimmy Carter's deputy secretary of state), to study the LAPD's past record of complaints regarding police misconduct. On April 2, Mayor Bradley called on Police Chief Gates, who had served on the LAPD since 1949 and had been police chief since 1978, to resign. In May, the LAPD suspended Sergeant Koon and officers Briseno and Powell without pay and dismissed officer Wind, a rookie without tenure, pending the outcome of their criminal trial. King then filed a civil rights lawsuit against the city of Los Angeles.

Several significant developments occurred as the officers awaited trial. On July 9, 1991, the Christopher Commission released the results of its investigation and its recommendations to the five-member Los Angeles Police Commission. The Police Commission employed the police chief and was responsible for the management of the LAPD. The Christopher Commission found that the LAPD, composed of 67.8 percent white officers in 1991, suffered from a "siege mentality" in a city where 63 percent of the population were people of color. The commission also found that a small but significant proportion of officers repeatedly used excessive force when making arrests and that the LAPD did not punish those officers when citizens filed complaints. Finally, the commission recommended measures to exert more control

Rodney King pleads for people to stop rioting on May 1, 1992, in Los Angeles. The riots were sparked by the acquittal of officers accused of criminal assault in connection with their handling of King's arrest.

over the LAPD's operations, including limiting the police chief's tenure to a five-year term, renewable by the Police Commission for one additional term only. After the release of the Christopher Commission report, Police Chief Gates announced his retirement, effective April, 1992 (which he later amended to July, 1992). On July 23, 1991, a California court of appeal granted the police defendants' request for a change of venue for the upcoming criminal trial.

The State of California Court Trial

The trial of the four officers began on March 4, 1992, in the new venue—the primarily white community of Simi Valley in Ventura County. The jury who heard the state of California's case against the four officers consisted of ten whites, one Latino, and one Asian. The officers' defense lawyers presented Holliday's videotape broken down into a series of individual still pictures. They asked the jury to judge whether excessive force—that is, force that was not warranted by King's "aggressive" actions— was employed at any single moment during the arrest. Referring often to the "thin blue line" that protected society from the "likes of Rodney King," the defense built a case that justified the police officers' actions. King's lawyer, Steven Lerman, a personal injury specialist, advised King not to testify at the trial out of concern that

King's "confused and frightened" state of mind since the beating might impair his memory of events and discredit his testimony. The Simi Valley jury acquitted the four officers of all charges of criminal assault, with the exception of one count against officer Powell on which the jury was deadlocked.

The acquittal of the four police officers on April 29, 1992, ignited widespread and destructive riots led by poor and angry black Angelenos. The riots affected areas throughout Los Angeles but particularly devastated parts of impoverished South Central Los Angeles. Fifty-three people died during the riots, which raged until May 2, and more than one billion dollars' worth of property was damaged. There had long been friction between Los Angeles' neighboring Korean and black communities, and the Korean American community bore the brunt of the rioters' destructive attacks.

The Federal Court Civil Rights Trial

On August 5, 1992, a federal grand jury indicted the four officers for violating King's civil rights. The grand jury charged Sergeant Koon with violating the Fourteenth Amendment, which obligated Koon, as the officer in charge of the arrest, to protect King while he was in police custody. Officers Briseno, Powell, and Wind were charged with violating the Fourth Amendment in using more force than necessary, and using that excessive force willfully, when they arrested King. King testified during the federal trial. On April 17, 1993, a jury of nine whites, two blacks, and one Latino found Koon and Powell guilty and Briseno and Wind not guilty. On August 4, 1993, Koon and Powell were sentenced to two-and-one-half-year prison terms. In May, 1994, a Los Angeles jury awarded King $3.8 million in compensatory damages in his civil rights lawsuit against the city, but on June 1, 1994, the jury denied King's request for additional punitive damages.   *Karen Garner*

Core Resources

For accounts of the Rodney King incident that are sympathetic to King, see H. Khalif Khalifah, ed., *Rodney King and the L.A. Rebellion: Analysis and Commentary by Thirteen Best-Selling Black Writers* (Hampton, Va.: U.B. & U.S. Communications Systems, 1992), and Tom Owens with Rod Browning, *Lying Eyes: The Truth Behind the Corruption and Brutality of the LAPD and the Beating of Rodney King* (New York: Thunder's Mouth Press, 1994). For an account of the police officers' point of view, see Stacey Koon with Robert Deitz, *Presumed Guilty: The Tragedy of the Rodney King Affair* (Washington, D.C.: Regnery Gateway, 1992). For a collection of essays that places the Rodney King incident in the context of race relations in the United States, see Robert Gooding-Williams, ed., *Reading Rodney King/Reading Urban Uprising* (New York: Routledge, 1993).

See also: Korean-African American relations; Los Angeles riots of 1992; Police brutality; Race riots of the twentieth century.

Know-Nothing Party

The Know-Nothing Party was a political organization that prospered in the United States between 1852 and 1856. During that period, the antiforeign and anti-Catholic feelings of Americans concerned about the large numbers of immigrants arriving in the United States, especially from Ireland, led to the creation of political organizations grounded in prejudice. The secret Order of the Star-Spangled Banner, informally known as the Know-Nothings because "I know nothing" was the response of members queried regarding the organization, emerged as the most prominent of the nativist organizations. The Know-Nothings eventually dropped their secrecy to become a force in U.S. politics. Under a new name, the American Party, the Know-Nothings surprised the nation with electoral victories in 1854 and 1855. The new party successfully shifted attention away from the issue of slavery in many parts of the country by playing on unrealistic fears of foreign and papal plots to control the United States. The American Party platform called for reforming immigration laws by limiting the number of immigrants and extending the time requirement for naturalization. Former president Millard Fillmore, the American Party candidate for president in 1856, received 21 percent of the popular vote but carried only the state of Maryland. Unable to emerge as a dominant force in national politics, the American Party split into factions over the issue of slavery.

Donald C. Simmons, Jr.

See also: Anti-Catholicism; Nativism; Xenophobia, nativism, and eugenics.

Komagata Maru incident

At the beginning of the twentieth century, the Sikhs (a religious community who originate in South Asia) became the targets of resentment, discrimination, and violence in Canada's British Columbia. In response to the anti-Sikh sentiment, in 1908 the Canadian government passed two orders-in-council specifically designed to stop East Indian immigration. The first raised the amount an immigrant had to have in his or her possession from twenty-five dollars to two hundred dollars. The second prohibited entry unless the person came directly from his or her country of birth or citizenship by continuous voyage; there were no direct or continuous voyage sea routes from India to Canada. Only East Indians were subject to these restrictions.

To enter Canada, a group chartered the Japanese ship *Komagata Maru* and made a continuous voyage from Calcutta to Vancouver with 346 Sikhs and 30 East Indians aboard. Even though the passengers satisfied all the immigration requirements, only a few, who were returnees, were allowed to disembark. After two months of negotiations, anti-Sikh demonstrations, and violence, the ship and her passengers were forced to leave.

Arthur W. Helweg

See also: Asian Indians in Canada; Asian Indians in the United States; Sikhs in Canada; Sikhs in the United States.

Korean-African American relations

Significance: Korean immigrants to the United States have tended to open small businesses, such as groceries, in central areas of American cities, where many of their customers have been African Americans. As a consequence, sometimes culture clashes and conflicts occur between members of these two minority groups.

Ownership of a small business is the most common job for people of Korean ancestry in the United States. Assisted by rotating credit associations (organizations that Koreans form to grant each other interest-free business loans requiring little collateral), Korean Americans have specialized in self-employment in small stores. The majority of Korean businesses in the United States are located in California and New York. In 1990, according to the U.S. Bureau of the Census, 44 percent of all Korean business owners lived in California and 12 percent of Korean business owners lived in New York. Within these states, they were concentrated in the Los Angeles-Long Beach area and in New York City.

Korean businesses are most often located in central areas of cities. During the 1970's and 1980's, owners of inner-city businesses began to leave, and Koreans, having access to business loans from their rotating loan associations but few job opportunities in established American businesses, began buying small urban shops. Although their businesses were in the city, the Koreans tended to settle in the suburbs. The people who do live in central urban areas and make up the majority of the customers in Korean businesses are African Americans. Korean shop owners are often looked upon by their inner-city customers as exploiters who come into neighborhoods to make a profit on the people and then take the money elsewhere. These customers complain about high prices, poor merchandise, and discourteous treatment. As new arrivals to the United States, Korean merchants sometimes have trouble with English and do not communicate well with those who come into their shops.

Korean businesspeople tend to hire other Koreans to work in their shops. Most of these shops are family enterprises, so family members frequently provide labor. As a result, Koreans not only live outside the communities where their stores are located but also hire few people who live in those communities. African Americans complain that Korean merchants do not hire black employees, do not buy from black suppliers of goods, and do not invest in the black neighborhoods in which they have located their businesses.

Although African American shoppers frequently view Koreans as outsiders and exploiters, the Koreans sometimes look with suspicion on those living in the neighborhoods where their businesses are located. Having little understanding of the history of U.S. racial inequality, Korean business owners may see low-income urban residents as irresponsible and untrustworthy. The high crime rates in these neighborhoods can lead them to see all members of the communities, even the most honest, as potential shoplifters or robbers.

Mistrust and Culture Clash

The cultural gap between African Americans and the Korean Americans who often own stores in black neighborhoods has resulted in a number of well-publicized clashes. In the spring of 1990, African Americans in Brooklyn began a nine-month boycott of Korean stores after a Korean greengrocer allegedly harassed an African American shopper. In 1992, trouble flared up again in the same neighborhood when an African American customer in a Korean grocery was allegedly harassed and struck by the owner and an employee. During 1995, an African American man was arrested while attempting to burn down a Korean-owned store, and both white and Korean store owners in Harlem received racial threats.

California, home to the nation's greatest number of Korean businesses, has seen some of the most serious conflicts between Koreans and African Americans. In April of 1992, a judge gave a sentence of probation to a Korean shopkeeper convicted in the shooting death of a fifteen-year-old African American girl, Latasha Harlins. Two weeks after

that, on April 29, riots broke out in South Central Los Angeles after the acquittal of police officers who had been videotaped beating an African American motorist, Rodney King. Although none of the police officers was Korean, Korean groceries and liquor stores in South Central Los Angeles became targets of the riots. The riots destroyed more than one thousand Korean businesses and an estimated twenty-three hundred Korean-owned businesses were looted.

Korean shop owners began leaving South Central Los Angeles in the years after the riots. Those who remained became even more wary of the local population than they were previously.

Efforts at Improving Relations

Korean and African American leaders have made efforts to improve relations between the two groups. In the days following the riots in Los Angeles, some African American and Korean leaders formed the Black-Korean Alliance to improve communication and find common ground. In New York, the Korean-American Grocer's Association has tried to find ways of bringing African Americans and Koreans together. These have included sending African American community leaders on tours of South Korea and providing African American students with scholarships to Korean universities.

It may be difficult to resolve the problems between Korean merchants and their African American customers as long as American central cities continue to be places of concentrated unemployment and poverty. Investment in low-income communities and the creation of economic opportunities for their residents are probably necessary in order to overcome the suspicion and resentment between members of these two minority groups.

Carl L. Bankston III

Core Resources

In *Caught in the Middle: Korean Merchants in America's Multiethnic Cities* (Berkeley: University of California

Jesse Jackson, second from right, meets with Korean community leaders in an attempt to improve relations between Korean and African Americans after the Los Angeles riots of 1992.

616 - Korean Americans

Press, 1996), sociologist Pyong Gap Min examines the situation of Korean businessmen in U.S. cities. Nancy Abelmann and John Lie discuss the consequences for Koreans of the 1992 Los Angeles riots in *Blue Dreams: Korean Americans and the Los Angeles Riots* (Cambridge, Mass.: Harvard University Press, 1995). Ivan Light and Edna Bonacich give a history of Korean American business in *Immigrant Entrepreneurs: Koreans in Los Angeles, 1965-1982* (Berkeley: University of California Press, 1988). Lauren Lee's *Korean Americans* (New York: Marshall Cavendish, 1995) provides a readable, in-depth description of this ethnic group.

See also: Harlins, Latasha, murder; King, Rodney, case; Korean Americans; Los Angeles riots of 1992; Middleman minorities.

Korean Americans

> **Significance:** Korean Americans are one of the fastest-growing ethnic groups in the United States. Korean American businesses and churches have become increasingly common, and members of other American ethnic groups frequently come into contact with Koreans.

Koreans first began settling in the United States in the 1950's, when American servicemen serving in Korea returned home with brides and war orphans. Korean migration to the United States continued at very low levels, however, until the U.S. Congress changed immigration laws in 1965, giving Asians the same opportunity as Europeans to settle in the United States. This triggered an almost immediate increase in Korean migration: Although only 10,179 Koreans immigrated from 1961 to 1965, the number jumped to 25,618 in the next half-decade, from 1966 to 1970. As more Koreans made their homes in the United States, more followed. During the period from 1986 to 1990, 172,851 Koreans immigrated. By 1990, according to the U.S. Census of Population and Housing, the Korean American population had reached 750,000.

After the 1965 change in immigration law, Korean immigrants were not only more numerous but also more likely to come as entire family groups. With large numbers of Koreans in the United States, they began to form Korean American communities instead of settling as isolated individuals. Korean businesses and Korean churches began to appear in American cities and suburbs.

California, with a 1990 Korean American population of 259,941, is home to the largest portion of Koreans in the United States. California is followed by New York,

which had a Korean American population of 95,648 in 1990. Illinois, New Jersey, Texas, Maryland, Virginia, and Washington also had large Korean populations.

Korean Businesses

As new immigrants, Koreans often have few job opportunities in the United States. However, Koreans do have a strong tradition of helping one another, and this has contributed to the growth of Korean-owned businesses in the United States. In the rotating credit system known as the *kye*, groups of Koreans pool money to make interest-free loans to group members.

Changes in the U.S. economy also encouraged the development of Korean businesses. During the 1970's and 1980's, as poverty became increasingly concentrated in American inner-city areas, many small business owners began closing or selling stores in these areas. New Korean immigrants, who had limited English-language abilities and few contacts to find jobs in established U.S. corporations, moved into ownership of small businesses. By the 1990's, Korean Americans had the highest rate of business ownership of any ethnic or racial group, and more than half of all first-generation Korean immigrants were self-employed.

Korean businesses have become the basis for many local and national Korean organizations. The Korean American Grocers' Association is one of the most important of the national business-based organizations, with local groups in most areas that have substantial Korean populations. The Korean Dry Cleaning and Laundry Association is another national Korean American organization based on small-business ownership.

The Korean pattern of employment has had consequences for the relations between Korean Americans and members of other groups. Koreans are often highly dependent on one another for financial and social support, sometimes creating the impression that they isolate themselves from the rest of American society. They tend not to live in the inner-city neighborhoods where they own their businesses, leading to cultural misunderstandings and conflicts between Korean business owners and their customers, many of whom are African American.

Korean Churches

Although Korean culture is traditionally Confucian and Buddhist, numerous Christian congregations, mostly Protestant, exist in South Korea. It is estimated that about 70 percent of Korean Americans are Christians and that the overwhelming majority of them are members of Korean churches. By the 1990's, there were more than two thousand Korean churches in the United States. Churches have become social centers for many Korean Americans, places where they can come together with others who speak their language and share their culture.

Korean American churches are places of worship, but they fulfill many other needs as well. Church members provide one another with information on available employment and housing. Language classes at churches teach English to new immigrants and Korean to U.S.-born children. The churches help to pass Korean culture on to children who may never have visited the home country of their parents.

Koreans and American Society

Korean businesses and churches both help to maintain Korean Americans as a separate group in American society. However, when U.S.-born Korean Americans become a larger proportion of the population, the separateness of Korean Americans is likely to diminish.

Many Korean American business owners do not pass on their businesses to their U.S.-born children. Instead, these children are typically encouraged to achieve high educational levels and obtain professional jobs in U.S. corporations. Over time, then, the distinctive employment patterns of Korean Americans are likely to disappear. Korean Americans have also shown increasing rates of marriage with members of other racial and ethnic groups, suggesting that members of this Asian ethnic group will gradually assimilate or blend into the larger American society. *Carl L. Bankston III*

Core Resources

From the Land of Morning Calm: The Koreans in America (New York: Chelsea House, 1994), by Ronald Takaki, uses documents on Korean immigration and oral histories of individual Korean Americans to help readers understand the background of this group. It is illustrated with photographs and contains a chronology of Koreans in the United States. *Caught in the Middle: Korean Merchants in America's Multiethnic Cities* (Berkeley: University of California Press, 1996), by Pyong Gap Min, looks at the situation of Korean businessmen in urban neighborhoods and how they are affected by racial and ethnic inequality in the United States. *Blue Dreams: Korean Americans and the Los Angeles Riots* (Cambridge, Mass: Harvard University Press, 1995), by Nancy Abelmann and John Lie, is a detailed examination of the impact of the 1992 riots on Korean Americans.

See also: Ethnic entrepreneurship; Harlins, Latasha, murder; Korean-African American relations; Los Angeles riots of 1992; Middleman minorities.

Korean Americans watch dancers from their booth at a 1991 marketplace festival in Ardmore Park in Los Angeles.

Korematsu v. United States

In *Korematsu v. United States*, the Supreme Court refused to rule in favor of the privacy rights of an American citizen of Japanese ancestry who was detained in a relocation camp during World War II. In 1942, American military authorities arrested Fred Toyosaburo Korematsu, an American citizen of Japanese ancestry, for remaining in San Leandro, California, a restricted region, in violation of a military order. The military acted under authority of President Franklin Roosevelt's Executive Order 9066, which authorized the secretary of war and appropriate military commanders to establish military areas from which persons might be excluded. The president issued this order on his authority as commander in chief of the army and navy. After being found guilty of violating the military order, Korematsu appealed his case to the U.S. Supreme Court.

On December 18, 1944, the U.S. Supreme Court ruled 6 to 3 in favor of the United States and in support of Korematsu's arrest. The majority opinion, written by Justice Hugo L. Black, sustained Korematsu's removal because "the properly constituted military authorities" feared an invasion of the West Coast and had decided that military urgency required the removal of persons of Japanese origin from the area. Black admitted that the exclusion order worked hardship on the Japanese American population, "but hardships are a part of war and war is an aggregation of hardships." Furthermore, Black reasoned, the exclusion program did not constitute racial discrimination as such; Korematsu had not been excluded because of his race but because of the requirements of national security. As to the question of loyalty, Black stated that there was insufficient time to separate the loyal from the disloyal Japanese. The only recourse, then, was for the military leaders to take such action as they deemed necessary to protect the country and its citizens from possible aggression. The section of Black's opinion that has most often been cited, however, states that "all legal restrictions which curtail the civil rights of a single racial group are immediately suspect" and must be given "the most rigid scrutiny."

Three justices differed from the majority and registered vigorous dissents. Justice Owen J. Roberts objected on the grounds of both loyalty and race. This was a "case of convicting a citizen as punishment for not submitting to imprisonment in a concentration camp, solely because of his ancestry," without evidence concerning his loyalty to the United States. Justice Frank Murphy was equally adamant in his dissent. He denounced the removal of Japanese citizens as "one of the most sweeping and complete deprivations of constitutional rights in the history of this nation in the absence of martial law." He concluded that the exclusion program itself "goes over the 'very brink of constitutional power' and falls into the very ugly abyss of racism."

The importance of *Korematsu v. United States* lies in the difficulty that the Court had in determining the dividing line between the constitutional rights of the citizen and the nation's power to defend itself. In this case, the Court did not rule on the constitutionality of the internment of someone on the basis of race, only that the presidential executive order and the subsequent military orders were deemed necessary for the defense of the nation and its citizens. While it took the United States more than forty years officially to rectify and repudiate the internment of Japanese Americans (reparations payments were authorized by Congress in 1988), many commentators have long believed that the United States acted improperly and in violation of the civil rights of American citizens by its use of the internment camp program.

Kevin F. Sims

See also: Civil Liberties Act of 1988; *Hirabayashi v. United States*; Japanese American internment; Redress movement.

Ku Klux Klan

Significance: A group of white supremacists, disaffected by the outcome of the Civil War, grew into an organization of institutionalized race hatred.

With the end of the Civil War and the emancipation of African American slaves in the South, tension arose between old-order Southern whites and Radical Republicans devoted to a strict plan of Reconstruction that required Southern states to repeal their black codes and guarantee voting and other civil rights to African Americans. Federal instruments for ensuring African American rights included the Freedmen's Bureau and the Union Leagues. In reaction to the activities of these organizations, white supremacist organizations sprouted in the years immediately following the Civil War: the Knights of the White Camelia, the White League, the Invisible Circle, the Pale Faces, and the Ku Klux Klan (KKK).

Beginnings

The last of these would eventually lend its name to a confederation of such organizations, but in 1866 it was born in Pulaski, Tennessee, as a fraternal order for white, male, Anglo-Saxon Protestants joined by their opposition to Radical Reconstructionism and an agenda to promote white, Southern dominance. This incarnation of the Klan established many of the weird rituals and violent activities for which the KKK became known throughout its history. They named the South the "invisible empire," with "realms" consisting of the Southern states. A "grand dragon" headed each realm, and the entire "empire" was led by Grand Wizard General Nathan B. Forrest. Positions of leadership were dubbed "giant," "cyclops," "geni," "hydra," "goblin." The white robes and pointed cowls stem from this era; these were donned in the belief that blacks were superstitious and would be intimidated by the menacing, ghostlike appearance of their oppressors, who thus also maintained anonymity while conducting their activities.

Soon the Klan was perpetrating acts of violence, including whippings, house-burnings, kidnappings, and lynchings. As the violence escalated, Forrest disbanded the Klan in 1869, and on May 31, 1870, and April 20, 1871, Congress passed the Ku Klux Klan Acts, or Force Acts, designed to break up the white supremacist groups.

Second Rise of the Klan

The next rise of the Klan presaged the period of the Red Scare (1919-1920) and the Immigration Act of 1921, the first such legislation in the United States to establish immigration quotas on the basis of national origin. In November, 1915, on Stone Mountain, Georgia, a second Ku Klux Klan was founded by preacher William J. Simmons, proclaiming it a "high-class, mystic, social, patriotic" society devoted to defending womanhood, white Protestant values, and "native-born, white, gentile Americans." Such an image of the Klan was perpetrated by the popular 1915 film *Birth of a Nation*, in which a lustful African American is shown attempting to attack a white woman, and the Klan, in robes and cowls, rides to the rescue.

The new Klan cloaked itself as a patriotic organization devoted to preserving traditional American values against enemies in the nation's midst. An upsurge of nationalist fervor swelled the ranks of the Klan, this time far beyond the borders of the South. This second Klan adopted the rituals and regalia of its predecessor as well as the same anti-black ideology, to which it added anti-Catholic, anti-Semitic, anti-immigrant, anti-birth-control, anti-Darwinist, and anti-Prohibition stances. Promoted by ad-man Edward Y. Clarke, its membership reached approximately 100,000 by 1921 and over the next five years, by some estimates, grew to 5 million, including even members of Congress.

The second Klan perpetrated more than five hundred hangings and burnings of African Americans. In 1924, forty thousand Klansmen marched down Pennsylvania Avenue in Washington, D.C., sending a message to the federal government that there should be a white, Protestant United States. Finally, the Klan's growing wave of violence alienated many of its members, whose numbers dropped to about 30,000 by 1930.

Klan activities increased again prior to World War II, and membership rose toward the 100,000 mark, but in 1944 Congress assessed the organization more than a half million dollars in back taxes, and the Klan dissolved itself to escape. Two years later, however, Atlanta physician Samuel Green united smaller Klan groups into the Association of Georgia Klans and was soon joined by other reincarnations, such as the Federated Ku Klux Klans, the Original Southern Klans, and the Knights of the Ku Klux Klan. These groups revived the agenda of previous Klans and were responsible for hundreds of criminal acts. Of equal concern was the Klan's political influence: A governor of Texas was elected with the support of the Klan, as was a senator from Maine. Even a Supreme Court justice, Hugo L. Black, revealed in 1937 that he had been a member of the Ku Klux Klan.

Challenges

In the 1940's, many states passed laws that revoked Klan charters, and many southern communities issued regulations against masks. The U.S. Justice Department placed the Klan on its list of subversive elements, and in 1952 the Federal Bureau of Investigation used the Lindbergh law (one of the 1934 Crime Control Acts) against the Klan. Another direct challenge to the principles of the KKK came in the 1960's with the advent of the Civil Rights movement and civil rights legislation. Martin Luther King, Jr., prophesied early in the decade that it would be a "season of suffering." On September 15, 1963, a Klan bomb tore apart the Sixteenth Street Baptist Church in Birmingham, Alabama, killing four young children. Despite the outrage of much of the nation, the violence continued, led by members of the Klan who made a mockery of the courts and the laws that they had broken. Less than a year after the bombing, three civil rights workers were killed in Mississippi, including one African American and two whites from the North involved in voter registration. This infamous event was later documented in the motion picture *Mississippi Burning*. Viola Lee Liuzzo was killed for driving freedom marchers from site to site. Such acts prompted President Lyndon B. Johnson, in a televised speech in March, 1965, to denounce the Klan as he announced the arrest of four Klansmen for murder.

After the conviction of many of its members in the 1960's, the organization became somewhat dormant, and its roster of members reflected low numbers. Still, as it had in previous periods of dormancy, the Klan refused to die. Busing for integration of public schools in the 1970's engendered Klan opposition in the South and the North. In 1979, in Greensboro, North Carolina, Klan members killed several members of the Communist Party in a daylight battle on an open street. Klan members have patrolled the Mexican border, armed with weapons and citizen-band radios, trying to send illegal aliens back to Mexico. The Klan has been active in suburban California, at times driving out African Americans who attempted to move there. On the Gulf Coast, many boats fly the infamous AKIA flag, an

The Ku Klux Klan, pictured in Chicago in 1924, aimed to intimidate African Americans, American Jews, and Catholics through cross burnings and other violent acts.

acronym for "A Klansman I Am," a motto that dates back to the 1920's. Klan members have tried to discourage or run out Vietnamese fishers. Klan leaders active since 1970 include James Venable, for whom the Klan became little more than a hobby, and Bill Wilkinson, a former disciple of David Duke. Robert Shelton, long a grand dragon, helped elect two Alabama governors. Duke, a Klan leader until the late 1980's, decided to run for political office and was elected a congressman from Louisiana despite his well-publicized past associations; in 1991, he ran for governor, almost winning. In the 1980's the Klan stepped up its anti-Semitic activities, planning multiple bombings in Nashville. Klan leaders in the 1990's have trained their members and their children for what they believe is an imminent race war, learning survival skills and weaponry at remote camps throughout the country.

A major blow was struck against the Klan by the Klanwatch Project of the Southern Poverty Law Center, in Montgomery, Alabama, when, in 1984, attorney Morris Dees began pressing civil suits against several Klan members, effectively removing their personal assets, funds received from members, and even buildings owned by the Klan.

Core Resources

Tyler Bridges's *The Rise of David Duke* (Jackson: University Press of Mississippi, 1994) is a thorough discussion of a notorious Klan member. David Mark Chalmers's *Hooded Americanism: The History of the Ku Klux Klan* (New York: F. Watts, 1981) is considered the bible of books about the Klan. Raphael Ezekiel's *The Racist Mind: Portraits of American Neo-Nazis and Klansmen* (New York: Viking Press, 1995) explores conditions of childhood, education, and other factors in an attempt to explain racist behavior. Bill Stanton's *Klanwatch: Bringing the Ku Klux Klan to Justice* (New York: Weidenfeld, 1991), by a former Klanwatch director, explains initiatives to disable the Klan, most of which have been effective. Wyn Draig Wade's *The Fiery Cross: The Ku Klux Klan in America* (New York: Simon & Schuster, 1987) recounts the Klan's history and episodes of violence.

See also: Aryan nation; Freedmen's Bureau; Hate crimes; Ku Klux Klan Acts; Reconstruction; Red Scare; White Aryan Brotherhood; White supremacist groups; Xenophobia, nativism, and eugenics.

Ku Klux Klan Acts

Also known as the Enforcement Acts, or Force Acts, these three laws were enacted by the U.S. Congress in response to the terrorist activities of the Ku Klux Klan and other groups committed to white supremacy in the South during the era of Reconstruction, immediately following the Confederate defeat at the end of the Civil War. The first act, passed in May, 1870, made night riding (the practice of riding on horseback at night and committing various acts of intimidation and harassment) a federal felony and reaffirmed the rights of African Americans provided for in the Fourteenth and Fifteenth Amendments. Congress passed a second act in February, 1871, which provided for election supervisors to ensure against fraud and racial discrimination. Two months later, Congress approved a third statute aimed specifically at the activities of the Ku Klux Klan. This law made it a federal offense to violate anyone's voting rights. In addition, it allowed the president to proclaim areas in which state governments failed to curb domestic violence to be in "rebellion" and authorized the use of military force and the suspension of the writ of *habeas corpus* to end rebellions. In October, 1871, President Ulysses S. Grant used the law to declare nine counties in South Carolina to be in rebellion. These laws proved effective in suppressing white supremacy organizations.

Thomas Clarkin

See also: Fifteenth Amendment; Fourteenth Amendment; Ku Klux Klan; Reconstruction.

This drawing depicts a visit by the early Ku Klux Klan. The Ku Klux Klan Acts (1870 and 1871) were designed to end the lynchings and other violent acts carried out by the Ku Klux Klan and other white supremacist groups.

L

Labor movement

> **Significance:** The history of the American labor movement has both reflected and influenced racial and ethnic relations.

An unusually diverse mix of racial and ethnic groups have formed and replenished the labor force of the United States since the Reconstruction era following the Civil War. Emancipated slaves and their descendants rapidly expanded the American labor ranks, with many entering agricultural and industrial production in both the North and the South. In a similar manner, immigration began to alter the appearance and form of American labor. In the late nineteenth century, the United States opened its doors to foreign migrants, in large part because the nation's rapidly expanding economy needed labor. Between 1880 and 1924, more than 25 million immigrants (primarily from Asia and Europe) poured into the country to join people of other nationalities working in factories and industries. Through their collective labor as workers, their actions as union members, and their varied responses to exploitation and insecurity, this varied ethnic mix was a crucial element in shaping the American economy and labor force through the twentieth century.

Such heterogeneity has had both negative and positive consequences for the American labor movement as a whole. It has produced interethnic and interracial conflict among working people; such conflict has often been purposefully exacerbated by employers to lessen the threat of worker solidarity. Yet this heterogeneity has also fostered strong ethnic identification and has been utilized toward worker mobilization for protection and advancement. Both tendencies can be seen within some of the key labor organizations that emerged during the United States' two "labor eras" (the 1880's and the 1930's) and in minority and immigrant labor activity in later decades.

Knights of Labor

The Noble Order of the Knights of Labor (KOL) was initially organized in Philadelphia in 1869; however, the period of its most successful accomplishment did not come until the 1880's. Led by Terence Powderly, a machinist from Scranton, Pennsylvania, the KOL aimed to unite all those who worked (except for liquor dealers, lawyers, gamblers, and bankers) into one huge union that would produce and distribute goods on a cooperative basis.

Recognizing the need for a broad-based labor solidarity to achieve this goal, the Knights of Labor opened its membership to men and women of all ethnic and racial groups. Powderly traveled the country gathering all those who advocated equal pay for equal work and the abolition of child labor. This recruitment campaign was quite successful, and more than thirty cooperative enterprises were established with membership that spanned national and racial boundaries. At its peak, the Knights of Labor included about seventy thousand black members and thousands of Asian and European laborers.

The results of such multiethnic labor solidarity can be seen in the strike against the Missouri Pacific Railroad in 1885. Through work stoppages and interruptions, certain unions affiliated with the Knights of Labor forced railroad mogul Jay Gould to restore wages he had cut the previous year and to rehire hundreds of fired union members. This victory so raised the KOL's standing that membership grew from about 100,000 to more than 700,000 within a year.

American Federation of Labor

The American Federation of Labor (AFL), formed in Philadelphia in 1886, was a very different organization. Its members were not individual workers but rather craft unions encompassing laborers from specific trades. Regular dues from these members provided the federation with money to fund strikes and to hire full-time organizers and labor-dispute negotiators.

Although the AFL provided these supportive labor services, it did so for a narrow spectrum of workers. The way in which AFL leader Samuel Gompers structured the organization made it racially and ethnically divisive and restrictive. In his recruitment campaigns, Gompers made membership appeals only to the elite males of the working class, the skilled workers. Few minority group members fit this description; even those who did were excluded from membership. Gompers's position was that allowing members of various ethnic and immigrant groups (especially blacks) to join the federation would embroil the organization in the controversial issue of race in the labor movement; he wished to avoid ethnic entanglements at all costs. Believing that the AFL had more "imperative" and "concrete" matters on which to focus, he closed the ranks of the AFL to minority workers. By the early 1920's, the AFL was the dominant workers' organization in the United States, but fewer than 10 percent of the nation's wage earners were organized into unions eligible for AFL membership.

The Twentieth Century
Evidence of the ways in which racial diversity can be utilized both to help and to hinder the labor movement is not restricted to the nineteenth century. Similar examples can be found in the second wave of labor organization that hit the United States in the 1930's.

The American Federation of Labor had survived into this decade despite the continuance of its strategies of labor elitism and racial division. The descendants of the craft union leaders who had come together in the federation of the 1880's sought to retain the legacy of their power and standing as the "aristocracy of labor." They continued to deny membership to unskilled or semiskilled immigrant labor from the mass-production industries; they also prohibited other leaders from organizing these workers in new unions.

AFL leaders doubted the ability of immigrant groups to provide valuable support for the labor movement. Racist and nativist ideologies led many to see these groups not as a possibly valuable coalition in the advancement of labor policies but as individual nationalities whose differences were potentially subversive to the labor movement. As a source of cheap labor, immigrant groups emerged as second only to capitalists themselves as organizers' and native workers' enemies.

Debate over this issue culminated between 1935 and 1938, when John L. Lewis and seven other AFL leaders broke from the Federation to form the Congress of Industrial Organizations (CIO). They asserted that the same defensive mindset that manifested itself within the AFL in exclusionary impulses could also impart great cohesion toward resistance to employers. To this extent, the CIO was organized to solidify those workers whom the AFL ignored or overlooked: the semiskilled and unskilled immigrant and minority ranks. Altogether, more than 1.8 million workers were organized by the CIO, and they proved to be a valuable tool toward labor advancement.

The CIO utilized its large membership (and the ethnic and ideological solidarity it often represented) to challenge repressive labor practices in the steel and automobile industries. In these challenges, the tool of the CIO was the sit-down strike: Instead of walking off the job and picketing, workers went to their posts in the plants and stayed there, making it difficult for others to replace them. In 1937, successful sit-down strikes against General Motors, Chrysler, and U.S. Steel won the CIO recognition as the bargaining agent for workers previously thought unorganizable.

The eventual merger of the AFL and the CIO in 1955 was of great interest to minority labor. CIO leader Walter Reuther and AFL leader George Meany worked declarations of opposition to racial discrimination into the new organization's merger agreement and subsequent constitution. Members of both organizations hailed these statements, but they still waited anxiously to see if the words would be backed by actions. These members would be both pleased and disappointed. The AFL-CIO won respect in the black community early in its career when its executive council called on President Dwight D. Eisenhower to comply with the U.S. Supreme Court's 1954 decision on school desegregation and deny school-construction funds to any state that defied the ruling. Yet it also antagonized the black community by remaining aloof during the great Montgomery bus boycott of 1955 and 1956.

The 1950's were charged with racial strife, and racial tensions often exacerbated difficulties in labor organization and negotiation. Specifically, most AFL-CIO union leaders feared regional political and economic repercussions and avoided adopting a stand clearly in favor of egalitarian racial principles. The ultimate result was the alienation of black workers from the AFL-CIO. Indeed, the National Association for the Advancement of Colored People (NAACP) issued a report in 1959 announcing that the AFL-CIO had not achieved its merger goals, having failed to unify racial and labor issues.

African Americans
Even before the CIO's split from the AFL, A. Philip Randolph had welded a powerful union from the many African Americans who worked on the nation's passenger railroads. Randolph's organization, the Brotherhood of Sleeping Car Porters, won significant concessions from the Pullman Company in the 1930's and later provided a solid base from which black labor could challenge discrimination on a variety of fronts. In 1941, Randolph organized a march on Washington to protest discrimination in the defense industry; he canceled the march when President Franklin D. Roosevelt agreed to issue an executive order forbidding employment discrimination by defense contractors. Further pressure by Randolph and the union helped prompt President Harry S Truman to end segregation in the armed forces

in 1948. After the AFL-CIO merger in 1955, Randolph became the only black member of the union's executive council.

The 1960's and 1970's saw more African American and Mexican American laborers attempt to assert their political, economic, and social identities. During these decades, a movement was begun to unify labor and civil rights issues and to extend that cause through the nation. Such a movement began locally, however, with significant labor strikes among black sanitation workers in Memphis, Tennessee, and black hospital workers in Charleston, South Carolina.

The strikes at Memphis and Charleston were among previously unorganized, heavily exploited, poverty-level workers who desired safer working conditions, better pay, and job security. Both strikes were bitterly opposed by the power structure in the communities involved, yet both were supported by top civil rights leaders, including Ralph Abernathy and Coretta Scott King. The strikes also won the support of powerful unions, including the United AutoWorkers' Union, the United Steelworkers of America, the United Rubber Workers, and the Tobacco Workers' International Union. Further, the black community at large bolstered the strikers through marches, mass meetings, boycotts, and financial aid. Despite their overall success, both strikes received only limited support from white workers.

Latinos

This struggle for black equality was paralleled by the rising aspirations of Hispanic Americans, including Cubans, Puerto Ricans, and Mexicans. Although these groups were linked by similar ethnic roots and by a common language and religious heritage, their labor experiences differed. Mexican American laborers, in particular, advanced under the leadership of César Chávez, the son of migrant farm workers. In the early 1960's, pressure from Chávez and other activists helped force the end of the Bracero program, a government-sponsored importation of Mexican laborers that had undercut the agricultural labor market since the early part of World War II. In 1965, Chávez's leadership launched the Delano Grape Strike, which brought national attention to the plight of migrant farm workers; he subsequently became head of the newly formed United Farm Workers. Chávez continued to use strikes and national boycotts against fruit- and vegetable-raising agribusinesses to win concessions from California grape growers. Yet as important as the victories of the United Farm Workers were, in both an economic and a cultural sense, the union, in an increasingly urbanized nation, could not become a major organizational base among the primarily rural Mexican American population as a whole.

Asian Americans

In recent decades, Hispanic and black workers have continued their struggle for labor and ethnic recognition and have been joined in this effort by other minority labor groups. One of the most active since the early 1990's has been the Asian Pacific American Labor Alliance (APALA), founded in 1992 to address the needs of the Asian and Pacific Island American labor community. APALA's commitment to labor includes the empowerment of all Asian Pacific workers through unionization on a national level and the provision of national support for individual, local unionization efforts. The organization actively promotes the formation of AFL-CIO legislation to create jobs, ensure national health insurance, and reform labor law. It also supports national governmental action to prevent workplace discrimination against immigrant laborers and to prosecute perpetrators of racially motivated crimes.

These efforts of the Asian Pacific American Labor Alliance are certainly not the final word on the relevance of racial and ethnic diversity to the labor movement. Their successes have not resolved the debate about the role of immigrant and minority workers in American labor, but they have ensured the continuance of discussion. Indeed, many of the same issues that have captured the attention of American labor organizers since the late nineteenth century continue to spark debate: the means to secure humane treatment, higher wages, and other improvements in working conditions, and the role of racial and ethnic workers in those efforts.

Thomas J. Edward Walker and Cynthia Gwynne Yaudes

Core Resources

Labor Divided: Race and Ethnicity in United States Labor Struggles, 1835-1960 (Albany: State University of New York Press, 1990), edited by Robert Asher and Charles Stephenson, is a collection of case studies that explores both the potential divisiveness of racial and ethnic heterogeneity in the American labor force and the ability of these diverse groups to coalesce toward united action. *Culture, Gender, Race and U.S. Labor History* (Westport, Conn.: Greenwood Press, 1993), edited by Ronald C. Kent et al., is a collection of essays unified through their "recollection of dissident historical movements—when individuals and collectives attempted to change perceived reality, to confront injustices in the general polity, and seek alternative paths to a shared future." Robert D. Parmet's *Labor and Immigration in Industrial America* (Boston: Twayne, 1981) describes the restrictionist attitudes and actions used in the attempt to prevent solidarity between "native" and "foreign" workers and discusses Samuel Gompers's role in promoting immigration restriction and exclusion. *Unions and Immigrants: Organization and Struggle* (New York: Garland Press, 1991), edited by George E. Pozzetta, is a collection of essays that discuss patterns of immigrant assimilation into the United States, their effect on American industrialization, and their role in creating an American working class. Thomas J. Edward Walker's *Pluralistic Fraternity: The History of the International Worker's Order* (New York: Garland Press, 1991) examines the seemingly unique ability of Communist-backed labor organizations to create worker solidarity across racial and national lines.

See also: Asian Pacific American Labor Alliance; Bracero program; Brotherhood of Sleeping Car Porters; Delano Grape Strike; Employment among African Americans; Employment among American Indians; Employment among Asian Americans; Employment among Latinos; United Farm Workers.

Latinas

> **Significance:** Within American society, Latinas face assimilation challenges because of their membership in a marginalized group and because their traditional secondary role in their own households has made access to rights and privileges beyond their home at times unimaginable.

The Latina population of the United States is a geographically, socially, culturally, and economically diverse one that is bound more than in any other way by commonality of language. The U.S. Census Bureau lists "Hispanic" as a single and legitimate racial category within American borders and estimates that the total Hispanic population of the United States was about 22.1 million, or about 8.8 percent of the population, in 1992. The category "Hispanic" comprises anyone whose ancestry includes Spanish-speaking people residing in Mexico, the Caribbean, Central or South America, or Spain. The terms "Latino" and "Latina" also describe linguistic heritage and may also include speakers of Portuguese, such as from Brazil and Portugal, or francophone peoples from Caribbean islands (although these are not the foremost associations made with the terms).

Since the mid-1980's, which saw the emergence of an important and particularly strong literary movement by women of Hispanic heritage, the word "Latina" seems to have been deemed the most appropriate designation for women with such a background for two main reasons: because of its potential inclusion of several groups, and because it does not carry the burdensome, racially charged connotation of ethnic undesirability.

Mexican Americans

In the United States, three groups of Latinos are dominant in the population. In the Southwest, Mexican Americans (Chicanos) make up a substantial portion of the demographic group; in California, 25 percent of the state's residents are Latino, the majority of these Chicano. Additionally, throughout the Southwest, in states such as Texas, New Mexico, Arizona, and even Colorado, the Chicano population constitutes the largest nonwhite demographic group. This figure serves as the legacy of the U.S. annexation of these states from Mexico at the conclusion of the Mexican-American War (1846-1848). Most Chicano residents of those regions did not actually immigrate to the United States, but rather were assumed into the country and suddenly became "foreigners" in the place of their birth. Resonance from this historic event echoed into the feminine experience recounted up to 140 years later, in short stories by Chicana writers who talk about linguistic and social assimilation that was particularly difficult for women whose role was mainly domestic.

Cuban Americans

In Florida, specifically Miami, Cuban émigrés make up a substantial percentage of the overall Cuban population of the United States. Miami is only 90 miles from the Cuban capital of Havana, and the city continues to receive waves of exiles from this Communist regime, which was formed after the takeover by Fidel Castro in 1959. The presence of Cubans in the United States is attributable principally to political circumstances in their homeland. Even under the circumstances of political exile, Cuban women in the United States for more than a generation begin to face the same issues that confront other ethnic groups on arrival to a new country. They must decide to what level of assimilation they are willing to aspire, a difficulty compounded by the traditional domestic role for women in this culture, which keeps them out of the economic, educational, and political spheres of life in their adopted country.

Puerto Ricans

For Puerto Ricans, the decision to adopt a new homeland was, in a sense, made for them. When Spain lost the Spanish-American War of 1898, it ceded Cuba and Puerto Rico to the United States. Cuba became an independent state, but Puerto Rico was made into a "free associated state," that is, a colony of the United States. Beginning in the 1930's, Puerto Rican migration to the mainland has been a steady and ongoing process, with the result that in New York, the Puerto Rican community dominates the Spanish-speaking landscape, taking a substantial lead over immigrants from the Dominican Republic, who have also established a community within

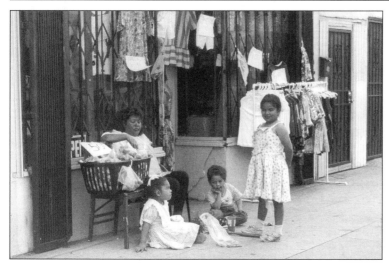

A Hispanic mother and her children gather at the side of the street in Los Angeles. The Latina's traditional role is one of wife and mother.

the city. In the Midwest, a number of immigrant groups of Hispanic origin have established thriving communities in cities such as Chicago and Milwaukee.

Marginalization of Latinas

Within this continually growing and dynamic establishment of Latin culture in North America, women had, until the 1960's, been relegated to a domestic role, as dictated by traditional practice. Such traditions developed under the influence of the Catholic church in Mexico and by Afro-Caribbean religion in Puerto Rico, Cuba, and the Dominican Republic, and they persisted in the new homeland. The Latina's role was that of wife and mother. Docile, self-abnegating, submissive, and subservient, she was reared to accept silently the confines of a patriarchal upbringing in preparation for a patriarchal marriage. When economic circumstance dictated, a woman was to work outside the home, but her primary responsibility was the wishes and demands of her husband and the service of her children. The women's movement in the United States in the 1970's gave Anglo women freedom and access to many institutions previously reserved only for men, but it fell short of opening those same doors for Latinas, whose culture was parallel to yet considerably different from that of their Anglo counterparts.

It is difficult to generalize about Hispanic culture in terms of social mores because of the rapidly evolving role of Latinas in society, both in Anglo-dominated North America and in Latin homelands, but some common features have been present among Latino groups. In 1976, a presentation to the Conference on Educational and Occupational Needs of Women discussed in detail the "cult of virginity" as a cornerstone of Latina upbringing, a cult that is undisputed in testimonials and in fictional accounts of short stories, novels, and plays. A young girl was reared to preserve and protect her chastity at all times. A woman who enjoyed sexuality was seen as "loose" or "modern," while one who adhered to the patriarchal prototype could be proud of her decorum and respect for traditional values and was considered a credit to her family and an honor to her household. The cult of the Virgin Mary in the Catholic Church played no small part in promoting this restrictive, often-silent role for women both in and outside of the home. A Latina who did not choose early marriage to a dominant man, who was not a virgin on the day of her marriage, or who had a knowledge and enjoyment of her sexuality could not live up to the ideal that would elevate her to an almost holy status within the family.

Education of a woman was often a release from her dependence on a man—her father, husband, brother, or son—and deemed a potentially dangerous pursuit, primarily from within the Latin culture but also from the Anglo perspective, which deemed manual labor the appropriate occupation for the Hispanic community. Education is the primary step in the emancipation of any group of people, especially a group at the margin of a dominant culture. Because of linguistic gaps, however, the education of Latinos requires another commitment to their assimilation into Anglo culture. In the 1960's, the Civil Rights movement and the War on Poverty waged by the administration of Lyndon B. Johnson yielded bilingual education opportunities that allowed many Latinas to enter the educational mainstream during that decade and to emerge some twenty years later with a dynamic new literary voice that described the Latina experience in the United States.

Helena Antolin Cochrane

Core Resources

Information about Latinas can be found in David T. Abalos's *The Latino Family and the Politics of Transformation* (Westport, Conn.: Praeger, 1993); *Breaking Boundaries: Latina Writing and Critical Readings* (Amherst: University of Massachusetts Press, 1989), edited by Asunción Horno-Delgado, Eliana Ortega, Nina M. Scott, and Nancy Saporta Sternbach; *Images and Identities: The Puerto Rican in Two World Contexts* (New Brunswick, N.J.: Transaction Books, 1987), edited by Asela Rodriguez de

Laguna; and Thomas Weyr's *Hispanic U.S.A.: Breaking the Melting Pot* (New York: Harper & Row, 1988).

See also: Cuban Americans; Ethnic identities of women; Family and socialization: Latinos; Immigrant women; Latinos in the United States; Women of color.

Latino literature

Significance: In the latter part of the twentieth century, Latino writers in North America established a strong literary reputation, enriching mainstream literature. Latino literature, characterized by impressive versatility, provides critical insights into the problematic issues of identity in terms of language, family, religion, education, acculturation, and artistic expression.

The term "Latino" includes a diversity of ethnic, racial, national, and cultural groups, with historic, economic, and social differences. However, these groups all share the use of the Spanish language. One of the most productive literary periods for Latinos began as a result of the cultural and political awakening that took place in the 1960's.

Two literary groups have been recognized: the native Hispanic and the migrated Hispanic. The definition for "migrated" and "native" are problematic, especially when dealing with Puerto Ricans, but both groups exhibit a polarized identity and a common sense of marginality. Through nostalgic remembrances and memories of their ancestors or their own countries, writers create an idealized homeland as a key source of reference. They write in Spanish, English, or in both, according to personal experiences and objectives. For example, Rosario Ferré, a leading Puerto Rican writer, wrote *The House on the Lagoon* (1995) in English; the migrated Puerto Rican Esmeralda Santiago translated her novel *When I Was Puerto Rican* (1993) into Spanish to reach more Latino readers.

Latino writers often indicate sociocultural hybridism and a need to preserve roots by including Spanish words and expressions in English text. Such switching from one language to another reflects the recognition of a double identity, Hispanic and Anglo, in New York-born Puerto Rican Nicholasa Mohr's *Nilda* (1973), New York-born Cuban Oscar Hijuelos's *Our House in the Last World* (1983), and Dominican Julia Alvarez's *How the García Girls Lost Their Accents* (1991). In these works, the rendering of growing up Latino in the United States includes self-exploration through writing as an act of artistic survival.

Puerto Rican Literature

Puerto Ricans migrated to the United States in search of a better life. Those who settled in New York became known as Nuyoricans. *A Puerto Rican in New York and Other Sketches* (1961), the landmark collection of essays and reminiscences by the Puerto Rican activist Jesús Colón, marks the birth of Nuyorican literature. Written in English with the inclusion of colloquial Puerto Rican Spanish, Colón's book depicts the brutal existence of young immigrants in the barrio. Piri Thomas, born in New York, documents dehumanizing life in urban streets and prison in the autobiographical classic *Down These Mean Streets* (1967).

Ed Vega's novel *The Comeback* (1985) offers a Puerto Rican interpretation of the American Dream. His *Casualty Report* (1991) chronicles the death of dreams in the face of racism, poverty, and crime. Victor Rodriguez's novel *Eldorado in East Harlem* (1992) depicts nostalgia for the island and dreams of making it on the mainland.

Nuyorican poetry, inspired by Caribbean rhythms of African origin, exhibits ethnic pride. One notable poet is Victor Hernández Cruz, who wrote *Mainland* (1973) and *By Lingual Wholes* (1982).

Cuban Americans

The major Cuban wave of immigration to the United States occurred after the 1959 Cuban Revolution. The older Cuban refugees, most of whom hoped to return home, wrote in Spanish of the exile experience. Younger writers who arrived in their teens or early twenties, such as Eliana Rivero, Achy Obejas, Rafael Catalá, and Dolores Prida, identified with the social struggles of minority groups. Spanish remained the primary language, and bilingual discourse captured their sense of a divided self, questioning the values of both cultures—the ancestral and the adopted one. Many of those who came on the 1980 Mariel boatlift focused on political and sexual persecution in Fidel Castro's Cuba and exile experiences, as exemplified in Reinaldo Arenas's works.

Virgil Suárez explores generational change in *Havana Thursdays: A Documentary Novel* (1995), noting that sorrow and joys transcend ethnicity. Roberto Fernández portrays the Cuban American experience in the satirical *Raining Backwards* (1988).

Hijuelos, born in New York, recalls the rich Afro-Cuban musical tradition in *The Mambo Kings Play Songs of Love* (1989). This novel, a 1990 Pulitzer Prize winner, was made into a film. Hijuelos depicts goodwill in ethnically divided urban America in *Mr. Ives' Christmas* (1995).

Latinas

Doubly marginalized as women and as Latinas, Latina writers approach myths of religion and marriage with a critical look at Catholicism. Prida, a Cuban American journalist, poet, playwright, actress, and director, addresses ethnic identity, assimilation, and women's sexuality with feminist satire—American style—in her musical *Beautiful Señoritas* (1977). Sandra María Esteves, a Nuyorican poet, painter, and actress, blends the realities of the urban poor with spiritual, blues, and women's poetics in *Bluestown Mockingbird Mambo* (1990). Alvarez explores life in exile and return to the homeland in the poems of *The Other Side-El Otro Lado* (1995).

Latino writers chronicling the Hispanic experience in the United States have taken center stage, receiving recognition through prizes and awards. The nature of the bilingual texts, giving voice to lives attempting to come to terms with intertwined cultures, has led to the consideration of a redefinition of the literary canon. Latino American writings, with differences of voice, style, and expression, have become part of American literary life, making it more representative and contributing to the cultural identity of North America.

Ludmila Kapschutschenko-Schmitt

Core Resources

Barrios and Borderlands: Cultures of Latinos and Latinas in the United States (New York: Routledge, 1994), edited by

Cuban American author Oscar Hijuelos is probably best known for his 1989 novel *The Mambo Kings Sing Songs of Love,* which was made into a 1992 film starring Armand Assante (left) and Antonio Banderas.

Denis Lynn Daly Heyck, presents readings from a variety of genres that form an excellent overview of the historical development of Latino literature. David T. Abalos's *Latinos in the United States* (Notre Dame, Ind.: University of Notre Dame Press, 1986) discusses literature as a means of politicizing and empowering Latino people. In *European Perspectives on Hispanic Literature of the United States* (Houston, Tex.: Arte Público Press, 1988), edited by Genevieve Fabre, American and European scholars compare visions of United States majority and minority cultures and identities, as reflected in literature.

See also: Code switching; Latinos and film; Latinos in the United States.

Latino stereotypes

To gain an understanding of the stereotyping of Latinos in the United States, one must consider issues of race and class inherent in the social structures of Latin American cultures as well as the multifaceted, often class-based biases held by various groups of Americans against persons of Hispanic origin. Historically, the roots of Latino stereotyping in the United States can be traced to early contact between Americans and Mexicans in what was to become the Southwest during the early nineteenth century. This initial interaction between cultures, frequently in the context of battle, left Anglo (non-Hispanic) Americans with both positive and negative images of the Spanish-speaking peoples they encountered: American settlers in Texas often characterized Mexicans as a backward people hampered by cowardice, laziness, and treachery, a perception that gained popular momentum during the Mexican-American War of 1846-1848; conversely, American explorers of modern-day California portrayed the Mexicans they encountered there as primitive, carefree, and romantic.

These early images of Mexican people endured through the twentieth century alongside modern stereotypes of Hispanics as illegal aliens with few interests or abilities other than unskilled labor, petty crime, gang violence, and the cultivation of large extended families. Much of this negative imagery can be attributed to generalized perceptions of nonwhite groups by a dominant white society; nevertheless, stereotypes specific to Latinos and Latino culture (such as the assumption that most Latinos are illegal aliens) abound. These stereotypes were perpetuated over time by white fears of crime, illegal immigration, welfare statism, and erosion of white majority status. In addition, white fears of increased Hispanic presence in the United States, and consequently white stereotypes of Latinos, were projected upon other minority groups such as African Americans, exacerbating tensions already present between these groups because of cultural differences and competition for jobs and housing.

Popular American stereotypes of Latinos have influenced and have been influenced by the self-perceptions of Hispanic Americans. Ethnic prejudices within Latino communities, originating in colonial caste systems that favored colonials over indigenous peoples, have contributed to coopting of Anglo American stereotypes by Hispanic Americans seeking to elevate their status in a white-dominated society by distinguishing themselves from other Latinos. For example, Hispanic peoples from South America and the Caribbean have resisted association with Mexicans because of the latter's association with illegal immigration, and Latinos in general historically have emphasized their Spanish heritage to dissociate themselves from "inferior" native peoples. Similarly, many Hispanic Americans have rejected the terms "Hispanic" and "Latino," arguing that they inaccurately portray Spanish-speaking peoples as a single ethnic group and thus encourage blanket stereotyping.

Increased emphasis upon ethnic heritage and identity in the 1960's accelerated the trend toward cultural distinctiveness among Hispanic Americans, sparking a renewed interest among young Latinos in preserving and nurturing previously disdained cultural traits and ethnic labels. For example, Mexican American youth adopted the term "Chicano," a contraction of the pejorative "Mexicano," as a manifestation of ethnic pride and often cultivated stereotypical portrayals of Mexicans as emotionally volatile, sexually aggressive, and given to excessive leisure. Ironically, the more redeeming traits of this cultural revival were often romanticized and exploited by white liberals, reviving paternalistic nineteenth century stereotypes of Latinos as "noble savages" best shielded from the "corrupting" influences of mainstream American society.   *Michael H. Burchett*

See also: Chicano movement; Hispanic vs. Latino; Latinas; Latino literature; Latinos and film; Latinos in the United States; Stereotype.

Latinos and film

> **Significance:** At the beginning of the twentieth century, the images of Latinos presented in American films were stereotypes heavily tinged with ethnic prejudice. Since then, Latino characters have acquired greater authenticity, and the superiority of Euro-Americans and their cultural values is no longer taken for granted.

Latinos portrayed in the early films were predominantly Mexicans or Mexican Americans, given the vast number of Westerns produced by the American film industry. Puerto Ricans, as an ethnic group, began to appear in later decades, generally in an urban setting.

Ethnocentrism in American Film

The target audience of the filmmakers in the first half of the twentieth century was predominantly white Anglo-Saxon and U.S.-born. Racial prejudice was the norm; nonwhites were not allowed to participate in film production and were unwelcome in motion picture theaters.

Western genre films were set in the Southwest, which is made up of the states ceded by Mexico in the Treaty of Guadalupe Hidalgo (1848). The narrative formula of nineteenth century dime novels was adapted to the screen with only minor variations. The Mexican-U.S. conflict was presented as a conflict of cultures: The Anglo (non-Hispanic) society values of thrift, hard work, and democracy were contrasted with the laziness, backwardness, and despotic power structures of Mexican society. In these films, the moral superiority of the Americans justified their overcoming the more primitive Hispanic society in their western expansion.

Some scholars distinguish the following types of Latino characters in early American films: the main male type is the greedy Mexican bandit, or greaser. The second type is the bumbling buffoon, usually an inept sidekick. Greasers or buffoons belong to the lower classes; not so the third type, the aristocratic caballero, a kind of Latino Robin Hood in colonial California, exemplified by Zorro, the Cisco Kid, and don Arturo Bodega. In the early 1930's, a fourth type appeared: the greaser gangster, who was a coward and a traitor. The fifth type is the Latin lover, a modern version of Don Juan.

Latinas had much more restricted roles: They existed in relationship to an Anglo hero. The usual types were the sexy cantina girl; the self-sacrificing, faithful señorita; and the vamp or seductress.

The 1930's

The heightened concern with social conditions brought about by the Great Depression was reflected in Hollywood's "social problem" films. The crude ethnic stereotypes of early films began to give way to stronger and more psychologically complex characters. The formula for these films was that sometimes American social institutions experienced problems that needed to be corrected by limited social change; therefore, the oppressed had to be patient and have faith that in the end justice would prevail.

The first Hispanic social problem film, *Bordertown* (1935), ends with the disillusioned Chicano protagonist returning to his barrio home, a suggestion that acceptance of the status quo is the right moral choice. However, the two best social problem films about Latinos, which were independently produced, *The Lawless* (1950) and *Salt of the Earth* (1954), portrayed Mexicans as real people who fought for their rights. Two important "historical message" films were *Juárez* (1939) and *Viva Zapata!* (1952), in which Mexican characters and Mexican history were treated much better than usual.

World War II

The Good Neighbor policy practiced by the United States toward Latin America during World War II as a way of securing alliances against Nazism resulted in two Disney animated films: *Saludos Amigos* (1943) and *The Three Caballeros* (1945), as well as a series of escapist Latin musicals, designed to improve hemispheric relations.

Many films depicting Latinos were produced in the 1980's. Edward James Olmos (left) and Lou Diamond Phillips star in the 1988 film *Stand and Deliver* based on the actual experience of a teacher in Los Angeles.

Some Latino actors were able to use stereotypical Hispanic roles, which were first played by American actors, as an effective vehicle to stardom. One of these actors was Lupe Vélez, the typical "Mexican Spitfire"; another was Leo Carrillo, who played gangsters and border bandits. When the star system began to dominate Hollywood, light-skinned Hispanic actors had to choose between being typecast in negative ethnic roles or anglicizing their names and their images to "reposition" themselves. Margarita Carmen Cansino became Rita Hayworth, and Raquel Tejada became Raquel Welch.

The 1960's and Beyond

In the 1960's, the liberalization of sexual mores, the emergence of the Civil Rights movement, and a growing Hispanic filmgoing audience profoundly affected the film industry. The classical Hispanic stereotypes were intensified by the explicit sex and violence of the new Westerns. Hollywood created new stereotypes such as the Hispanic avenger and youthful Hispanic gang member. Notable examples of the latter are *West Side Story* (1961) and *The Young Savages* (1961); *Boulevard Nights* (1979) and *Colors* (1988) treat the theme with more realism. Films of this genre usually presented Puerto Rican main characters as gang members involved in violent acts, thus reinforcing the notion that all Hispanics are law breakers.

In the 1970's and 1980's, two parallel phenomena fundamentally altered the position of Hispanics in the film industry. Members of the Chicano movement, determined to present their own view of the Chicano experience, began independently to produce and direct

documentaries and docudramas, and later, feature films, some of which were aired on television and some supported and distributed by Hollywood. Outstanding examples are *Alambrista!* (1977, Robert Young), *The Ballad of Gregorio Cortez* (1982, Moctesuma Esparza and Robert Young), *Seguín* (1981, Jesús Salvador Treviño), and *El Norte* (1983, Gregory Nava).

The second phenomenon, known as "Hispanic Hollywood," resulted from the greater participation of Latinos as producers and directors in Hollywood films since the 1980's, which was believed to be a result of the pressure exerted on the studios by Hispanic civil rights organizations to open more jobs to Latinos. *La Bamba* (1987), *Born in East L.A.* (1987), *The Milagro Beanfield War* (1987), and *Stand and Deliver* (1988) were some or its most successful products.

Puerto Rican Films

After several failed attempts by private companies and the government to develop film production on the island, Viguié Film Productions, founded in 1951, and the Division of Community Education, established in 1949, began to turn out an ever-increasing number of films. In the 1970's and 1980's, the political climate spurred the production of documentaries, some of which were made by Puerto Rican filmmakers working in Boston, New York, and Philadelphia. Among feature films, one of the finest is *Hangin' with the Home Boys* (1991), directed by Joseph B. Vásquez.   *Graciela Bardallo-Vivero*

Core Resources

Hispanics and United States Film: An Overview and Handbook (Tempe, Ariz.: Bilingual Press, 1994) and its companion volume, *A Biographical Handbook of Hispanics and United States Film* (Tempe, Ariz.: Bilingual Press, 1997), both by Gary D. Keller, offer a comprehensive review of the portrayal of Latinos in films and their participation in the film industry. Also useful are *The Latin Image in American Film* (Los Angeles: University of California, Los Angeles, Latin American Center Publications, 1980), by Allen L. Woll; *Chicanos and Film: Essays on Chicano Representation and Resistance* (New York: Garland, 1992), edited by Chon Noriega; and *Images of the Mexican American in Fiction and Film* (College Station: Texas A&M University Press, 1980), by Arthur G. Pettit.

See also: Latinas; Latino literature; Latino stereotypes; Latinos in the United States.

Latinos in the United States

> **Significance:** The large and growing Latino minority has had a significant impact on the United States, both culturally and economically. Although linked by language, Latinos are a diverse group, consisting of many different races and nations of origin.

The Latino minority, also often referred to as the Hispanic American sector of United States society, continues to increase proportionately to the total population with each succeeding decade. In 1996, some 25 million (9.7 percent) of residents of the United States traced their cultural, racial, or ethnic origins to some Spanish or Portuguese antecedents. Included in this group are recent immigrants, those who have arrived from Latin American nations both legally and illegally, and U.S. citizens whose families have been residents of the United States for many generations. The combination of this group's high birthrate coupled with the constant influx of immigrants into the United States has led to the prediction that by the year 2020 the Latino population will exceed 51 million, representing 15.7 percent of the estimated total U.S. population of 326 million. A July, 1998, federal government report estimates that Latinos will be the largest U.S. minority as early as the year 2005. Already the number of Latino schoolchildren in the United States exceeds that of the country's African American schoolchildren.

Nationalism
Nevertheless, the Latino population described above is far from a homogeneous cultural group. Its members can be characterized better by their diversity than by their similarity. Strong nationalistic identification with their countries or regions of origin serves to divide Mexican Americans from Cuban Americans from Puerto Ricans—and a host of other nationals—and to mitigate against their acting in concert politically, economically, or socially. For example, the large Cuban American colony in greater Miami, Florida, tends to be highly conservative politically, while the Puerto Ricans of New York state and the Mexican Americans of California generally are Democratic or liberal in political affiliation.

Race and Ethnicity
Members of the Latino community run the gamut of virtually every racial and ethnic group found in the world. The initial voyages of exploration and discovery of the Western Hemisphere by Europeans from Spain, England, Portugal, France, and the Netherlands led quickly to a racial amalgamation of these primarily Caucasian peoples with the bronze-skinned indigenous peoples mistakenly called "Indians" (under the false belief that they occupied the Asian continent). This admixture of races resulted in what has been referred to as the *mestizo*, soon to become the predominant racial entity throughout much of Central and South America, as well as what would ultimately become the U.S. Southwest.

When the European settlers in Mexico, Central America, and South America found that they could not successfully exploit the indigenous peoples in mining and agriculture, they turned to the importation of Africans, initially as indentured servants but ultimately as slaves. England, France, Portugal, Spain, and the Netherlands entered into an extensive and lucrative transhipment of Africans to the Western Hemisphere, where they were sold as labor for the mining of precious metals and the manufacture of sugar, cotton, rice, and a wide variety of other marketable crops.

Owners of black slaves bred their human chattels with other slaves as part of the existing economic system, and soon blacks—now typed as mulattos, quadroons, octoroons, and other racial mixtures—became part of a gene pool already containing a mixture of Caucasian and American Indian strains. In the course of the centuries that followed, Asians joined the heterogeneous racial population that spread throughout the Western Hemisphere. Chinese settled in substantial numbers along the borders of Mexico's northernmost states. Faced with persecution by warring factions during Mexico's Revolution of 1910, they migrated to the United States in large numbers.

Religion
When Europeans landed in what became Mexico in the sixteenth century, they encountered a highly civilized society that was in many ways more advanced than that

of Europe at the time. Spaniards, however, did not perceive or value the cultural sophistication of the newly discovered civilization—considering it their responsibility, on the contrary, to replace what they perceived as a heretic religion (in which the Aztec emperor was revered as a demigod) with Catholicism. The Europeans therefore adopted a program of ruthless destruction of what they considered idolatry. Similarly, in other parts of the continent, Portuguese, French, and English forced their own brands of Christianity on the natives whom they conquered and exploited. In the initial four centuries following the opening of the hemisphere, Catholicism and Protestantism became the dominant religions throughout North, South, and Central America.

Nevertheless, some indigenous peoples attempted to retain their identification with their old gods. Often this took the form of hiding their ancient sacred images behind the altars of European places of worship. Today, in more tolerant times, native and European religions are often practiced side by side, venerating gods and saints together, although by different names, as can be seen in contemporary Guatemala.

African slaves, seized and transported from their native lands to the Western Hemisphere, often brought their native religions with them, a source of comfort and hope under truly trying conditions. These African religions, sometimes modified by exposure to Christian sects, have open, active communicants in countries such as Haiti, Cuba, the Dominican Republic, and Brazil. Immigrants to the United States from these nations often bring these ancestral religious practices with them. These religious societies play an active role in the daily lives of their followers in the United States.

Language

Most second- and third-generation Latinos in the United States have a good command of English. Newcomers, however—like most immigrants from non-English-speaking nations—often lack basic English-language skills, severely limiting their ability to progress economically, politically, and socially. In a few areas, there are neighborhoods large and insular enough in their organization, where Spanish is so widely spoken among commercial establishments that English is unnecessary to carry on daily activities. Opportunities exist in most areas for newcomers to acquire basic English skills necessary to move into the mainstream of U.S. culture. Nevertheless, immigrants from isolated communities to the south, often still committed to tribal mores and language, find it difficult to blend into the larger culture. Some do not even speak Spanish but depend on their native dialects such as Mayan, Quechua, or Nahuatl for communication. Lacking either English or Spanish, quite often these small, essentially tribal, groups are subject to exploitation by unscrupulous business interests and often are forced to work for miserably low wages and threatened with being turned into U.S. immigration authorities if they seek redress under the law.

Mexico

Mexico leads all other nations both in the number of foreign-born living in the United States and in the quantity of new arrivals each year. With a population approaching 100 million, Mexico cannot provide enough jobs for those entering its workforce every year. This pool of surplus labor, combined with the availability of unskilled or entry-level jobs in the United States, has accounted for Mexico's primary position in terms of immigrant influx.

Included in this wave of new arrivals are members of Mexico's Indian communities, who speak a variety of tribal tongues as their first language. Primarily from rural areas and with a minimum of education, they are subject to economic exploitation to a greater degree than are other immigrants.

Mexicans have lived in areas in what is now the United

U.S. transportation secretary Federico Peña, a Latino, speaks in Spanish to fellow Latino riders on the New York subway. Latinos are a very diverse group, encompassing a number of races and a wide range of socioeconomic levels.

States before they were incorporated into the Union. Texas, New Mexico, Arizona, and California were under the Mexican flag until the Mexican-American War of 1846-1848. The Treaty of Guadalupe Hidalgo signed in 1848 between the two countries ceded this territory to the United States for $15 million—a cheap price for the Americans.

Puerto Rico

The United States defeated Spain in a brief war in 1898. In the ensuing Treaty of Paris, Spain gave up Puerto Rico, the Philippine Islands, and Guam to the victorious Americans. The United States also reluctantly agreed to the island of Cuba's independence under that treaty. However, the Americans retained sovereignty over Puerto Rico, viewing it as critical to U.S. defenses in the event of an attack from the Caribbean. In 1953, Puerto Rico achieved Commonwealth status, becoming a self-governing territory.

Following World War II, thousands of Puerto Ricans moved to the continental United States. In the immediate postwar period, airplane fares to the mainland sold for as little as seventy-five dollars. Almost three million Latin American citizens now live in the Northeast, mostly in the New York area. Because they are by law U.S. citizens, immigrants from the island are required only to demonstrate proof of birth in Puerto Rico before entering the continental United States.

Cuba

The takeover in 1959 of the island of Cuba by Fidel Castro and his supporters resulted in a mass exodus of much of the country's upper-class and middle-class professional and business interests, who did not agree with the imposition of what eventually became a socialist, Communist-supported, regime. Numbering close to one million, most of these refugees established themselves initially in the greater Miami area. In the spring of 1980, a second wave of refugees, called Marielitos and numbering perhaps one hundred thousand, managed to immigrate, with the permission of both the Castro regime and the administration of President Jimmy Carter, to the United States. The Cuban community, still centered in southern Florida, developed into a powerful economic and political force. In the 1990's, desperate Cubans continued to attempt to escape to the United States utilizing primitive boats, rafts, and even inner tubes.

Central America

Throughout the 1970's and 1980's, the countries of El Salvador, Guatemala, and Nicaragua were plagued by civil wars. As a consequence of those unsettled political times, between one million and one and a half million Central American refugees entered the United States. Nicaraguans had easy access, since the United States compared the leftist government of Daniel Ortega to

Latin American Migration to the United States

Year	Event	Impact
1910-1920	Mexican Revolution	Ten years of political and economic chaos force a quarter million Mexicans to resettle north of the U.S.-Mexico border.
1942-1964	Bracero program	Wartime labor shortages create a need for farmworkers that is filled by a Mexican and U.S. program that brings Mexicans to the United States to work the fields. The program establishes a pattern of migration of farmworkers.
1945-1950	Puerto Rican immigration	Following World War II, seventy-five-dollar economy air flights permit thousands of Puerto Ricans to resettle in the New York area. Since Puerto Ricans are U.S. citizens, no official entry papers are required.
1957-1960	Cuban Revolution	The takeover by the leftist Fidel Castro sends more than one million Cuban businesspeople and professionals to Miami.
1980-1990	Central American conflicts	Civil wars in El Salvador, Nicaragua, and Guatemala send more than one million political and economic refugees north, mostly to California and the East Coast.
1981-1990's	Mexican economic crises	The continuing erratic behavior of the Mexican economy, in addition to the inability of the country to provide employment for those entering the workforce each year, sends a constant wave of Mexican immigrants north to find work.

Castro's regime in Cuba. U.S. supporters of Salvadoran and Guatemalan refugees insisted on the same opportunity for victims of political oppression in those countries as well.

Most of these three groups have continued to remain in this country through one form of amnesty or another, concentrating in California, Florida, and communities on the Eastern seaboard.

Dominican Republic
As has been the case with so many of the small Caribbean island nations, the Dominican Republic cannot furnish enough job opportunities for all its citizens. Depending primarily on the export of sugar, some mining, and the attraction of cruise ships to its ports, this country, which shares the island of Hispaniola with Haiti, exports a substantial number of its working-class citizenry as well.

Many Dominican immigrants seeking illegal entry into the United States have used Puerto Rico as a staging area. False documents are obtained to establish a Puerto Rican identity. Most Dominican Republicans have gravitated to the New York area after arriving in the United States. The little island nation ranked fourteenth in recent figures on immigration to the United States.

Other Latin Americans
The balance of the Western Hemisphere's Latin American countries have contributed immigrants as well, although generally as smaller percentages of their total populations. For example, the drug trade and the resulting political unrest has caused Bolivians, Peruvians, and Colombians to seek asylum in the United States, which continues to represent a beacon of hope to citizens of those countries where political disorder or economic deprivation threaten the lives of their citizens.

Diversity vs. Unity
Despite the formidable growth of the Latino element in U.S. society, its diversity has prevented this group from reaching its potential as a unitary political force. Instead, the members of each particular ethnic entity have shown a preference to confine their organizational efforts to members of their own particular community—to establish themselves as Mexican American, Cuban American, or Puerto Rican political associations, with membership confined to their own ethnic group. Nevertheless, should there come a time when diverse organizations such as these come to realize the potential strength that their combined numbers represent, the fast-growing Latino contingent could become a major factor in determining the course of the future of the United States. In the interim, the Latino sons of immigrants have followed the paths of other racial and ethnic minorities in U.S. society in past decades. Many, showing a high degree of

individual initiative, have worked their way into positions of greater responsibility in business and the professions.

Carl Henry Marcoux

Core Resources
Robert M. Levine, in *Race and Ethnic Relations in Latin America and the Caribbean* (Metuchen, N.J.: Scarecrow Press, 1980), provides an extensive dictionary of Latino terms as well as their historical origins. Geoffrey Fox, in his *Hispanic Nation* (Secaucus, N.J.: Carol Publishing Group, 1996), argues that the old political and cultural differences that divided various Latino groups have already begun to diminish and that Latinos in the twenty-first century will become the United States' largest and most influential minority. Niles Hansen's *The Border Economy* (Austin: University of Texas Press, 1981) discusses the role of the Mexican immigrant in today's economic picture. Tad Szulc's *Fidel: A Critical Portrait* (New York: Avon Books, 1986) outlines the Castro takeover and the conflict with the American government. Raymond Carr, in *Puerto Rico: A Colonial Experiment* (New York: Vantage Books, 1984), furnishes background on the U.S. acquisition of Puerto Rico. Walter La Feber's *Inevitable Revolutions* (New York: W. W. Norton, 1983) analyzes the U.S. role in Central American politics.

See also: Chicano movement; Cuban Americans; Cuban Revolution; Dominican Americans; Family and socialization: Latinos; Guadalupe Hidalgo, Treaty of; Haitians and Haitian refugees; Hispanic vs. Latino; Illegal aliens; Little Havana; Mariel boatlift; Mestizo; Miami riots of 1980; Missions, missionaries, and American Indians; Puerto Rico; Sanctuary movement; Self-identification among Latinos; Slavery: history.

Lau v. Nichols

> **Significance:** On January 21, 1974, the U.S. Supreme Court ruled that school districts must provide bilingual education to limited-English-speaking students.

In 1954, the Supreme Court ruled in *Brown v. Board of Education* that the Fourteenth Amendment to the U.S. Constitution forbade school systems from segregating students into separate schools for only whites or African Americans. The decision effectively overturned a previous Court ruling, in *Plessy v. Ferguson* (1896), that such facilities could be "separate but equal." Instead of desegregating, however, Southern school systems engaged in massive resistance to the Court's order during the next decade. Congress then passed the Civil Rights Act of

1964, which prohibits many types of discrimination. Title VI of the law bans discrimination by recipients of federal financial assistance, including school systems.

Chinese-Speaking Students

In 1965, Congress adopted the Immigration and Nationality Act, under which larger numbers of Asian immigrants arrived in the United States than ever before. Their non-English-speaking children were enrolled in public schools. In the San Francisco Unified School District, students were required to attend school until sixteen years of age, but in 1967, 2,856 students could not adequately comprehend instruction in English. Although 433 students were given supplemental courses in English on a full-time basis and 633 on a part-time basis, the remaining 1,790 students received no additional language instruction. Nevertheless, the state of California required all students to graduate with proficiency in English and permitted school districts to provide bilingual education, if needed. Except for the 433 students in the full-time bilingual education program, Chinese-speaking students were integrated in the same classrooms with English-speaking students but lacked sufficient language ability to derive benefit from the instruction. Of the 1,066 students taking bilingual courses, only 260 had bilingual teachers.

Some parents of the Chinese-speaking children, concerned that their children would drop out of school and experience pressure to join criminal youth gangs, launched protests. Various organizations formed in the Chinese American community, which in turn made studies, issued proposals, circulated leaflets, and tried to negotiate with the San Francisco Board of Education. When the board refused to respond adequately, a suit was filed in federal district court in San Francisco on March 25, 1970. The plaintiffs were Kinney Kinmon Lau and eleven other non-English-speaking students, mostly U.S. citizens born of Chinese parents. The defendants were Alan H. Nichols, president of the San Francisco Board of Education, the rest of the Board of Education, and the San Francisco Board of Supervisors.

Findings and Rulings

On May 25, 1970, the Office for Civil Rights (OCR) of the U.S. Department of Health, Education, and Welfare issued the following regulation pursuant to its responsibility to monitor Title VI compliance: "Where inability to speak and understand the English language excludes national-origin minority group children from effective participation in the educational program offered by a school district, the district must take affirmative steps to rectify the language deficiency in order to open its instructional program to these students." OCR had sided with the Chinese-speaking students.

One day later, the court ruled that the school system was violating neither Title VI nor the Fourteenth Amendment; instead, the plaintiffs were characterized as asking for "special rights above those granted other children." Lawyers representing the Chinese Americans then appealed, this time supported by a friend-of-the-court brief filed by the U.S. Department of Justice. On January 8, 1973, the Court of Appeals also ruled adversely, stating that there was no duty "to rectify appellants' special deficiencies, as long as they provided these students with access to the same educational system made available to all other students." The appeals court claimed that the children's problems were "not the result of law enacted by the state . . . but the result of deficiency created by themselves in failing to learn the English language."

On June 12, 1973, the Supreme Court agreed to hear the case. Oral argument was heard on December 10, 1973. On January 21, 1974, the Supreme Court unanimously overturned the lower courts. Justice William O. Douglas delivered the majority opinion, which included the memorable statement that "There is no equality of treatment merely by providing students with the same facilities, textbooks, teachers, and curriculum; for students who do not understand English are effectively foreclosed from any meaningful education." The Court returned the case to the district court so that the school system could design a plan of language-needs assessments and programs for addressing those needs. In a concurring opinion, Chief Justice Warren E. Burger and Justice Harry A. Blackmun observed that the number of underserved non-English-speaking, particularly Chinese-speaking, students was substantial in this case, but they would not order bilingual education for "just a single child who speaks only German or Polish or Spanish or any language other than English."

The Supreme Court's decision in *Lau* ultimately resulted in changes to enable Chinese-speaking students to obtain equal educational opportunity in San Francisco's public schools, although it was more than a year before such changes began to be implemented. The greatest impact, however, has been among Spanish-speaking students, members of the largest language-minority group in the United States.

Recognition of Bilingualism

Subsequently, Congress passed the Equal Educational Opportunities Act in 1974, a provision of which superseded *Lau* by requiring "appropriate action to overcome language barriers that impede equal participation," which a federal district court later applied to the need for new methods to deal with speakers of "Black English" in *Martin Luther King, Jr., Elementary School Children v. Michigan Board of Education* (1979). Also in 1974, the Bilingual Education Act of 1968 was amended to provide more federal funds for second-language instruction so that school districts could be brought into compliance with *Lau*. Bilingualism was further recognized when Congress passed the Voting Rights Act of 1975, which established guidelines for providing ballots in the languages of certain minority groups.

In 1975, OCR established informal guidelines for four bilingual programs that would enable school districts to come into compliance with the Supreme Court ruling. The main requirement was first to test students to determine language proficiency. Students with no English proficiency at all were to be exposed to bilingual/bicultural programs or transitional bilingual education programs; secondary schools also had the option of providing "English as a second language" or "high intensive language training" programs. If a student had some familiarity with English, these four programs would be required only if testing revealed that the student had low achievement test scores.

Because the OCR guidelines were not published in the *Federal Register* for public comment and later modification, they were challenged on September 29, 1978, in the federal district court of Alaska (*Northwest Arctic School District v. Califano*). The case was settled by a consent decree in 1980, when the federal agency agreed to publish a "Notice of Proposed Rulemaking"; however, soon after Ronald Reagan took office as president, that notice was withdrawn. By 1985, a manual to identify types of language discrimination was compiled to supersede the 1975 guidelines, but it also was not published in the *Federal Register* for public comment. Meanwhile, methods for educating limited-English-speaking students evolved beyond the OCR's original conceptions, and further litigation followed. In 1981, a U.S. circuit court ruled in *Castañeda v. Pickard* that bilingual educational programs are lawful when they satisfy three tests: (1) the program is recognized by professionals as sound in educational theory; (2) the program is designed to implement that theory; and (3) the program actually results in overcoming language barriers.

During the presidency of Ronald Reagan, civil rights monitoring focused more on "reverse discrimination" than on violations of equal educational opportunities. Congressional hearings were held to goad OCR into action. Although in 1991 OCR's top priority was equal educational opportunities for national-origin minority and Native American students with limited-English proficiency (LEP) or non-English proficiency (NEP), results were difficult to discern, and a movement to make English the official language of the United States (the "English-only" movement) threatened to overturn *Lau* and related legislation. Moreover, by the late 1990's the controversy over bilingual education had revived, as many teachers, parents, policymakers, and legisla-

tors—including a significant number of Latinos—acknowledged the disappointing results of bilingual programs and sought solutions through legislation. In 1998, for example, California voted to curtail bilingual education by passing Proposition 227. Such measures were perceived as appropriate means of forcing quick English-language acquisition by some, but as simplistic and counterproductive by others. *Michael Haas*

Core Resources
Barry L. Bull, Royal T. Fruehling, and Virgie Chattergy's *The Ethics of Multicultural and Bilingual Education* (New York: Columbia University Teachers College Press, 1992) contrasts how liberal, democratic, and communitarian approaches to education relate to bilingual and multicultural education. Carlos J. Orlando and Virginia P. Collier's *Bilingual and ESL Classrooms: Teaching in Multicultural Contexts* (New York: McGraw-Hill, 1985) discusses the need for bilingual education, alternative approaches available, and resources required. The U.S. Commission on Civil Rights's *A Better Chance to Learn: Bilingual-Bicultural Education* (Washington, D.C.: Author, 1975) assesses the national impact of *Lau*; contains the text of the Supreme Court decision and related documents. L. Ling-chi Wang's "*Lau v. Nichols*: History of the Struggle for Equal and Quality Education," in *Asian-Americans: Social and Psychological Perspectives* (Palo Alto, Calif.: Science & Behavior Books, 1980), edited by Russell Endo, Stanley Sue, and Nathaniel N. Wagner, describes how the *Lau* case was pursued, especially the resistance to implementation.

See also: Bilingual education; Bilingual Education Act; *Brown v. Board of Education*; Civil Rights Act of 1964; English-only and official English movements; Immigration and Nationality Act of 1965.

League of United Latin American Citizens

> **Significance:** The League of United Latin American Citizens is one of the oldest Hispanic advocacy organizations.

The League of United Latin American Citizens (LULAC) was formed in order to unite all Latin American organizations under one title. In 1927, the main Latin American groups were the Sons of America, the Knights of America, and the League of Latin American Citizens, and there were other less well-known groups. The Sons of America had councils in Sommerset, Pearsall, Corpus

Christi, and San Antonio, Texas; the Knights of America had a council in San Antonio; the League of Latin American Citizens had councils in Harlingen, Brownsville, Laredo, Peñitas, La Grulla, McAllen, and Gulf, Texas.

As more Anglo-Americans moved into Texas in the early 1800's, persons of Spanish or Mexican descent experienced open discrimination and segregation that placed them in the position of second-class citizens. They had been under the rule of six different countries before Texas entered the Union in 1845. Most continued to live and work as they always had, without being assertive about their rights. As time progressed, many Hispanics found that prejudice and discrimination were becoming less tolerable. Groups began to form to give more impact to requests that these practices cease. The Sons of America Council No. 4 in Corpus Christi, led by Ben Garza, originated a unification plan, believing that if all Hispanic organizations would regroup into one strong, unified, and vocal organization, more attention would be brought to the plight of those who were being discriminated against.

On August 14, 1927, delegates from the Sons of America, the Knights of America, and smaller groups met in Harlingen, Texas, to form LULAC. The resolution that was presented was adopted by those in the meeting. It was expected that the leaders of the major groups—Alonso Perales, Luz Saenz, José Canales, and Juan Lozano of the Rio Grande Valley of south Texas—would be invited by the president general of the Sons of America to begin the unification process. In response to concerns about the merger expressed by some members, Council No. 4 of the Sons of America drafted an agreement between itself and the Knights of America to unite. These two groups waited a year for the merger to be completed. Perales, president general of the Latin American League, stayed in close contact with Garza to maintain interest in the merger among the three main groups. However, the president general of the Sons of America never called the convention. After the long wait, Council No. 4 withdrew from the Sons of America on February 7, 1929. Participants at this meeting again voted to have a general convention for the purpose of unification. On February 17, 1929, invitations were sent to all the groups to meet in Corpus Christi, Texas, to vote on the merger.

Along with interested members of the Hispanic groups, Douglas Weeks, a professor at the University of Texas, attended not only to study the merger but also to open the convention as a nonaligned attendee. Ben Garza was elected chairman pro tem. His popularity as an energetic and fair civic leader made him a good spokesperson for the new group. The assembly had to choose a chairman, plan a single constitution, and select a name that would encompass the goals of the previously

separate groups. The committee chosen to select a name included Juan Solis and Mauro Machado of the Knights of America, Perales and Canales of the Latin American League, E. N. Marin and A. de Luna of Corpus Christi, and Fortunio Treviño of Alice, Texas. Machado, of the Knights of America, proposed "United Latin American Citizens." This was amended to read "League of United Latin American Citizens," which was seconded by Canales. On February 17, 1929, LULAC formally came into being at Corpus Christi, Texas.

The naming committee undertook other proposals before coming back to the general convention. Canales proposed a motto, "All for One and One for All," as a reminder of their purpose in uniting and as a basis for their future activities. They set some basic rules to guide the league until the constitutional convention could be held. This meeting was called for May 18 and 19, 1929, with an executive committee made up of Garza, M. C. Gonzales as secretary, and Canales and Saenz as members at large. On May 18, the first meeting under the new title was called. The constitution proposed by Canales was adopted, and new officers were elected. The officers were Garza, president general; Gonzales, vice president general; de Luna, secretary general; and Louis C. Wilmot of Corpus Christi, treasurer general. George Washington's prayer was adopted from the ritual of the Sons of America, and the U.S. flag was adopted as the group's official flag. Now, in union, the new group could work to remove the injustices that had been building for many years. LULAC was chartered in 1931 under the laws of the State of Texas and later in New Mexico, Arizona, California, and Colorado, as other councils were formed. LULAC began issuing *LULAC Notes*, but in August, 1931, the first issue of *LULAC News* was published. In the 1990's, this magazine carried the subtitle *The Magazine for Today's Latino*.

Evolution

In the formative years, auxiliaries were started by women whose husbands were active LULAC members. In August, 1987, LULAC amended its constitution to admit women into the organization. Between 1937 and 1938, junior LULAC councils were formed under the sponsorship of adult councils. In 1940, LULAC councils peaked, but with the beginning of World War II, the councils weakened with the departure of the men to military service. In 1945 and 1946, LULAC began to make great strides as educated, trained men returned from the service. Prestigious positions were filled by Hispanics and discrimination lessened. Non-Hispanics were joining, and LULAC was moving toward its objectives.

When the Civil Rights movement of the 1960's began, other Hispanic groups with a more militant response to discrimination began to form. Leaders such as the charismatic preacher, Reies López Tijerina in New Mexico and Rodolfo Gonzales in Denver marched in protest of the treatment Hispanics were receiving. César Chávez led farm groups in California on peaceful marches, which frequently erupted into violent confrontations as the number of militant members rose. LULAC did not totally support all these movements. It preferred mediation to resolve serious disagreements and education for all Hispanics as better ways of blending peacefully into the U.S. mainstream.

LULAC has evolved to stress education. Parents are encouraged to prepare their children well to enter school. English is encouraged as the primary language, Spanish as the second language. As students mature, they are encouraged to finish high school and enter college. For those who aspire to higher learning, LULAC sponsors many scholarships; it also offers other forms of financial aid and counseling. LULAC Education Centers are located in sixty cities in seventeen states to provide this help. With corporate and federal aid, these centers have made it possible for disadvantaged Hispanic American youth to become productive members of their American communities. *Norma Crews*

Core Resources
Latinos and the Political System (Notre Dame, Ind.: University of Notre Dame Press, 1988), edited by F. Chris Garcia, discusses some of the political problems that prompted the formation of organizations such as LULAC. Mario T. Garcia's *Mexican-Americans: Leadership, Ideology, and Identity 1930-1960* (New Haven, Conn.: Yale University Press, 1989) is a thorough treatise on Hispanic assimilation into the mainstream of U.S. business and community. Earl Shorris's *Latinos: A Biography of the People* (New York: W. W. Norton, 1992) is a collection of information on Hispanics in the United States, and a general overview of those Hispanics who immigrated and settled during the 1900's.

See also: Bilingual Education Act; Bracero program; Chicano movement; Delano Grape Strike; Latinos in the United States; Mexican American Legal Defense and Education Fund; Operation Wetback; *Plyler v. Doe*; United Farm Workers.

Liberator, The

Significance: The weekly newspaper *The Liberator* served as a major vehicle for advocacy of the immediate abolition of slavery.

The initial publication of white abolitionist William Lloyd Garrison's weekly newspaper, *The Liberator*, in Boston, on January 1, 1831, helped to transform the antislavery movement in the United States. It symbolized the beginning of a radical effort to abolish slavery and secure equal rights for African Americans throughout the country.

Garrison and his newspaper were products of the religious revival called the Second Great Awakening, which transformed Protestant theology in the United States. The Awakening engendered moral reform movements in New England and other parts of the North during the early decades of the nineteenth century. Unlike their Calvinist predecessors, those who engaged in moral reform assumed that human beings, by their actions, could create a perfect society and bring about the millennial return of Jesus Christ. In his perception of the sinfulness and criminality of slaveholding, which he believed deprived both slaves and masters of a chance for salvation, Garrison went beyond most of the other reformers of his time.

Garrison's Beliefs
Garrison was born in Newburyport, Massachusetts, in 1805. Deserted by his seafaring father in 1808, Garrison was raised in poverty by his devout Baptist mother, who instilled in him her strict moral code. At thirteen years of age, he apprenticed with a printer at the *Newburyport Herald*, where he learned the newspaper business. By 1828, he was in Boston as the editor of *The National Philanthropist*, advocating the temperance movement. Garrison also supported what he and others perceived to be the antislavery efforts of the American Colonization Society (ACS), founded in 1817. As the dominant antislavery organization of the 1820's, the ACS advocated the gradual abolition of slavery, combined with the colonization of free black Americans in Africa.

It was Garrison's decision, later in 1828, to join Quaker abolitionist Benjamin Lundy in Baltimore as coeditor of Lundy's weekly newspaper, *The Genius of Universal Emancipation*, that led to *The Liberator* and a more radical antislavery movement. In Baltimore, Garrison observed slavery in practice. Influenced by members of Baltimore's African American community, Garrison came to believe that gradualism would never end the "peculiar institution." African American influences also led Garrison to conclude that the ACS perpetuated a racist assumption that blacks and whites could not live together as equals in the United States.

Garrison's increasing militancy made cooperation with the more conservative Lundy difficult. Garrison's radicalism also led to his imprisonment for libel in the Baltimore jail and to his decision to return to New England to begin his own antislavery newspaper.

Garrison Makes a Statement

In the first issue of *The Liberator*, Garrison proclaimed his conversion to immediate abolitionism. Harshly condemning slaveholders as sinners and thieves, he pointed out that one did not ask sinners to stop sinning gradually or require that thieves gradually stop committing crimes. Christian morality and justice, he insisted, required that slaveholders immediately and unconditionally free their bondspeople.

Garrison was not the first to advocate immediate emancipation. What was significant was his rejection of moderation and his linkage of immediatism with a demand that the rights of the formerly enslaved be recognized in the United States. In his most famous statement, Garrison proclaimed, "I am in earnest—I will not equivocate—I will not excuse—I will not retreat a single inch— AND I WILL BE HEARD."

The initiation of *The Liberator* also is significant for its reflection of biracial cooperation in the antislavery movement. Although Garrison, like other white abolitionists, never entirely escaped the racial prejudices of his time, he and his newspaper enjoyed the strong support of African Americans. Wealthy black abolitionist James Forten of Philadelphia provided crucial financial support to *The Liberator* in its early years. During the same period, Garrison employed black subscription agents, and three-quarters of the newspaper's subscribers were black. In Boston, where white antiabolition sentiment could produce violent confrontations, Garrison enjoyed the physical protection of African Americans.

The Paper's Effects

Meanwhile, Garrison and *The Liberator* played an essential role in the formation of the American Anti-Slavery Society (AASS). Founded in December, 1833, under the leadership of Garrison and New York City businessmen Arthur and Lewis Tappan, the AASS united immediate abolitionists in the United States during most of the 1830's. Reflecting the pacifistic views of Garrison, the Tappans, and others, the society pledged in its Declaration of Sentiments (modeled on the Declaration of Independence) to use peaceful means to bring about the immediate, uncompensated emancipation of all U.S. slaves, without colonization. Promoted by *The Liberator*, dozens of other antislavery newspapers, and thousands of antislavery pamphlets, the AASS grew exponentially. By 1838, it had a membership in the North of approximately one-quarter million and as many as 1,350 local affiliates.

By the late 1830's, however, internal tensions were tearing the AASS apart. The essential problem was that Garrison and his closest New England associates, including Maria Weston Chapman, Wendell Phillips, and Henry C. Wright, had concluded that the spirit of slavery had so permeated the nation that the North—not just the South—had to be fundamentally changed.

Although other abolitionists were reaching similar conclusions in the late 1830's, many of them objected to the specific policies advocated in the columns of *The Liberator* to effect those changes. In particular, an increasingly unorthodox Garrison antagonized church-oriented abolitionists by his wholesale condemnation of organized religion. He also seemed to threaten traditional concepts of patriarchy by his championing of women's rights and, specifically, female equality within the AASS. He appeared to threaten government through his advocacy of nonresistance, the pacifist doctrine that physical force is never justified, even in self-defense or on behalf of law and order. He frustrated those who desired a separate abolitionist political party by condemning political parties as inherently corrupt.

As a result, the abolitionist movement splintered in 1840. Garrison, his New England associates, and a few others across the North retained control of the AASS, but the great majority of abolitionists left the organization. Lewis Tappan began the American and Foreign Anti-Slavery Society, which, until 1855, maintained a church-oriented antislavery campaign. Politically inclined abolitionists organized the Liberty Party. By the 1850's, a majority of non-Garrisonian abolitionists had come to support the Republican Party, which advocated neither immediate abolition nor equal rights for African Americans.

In the 1840's and 1850's, Garrison, in *The Liberator* and elsewhere, continued to promote anticlericalism, women's rights, and nonresistance, as well as immediate emancipation and equal rights for African Americans. Although he and his former AASS colleagues remained in agreement on many points, there was also considerable mutual antagonism. Chances for reconciliation among them diminished in 1842, when Garrison began to call on the people of the North to dissolve the Union. He argued that it was Northern support that kept slavery in existence in the South, implying that, when the North withdrew its support through disunion, the slaves could free themselves. His abolitionist critics responded that disunion was tantamount to the North's exculpating itself from the slavery issue.

When the South, rather than the North, initiated disunion in 1860 and 1861, however, changing circumstances caused Garrison to draw back from some of his more radical positions. He compromised his pacifism and his opposition to party politics by supporting Republican president Abraham Lincoln's war to preserve the Union and free the slaves. When the war ended successfully for the North and slavery was formally abolished, Garrison, old, tired, and seeking vindication, announced that his work was done—although it was clear that black equality had not been achieved with the end of slavery. The last issue of *The Liberator* rolled off its press on December 29, 1865.   *Stanley Harrold*

Core Resources

Robert H. Abzug's *Cosmos Crumbling: American Reform and the Religious Imagination* (New York: Oxford University Press, 1994) demonstrates Garrison's radicalism in the context of early nineteenth century U.S. Protestantism. Lawrence J. Friedman's *Gregarious Saints: Self and Community in American Abolitionism, 1830-1870* (New York: Cambridge University Press, 1982) includes a description of Garrison's circle of abolitionists and his leadership style. Aileen S. Kraditor's *Means and Ends in American Abolitionism: Garrison and His Critics on Strategy and Tactics, 1834-1850* (New York: Vintage Books, 1970) is a probing analysis of Garrison's tactics in comparison with those of other abolitionists. Walter M. Merrill's *Against Wind and Tide: A Biography of William Lloyd Garrison* (Cambridge, Mass.: Harvard University Press, 1963) is the most detailed biography of Garrison to date. James Brewer Stewart's *William Lloyd Garrison and the Challenge of Emancipation* (Arlington Heights, Ill.: Harlan Davidson, 1992) explores the personal choices that initiated and maintained Garrison's career as an abolitionist. John L. Thomas's *The Liberator: William Lloyd Garrison, A Biography* (Boston: Little, Brown, 1963) portrays Garrison as a romantic individualist who defied authority for psychological reasons.

See also: Abolition; American Anti-Slavery Society; Lincoln-Douglas debates; Proslavery argument; Turner's slave insurrection.

Lincoln-Douglas debates

The most famous and consequential campaign debates in American history, the dialogue between Abraham Lincoln and Stephen A. Douglas, clarified how Democratic and Republican conceptions of justice differed and laid a foundation for a renewed national commitment to principles of freedom.

In 1858, Lincoln, a leader of Illinois' recently formed Republican Party and a former one-term member of the House of Representatives, ran for the Senate against incumbent Douglas. A national leader of the Democratic Party, Douglas based his campaign, and his future presidential ambitions, on "the great fundamental principle" of "self-government," or "popular sovereignty." People of the federal territories, he argued, had the right to vote for or against allowing slavery, as they saw fit, and no outsiders had a right to interfere with their decisions. To Douglas, no principle was more fundamental to Ameri-

can democracy than this right of self-government, even if it meant countenancing slavery.

Lincoln viewed Douglas's position as a repudiation of the principles of freedom enshrined in the Declaration of Independence, which, if they meant anything, meant that slavery was wrong. Slavery had existed in the nation since before it began, but Lincoln echoed Thomas Jefferson in recognizing that the founders had been keenly aware of its incompatibility with principles of freedom and that they hoped for its eventual end. For Lincoln and other Republican Party leaders, the issue of extending slavery into the territories—the dominant political controversy of the 1850's—demanded that the nation make a choice. It must either recommit itself to the principles of freedom by refusing to extend this odious institution to new areas or adopt a position of moral neutrality toward slavery, thereby allowing it to spread into the territories and eventually into the free states. At stake was not only the fate of African Americans but also the freedom of all Americans. If the American credo

Slavery was discussed during the 1858 debates between Abraham Lincoln (pictured standing in this print from an early 1900's book) and Senator Stephen A. Douglas.

were to abandon the idea that "all men are created equal," tyranny of one form or other would surely follow.

These issues focused the seven debates that Lincoln and Douglas conducted throughout Illinois between August and October of 1858. In a format quite unlike modern political "debates," one man spoke for an hour, the other responded for an hour and a half, then the first finished with a half-hour rejoinder. They alternated speaking first.

Although Douglas was reelected to the Senate (the actual vote was by state legislators, who had pledged themselves to either Lincoln or Douglas in their own election campaigns), Lincoln's forceful defense of the antislavery position won him fame outside Illinois and greatly contributed to his election to the presidency in 1860. His elevation to the presidency, in turn, marked the political defeat of Douglas's position of moral indifference to slavery and led to a national reaffirmation that American justice would remain rooted in freedom and equality.

Joseph M. Bessette

See also: Abolition; Civil War; Free-Soil Party; Kansas-Nebraska Act; *Liberator, The*; Missouri Compromise; Proslavery argument; *Scott v. Sandford*; Slavery: history.

Literacy tests

In an election, a citizen is expected to be literate enough to read a printed ballot in order to cast a vote. It is unnecessary to exclude illiterates from voting, as their marks are likely to be random and therefore will not influence the outcome of an election.

After the Civil War (1861-1865), tests for literacy were adopted as voting requirements in many states. The aim was to exclude marginally literate persons from voting, in particular African Americans and recent immigrants. The way to exclude marginally literate persons was either to reject those applying to register to vote who had errors on their application forms or to ask such persons to explain esoteric provisions in the Constitution of the United States or other text to a voter registrar, who would turn down their application.

The Voting Rights Act of 1965 suspended all literacy tests in states in which less than 50 percent of the voting-age population had been registered or had voted in the 1964 election. The law had an immediate impact. By the end of 1965, a quarter of a million new black voters had been registered, one-third by federal examiners. In the Voting Rights Act of 1970, Congress prohibited the use of all literacy tests and similar tests as preconditions for voter registration.

Michael Haas

See also: Poll tax; Voting Rights Act of 1965.

Little Bighorn, Battle of the

Significance: The stunning defeat of the Seventh Cavalry on June 25-26, 1876, unleashed relentless pursuit of the victorious Indians, culminating in their surrender, their exile to reservation life, and the end of traditional Plains culture.

The Treaty of Fort Laramie (1868) guaranteed the Sioux a permanent reservation that encompassed all of present South Dakota west of the Missouri River and from which encroaching white settlers were forbidden. The Sioux were also guaranteed the right to hunt in a larger unceded territory, also closed to whites. About three thousand free-roaming Sioux lived on these lands and despised the thought of reservation life. Crazy Horse and Sitting Bull were the most famous of these Sioux.

Background to the Battle

The terms of the treaty, however, were blatantly violated. From 1871 to 1874, surveying parties with army escort trespassed on both the reservation and unceded territory, charting routes and finding gold in the sacred Black Hills. By mid-1875 hordes of white prospectors and adventurers were poised to invade Sioux territory, held back only by the army.

The government tried through persuasion and threats to induce the Sioux to sell the Black Hills but were unequivocally rebuffed. This led President Ulysses S. Grant to devise a plan to justify a war against the Sioux. Their defeat would remove the free-roaming Sioux from the unceded territory and place them on the reservation. The Black Hills and unceded territory would be opened for settlement and prospecting. The plan began with a decision not to enforce the ban on prospectors entering the Black Hills. Lies about Sioux misdeeds and crimes were publicly circulated. Then in December, 1875, the government gave an ultimatum to the free-roaming Northern Cheyenne and Sioux to surrender at their agencies by January 31, 1876, or be forced there by military action.

The Indians bitterly resented this ultimatum. It violated the 1868 treaty, and the free-roaming groups were determined to maintain their traditional way of life and not go to reservations. Resentment was further fueled by a famine on the reservation caused largely by negligence and graft in the distribution of guaranteed rations. In addition, the sale of firearms to hunt needed food was prohibited. The Platte Sioux had been arbitrarily removed from their reservation to save on freight charges for their rations.

General George Custer (upper right) died in the Battle of the Little Bighorn. Although the Sioux were victorious, the resulting Euro-American backlash ended their way of life.

Annihilation of Custer's Forces

The Indians ignored the ultimatum, and the army was ordered to capture or disperse them. On June 24 the Seventh Cavalry, under the command of General George Armstrong Custer, found an Indian camp (predominantly Sioux but including some Northern Cheyenne and Arapaho) on the south bank of the Little Bighorn River. In the mid-afternoon of June 25, 1876, the Battle of the Little Bighorn commenced. Major Marcus Reno and his three companies of 175 soldiers and Indian scouts attacked the southern end of the camp. Reno aborted the attack, however, when he realized the number of Indians he would engage. He took cover in timber along the river but was forced to withdraw to a more defensible hilltop on the bluffs across the river when set upon by an overwhelming force of Indians. The withdrawal turned into a panic and a rout. Seven officers and 84 men made it to the hill. Forty were killed, 13 were wounded, and several were missing.

Custer observed Reno's charge from Weir Point, a high bluff. He searched for an opening that would permit him and his 210 troops to join the battle as soon as possible. Custer made contact with the Indians at around 3:45 P.M., near the river. What then happened is not exactly clear, but Custer moved away from the river and ended up on Custer Hill, about four miles from Reno's hill. Almost 2,000 Indians attacked Custer's force and completely surrounded it. Within about an hour Custer and all his men were annihilated.

The third unit of Custer's force, 5 officers and 110 soldiers, was commanded by Captain Frederick Benteen. Benteen was under orders to search for hostiles to the left of Custer's force and then hurry back and join Custer. Benteen, however, contrary to orders, dawdled behind, probably in the belief that there were no Indian warriors in the area. Benteen did not get to the battlefield in time to help Custer. The fourth unit of Custer's force, the pack train carrying supplies, was manned by 2 officers and 134 soldiers. It languished in the rear and could not be of assistance when Custer was attacked.

When Benteen and the pack train arrived at the Little Bighorn they joined Reno on Reno Hill. This total force of 367 was able to withstand Indian attacks on the morning of June 26, with a loss of 7 men killed and 40 men wounded. The Indians were gone by June 27, and the battle was over. Total army casualties numbered 263 killed and 59 wounded.

The army's defeat was the result of several factors. Inadequate intelligence led Custer to underestimate the strength and temper of his foe: 2,000 battle-tested warriors resolved to defend their way of life against 597 cavalry. Custer's troops were divided into four units, only two of which fought, and then at different times and places and against overwhelming odds. Another factor was the strength of the Indians' leadership; Crazy Horse, Gall, and Rain-in-the-Face were all actively involved in the fighting.

The Indians' victory was short-lived. An angry American public, Congress, and military demanded revenge. The Indians were relentlessly pursued in 1877, and by the end of the 1870's nearly all Plains Indians had been killed or confined to reservations; the traditional Plains culture passed into history. *Laurence Miller*

Core Resources

Useful sources on Custer's defeat include Richard H. Dillon's *North American Indian Wars* (New York: Facts on File, 1983); John S. Gray's *Centennial Campaign* (Ft. Collins, Colo.: Old Army Press, 1976); Bruce A. Rosenberg's *Custer and the Epic of Defeat* (University Park: Pennsylvania State University Press, 1974); Don Russell's *Custer's Last Stand* (Fort Worth, Tex.: Amon Carter Museum of Western Art, 1968); and Jesse W. Vaughan's *Indian Fights* (Norman: University of Oklahoma Press, 1966).

See also: Indian-white relations: United States; Reservation system of the United States.

Little Havana

The term "Little Havana" was originally coined by the English-speaking community in Miami in the late 1920's and early 1930's to describe the small enclave of Cubans that lived in the Eighth Street and Flagler Avenue area. After the Cuban Revolution of 1959 led by Fidel Castro, a large number of Cuban refugees arrived in Miami. They, and more than a half million Cubans who arrived during the 1960's, settled in the Little Havana area of Miami. Though many Cuban immigrants have dispersed to other U.S. cities, the enclave of Little Havana has remained.

Little Havana encompasses an area of about four square miles. It is located in the southwest portion of Miami, hence the Cuban name for the area, *Souwesera*. Upon the arrival of the immigrants in the 1960's, the area took on a distinct Cuban flavor. Cuban businesses sprang up everywhere, especially on Eighth Street (also known as *Calle Ocho*). Most store signs were in Spanish; later signs reading "English spoken here" were placed in many storefronts in an attempt to avoid alienating other Miami residents. However, anyone living and doing business in Little Havana did not need to speak English.

The first wave of Cubans fleeing the 1959 revolution arrived with nothing except the clothes on their backs and nearly empty suitcases. Because they were often unfamiliar with the language or the culture, they tended to congregate with fellow Cuban Americans, much as the Irish, Swedish, Norwegians, and Italians had done during their mass migrations in the final third of the nineteenth century.

The Cubans accepted almost any employment they could find, which created racial conflict with other economically challenged groups in Miami, especially the African American community. The African American community felt that the Cuban refugees were taking many of the jobs and positions to which they aspired. Tensions ran high and finally boiled over with the Miami riots of 1980. Although these riots were the direct result of a Hispanic police officer being acquitted in the shooting of an African American, the underlying cause was all the years of tension between the two communities.

As time passed, many of the residents of Little Havana, some of whom had become prosperous, moved to suburbs such as Hialeah and Coral Gables and other Florida cities. Though this lessened the tensions between Cuban Americans and other ethnic and racial groups in Miami, it created problems between the Cuban Americans and the white, European American populace. The tensions were largely cultural: The white community resented the Cubans' use of Spanish, even among themselves, and attempted to legislate that they use only English. Though the "English only" proponents failed, they are likely to try again. Unlike other minorities or ethnic groups that migrated to the United States, the Cuban community has sought to preserve its cultural heritage more vigorously and openly. This in itself has created tensions with the U.S. population as a whole.   *Peter E. Carr*

See also: Cuban-African American relations; Cuban Americans; Cuban Revolution; Ethnic enclaves; Mariel boatlift; Miami riots of 1980.

Little Italies

Millions of people from 1880 to 1930 came to the United States with the hope of finding a life better than the one they had left in their country of origin. The U.S. census indicates that during this fifty-year period more than four million Italians (mostly from poor backgrounds) migrated to U.S. cities such as New York, Boston, Philadelphia, and Chicago. In these cities, the Italian immigrants moved to areas that contained other Italians, specifically their *paesani*, or people from the same village in Italy. Italian communities known as Little Italies developed as an outcome of this migration.

The Italian Americans (1970), by Joseph Lopreato, indicates that Little Italies separated Italian immigrants from the mainstream American society and enabled them to maintain their ways of life, eating familiar foods, speaking their native language, and maintaining their close-knit family organization and religious practices. Lopreato demonstrates that the Little Italies shielded Italian immigrants from the ways and demands of American society. He points out that these immigrants, having distanced themselves from the old culture in Italy, needed a certain amount of time to understand and participate in the social organizations of the new society in the United States. The Little Italies acted as bridges between the old life in Italy and the new life in the United States.

Works such as *Italian Americans into the Twilight of Ethnicity* (1985), by Richard Alba, and *The Italians* (1976), by Patricia Snyder Weibust, Gennaro Capobianco, and Sally Innis Gould, describe the growth and decay that Little Italies have undergone in U.S. cities. Between the 1880's and early 1940's, the Little Italies flourished, giving birth to many Italian American-owned businesses (including restaurants, bakeries, groceries, clothing shops, butcher shops, and pasta shops), Italian-language newspapers, and mutual benefit societies (organizations involved in helping Italian immigrants deal with sickness, death, and loneliness). Moreover, these communities were host to celebrations of *festa* (Italian religious festivals) and other religious activities. Before World War II, Little Italies reached their peak in development and activities. However, after the 1940's, these communities began to shrink, partly because second- and third-generation Italian Americans were becoming wealthier and leaving the Little Italies for the suburbs. In addition, few Italians were immigrating to the United States. Since the 1970's, the bulk of Italian Americans have lived outside the Little Italies, where only a semblance remains of the old order. The number of Italian American-owned businesses, Italian-language newspapers, and mutual benefit societies in these communities has decreased tremendously. Certain activities, such as the *festas*, have continued to be held in Little Italies, some as simple appearances and others to keep the memories alive of an earlier time.   *Louis Gesualdi*

See also: Ethnic enclaves; European immigration to the United States: 1892-1943; Italian Americans.

Little Rock school desegregation

In the *Brown v. Board of Education* decision of 1954, the Supreme Court declared segregation unconstitutional, but its 1955 implementation order allowed the lower courts to develop plans to desegregate. It was the first time that the Court had not ordered immediate establishment of a constitutional right. In a state such as Arkansas, moderate and reluctantly willing to accept political and legal (though not social) equality, this approach seemed to suggest that a gradual process would be possible. Trouble seemed unlikely.

Little Rock school superintendent Virgil Blossom planned to start by enrolling a few black students at Central High School in 1957 and working down the grades year by year. The children, eventually pared down to nine, were chosen for strong scholarship and character; they were from middle-class families. When school opened on September 3, however, these children met serious resistance.

Governor Orval Faubus had decided that his best bet for future political success—most immediately a third term—lay in making himself the leader of the lower-class white segregationist element in the state. Despite the fact that he had not previously been particularly (or at least overtly) racist, Faubus announced that he could not keep the peace and called out the National Guard to keep order.

Daisy Bates, head of the local chapter of the National Association for the Advancement of Colored People (NAACP), realized that families served by Central High School were predominantly lower class and were likely to be stirred to resistance by the governor's statements. She organized the students to arrive in a group. They were turned away at bayonet point. One student, Elizabeth Eckford, did not get the message and arrived alone to face a mob of angry whites. Blocked from the school by armed Guardsmen and cursed and reviled by the mob, she was rescued by a reporter from *The New York Times* and an older white woman. Such scenes as these were reported by the press and broadcast on television. The nation was forced for the first time to face the true ugliness of its prejudice.

President Dwight D. Eisenhower met with Faubus on September 14 and got what he thought was a promise to abide by the Supreme Court decision. When Faubus reneged, the president, on September 25, ordered elements of the 101st Airborne to Little Rock. The soldiers escorted the black children to school and protected them for several weeks. Then the state National Guard, placed under federal authority, took over. Despite continuing harassment by white students, all but one of the nine was graduated from Central High.

In Little Rock, the *Brown* decision had been enforced, but resistance to school integration continued in many areas of the South. Faubus, who continued to fight, won a total of six terms as governor. The Little Rock crisis was a vital first step in desegregation, but it was no more than that.   *Fred R. van Hartesveldt*

Fifteen-year-old Elizabeth Eckford walks as calmly as possible as angry students shout insults at her. Eckford and others participated in the integration of Central High School in Little Rock, Arkansas, in 1957.

See also: *Brown v. Board of Education*; Busing and integration; Civil rights; Civil Rights movement; Desegregation: public schools; National Association for the Advancement of Colored People; *Sweatt v. Painter*.

Little Tokyos

In Los Angeles around 1885, Japanese immigrants gradually populated a small section of the city that became known as Little Tokyo. By 1910, Japanese shops, restaurants, language schools, and shrines were established, and Little Tokyo became the home of nearly 37,000 Japanese. Before World War II, Little Tokyos were also established in Seattle (almost 11,700 Japanese immigrants) and in San Francisco, where the Japanese ethnic community was the third largest in the United States, at about 5,000. Other Little Tokyos of more than 1,000 were in Sacramento and Stockton, California, Portland, Oregon, and New York City.

Although Japanese began immigrating as early as the mid-1850's, Little Tokyos were not established until the early twentieth century. They took much longer to be established than Chinatowns, probably because of the cultural differences between the two groups. The Japanese traditionally believed that agriculture was the most virtuous occupation and that people who made their living as merchants were less respectable. As a result, the majority of the early Japanese immigrants gravitated to rural areas to be farmers, as opposed to the Chinese immigrants, who were usually merchants in the city.

In Canada, before World War II, more than 97 percent of Japanese immigrants resided in the province of British Columbia. By 1931, nearly one-third of the Japanese population (about 8,300) lived in Vancouver, and more than half of them were in the district known as Little Tokyo. This was the only Japanese ethnic community in Canada in those days. However, no physical structures or symbolic buildings such as shrines were built because of severe anti-Asian sentiment.

During World War II, Little Tokyos practically disappeared from North America following the incarceration of people of Japanese descent in internment camps. In the 1970's and 1980's, when the political and economic relationships between the United States and Japan flourished, Japanese Americans began to revitalize Little Tokyos. However, by then, Little Tokyos had become more tourist attractions than residential areas. Today new generations of Japanese Americans tend to live in all parts of the city and suburbs.

In Canada, after World War II, Japanese internees were not allowed to return to their homes in British Columbia. They had to choose between going to Japan or relocating to other provinces east of the Rocky Mountains. In 1949, Japanese Canadians were finally permitted to return to British Columbia. Some people returned and reestablished Little Tokyo in Vancouver. However, new generations of Japanese Canadians, like Japanese Americans, tend to live in the suburbs. Although Vancouver's Little Tokyo still maintains shops and restaurants along with cultural activities, people who work there do not live in that area.

Since the 1970's, Japanese corporations have sent many nationals to work in the United States and Canada. These workers are often encouraged to live among North Americans in order to become more proficient at speaking English and to avoid creating a threatening Japanese "ghetto." Japanese supermarkets, bookstores, and restaurants have sprung up in various cities where many Japanese nationals work, including Seattle, Portland, Chicago, New York, and Vancouver. These new "Little Tokyos," which are smaller in size than the prewar Little Tokyos and may not be as concentrated, are usually just shopping centers.   *Nobuko Adachi*

See also: Ethnic enclaves; Japanese American internment; Japanese Americans; Japanese Canadians.

Lone Wolf v. Hitchcock

Lone Wolf v. Hitchcock established the precedent that congressional plenary power over tribal property was virtually unlimited and that Indian treaties were subject to unilateral abrogation. Lone Wolf, a principal chief of the Kiowa Nation, sought a perpetual injunction against congressional ratification of a 1900 agreement that allotted tribal lands and led to a direct loss of more than two million acres of Indian territory. The tribes contended that the forced allotment of their lands violated Article Twelve of the 1867 Treaty of Medicine Lodge. This article explicitly stated that no cession of tribal lands would be valid without the consent of "three-fourths of all the adult male Indians."

In 1892 the Jerome Commission concluded an allotment agreement with certain representatives of the Kiowa, Comanche, and Apache (KCA) tribes. Although the commissioners secured a number of Indian signatures, the three-fourths provision was unfulfilled. Nevertheless, the agreement was rushed to Washington, D.C., for congressional ratification. Almost immediately upon hearing about the allotment agreement, more than three hundred KCA tribal members urged the Senate to disapprove the 1892 agreement because "misrepresentations, threats, and fraudulent" means had been used by the government's commissioners to secure Indian signatures. Tribal consent, in other words, had not been legitimately secured.

More important, as the 1892 agreement wound its way through the ratification process, Congress substantially revised the agreement. These revisions were never submitted to the KCA tribes for their approval. Nevertheless, on June 6, 1900, and despite the protestations of the tribes concerned, Congress ratified the amended agreement.

Justice Edward D. White wrote the opinion, which was, shortly after its pronouncement on January 5, 1903, called the "Dred Scott decision number two" because it inculcated the doctrine that Indian treaty rights, although the "supreme law of the land," could be disregarded with the passage of virtually any federal law. White stated that the 1867 treaty provision had been abrogated by the 1900 agreement even though the later statute contradicted the treaty provision and lacked tribal consent. This, White said, was in keeping with "perfect good faith" toward the Indians.

White inaccurately stated that Congress had exercised plenary authority over tribes "from the beginning" and that such power was "political" and therefore not subject to judicial review. These statements were legal rationalizations, yet they were also in line with the reigning policy view of Indians at the time held by the federal government: Indians were dependent wards, subject to their sovereign guardian—the United States.

Lone Wolf v. Hitchcock was a devastating blow to tribal sovereignty. The Court's brazen refusal to examine congressional acts that abrogated treaty-acknowledged property rights was particularly oppressive because the lion's share of tribal sovereign, political, and property rights was defined by the hundreds of ratified treaties and agreements tribes negotiated with the United States. Indian rights, in short, were not created by or included in the federal Constitution. As a result of this decision, treaties as legal contracts were no longer enforceable if Congress decided to act in a manner that violated their provisions.

David E. Wilkins

See also: Allotment system; General Allotment Act; Indian Rights Association; Indian-white relations: United States.

Long Walk

> **Significance:** The unsuccessful relocation of Mescalero Apaches and Navajos from their ancestral lands to Bosque Redondo (Fort Sumner), New Mexico, caused the U.S. government to reassess its policy toward southwestern Indian tribes.

In early March, 1864, 1,443 Navajos (*Dineh*, meaning "the people," "men," or "earth people" in the Navajo language) began the Long Walk, as they described their journey, of 250 miles from their ancestral homes in northeastern Arizona and northwestern New Mexico to the Bosque Redondo reservation, located on New Mexico's eastern plains at Fort Sumner. Bosque Redondo, named by Spanish explorers for a round grove of cottonwood trees situated on the Pecos River, and adjacent Fort Sumner were viewed by the American military as appropriate locales for the forced assimilation into American life of the 8,354 Navajos and 405 Mescalero Apaches confined there by December, 1864. Although most Navajos made the journey in 1864, smaller groups had made the journey the year before.

Historical Background

Following the Mexican government's cession of 1.2 million square miles of territory to the United States by the Treaty of Guadalupe Hidalgo, February 2, 1848, relations between Americans and Navajos became increasingly tense as the United States government exerted control over the Southwest, land now under United States sovereignty. This increased tension characterized Colonel James Macrae Washington's expedition into *Dinetah* (Navajo land) in August, 1849, an invasion which resulted in the death of a respected Navajo headman (*naataani*), Narbona, August 31, 1849. Narbona was "shot in four or five places and scalped," according to an eyewitness. Ostensibly undertaken to assure Navajos of American "peaceful" intentions in constructing forts in and settling Navajo land, Washington's expedition had the opposite effect. Angered by Narbona's murder, his son-in-law, Manuelito, vowed to drive all white men from Navajo country. With the aid of another Navajo headman, Barboncito, on the night of April 29, 1860, Manuelito launched an offensive against Fort Defiance, built by Colonel Edwin Vose Sumner in 1851. Fort Defiance and its nearby canyon, Cañoncito Bonito (both adjacent to present-day Window Rock, Arizona, capital of the Navajo Nation), became central staging areas for the Long Walk.

Carleton's War, 1862-1864

Tensions with the Mescalero Apaches, evidenced in the murder of Nodnhi Apache chief Mangas Coloradus in January, 1863, and the incursions of New Mexican raiding parties on Navajo land to purchase Navajo slaves resulted in a planned effort to exterminate both Mescalero Apaches and Navajos. Another impetus was Union brigadier general James H. Carleton's view that Apache and Navajo country contained gold and other minerals. Appointed commander of the New Mexico military department, Carleton reasoned that, following his successful 1862 recapture of Tucson for the Union, he could destroy Confederate designs on New Mexico by removing Indians from their ancestral homes and opening their lands to Anglo-American prospectors.

To realize this ambition, General Carleton's Indian policy (approved by Mauhuache Ute agent Christopher "Kit" Carson; James L. Collins, Superintendent of Indian Affairs in New Mexico; and New Mexico territory's new governor, Henry Connelly) called for his fifteen hundred California volunteers to force New Mexico's non-slave Indians to surrender and to relocate at Bosque Redondo, situated on the alkaline Rio Pecos, 175 miles southeast of Santa Fe. There the Mescalero Apaches and Navajos would be taught agriculture and Christianity. Not without his misgivings about Carleton's policy, Kit Carson, now a colonel in the New Mexican territorial militia, waged war against the Mescalero Apaches and their chief, Cadete, during the 1862-1863 winter. By March, 1863, more than 400 Mescalero Apaches—men, women, and children—were confined to Bosque Redondo in an experiment in agricultural self-sufficiency

from which they would flee in the autumn of 1865. Carson turned the attention of Carleton's California volunteers to the Navajos.

During the summer of 1863, General Carleton ordered a campaign of subjugation against the Navajos, an offensive begun August 5, 1863. From Forts Defiance and Wingate, Colonel Carson and his one thousand volunteers vied with Governor Connelly's companies of civilian volunteers to take Navajo captives. Connelly's civilians assumed that, if the Navajos surrendered to Carson, opportunity to profit from Navajo slavery was impossible. Carson urged his Ute guides to take Navajo captives, thus destroying the "collectiveness" of Navajo tribal interest.

Carson's War, 1863-1864

Navajos eluded capture by Carson's volunteers, headquartered at Fort Defiance (renamed Fort Canby by Carson in July, 1863). General Carleton reported to the federal government at the beginning of September, 1863, that a mere 51 Navajos, including children and

Long Walk of the Navajos

women, had been rounded up and sent to the Bosque Redondo reservation. Carleton ordered Carson to tell Navajo males: "Go to the Bosque Redondo, or we will pursue and destroy you." In the harsh 1863-1864 winter, Carson's pursuit of the impoverished Navajos, now scattered in small bands throughout Navajo country, was successful.

Carson's destruction of Navajo crops and livestock between Fort Canby and Canyon de Chelly resulted in the surrender of 188 Navajos and their Long Walk to Bosque Redondo in the autumn of 1863. The captured included Delgadito, a prominent Navajo headman, who agreed to Carleton's request to convince other headmen to relocate to the Bosque Redondo. Repeated American forays into the Navajo stronghold, Canyon de Chelly, resulted in the surrender of 1,200 Navajos at Fort Canby by mid-February, 1864. Many of this group and the 700 Navajos surrendering to Fort Wingate authorities on Delgadito's advice formed the main part of the Long Walk of the Navajos to Fort Sumner and the Bosque Redondo in March, 1864, accompanied by nearly five hundred horses and about three thousand sheep. Of the 1,443 Navajos on this trek, 10 died during the Long Walk and 3 children were kidnapped for use as slaves by New Mexican members of the soldier escort.

The Long Walk
In the mid-1860's approximately 9,000 Navajos were forced to live in imprisonment at Bosque Redondo. Navajo deaths among Long Walk participants were steep. On March 4, 1864, 2,400 Navajos, their numbers reduced by the deaths of 126 from dysentery the preceding week, left Fort Canby for the Bosque Redondo reservation. On reaching Fort Sumner, 197 remained behind, either dead or dying. The 800 Navajos leaving Fort Canby for their new home on March 20, 1864, experienced a four-day snowstorm, the kidnapping of many Navajo children, the loss of twenty-three wagons used to transport the infirm and elderly, and the loss of supplies at Los Pinos (south of Albuquerque). By the time the group reached Fort Sumner and Bosque Redondo on May 11, 1864, 110 had perished. By July, 1864, some 5,900 Navajos were resettled at Bosque Redondo. General Carleton, guessing that only 2,000 Navajos remained in *Dinetah*, advised Kit Carson that Bosque Redondo could feed 7,500 Navajos.

Navajo leaders Barboncito and Ganado Blanco, son of Ganado Mucho, temporarily fled Bosque Redondo in July, 1865. Their later return left two headmen, Ganado Mucho and Manuelito, remaining free in Navajo country. Manuelito had participated in the Long Walk but quickly returned home, informing a delegation of Navajo headmen sent by Carleton from Bosque Redondo that he would not return. On September 1, 1866,

however, forty-eight-year-old Manuelito surrendered at Fort Wingate, arriving at Bosque Redondo one month later. In the autumn of 1865, Ganado Mucho and his band surrendered at Fort Wingate, New Mexico. Preceded on their Long Walk to Bosque Redondo by women and children, Ganado Mucho and the men of his band who herded his livestock learned in reaching Fort Sumner that Mucho's two daughters had been kidnapped near the Rio Grande. This tragedy was compounded by the tragedies of Navajo resettlement at Bosque Redondo.

End of the Long Walk
Brigadier General Carleton's plan for the resettlement of Mescalero Apaches and Navajos at the Long Walk's terminus, Bosque Redondo, was not achieved. Indian self-sufficiency in agrarian pursuits was overshadowed by traditional animosity between Mescalero Apaches and Navajos, corn crop failures caused by cutworm invasions, Comanche attacks, smallpox epidemics, and increased criticism of Carleton's policies from a number of quarters. Secretary of War Edwin M. Stanton removed Carleton from his command on September 19, 1866. The 7,304 Navajos living at Bosque Redondo were promised a return to a new 3.5-million-acre reservation on their homeland by the terms of a June 1, 1868, peace treaty signed by United States representatives William T. Sherman and Colonel Samuel F. Tappan and by 9 Navajo headmen. The U.S. Congress appropriated $150,000 for Navajo travel expenses from Bosque Redondo. Escorted by four companies of U.S. cavalry, they began their long walk home on June 18, 1868.   *Malcolm B. Campbell*

Core Resources
Sources on the Long Walk include Norman J. Bender's *"New Hope for the Indians": The Grant Peace Policy and the Navajos in the 1870's* (Albuquerque: University of New Mexico Press, 1989); Peter Iverson's *The Navajo Nation* (Albuquerque: University of New Mexico Press, 1983) and *The Navajos* (New York: Chelsea House, 1990); Raymond Friday Locke's *The Book of the Navajo* (Los Angeles: Mankind Publishing, 1976); and Ruth Underhill's *The Navajos* (rev. ed., Norman: University of Oklahoma Press, 1967).

See also: Guadalupe Hidalgo, Treaty of; Navajo War.

Longest Walk

The Longest Walk, one of the several major American Indian protest movements of the 1970's, was an attempt to persuade the U.S. government to recognize and protect Indian treaty rights and Indian sovereignty. The

In 1978, Chief Onandaga of the Iroquois Confederacy addresses some of the nearly eight hundred American Indians who took part in a march from California to Washington, D.C., to protest proposed legislation that would damage their way of life.

See also: American Indian Movement; Indian-white relations: United States; Long Walk; Pan-Indianism; Treaties and agreements with Indians: United States.

Loo, Ming Hai, murder

Asian Americans have been the victims of discrimination and violence throughout the course of U.S. history. This was especially true during periods of significant Asian immigration and also during and after wars in which Asians were the United States' adversary.

One such instance of violence involved the murder of a Chinese American, Ming Hai Loo, in Raleigh, North Carolina, in July, 1989. Two brothers, Robert and Lloyd Piche, who had lost relatives in the Vietnam War, mistakenly thought that Loo was Vietnamese and held him responsible for their relatives' deaths. They attacked Loo and killed him.

One of the killers, Robert Piche, was offered a plea bargain and a minimal sentence, but he opted for a trial. Although he expected an acquittal from a hometown jury, he was found guilty and sentenced to thirty-seven years in prison. His brother, Lloyd, was convicted of a misdemeanor and was sentenced to only six months in jail.

The media had reported on this case in a manner consistent with other murder trials; however, after Lloyd Piche's lenient sentence was handed down, the media joined Asian American civil rights organizations in urging the federal government to intercede and charge Lloyd with conspiracy to violate Loo's rights. An appeals court ordered a resentencing for Lloyd, and he was sent to prison for six years.

Loo's death clearly demonstrated the existing prejudice toward Asian Americans as exemplified by the expression, "They all look alike." Loo was killed not because he had done anything wrong but rather because he "looked" Vietnamese. *Stephen Schwartz*

protest was a five-month cross-country demonstration by Indian people to protest federal bills in Congress that were seen as destructive of the Indians' very existence. About two hundred Native Americans began the walk from the once Indian-occupied Alcatraz Island, in San Francisco Bay. Thousands of Indians participated along the way, ultimately arriving in Washington, D.C., on July 15, 1978. One of the demonstrators was Russell Means of the American Indian Movement. The protesters set up a camp at the Mall, hoping to convince lawmakers not to pass the bills.

The pending legislation would have weakened Indian rights to land, resources, and self-government. For example, one bill proposed to limit Indian water rights, while others threatened to cancel Indian hunting and fishing rights and terminate all treaties between the United States and Indian tribes.

Congressional supporters and others assured the Indians that the anti-Indian bills would not pass. Nevertheless, they agreed with the Indian demonstrators that Congress and the American public should be aware that such legislation had been proposed. The Longest Walk was a symbolic victory for Indian people. It also demonstrated a solidarity among Indians. *Raymond Wilson*

See also: Asian American stereotypes; Chin, Vincent, murder; Chinese Americans; Orientalism; Vietnamese Americans.

Los Angeles riots of 1992

> **Significance:** The acquittal of four police officers charged with police brutality sparked the worst violence in the city's history from April 29 to May 1, 1992.

Before the Rodney King beating on March 3, 1991, many in the Los Angeles community believed that the Los Angeles Police Department (LAPD) had demonstrated a pattern of excessive force, particularly against minority groups. One significant example was Operation Hammer, begun in 1989, during which the LAPD allegedly rounded up African Americans and Hispanics without probable cause that they had had committed a crime, simply because of the way the suspects looked and because the police wanted to avert the threat of gang violence. As a result, the chief of the LAPD, Daryl Gates, was despised by many in the African American community. The videotape of Rodney King's beating by members of the LAPD, therefore, came as no surprise to the African American community of Los Angeles. It merely confirmed what they already thought: that police brutality and use of excessive force against minorities was a common practice.

The Beating of Rodney King

The videotape, recorded by private citizen George Holliday in the morning hours of March 3, 1991, contained eighty-one seconds of footage. The footage that was seen throughout the United States was of King, a six-foot, three-inch African American weighing 225 pounds, prone on the ground, sustaining blows to his head, neck, kidney area, and legs from four policemen, who were kicking and smashing at him with their truncheons. Not in full view on the videotape were nineteen other police officers surrounding the four who were administering the beating. Also not in view were the onlookers who were pleading that the beating stop. The police paid no attention to them. As a result of the beating, King sustained eleven fractures to his skull, a crushed cheekbone, a broken ankle, internal injuries, a burn on his chest, and some brain damage.

Television viewers also did not see what preceded the beating. During the evening, King had consumed the equivalent of a case of beer. His blood alcohol level was twice the legal limit.

He was on parole at the time and ran the risk of landing back in jail if he were caught speeding. Police, led by Stacey Koon, started chasing King as he sped through the streets of Los Angeles. The chase escalated to one hundred miles per hour at one point, before the police were able to stop King and force him out of his car. Nor did television viewers see King fighting with the police, even standing up after being stunned twice with a Taser gun. People saw only the prone body of an African American man being assaulted repeatedly by white police officers.

The Trial

Four of the officers, including Koon, were charged with the beating at the end of March, 1991, in Los Angeles. Their attorneys moved for a change of venue for the trial, which was granted. The trial was held in the spring of 1992 in Simi Valley, a suburban town an hour's drive north of Los Angeles. The town was the home for a large proportion of LAPD officers and retirees and was dominated by law-and-order conservatives. Six men and six women, none of whom was African American, made up the jury. According to those who were present, the prosecution presented a weak and diffuse case. The defense, however, was strong. It played the videotape in slow motion over and over until its effect became trivialized. The defense also emphasized how King presented a threat to the police. Koon testified about King's "hulk-like strength and how he groaned like a wounded animal," conjuring up for the jury the image of police representing the "thin blue line" that protects the forces of civilization from the savagery represented by King. To those who had likely settled in Simi Valley to get away

Many buildings in Los Angeles burned during the 1992 riots. Here, a day after the riots ended, Department of Water and Power employees try to restore power.

from the alleged evils and crime of the inner city, the message resounded. After thirty-two hours of deliberation, on April 29, 1992, the jury acquitted the four officers. The verdict was announced on television at 2:50 P.M.

The Riots

At 4:00 P.M., in the South Central Los Angeles district near Florence and Normandie Boulevards, five African American gang members went to get some malt liquor at the Payless Liquor Store. They started to take it without paying, and the owner's son tried to stop them. One of the gang members smashed the son on the head with a bottle and allegedly said, "This is for Rodney King." Other gang members hurled the bottles they held through the store windows, while the owner pressed the alarm for the police. When two officers came, the suspects were not there.

At 5:30, at the corner of Florence and Normandie, eight black men wielding baseball bats started breaking the car windows of passing motorists. Eighteen police cars and thirty-five officers from the LAPD sped to the area. They arrested three suspects but left at 5:45. In the next hour, the crowd attacking cars grew to two hundred people. One of the victims was Reginald Denny, a white truck driver, who was pulled from his truck and beaten by African Americans, including Damien Williams, with a fire extinguisher. The police from the 77th district of the LAPD still stayed away. Chief Gates had left police headquarters at 6:30 to attend a fund-raising event in the affluent suburb of Brentwood.

By 7:30, the crowd at Florence and Normandie had started lighting fires. An hour later, the LAPD finally returned to the area and began to disperse the crowd. By that time, the fires, rioting, and looting had spread to other parts of the city. The riots continued for two more days; local news coverage flooded the airwaves with helicopter views of hundreds of fires throughout the city and normally law-abiding citizens looting goods from stores. On Friday, May 1, 1992, Rodney King appeared on television with the plea, "Can't we all get along?" When the riots ended that day in Los Angeles, more than fifty people had died, more than twelve thousand people had been arrested, and the property damage was estimated to be $1 billion. Throughout the nation, uprisings had started in Atlanta, Las Vegas, Minneapolis, New York, Omaha, and Seattle.

The riots in Los Angeles following the King trial caused more damage and spread across a wider area than those of the 1960's. Gates subsequently was replaced by an African American chief of police, Koon and a fellow officer were convicted of violating King's civil rights in federal court, Williams was acquitted of most of the charges in the beating of Denny, and King won a civil suit against the city of Los Angeles. These actions rein-

forced the perception of many that the criminal justice system treats whites and African Americans differently, whereas others argued that the riots were less the result of racial tensions than of a widening gap between "haves" and "have-nots" in U.S. society.   *Jennifer Eastman*

Core Resources

"Can't We All Get Along?" "The Fire This Time," and "Anatomy of an Acquittal" (*Time* 139, May 11, 1992), give a good overview of the events on April 29, 1992, and following. "Los Angeles, April 29, 1992, and Beyond: The Law, Issues, and Perspectives" (*Southern California Law Review* 66, May, 1993) contains a panoply of views on the trial and the riots. "Symposium—The Urban Crisis: The Kerner Commission Report Revisited" (*North Carolina Law Review* 71, June, 1993) discusses how the riots of 1992 differed from those of the 1960's.

See also: King, Rodney, case; Miami riots of 1980; Newark race riots; Race riots of the twentieth century; Watts riot.

Lynchings

> **Significance:** Lynchings were a primary means of intimidation and control of blacks in the American South.

Lynching, the deadliest form of vigilantism, has a long history in America. At the time of the American Revolution, lynchings were used to punish Tories or British sympathizers. Until the 1850's, lynchings were associated with nonlethal forms of punishment such as beatings and tarring and feathering. In the years immediately before the Civil War, lynching took on its fatal connotation as it was used to suppress slave insurrections. Although lynching is often associated with hanging someone, lynching includes all sorts of violent acts, including flogging, dismemberment, torture, burning, and shooting.

History of Lynching

After the Civil War, lynching became more widespread as former slaves came to be viewed as a threat by their former slavemasters. Accurate numbers on lynching are hard to come by, and it was not until 1872 that there was a systematic effort to obtain reliable data. Records kept by the Tuskegee Institute indicate that there were 4,743 lynchings in the United States between 1882 and 1968. Of those lynched, 3,446 (73 percent) were blacks and 1,297 (27 percent) were whites. Even these numbers underestimate what most scholars believe to be the actual number of lynchings. A more accurate estimate would be close to 6,000 lynchings.

Lynchings were most prevalent from the 1880's to the 1920's. During the last two decades of the nineteenth century, there was an average of 150 lynchings per year, with a high of 230 in 1892. Between 1901 and 1910 there was an average of 85 lynchings per year, and from 1911 to 1920 there was an average of 61 per year. Lynchings declined to an average of 28 per year during the 1920's, to 11 per year during the 1930's, and to 3 per year during the 1940's. From 1951 to 1985 a total of 10 lynchings were reported in the United States. Although almost every state experienced lynchings, 82 percent occurred in the South. Mississippi ranks first with 581, followed by Georgia with 530 and Texas with 493.

Grounds for Lynching

Although lynching was often justified as a method of protecting white women from black rapists, only 25 percent of lynching victims were suspected of rape or attempted rape. In most cases, lynching victims were summarily executed before receiving any trial. Their guilt was never established at all, let alone beyond a reasonable doubt. The justification for lynching in the cases of rape was to protect the white woman from the agony of testifying in court.

Approximately 40 percent of lynchings involved murder or attempted murder allegations. Nine percent involved assault or robbery charges, certainly not capital offenses, and 2 percent involved blacks insulting whites, particularly white women. The most famous example of a black who was lynched for insulting a white woman was Emmett Till. Till, a fourteen-year-old Chicago native, was visiting relatives in Mississippi in 1955. Prodded by some friends, Till asked a white woman for a date. The woman immediately rejected Till and went to get a pistol. Till walked out of the store saying, "Bye, baby," and "wolf whistled" at her. Till's actions violated one of the major cultural taboos in the South, and he would pay with his life. That same day, the woman's husband and her half-brother abducted Till from the home he was visiting. Three days later, Till's decomposing body was found floating in the Tallahatchie River. Till had been beaten and shot before his weighted-down body was thrown into the river. The two white men who abducted Till were charged with his murder, but it took an all-white jury less than one hour to acquit them.

The Campaign Against Lynching

Few individuals who participated in lynchings were ever prosecuted. Coroners' juries repeatedly concluded that the death had come "at the hands of parties unknown." Seldom was anything further from the truth. Often lynchings took on a festive air, and local newspapers provided complete coverage, sometimes including photographs. In the event someone was arrested for the

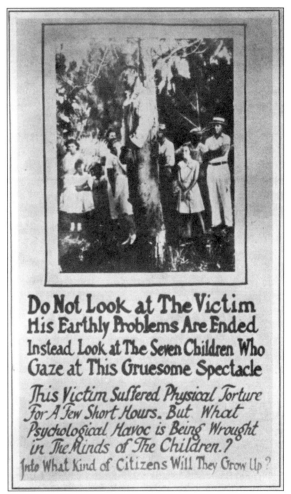

The National Association for the Advancement of Colored People created this poster to demonstrate the horrors of lynching.

crime, such as the two white men accused of murdering Emmett Till, they would be found not guilty by all-white juries.

Leading the effort to abolish lynchings were the Commission on Interracial Cooperation, headed by Will Alexander, and Southern Women for the Prevention of Lynching, led by Jessie Daniel Ames. Ames, one of the leading social reformers in the South, had forty thousand members in her organization within nine years of its establishment in 1930. When alerted about a possible lynching, Ames contacted women in the area who were members of her organization or sympathetic to its objectives.

One of the earliest objectives of the National Association for the Advancement of Colored People (NAACP), a civil rights organization established in 1909, was to pressure the U.S. Congress to pass a federal antilynching bill. On several occasions, the House of Representatives passed such legislation, but it was always filibustered by southern senators when it reached the Senate. In the late 1940's President Harry Truman appointed a President's Committee on Civil Rights (PCCR). The PCCR urged Congress to pass a federal antilynching law, but without success.

The NAACP met with greater success in attempting to mobilize public opinion against lynching. The NAACP investigated lynchings and often sent special investigators into areas where a lynching had occurred. The NAACP prepared written narratives of the lynchings, including photographs if available, and distributed them to any media outlet that would publicize the lynching. The effort was to try to shame the South into stopping this despicable practice.   *Darryl Paulson*

Core Resources

Among the best studies on lynching are Ray Stannard Baker's *Following the Color Line: An Account of Negro Citizenship in the American Democracy* (New York: Doubleday, Page, 1908); Richard M. Brown's *Strain of Violence: Historical Studies of American Violence and Vigilantism* (New York: Oxford University Press, 1977); James Chadbourn's *Lynching and the Law* (Chapel Hill, N.C.: University of North Carolina Press, 1933); Arthur Raper's *The Tragedy of Lynching* (Chapel Hill, N.C.: University of North Carolina Press, 1933); Walter White's *Rope and Faggot* (New York: Alfred A. Knopf, 1929); Stephen Whitfield's *A Death in the Delta: The Story of Emmett Till* (Baltimore: The Johns Hopkins University Press, 1988); and Robert Zangrando's *The NAACP Crusade Against Lynching, 1909-1950* (Philadelphia: Temple University Press, 1980).

See also: Dyer antilynching bill; Frank, Leo, lynching; Hate crimes; Ku Klux Klan; National Association for the Advancement of Colored People.

Lyng v. Northwest Indian Cemetery Protective Association

In 1982, the United States Forest Service prepared an environmental impact report for construction of a paved road through federal lands in the Six Rivers National Forest in California. The study reported a section of this land was historically used for religious purposes by Yurok, Karok, and Tolowa Indians, and because the site was integral to the religious practices of these people, it recommended the road not be completed. That same year, despite its own report, the Forest Service decided to build the road. After exhausting administrative remedies, a coalition of Indian organizations filed suit in federal court, challenging the decision based on the right to free exercise of religion under the First Amendment and on similar guarantees in the American Indian Religious Freedom Act (1978).

In 1987, the U.S. Supreme Court ruled against the Indian coalition even though the Court admitted the road would severely affect tribal religious practices. The Court declared that although the free exercise clause affords individual protections, it does not afford an individual right "to dictate the conduct of the government's internal procedures." Additionally, it ruled that the American Indian Religious Freedom Act has no enforcement mechanisms that could compel the government to halt construction on the road. This case severely reduced both the intent of the American Indian Religious Freedom Act and the protections it afforded Indian people, and it raised questions about basic protections afforded American Indian citizens of the United States.   *Carole A. Barrett*

See also: American Indian activism; American Indian civil rights; American Indian Religious Freedom Act.

M

McCleskey v. Kemp

In *McCleskey v. Kemp*, the Supreme Court on April 22, 1987, rejected a death row inmate's claim that Georgia's system of sentencing people to death was unconstitutional because it discriminated on the basis of race.

In 1978, Warren McCleskey, a black man, was convicted of killing a white police officer during an armed robbery of a store in Atlanta, Georgia. McCleskey's jury—which consisted of eleven whites and one black—sentenced him to die in Georgia's electric chair. McCleskey sought a writ of *habeas corpus*, arguing, among other things, that the Georgia capital sentencing process was administered in a racially discriminatory manner and violated the United States Constitution. According to McCleskey, the jury's decision to execute him violated the Eighth Amendment because racial bias rendered the decision arbitrary and capricious. Also, the equal protection clause of the Fourteenth Amendment was violated because McCleskey, a black man, was treated differently from white defendants in the same position.

To support his claim of racial discrimination, McCleskey offered as evidence a sophisticated statistical study performed by Professor David B. Baldus and his colleagues at the University of Iowa (the Baldus study). The Baldus study showed that race played a dual role in deciding whether convicted murderers in Georgia would be sentenced to death. First, the race of the murder victim played a large role in whether a defendant would be sentenced to die. According to the study, defendants charged with killing whites received the death penalty in 11 percent of the cases. Defendants charged with killing blacks received the death penalty in only 1 percent of the cases. After taking account of thirty-nine variables that could have explained the disparities on nonracial grounds, the Baldus study concluded that, in Georgia, defendants charged with killing white victims were 4.3 times as likely to receive a death sentence as defendants charged with killing blacks.

Second, the race of the defendant played an important role during capital sentencing. According to the Baldus study, black defendants were 1.1 times as likely to receive a death sentence as other defendants. Thus, the study showed that black defendants such as McCleskey who had killed white victims had the greatest likelihood of receiving the death penalty.

By a 5 to 4 vote, the Supreme Court ruled against McCleskey. The Supreme Court accepted the validity of the Baldus study but held that McCleskey failed to prove "that decisionmakers in his case acted with discriminatory purpose." In other words, McCleskey failed to show that his constitutional rights were violated because he did not prove that anyone involved in his particular case intentionally discriminated against him based on his race. Justice Lewis Powell's opinion for the majority expressed special concern that if the Court accepted McCleskey's argument—that racial bias impermissibly tainted capital sentencing proceedings—all criminal sentences would be subject to attack based on allegations of racial discrimination. The *McCleskey* decision is a landmark ruling in the modern era of capital punishment.

Warren McCleskey died in Georgia's electric chair on September 25, 1991. That same year Justice Powell, whose 5 to 4 majority opinion had sealed Warren McCleskey's fate, told a biographer that he would change his vote in that case (thus sparing McCleskey's life) if he could. Also, although executions had resumed in the United States in 1977, 1991 marked the first time in the modern era of American capital punishment that a white defendant (Donald "Pee Wee" Gaskins) was executed for killing a black person.   *Randall Coyne*

See also: Discrimination: racial and ethnic; *Furman v. Georgia.*

Machine politics

In Ireland, several potato crops failed during the 1830's, resulting in a devastating famine that sent millions of immigrants to U.S. shores. Like most of the refugees who came in the nineteenth century, the Irish expected to achieve fame and fortune—the American Dream. Instead, they found poverty and discrimination. One sign that appeared in the windows of many businesses read "Irish need not apply." Seeking a way out, many Irish Americans tried to climb the political ladder, thus creating an American phenomenon known as machine politics.

Early Irish bosses played an extremely important role in serving the immigrants' needs. In the days before Social Security, welfare, Medicare, and Medicaid, the bosses (or their agents) met the immigrant ships at the docks, helped the weary travelers find a place to live and a job and provided them with most of life's necessities. The urban machines served as a quasi-welfare agency. At Christmas, they delivered huge baskets of food to the poor who lived in the squalor of the slums. The machine provided patronage—jobs, housing, and other necessities—and in return, the immigrants supplied the votes to keep the machine in power.

It took a great deal of money to fuel these machines. Money came from profit-seeking businessmen and paycheck kickbacks from machine members. Irish bosses such as Daniel P. O'Connell of Albany, New York, James Michael Curley of Boston, and Patrick A. Nash and Edward J. Kelly of Chicago enraged middle-class, white Anglo-Saxon Protestant reformers by encouraging vote fraud, intimidation, graft, bribery, and many other forms of vice, sin, and corruption that sullied the image of U.S. democracy.

Two of the most famous Irish bosses played an important role in electing a president. Harry S Truman emerged from the ranks of Thomas J. Pendergast's Kansas City, Missouri, organization. The Pendergast machine ran Kansas City with an iron hand from 1911 to 1938. The big boss provided the jobs and delivered the votes (many of them fraudulent) that sent Truman to the U.S. Senate. Pendergast eventually received a prison sentence for income tax evasion.

Another boss, Chicago mayor Richard J. Daley, provided crucial support in shifting Illinois' electoral vote to John F. Kennedy during the 1960 presidential election. Daley, the last of the bosses, ran the "Windy City" from the 1950's to the 1970's and died while still in office in 1976. Before the mayor's death, he created the image of Chicago as a highly efficient city where the streetcars ran on time, garbage trucks routinely picked up the trash, and the police strictly maintained law and order.

For many years, white Anglo-Saxon Protestants viewed the Irish with distrust. Poverty in the Irish shanties seemed to produce myriad problems: juvenile delinquency, drug and alcohol abuse, unemployment, and other factors that led to the rise of the boss and his machine. Eventually, as the Irish moved up the socioeconomic ladder, they gained respectability. They gained acceptance from many segments of society, and the boss came to symbolize a stabilizing era in the history of the cities.

Eventually African American and Hispanic political leaders replaced the Irish bosses. Although the Irish machine tolerated or encouraged corruption, it played an important role in bringing order to the confusion and disorganization that characterized the American city in its formative stages.   *J. Christopher Schnell*

See also: Irish American stereotypes; Irish Americans; Irish Catholic "race."

Mainstreaming

The practice of mainstreaming began with national attention to the right of physically and mentally challenged individuals to attend the same public schools and be in the same classrooms as traditional students. In the area of race and ethnic relations, however, mainstreaming has come to mean something else.

Primarily, mainstreaming refers to the integration of ethnic minority students, mostly Spanish-speaking children, into traditional English-speaking classrooms. Since 1975, many Hispanic children have been taught through bilingual education. English as a Second Language (ESL) programs have been suggested as a way to transition students from bilingual education to an English-only school environment. In the 1990's, some efforts for legislation favoring ESL immersion succeeded in California (Proposition 227), and these developments appeared to be the leading edge of a national trend.

A fierce debate surrounds the various ways of achieving mainstreaming. Proponents argue that all public school instruction should be in English and that children who do not speak the language should be rapidly immersed in traditional classrooms. Critics argue that this is mere assimilationist rhetoric. They believe that children should have the opportunity to speak their own language while learning English and that cultural pluralism should be preserved in public schools.

Christopher Guillebeau

See also: Assimilation: cultural and structural; Bilingual education; Cultural pluralism; English-only and official English movements.

Majority and minority

In general, the value placed on different racial and ethnic backgrounds is determined by the majority, those who hold power in a society. By establishing the values and norms of society, the majority consciously and unconsciously create a social structure that operates in their favor. Their positions of power allow them to enjoy certain privileges, including better housing, better schools, and higher incomes.

Because the resources and rewards found in society

are limited, the privileged position of the majority is often gained at the expense of the opportunities available to minority groups within the society. Although the term minority often means less than half of the whole, when applied to people it does not necessarily refer to numerical proportion. Some minority groups, such as African Americans in some cities in the United States, have more members than the majority but receive fewer economic and political opportunities.

If a minority group has economic resources or a good education, its acceptance by the majority is typically easier. This is especially so in the United States, where class is largely defined by economic success. Although extreme economic and social inequalities continue to divide Americans into majority and minority groups, the divisions tend to be more a reflection of economic class than of ethnicity.   *Alvin K. Benson*

See also: Dominant group; Racial and ethnic relations: race-class debate; Subordinate group.

Malcolm X assassination

> **Significance:** The February 21, 1965, murder of Malcolm X silenced an inspiring militant spokesman for African American rights.

Perhaps no twentieth century African American leader better expressed the anger and frustrations of urban African Americans than Malcolm X. During the 1960's Civil Rights movement, Malcolm X, the national spokesman of a black separatist Muslim sect known as the Nation of Islam, articulated in militant language the effects of the nation's historical pattern of racism against African Americans and the social consequences the country faced if significant change did not occur. Before his assassination in 1965, Malcolm X had come to symbolize the disenchantment of African American ghetto residents, a group who were disillusioned about the benefits of racial integration and becoming increasingly impatient with the dominant nonviolent philosophy of the Civil Rights movement.

Malcolm's Early Life
Malcolm X was born Malcolm Little on May 19, 1925, in Omaha, Nebraska, to Louise Norton Little and J. Early Little. His father, a Baptist preacher, worked as an organizer for the Universal Negro Improvement Association, the black nationalist organization led by Marcus Garvey. In his later life, Malcolm too would consider himself a black nationalist. In 1931, Malcolm's father died mysteriously in East Lansing, Michigan, where the family had relocated. Thereafter, Malcolm's life was marked by a series of crises.

The impoverished family, now comprising Malcolm, his mother, and six siblings, was soon separated: Malcolm's mother was committed to a mental hospital and no longer influenced his development. Malcolm was placed in a foster home and began to get into trouble as he grew older. Hoping to change the direction of the troubled teen's life, Ella, an older half sister, brought him to live with her in Boston, Massachusetts. Although he possessed a good mind, he did not find school rewarding and dropped out to work at odd jobs. An attraction to street life overcame his interest in legitimate employment, however, and he gradually gravitated toward hustling, drugs, and petty crime.

For a time, Malcolm loved the culture of urban street life and seemed to flourish in it. In the 1940's, he wore the zoot suit and wide hat popular among young African American and Hispanic hipsters and patronized the night spots in Boston's Roxbury and New York's Harlem ghettoes. The seedy side of this life proved to be his downfall. His graduation to the more serious crime of burglary eventually landed him in prison, and at twenty years of age, he began serving six years of a ten-year sentence in Massachusetts' Charlestown and Norfolk penitentiaries.

Initially, Malcolm was hardly a model prisoner. In many ways, however, prison proved to be his redemption, for it was in prison that Malcolm converted to a version of Islam that changed his life. Largely through the efforts of his sisters and brothers, who visited him regularly, Malcolm was introduced to the ideas and philosophy of a little-known Muslim sect, the Nation of Islam, headed by Elijah Muhammad. Gradually, Malcolm abandoned his aggressive behavior, adopted Muslim prayer and life practices, and enmeshed himself in the teachings of Muhammad.

Malcolm as a Muslim
Malcolm absorbed the Muslim interpretation of the history of races, an interpretation that explained how and why white people came to be regarded as "devils" and the oppressors of black people throughout the world. Based on Muhammad's teaching, Malcolm's own life experiences, and wide reading in history, politics, and economics, Malcolm came to understand how central the role of white people had been in causing the lowly conditions of African Americans. Muhammad could not have found another adherent with a wider breadth of knowledge about black and white race relations than Malcolm. Their attraction to each other and Malcolm's commitment to spreading Muhammad's message placed Malcolm in an ideal position for elevation

Black nationalist and Muslim Malcolm X was assassinated on February 21, 1965, by three members of the Nation of Islam.

to a more visible role in the Islamic organization.

Shortly after his parole in 1952, Malcolm was appointed minister of Temple No. 7 in Harlem by the Muslim leader. Articulate and intellectually gifted, Malcolm undertook his duties with a passion and energy unmatched by his peers. He increased the membership in his own temple and traveled throughout the country organizing new mosques. By 1959, the sect could boast of forty-nine temples nationwide and more than forty thousand members. In six years, temple establishment increased nearly tenfold, and Malcolm almost single-handedly accounted for this.

By 1960, Malcolm clearly had emerged as the second most influential man in the Nation of Islam, and was the national spokesman for Elijah Muhammad. Malcolm was heard on the radio and seen on national television. Converts and sympathizers read about his views through the columns of the newspaper that he established, *Muhammad Speaks*, and in other African American urban newspapers for which he regularly wrote. In his Harlem street meetings, he railed against police brutality, and he quelled potentially explosive confrontations between African Americans and law enforcement officials. He continued to "fish" on the ghetto streets for new converts, appealing to them with a mastery of oratory that condemned white racism and the failure of liberal black and white leaders to address the real needs of the African American community. In no uncertain terms, he told listeners that African American men sought to present and defend themselves as men, violently if necessary. Change would occur in the United States, he said, either by the ballot or by the bullet.

Speaking Out

In the span of a few short years, Malcolm's name was as familiar as that of Martin Luther King, Jr. Malcolm's national notoriety and influence sparked rivalry and jealousy within the ranks of the Nation of Islam, however. Even Elijah Muhammad, who had warned Malcolm of potential internal dangers from becoming too powerful, grew envious of his national prominence. Rival factions looked for ways to bring him down.

The opportunity occurred in December, 1963, following President John F. Kennedy's assassination, when Malcolm violated Muhammad's order for Muslims to remain silent about the murder. In an interview, Malcolm equated the president's death to "chickens coming home to roost," an impolitic remark that provided the excuse for Muhammad to punish him. Discredited and officially silenced for ninety days, Malcolm's influence within the Nation of Islam waned precipitously.

Unable to forge an effective reconciliation with Muhammad and increasingly determined to speak more broadly for African Americans independent of Nation of Islam constraints, Malcolm left the organization in early 1964 to form his own group, Muslim Mosque, Inc. A pilgrimage to Mecca, the Hajj, and subsequent travel to Africa expanded his understanding about the true nature of Islam, validated his status as an international personality, and helped him to define new agendas in his fight for black people worldwide. A new Malcolm with a new Islamic name, El-Hajj Malik El-Shabazz, hoped to accomplish his agenda through a more politically oriented organization of his making, the Organization of Afro-American Unity.

The Assassination

Malcolm remained a marked man, however, and was unable to escape the vilification of enemies in the Nation of Islam. Privately and publicly, they denounced him as a traitor to Elijah Muhammad and placed him under surveillance. From many quarters, those threatened by Malcolm's mass appeal and influence called for violent retribution. In February, 1964, he and his family escaped death from a bomb that destroyed their home.

Malcolm's pleas for peace with the Nation of Islam could not stave off another attempt on his life. On February 21, 1965, while speaking before a crowd of several hundred followers in Harlem's Audubon Ballroom, Malcolm was felled by a fusillade of bullets. In

March, 1966, a racially mixed jury found three men—Talmadge Hayer, Norman 3X Butler, and Thomas 15X Johnson—guilty of first-degree murder in Malcolm's death. Despite their conviction, conspiracy theories about Malcolm's death have remained, including theories implicating non-Muslims and even the U.S. government.   *Robert L. Jenkins*

Core Resources
George Breitman, Herman Porter, and Baxter Smith's *The Assassination of Malcolm X* (New York: Pathfinder Press, 1976) investigates the authors' claim of a cover-up regarding Malcolm's death. Karl Evanzz's *The Judas Factor: The Plot to Kill Malcolm X* (New York: Thunder's Mouth Press, 1992) is a detailed, documented account revealing the author's theory that the intelligence community was involved in Malcolm's death. Michael Friedly's *Malcolm X, the Assassination* (New York: Carroll & Graf, 1992) explores the various conspiracy theories advanced about Malcolm's murder and gives extensive coverage of his relationship with Elijah Muhammad. Bruce Perry's *Malcolm: The Life of a Man Who Changed Black America* (Barrytown, N.Y.: Station Hill, 1991) revises earlier images of Malcolm's life and public career, presenting a man whose childhood was burdened with hardship and violence and who was driven by the need for acceptance by the society he condemned as racist.

See also: Black Power movement; Civil Rights movement; King, Martin Luther, Jr., assassination; Nation of Islam.

Maquiladoras

Maquiladoras are the assembly plants, mainly foreign-owned, that have been operating in Mexico since 1965, mostly along the northern border with the United States. From Tijuana on the Pacific Coast to Matamoros on the Gulf of Mexico, these tariff-free plants experienced their biggest boom in the 1990's. Between 1994 and 1995, the maquiladoras created an additional 400,000 jobs.

The racial and gender dimensions of the maquiladora industry are complex. In some Mexican cities, Asian companies own the majority of the maquiladoras. In Mexicali, for example, 62 percent of all assembly plants are owned by Asians, mainly Taiwanese and Japanese investors. It took a long time for Asians to accept Mexican attitudes toward punctuality, company loyalty, and absenteeism, which run counter to those of the more disciplined Asian workforce. After several adjustments, Mexican laborers and Asian managers worked out compromises that were mutually acceptable.

In most factories, a large majority of the workers are women. These women have a median age of twenty-five and are more likely to possess a secondary education than other women their age. Most women working in maquiladoras are single and usually migrated to wherever they found employment. For the most part, these women are satisfied with their steady paychecks and health benefits, although many find that their jobs alienate them from family expectations. When they leave employment in the maquiladoras, it is normally because of family necessities, transportation problems, or disappointment with their jobs.

Many of these women undergo a transformation in their relationships with the men in their families. The fact that maquiladora workers contribute an average 40 percent to household budgets has a stressful impact on these women's relationships with men in the traditionally authoritarian Mexican family. However, it is usually a younger daughter who works in the factory, not the family's main provider. Many young women give their earnings to their mothers, keeping only a small amount for themselves. Some women do become financially independent and therefore experience personal freedom; however, the family continues to maintain a substantial influence over them. Because interaction between men and women on the factory floor is limited, the large number of women has not significantly altered gender attitudes. Although most assembly-line supervisors are women, generally women do not seek out these positions. Accepting a supervisory role moves the women out of the work group and creates suspicion about their association with management.

Critics of maquiladoras have pointed out that the low wages paid to their employees constitute raw exploitation. Even with the numerous bonuses and benefits required by Mexican law, a large multinational maquiladora might pay its assembly-line workers a base of 50 to 60 cents per hour. With benefits, which include bonuses, social security, and health care, the total compensation rises to $1.50. The minimum wage in the United States in 1998 was well over $5.00 per hour.

Another controversy is the accusation that unless maquiladora wages rise substantially, the low-wage factories will constitute unfair competition and attract large numbers of U.S. companies with a resultant loss of jobs in the United States. Nevertheless, manufacturers believe that higher wages could bite into the competitive edge that brought them to Mexico in the first place; maquiladora owners believe they are saving up to $25,000 per worker per year. Many African Americans and Mexican Americans who lost their jobs in the United States have become bitter and resentful against Mexican policies that continue to lure manufacturers from the United States. The end result is that displaced white and African American workers sometimes regard Mexican immigrants as the problem, heightening racial as well as ethnic tensions within the United States.

Douglas W. Richmond

See also: Economics and race; Employment among African Americans; Labor movement.

Mariel boatlift

> **Significance:** This massive influx of Cuban refugees provoked an agonizing reappraisal of U.S. refugee policy.

After Fidel Castro became dictator of Cuba in January, 1959, relations between the United States and Cuba steadily deteriorated, as Castro turned his country into a communist state allied with the Soviet Union, the United States' rival in the Cold War. Diplomatic relations with Cuba were broken, and an economic embargo was imposed upon the country.

The communization of Cuba alienated Cubans as well. From 1959 to 1962 (when Castro halted all further airplane flights from the island), about two hundred thousand Cubans fled their homeland, most of them settling in Miami. In late 1965, special freedom flights of refugees were organized with the cooperation of the Castro government; although registration for these flights was closed off in 1966, the flights themselves continued until 1973. The early refugees were disproportionately from Cuba's professional and white-collar classes; with extensive financial assistance from the U.S. government, and their own hard work, they achieved a remarkable level of prosperity in the United States in a short time.

Hopes for rapprochement with Castro rose in 1977, when Jimmy Carter became president of the United States. A United States Interests section of the Swiss embassy was established in Havana, under a State Department official, Wayne Smith, to handle relations between Cuba and the United States. When Castro persisted in his military intervention in the African nation Angola, however, plans for lifting the U.S. embargo were shelved indefinitely. In October, 1979, relations with Castro deteriorated when Washington, D.C., welcomed the hijacker of a Cuban boat as a freedom fighter.

Between January and March, 1979, Castro, to polish his image abroad and to gain badly needed foreign currency, allowed more than 115,000 Cuban Americans to visit their relatives in Cuba. The apparent prosperity of the Cuban Americans caused discontent among Cubans on the island because of the austerity and lack of consumer choices in the island's socialist economy.

Mariel Refugees

On April 1, 1980, six Cubans commandeered a city bus and drove it through the gate of the Peruvian embassy, demanding asylum; in the ensuing melee, one Cuban guard was killed. Castro responded by removing the police guards from the embassy. By April 9, 1980, about ten thousand more Cubans had crowded into the embassy, demanding the right of political asylum. On April 16, with Castro's permission, airplane flights began to take asylum-seekers to Costa Rica; on April 18, however, Castro, embarrassed by the blow to his image abroad, suddenly canceled these flights. On April 20, he opened the port of Mariel to all those who wished to leave the island and to anyone who wished to ferry discontented Cubans to Florida.

Persons sympathetic to the plight of the would-be emigrants chartered boats to sail to Mariel, pick up those who wanted to leave, and bring them to Key West, Florida. Once in Mariel, the boats' skippers were forced to accept everyone whom Cuban authorities wanted to be rid of, including criminals, the mentally ill, and homosexuals. Because some of the boats were not seaworthy, a tragic accident was always a possibility; and the U.S. Coast Guard sometimes had to rescue refugees from boats in danger of sinking.

President Carter, distracted by the Iranian hostage crisis and the worsening of relations with the Soviet Union after the latter's occupation of Afghanistan, vacillated in regard to the boatlift. In a speech given on May 5, Carter urged the people of the United States to welcome the refugees with open arms. On May 14, however, he threatened criminal penalties for those who used boats to pick up Cubans, and ordered the Coast Guard to stop the boatlift by arresting and fining the skippers and seizing the boats. Without cooperation from Castro, this order was largely ineffective. It was not until September 25, after hard bargaining between Castro and State Department negotiators Wayne Smith and Peter Tarnoff, that Castro ended the boatlift; several hundred would-be refugees who had missed the boatlift were allowed to take air flights out of Cuba in November.

Between April and September, 1980, south Florida bore the brunt of the tidal wave of refugees, which is estimated to have reached as many as 125,000. In the Miami area, social services, health services, schools, and law enforcement authorities found their resources strained to the breaking point by the sudden influx. Housing was suddenly in short supply; quite a few Mariel refugees in Florida had to sleep in the Orange Bowl, underneath a highway overpass, or in tent cities. On May 6, Carter, in response to pleas from Florida governor Bob Graham, declared Florida a disaster area and authorized ten million dollars in relief for that state to help defray the cost of the refugee influx; U.S. Marines were sent to Florida to help process the refugees.

Camps and Discrimination

In June, 1980, President Carter ordered all those refugees who had not found relatives or others willing to sponsor them placed in detention camps in Wisconsin, Pennsylvania, and Arkansas. In Pennsylvania and Arkansas, the refugees, bored and fearful about their future, rioted. By October, the majority of the Marielitos had been released into various communities, and the detention camps were closed.

News of the riots fueled a growing backlash in U.S. public opinion against the Mariel refugees. The much-publicized presence of criminals among the refugees also helped generate a feeling of revulsion against the entire group: Marielitos were blamed for the upsurge in violent crime in Miami in 1981. In 1980, a year of economic downturn, many people in the United States feared that more Cuban refugees would mean higher unemployment.

Once released from custody, Marielitos faced a difficult adjustment. Unlike earlier Cuban refugees, the Marielitos did not arrive in the midst of general prosperity; they came when the twin plagues of inflation and recession were besetting a U.S. economy still struggling to absorb refugees from Vietnam, Laos, and Cambodia. Hence, Marielitos did not receive as much financial assistance from the federal government as earlier Cuban refugees. In addition, more of the Marielitos were poorly educated people from blue-collar backgrounds; more of them were single men without family ties; and a larger percentage of them were black or mulatto. Marielitos of all colors faced prejudice and discrimination, not merely from Euro-Americans but also from longer-settled Cuban Americans, who saw the Marielitos as insufficiently hardworking and feared that popular U.S. resentment of the Marielitos might rub off on them. In 1983, Marielitos in Miami had an unemployment rate of 27 percent; although the rate had been cut to 13 percent by 1986, they still lagged behind longer-settled Cuban Americans in employment and income.

Marielitos who ran afoul of the law quickly discovered that, however minor their offenses, they had fewer rights than native-born U.S. criminals. Marielitos who had criminal records in Cuba or who committed crimes in the United States faced incarceration for an indefinite term in federal prisons. In 1985, President Ronald Reagan secured a promise from Castro to take back Marielito criminals; only a few hundred had been deported when Castro, enraged by U.S. sponsorship of Radio Martí—an anti-Castro radio broadcast—canceled the agreement. In November, 1987, a new agreement provided for the deportation to Cuba of Marielito criminals in return for the acceptance by the United States of Cuban political prisoners; upon hearing of the agreement, Marielitos held in federal prisons in Oakdale, Louisiana, and Atlanta, Georgia, rioted, taking hostages. The riots ended only when the Reagan administration promised that no prisoner would be sent back to Cuba without individual consideration on his or her case, and that some of those whose offenses were relatively minor would be released into the community. In 1995, however, eighteen hundred Marielitos were still incarcerated in federal prisons.

The American Reaction

When the Mariel boatlift began, Islamic militants in Iran had already publicly humiliated the United States government by seizing and holding captive U.S. diplomatic personnel. The seemingly uncontrollable Cuban refugee influx came to be seen as a symbol, not of the bankruptcy of Communism, but of Carter's alleged ineptitude in conducting U.S. foreign policy. U.S. voters' anger over the refugee influx, together with widespread frustration over economic recession and the Iranian hostage crisis, helped doom Carter's bid for reelection in November, 1980.

The Mariel boatlift of 1980 revived xenophobia among people in the United States. Until 1980, much of the U.S. public had seen Cuban refugees as courageous freedom fighters, comparable to Czechs or Hungarians fleeing Soviet tanks rather than to Puerto Ricans or Mexicans fleeing poverty; the presence of criminals and misfits among the Marielitos shattered the benign Cuban stereotype. After 1980, sentiment would build steadily for reducing the number of immigrants and refugees admitted into the United States. The ultimate consequence of the Mariel boatlift of 1980 was President Bill Clinton's decision in August, 1994, when faced with a new exodus from Cuba, to eliminate the privileged status of Cuban asylum-seekers.   *Paul D. Mageli*

Core Resources

Mark S. Hamm's *The Abandoned Ones: The Imprisonment and Uprising of the Mariel Boat People* (Boston, Mass.: Northeastern University Press, 1995) is the best study of the Marielito prison riots of 1987; also contains much information on the 1980 boatlift. Alex Larzelere's *Castro's Ploy, America's Dilemma: The 1980 Cuban Boat Lift* (Washington, D.C.: National Defense University Press, 1988) is a detailed study on the boatlift, especially valuable for its look at the decision-making process within the Carter administration. Gil Loescher and John A. Scanlan's *Calculated Kindness: Refugees and America's Half-Open Door, 1945-Present* (New York: Free Press, 1986) examines the effect of the Mariel boatlift on the shaping of U.S. refugee policy in general. Silvia Pedraza-Bailey's *Political and Economic Migrants in America: Cubans and Mexicans* (Austin:

University of Texas Press, 1985) compares the demographic portrait of the Marielitos with that of earlier Cuban refugees. Alejandro Portes and Alex Stepick's *City on the Edge: The Transformation of Miami* (Berkeley: University of California Press, 1993) is one of the few deep studies of the Marielitos' adjustment problems.

See also: Cuban Americans; Miami riots of 1980; Refugees: U.S. policy.

Marital assimilation

In 1964, while attempting to analyze the general process of assimilation, sociologist Milton Gordon developed the notion of marital assimilation. He argued that marital assimilation has occurred in a society when intermarriage between two groups is widely accepted. Although this type of acceptance is likely to lead to a high level of intermarriage, the actual rates of intermarriage are not the proper gauge of marital assimilation. Instead, marital assimilation is measured by the support the interracial or interethnic couple receives from the rest of society. Gordon conceptualized marital assimilation as the third stage of a seven-step process by which minority groups eventually become assimilated into the culture of the dominant American society. He argued that marital assimilation can occur only after structural assimilation has taken place and that such assimilation precedes what he terms identification assimilation. Some scholars have argued that marital assimilation may also be the most critical stage of this process because if it lasts for an extended period of time and there are a high number of intergroup marriages, then both groups will begin not to think of themselves as separate groups. This may lead to the development of common values and shared identities. *George Yancey*

See also: Anglo-conformity; Assimilation: cultural and structural; Assimilation theories; Attitude-receptional assimilation; Behavior-receptional assimilation; Civic assimilation; Identification assimilation; Interracial and interethnic marriage; Structural assimilation.

Marranos

As a result of the Spanish Inquisition, by 1492 all the Jews in Spain had either converted to Catholicism (about 100,000), had been murdered (about 30,000), or had been forced into exile (about 200,000). Expulsion or conversion was enforced in Portugal in 1497. As a result, Jews remaining in these nations subverted their religious beliefs but remained "secret Jews." Marranos were the

secret Jews of Spain and Portugal. The word *marrano* generally is believed to be a derisive Spanish word meaning "swine" and is rejected by most descendants of secret Jews. In the 1990's, the term "Crypto Jews" was furthered by the Society for Crypto-Judaic Studies, which based its research primarily in the southwestern United States. *Anusim*, Hebrew for "forced one," also is a positive term that is often used. *Conversos* historically has referred to either sincere or insincere Jewish converts to Christianity, and "New Christians" has differentiated Jewish converts to Catholicism from Old Christians (Spanish Catholics).

Brazil had the largest number of secret Jews in the Americas, and a few overt and secret Jews escaped the Inquisition there to begin the first Jewish settlement in the United States in 1654 in New Amsterdam (later New York City). The Dutch governor of New Amsterdam applied restrictions that were rapidly removed because of pressure from the Jewish community in Holland.

Small numbers of descendants of secret Jews who settled in Protestant areas in the eastern United States usually were openly Jewish and relatively accepted. However, most secret Jews in North America were in Mexico, where the Inquisition also existed. They mostly moved into isolated parts of present-day New Mexico and other Mexican territories in order to minimize threats from the Inquisition's headquarters in Mexico City. Frequently they remained secretly Jewish but openly practiced Catholicism because of fears of the Inquisition, Spanish Catholicism's generally negative attitude toward Jews, and the pervasiveness of Catholicism. Over several centuries, most became Catholics in belief as well as practice; however, specific Jewish rituals sometimes remained. Some practitioners knew that the customs were Jewish, and others continued these practices but over time lost knowledge of their Jewish meaning. In the southwestern United States, beginning in the 1980's, a noticeable number of descendants of Crypto Jews began returning to Judaism. In many cases, they were strongly criticized by members of their families because of strong Catholic family identities, family fears of stigmatization, or anti-Semitism.

Traditional (Orthodox) Judaism has rigid rules requiring that a person's mother be Jewish or that an Orthodox conversion take place before an individual is considered Jewish. Therefore, descendants of the Crypto Jews are not accepted as Jewish unless they undergo an Orthodox conversion. Conservative Judaism and Reform Judaism have some religious flexibility, but most North American Jews have backgrounds in Eastern Europe (Ashkenazim) and know little about Crypto Jewish history and survival. This lack of knowledge, a tendency to define Jewishness (customs, foods, language, and so on) in Eastern European terms, and some traditional religious objections have hindered under-standing of and acceptance of descendants of Crypto Jews who have returned openly to Judaism. Sephardim (Jews descended from the Jews of Spain and Portugal) are more knowledgeable about Crypto Jewish history and practices, but traditional religious beliefs have pre-vented full acceptance of Crypto Jews. A few rabbis in the southwestern United States accept Crypto Jewish descendants as Jews without conversions, viewing them as returning Jews.   *Abraham D. Lavender*

See also: Anti-Semitism; Ashkenazic and German Jews; Eastern European Jews; Religion-based ethnicities; Sephardic Jews.

Marxist models

There are two models of race relations that are held by interpreters within the Marxist tradition. The first and oldest view is quite similar to the social class theory of race relations proposed by the sociologist Oliver Cox in *Race Relations: Elements and Social Dynamics* (1976) and by the historian Herbert Aptheker, in works such as *American Slave Revolts* (1943). This interpretation sees racism as part of the method used by the wealthy, ruling class to divide the working class. If African American and white workers hate each other because of their skin color, they are less likely to join together to challenge the capitalist system. Racial consciousness is another aspect of "false consciousness," which for Marxists refers to the totally false and misleading view of how the world works that is presented to the victims of exploitation by the ruling elite. This false consciousness, which says that African Americans are biologically and culturally inferior to whites, prevents workers from seeing their common interest, which is the destruction of capitalism.

A newer Marxist perspective does not deny the earlier interpretation but adds a significant new factor to it. The best explanation of this view is found in the work of historian Eugene Genovese, especially in *Roll, Jordan, Roll: The World the Slaves Made* (1974). The new factor is the creation of a racial consciousness among the ex-ploited population that challenges the supremacist ideas of the ruling class. This spirit of nationalism among the victims of racist thought helps them create a sense of purpose and dignity. These values help them eventually come together to challenge the economic and political power of the dominating elite.

Both Marxist views describe black-white relations within the context of a capitalist economy. Capitalist society is already divided into social classes that have unequal power, so the division of the lowest class, the workers, into racially hostile camps makes the task of organizing a revolution just that much more difficult. For Marxists, a revolution led by workers is the only way to eliminate inequality. Racism, like low wages and child labor, is another form of inequality. The question is how attitudes based on white supremacy can be overcome.

One proposal calls for all workers to unite in a color-less, raceless, revolutionary struggle simply by recogniz-ing the absurdity of racist pronouncements. The other model for change calls for workers to discover the con-tradictory nature of racism. They need to understand that racism is a source of oppression and division that prevents workers from joining together in the fight for equality. However, at the same time, the horrors of white society's racist past have stimulated an ideology of libera-tion and unity among the people most severely injured by that past. Eventually that new spirit of revolt (black nationalism) will help lead the way toward the destruc-tion of capitalist society itself. Marxists generally believe that once economic exploitation is ended, racism, too, will disappear, because there will no longer be a need for it.   *Leslie V. Tischauser*

See also: Class theories of racial/ethnic relations; "Class-less" society; Social stratification theories.

Massie case

One evening in 1931, Thalia Massie, wife of naval lieu-tenant Thomas Massie, walked home from a nightclub in Waikiki, Honolulu, Hawaii. Arriving home with her face bruised and her lips swollen, she claimed that she had been raped by dark-skinned local men. After police arrested five young men who were having an altercation with a couple in another car, they took the five men to her hospital room, where she identified the five as her rapists but only after police brought them into her hospital room four or five times. The evidence was so slim that a jury of local residents refused to bring in a verdict in *Hawaii v. Ahakuelo* (1931).

Incensed that justice had not prevailed, the Massies sought revenge. With the aid of two subordinate naval officers, the Massies arranged to abduct one of the defendants, who was tortured and accidentally shot. In *Hawaii v. Massie* (1932), the conspirators were convicted of murder despite an eloquent defense by their attorney, Clarence Darrow. After sentence was passed, Governor Lawrence Judd commuted the sentence to one hour of detention in the office of the governor. For Asian Ameri-cans and native Hawaiians, the Massie case became the symbol of white misrule over nonwhites.   *Michael Haas*

See also: Chin, Vincent, murder; Hawaiian and Pacific Islander Americans; Loo, Ming Hai, murder.

Meech Lake Accord

Fears that Quebec might break away from the rest of Canada led Canadian prime minister Brian Mulroney and the ten provincial premiers in 1987 to propose a set of amendments to the 1982 Constitution Act. The proposal, known as the Meech Lake Accord after the site of the meeting, recognized French-speaking Quebec as one of the founding nations of Canada and as a distinct society with its own language and culture. The accord, however, granted no such courtesy to the aboriginal peoples of Canada. In order for the accord to become law, it required ratification by all ten provinces before June 23, 1990.

An additional provision of the Meech Lake Accord dealt with admission of a new province to the Confederation. That provision required the unanimous consent of the ten existing provinces in order to establish a new province. Since many of the provinces have territorial desires to extend their borders north, this virtually ensured that the Yukon and Northwest territories, as well as the proposed Nunavut Territory, would be precluded from ever achieving provincial status. Unlike the rest of Canada, the two regions have overwhelmingly native populations.

Native organizations fought bitterly against ratification of the accord. Their leaders insisted that native cultures were no less distinct than Quebec's and that aboriginal rights also deserved formal recognition in the body of the constitution. Since the courts had held that despite the addition of the Charter of Rights and Freedoms to the constitution, aboriginal rights were not assured, the natives' concerns were well justified. The leaders further demanded guarantees that they would be given a role in all future First Ministers' conferences affecting natives. George Erasmus, national chief of the Assembly of First Nations, was especially vocal.

Thinking that a looming deadline would help assure passage, Prime Minister Mulroney delayed pushing for ratification of the accord until the very end of the ratification period. That delay proved fatal to the proposal. It allowed Elijah Harper, Manitoba's only native legislator, to prevent consideration of the Meech Lake Accord by the Manitoba Legislative Assembly. Supported by native organizations, Harper exploited a procedural error made by Manitoba Premier Gary Filmon. Manitoba law required unanimous consent of the legislators to begin public hearings on any issue with less than a forty-eight-hour notice. Harper withheld his consent, and the deadline for ratification passed without the Meech Lake Accord ever being considered by the Manitoba Legislative Assembly.

Richard G. Condon and Pamela R. Stern

See also: Aboriginal Canadians; Declaration of First Nations; Distinct society concept; Indian Act of 1876; Indian Act of 1951; Indian Act of 1989; Indian-white relations: Canada.

Melting pot theory

At the beginning of the twentieth century, the playwright Israel Zangwill described the United States as a society in which cultural, ethnic, and racial differences would disappear, and people would become amalgamated. His vision was of people from many different racial and ethnic groups socializing freely with one another, sharing customs and values, intermarrying, and creating one uniquely American culture. This vision was called the "melting pot ideal."

Many Americans share a melting pot ideal, but some ethnic groups have "blended in" far more easily than others. Immigrant ancestors of some white ethnic groups, including the Irish and Jews, experienced much prejudice and discrimination. Over time, however, whites have been better able to gain access to the power structure than nonwhites, enabling them to blend in and shape the dominant American culture. White Americans whose families have been in the United States for many generations usually are not viewed as "hyphenated" Americans—Swedish Americans or German Americans—and major cultural distinctions among descendants of most white ethnic groups have "melted" away over time. These groups have intermarried, have learned the English language, have worked to achieve higher socioeconomic standing, and have become acculturated. Most whites, therefore, epitomize the melting pot ideal.

Discrimination and poverty, however, have prevented many members of nonwhite ethnic groups from blending in with the rest of the society. Only with the passage of civil rights legislation in the 1960's were many nonwhites even allowed to vote. For example, black slaves and most of their descendants were denied opportunities to achieve higher education, obtain jobs, enter the middle class, live in white neighborhoods, gain access to power structures, and be recognized for personal achievements and their contributions to the United States. One consequence is that almost one-third of African Americans live below the poverty line, compared with one-tenth of whites. African Americans, historically, have been one of the least successful groups at blending into the great melting pot of mostly middle-class Americans.

In the second half of the twentieth century, immigrants have been far more likely to come from a variety of Latin American and Asian countries rather than European nations. Many find it difficult to assimilate because of anti-immigrant attitudes among some long-established

The melting pot theory–the idea that all immigrants would blend into American society–was based largely on the experience of European immigrants such as these viewing the Statue of Liberty from a ship in 1887. The theory breaks down when applied to the experiences of African and Asian Americans.

Meritocracy myth

The myth of meritocracy assumes that those at the pinnacle of society's institutions have achieved their status solely through merit. Many elites possess meritorious criteria: intelligence, prestigious degrees, and high scores on "objective" tests. Therefore, proponents of meritocracy argue that stratification is the legitimate result of talented, hardworking individuals besting lackluster or lazy ones. Some even argue that those who fail to achieve are either genetically or culturally inferior. Critics of meritocracy ask whether racial and ethnic minorities have an equal chance to compete, that is, whether there is equality of opportunity in the United States. They point out that social circumstances, from the onset of life to its end, are profoundly unequal. Some children are born into families through which they inherit privileges. Familial advantages are augmented by institutional discrimination, as is the case with education in the United States. Critics argue that as a myth, or moral fiction, meritocracy justifies racial and ethnic (and class and gender) stratification and masks power and privilege; moreover, opponents submit that the measures of merit (for example, IQ tests) are culturally biased. One policy question since 1965 (affirmative action) has been debated by those who, opposing the myth, want to implement more inclusive, multicultural standards, and merit fundamentalists who contend that merit is untainted and should prevail as the undiluted justification of status.

Gil Richard Musolf

See also: Ability testing; Affirmative action; Equality of opportunity; Intelligence testing; Social stratification theories.

Americans who sometimes claim that immigration means fewer jobs and more taxation for themselves. Welfare stereotypes have also contributed to xenophobia, or hatred of foreigners. As a result, some politicians have proposed public policies that deny immigrants and their children access to schools, jobs, citizenship, and basic social services. Even when those proposals do not become law, a hostile climate for nonwhite ethnic groups develops, making a true melting pot impossible.

Moreover, not all Americans wish to completely blend into the dominant culture, believing that the United States is enriched by celebrating diverse cultural traditions, and not by asking or forcing people to completely assimilate. Proponents of this position prefer the metaphor of the mixed salad bowl, in which each ingredient (ethnic group), makes a unique and important contribution to the taste of the entire "salad." It is further argued that idealizing the United States as a melting pot merely provides justification for members of the power structure to impose their cultural values on others—for example, with English-only initiatives. Still others argue that more "melting" must take place among the ethnic groups before a true sense of unity can be attained among all Americans. *Grace Maria Marvin*

See also: Assimilation: cultural and structural; Assimilation theories; Pluralism vs. assimilation.

Mestizo

"Mestizo" is a Spanish word that comes from the Latin *mixtus*, meaning mixed, and it refers to any person of mixed ancestry. The term always implies that the mestizo speaks either Spanish or Portuguese fluently, and there have also been implications of biological superiority and inferiority associated with the term. In Latin America, the definition of "mestizo" varies from country to country, and it must be understood in its cultural context. In Central and South America, it designates a person of combined Indian and European extraction. In Mexico, the word was originally used to indicate any person of mixed Indian and white ancestry, but the definition has become so vague and variable that it is no longer used in census reports in Mexico. The upper-class people of mixed ancestry in Mexico are now called Creole or *cruzado* rather than mestizo. In some countries, particularly Ecuador, mestizo has taken on social and cultural connotations, referring to pure-blooded Indians who have adopted European dress and customs. In Brazil, a person who speaks Portuguese, lives as a storekeeper or trader in the backwoods, and deals with the Indians is typically referred to as a mestizo; however, in the Philippines, the term denotes any person of mixed foreign and native ancestry. *Alvin K. Benson*

See also: Biracialism; Creole; Multiracial identity.

Metis

> **Significance:** The Metis, or métis, are people of mixed European and North American Indian ancestry. They played a vital but unrecognized role as cultural brokers in the settling and governing of North America. In Canada, they have developed a distinctive way of life and think of themselves as a nation with rights.

In the broadest sense, *métis* (pronounced mahTEE), with a small *m*, refers to people of a dual North American Indian and white ancestry. *Metis*, with a capital *M*, indicates a distinctive ethnic group with a particular sociocultural heritage and/or political or legal category. In Canada, Metis usually refers to people who are descendants of Scottish or French fur traders who married Cree or Ojibway women. The French traders operated along the St. Lawrence River in Acadia (New France) and the English in the Hudson Bay region, creating two groups of Metis, those with French ancestry along the Ottawa River and Upper Great Lakes and those of Scottish ancestry in the Hudson Bay region from the Rupert River to Churchill.

French Metis
The French contingent of the Metis is older and more populous than its Scottish counterpart. Initially, French officials supported intermarriage,

hoping to forge trading and kinship ties, encourage conversion to Christianity, and populate Acadia. In the 1600's, Metis families and communities developed from Acadia to Labrador. The union was usually between a French man and a native woman. During this period, Metis were used as interpreters, intermediaries, and distributors of gifts from French officials.

By the eighteenth century, partly because of the increased presence of white women, policy and opinion shifted against mixed marriages, especially those not sanctioned by the church. The official policy of discouraging mixed unions was probably one of several factors that led to the formation of distinct Metis communities in New France. Numerous American and Canadian communities around the Great Lakes originated as biracial communities, namely Detroit and Michilimackinac in Michigan; Sault Sainte Marie in Ontario; Chicago and Peoria in Illinois; Milwaukee, Green Bay, and Prairie du Chien in Wisconsin.

These communities developed a culture of their own, which included an attenuated form of French Catholicism. Family and daily life was largely based on the norms of Indian society. Metis worked as guides, interpreters, voyagers, or suppliers to the forts. The region was rich in game, fish, wild rice, and maple sugar, and the climate and environment were conducive to a slash-and-burn style of farming. In essence, the Metis of French ancestry followed the Indian way of life. An Indian woman was indispensable, because in that society, a man lost position and respect if he did any tasks considered women's work, such as cooking or sewing.

Scottish Metis
The Metis of Scottish ancestry developed quite differently. After the Treaty of Utrecht in 1713, Hudson Bay Company posts were established north of the Great Lakes watershed, the region draining into Hudson Bay. Enclaves of Cree Indian formed around the trading posts, and the Indians became provisioners who were crucial for the survival and success of the company. To consolidate trade and ensure a lasting friendship, the

Metis and Overall Population in Canada, by Sex, 1996

	Metis	Non-Metis	Total Population Canada
Both sexes	210,190	28,317,935	28,528,125
Male	104,470	13,942,405	14,046,875
Female	105,720	14,375,530	14,481,250

Source: Census of Canada, 1996

Metis and Overall Population in Canada by Age Groups, 1996

	Metis	Non-Metis	Total Population
0-4 years	22,955	1,894,470	1,917,425
5-9 years	22,025	1,967,775	1,989,800
10-14 years	21,050	1,970,930	1,991,980
15-19 years	20,130	1,935,985	1,956,115
20-24 years	18,390	1,874,520	1,892,910
25-34 years	36,050	4,445,265	4,481,315
35-44 years	31,230	4,811,795	4,843,025
45-54	19,590	3,678,380	3,697,970
55-64	10,760	2,467,055	2,477,815
65 years and older	8,005	3,271,765	3,279,770

Source: Census of Canada, 1996

Cree offered women as wives to the Europeans. No white women were at the trading posts, but the Hudson Bay Company had strict rules prohibiting its employees from marrying Indians. The company believed it necessary to prohibit white-Indian unions because it wanted to maximize security, minimize expenses (such as those incurred by dependents of the employees), and decrease friction with the Indians. Despite the prohibition, unions occurred. By 1810, the company began to take responsibility for educating the progeny of its trading post employees; however, it also discouraged the formation of communities dependent on the trading post by removing from the Hudson Bay region all retired and dismissed employees and encouraging the Indians to disperse to their hunting grounds each winter. Except for a few children who became servants for the company, the mixed-race offspring were absorbed by the Cree.

Establishing a Metis Identity

With the British conquest of New France in 1760, a sense of separateness began developing among the Metis. Francophones were relegated to lower ranks, and in the United States, after the Canadian-United States boundary was established in 1794, American white settlers and governments displaced numerous Metis communities in the lower Great Lakes region. These refugees migrated northwest to Manitoba and Minnesota.

In the northwest, the Metis evolved a distinct way of life that was neither Indian nor European but uniquely Metis. When conflict erupted in the region, the North West Company argued that the Metis were defending an identity and interest of their own. The company policy had the side effect of helping the Metis develop a sense of unity. Catholic missionaries encouraged the Metis to maintain their French language and Catholic faith.

Group identity was further fostered when a large group of Metis settled at Red River, attracted by the mission of Bishop Joseph Provencher and led by Cuthbert Grant, who was of mixed ancestry. However, it was the buffalo hunt that brought the Metis together. The excitement of hunting buffalo and profits from selling pemmican and buffalo meat were preferred over the dullness and low profitability of agriculture. Hunting for buffalo and working on boat brigades to St. Paul encouraged Metis to remain nomadic.

Decline of the Metis

Change for the Metis came fast when Canada began annexing the northwest. The buffalo hunt was ending, and railroads were replacing boats and carts. An attempt by the Canadian government to survey the Red River without respecting the land held by the Metis resulted in the Riel Rebellion (also known as the Red River Rebellion) of 1869-1870. The Metis, led by Louis Riel, Jr., set up a provisional government to fight for their collective rights. Negotiations that followed promised a land base for the Metis, but the promises were not kept, and European Canadian settlers and troops who arrived in the area from 1870 on were hostile to the Metis. Although some Metis went south to the United States and others went north, most went west to the Catholic mission near Fort Edmonton. While the government was negotiating treaties with the Indians and land rights with the railroads, the Metis sought clear land titles but were ignored. In frustration, the Saskatchewan Metis took up arms under Riel and Gabriel Dumont in the Second Riel Rebellion of 1885 (also known as the Northwest Rebellion). They were defeated at Batoche, Riel was executed, and the Metis dispersed, particularly to Alberta, weakened politically and cohesively.

From 1885 to the mid-1900's, the Metis were impoverished and demoralized. Some lived on reservations with the Indians, but others did not identify as strongly with this part of their heritage. During this time, they formed some associations, including the Union Nationale Métisse St. Joseph de Manitoba, which collected documents and testimony that led to A. H. de Tremaudan's History of the Metis Nation in Western Canada. In addition, new leaders, such as Patrick "Jim" Brady and Malcolm Norris, emerged to build a political base to defend Metis interests. Provincial organizations then developed, and the Metis eventually were successful in obtaining some land for their group and passage of the Metis Betterment Act of 1938.

Metis Culture in the 1990's

Of the more than 200,000 Metis in Canada, most reside in Northern Alberta on more than 500,000 hectares of land. The Metis have a distinct culture, often combining Indian and Euro-Canadian culture. For example, "jigging," a form of Metis dance, combines the reels of Scotland and France with the chicken dance of the Cree. The Metis language combines English, French, and Cree words and is spoken in addition to English. Most in the settlements retain Indian spiritual beliefs and customs. The Metis are working to make schools in their region more responsive to their culture.

The economy is dominated by ranching, logging, farming, and energy products. The Metis have developed a mixed plan that combines traditional economic activities with industrial and other commercial ventures. Also, efforts are progressing to grant land titles to the Metis. *Arthur W. Helweg*

Core Resources

D. Bruce Sealely's and Antoine Lussier's *The Metis: Canada's Forgotten People* (Winnipeg: Pemmican Publishers, 1981) sets forth the origins and history of the Metis and describes the hardships they still face. Normand Josee's *A Profile of the Metis* (Ottawa: Statistics Canada, 1996) examines the cultural distinctiveness of the Metis in the historical, legal, political, linguistic, and cultural categories. Ken and Victoria Zeilig's *Ste. Madeleine: Community Without a Town* (Winnipeg: Pemmican Publishers, 1987) describes a 1930 incident in which Canadian government officials turned a Metis community of thirty large families into a pasture.

See also: Biracialism; Indian-white relations: Canada; Multiracialism.

Mexican American Legal Defense and Education Fund

Founded by San Antonio lawyer Pete Tijerina in 1968, the Mexican American Legal Defense and Education Fund (MALDEF) works through litigation and other legal avenues to battle discrimination and integrate Mexican Americans into the U.S. mainstream. Headquartered in Los Angeles, MALDEF maintains regional offices in Fresno, Sacramento, San Francisco, and Santa Ana, California; El Paso and San Antonio, Texas; Detroit, Michigan; Chicago, Illinois; and Washington, D.C. The organization has a professional staff of about sixty-five and relies on volunteers to perform the bulk of its work. *Frederick B. Chary*

See also: Chicano movement; Immigration and emigration; Latinos in the United States.

Mexican American Women's National Association

The Mexican American Women's National Association (MANA) began in 1974 in Washington, D.C., as a feminist organization associated with the women's movement. Because other feminist groups were not addressing concerns of Mexican Americans, and because male-dominated Hispanic groups spoke for women in Congress, women with Chicana backgrounds formed MANA. Dedicated to their cause, MANA leaders volunteer their service in order to handle all the tasks normally done by paid staff.

MANA goes into Mexican American communities, where it forms a network to encourage leadership and to promote public awareness of the issues that concern Mexican American women. Its members have testified before Congress and have campaigned for the Equal Rights Amendment (ERA) and family leave and against sterilization abuse.

Considering education a top priority, MANA started a project called Hermanitas (meaning "little sisters") to help junior high and high school girls with future career choices and to guide them through the requirements needed for high school graduation and college.

In the early 1990's, MANA had chapters in sixteen states and members in thirty-six, many of whom were not Mexican American. Their concerns have grown to include pay equity, teen pregnancy, and children in poverty. Information is transmitted to members through a quarterly newsletter, issue updates, and conventions. Through the group's efforts, many Mexican American women have broken through barriers to become leaders in their communities. *Marilyn Elizabeth Perry*

See also: Ethnic identities of women; Immigrant women; Latinas; Women of color.

Mexican deportations

Significance: Massive unemployment during the Depression prompted deportation of immigrant workers in order to redistribute jobs to U.S. citizens.

In the early decades of the twentieth century, immigration of Mexican nationals into the United States was a growing phenomenon. It was not viewed as a problem because cheap labor was welcomed, particularly on farms and ranches. U.S. immigration laws generally were enforced selectively with regard to Mexicans. During

World War I, at the request of U.S. businesses, the provisions of the Immigration Act of 1917 that required immigrants to pay an eight-dollar "head tax" and prove literacy were waived for Mexican laborers. This special order legitimized U.S. dependence on cheap Mexican labor and institutionalized Mexico's special status.

At the end of World War I, the order was not rescinded; in fact, U.S. companies intensified their recruitment of Mexican farmworkers. Industrial companies in the Northeast and Midwest, such as steel mills and automobile manufacturers, also began recruiting Mexicans from the Southwest, resulting in an expanding migration in terms of both numbers of immigrants and their geographic spread. The Emergency Immigration Act of 1921 and the National Origins Act (Immigration Act of 1924) had each limited immigration from Europe, but no restrictions were imposed on the number of immigrants from countries in the Western Hemisphere. Thus, a large and growing population of Mexican immigrants had established itself in the United States in the first decades of the twentieth century.

A Change in Attitude
In the 1920's, the U.S. government's attitude toward Mexican immigrants gradually changed from lax enforcement to severe restrictions. As social and economic conditions deteriorated on a global scale, the great pool of cheap Mexican labor was increasingly resented by unemployed U.S. citizens. Despite pressure from businesses, laws restricting entry—that is, the head tax and literacy test—began to be strictly enforced against Mexicans by immigration authorities. Two new laws also were passed that had a further chilling effect on Mexican immigration to the United States: the Deportation Act of March 4, 1929, which made illegally entering the United States a misdemeanor punishable by a year in prison or a fine of as much as one thousand dollars, followed by the May 4, 1929, law making it a felony for a deported alien to reenter the United States illegally. These laws, followed by the October, 1929, stock market crash that marked the onset of the Great Depression in the United States, set the stage for a period of repressive measures against Mexican nationals in the United States.

As the Depression caused more unemployment, the caseloads of social welfare agencies increased. By 1931, as the pool of unemployed immigrants requiring assistance grew, local agencies intensified their efforts to force repatriation; on the federal level, calls to deport immigrants increased also. President Herbert Hoover endorsed the aggressive efforts to expel aliens, restrict legal immigration, and curtail illegal entry. William N. Doak, who took office as Hoover's secretary of labor in December, 1930, proposed that any alien holding a job be deported. The Bureau of Immigration, at that time a

part of the Department of Labor, began an aggressive campaign of rooting out illegal aliens, with the objective of reducing unemployment and thus hastening the end of the Great Depression. Many of the aliens deported under this program, however, were already unemployed.

Although Mexicans were not specifically targeted by the immigration authorities, they were numerically the most affected as a group. The response of the Mexican government to the problem varied: At times, land reform programs were established for repatriating Mexican citizens; at other times, Mexico feared the addition of more unemployed citizens to its labor surplus. Opportunities for Mexican Americans to obtain land in Mexico usually required money to be invested, although occasionally there were programs that offered land to destitute repatriates.

California's Response
In the southwestern states, particularly, immigration officials aggressively sought deportable Mexicans, and social service agencies encouraged Mexicans to volunteer for repatriation. The most ambitious of these programs was undertaken in Los Angeles County, California, but cities such as Chicago and Detroit, where Mexicans had been recruited by industry in the early 1920's, also were actively attempting to get even legal Mexican residents to leave in the 1930's.

The Los Angeles Citizens Committee on Coordination of Unemployment Relief, headed by Charles P. Visel, had been charged with assisting the unemployed residents of the city, especially through creation of jobs, for which longtime local residents would be given preference. Inspired by Labor Secretary Doak's earlier pronouncements that some 400,000 deportable aliens were believed to be in the country, Visel set out to identify and deport as many illegal aliens as possible from the city of Los Angeles. Visel contacted Doak and requested that a sufficient number of immigration agents be deployed in Los Angeles to create a hostile environment, from which he hoped aliens would flee voluntarily. Visel planned to open his campaign with press releases and a few well-publicized arrests.

Although the plan was not aimed specifically at Mexicans, some statements made by Visel did mention Mexicans as a group to be targeted. The Spanish-language newspapers in Southern California stirred up the Mexican community, both in Los Angeles and in Mexico, by publishing inaccurate stories that virtually all Mexicans were being targeted for deportation. In the first three weeks of February, 1931, immigration agents had investigated several thousand people, 225 of whom were determined to be subject to deportation. Figures released by Visel's committee in March, 1931, indicated that 70 percent of the persons deported up to that time in the Los Angeles campaign were Mexicans. According to the Mexican Chamber of Commerce, an estimated 10,000 of the more than 200,000 Mexicans thought to be living in Los Angeles prior to 1931 had left; many of these repatriates owned businesses and homes in Southern California. It should be noted, however, that the Chamber of Commerce would be more likely to have contact with the more prosperous members of the population than with the unemployed or laborers.

Concurrent with the federal and local campaigns to deport illegal aliens, Los Angeles County officials began attempting to repatriate destitute Mexicans. Many Mexican nationals had entered the United States at a time when penalties for illegal entry were nonexistent or seldom enforced against Mexicans; thus, their legal status was uncertain. With chances of unemployed Mexicans finding employment in the United States slim, welfare officials were beginning to put pressure on alien relief recipients to return to Mexico, at times leading them to believe that if they did not leave voluntarily, they would be cut off from aid immediately.

Frank Shaw, a member of the Los Angeles County Board of Supervisors, was the first area official to propose paying the cost of transporting families back to Mexico by train. In March, 1931, 350 Mexicans signed up for the first trip. Many more trips were made, but statistics on the numbers who were repatriated under the county program are clouded by the fact that the same trains that carried county-aided Mexicans also carried deportees and Mexicans who had made their own arrangements to leave, and accurate records were not kept. Overall, the various efforts to reduce the number of immigrants in Southern California in the early 1930's caused a noticeable, but temporary, reduction of the Mexican population in the area.   *Irene Struthers*

Core Resources
Lawrence A. Cardoso's "The Great Depression: Emigration Halts and Repatriation Begins," in *Mexican Emigration to the United States, 1897-1931* (Tucson: University of Arizona Press, 1980) discusses federal deportation efforts and local repatriation efforts in the early 1930's. Abraham Hoffman's *Unwanted Americans in the Great Depression: Repatriation Pressure 1929-1939* (Tucson: University of Arizona Press, 1974) is a comprehensive look at the deportation and repatriation of Mexicans, particularly from Los Angeles County, in the 1930's. Matt S. Meier and Feliciano Ribera's *Mexican Americans and American Mexicans: From Conquistadors to Chicanos* (New York: Farrar, Straus & Giroux, 1993) is a comprehensive history of the Mexican presence in the United States.

See also: Bracero program; Immigration Act of 1924; League of United Latin American Citizens; Operation Wetback; United Farm Workers.

Miami riots of 1980

Significance: The Miami riots of 1980 constituted one of the most violent urban disorders in the United States since the 1960's. The random killing of whites, not merely the looting of stores, was the goal of the rioters. Yet if the excesses of the rioters were terrible, the provocation that moved them to these acts was also severe.

On December 17, 1979, Arthur McDuffie, a thirty-three-year-old African American insurance agent with no criminal record, was riding along the highway on his motorcycle when several officers of the Public Safety Department of Dade County ordered him to stop. When he refused to do so, he was pursued; when captured, he was beaten severely with nightsticks and heavy flashlights. McDuffie died a few days later from the injuries he had sustained at the hands of the police. This was the last of several incidents of alleged police brutality in the county in 1979: These included the shooting death of a teenager in Hialeah; the alleged sexual abuse of a prepubescent African American girl by a white police officer; and the severe beating administered by police to a black schoolteacher, after the police had raided his house in search of illegal drugs.

The Trial and Aftermath
The state attorney for Dade County, Janet Reno, prepared a case against four Dade County police officers who had beaten McDuffie. The case was brought to trial on March 31, 1980, in the town of Tampa, on the state's gulf coast; it was believed that the officers could not get a fair trial in Miami. Because of peremptory challenges by the defense attorney, the jury before which the case was tried was all white. The jury's decision, handed down on Saturday afternoon, May 17, 1980, shocked Miami's African American community: The police officers were acquitted of all charges.

In the early evening hours of May 17, the anger of the black Miamians boiled over into violence; rocks began to fly, and mobs began to attack individuals. Later that evening, after a mob attempt to set fire to the Metro Justice Building was barely repulsed, the governor of Florida, Bob Graham, ordered the National Guard to Miami; it did not arrive in full force, however, until Tuesday. It was not until May 23 that the situation was returned to normal. As a result of the riots, 18 people died and hundreds were injured. There was eighty million dollars' worth of property damage and 1,100 people were arrested. Many Miami businesses were burned: African American, Cuban, and native-born white business owners all suffered.

Major arteries of traffic, used by motorists of all races

and ethnic backgrounds, ran through Liberty City, a black area near Miami. In the evening hours of May 17, several white motorists, presumably unaware of the verdict, drove through that neighborhood, where they encountered maddened crowds, composed mostly of young people, bent on revenge. About 250 whites were injured that night in attacks by rioters; 7 whites died as a result of the injuries sustained. Of those who died, one middle-aged woman perished from severe burns when her car was set afire; a young sales clerk, a teenager, and a sixty-three-year-old Cuban refugee butcher died as the result of severe beatings. The reign of terror that night was mitigated only by the willingness of some courageous African Americans to rescue persons threatened by the mobs. The deliberate attacks on whites distinguished the Miami riot from the urban riots of the late 1960's, in which most deaths had occurred by accident.

In the days following that bloody Saturday, blacks were riot victims as well. Some of those killed were rioters; others were law-abiding individuals mistaken for rioters by the police; still others appear to have been random shooting victims of unknown white assailants. Most Miami-area African Americans were neither rioters nor heroes nor victims; they simply waited for the disturbances to end.

For the United States, the Miami riot of 1980 ended twelve years of freedom from major urban riots. Riots broke out again in Miami's African American ghetto in December, 1982; in January, 1989 (when a Hispanic police officer, William Lozano, shot and killed an African American motorcyclist); and in July, 1995. The later riots, however, were not as costly in lives or property as the 1980 outburst. In May, 1993, Lozano's acquittal by a jury in Orlando was not followed by violence.

The Miami riot of 1980 was an alarm bell, warning the United States of the sharp tensions between the races that still persisted a decade and a half after the legislative victories of the Civil Rights movement, and of the combustible possibilities that existed wherever blacks, native-born whites, and Hispanic immigrants lived side by side. The triggering of the Miami riot by an unpopular jury verdict rather than by immediate actions by the police foreshadowed the trajectory of the disastrous riot of April 29-May 1, 1992, in Los Angeles, California. *Paul D. Mageli*

Core Resources
Paul Anderson's *Janet Reno: Doing the Right Thing* (New York: John Wiley and Sons, 1994) offers insights into the character and personality of a key player in the 1980 events. Raymond A. Mohl's "On the Edge: Blacks and Hispanics in Metropolitan Miami Since 1959" (*Florida Historical Quarterly* 69, July, 1990) traces the riots of 1980, 1982, and 1989 back to African American anger at Cuban success. Bruce Porter and Marvin Dunn's *The Miami Riot*

of 1980: Crossing the Bounds (Lexington, Mass.: D. C. Heath, 1984) is a detailed book-length account of the 1980 riot. Alejandro Portes and Alex Stepick's *City on the Edge: The Transformation of Miami* (Berkeley: University of California Press, 1993) presents the May, 1980, riot as part of a long process by which Miami-area blacks came to see Cuban refugees, as well as native-born whites, as their oppressors. Jerome H. Skolnick and James J. Fyfe's *Above the Law: Police and the Excessive Use of Force* (New York: Free Press, 1993) compares the McDuffie incident with cases of police brutality in other U.S. cities and provides a good account of efforts within the Dade County police department, after 1980, to control the use of force by police.

See also: Cuban-African American relations; Cuban Americans; King, Rodney, case; Los Angeles riots of 1992; Mariel boatlift; Race riots of the twentieth century; Watts riot.

Middleman minorities

> **Significance:** Middleman minorities stand, economically and socially, midway between majority groups and other minority groups. They typically engage in brokering occupations; because of their occupations and presumed characteristics (they are often said to be thrifty and clannish), they are often the object of resentment or even hatred.

"Middleman" minorities, or middle minorities, are groups that, in a number of societies around the world, act as intermediaries between producers and consumers. This intermediary position frequently causes conflict with dominant and subordinate groups and includes (primarily) such functions as moneylending, trading, and shopkeeping. Historically, many groups have occupied this niche. They include Jews, the "overseas Chinese," Indians in East Africa, the Lebanese in West Africa, and Armenians in Ethiopia. The fact that such diverse groups, operating in very different societies, exhibit similar traits has led to much theorizing about middleman minorities. According to sociologist Robin Ward, these theories seek to answer three key questions: why particular groups become middleman minorities, why these groups enter into the specific occupations characteristic of middleman minorities, and what causes hostility toward them?

Reasons for Becoming Middlemen
The first question is, in fact, two questions, because social scientists must not only account for why particular groups become middleman minorities but also explain why others do not. Answers to the first part of this question fall into two broad categories: structural factors and cultural attributes.

Structural factors refer to the economic opportunities that unfold before certain groups, thereby enabling them to become traders, moneylenders, or any of the other occupations characteristic of middleman minorities. For example, in "The Koreans: Small Business in an Urban Frontier" (1987), sociologist Ilsoo Kim argues that as Jewish and Italian small business owners have retreated from inner cities, Korean immigrants, using readily available cash, have bought their stores. This option is attractive because, though many are highly educated, their difficulties with English hinder advancement in the professions. Moreover, the Korean community possesses a variety of institutions, both religious and social, that facilitate the immigrants' transition into American life. To these structural factors must be added such cultural traits as frugality (which includes hiring relatives at low wages), clannishness, and hard work. Thus, Koreans' success as small-business owners has resulted from a combination of structural and cultural factors. The same is true of other groups, such as the Chinese and Japanese.

In the United States, the success of these groups in small business has been contrasted to the relative lack of success by African Americans. This difference is heightened because African Americans have a much longer history in the United States and because many Asian (especially Korean) small businesses operate in black enclaves of the larger American cities. The answer appears to lie in a combination of structural and cultural barriers. Historically, racial discrimination in obtaining start-up capital has been the chief structural barrier faced by would-be African American businesspeople. Yet, as sociologist Ivan Light argued in *Ethnic Enterprise in America* (1972), this explanation by itself is inadequate, since black West Indian immigrants have played the role of middleman minorities in Harlem. He attributes success in this role to West Indians' continuation of the African cultural tradition of rotating credit associations, which allowed them to generate start-up capital within the immigrant community, thereby partially bypassing discriminatory treatment by banks. In contrast, this practice has died out among African Americans; consequently, they have had fewer nondiscriminatory resources on which to draw to start small businesses.

Occupational Choice

There are a variety of reasons why middleman minorities enter into particular occupations, some of which have already been discussed. For the sake of convenience, these may be placed into three categories: economic, historical, and sociocultural. Economic factors include situations (as noted for Koreans in the United States) in which groups find that a demand exists in certain areas of society and take advantage of it. This suggests a certain element of chance. As sociologist Donald L. Horowitz

has shown in *Ethnic Groups in Conflict* (1985), however, colonial policy in some developing countries steered some groups into particular occupations. Over time, a pattern of ethnic recruitment occurred, and folk beliefs justifying why some groups are more "suitable" to certain occupations arose. Examples include Chinese traders in Malaysia and Sikh artisans in India. In these examples, historical and sociocultural factors overlap to create middleman minorities.

Violence and Middleman Minorities

A third key question with respect to middleman minorities is why they are so often the victims of deliberate violence. The reasons for this violence are many, and violence toward middleman minorities originates from both the dominant and subordinated groups in society. Economist Thomas Sowell argues that a general reason for this violence is the view that, despite their usefulness, middleman minority occupations are inherently degraded. Hence, different groups performing the same role in different societies will face similar criticisms. A second reason is that middleman minority occupations become identified with all members of the group regardless of the actual occupations of individual members. This ethnocentric response identifies and intertwines despised minorities with despised roles. Sowell notes that a third reason for conflict is the ability of middleman minorities to achieve success in the professions. They come to be seen as formidable competitors and are resented, especially by subordinated minorities who view this success as coming at their expense. Political manipulation of latent antimiddleman minority sentiments is yet another reason for violence against middleman minorities. Horowitz shows that this occurs, for example, where subordinated minority groups, seeking to start businesses but finding middleman minorities as competitors, stir up trouble in an attempt to gain a competitive advantage.

Historical Context

The middleman minority concept has had a long history, rooted in the similar experiences of a number of groups around the world. Particularly important is the experience of Jews in Europe, for as social scientist Walter P. Zenner has pointed out, many of the theories of middleman minorities originated as attempts to explain anti-Semitism. Historically, European Jews have closely matched the profile of the middleman minority. They stood as intermediaries between nobles and serfs, performing such occupations as moneylending and merchandising. They tended to be frugal, hardworking, clannish, and highly educated. The result was economic success but at the cost of great hostility from their non-Jewish neighbors. A variety of negative stereotypes about Jews developed. These included charges of disloyalty (for refusing to assimilate), deviousness, and dishonesty in business. Additionally—and significantly, in societies dominated by Catholicism—they were accused of being anti-Christian. Stereotypes such as these resulted in the ghettoization of Jews and repeated pogroms, culminating in the Holocaust of World War II. Thus, both Jewish economic success and the persecution of Jews in Europe were intimately tied to their peculiar status as middleman minorities.

The historical experiences of Jews closely match those of a number of other such groups, which points to the need for a concept to tie a minority group's experiences to its economic function relative to dominant and subjugated groups. For example, sociologist D. Stanley Eitzen has shown the existence of close historical similarities between the Jewish experience and that of the Chinese in the Philippines. As is the case with the Jews in Europe, Chinese contact with the Philippines dates back hundreds of years. By the time the Spanish took control of the Philippines in 1571, the Chinese had already established themselves as craftsmen, merchants, and moneylenders. Initially welcomed by the Spanish for their useful economic function, they soon experienced ghettoization and mass killings (by the Spanish) because of their new economic power. This hostility has lasted through the period of American occupation (from 1898 to 1946) to the present. In the post-1946 independence period, nationalistic fervor combined with anti-Chinese sentiment to limit opportunities for the Chinese in the Philippines. For example, the Filipino government has made it difficult for Chinese to become citizens, limited their ownership of land, and prevented their entrance into certain industries.

The historical similarities between groups are the result of the economic roles they occupy in society rather than of who they are. It seems that a particular combination of brokering occupations and values that enhance economic success in these occupations always leads to hostility. The historical evidence suggests that as long as some groups exist in this mode they will to some degree remain outsiders to the societies in which they live and will suffer success mixed with persecution.   *Milton D. Vickerman*

Core Resources

Edna Bonacich's "A Theory of Middleman Minorities" (*American Sociological Review* 38, October, 1973) attributes middleman minorities' occupational choices and values (for example, clannishness) to their "sojourner" status. Donald L. Horowitz's *Ethnic Groups in Conflict* (Berkeley: University of California Press, 1985) downplays the idea that middleman minority occupations cause conflict. Illsoo Kim's "The Koreans: Small Business in an Urban Frontier," in *New Immigrants in New York* (New York: Columbia University Press, 1987), edited by Nancy Foner, argues that a combination of economic

opportunity, fiscal preparedness, education, community organization, and values have helped Koreans achieve success in the United States. Ivan Light's *Ethnic Enterprise in America* (Berkeley: University of California Press, 1972) investigates the factors making for success—or the lack of it—among minorities. Thomas Sowell's "Middleman Minorities" (*The American Enterprise* 4, May/June, 1993) argues that the possession of certain values is the central characteristic of middleman minorities.

See also: Assimilation: cultural and structural; Economics and race; Jewish Americans; Korean Americans; Melting pot theory.

Migrant superordination

Migrant superordination refers to the process whereby an immigrant group of "foreigners" subdues the native people of a territory. The classical form of this relationship is colonization, in which the migrant group uses force to dispossess the indigenous group of land, resources, or work. The resulting superordinate/subordinate relationship can take economic, political, and cultural forms. This relationship is characterized by the institutionalization of dominant-minority relations in which the migrants enjoy disproportionate power, resources, and prestige. The power relationship is then justified by a system of beliefs that rationalizes the superiority of the immigrant group in relation to the indigenous people. Reactions on the part of the indigenous people range from resistance and rebellion to accommodation and assimilation. Examples of migrant superordination include the European conquest of Native Americans in the Western Hemisphere and of Africans in South Africa.   *M. Bahati Kuumba*

See also: British as dominant group; Colonial model of racism; Dominant group; External colonialism; Minority and majority groups; Subordinate group.

Military and racial/ethnic relations

> **Significance:** Racial and ethnic relations in the U.S. military became the center of attention with the integration of the armed forces in 1948 and the shift to an all-volunteer service in 1973. Sociological, ethical, and political concerns revolve around recruitment, promotion, and official military policy regarding race.

The regular service of minorities, especially African Americans, in the U.S. military is a relatively recent phenomenon. Before the Civil War (1861-1865), the U.S. military tradition was one of erratic militia-based service and sanctioned prejudice. Therefore, minorities played very little role in U.S. military life. The Civil War saw the first real attempt to incorporate blacks into the service, strangely enough, on both sides of that conflict. However, they were largely used in noncombat roles, especially in the South, and their use, though playing a marginally important part in the Union's victory, was hotly debated and carefully segregated. This segregation continued well into the twentieth century through two world wars.

The years immediately after World War II saw the first impetus for change. Various segregated black units and a few individual black servicemen (such as Dorrie Miller, a Navy hero at Pearl Harbor) had distinguished themselves in battle, and this opened the debate on the desegregation of the armed forces. President Harry S Truman initiated new policies on race relations in the military, and the services were mostly integrated by the start of the Korean War in 1950. The U.S. Navy, previously the most conservative branch, actually took the early lead in promoting equality within the ranks. Gradually, African Americans began gaining some ground, a few even rising to officer status. During the Vietnam War (1957-1975), a multitude of problems arose, many of which concerned black troops.

From Conscription to the All-Volunteer Force

The United States' modern wars, from the Civil War to the Vietnam War, were largely fought by conscripts or draftees. In the two world wars, conscription and segregation went hand in hand. The wars in Korea and Vietnam, especially the latter, were the United States' first experience with draftees fighting in an integrated service. Although conscription was designed to promote equitable social and ethnic representation in the services, it was often alleged that blacks were overly represented and burdened with the risks of combat during the Vietnam War. Indeed, the poor and minorities appear to have suffered from the inequities of the draft, in large part because middle-class and more affluent people could more easily be excused from service or obtain deferments. This discrepancy was also caused by the war's increasing unpopularity. As the combat effectiveness of conscripts declined in the later years of the Vietnam War, the debate ensued as to the desirability of having an all-volunteer force (AVF).

Initially, opposition to ending the draft arose from many quarters. This opposition was based on notions that a large, all-volunteer force would be mercenary, ineffective, socially unrepresentative, and costly. Never-theless, in 1970, a presidential task force known as the Gates Commission forwarded recommendations that an AVF was possible if military pay and benefits were raised to meet civilian standards. By 1973, the AVF was in place as the last U.S. troops left Vietnam. This AVF seemed to function well at first, but problems arose that led to a decline in quality of personnel for the next decade. The 1980's, however, saw two important changes occur: the onset of serious effort and spending to upgrade the AVF and the implementation of solid racial policies in the U.S. military.

The AVF and Race Relations

The 1980's saw a marked improvement in the overall effectiveness of the AVF. Higher pay, better benefits, and more effective advertising have been cited as the cause. Enlistment eligibility requirements were raised considerably during this time. The number of blacks enlisting in the service continued to rise, reaching 22 percent in 1989. The greatest increase in black recruits occurred in the U.S. Navy, where enlistment doubled. Because of the higher eligibility standards, the educational and aptitude levels of all recruits, including minorities, continued to rise into the 1990's. With this higher-quality recruit came a concerted effort at improving race relations and the advancement prospects of minorities in the services. In some respects, an outward attempt was made to make the AVF not only combat effective but also an ideal model in the areas of cost-efficiency, team effort, and race relations. Efforts to improve recruits' sensitivity to race began as early as 1973, but the U.S. military consistently added policies throughout the years that have achieved a remarkable level of color-blind professionalism. Racial incidents underwent a steady decline and have been dealt with sternly. The military maintains a complex system of grievance procedures and racial protocol. Indeed, the U.S. military's record on race is, by most accounts, far better than its record on gender and other issues.

The issue of race and social representation is also a factor in both vocational placement and promotion through the ranks. For active-duty personnel, there appears to be equal representation in combat roles, while blacks occupy larger numbers of clerical, administrative, and logistical positions. A few experts have even suggested capping minority recruitment in some areas, although this would revive the issue of discrimination. The U.S. military boasts the largest percentage of minorities in command roles in its entire history, and an African American officer, General Colin Powell, served as chairman of the Joint Chiefs of Staff during the critical period of the Persian Gulf War. When that conflict erupted in early 1991, it was seen as a major test of the effectiveness of the AVF. Smart bombs and other high-tech weaponry may have garnered the attention of most viewers, but professional military men were quick to point out the readiness and steady professionalism of the men and women of the all-volunteer force that handily won the Gulf War. *Gene Redding Wynne, Jr.*

Core Resources
S. A. Stouffer's *The American Soldier* (Princeton, N.J.: Princeton University Press, 1949) offers an account of the motives behind integration of the services. Bowman, Little, and Sicilia's *The All-Volunteer Force After a Decade* (Washington, D.C.: Pergamon-Brassey's, 1986) sheds some positive light on the emerging professional army of the period. D. Bandow's "An Involuntary Military: Paying More for Less," in *The Anthropo Factor in Warfare: Conscripts, Volunteers, and Reserves* (Washington, D.C.: National Defense University, 1988), edited by Lee Austin, clearly expresses some doubts. David R. Segal, in *Recruiting for Uncle Sam* (Lawrence: University Press of Kansas, 1989) deals with the attraction of new recruits to the service. For a firsthand look at the role of black troops in the new military, see Ronald Walters's *African-American Participation in the All-Volunteer Force*, testimony before the Committee on Armed Services, U.S. House of Representatives, March 4, 1991.

See also: African Americans in the Civil War; Desegregation: defense; Military desegregation; Tuskegee Airmen.

Military desegregation

On July 26, 1948, President Harry S Truman established a major precedent in the history of equal opportunity for all races when he issued two executive orders. The first, 9980, allowed governmental employees to appeal discriminatory employment procedures to the Fair Employment Board, a subdivision of the Civil Service Commission. The second, 9981, potentially revolutionized race relations in the United States by integrating the armed forces of the United States.

The president's military desegregation order exhibited a characteristic bluntness that came to symbolize his presidency. "It is hereby declared," he commanded, "to be the policy of the president that there shall be equality of treatment and opportunity for all persons in the armed services without regard to race, color, religion, or national origin."

Critics immediately lambasted the order. The *Baltimore Sun* accused Truman of trying to win African American votes. There may have been some merit to this charge: African American leader A. Philip Randolph quickly announced the cancellation of a civil disobedience campaign planned for August 18, 1948. However, when General Omar Bradley insisted that the U.S. Army would not participate until "the nation as a whole" joined the effort, Truman struck back. He would not equivocate on this issue; he would not retreat a single inch. The military was to obey. Unlike other presidents who tried but failed to protect civil rights in the military, Truman personally ensured the end of racial discrimination and segregation in the armed forces.

By January, 1950, Executive Order 9981 effectively integrated most of the military. For example, blacks and whites were working together in the U.S. Air Force, and some black officers now commanded white enlisted airmen. Changes in the Air Force did not attract much

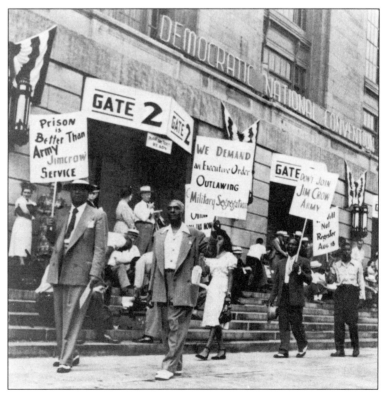

African Americans demonstrate outside the Democratic National Convention, demanding desegregation of the U.S. military. In 1948, President Harry S Truman issued Executive Order 9981, desegregating the military.

attention, however, since only 351 African American officers served in the corps, constituting less than 1 percent of the entire branch.

Similar advances, despite stubborn resistance by some officers, occurred in the U.S. Navy. By December 22, 1949, all black U.S. Marines experienced integrated basic training. The Navy also increased its promotional campaign to recruit more African Americans into its Reserve Officer Training Corps. African Americans previously relegated to the lowly rank of steward now found themselves being promoted to petty officer.

In the Army, however, integration proceeded at a slower pace. On June 7, 1949, Secretary of the Army Louis Johnson ordered the tempo increased. When that failed, African American newspapers called upon the president to intervene. Truman, however, allowed the process to develop at a natural rate, and the Army adhered to a 10 percent quota of African American troops until the beginning of the Korean War. As part of the war effort, the quota was removed, and African American enlistments dramatically increased, prompting Army commanders to desegregate basic training camps. African Americans increased to 11.4 percent of the Army within sixty days after North Korean troops invaded South Korea in June, 1950.

By the time Truman left office in January, 1953, he had reached his goal of nearly total integration of the U.S. military. Although his personal popularity with the U.S. public reached new lows in presidential polls, African American voters remained loyal to the Democratic Party. Executive Order 9981 no doubt played a major role in this significant development.

J. Christopher Schnell

See also: African Americans in the Civil War; Military and racial/ethnic relations.

Milliken v. Bradley

In *Milliken v. Bradley* (1974), the U.S. Supreme Court decided that courts did not have the authority to order school desegregation plans that required moving schoolchildren across school district lines unless it could be shown that school district lines had been constructed in a manner designed to preserve segregation.

By the early 1970's, many urban school districts continued to operate schools with a majority black population because of the dearth of white students in those school districts. In 1971, the U.S. Supreme Court in *Swann v. Charlotte-Mecklenburg Board of Education* had held that urban school boards could be required to engage in extensive school busing to integrate their schools. The *Swann* decision, however, did not address the issue of how to integrate urban school districts that had few white students.

In the early 1970's, a group of black parents, with the assistance of the National Association for the Advancement of Colored People Legal Defense and Educational Fund, brought suit seeking to desegregate the Detroit school system. In 1972, federal district court judge Stephen Roth ruled that the Detroit schools were in fact illegally segregated and ordered a multidistrict desegregation plan involving the Detroit city school district along with fifty-three surrounding suburban school districts. One year later, the U.S. Court of Appeals for the Sixth Circuit affirmed, holding that the Detroit schools could not be adequately desegregated without such a multidistrict plan. Shortly thereafter, the U.S. Supreme Court agreed to hear the case.

In 1973, the Supreme Court had considered a similar multidistrict desegregation plan involving the Richmond, Virginia, schools. In that case, the Court had divided 4 to 4, with Justice Lewis Powell recusing himself because of his prior membership on the Richmond School Board. The Court took the Detroit case to decide the question of whether multidistrict desegregation plans were required when inner-city school districts could not otherwise be desegregated. In the meantime, the specter of multidistrict desegregation prompted a firestorm of activity in Congress, as many members of Congress backed both legislation and amendments to the Constitution restricting the ability of federal courts to order extensive desegregation plans.

The Supreme Court held in the *Milliken v. Bradley* decision, with a 5-4 vote, that a district court should not order an interdistrict remedy unless it could be shown that the school district lines had been constructed in a manner to preserve segregation or unless state government officials had taken other action that contributed to the interdistrict segregation. This was a burden of proof that would prove difficult to meet. The *Milliken* decision marked the first time that the Supreme Court had declined to refine existing school desegregation jurisprudence to further integrationist goals.

In the wake of the *Milliken* decision a few metropolitan areas did adopt interdistrict desegregation remedies, but, for the most part, the decision undermined desegregation efforts in America's cities. Unable to utilize an assignment plan that included children from surrounding suburban school districts, inner-city school boards were greatly restricted in their efforts to desegregate their schools.

Davison M. Douglas

See also: *Brown v. Board of Education*; Busing and integration; Discrimination: racial and ethnic; Segregation: de facto and de jure; *Swann v. Charlotte-Mecklenburg Board of Education*.

Million Man March

> **Significance:** In October, 1995, an event known as the Million Man March took place in Washington, D.C. The march was significant in that it was successful in assembling more than one million African American men in the nation's capital for a day of reckoning. Although the march's controversial sponsors, Louis Farrakhan and Benjamin Chavis, caused many Americans, particularly certain black leadership, to question the legitimacy of the event, the march did require the nation to focus on the various predicaments that confronted black men in the United States.

On October 16, 1995, more than a million men of African descent converged on Washington, D.C. They came from all over the United States. The majority were poor and working class, a sizable number were middle class, and some were affluent. They all came with the intention of becoming better men once they returned to their homes. The event was known as the Million Man March, and it was one of the major media stories of 1995.

Led by the controversial Nation of Islam leader, Louis Farrakhan, and a former National Association for the Advancement of Colored People (NAACP) leader, Benjamin Chavis, the march generated an ample amount of positive and negative publicity. Farrakhan is well known for his virulent anti-Semitic remarks, and Chavis was voted out of his position as NAACP president after it was disclosed that he had paid $332,400 in organizational funds to his former mistress. Farrakhan, by addressing the deepest concerns of many African Americans at a time when many other black politicians were alarmingly silent, managed to insert himself into the center of what was (and still is) an ongoing racial debate in the United States. Because of the march's success, many mainstream media pundits conceded that Farrakhan was a force to be acknowledged. Ted Koppel, on ABC's *Nightline*, stated that Farrakhan could be called "one of the most influential leaders in black America." During the march, Farrakhan advocated pride, love, and black self-reliance.

Dissenters

From the outset, the event was mired in controversy. Many leaders, black and white, questioned the ability and/or sagacity of Farrakhan and Chavis to cosponsor a march that called for equality and brotherhood. Critics of Farrakhan pointed to his virulent anti-Semitic attacks on Jews and other minorities; critics of Chavis noted his larceny and infidelity. Both men were chided by many women and women's rights organizations for their deeply ingrained sexism.

Mary Francis Berry, chairperson of the U.S. Commission on Civil Rights, wrote a letter in the October, 1995, issue of *The Washington Post* in which she stated, "I do not trust Louis Farrakhan or Benjamin Chavis to lead us to the Promised Land." More than a few African Americans endorsed Berry's sentiments. A *U.S. News & World Report* poll taken in 1995 found that 31 percent (almost a third) of African Americans harbored an unfavorable impression of Farrakhan. Such disdain was echoed by many Jewish leaders as well. On September 19, 1995, the Anti-Defamation League of B'nai B'rith (a Jewish civil rights organization) took out a full-page advertisement in *The New York Times* aggressively denouncing Farrakhan. The advertisement stated, "This march will be led by the most mainstream anti-Semite in recent American history." Alvin Poussaint, a leading black psychiatrist at Harvard University Medical School, said that Farrakhan had to confront his controversial racist past. Poussaint argued that Farrakhan could not continue to speak out of both sides of his mouth and fail to take into account how his own remarks were interpreted.

The Million Man March also exposed the tension that existed between men and women in the African American community. Syndicated columnist Julianne Malveaux; Gloria Watkins, distinguished professor of English at City College in New York; and other prominent African American women denounced the event because of what they saw as the endemic paternalism and sexist message that the march promoted. Other African American women raised similar arguments. With the exception of poet Maya Angelou and the late Betty Shabazz (widow of Malcolm X), virtually no African American women were present at the march.

Supporters of the "no women allowed" policy argued that by prohibiting African American women from attending the march, African American men would be able to concentrate on themselves as individuals and their responsibilities as men, and would not be distracted. Opponents of excluding women from the march argued that such a decision demonstrated the lack of sensitivity that has always been a part of the Nation of Islam regarding women. By engaging in such an act, Farrakhan and his supporters had ignored the crucial role that African American women have played in the struggle for freedom. By relegating African American women to a secondary role, Farrakhan demonstrated either his historical ignorance or gross insensitivity toward his female brethren.

Economic Class

Other supporters of the march participated out of a spirit of defiance. Although a sizable number of middle-class men attended the march, the majority of the men came from working-class backgrounds. These were men

Nation of Islam leader and march sponsor Louis Farrakhan (on screen) addresses the crowd of African American men gathered in Washington, D.C., for the Million Man March in October, 1995.

black and white, harbored toward Farrakhan. In the October 23, 1995, article "A Million Men, Minus One," *Time* magazine journalist Jack White criticized and dismissed Farrakhan and discussed his boycotting of the event. In the October 16, 1995, article "Marching to Farrakhan," *Time* magazine journalist David Van Biema talked about the events surrounding the Million Man March. Eric Pooley in his *Time* magazine article, "To the Beat of His Drum" (October 23, 1995), argued that Farrakhan had forced the nation to acknowledge the force he has in black America. The *Time* magazine piece "I, Too, Sing America" (October 30, 1995) examined the sociological impact that the march had on African American men. The October 9, 1995, *Newsweek* magazine article "Farrakhan on the March," written by Vern E. Smith and Steven Waldman, discussed how Farrakhan attempted to give exposure to the voice of a silent majority, the black underclass.

See also: African American women; Black nationalism; Family and socialization: African Americans; Million Woman March; Nation of Islam.

Million Woman March

The Million Woman March took place in Philadelphia, Pennsylvania, on October 25, 1997, and provided African American women the opportunity to discuss some key racial issues. The streets were filled with women pushing baby strollers, beating drums, and walking with the determination to be counted among the several hundred thousand women who attended the historic gathering. Participants carried the red, black, and green flag of the national African American movement and banners that showed the many areas from which they had traveled. The event was organized by activist and bookstore owner Phile Chionesu and was attended by many African American celebrities, including actors Blair Underwood, Margaret Avery, and Jada Pinkett, as well as Winnie Mandela, former wife of South African president Nelson Mandela.

The women marched to draw strength from one another and to focus on their common problems. The event provided a forum to address many issues that are not typically dealt with by women's groups. Some of the main issues discussed were human rights abuses against

who had seen their economic prospects falter and had become increasingly distrustful of many successful people, white or black. This was also the group within the African American community that has most recently responded to the message of manhood, greater family responsibility, and black pride.

Farrakhan provided hope for many working-class blacks, who used the march to demonstrate their rage against and resentment of many mainstream Americans, black and white, who argued that African Americans should stay away from the march and that Farrakhan and Chavis were nothing more than two racist and sexist hatemongers who epitomized everything that was negative about black nationalism. On the contrary, for many blacks in this socioeconomic class, these two men embodied all that was absent in their lives. Farrakhan and Chavis were able to tap into the hopelessness, despair, and uncertainty that many of these men felt. Despite opposition, even the Million Man March's detractors conceded that the event was a success. The march put the spotlight on African American men and gave Farrakhan a renewed sense of visibility and importance.

Elwood David Watson

Core Resources

Scott Minerbrook's article in *U.S. News & World Report*, "The Right Man for the Job?" (October 16, 1995), debated whether Farrakhan had the moral and political resources to be a spokesperson for a march of one million men. Sylvester Monroe, in his *Time* magazine article "The Mirage of Farrakhan" (October 30, 1995), discussed the ambivalence that many Americans, both

African Americans, the start of independent African American schools, and a demand for an investigation into allegations of Central Intelligence Agency involvement in the crack cocaine trade in African American neighborhoods. Most of the women left inspired to make changes in their communities, and Chionesu planned to hold a second Million Woman March.   *Alvin K. Benson*

See also: Ethnic identities of women; Million Man March; Women of color.

Minority and majority groups

> **Significance:** Minority groups are defined by their powerlessness relative to other groups in a society, and majority groups are the reverse: They dominate other groups. This concept helps explain why and how conflict occurs in ethnically stratified societies.

"Minority group" and "majority group" are complementary concepts (one implies the other) that denote a hierarchical relationship of dominance and subjugation between groups. The terms carry much emotional and political baggage because of their association with two related concepts, "race" and "ethnicity." To understand minority and majority groups, one needs to distinguish between the sociological viewpoint just outlined and the meanings attributed to the terms by the ordinary person in the street. Sociologists tend to define the concepts strictly, whereas nonacademics define them loosely. This lack of precision lends itself to misconceptions, but it is also true that the sociological viewpoint has inherent problems.

Scholarly vs. Popular Definitions
Anthropologists Charles Wagley and Marvin Harris have put forward a widely accepted definition of the term "minority group." In *Minorities in the New World: Six Case Studies* (1958), they argued that five characteristics identify these groups. First, they are relatively powerless compared with members of the dominant group. Second, they share distinctive cultural and/or physical characteristics that distinguish them from the dominant group. This fact, along with their powerlessness, exposes them to unequal treatment. Third, their distinctive traits cause minority groups to become self-conscious social units. Fourth, an established rule of descent exists for transmitting membership in minority groups across generations. Fifth, members of minority groups tend to marry within their groups.

Most social scientists agree that these criteria are not equally important. They view minority groups' relative

powerlessness as the most important criterion distinguishing them from majority groups. For example, in *Majority and Minority: The Dynamics of Race and Ethnicity in American Life* (1991), sociologist Norman Yetman argues that "minority group" is synonymous with the term "subordinate," and "majority group" is synonymous with "dominant." The main implication of this viewpoint is that, contrary to what one might assume, members of minority groups can constitute a numerical majority in their society, and majority group members might be a numerical minority. The classic example of this is South Africa, where blacks, although they constitute approximately 75 percent of the population, were powerless under apartheid, while whites, constituting approximately 14 percent of the population, were dominant.

Sociologists distinguish between racial, ethnic, religious, and gender groups, on one hand, and minority and majority groups on the other. They view the latter twin concepts as subsuming the others. That is, majority groups and minority groups may consist of distinct races, ethnic groups, religious groups, and gender groups. These various types of majority/minority groups differ from each other symbolically. Thus, racial majority/minority groups are set apart by physical features, ethnic majority/minority groups by their unique cultural attributes, religious majority/minority groups by unique spiritual beliefs, and gender majority/minority groups by societal expectations of sex-linked characteristics. A minority and majority group might display a number of these characteristics simultaneously. An example of an overdetermined minority group would be black, Haitian, female Catholics.

Nonacademics often adopt a loose definition of minority and majority groups. They tend to ignore the latter concept and focus on the former. In this focus, "minority group" becomes synonymous with specific racial and/or ethnic groups, and the term "minority" is often used to refer to individuals belonging to these groups. Thus, in the United States, the term "minorities" is often understood to mean blacks and/or Hispanics. This is controversial, because such usage often occurs in a pejorative context and may be viewed as a way of attacking those two groups. Used in this way, the term "minority" can become a weapon in intergroup conflict.

Problems with Definitions
Adopting the sociological viewpoint on majority/minority groups leaves less room for confusion. Nevertheless, this viewpoint also has problems. To begin with, it seems counterintuitive to suggest that numerical majorities can be, in fact, "minorities." This is not a problem when a group—for example, African Americans—is both numerically smaller and less powerful than the dominant group. As sociologist Pierre L. van den Berghe (*Dictionary*

of Race and Ethnic Relations, 1988) has suggested, however, that colonial subjects who vastly outnumber their colonial rulers might take umbrage at the notion that they constitute a "minority." The problem is that the commonsense understanding of "minority" conflicts with sociological usage; therefore, the potential for confusion exists.

Van den Berghe even argues that this confusion is deliberate, since it serves useful political purposes. In pluralistic societies—such as the United States—that have instituted affirmative action programs to aid historically disadvantaged groups, being identified as a "minority group" can prove beneficial in some instances. The problem lies in deciding which groups are minority groups. Blacks and Hispanics are uncontroversial choices, but whether Jews, Japanese Americans, and Chinese Americans should be considered minority groups is more problematic and controversial. These groups, though numerical minorities, enjoy a level of socioeconomic success which far outstrips that of blacks and Hispanics. Thus, the term "minority group," with its connotation of powerlessness and relative deprivation, seems somewhat inappropriate. A fuzzy definition of "minority group," however, would give these economically successful groups a firmer claim to minority status and, with it, even greater access to societal resources. Van den Berghe suggests that similar confusion over the term "majority group" allows the tiny elite who exercise hegemony over the United States to cloud their identity and escape criticism by being lumped into a larger category—white Anglo-Saxon Protestants—who are perceived, mistakenly, as the dominant group.

Use of the Concept
The concept of minority groups has long been used in Europe to describe national groups who, for whatever reason (for example, through conquest by another group), have come to form small enclaves in societies dominated by other groups. Early in the twentieth century, the concept was adopted by American sociologists seeking a comprehensive term to describe the multifaceted intergroup conflict that has been a recurring theme in American history. With respect to blacks, American Indians, the Chinese, and the Japanese, the conflict seemed to be racial; with respect to groups such as Eastern European Jews, the Irish, and Italians, the conflict seemed to revolve around religious and cultural differences. As noted above, the unifying thread was domination by one group (native whites) of these various other groups. This suggested to sociologists such as Donald Young the need for a word to encapsulate all these various conflicts. In *American Minority Peoples* (1932), he suggested that the term "minority groups" be used to describe the distinctive groups who found themselves in conflict with the white majority.

Since the time of Young's proposal, the minority group/majority group concept has gained widespread acceptance because of the universality of intergroup conflict following European decolonialization. This process created new states such as India and Pakistan, but it also led to widespread racial, ethnic, religious, and nationalistic conflicts. Not all of these can be described as minority group/majority group situations, but many are. Examples include the Rodiya and Sinhalese in Sri Lanka, the Hutu and Tutsi in Burundi, and the Osu and Ibo in Nigeria. In *Ethnic Groups in Conflict* (1985), Donald Horowitz gives numerous examples of such conflict occurring in formerly colonized areas.

The more industrially developed areas of the world are also the scene of numerous minority group/majority group conflicts. The conflict between blacks and whites in the United States is perhaps the best known, but to this could be added French Canadians and English-speaking Canadians, aboriginal Canadians and white Canadians, Australian aboriginals and white Australians, white New Zealanders and Maoris, and nonwhite immigrants and whites in the United Kingdom. Even more pressing examples are to be found in Eastern Europe, where the breakup of the former Soviet Union has allowed long-standing racial, ethnic, religious, and nationalistic hatreds to flare into open warfare. This breakup has combined with economic recession in Western Europe to reawaken antiminority fervor. Thus, in West Germany, Eastern European, Turkish, Vietnamese, and African immigrants have been repeatedly attacked by neo-Nazi groups. In France, agitation against Arab and African immigrants led the government to pass laws making it easier to track the movement of these immigrants. Even traditionally tolerant countries such as Denmark have experienced anti-immigrant sentiment. The prevalence of this type of conflict illustrates why the twin minority/majority group concept is likely to retain its utility. *Milton D. Vickerman*

Core Resources
Donald Horowitz's *Ethnic Groups in Conflict* (Berkeley: University of California Press, 1985) contains numerous examples of intergroup conflict involving majority/minority situations. Peter I. Rose's *They and We* (4th ed., New York: McGraw-Hill, 1990) is a well-written and accessible book on racial and ethnic relations in the United States. George Simpson and J. Milton Yinger's *Racial and Cultural Minorities* (5th ed., New York: Plenum Press, 1985) presents an encyclopedic discussion of issues related to race and ethnicity. *Majority and Minority: The Dynamics of Race and Ethnicity in American Life* (5th ed., Boston: Allyn & Bacon, 1991), edited by Norman Yetman, is a collection of twenty-nine articles that gives a comprehensive overview of the field of race and ethnicity. Donald Young's *American Minority Peoples* (New York:

Harper & Brothers, 1932) is an early book devoted to the subject of minority/majority relations; Young is said to have introduced the concept of minority groups into the sociological literature.

See also: Dominant group; Ethnicity and ethnic groups; Oppositional culture; Racial hierarchy; Resistance, cultures of; Subordinate group.

Minority voting districts

The 1965 Voting Rights Act prohibited limiting the rights of all people to vote and called on the federal government to examine suspect elections. Specifically, it addressed efforts by whites in the American South to keep African Americans from voting. The act was successful in eradicating exclusionary practices and resulted in substantial increases in the numbers of African Americans who voted, but minority political disfranchisement still existed. Minorities remained proportionally underrepresented in elected offices nationwide.

The 1982 amendment mandated the creation of "majority-minority" voting districts in states with a history of racial disfranchisement. Such districts contain populations of minorities large enough to constitute a majority or elect a candidate of their preference. This is achieved through reapportionment, a process whereby districts are periodically redrawn by state legislatures, typically following the decennial U.S. census. Reapportionment ideally reflects the changes in population occurring since the last census count. However, districts were "gerrymandered" during reapportionment to preclude the election of minorities by dividing minority populations across districts. Such gerrymandering for political self-interest is commonplace and was named after Massachusetts governor Elbridge Gerry, who, in 1812, advocated a salamander-shaped voting district.

Redistricting to create minority voting districts has been successful if measured by the numbers of minorities elected to office in such districts. However, minority districts face constitutional challenges.

Robert P. Watson and Claudia A. Pavone Watson

See also: Disfranchisement laws in Mississippi; Reapportionment cases; Redistricting; Representation: gerrymandering, malapportionment, and reapportionment; Voting Rights Act of 1965.

Miscegenation laws

State miscegenation laws were examples of explicit racial discrimination in U.S. statutory law; they criminalized and penalized the unions of persons of differing racial heritages and denied legal legitimacy to mixed-race children born to such interracial couples.

Thirty-eight U.S. states at one time had miscegenation laws in force; seven of those thirty-eight repealed their laws before 1900. All southern states (not including the District of Columbia) had miscegenation statutes. Many western states (including Arizona, California, Montana, Nevada, Oregon, Utah, and Wyoming), in addition to forbidding intermarriage between blacks and whites, also specifically prohibited unions between whites and Native Americans or whites and Asian Americans. Penalties upon conviction varied from a maximum imprisonment of more than two years in most of the South and some other states (ten years in Florida, Indiana, Maryland, Mississippi, and North Carolina) to sentences ranging between a few months and two years in other states. Enforcement of the laws was random and irregular.

The key case in ending miscegenation laws was *Loving v. Virginia* (1967). At the time that the U.S. Supreme Court heard the *Loving* case, sixteen states still had miscegenation laws in force. Virginia's laws dealing with racial intermarriage were among the nation's oldest. They stemmed from statutes formulated in the colonial period (1691) and had been strengthened by more stringent miscegenation legislation passed in the mid-1920's in which whiteness was very narrowly defined. The codes that became law in 1924 were aimed primarily at discriminating against people of mixed African American and white heritage and/or of American Indian background.

In the *Loving* case, Richard Perry Loving, who was white, had married Mildred Delores Jester, who was African American, in Washington, D.C., in June, 1958. The Lovings made their home between Fredericksburg and Richmond in Caroline County, Virginia. They were issued warrants of arrest in July, 1958, and in January, 1959, they were convicted before the Caroline County court of violating Virginia's antimiscegenation statute. Their minimum sentences (of one year imprisonment each) were suspended on agreement that they would leave the state. They moved to Washington, D.C., until 1963, when they returned to their farm in Virginia and worked with attorneys Bernard Cohen and Philip Hirschkop of the American Civil Liberties Union (ACLU), who placed their case under appeal. The miscegenation law and the Lovings' convictions were upheld by the Virginia Supreme Court of Appeals in March, 1966, but in June, 1967, the U.S. Supreme Court overruled the appellate finding. The Supreme Court ruled that use of race as a basis for prohibiting marriage rights was unconstitutional under the Fourteenth Amendment's equal protection and due process provisions. The ruling nullified all remaining laws forbidding interracial marriage. Previous to the unanimous 1967 ruling, the U.S. Supreme Court had taken a conservative approach to this civil rights issue. It had repeatedly avoided reviewing lower court convictions based on state antimiscegenation laws (*Jackson v. Alabama*, 1954; *Naim v. Naim*, 1955; *McLaughlin v. Florida*, 1964).   *Barbara Bair*

See also: Biracialism; Blackness and whiteness: legal definitions; Hypodescent; Hypogamy; Interracial and interethnic marriage; Multiracial identity; One-drop rule; Race as a concept.

Missions, missionaries, and American Indians

> **Significance:** Missionaries and their missions provided American Indians with their first concentrated contact with white culture. Missionaries helped implement the policies of assimilation, agrarianism, and cultural extermination.

From the 1500's, when Spanish and French explorers brought Roman Catholic priests to North America, until the 1950's, missionaries influenced both American Indians and U.S. policy toward Indians. Missionaries taught English, built schools and churches, and created pan-tribal connections. They also, however, spread disease and forced assimilation and Christianization on Indians. Most missionaries were well-meaning, but their efforts were often misguided. Some were so convinced of the correctness and superiority of their own culture and belief system that they tried to suppress and destroy those of the Indians. Missionary work supported by various denominations continues today, but since the 1950's, missionaries have been more sensitive than their predecessors to Indian culture. Missionaries and their missions remain controversial in most American Indian communities today.

Sixteenth Century Through Eighteenth Century
Missionaries first entered North America through the Spanish Empire in Mexico and through French trading posts in Quebec. The Spanish viewed Christianization as their holy duty to God and used it to rationalize conquest. State-sponsored Catholic missionaries developed missions in New Mexico, Texas, Arizona, and California. They provided protection, food, and shelter to the weaker tribes, such as the Pueblo Indians, while being constantly threatened by the stronger tribes, such as the Apaches and the Navajos. This system suffered a setback in the 1680 Pueblo Revolt (also known as Pope's Revolt),

when tribes rose up and chased the missionaries and the Spanish settlers out of New Mexico. The Spanish reestablished the missions within fifteen years.

The French allowed Catholic missionaries into their territory, but they were not state-sponsored as they were in the Spanish Empire. Jesuits attempted to Christianize the Hurons, but instead they brought smallpox, which decimated the tribe. This upset the tribal balance of power, and the Iroquois attacked and killed off most of the Hurons. The Jesuits retreated and simply kept missions at trading posts until the 1790's.

The English Protestants also saw Christianization of the Indians as part of their role in North America. In the seventeenth century, John Eliot of Massachusetts established praying villages where Indians lived "as white men": They wore English clothes, learned farming techniques, and became Christians. As disease decimated many of the Northern Woodlands tribes, the remaining members joined the praying villages for survival. The villages appeared to be successful at attracting converts. Though many of the Indian residents did convert, most died from diseases spread by the whites within the praying villages.

David Brainerd, an Eliot student, began a mission among the Cherokee in Tennessee. The Cherokee used the mission to learn English and to learn about white culture. The high attendance rate made the school appear to be a success, which inspired other Protestant groups to send missionaries among the Indians. All these early missionaries—Spanish, French, and English—believed in the power of Christianity, the importance of sedentary farming, and the necessity of extinguishing Indian culture.

Nineteenth Century
Mission work exploded with the development of large missionary societies between 1830 and 1850. Presbyterian, Methodist, Baptist, and Catholic societies sponsored hundreds of missionaries, both male and female, to work with Indians. Missionaries built schools and churches to attract Indians to Christianity and white civilization. They expected Indians to convert in large numbers and to support their own missions financially (as the natives of India and Africa had done). Despite these efforts, the Indians showed little interest in converting to Christianity.

In the 1850's, the missionary societies grew impatient with the lack of progress. They accepted money from the American government to help support their missions. In return, the government demanded that the missionaries increase their efforts to Christianize and "civilize" the Indians. Money was supplied to help assimilate all Indian groups to sedentary farming and Christianity. This method was a general failure, perhaps most conspicuously with Plains and Northwest Coast groups.

By the 1870's, missionary societies lost patience with the lack of success and cut off funding for missionaries. Individual missionaries became responsible for their own financial support. Many entered into agreements with the U.S. government that tied them to conversion quotas. The government wanted a certain number of "pacified" Indians in exchange for its invested dollars. Additionally, missionaries wrote pamphlets and books about the "wretched condition" of specific Indian groups. These writings influenced public views of the condition of the American Indian. Many of these missionary works formed the basis for anthropological studies of the Sioux, the Cheyenne, the Navajo, the Salish, and other native groups.

Despite their funding problems, missionaries continued their program of assimilation, agrarianism, and cultural extermination. The height of this policy occurred during the 1870's when the government's "peace policy" allowed missionaries to administrate the Bureau of Indian Affairs (BIA). At this time, residential schools became popular. Missionaries removed Indian children from their parents and sent them away to be acculturated into white society. Missionaries forbade the children to speak their own language, wear their own clothes, or practice any aspect of their own culture. At this point, missionary and government policy coalesced into one united front against Indian culture. By the end of the nineteenth century, missionaries had fallen out of favor with the government, which saw their attempts at fostering assimilation as failures. Few Indians had converted to Christianity; most had developed a resentment of missionaries and saw them as agents of cultural genocide.

Missionaries remained part of Indian policy through the 1950's. They ran schools, wrote reports, and continued to act as agents and intermediaries for the government.

Positive Contributions

Though missionaries generally attempted to destroy Indian cultures and societies in their efforts to help Indians, they made some positive contributions. First, education and acculturation provided Indian groups with a common language—English. Second, the residential school system provided a common experience for native leaders and gave them the opportunity to meet people from different tribal groups. Finally, education created bicultural natives who understood their own culture and white culture. This development helped

many tribal groups in their legal battles against white governments. *C. L. Higham*

Core Resources

The relations between missionaries and American Indians are explored in Robert Pierce Beaver's *Church, State, and the American Indians* (St. Louis: Concordia, 1966); Robert Berkhofer, Jr.'s *Salvation and the Savage* (Lexington: University Press of Kentucky, 1965); Carol Devens's *Countering Colonization: Native American Women and Great Lakes Missions, 1630-1900* (Berkeley: University of California Press, 1992); John Webster Grant's *Moon of Wintertime: Missionaries and the Indians of Canada in Encounter Since 1543* (Toronto: University of Toronto Press, 1984); and Robert Kelley's *American Protestantism and United States Indian Policy* (Lincoln: University of Nebraska Press, 1983).

See also: Carlisle Indian School; Education and American Indians; Indian Rights Association; Indian-white relations: Canada; Indian-white relations: United States.

Mississippi Freedom Democratic Party

The Mississippi Freedom Democratic Party (MFDP) was founded to bring attention to the lack of political freedom in Mississippi. The Freedom Summer project had registered only sixteen hundred voters in Mississippi in 1964, and the ruling Democratic Party barred civil rights activists from attending party conventions. The Council of Federated Organizations (COFO) therefore created a new party and selected sixty-eight delegates and alternates to attend the Democratic Party's national conven-

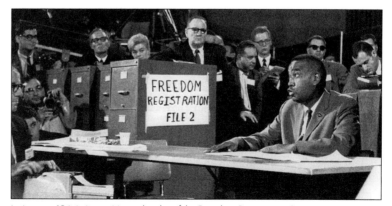

In August, 1964, Aaron Henry, leader of the Freedom Democratic Party, tries to convince the credentials committee to give seats at the Democratic National Convention to his party members instead of to the all-white Mississippi delegation.

tion in Atlantic City, New Jersey. Their mission was to contest the seats held by Mississippi's all-white delegation, arguing that the MFDP was the only truly democratic party in the state.

Civil rights workers testified before the national Democratic Party's Credentials Committee about conditions in Mississippi. Fannie Lou Hamer, a sharecropper's daughter, delivered a riveting account of being threatened and beaten for attempting to register to vote. President Lyndon B. Johnson feared losing the support of white Democrats and tried to arrange a compromise that would allow the MFDP token representation. Even though white liberals and moderate civil rights leaders such as Martin Luther King, Jr., were willing to accept this compromise, a majority of the MFPD's members were not. This disagreement solidified the split in the Civil Rights movement between integrationist moderates and separationist radicals.   *Robert E. McFarland*

See also: Civil Rights movement; Council of Federated Organizations; Disfranchisement laws in Mississippi; Freedom Summer.

Missouri Compromise

> **Significance:** The Missouri Compromise of 1820 was an attempt to pacify both northern and southern sectional interests by allowing slavery to exist in the southern part of the Louisiana Purchase territory.

Between 1818 and 1819 both the territories of Missouri and Maine petitioned the U.S. Congress to be admitted as new states. The Missouri Territory had been created from the Louisiana Purchase (1803) and was promised constitutional protection. However, Congress could not decide if the right of property applied to the institution of slavery. Should it be allowed in Missouri and the rest of the Louisiana Purchase, or did Congress have the moral responsibility to rectify the issue of slavery that had been avoided since the Constitutional Convention of 1787? It would take three sessions of Congress between 1818 and 1821 before Missouri was fully admitted as a state. The issue of slavery sparked by the ensuing debate spread throughout the country and threatened to cause disunion between the northern and southern regions.

The Issue of Slavery
At the time that Missouri and Maine applied for statehood, the United States consisted of eleven free states and eleven slave states. This political balance had been

achieved since 1789 by admitting a slave state and then a free state determined by geographical location and each region's past history with regard to slavery. This arrangement supplied each section with an equal number of senators (two per state) and attempted to equalize representation in the House of Representatives through the three-fifths clause.

The three-fifths compromise, added to the final draft of the Constitution, allowed slave states to count each slave as three-fifths of a person to balance their representative power against that of the more densely populated North. Nevertheless, the North had a majority of representatives in Congress (105 to 81). Missouri's admission as a free or slave state therefore became an important issue in the very body that would resolve it. Missouri threatened to extend the influence of the industrial free North in the Senate or provide the majority to the agrarian slaveholding South.

In 1818, Missouri's boundaries were approximately the same as those of today, and the territory was estimated to have 2,000 to 3,000 slaves. Slavery was a historical by-product of prior French and Spanish colonial policies. Missouri reasoned that slavery should be allowed to continue as it had in other territories that had been granted statehood since 1789.

In February, 1819, the House of Representatives responded to this debate by adopting the Tallmadge amendment. Representative James Tallmadge of New York proposed an amendment to the bill allowing Missouri to frame a state constitution. The two clauses in the amendment would restrict the further introduction of slavery into Missouri and provide that all children born to slaves would be free at age twenty-five. Both clauses passed the House. Southern senators were shocked by the bitterness of the debate in the House and the ability of the North to muster votes. They saw the Tallmadge amendment as the first step in eliminating the expansion of slavery. Voting along sectional lines, the Senate rejected both clauses.

Congress adjourned session until December 6, 1819. During this interim, Maine formed a constitution and applied for admission as a free state. Maine had been incorporated into the Massachusetts Bay Colony in 1691 but had started to agitate for separate statehood during and after the War of 1812. Its application for statehood as a free state seemed to provide a possible solution to the Missouri debate that threatened the stability of the young nation. On February 18, 1820, the Senate Judiciary Committee joined the two measures and the Senate passed Maine's and Missouri's applications for statehood but without mentioning slavery. This infuriated Maine, which had, as part of Massachusetts, outlawed slavery in 1780. What should have been a routine confirmation of new states became part of the most explosive issue to face the country. Maine would be allowed to separate from Massachusetts and gain statehood as long as Congress approved it by March 4, 1820, or the nine counties would revert back to Massachusetts. Even so, many of Maine's constituency urged that Maine's application fail so that slavery would not spread into Missouri.

Sectional Polarization
Senator J. B. Thomas of Illinois offered a compromise amendment to the Senate bill that would admit Missouri as a slave state with the proviso that the remaining territories in the Louisiana Purchase above 36°30′, Missouri's southern border, would be free of slavery. The Northern-controlled House responded by rejecting this Thomas amendment and passed a proviso prohibiting the further introduction of slavery anywhere. The result was polarization along sectional lines. In turn, the Senate struck out the antislavery provision and added the Thomas amendment. Thus began the final debate over whether slavery would be allowed to expand.

Senator Rufus King of New York continued the debate by stating that Congress, under Article IV, section 3 of the Constitution, was empowered to exclude slavery from the territory and to make slavery an issue for statehood. "New states *may be* admitted by the Congress into this Union." A precedent had been established under Article IV, section 3 of the Constitution which forbade slavery in lands above the Ohio River in the Northwest Ordinance of 1787. Therefore, in the minds of many of the northern congressmen, they should take this opportunity to eliminate slavery from any point west of the Mississippi. In response, Senator William Pickering of Maryland stated that the United States was composed of an equal number of slave states and free states; Missouri should be allowed to determine its own fate.

Missouri responded with anger and frustration, asserting that the issue was not about slavery but rather the issue of state sovereignty. Congress had delayed its admission for years. Missouri, like other states, had the right to choose its property laws. In Missouri as well as the rest of the South, the issue swung from one dealing with slavery to one dealing with property rights and the equality of states within the United States. These issues captured the attention of citizens throughout the country and led to heated debates on all levels. For the first time, slavery was being justified and defended as a good way of life by not only southern politicians but also the southern clergy. Would the country be influenced by restrictionists who sought to control this institution, or would states' rights be preserved?

The Compromise
A compromise between the two houses was eventually reached in a conference formed to break the deadlock.

Speaker of the House Henry Clay of Kentucky stated that he would not support Maine's admission unless Missouri was admitted with no restrictions. The Senate took the House bill and inserted the Thomas amendment. The House under Henry Clay's leadership voted to admit Maine as a free state and Missouri as a slave state and restricted slavery north of 36°30′. It is interesting to note that seven of Maine's nine representatives in the Massachusetts delegation voted against Maine's admission so that their state would not be used to provide a solution to the slavery issue.

Missouri continued to be an issue when it presented a state constitution in November, 1820. As if to get the final word, the Missouri Constitutional Convention had incorporated into its constitution a provision excluding free blacks and mulattoes from the state. This provision incited the antislavery factions in the Senate and House and threatened to destroy the fragile compromise. A "Second Missouri Compromise" was needed which stated that Missouri would not gain admission as a state unless its legislature assured Congress that it would not seek to abridge the rights of citizens. The Missouri legislature agreed to this in June, 1821. On August 10, 1821, President James Monroe admitted Missouri as the twenty-fourth state. After waiting a short time, Missouri's state congress sought to have the last say when it approved statutes forbidding free blacks from entering the state.

The Missouri Compromise would stand for the next three decades. During that time it served to mark a clear delineation between the growing regional and sectional problems of the North and South and made states' rights the rallying cry for the South until the Civil War.

Vincent Michael Thur

Core Resources
Richard H. Brown's *The Missouri Compromise: Political Statesmanship or Unwise Evasion?* (Boston: D.C. Heath, 1964) contains primary source material showing views of contemporary leaders and varying perspectives of historians. R. Douglas Hurt's *Agriculture and Slavery in Missouri's Little Dixie* (Columbia: University of Missouri Press, 1992) is a study of the political and legal impact of the Missouri Compromise in a seven-county area along the Missouri River. Glover Moore's *The Missouri Controversy, 1819-1821* (Gloucester, Mass.: Peter Smith, 1967) is a significant monograph on the political compromise that signaled nineteenth century sectional controversies during the antebellum era.

See also: Civil War; Bleeding Kansas; Compromise of 1850; Lincoln-Douglas debates; Proslavery argument; Slavery: history; Three-fifths compromise.

"Model" minorities

Significance: The term "model minority" generally refers to a minority group that has attained educational and economic success and has achieved a high degree of assimilation into a dominant society. It has most often been applied to Asian Americans, notably Japanese and Chinese Americans.

The concept of the "model" minority has been studied and debated since the 1960's, when the term first appeared. Its validity has been both defended and attacked, and the possible harmful effects of the concept as an accepted and unquestioned stereotype have been argued. Another particularly contentious issue is that the suggestion that certain minorities are "model" implicitly contains the opposite idea: Other minorities are less than "model" and are perhaps even deficient in some way.

Definition and History of the Term
A "model" minority is any minority group (typically of non-European background) that does well despite having faced discrimination. The criteria by which a minority group is judged as doing well or not doing well vary, but they have included average family income; success in entrepreneurship; children's educational achievement (for recently settled groups); and extent of symptoms of deviance or social pathology. The higher the first three, and the lower the last one, the likelier a group is to be considered a model minority. Since every ethnic or minority group in the United States has produced at least a few high achievers and at least a few failures and criminals, social scientists' judgments of ethnic group success or failure are always statements of averages; they are often based on census data.

The term first appeared in an article in *The New York Times Magazine* of January 9, 1966, entitled "Success Story, Japanese-American Style," by white American sociologist William Petersen. Before World War II, Petersen points out, those Japanese Americans born in Japan could neither own land in California nor become naturalized American citizens; their American-born children (the Nisei) were barred from many types of employment. During World War II, Japanese Americans living in the Pacific coast states were herded into internment camps. Yet in the two decades after World War II, Japanese Americans achieved a level of education higher than that of white Americans; a level of family income at least equal to that of whites, and a level of social pathology (such as juvenile delinquency) lower than that of whites. Hence, Petersen calls Japanese Americans "our model minority."

In *Japanese Americans: The Evolution of a Subculture* (1969), Harry L. Kitano, a Japanese American sociologist, also uses the term "model minority," acknowledging its origin with Petersen. Kitano expresses ambivalence about the term, which he regards as an ethnocentric white majority's view of a racial minority. Yet, like Petersen, Kitano ascribes the economic success of Japanese Americans after World War II to ethnic Japanese cultural values.

Model Groups
Japanese Americans are not the only Asian American ethnic group that has been noted by social scientists for its level of achievement since the 1960's. Chinese Americans have also been so identified. The business success of both Chinese and Japanese Americans has been attributed by some sociologists and historians to ethnic cultural values, as exemplified by the rotating credit systems that immigrants established to help provide one another with funds to start businesses. Korean business success has been similarly explained. The academic success of Indochinese refugee schoolchildren has been ascribed to the congruence of the refugees' Confucian ethic with the ethic of the American middle class. Louis Winnick, a scholarly expert on urban neighborhoods, went so far as to lump all Asian Americans together as a model minority.

Some non-Asian groups have been viewed as model minorities as well. In the early 1970's, post-1959 Cuban refugees were praised in the mass media for having overcome adversity quickly. Thomas Sowell, a black conservative intellectual, asserts that British West Indian immigrants (who are mainly black) outperform native-born black Americans economically and educationally. Similarly, Ivan Light argued in 1972 that British West Indian immigrants do better in small business than native-born black Americans; they do so, he said, because of their rotating credit system. Writing in 1993, two journalists (white New Yorker Joe Klein and Haitian émigré Joel Dreyfuss) contended that Haitian immigrants exhibit fewer social pathologies and more signs of economic and educational advance than native-born black Americans. Social scientist Kofi Apraku has described post-1965 African immigrants (such as refugees from Ethiopia) as above average in occupational and entrepreneurial attainment.

Sociological Viewpoint
Sociologists who employ or support the model minority concept usually adhere to the assimilation model of interethnic relations. According to this theoretical model, the ultimate destiny of any American ethnic or minority group is to climb upward into the broad middle class. Such thinkers tend to see the progress of any ethnic or minority group as a function of its cultural values

rather than of the extent of the discrimination it suffers. The relative slowness of any particular group to overcome poverty and win the acceptance of the majority is ascribed, at least in part, to that group's cultural values; hence, one can regard some minorities as "model" and others as less exemplary.

Such structural theorists as sociologist Stephen Steinberg, by contrast, argue that it is not cultural deficiencies that retard minorities' progress but discriminatory barriers erected by the majority. These barriers can be far more widespread and insidious than is first apparent. Such theorists also contend that the seemingly miraculous progress of some model minorities can be explained by the social class background of the immigrants and by the opportunity structure that they found upon arrival rather than by any alleged superiority of those minorities' cultural values.

Implications

The model minority concept has most often been applied in discussions of the relative success of certain Asian ethnic immigrant groups in the United States. The term has engendered much debate because of its implicit criticism of other groups—if these "model" groups could succeed, it suggests, then others should be able to as well. This implication then leads to the question: If certain groups cannot succeed as well as others in American society, where does the problem lie—with discrimination, with the attitudes of the dominant culture, or with the cultural attributes and attitudes of the minority groups themselves?

The model minority concept has surfaced repeatedly in debates over the status of African Americans, the minority group that has been in the United States the longest but that has arguably assimilated least effectively. In the late 1950's and the 1960's, many white Americans felt anxieties about the Civil Rights movement; the urban unrest of the late 1960's exacerbated fears and uncertainties about the future of race relations. Then, in the late 1970's and 1980's, white resentment of affirmative action programs, which primarily benefited African Americans, grew. At the same time, there was some bewilderment that inner-city black poverty persisted despite affirmative action. The model minority concept, with its evidence of Asian American success, seemed to suggest that such programs might be, or should be, unnecessary.

Hence, from 1966 onward, the notion of Asian Americans as a model minority found receptive ears among conservative white Americans. By the middle and late 1980's, it was being purveyed in a speech by President Ronald Reagan (in 1984), in magazine articles, and on television news programs (which placed special emphasis on the scholastic achievements of Asian American youth). Although most blacks in the 1980's resented being compared unfavorably with Asian Americans, some conservative black intellectuals, Thomas Sowell, Walter E. Williams, and Shelby Steele among them, defended the concept and pointed to Asian American success as an example for blacks to follow.

Controversy and Challenges

Because of its use in arguments over public policy, the model minority thesis is hotly disputed. Thus a laudatory report on Indochinese refugee schoolchildren by Caplan, Whitmore, and Choy was criticized by sociologist Rubén Rumbaut for having covered only the Vietnamese, Sino-Vietnamese, and Lao, omitting data on the less successful refugees, the Hmong and the Cambodians. The overall high Asian American average in income and education, Asian American scholars Ronald Takaki, Deborah Woo, Peter Kwong, and Arthur Hu point out, hides a bipolar distribution: Chinese immigrants, for example, include both sweatshop laborers and scientists. Many of the Asian American youth who excel in school, it is emphasized, are children of well-educated immigrants who either hold professional jobs in the United States or did so in Asia; Asian immigrant teenagers from poorer, less well-educated families are not always high achievers, and they are sometimes members of urban juvenile gangs. Asian American family incomes, it is conceded, may equal or surpass those of whites, but only because of a larger number of earners per family. Per capita income is less than that of whites; moreover, Asian Americans tend to live in areas with a higher than average cost of living, such as Hawaii, New York, and California. Also, Asian Americans statistically must achieve higher education levels than white Americans to equal their incomes.

Sowell's portrait of British West Indian immigrants to the United States as an ethnic success story has also been challenged. These immigrants, economist Thomas Boston argues in *Race, Class, and Conservatism* (1988), exceed both the average British West Indian and the average native-born black American in educational level; hence, the superior West Indian economic performance in the United States is no simple rags-to-riches story. Sociologist Suzanne Model, using census data, asserts that any West Indian socioeconomic lead over American-born blacks had disappeared by 1990.

If the "model" part of "model minority" has been criticized, so has the "minority" part, at least regarding Asian Americans. Although everyone agrees that certain Asian American groups have been unjustly persecuted, some scholars, such as political scientist Lawrence Fuchs, argue that no Asian American group was ever discriminated against as consistently, or for as long a time, as black Americans were.

Some view the Asian American model minority stereotype as potentially harmful to Asian Americans themselves. Writing in the late 1980's, Takaki and Woo warned that widespread acceptance of the stereotype might lead to governmental indifference to the plight of those Asian Americans who are poor and to neglect of programs that would help Asian immigrants learn English and find jobs. Takaki, worried about the loss of legitimate minority status, points to examples of low-income Asian American university students being denied aid under educational opportunity programs. He also thinks that the envy generated among black and white Americans by the model minority stereotype partially explains the violent anti-Asian incidents of the 1980's.   *Paul D. Mageli*

Core Resources
Herbert R. Barringer, Robert W. Gardner, and Michael J. Levin's *Asian and Pacific Islanders in the United States* (New York: Russell Sage, 1993) compares Asian Americans' income, education, and family structure with those of whites and blacks. Margaret A. Gibson's *Accommodation Without Assimilation: Sikh Immigrants in an American High School* (Ithaca, N.Y.: Cornell University Press, 1988) examines the excellent academic performance of American-born Sikh youth in the face of majority prejudice. Harry L. Kitano's *Japanese Americans: The Evolution of a Subculture* (Englewood Cliffs, N.J.: Prentice-Hall, 1969) is a classic exposition of the model minority thesis that ascribes the economic success of Japanese Americans after World War II to specific cultural traits inherited from Japan. Willima Petersen's *Japanese Americans: Oppression and Success* (New York: Random House, 1971) is an elaboration and expansion of the model minority thesis propounded in Petersen's 1966 article in *The New York Times Magazine*. Ronald Takaki's "Breaking Silences," in *Strangers from a Different Shore: A History of Asian Americans* (Boston: Little, Brown, 1989), is one of the most eloquent and easily accessible critiques of the Asian American model minority thesis.

See also: Asian American stereotypes; Assimilation: cultural and structural; Assimilation theories; Economics and race.

Molly Maguires

The Molly Maguires were an Irish American secret terrorist society that operated in the anthracite coal region of eastern Pennsylvania from 1854 to 1877. The Molly Maguires of America adopted their name from one of the Ribbon societies of Ireland that had waged a campaign of intimidation and attacks against landlords and process servers between 1835 and 1855. The Pennsylvania Molly Maguires consisted of similarly disfranchised Irishmen, but there was no direct connection between the two organizations. The American organization was associated with the Ancient Order of Hibernians, a benevolent society having branches throughout North America and Great Britain. Membership in the order required a person to be of Irish birth or descent and a Roman Catholic with Roman Catholic parents. Despite its links to Catholicism, the Order of Hibernians was a secret society and thus under official ban of the Catholic Church.

In the eastern mining district of Pennsylvania, the Order of Hibernians eventually came under control of militants who created an inner order of Molly Maguires, with the intention of improving living and working conditions in the mining industry. To achieve their goals, the Mollies waged a violent terror campaign, harassing, intimidating, and murdering mine owners and supervisors, mine-owner-dominated police officers and judges, and miners of non-Irish descent. By plan, violent acts of arson, thuggery, and assassination were carried out in one district by Mollies from another district so the crimes were always perpetrated by non-locals, making criminal identification more difficult.

The Molly Maguires grew in strength during the Civil War when the increased demand for coal caused an influx of Welsh, English, and German miners to eastern Pennsylvania, displacing Irish American miners. During the war, the Mollies opposed enlistment in the Union Army and harassed federal recruitment officers. During the postwar years, between 1865 and 1875, the Molly Maguires' violent activities increased as wages and living conditions deteriorated for mining families in eastern Pennsylvania. During this time, the group organized a union and initiated several coal strikes. Eventually, members of the group ran for public office to advance mine workers' interests.

In 1873, after repeated efforts to bring the Molly Maguires to justice had failed, and the ongoing threat of the group became intolerable to mine owners, Franklin B. Gowen, president of the Philadelphia and Reading Railroad and its affiliated Coal and Iron Company hired the Pinkerton Detective Agency to eradicate the group. James McParlan, an Irishman and Pinkerton detective, infiltrated the Molly Maguires and for more than two years was a member of the Shenandoah division, one of the most violent of the Molly Maguire lodges. McParlan collected enough evidence to break the organization through a series of murder trials lasting from 1875 through 1878. McParlan's evidence and testimony aided in convicting twelve of the nineteen Mollies eventually found guilty and hanged. Of historical and legal interest is the fact that the destruction of the Molly Maguires was initiated by a private corporation with the aid of a private police force, and the defendants on trial were prosecuted by mining company attorneys, then executed: All of this took place outside the confines of the U.S. judicial system. *Randall L. Milstein*

See also: Ancient Order of Hibernians; Irish American stereotypes; Irish Americans.

Mongrelization

The term "mongrelization" was adopted by racist proponents of immigration restriction in the early decades of the twentieth century to dramatize their fear of the consequences of permitting unlimited immigration into the United States. A leading exponent of these ideas was Madison Grant, a distinguished naturalist who was a founder and president of the New York Zoological Society. In *The Passing of the Great Race* (1916), he classified national and ethnic groups as "races" and arranged them in an evolutionary order, with the "Nordic" peoples of northern and western Europe considered the most highly evolved, and the peoples of eastern and southern Europe, especially Jews, Italians, and Slavs, ranked as markedly inferior. Grant believed that it had been scientifically established that mental as well physical traits were genetically determined and could not be significantly altered by the environment. He also believed that in any mixture, inferior genes would triumph and "produce many amazing racial hybrids and some ethnic horrors that will be beyond the powers of future anthropologists to unravel." Grant was sure that "the surviving traits will be determined by competition between the lowest and most primitive elements and the specialized traits of Nordic man; his stature . . . and his splendid fighting and moral qualities, will have little part in the resultant mixture." *Milton Berman*

See also: Biosocial theories; Biracialism; Multiracial identity; Multiracial movement; Social Darwinism and racism.

Montgomery bus boycott

Significance: The Montgomery bus boycott of 1955 and 1956, the first major effort by African Americans to fight entrenched discrimination through economic sanctions, sparked the early Civil Rights movement.

When the Supreme Court issued its decision in *Brown v. Board of Education* in May, 1954, ruling that racial segregation in public schools was unconstitutional, it marked the beginning of a period of dramatic change in the relationships between African Americans and whites. Until the mid-1960's, that change was hastened by the organized nonviolent resistance by many African Americans to laws and conditions that they regarded as discriminatory. The first occasion in which such tactics proved successful was a boycott of public buses in Montgomery, Alabama.

Although African Americans had achieved some hard-fought successes before 1954—most notably the desegregation of the armed forces—in many respects they remained a separate community, enjoying fewer rights and opportunities and less legal protection than whites. This was especially true in the Deep South, where the doctrine of "separate but equal" was held to apply to most areas of daily life and was used to justify a decidedly unequal segregation. Hundreds of laws, many of them passed in the late nineteenth century, restricted the rights of black southerners to eat, travel, study, or worship with whites.

The school desegregation ruling brought no immediate change to race relations in Montgomery. Once the capital of the Confederacy, this city of about 130,000 people—50,000 of whom were African American—continued resolutely in the old pattern of racial separation. The African American community of Montgomery had undertaken initial steps to challenge certain local segregation practices that were particularly offensive. E. D. Nixon of Montgomery headed the National Association for the Advancement of Colored People (NAACP) in Alabama. Because he worked as a sleeping-car porter, a unionized profession, he was less susceptible to attempts by the white establishment to control his behavior by threatening his job. Jo Ann Robinson helped lead the African American clubwomen in Montgomery, who provided a powerful organizational backbone among the small African American middle class in Montgomery. This nascent movement still lacked both a unified structure and a single issue to mobilize the African American community to push for civil rights.

Rosa Parks's Arrest
The issue came to a head on December 1, 1955, when Rosa Parks, a seamstress at a Montgomery department store and formerly the secretary of the local NAACP chapter, refused to give up her seat to maintain a row of vacant seats between white and black riders on the public bus system in Montgomery, as required by law. She was arrested and charged with violating the segregation ordinance. Parks's action was in part spontaneous—she had not boarded the bus with the intent to violate any segregation ordinance. Yet she had attended the Highlander Folk School in Tennessee, where members of the

community learned to become more effective, and a lifetime of enduring racial indignities had made her acutely aware of the evil nature of segregation.

Immediately, Montgomery's African American community sprang into action. Fred Gray, one of but four black lawyers in Alabama, contacted Clifford Durr, a liberal white attorney, to post bail for Parks. Nixon brought together two ministers, Ralph David Abernathy and Martin Luther King, Jr., with Jo Ann Robinson to plan for a massive boycott of Montgomery public buses, a majority of whose riders were African American. It would be necessary to arrange for transportation for scores of African Americans who did not own cars. To coordinate the massive undertaking, Montgomery's African American leaders created the Montgomery Improvement Association (MIA), presided over by King, the twenty-six-year-old pastor of Dexter Avenue Baptist Church. The boycott began on December 5, 1955.

The Response to the Boycott
At first, whites reacted with indifference or amusement, until the bus company's revenues dropped by 75 percent. A series of meetings between the city commissioners, representatives of the bus company, and the MIA failed to produce any agreement on the African Americans' demands—courteous treatment by bus drivers; a first-come, first-served seating arrangement, with blacks filling the rear and whites the front of the bus; and the employment of African American drivers on routes that served predominantly African American neighborhoods of Montgomery. Instead, the city police department began to harass the carpools that had been set up by the

MIA to provide alternative transportation, and they arrested some of the drivers. Police officers arrested King himself for speeding, and on January 30, persons unknown blasted King's house with dynamite. The houses of two other boycott leaders met a similar fate.

These acts of violence and intimidation affected the course of events in several ways. First, they united the African Americans in Montgomery, inspiring them to continue the boycott for more than a year. The violence also attracted national attention to Montgomery and led to substantial outside support for the boycott, assistance vital to its success. Finally, the violence served as a foil for the rhetoric of nonviolent resistance that King so eloquently articulated. In one mass meeting after another, he urged his followers to ignore hostile provocations, to confront their persecutors passively, and to refuse to fight back, relying on the moral authority of their actions to sway the hearts and minds of their antagonists.

While the boycott continued, the legal issues it raised were argued in federal courts. On February 1, 1956, five Montgomery women filed suit to have the Court strike down the city bus seating ordinance. The case was heard on May 11, by which time eighty-nine MIA members faced local charges for conspiracy to interfere with normal business. In November, city officials obtained an injunction against the MIA officials for running a carpool, which nearly brought the boycott to a halt. Nevertheless, the federal suit received a favorable hearing and was affirmed by the Supreme Court in *Browder v. Gayle* in November, and the Court ordered the seating on Montgomery buses desegregated on December 17, 1956. Four days later, King, Abernathy, and Nixon rode the bus downtown and were able to sit wherever they wanted.

Results of the Boycott
The boycott succeeded for a number of reasons, not the least of which was the timely court ruling. It also benefited from fissures in the white community across gender, age, and economic lines. White, middle-class women often transported their black maids to and from work, unwittingly aiding the boycott. Within the Chamber of Commerce, a coalition of young businessmen called the Men of Montgomery demanded that the city fathers end the boycott because the city's tarnished image made it difficult to attract outside businesses.

Successful in its immediate objective, the boycott established a precedent for other economic protests over

After the U.S. Supreme Court's integration order went into effect in Montgomery, Alabama, in December, 1956, the Reverend Ralph D. Abernathy (front, left) and the Reverend Martin Luther King, Jr., (second row, left) were among the first to ride the buses.

the next decade. Because of his role in the boycott, Martin Luther King, Jr., emerged as the most important spokesperson for African Americans. His tactics of non-violent passive resistance remained the major tool of the Civil Rights movement until the mid-1960's. Shortly after the boycott's conclusion, King was instrumental in founding the Southern Christian Leadership Conference, which applied the Montgomery formula to other southern cities. African American leaders tried nonviolent resistance and economic protests in Birmingham, Alabama, and Albany, Georgia. The Montgomery bus boycott was an important harbinger of the most profound social changes in the United States during the 1960's, in that it marked a change in the attitudes and strategies of African Americans to confront racial indignity. *Courtney B. Ross, updated by Edward R. Crowther*

Core Resources

David J. Garrow's *Bearing the Cross: Martin Luther King, Jr., and the Southern Christian Leadership Conference* (New York: William Morrow, 1986) is a thorough, detailed biography of King that provides an excellent account of King's Montgomery days. Martin Luther King, Jr.'s *Stride Toward Freedom: The Montgomery Story* (New York: Harper & Row, 1958) is King's own account of the boycott. Jo Ann Gibson Robinson's *The Montgomery Bus Boycott and the Women Who Started It: The Memoir of Jo Ann Gibson Robinson* (Knoxville: University of Tennessee Press, 1987) provides a powerful portrait of the world of middle-class women in Montgomery and the essential role they played in the boycott strategy.

See also: *Brown v. Board of Education;* Civil Rights movement; King, Martin Luther, Jr., assassination; Little Rock school desegregation.

Moose Lodge No. 107 v. Irvis

In *Moose Lodge No. 107 v. Irvis,* the Supreme Court on June 12, 1972, ruled that a state did not deny the equal protection of the law when it granted a license to serve alcohol to a racially discriminatory private club.

Moose Lodge No. 107 was a private club in Harrisburg, Pennsylvania, that served both food and alcohol, the latter under a license granted by the Pennsylvania Liquor Control Board. The club was often used by members of the state legislature for lunch breaks and after-hours relaxation. A white member of the lodge brought an African American fellow legislator, K. Leroy Irvis, into the club's dining room and bar, where the pair were refused service on the grounds of Irvis's race.

The Fourteenth Amendment to the Constitution forbids state action in furtherance of racial discrimination.

Since the lodge's refusal to serve Irvis amounted to racial discrimination, the Supreme Court was asked to determine whether Pennsylvania's granting of a liquor license constituted state action in furtherance of that discrimination.

The Court ruled in a 6-3 vote that mere state licensing of a private club on private land did not make every action of the club an action of the state. The majority noted that the impetus for discrimination did not have to originate with the state in order for there to be state action, so long as the state was involved in enforcing private discrimination in a significant way. If the lodge had been a tenant in a state-owned building and had opened its facilities to all members of the public except African Americans, the state would have been engaged in a joint venture with the club, and the club's discrimination would have been state action. In this case, however, the building was privately owned, it rested on privately owned land, and its facilities were open not to the public in general, but to members only. The Court observed that the state provided many services, among them water, electricity, licensing, and police and fire protection. The mere provision of such services was not enough to convert every action of the beneficiary into state action.

The dissenters argued that there was state action, since the liquor regulatory scheme was pervasive, regulating "virtually every detail of the operation of the licensee's business." They also observed that since the quota for liquor licenses had been exceeded in Harrisburg, the state's renewal of the Moose Lodge's license prevented a different facility with nondiscriminatory policies from opening.

This important case limited the reach of the Fourteenth Amendment by defining state action narrowly. It remained possible for victims of discrimination to find recourse in federal and state antidiscrimination statutes. Leroy Irvis was able to do just that when he brought suit against Moose Lodge No. 107 under Pennsylvania's public accommodations law. He eventually gained admission to the club's facilities and was later elected speaker of the Pennsylvania House of Representatives. *William H. Coogan*

See also: Restrictive or racial covenants; Segregation: de facto and de jure; *Shelley v. Kraemer.*

Morrill Land Grant Act of 1890

In 1862, the United States Congress passed the first Morrill Land Grant Act to authorize the establishment of a land-grant institution in each state to educate citizens in agriculture, mechanic arts, home economics, and other practical professions. Because of the emphasis on agriculture and mechanic arts, these institutions were referred to as A&M colleges. Because of the legal separation of the races in the South, African Americans were not permitted to attend these original land-grant institutions. This situation was rectified in 1890, when Congress passed the second Morrill Land Grant Act, expanding the 1862 system of land-grant colleges to provide support for the establishment of African American institutions of higher learning in states that lacked such facilities.

Each of the southern states that did not have an African American college by 1890 established one or more under the second Morrill Land Grant Act. The 1890 institutions evolved into a major educational resource for the United States. For more than a century, these institutions have provided the principal means of access to higher education for African Americans. They continue to be a major source of African American leaders who render valuable service to their communities, the nation, and the world.   *Alvin K. Benson*

See also: Black colleges and universities; College admissions; Desegregation: public schools; Education and African Americans.

Motown Records

Named after Detroit, Michigan, the "Motor City," Motown Record Company was founded in 1959 by Berry Gordy, Jr. His record company brought African American performers and music to mainstream popular music charts by fusing gospel and popular music into an appealing, melodic sound. Motown Records brought great pride to the African American community by demonstrating that blacks could become superstars and perform worldwide. Some of Motown's greatest artists and groups were Smokey Robinson and the Miracles, Gladys Knight and the Pips, the Four Tops, Martha and the Vandellas, Stevie Wonder, Marvin Gaye, Diana Ross and the Supremes, the Temptations, and the Jackson Five.

The music from Motown Records has made it possible for generations of African Americans to have hope for a better economic future and to share great times together. To African Americans, the music of Motown holds uplifting, identifiable messages that translate into working-class dance music. This music has inspired not only African Americans but also many white Americans. By generating love, soul, and inspiration through their music, Motown entertainers became heroes and heroines to the African American people, and the Motown style and messages crossed race barriers, providing a common bond between blacks and whites.   *Alvin K. Benson*

See also: African Americans and music; Soul.

In 1959, Berry Gordy, Jr., founded Motown Records, a Detroit, Michigan, recording label that popularized black music among mainstream listeners.

Moynihan Report

One explanation for high levels of impoverishment in black communities was published in *The Negro Family* (1965), by Daniel Patrick Moynihan, a white social scientist of Irish descent who later became a U.S. senator. By postulating that "the family structure of the lower-class Negroes is highly unstable," the Moynihan Report argued that family deterioration was at the heart of high unemployment, welfare dependency, low achievement, and crime. In Moynihan's view, black communities were enmeshed in a "tangle of pathology." The report relied heavily on earlier observations by E. Franklin Frazier (1932), who conceptualized lower-class culture as disorganized and pathological. This thesis has since been used by others who contend that disadvantaged poor and minority groups encourage cultural practices that fuel their continued poverty.

Reaction to the Moynihan Report was generally negative on the part of leaders of the Civil Rights movement—especially clear when the report's conclusions were dismissed by those participating in the November, 1965, meeting of the White House Conference on Civil Rights. The idea that poverty is caused by subcultural patterns has implications for public policy. Instead of focusing on federal efforts to ensure good jobs, housing, education, health care, and income maintenance, those who hold this view focus on improving the character of individuals and families. Critics of the report said that this culture-of-poverty theory was a form of victim blaming that ignored societal and institutional structures—such as unequal access to jobs, segregated education, and unaffordable, deteriorating housing—that make groups who are discriminated against more susceptible to poverty and the problems it causes for families and communities. Poor and minority people have the same values as those in more advantaged sectors of society, but their barriers to achievement are much greater.

This perspective continues to offend and enrage many people, including African Americans, civil rights workers, and progressive community and government activists.
Eleanor A. LaPointe

See also: Culture of poverty; Economics and race; Poverty and race.

Mulattoes

Before the Civil Rights movement of the 1950's and 1960's, white supremacy was a prevalent concept in U.S. society. White supremacists held that Caucasians, or whites, were better than people of other races. Laws passed by white legislators usually discriminated equally against mulattoes (people of mixed white and black ancestry) and people of unmixed African ancestry. However, white leaders were generally more willing to interact with mulattoes than with darker-skinned African Americans. Consequently, blacks and whites alike saw having light skin as an asset; most African American leaders were mulattoes.

This began to change, however, during the Civil Rights movement. African Americans began to exhibit a new awareness of their racial identity and increased sense of self-worth—"black pride"—and to emphasize their African culture in their hairstyles, manner of dress, language, and artistic expression. Many African Americans began to think that mulattoes should be discriminated against because their physical characteristics were not more obviously African.

In time, however, as white supremacy became a thing of the past in U.S. society, African Americans began to view mulattoes the same way that whites had earlier—as simply African Americans with light skin. The U.S. Census Bureau, which had earlier counted blacks and mulattoes separately, combined the two designations. Consequently, the word "mulatto" lost both its social and legal significance and has slipped from general usage in the United States.
Roger D. Hardaway

See also: Biracialism; Blackness and whiteness: legal definitions; Multiracial identity; Passing; White supremacist groups.

Multiculturalism

> **Significance:** Multiculturalism is an approach to education, public policy, and other areas of social life that affirms the cultural diversity of a multiracial and multiethnic society.

The word "multicultural" first emerged after World War II; its derivative, "multiculturalism," came into use during the Civil Rights movement and gained currency in the 1980's. Whereas "multicultural" is a descriptive term referring to the presence of many cultures in a multiethnic and multiracial society such as the United States, "multiculturalism" is a prescriptive concept that entails attitudes, value judgments, public policies, and controversies with regard to the diverse cultures present, especially as to how such cultures are to be identified and represented. Although differences in race, ethnicity, gender, age, ability, and sexuality are subsumed under the term "multicultural," multiculturalism has often been seen in particular as the antithesis of Western civilization or the culture of the white Anglo-Saxon Protestant (WASP) male. Encoded as the identity politics of ethnic minorities, women, and gays and lesbians, in the 1990's it became the major issue of the "culture wars"—the struggle to control the symbols and interpretations of American culture—and hence the definition of the national identity and the exercise of political power.

The U.S. Reality

In the United States, Americans contemplating the history and reality of their country as well as their own identities must come to terms with the fact that their nation was shaped not only by the settlement of Europeans but also by other circumstances, including the deprivation of indigenous tribes, the slavery of Africans, the conquest of the Southwest (which once was a Mexican territory), the colonization of other countries (Puerto Rico, Hawaii, and the Philippines prior to its independence), military interventions in the politics of other regions (Korea, Vietnam, the Middle East, and South America), the immigration of peoples from all over the world, the contribution of American women from all races, and the global contexts of American politics and economy. This fundamentally multicultural fact, which is reflected in the nation's motto, *e pluribus unum* (out of many, one), has been either suppressed (as in segregation and discrimination) or recognized at different historical junctures, usually after political conflicts of vary- ing magnitudes ranging from the Civil War to racial riots and civil rights demonstrations. On the legal level, such recognition came in the form of constitutional amend- ments, Supreme Court decisions, and civil rights legisla- tion. The counterpart of such recognition in the domain of culture production, ideological discourse, and educa- tion is multiculturalism.

As a loosely defined set of principles meant to orient the social behavior of Americans, multiculturalism is closely related to the concept of "cultural pluralism," a doctrine that encourages the recognition and coexis- tence of differences. What sets multiculturalism apart from the assimilation and integration of ethnic minori- ties into the mainstream is its explicit criticism of the dominant culture as a kind of ethnocentricity, xenopho- bia, and oppression—hence the rejection of the melting pot model of acculturation in favor of the promotion of difference, self-esteem, and ethnic pride. As the cultural extension of the Civil Rights movement, multicultural- ism became a celebrated cause in itself. Gaining support from educators, cultural workers, and various agencies across the nation, it was gradually implemented in the curricula of schools and colleges. The cultural sector, especially publishers, also began to respond to the needs of multiculturalism; results of this include the emer- gence of ethnic writers and artists, the sensitive portrayal of minorities in the mass media, and the reassessment of

historical events such as the arrival of Christopher Co- lumbus in the "New" World.

Multiculturalism and Education

Multiculturalism at the school level is often seen to be instrumental in the successful education of an increas- ingly diverse student population in terms of their scho- lastic proficiencies, civic aptitudes, and comprehensive preparation for the global economy of the twenty-first century. Important themes and issues in multicultural education include the cultural heritages of different ethnic groups, bilingual education, cultural sensitivity, tolerance of difference, overcoming prejudice and rac- ism, heroes from other cultures, self-esteem, and the strength of diversity. Some educators suggest that by means of multicultural education, an individual should be transformed intellectually and emotionally into a person who is capable of seeing things from another's perspective, committed to the unity and equality of the human race, and ultimately ready to take action in bringing about social justice.

In higher education, the adoption of multicultural- ism is reflected in the curriculum, especially the creation of programs and departments, the transformation of core requirements, the diversification of course offer- ings, and the incorporation of texts addressing the his- tory and culture of African Americans, Latinos, Asian Americans, American Indians, women, gay men and lesbians, and other identifiable groups. Initially, curricular expan- sions of this kind were sometimes ac- complished through the activism of minority students, but gradually they have been institutionalized. One im- portant result of this curricular re- form in the humanities is the revision of the "canon"—that is, the inclusion of previously silenced or ignored texts (usually by women, minorities, and non-Western authors) and their dis- placement of certain other privileged classics (books by European male authors). Another effect is the critical rereading of canonized texts from the perspectives of race, ethnicity, gen- der, and sexual orientation.

As publicized—sometimes sensa- tionalized—in national magazines, at the height of the multicultural movement (late 1980's to early 1990's), its advocates began to draw the critical attention of the public. Some critics were alarmed at the ero- sion of Americans' "cultural literacy"

Many of the major cities of the United States and Canada have become multicultural, as this Toronto street scene attests. However, of these two nations, only Canada has adopted a policy of multiculturalism.

(E. D. Hirsch, Jr.), "the closing of the American mind" (Allan Bloom), and the "disuniting of America" (Arthur M. Schlesinger, Jr.) as a result of multiculturalism. The "victims' revolution" (Dinesh D'Souza) behind the politics of multiculturalism was also questioned. Complicating such controversies are certain policies regulating the multicultural reality of college campuses, for example, affirmative action admissions and hirings, the distribution of scholarships and funds, the treatment of ethnic student bodies, and sexual conduct. One particular controversy that captured the public's imagination was related to codes of proper behavior and speech with regard to women, minorities, and people with disabilities. Ridiculed as "politically correct" (PC), such codes have come to be seen as an extremist form of multiculturalism that reproduces rather than ameliorates the tensions of the multiracial, multiethnic, and multicultural society at large. On a further radicalized front, the dangers of the co-optation and institutionalization of multiculturalism have also been called into question as the debate continues.   *Balance Chow*

Core Resources
Sources on multiculturalism include James A. Banks's *Multiethnic Education: Theory and Practice* (2d ed., Boston: Allyn & Bacon, 1988); Allan Bloom's *The Closing of the American Mind: How Higher Education Has Failed Democracy and Impoverished the Souls of Today's Students* (New York: Simon & Schuster, 1987); Dinesh D'Souza's *Illiberal Education: The Politics of Race and Sex on Campus* (New York: Free Press, 1991); Henry Louis Gates, Jr.'s *Loose Canons: Notes on the Culture Wars* (New York: Oxford University Press, 1992); E. D. Hirsch, Jr.'s *Cultural Literacy: What Every American Needs to Know* (Boston: Houghton Mifflin, 1987); James Davison Hunter's *Culture Wars: The Struggle to Define America* (New York: Basic Books, 1991); Arthur M. Schlesinger, Jr.'s *The Disuniting of America* (New York: W. W. Norton, 1992); and Ronald Takaki's *A Different Mirror: A History of Multicultural America* (Boston: Little, Brown, 1993).

See also: Affirmative action; Assimilation theories; Cultural pluralism; Diversity; Multiculturalism Act; Multiculturalism in Canada; Multiracial movement.

Multiculturalism Act

On October 8, 1971, Prime Minister Pierre Trudeau established multiculturalism as the official social policy of Canada, making the nation the first and only one to have such a policy. On July 21, 1988, Canada passed a national multiculturalism law, which made multiculturalism a fundamental component of Canadian society and gave it an integral place in the decision-making process of the federal government. The core of multiculturalism is the idea that differing cultural or ethnic groups can coexist harmoniously in a pluralistic society. Canada has made multiculturalism its official doctrine and instituted corresponding policies that formally promote and incorporate ethnic and racial differences as integral components of the political, social, and symbolic order. Whereas American society has been compared to a melting pot, promoting conformity to a particular norm, Canadian society is likened to a patchwork quilt where ethnic boundaries are encouraged and supported by government policies and monetary resources. Just as the patches of a quilt determine its unique pattern, the different cultures in Canada determine its unique character.

For a policy of multiculturalism to work, a nation's policies and ideologies must promote minority rights to social equality and cultural identity within a pluralistic environment. Although Canada was initially oriented toward Anglo-conformity, diversity was a part of some of its laws and given some consideration. Aboriginal people had a special status, and the French and English were established as charter groups. Also, to encourage settlement of the prairie before World War I, the Canadian government promised to protect the immigrants' languages and cultures. The Citizenship Act of 1947 gave immigrants and native-born people similar status and rights in Canadian society.

During the 1960's, Canada's aboriginals became more assertive, the Québécois resented exclusion from central political institutions, and other ethnic minorities feared losing their culture and becoming second-class citizens. It was in this context that the policy of multiculturalism was implemented, allowing all Canadian citizens to choose to live according to their preferred culture while respecting the rights of others. The multiculturalism law of 1988 focused equally on cultural maintenance and social integration within a framework of equal opportunity.

The Multiculturalism Act has affected many aspects of Canadian society. Schools developed programs to accommodate more than sixty language groups and seventy ethnocultural communities and implemented multicultural and antiracism programs. Media have also experienced growth. Toronto has more than one hundred non-English newspapers, and more than forty cultures are represented in Canada's ethnic press. Ethnic radio and television programs are thriving. Programs have been developed on the community level, and at the federal level, supportive laws and policies have been instituted to help create additional multicultural and ethnic heritage programs.

Critics of multiculturalism argue that it is divisive,

creates social and cultural ghettos, and in the long run inhibits opportunities for minorities. Others see antiracism and multiculturalism as being incompatible. However, multiculturalism appears, for the most part, to be working in Canada.   *Arthur W. Helweg*

See also: Bilingualism in Canada; Citizenship Act; French Canadians; Multiculturalism in Canada; Official Languages Act; Pluralism vs. assimilation.

Multiculturalism in Canada

> **Significance:** Canada, in its efforts to find a means of harmonizing the diverse cultural backgrounds of its population, which includes immigrants from Europe, Asia, Latin America, and Africa, without imposing one dominant societal norm on all of them turned to multiculturalism. This policy is designed to enable immigrants to blend into Canadian society while retaining certain distinctive traditions from their countries of origin.

The idea behind multiculturalism, a term that developed in the 1960's, is to find unity in diversity, to enable immigrants to assimilate linguistically, politically, and into the labor force while retaining some affinity with their countries of origin via public endorsement and funding of their cultural and linguistic heritage. Multiculturalism has frequently been contrasted with the melting pot concept more prevalent in the United States, whereby some groups have assimilated into the dominant culture in about two or three generations following immigration. The aim of Canadian multiculturalism is to build a rich social tapestry of different traditions that combine to create a unique Canadian identity. Ideally, being "Canadian" would imply identification with many cultural systems, loyalty to an individual's own roots, tolerance for different peoples, and mutual respect. In reality, multiculturalism is a work in progress with as many setbacks as advances.

Multiculturalism was perhaps inevitable given that when Canada became a confederacy in 1867, the country already contained three distinctive societies, dominated by British immigrants (60 percent), French immigrants (30 percent), and indigenous peoples. By the early 1990's, nearly 42 percent of the population of Canada had an ethnic origin that was neither British nor French.

Government Policy
In October, 1971, the government of Canada announced its ethnocultural policy with the objectives of (1) assisting groups to retain an identity based on origin; (2) enabling ethnic minorities to participate as equals within Canadian society; (3) encouraging cultural exchanges within the country; and (4) helping immigrants learn one of the two official languages. The policy was funded with an initial grant of $200 million (Canadian) for a decade. The establishment of a Multicultural Directorate (1972) expanded the mandate to assist minorities with human rights problems and to promote freedom from racial discrimination. In 1973, multiculturalism acquired its own ministry within the federal bureaucracy, and linkages were encouraged with a variety of ethnic associations.

The "institutionalization" of multiculturalism continued when the concept was enshrined in the Canadian Charter of Rights and Freedoms (1982). Section 27 of the charter directs that its interpretation shall be consistent with the preservation and enhancement of Canada's multicultural heritage. The charter also guarantees equality before the law regardless of national or ethnic origin.

Of considerable significance was the passage by Parliament of the Multiculturalism Act in 1988, because Canada became the first country to convert this concept into a national law. The act provided for full participation in all aspects of Canadian society but recognized the right of every Canadian to choose and identify with the individual's cultural heritage. The legislation concentrated on the need to end racism (especially systemic racism), to eradicate discrimination in Canadian society, and to promote minority involvement in Canada's institutions.

The short-lived Department of Multiculturalism and Citizenship (1989) undertook the task of implementing the act with community involvement in a variety of programs to enhance appreciation and acceptance of the growing diversity of Canada's population. Although the department was disbanded in 1993, the objectives of seeking fairness and participation for all minorities were incorporated in new programs headed by a secretary of state for multiculturalism.

Perceptions of Multiculturalism
There are probably as many opinions on multiculturalism as there are ethnic groups in Canada. This is because Canadians are not certain about the precise meaning or application of multiculturalism or the cost of being part of a multicultural society. A 1991 Angus Reid poll showed that 78 percent of Canadians supported the concept. The majority anglophone population (people whose mother tongue is English), while espousing multiculturalism in principle, found practical difficulty in reconciling diverse cultures into the Canadian mainstream. Researchers have found the strongest support for multiculturalism among well-educated, young Canadians.

The francophone population of Quebec (those whose mother tongue is French) is so focused on its own distinct identity that it often fears an erosion of its French influence if so many cultures are given recognition within Canadian society. Through the 1990's, there has been consistent criticism of multiculturalism for diluting Canadian identity from its original British/French cultural orientation, for encouraging minorities to reject assimilation into the prevailing cultural mainstream, for fostering division rather than unity, and for diverting Canadian attention from more pressing considerations such as the economy and the national debt.

The reaction of allophones (those whose mother tongue is something other than English or French) in Canada is varied. While applauding the verbal and written guarantees of racial equality, they point to the all-too-frequent problems encountered by visible minorities in crucial areas such

Diverse cultures mix in this Canadian Italian and Greek bakery in Toronto. Multiculturalism encourages diversity.

as employment, housing, and education as a sign that multiculturalism has progressed institutionally and bureaucratically as a notion but has a long way to go with respect to effective implementation in Canadian society. The policy's inability to stem racism has provoked much of the criticism from visible minorities.

Other allophones are skeptical of the whole process, which provides funding for ethnic festivals complete with food and dancing in colorful costumes while visible minorities continue to be grossly underrepresented in federal and provincial civil service positions and still encounter racism in numerous cities and towns in Canada. Critics also suggest that fostering diversity encourages a psychology of separateness and isolation among immigrants and that this imperils the already threatened political unity of Canada. Interestingly, multiculturalism has made Canada a far more popular tourist destination, and this has generated considerable revenue.

The concept of multiculturalism has been a positive ideal for a nation composed largely of immigrants from a variety of backgrounds. Canada's contribution has been in enshrining this concept within its constitution, in giving it the force of law, and in promoting, to a limited extent, its implementation. The many setbacks to the creation of Canada as a tolerant society free of racial discrimination cannot obscure the fact that the constitutional and legal guarantees provide a direction and a guide for all Canadians to follow. Although it has been extensively criticized by politicians, journalists, academics, and writers, multiculturalism continues to be one path to forging a more harmonious Canadian identity.

Ranee K. L. Panjabi

Core Resources

Three sources of additional information on multiculturalism in Canada are Jeffrey Reitz and Raymond Breton's *The Illusion of Difference: Realities of Ethnicity in Canda and the United States* (Toronto: C. D. Howe Institute, 1994), Neil Bissoondath's *Selling Illusions: The Cult of Multiculturalism in Canada* (Toronto: Penguin Books, 1994), and *Canadian Multiculturalism: Issues and Trends* (Ottawa: Library of Parliament, Research Branch, 1997).

See also: Anglophone; Bilingualism in Canada; Charter of Rights and Freedoms; Francophone; Multiculturalism Act; Official Languages Act; Racial/ethnic relations in Canada; Visible minority allophones in Canada.

Multiracial identity

Significance: In the United States, racial boundaries have historically been drawn so that racial groups and identities are viewed as mutually exclusive, or "monoracial," categories of experience, forcing the children of interracial unions to identify with only one of their backgrounds. During the 1990's, however, growing numbers of individuals began to view themselves as "multiracial," or belonging to more than one racial group.

The growth in the multiracial population can be traced back to changes that took place since the dismantling of Jim Crow laws—particularly the 1967 removal of the last

696 – Multiracial identity

laws against miscegenation in *Loving v. Virginia*—and the implementation of civil rights legislation during the 1950's and 1960's. The comparatively more fluid intergroup relations led to increased interracial marriage. Census data indicate that the number of children born of interracial marriages grew from less than 500,000 in 1970 to about 2 million in 1990. The majority of these children have one parent who is European American. Interracial couples have used various terms to describe their offspring, including "rainbow," "brown," "melange," "blended," "mixed," "mixed-race," "biracial," "interracial," and "multiracial."

The Multiracial Identity Paradigm
A multiracial identity is not, however, indicative of someone who simply acknowledges the presence of various ancestries in his or her background. This identity, therefore, differs from that of other racial groups that may have multiple racial backgrounds but have monoracial identities, such as African Americans and Latino Americans. Multiracial individuals seek to replace these one-dimensional identities with multidimensional configurations. A multiracial identity is similar to, yet not synonymous with, an identity that is multiethnic in nature. A multiethnic identity is displayed by individuals who consider themselves to be members of several groups that are thought to be racially similar but culturally different, for example, individuals who are English and German American or Chinese and Japanese American. Social inequality in the United States has been determined more by notions of racial difference than by differences that are cultural in nature.

A multiracial (or multiethnic) identity is not the same as a multicultural identity. A multicultural identity is applicable to any individual who, irrespective of genealogy or ancestry, displays a general temperamental openness and sensitivity to racial and cultural differences.

Children with One White, One Nonwhite Parent, by Race
(1990 census, percentage of interracial households)

Native American and white	34
Asian American and white	45
African American and white	20

Source: Data are calculated from U.S. 1990 Census of Population and appear in "Recommendations from the Interagency Committee for the Review of the Racial and Ethnic Standards to the Office of Management and Budget Concerning Changes to the Standards for the Classification of Federal Data on Race and Ethnicity; Notice," *Federal Register,* 62:36901, July 9, 1997.

These individuals have an affinity with the values, beliefs, and customs of more than one racial or cultural group because of exposure to multiple racial and cultural groups. Multiethnic individuals feel a sense of kinship with several groups in direct response to the multiple cultural backgrounds in their genealogy. Similarly, multiracial individuals feel a sense of kinship with those groups directly in response to the multiple racial backgrounds in their genealogy. Exposure to these backgrounds enhances this feeling of kinship. Simple awareness of those backgrounds, however, can also bring about this sentiment. A lack of contact does not prevent it from being present.

Impact on Theories of Marginality
Because of the multidimensional nature of their identity, multiracial individuals operate on the margins of several racial groups. However, this marginality, or sense of being "betwixt and between," does not necessarily result in the personal alienation traditionally ascribed to this phenomenon. Those traditional frameworks (particularly misinterpretations of sociologist Robert Ezra Park's theories) were formulated before the 1970's. They argued that marginality itself is necessarily pathological and the source of lifelong personal conflict. Consequently, multiracial individuals supposedly felt divided and ambivalent about their group loyalties. This interpretation is largely a result of the mutually exclusive nature of United States racial identities and a society that historically has been hostile to the idea of a multiracial identity. These theorists paid little attention to the sociological forces that made psychological functioning difficult for multiracial individuals and instead characterized them as "psychologically dysfunctional" because this image was acceptable to then current beliefs that sought to discourage miscegenation. These theorists thus distorted, or at least misinterpreted, Park's theory of marginality. They also overshadowed other contemporary theorists who argued that marginality could provide individuals with a broader vision and wider range of sympathies because of their ability to identify with more than one racial or cultural group.

The traditional theories of marginality were further challenged by data collected beginning in the 1980's. A consensus was developing that multiracial-identified individuals, in their journey to reach racial and cultural wholeness, may experience various ambiguities, strains, and conflicts. These phenomena come "naturally" with marginality in a society that views racial identities as mutually exclusive categories of experience. However, the negative feelings associated with marginality can be counterbalanced by an increased sensitivity to commonalities and appreciation of racial and cultural differences in interpersonal and intergroup situations.

Impact on Intergroup Relations

The models of multiracial identity that have emerged since the dismantling of segregation laws in the 1950's and 1960's challenge traditional U.S. racial boundaries and categories in much the same way that their historical predecessors did. These historical manifestations of multiracial identity include integration through "passing" for a white person and the formation of rural enclaves and pluralistic urban elites, such as blue-vein societies and Louisiana Creoles of color. However, those identities were motivated by the legal system of segregation, which sought to control the potential "threat" to white dominance posed by individuals of color. Consequently, they were not so much a response to the forced denial of European ancestry or cultural orientation as they were a reaction to being subordinated and to being denied the privileges that these criteria implied. These traditional identities also maintained the hierarchical value attached to racial differences by the larger society. Such attitudes were the products of Eurocentrism and were responsible for colorism among Americans of color. Colorism involves the preferential treatment of individuals who more closely approximate whites in terms of consciousness, behavior, and phenotype within the various communities of color as well as the larger society.

The "new" multiracial identity is not premised on the desire to gain privileges that would be precluded by identifying as a person of color and therefore is not synonymous with the psychosocial pathology of colorism. This identity instead contests the mutually exclusive nature of American racial boundaries and challenges the hierarchical valuation of racial (and cultural) differences. A multiracial identity thus recognizes the commonalities among various communities (integration) and, at the same time, appreciates the differences (pluralism). More important, this identity is premised on an egalitarian dynamic between pluralism and integration, which are viewed as relative, rather than absolute extremes, on a continuum of grays.

G. Reginald Daniel

Core Resources

Paul R. Spickard's *Mixed Blood: Intermarriage and Ethnic Identity in Twentieth-Century America* (Madison: University of Wisconsin Press, 1989) examines intermarriage and multiple racial and ethnic identities as these topics relate to Jewish, Japanese, and African Americans. *Racially Mixed People in America* (Thousand Oaks, Calif.: Sage Publications, 1992) and *The Multiracial Experience: Racial Borders as the New Frontier* (Thousand Oaks, Calif.: Sage Publications, 1996), both of which were edited by psychologist Maria P. P. Root, are groundbreaking volumes that include research by scholars and other experts on the multiracial experience in the United States. *American*

Mixed Race: The Culture of Microdiversity (Lanham, Md.: Rowman & Littlefield, 1995), edited by Naomi Zack, is a collection of essays on the topic of multiracial identity including autobiographies, art, social science, public policy, and identity theory. Lise Funderburg's *Black, White, Other: Biracial Americans Talk About Race and Identity* (New York: William Morrow, 1994) is a collection of powerful oral histories of racially blended individuals of primarily white and black backgrounds.

See also: Biracialism; Creole; Ethnicity and ethnic groups; Ethnic identities of women; Interracial and interethnic marriage; Marital assimilation; Miscegenation laws; Mongrelization; Mulattoes; Multiracial movement; One-drop rule; Options for ethnic identity; Panethnicity; Passing; Race as a concept; Self-identification among Asian Americans; Self-identification among Latinos; Transnationalism and ethnonationalism; Transracial adoption.

Multiracial movement

Significance: The multiracial movement originated in the growing numbers of individuals in the United States who identify with more than one racial background. Its impact was most evident in challenges to official racial classifications, particularly on the decennial census, which have traditionally required individuals to identify with only one racial background.

In 1979, interracial couples in Berkeley, California, founded I-Pride (Interracial/Intercultural Pride) in order to provide general support for interracial families. However, its specific goal was to get the Berkeley public schools to reflect the identity of their offspring accurately by including a multiracial designator on school forms. During 1979-1980, the Berkeley public schools added "interracial" to school forms, the first time such a classification had been used in modern United States history. By the 1990's, I-Pride had become part of a coalition of more than fifty grassroots organizations that had come into existence since the 1970's. The coalition began pressuring for the addition of a multiracial identifier to the decennial census. These organizations included groups such as Multiracial Americans of Southern California in Los Angeles (MASC), the Biracial Family Network in Chicago (BFN), the Interracial Family Alliance in Atlanta (IFA), the Interracial Family Circle in Washington, D.C. (IFC), and a national umbrella organization called the Association of Multiethnic Americans (AMEA). This coalition also included A Place

U.S. Census Bureau Assignment of Multiracial Responses in the Other Category
(1990 census, ten most frequently used responses)

Response	Assigned Category	Total
Black and white	Black	47,835
Mixed, multiracial (or multiethnic)	Other	32,505
Mulatto (or quadroon, octoroon)	Other	31,848
White and black	White	27,926
Eurasian	Asian	19,190
Amerasian	Asian	18,545
Biracial (or interracial)	Other	17,202
White and Japanese	White	9,329
White and Filipino	White	7,081
Creole	Other	6,244

Notes: In 1990, Amerasian and Eurasian were reassigned from the other category to the Asian category. That same year, Creole was reassigned to the other category although in 1980 it had been recoded as black. Also, individuals who used terms such as mulatto, quadroon, or octoroon remained in the other category; previously they had been reassigned to the black category. Those individuals who listed themselves as two or more racial groups were reassigned to the first racial group listed.

Source: Data are from the U.S. Bureau of the Census. 1990 Census.

for Us/National, which is a national nondenominational religious support network for interracial families, organizations such as the Georgia-based activist, informational, and educational Project RACE (Reclassify All Children Equally), and *Interracial Voice*, an advocacy journal on the Internet that provides a public forum for the discussion of issues related to multiracial-identified and interracially married individuals.

This network of organizations encompasses individuals from various racial backgrounds; however, it has attracted a significant number of black and white couples and their children, largely because of the one-drop rule of hypodescent, which designates everyone of African descent as black. The network also has attracted a smaller number of "multigenerational" individuals who have backgrounds that have been blended for several generations. Although they have been socially designated as members of the various traditional United States racial groups (European American, African American, Native American, Latino American, and so on), they have resisted identifying solely with those socially assigned communities.

The 1990 Census

The controversy over the issue of multiracial identity became intense in 1988. On January 20 of that year, the Office of Management and Budget (OMB), the branch of the government responsible for implementing changes in federal statistical surveys, published in the Federal Register a notice soliciting public comment on potential revisions in Directive No. 15. This directive was implemented in May, 1978, as the government-wide guide for conducting racial/ethnic surveys. The revisions would permit individuals to identify themselves as "other" if they believed they did not fall into one of the four basic official racial categories—black, white, Asian/Pacific Islander, American Indian and Alaska Native—or in the so-called "ethnic" category, Hispanic. Heretofore, the OMB advised that the category that most closely reflected how the individual was recognized by the larger community should be used in cases where there was any uncertainty. (Although an "other" category has not been used on all statistical surveys, it has been provided on each census since 1910 to increase the response rate to the race question. However, write-in responses in the "other" category are reassigned to one of the traditional racial categories.)

Many interracial couples and multiracial-identified individuals requested that a multiracial or biracial identifier, instead of "other," be added to the five categories. (On the 1970 census, multiracial offspring were classified in terms of the father's racial identity; in 1980, the Census Bureau shifted to a formula relying on the identity of the mother. However, a "biracial" or "multiracial" designation was not permitted.) The OMB received overwhelmingly negative responses from the public to the proposed changes to Directive No. 15, particularly the addition of a multiracial identifier. This included some federal agencies, such as the Civil Rights Division of the Department of Justice, the Department of Health and Human Services, the Equal Employment Opportunity Commission, the Office of Personnel Management, and several large corporations. Some of this opposition was based on logistical and financial concerns about the increase in data collection, paperwork, changes in the format of forms and computer programs for data analysis, and data burden on respondents.

Various African American leaders and organizations in particular voiced their opposition to the change. They argued that most, if not all African Americans, have some European, and in many cases, Native American ancestry (although most identify solely with the black community). Consequently, they feared that many individuals would designate themselves as "multiracial" rather than black in order to escape the continuing negative social stigma associated with African Americans. Similar concerns were expressed by individuals and organizations representing other traditional communities of color, including Latinos, Native Americans, and Asian Americans. In addition, opponents argued that the rule of hypodescent, if originally oppressive, has also been a means of mobilizing communities of color in the struggle against white racial privilege. More important, this mechanism has prevented a reduction in the number of individuals who would be counted as members of the traditional communities of color. These numbers were needed to enforce and support civil rights legislation and claims aimed at tracking historical and contemporary patterns of discrimination. They were particularly important in arriving at goals for achieving social and economic equity in the manner of affirmative action.

On November 12, 1988, the AMEA was formed in Berkeley to serve as a national network for the various independent support groups. Its overall goal was to promote healthy images of interracial couples and multiracial individuals. More specifically, its purpose was to increase public awareness about the importance of adding a multiracial identifier to the decennial census. A flurry of telephone calls and correspondence between officials at the OMB and the Census Bureau and various individual groups affiliated with the AMEA ultimately resulted in some clarity as to how multiracial individuals might be accommodated on the 1990 census. Officials said they would specifically code write-in responses in the "other" category as "biracial," "multiracial," or some other designation that clearly indicated a blended identity. This would help determine what, if any, changes should be made on the year 2000 census. This was a departure from policy on previous censuses. However, none of the approximately 253,000 multiracial responses in the other category on the 1990 census can be used as a accurate estimate of the actual number of individuals who identify as multiracial. Also, vast numbers of individuals followed the tradition of circling one box because they were unaware of any other alternative.

The Year 2000 Census
Efforts to get the U.S. Census Bureau to make "multiracial" an acceptable means of self-identification were unsuccessful for the 1990 census. Nevertheless, forms for the Operation Desert Shield/Storm Deployment Survey included a multiracial designator for the offspring of returning intermarried veterans. Under the guidance of Project RACE, several states included "multiracial" as an acceptable official means of self-identification. Georgia, Ohio, Illinois, Michigan, Indiana, and Maryland made

this option available on all official state forms. Florida and North Carolina included a multiracial identifier on all school forms. A 1994 survey of eight hundred public school districts, conducted by the Education Office for Civil Rights, found that approximately 30 percent of the school districts use a special separate category. Other districts simply use the mother's racial designation; some use the father's. The American College Test (ACT), which is the alternative to the Scholastic Aptitude Test (SAT) college entrance exam, included "multiracial" as an acceptable means of identification. Most universities were resistant to any changes in the collection of racial data; however, Williams College in Williamstown, Massachusetts, included a multiracial identifier on its official forms. Beginning in 1989, reports prepared by the Center for Assessment and Demographic Studies at Gallaudet University in Washington, D.C., counted individuals who indicated identification with a multiracial background. Nevertheless, these data were reassigned at the federal level to one of the four official racial categories (along with the Hispanic identifier, when it was given as an option) or added into the figures for each of the racial groups with which multiracial individuals identified. This second method is especially useful when trying to track those whose background includes historically underrepresented groups of color for the purposes of affirmative action.

"Multiracial" was not accepted as a means of self-identification on federal forms during the early 1990's. However, the OMB began a comprehensive review process in 1993 to discuss possible changes in this direction on the year 2000 census. After extensive cognitive research and field testing of sample households, the OMB on October 30, 1997, approved changes that would allow multiracial individuals to identify themselves as such on official forms. (The key findings based on the comprehensive review were that between 1 percent and 1.5 percent of the public would select a multiracial identifier when offered an opportunity to do so.)

Most activists had hoped for a combined format that would include a separate multiracial box but would also allow individuals to check the other boxes representing the various components of their background. The OMB proposed a format that read: "What is this person's race? Mark[X] one or more races to indicate what this person considers herself/himself to be." This format was chosen partially in response to the unanimous support it received from the various federal agencies that require data on race and ethnicity. These agencies argued that the mark-one-or-more alternative—unlike the combined format—would require fewer changes in formatting on existing forms and allow for data continuity. More important, the data could be counted in each of the existing official racial categories with which multiracial individuals identified, thus including the historically underrepresented racial components in their background. This would be especially important for the purposes of the continued enforcement of civil rights legislation and in meeting affirmative action guidelines. This format is similar to the one that appears on the Canadian census. Since the 1980's, Canada has allowed individuals to check more than one box on the census race/ethnic ancestry question. In addition, Canadian census data have been used for the purposes of achieving "job equity" in a manner similar to affirmative action and other civil rights mandates in the United States.

The mark-one-or-more format also received strong support from traditional civil rights organizations such as the National Association for the Advancement of Colored People (NAACP), the National Urban League, the Congressional Black Caucus, and the Mexican American Legal Defense and Education Fund (MALDEF). These groups argued that a stand-alone multiracial identifier would lead to a decline in their numbers. (It should be noted, however, that the combined format would have prevented this loss. In addition, that format would have had the advantage of making it possible to count the data in each of the racial groups with which multiracial individuals identify as well as specifically acknowledging the identity of multiracial individuals.) Furthermore, the traditional communities of color expressed concerns about the potential divisiveness of even the appearance of a multiracial box, whether as a stand-alone identifier or in combination with checking multiple boxes. These concerns were very influential in prompting the OMB officials to chose the mark-one-or-more format. In addition, various representatives from traditional communities of color expressed concerns about how the data would actually be tabulated even though they supported the mark-one-or-more format. The OMB officials indicated that they would make recommendations and provide additional guidance with respect to this question before the year 2000 census after consulting with officials from various federal agencies, interested groups, demographers, planners, and social scientists.

G. Reginald Daniel

Core Resources

Racially Mixed People in America (Thousand Oaks, Calif.: Sage Publications, 1992) and *The Multiracial Experience: Racial Borders as the New Frontier* (Thousand Oaks, Calif.: Sage Publications, 1996), edited by psychologist Maria P. P. Root, are groundbreaking volumes that include research by scholars and other experts on the multiracial experience and movement in the United States. *American Mixed Race: The Culture of Microdiversity* (Lanham, Md.: Rowman & Littlefield, 1995), edited by Naomi Zack, includes several essays that discuss the multiracial movement and its impact on public policy. Jon Michael

Spencer, in *The New Colored People: The Mixed-Race Movement in America* (New York: New York University Press, 1997), examines the potential dangers of the multiracial movement in the United States by comparing it with the multiracial identity of South African coloureds.

See also: Affirmative action; Biracialism; Censuses, U.S.; Hypodescent; Multiracial identity; One-drop rule; Self-identification among Asian Americans; Self-identification among Latinos.

Muslims in North America

> **Significance:** By the late 1900's, Muslim American communities of significant size and number had developed in the United States and Canada. However, some people felt threatened by the rise of Islam in North America.

In March, 1998, *Newsweek* magazine estimated that six million Muslim Americans live in the United States. It found that 42 percent of these Muslims are African American, 24.4 percent are South Asian American, 12.4 percent are Arab American, and 21.2 percent are of other ancestry. According to the article, although the Muslim community faces many hostile stereotypes, it had enough political clout for First Lady Hillary Rodham Clinton to host a Ramadan party for Muslims, who overwhelmingly supported her husband over Senator Robert Dole in the 1996 presidential election.

Newsweek found that the children of Muslim immigrants are adopting mainstream American ways. Muslim women have active mosque and professional roles, and some young people are dreaming of becoming Muslim American politicians. Muslims actively opposed the United States' bombing of Iraq, and the American Muslim Council organized a lobbying campaign against this bombing.

In December, 1997, the Muslim crescent and star, the Christian cross, and Jewish Hannukah lamps were featured in Washington, D.C., holiday displays, but vandals painted a swastika on the Muslim display. Like the Muslim symbols in the display, the religion of Islam has gained some level of recognition and influence in the United States but has not yet gained acceptance. Many Americans and Canadians see Islam as a threatening, foreign religion that inspires vicious acts of terrorism. This impression, reinforced by the 1993 bombing by foreign-born Muslims of the World Trade Center in New York, led many Americans to suspect that Muslims were behind the April, 1995, bombing of the federal building in Oklahoma City, Oklahoma. Some committed hate crimes against innocent Muslim Americans. Later it was determined that the Oklahoma bombings had been committed by a white American man, Timothy McVeigh. If Islamic terrorism—some of which is related to the *jihad*, or "holy war" against Israel—grows, many American Muslims fear that their civil rights may be ignored. Some experts, such as former attorney general Ramsey Clark, have expressed doubts about the guilt of Sheikh Omar Abdel-Rahman, an Egyptian-born cleric convicted of terrorism in the World Trade Center bombing.

Practical Problems

Being a practicing Muslim is not easy in the United States and Canada. Muslims do not eat pork or pork products or consume alcohol and often find it hard to obtain meat butchered according to Islamic tradition. Required to pray five times per day, Muslims sometimes find it difficult to fit their prayers into schedules designed for non-Muslims. Schools and businesses generally do not recognize Islamic holidays, and not every community has a mosque. The practical problems that are experienced by devout Muslims are in many respects similar to those experienced by Orthodox Jews.

During Ramadan (the ninth month of the Islamic calendar, which falls in the spring), Muslims and their families fast during the day. This makes it difficult for Muslims to entertain non-Muslim business clients and social guests. During their holiest month, observant Muslims suffer from heightened isolation.

This Muslim family celebrates the graduation of one of its members from college. Muslims in the United States face many negative stereotypes partly because of the nation's conflicts with Middle Eastern countries.

Future Projections

The Muslim population in North America is increasing. Muslim Americans will almost certainly outnumber Jewish Americans within the first quarter of the twenty-first century, and the Muslim Canadian population is also growing rapidly. Therefore, both Muslims and the larger society have a strong interest in Muslim participation in interfaith relations. In addition, religious scholars are beginning to document New World changes in Islam to illustrate the impact of democracy and multiculturalism on a nearly fourteen-hundred-year-old religious tradition.

Susan A. Stussy

Core Resources

Kambiz Ghanea Bassiri's *Competing Visions of Islam in the United States: A Study of Los Angeles* is a scholarly community study by a Muslim author (Westport, Conn.: Greenwood Press, 1997). Bassiri covers the African American, Arab, Pakistani, and Persian elements of the Los Angeles Muslim community and the differences in belief and practice among the groups. *Islam in North America: A Sourcebook*, edited by Michael A. Koszegi and J. Gordon Melton (New York: Garland, 1992), is an impressive collection of essays on Islam in the United States and Canada. Chapter 7 includes a useful directory of Islamic organizations. Aminah Beverly McCloud's *African American Islam* studies Islam as part of the black American experience. Her work illustrates the tensions between African American Muslims regardless of their religious orthodoxy and members of Muslim immigrant groups. In *Neighbors: Islam in North America*, Elias D. Mallon presents a collection of interviews of ordinary American and Canadian Muslims. Richard Brent Turner's *Islam in the African American Experience* (Bloomington: Indiana University Press, 1997) traces the development of Islam in the United States from colonial days, when Muslim slaves tried to preserve their religion in the African diaspora, to the present Muslim expressions of faith in the African American community.

See also: Arab American intergroup relations; Arab Americans; Arab Canadians; Iranian Americans; Jewish-African American relations; Jewish-Arab American relations; Nation of Islam; Nativism; Religion-based ethnicities.

N

Naïveté explanation of racism

Paul Sniderman, professor of political science at Stanford University, concluded that most white Americans are not racists. Although Americans may sometimes express a simple-minded, naïve, prejudiced view of blacks, this disappears when researchers delve more deeply into their true beliefs concerning equality. Sniderman's views are found in *Reaching Beyond Race* (Cambridge, Mass.: Harvard University Press, 1997). Sniderman discovered that about as many white Americans believe in equality for blacks as are opposed to the concept. Sniderman's surveys led him to conclude that current conflicts over racial policies are driven as much by a white person's view of what the government should try to do as by any deep prejudice or racial hatred of African Americans. Sniderman finds that many Americans, white and black, share the basic values of liberalism: a belief in the equality of all human beings, a belief that government can be a positive force for social change, and a deep commitment to help those in society who are not well off. His surveys show that it is a mistake to believe that before equality can be achieved white values, based on prejudice, must be changed. It is not the prejudice of whites that prevents change because many whites no longer express or hold racist views of black inferiority. The overall impact of racial prejudice on political choices made by whites is very "modest," according to Sniderman.

Instead, Sniderman concluded, the programs advocated by civil rights groups are the biggest obstacles to equality because they seem to be opposed to another basic American value: fairness. Programs dedicated to creating equal opportunity, such as affirmative action, are seen as condoning unequal treatment under the law. Race-conscious policies aimed at overcoming prejudice blame people living now for crimes committed many years and generations ago. Many white Americans who are not prejudiced against African Americans see this as unfair. Similarly, laws outlawing hate speech bother many whites who see them as preventing free discussion and free speech.

Surveys of racial attitudes conducted by Sniderman show an increase, even since 1993, in the number of whites who bear goodwill toward blacks. He finds two forces at work in white America: a diminishing core of citizens who hate blacks fully and completely and a growing number who wish to see improvement in the quality of lives led by African Americans.

Sniderman suggests that it is no longer necessary to change the "hearts and minds" of whites to bring about full equality. What should be done is to change the terms of the debate. Political leaders who support programs aimed at helping impoverished black families should broaden their views to include help for all poor families. They should base their appeals for help on the moral principle of fairness, that all people who need help should get it, regardless of race. According to Sniderman, a platform calling for social justice, rather than racial justice, would end racial divisions in the United States and bring about a true biracial coalition that would change America forever. *Leslie V. Tischauser*

See also: Affirmative action; Hate speech; Racism: changing nature of; Racism: history of the concept.

Nation of Islam

> **Significance:** The Nation of Islam is a Muslim religious organization that inculcates black pride and helps elevate African Americans' social and economic status.

The Nation of Islam (NOI) is a religious organization that has successfully melded orthodox Islam, black nationalism, and a set of social and economic principles to produce a highly structured way of life for its African American membership. Founded in 1930 in Detroit, Michigan, the NOI crystallized around three leaders: W. D. Fard, Elijah Muhammad, and Malcolm X.

Beliefs
The Nation of Islam embraces the essential teachings of orthodox Islam. Both groups stress cleanliness and a strict moral code, and shun alcohol, drug abuse, and eating pork. Early NOI leaders, however, expanded orthodox Islam because of the historic oppression of Afri-

can Americans. The Nation of Islam is orthodox Islam customized for the African American experience, with solidarity and racial pride being key added features. Black Muslims are required to drop their European last names, associated with enslavement, and adopt the "X" until they earn an Islamic surname. Additional elements, such as advocating a separate nation for its members and teaching about the racist deeds of the "white man," were the source of much outside criticism and prevented the NOI's acceptance into the official fold of orthodox Islam.

History

In the midst of Great Depression woes and the past specter of slavery, many African Americans were disillusioned and susceptible to philosophies and leaders who promised improvements. Consequently, a number of nationalistic and religious movements developed. In 1930, W. D. Fard formed the Nation of Islam, which espoused the political nationalism of Jamaican-born Marcus Garvey, who amassed thousands of followers in the United States from 1916 until his imprisonment in 1923 and subsequent deportation. Garvey advocated a separate African American nation, economic and political solidarity, and racial pride.

Fard, the first prophet of the Nation of Islam, is shrouded in mystery. Although believed to be from Mecca, his national origins, his real name, and the circumstances of his 1934 disappearance are not known. Fard's achievements, however, are well documented. In four years during the Great Depression, Fard established the church's basic philosophy, created a security force known as the Fruit of Islam, opened the University of Islam, built its first temple, and amassed about eight thousand followers. Many of his followers, including Elijah Muhammad, thought Fard to be an incarnation of Allah. After Fard's sudden disappearance Elijah Muhammad became the group's leader.

Elijah Muhammad was born Elijah Poole in Sandersville, Georgia. His parents had been slaves and sharecroppers. He married Clara Evans in 1919, and during the 1920's he and his family migrated to Detroit, where he met Fard and became one of his most devoted converts. He was rewarded by being chosen as Fard's successor, and he transformed Fard's sincere project into a thriving organization.

Elijah Muhammad

After Fard's disappearance, rivalry caused some factionalism and a sharp decrease in NOI membership. Muhammad, often the victim of harassment and death threats, was imprisoned. Consequently, he moved the NOI headquarters from Detroit to Chicago, where he was able to rebuild and strengthen the organization. When Muhammad died in 1975, the Nation of Islam had

Elijah Muhammad, who died in 1975, was a major force in the development of the Nation of Islam.

temples and schools from coast to coast; owned a string of restaurants, apartments, and other businesses and real estate; operated a major printing press; and had a membership of more than one hundred thousand. Much of Muhammad's success, however, can be attributed to one of his ministers, Malcolm X.

Malcolm X

Malcolm X was born Malcolm Little in Omaha, Nebraska. His parents, Earle and Louise Little, were organizers for Marcus Garvey's Universal Negro Improvement Association. Because of their views, the Littles were forced to move. They eventually settled in East Lansing, Michigan, where Earle apparently was murdered and Louise had a breakdown. Malcolm wandered between odd jobs and engaged in petty crime. He was imprisoned from 1946 to 1952, and he married Betty Shabazz in 1958. He was murdered in New York on February 21, 1965.

In prison, Malcolm became self-educated and converted to Islam. After his release, he met Elijah Muhammad, received his X, and trained for the NOI ministry. He headed temples in several cities before becoming the primary spokesperson for the Nation of Islam. His frank speeches and numerous public appearances catapulted the NOI into the national forefront. Membership swelled due to Malcolm's visibility, but his enemies increased also. For unauthorized remarks made about President John F. Kennedy's assassination, Malcolm was suspended from the NOI. Around that time, he changed his name to El Hajj Malik El-Shabazz. He left the NOI in

March, 1964, and formed two new organizations, which were curtailed by his death.

After Elijah Muhammad's death, his son, Warith, also known as Wallace, became the NOI leader. Warith's changes forced another NOI split, spearheaded by Louis Farrakhan. The NOI expanded under Farrakhan, a controversial figure for some of his adamant and at times incendiary statements. His nondenominational Million Man March in October, 1995, immensely added to his visibility and to some extent mitigated his controversial image. *Linda Rochell Lane*

Core Resources

Clayborne Carson's *Malcolm X: The FBI Files* (New York: Carroll & Graff, 1991) extracts data from Federal Bureau of Investigation files and provides information on Malcolm X, his family, and the Nation of Islam from 1919 to 1980. John Henrick Clark edited *Malcolm X: The Man and His Times* (Trenton, N.J.: African World Press, 1990), which contains essays by scholars and personal acquaintances and a chapter in Malcolm's own words. E. Franklin Frazier's *The Negro Church in America* (1963, reprint, New York: Schocken Books, 1974) and C. Eric Lincoln's *The Black Church Since Frazier* (New York: Schocken Books, 1974) provide critical background on African American religion. Lincoln's *The Black Muslims in America* (Boston: Beacon Press, 1961) is the first complete academic analysis of the Nation of Islam. Thomas W. Lippman, in *Understanding Islam* (New York: Signet Books, 1982), provides a good start for those with little knowledge of orthodox Islam. In *The Autobiography of Malcolm X* (New York: Ballantine Books, 1965), Malcolm X and Alex Haley tell the story of the African American revolutionary and Black Muslim leader.

The beliefs of the Nation of Islam are explained by Elijah Muhammad in *The Supreme Wisdom* (2 vols., Brooklyn: Temple of Islam, 1957).

See also: Malcolm X assassination; Million Man March; Muslims in North America; Religion-based ethnicities; Separatism; Universal Negro Improvement Association.

National Advisory Commission on Civil Disorders

The National Advisory Commission on Civil Disorders was created by executive order in 1967 with Governor Otto Kerner of Illinois as chairman and Mayor John V. Lindsay of New York City as vice chairman. The commission had eleven members, including four members of Congress as well as labor, civil rights, and law enforce-ment leaders. Other public officials and private citizens participated on advisory panels studying such things as private enterprise and insurance in riot-affected areas.

Racial violence had escalated with the riots in Watts in 1965 and, by the summer of 1967, was spreading to other American cities. After extensive study, the commission recommended new and expanded employment and educational opportunity programs, national standards for welfare programs, and increased access to housing. The commission's report stated that the United States was becoming "two societies, one black, one white—separate and unequal." It was the first major study to place the blame for creating black ghettos on white society.

The commission studied the major race riots, identified patterns in the violence, developed profiles of participants, and analyzed the conditions prior to and following the disorders. Despite concern among some officials that the violence was being encouraged by radical groups, the commission determined that the principal causes were widespread discrimination and segregation and the increasing concentration of the black population in inner-city ghettos offering little opportunity. These conditions, according to the report, led to pervasive frustration, the acceptance of violence as a means of retaliation, and growing feelings of powerlessness. A spark was all that was necessary to ignite violence, and the police often provided it.

The commission recommended new federal programs to address the problems of poverty, unemployment, education, and housing and the expansion of existing urban programs, such as the Model Cities Program, to provide economic opportunity to residents of the inner city. Guidance was also offered to state and local officials for identifying potentially violent conditions, reducing the likelihood of violence, providing training to police to lessen tensions in minority communities, and organizing emergency operations in response to escalating violence.

See also: Civil rights; Detroit riot; Kerner Report; Newark race riots; Race riots of the twentieth century; Watts riot.

National Association for the Advancement of Colored People

Significance: Founded in 1910, the NAACP has been at the center of the struggle for civil rights and social, political, and economic equality for African Americans.

The Niagara Movement, founded in 1905, was the fore-runner to the National Association for the Advancement of Colored People (NAACP). A group of African American leaders headed by W. E. B. Du Bois and William Monroe Trotter met at Niagara Falls, Canada. Their chief purpose was to develop an aggressive campaign for the full citizenship of African Americans. They were dissatisfied with the approach of Booker T. Washington, who advocated black achievement while submitting to the injustice of segregation. Race riots, in which a number of African Americans were shot, beaten, burned, or hanged by lynch mobs in the early twentieth century, served as the backdrop for the meeting. Among the primary goals of the Niagara Movement were erasing all distinctions based on race, gaining respect for all working men, and attaining black suffrage. The Niagara Movement was the first attempt to organize African Americans after the Reconstruction Era (1863-1877).

Open-minded whites, moved to action by the race riots, called for a national conference on Lincoln's birthday in 1909 and invited Niagara Movement members. The NAACP was formally founded in May of 1910, and the Niagara Movement was incorporated into it. Most charter members were white rather than people of color. They had a wide range of expertise and resources. One of its most notable African American members was W. E. B. Du Bois, the great African American leader and scholar. The new organization vowed to fight de jure (legal) segregation and to work for equal education for white and black children, complete suffrage for African Americans, and the enforcement of the Fourteenth and Fifteenth Amendments. During its first year, the NAACP established programs for blacks in economic development and job opportunities. It pushed for more police protection in the South and for antilynching and lawlessness initiatives in the nation. *The Crisis*, the official publication of the NAACP, served as the "cutting edge" of critical thought regarding the "race question," publicizing injustices against African Americans. Du Bois served as editor.

Civil Rights or Economic Advancement?

Early tension within the NAACP centered on the question of whether the budding organization should focus primarily on civil rights or should tackle economic issues as well. Noneconomic liberalism became the guiding light for the organization, since a consensus could not be reached over the importance of economic issues. The liberal white who served as president starting in 1930, Joel E. Spingarn, believed that once the racial issue in the United States had been resolved, African Americans would be able to compete on an equal footing in the economic and educational arenas. Future leaders of the NAACP would include Walter White, Roy Wilkins, Ben-

jamin Hooks, and Benjamin Chavis.

There was considerable debate over whether African Americans should pursue a social agenda of equality and civil rights as opposed to economic development and independence. In its most acute form, this involved public debate between W. E. B. Du Bois and Booker T. Washington. Washington was renowned as the founder and president of Tuskegee Institute (now University) in Alabama. He was often consulted by presidents and invited to the White House. Washington argued that African Americans should focus on vocational education and training. He viewed politics as secondary and social equality for blacks as less important—a philosophy that pleased white southerners and presidents. Civil rights, to his way of thinking, would gradually evolve as African Americans developed their own business enterprises. Until then, African Americans should not be too pushy, for fear of alienating whites. In short, blacks should remain subservient to whites and, particularly in the South, reconcile with the prevalent racism.

Du Bois, on the other hand, argued that Washington's approach was inadequate and asked African Americans to give up too much. Du Bois held that African Americans needed higher education. He held that a "talented

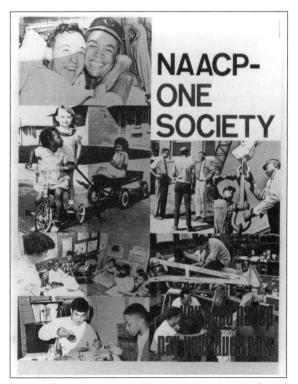

Since its foundation in 1910, the National Association for the Advancement of Colored People has worked to secure the social, political, and economic rights of African Americans.

tenth," meaning those with higher education, would be in the position to lead the masses and working class. Unlike Washington, Du Bois maintained that economic progress was irrelevant without political participation and political power. To his way of thinking, political power would nurture economic development, not vice versa.

The failure of noneconomic liberalism can be seen in the results of the Great Depression. While the NAACP focused on social status and targeted race and racism, African Americans were devastated by the Depression. Already on the bottom of the economic ladder, many African Americans began to migrate to northern industrial cities in search of job opportunities and an improved standard of living relative to that in the South. The timing of their migration, however, collided with the Great Depression. African Americans in the South still survived at a subsistence level, trying to make a living as sharecroppers in an agricultural economy. The arrival on the political stage of Marcus Garvey in the early 1920's stirred the black masses. Preaching black nationalism and economic independence, Garvey urged African Americans to return to the Mother Country (Africa), emphasizing self-determination and independence. Garvey developed a large following in a short period of time between 1919 and 1925. Du Bois realized that the Garvey phenomenon, combined with the effects of the Depression of the 1930's, revealed a critical flaw in the thinking and philosophy of the NAACP. In 1934 Du Bois challenged the NAACP to question its organizational philosophy of noneconomic liberalism and to stress economic development and issues. The organization, still with Spingarn and a board of directors dominated by whites, failed to heed the call. Their agenda remained centered on racial equality. It was at this point that Du Bois broke with the NAACP.

Role in Justice and Equality

A black and white team of lawyers of the NAACP, constituting its legal committee, won three significant legal cases during the first fifteen years of the NAACP's existence. In *Guinn v. United States* (1915) the Supreme Court invalidated the grandfather clause in Maryland and Oklahoma, ruling that it was unconstitutional under the Fifteenth Amendment. Two years later, in the case of *Buchanan v. Warley* (1917), the Court voided a Louisville ordinance requiring African Americans to live in certain sections of the city. In the case of *Moore v. Dempsey* (1923), the Court ordered a new trial in a case in which an African American had been convicted of murder in Arkansas. The poverty-stricken defendant had been tried before an all-white jury. As a result of these early victories, the NAACP soon realized that the court system could be a valuable ally in the fight against racial injustice and the struggle for equality.

In addition, the NAACP supported or provided the legal expertise in a number of cases that successfully challenged aspects of the "separate but equal" doctrine of racial segregation established in *Plessy v. Ferguson* (1896). This doctrine was premised on the notion that it was legal to have separate facilities for blacks and whites as long as those facilities were equal. Successful challenges included restrictive covenants in the case of *Corrigan v. Buckley* (1926) and the legality of the white primary in *Nixon v. Condon* (1927, 1932). In the wake of *Smith v. Allwright* (1944), which finally sounded the death knell for the white primary, the NAACP began to organize local voter leagues in the South. Repression from local governments and the White Citizens' Council, however, led to the decrease of the NAACP's influence in the South in the 1950's, to be replaced by younger organizations such as the Southern Christian Leadership Conference.

The 1954 U.S. Supreme Court case of *Brown v. Board of Education* gained the greatest attention for the NAACP and its sister organization, the NAACP Legal Defense and Educational Fund. Thurgood Marshall argued this landmark case. In its decision, the Court ruled that the pernicious "separate but equal" doctrine of racial segregation in the public schools was unconstitutional, stating that separate schools for whites and blacks were inherently unequal. The *Brown* case served as the defining moment for the NAACP and the Civil Rights movement in the 1950's.

Legal Defense and Educational Fund

The NAACP Legal Defense and Educational Fund (LDEF) was founded in 1939. It was designed to be the chief legal arm of the NAACP. It claimed to be a non-profit entity, yet it had an interlocking membership with the NAACP. As a result of objections by the Internal Revenue Service in 1957, the legal and educational arm formally separated from the NAACP. Thus, the NAACP Legal Defense and Educational Fund developed its own staff, board of directors, budget, and policies. Thurgood Marshall became the first director-counsel until 1961, followed by Jack Greenberg, who served in this capacity until 1984, when Julius L. Chambers took over. The LDEF had represented thousands of cases in education, employment, prisoners' rights, housing, health care, voting rights, and other areas by the end of the 1980's.

The NAACP continued to push for civil rights and racial integration in the 1950's and 1960's as the Civil Rights movement intensified its efforts to overcome racial segregation in every phase of American society. Like other civil rights organizations of the time, the NAACP engaged in a number of nonviolent activities. The NAACP, along with a number of other organizations, was partly responsible for the Civil Rights Act of

1964. The NAACP, and the Civil Rights movement as a whole, reached its zenith in this decade, as the 1964 Civil Rights Act, the 1965 Voting Rights Act and the 1968 Civil Rights Act were passed. In the 1970's and 1980's, the organization became increasingly irrelevant, since constitutional civil rights guarantees were in place and had been upheld by the courts. At the same time, the social movement in African American communities switched increasingly toward community control, black nationalism, and separatism, which were diametrically opposed to the organizational goals of the NAACP. In the 1980's, as the federal government and the Reagan administration was less supportive of civil rights and previous black gains, the NAACP Legal Defense and Educational Fund continued to play an important role in the legal arena.

Mfanya D. Tryman

Core Resources
Informative sources include Gerald David Jaynes and Robin M. Williams, Jr., eds., *A Common Destiny: Blacks and American Society* (Washington, D.C.: National Academy Press, 1989); Harold Cruse, *Plural but Equal* (New York: William Morrow, 1987); John Hope Franklin, *From Slavery to Freedom* (New York: Alfred A. Knopf, 1967); Jack Greenberg's article "NAACP Legal Defense and Educational Fund," in *Civil Rights and Equality*, edited by Leonard W. Levy, Kenneth L. Karst, and Dennis J. Mahoney (New York: Collier Macmillan, 1989); Talcott Parsons and Kenneth B. Clark, eds., *The Negro American* (Boston: Houghton Mifflin, 1966). Additional information on the NAACP will be found in Mimmi Finch, *The NAACP: Its Fight for Justice* (Metuchen, N.J.: Scarecrow Press, 1981); Charles Flint Kellogg, *NAACP: A History of the National Association for the Advancement of Colored People* (Baltimore: The Johns Hopkins University Press, 1964); and Robert Zangrando, *The NAACP Crusade Against Lynching, 1909-1950* (Philadelphia: Temple University Press, 1980).

See also: *Brown v. Board of Education*; Civil rights; Civil Rights Act of 1964; Civil Rights movement; Congress of Racial Equality; Equality of opportunity; National Association for the Advancement of Colored People Legal Defense and Educational Fund.

National Association for the Advancement of Colored People Legal Defense and Educational Fund

The National Association for the Advancement of Colored People Legal Defense and Educational Fund (LDF or LDEF) was established in 1939-1940 as a tax-exempt corporation by the National Association for the Advancement of Colored People. Its charter was handwritten in March, 1940, by Thurgood Marshall, who stated the new organization's dual purpose: to provide legal aid to African Americans "suffering legal injustices by reason of race or color" and to create education opportunities for African Americans that had been denied them by reason of race or color.

The LDF was founded to carry on litigation in the spirit of the social change agenda already established by the actions of NAACP attorneys in the American courts. It provides or supports legal representation on behalf of African Americans and other people of color in defending their legal and constitutional rights against discrimination in education, employment, land use, recreation, transportation, housing, voting, health care, and other areas. It has successfully argued against grandfather clauses, restrictive housing covenants in city ordinances, white primaries, white juries, capital punishment, and segregation of public facilities.

Since the 1950's the LDF has operated independently from its parent organization, which maintains its own legal department, and at times the relationship between the LDF and NAACP has involved some conflict. The LDF both represents individuals and brings suit on behalf of civil rights groups. It has been based in New York City since its formation and also maintains a center in Washington, D.C.

Barbara Bair

See also: *Brown v. Board of Education*; Civil Rights Act of 1964; Civil Rights movement; Little Rock school desegregation; National Association for the Advancement of Colored People; Voting Rights Act of 1965.

National Association of Colored Women

Near the end of the eighteenth century, grave concerns about African Americans being treated as second-class citizens compelled a group of African American women to move beyond their local and state associations to devise plans for the formation of a national body that would systematically and professionally address the problems that they believed threatened the very survival of African Americans. Economic disparities, political disfranchisement, and social ostracism presented the greatest threats to African American aspirations for freedom and inclusion in the American system of democracy. Meeting at the Nineteenth Street Baptist Church in Washington, D.C., in July, 1896, the National Federation of Afro-American Women and the National League of Colored Women joined forces to form a national organization known as the National Association of Colored Women (NACW).

Operating through a series of departments and a strong executive cabinet, the NACW became an umbrella group for African American women's organizations at both state and local levels. The organization's official publication, *National Notes*, served as an instrument to unite the women and to educate them in the concepts and techniques of reform, advocating racial uplift, improved race relations, and protection of women. From its inception, the NACW has worked to improve the lives of African American people in the United States and to help them achieve full citizenship rights.   *Alvin K. Benson*

See also: African American women; Ethnic identities of women; Women and racism; Women of color.

National Black Women's Political Leadership Caucus

Founded in 1971, the National Black Women's Leadership Political Caucus is committed to helping African American women work toward equality and increase their knowledge of the role of women in the political process. The organization has its headquarters in Washington, D.C., but it also has groups in three regions and thirty-three states throughout the United States. Aside from its primary members, the caucus has an auxiliary membership that includes men, senior citizens, and youth. The organization encourages African American women and youth to participate in the country's economic and political systems. In addition, the caucus enables women to familiarize themselves with the functions of city, state, and federal government. The group is also involved in research, conducting studies in the areas of African American families, politics, and economics. A variety of other services are provided by the National Black Women's Political Leadership Caucus, such as training in public speaking; legislative federal, state, and local workshops; children's services; charitable programs; awards for humanitarianism; and placement services. The organization publishes a semiannual newsletter and has published election tabloids.   *K. Sue Jewell*

See also: African American women; Women of color.

National Coalition of Blacks for Reparations in America

The National Coalition of Blacks for Reparations in America (N'COBRA) is a coalition of organizations across the United States that support reparations for African Americans. African Americans were supposed to receive "forty acres and a mule" from the U.S. government upon emancipation in reparation for the time they spent in slavery, but this proposal was never actually made law. The newly freed blacks lacked property, capital, education, and job experience, giving them a severely disadvantaged start. In addition, not long after slavery was made illegal, a system of segregation known as Jim Crow took effect. Segregation blocked equal access to home ownership, which is the main source of capital for most Americans, and this government-sanctioned inequality can be seen as the root cause of the wealth gap between black and white Americans in modern times, according to Melvin Oliver and Thomas Shapiro in *Black Wealth/White Wealth* (1995). N'COBRA supports and lobbies for HR 40, a congressional bill introduced every year since 1989 by John Conyers, a Democratic representative from Illinois, that demands reparations for blacks not unlike those received by Native Americans for land seized by the government and by Japanese Americans for time spent in internment camps during World War II.   *Eileen O'Brien*

See also: Emancipation Proclamation; Jim Crow laws; Redress movement; Slavery: history.

National Congress of American Indians

The National Congress of American Indians (NCAI), organized in 1944, is a coalition of sovereign nations recognized by the United States through treaty and executive agreement. Its purpose is to protect the rights of American Indians as citizens of nations and tribes within the boundaries of the United States. It is supported through annual membership dues and special fund-raising endeavors. It is organized as a congress, with American Indian governments voting to participate and selecting delegates and alternates to represent them in the NCAI convention and executive council, where they have blocks of votes.

American Indian delegates representing fifty tribes with homes in twenty-seven western states met in Denver, Colorado, in 1944. The NCAI's initial stated goals included pursuit of American Indian rights within the United States, expansion and improvement of Indian education, preservation of Indian values, and equitable settlement of Indian claims. During the 1950's, it aided in the struggle against termination and relocation. More recently, it has been in the forefront of the struggle for Native American cultural rights legislation, which has brought on more reasonable approaches to repatriation of Indian remains and artifacts.   *Howard Meredith*

See also: American Indian activism.

National Council of American Indians

In the early part of the twentieth century, a movement known as the Red Progressive movement called for American Indians to assimilate to the general American lifestyle. It was led by Indians who were well educated and had achieved success in mainstream American society. Among its leaders were Henry Roe Cloud, Thomas L. Sloan, Arthur C. Parker, physicians Charles Eastman and Carlos Montezuma, and Gertrude Simmons Bonnin, a Sioux writer and musician.

The Red Progressives united at first under the Society of American Indians (SAI), but by the early 1920's that organization had split into several rancorous factions. A number of new organizations appeared, including the National Council of American Indians, founded in 1926 by Gertrude Bonnin and her husband. The organization was closely aligned with the General Federation of Women's Clubs, a mostly white and black organization of successful women. Bonnin had served as secretary of the Society of American Indians and in 1924 had coauthored *Oklahoma's Poor Rich Indians: An Orgy of Graft and Exploitation of the Five Civilized Tribes—Legalized Robbery*, a muckraking exposé of graft and greed involving Oklahoma lawyers, judges, and politicians.

The slogan of the National Council of American Indians was "Help the Indians Help Themselves in Protecting Their Rights and Properties." Its major early emphasis was promoting voting and participation in politics after the passage of the Indian Citizenship Act in 1924. It was most successful in these efforts in Oklahoma and South Dakota. The organization also advocated banning peyote use and the Native American Church; it took a moderate stance toward the Bureau of Indian Affairs.

In January, 1934, representatives of several organizations were called together in Washington, D.C., to confer with President Franklin Roosevelt's commissioner of Indian affairs, John Collier, on reforms needed to ameliorate the living conditions of Indians. The Bonnins represented both the National Council of American Indians and the General Federation of Women's Clubs. They strongly supported the Indian Reorganization Act, which was adopted by Congress the same year. The council successfully pushed for a requirement for majority rule elections for tribal offices.

Gertrude Simmons Bonnin, a Sioux writer and musician, and her husband founded the National Council of American Indians in 1926.

The National Council of American Indians, like its predecessors, was torn by factionalism; the Bonnins were its major support. With the coming of World War II, the council faded from existence, but it left behind a strong heritage of Indian political participation. *Fred S. Rolater*

See also: American Indian Defense Association; Indian Citizenship Act; Indian Reorganization Act; Society of American Indians.

National Council of Colored People

> **Significance:** The National Council of Colored People was one of the first groups concerned with the advancement of African Americans and the cause of abolition.

Richard Allen, founder of the AME Church, organized Negro Conventions that led to the formation in 1853 of the National Council of Colored People.

On July 6, 1853, more than one hundred delegates from around the country assembled in Rochester, New York, for a three-day convention to form the National Council of Colored People. This organization was an outgrowth of the Negro Convention movement, which had begun during a meeting on September 20-24, 1830, in Philadelphia. Richard Allen formed the convention with the intention of improving the lives of African Americans by raising their social status through education and, possibly, emigration. The convention met many times in many cities, discussing plans for improvement, and the group thrived on the increasing solidarity among its members. It was at one of the convention meetings, in Rochester, New York, that the plan for the National Council of Colored People was adopted. The meeting in Rochester drew many prominent African American leaders, including Frederick Douglass, James McCune Smith, and James Pennington.

Formation of the Council
At the meeting in 1853, a constitution was drawn up for the new organization, and a president and several vice presidents were chosen. The group discussed the rampant racial oppression of the African American people. Members of both the convention and the newly formed

National Council of Colored People believed that, in order to increase the rate of improvement of the social status of African Americans, it was necessary to create a new institution for the education of African American youth. The new institution would be an industrial school that concentrated on agriculture and the mechanical arts. On the second day of the convention, the council elected to withdraw the proposed school plan because of the exclusive nature of the school. In the final hours of the last day of the convention, the council endorsed two seminaries as places for the education of African Americans—McGrawville College and Allegheny City College.

On November 15, 1853, elections were held in several cities to elect delegates for the formation of new state councils that would act in accordance with the National Council of Colored People. The leading delegates would attend the national council meetings as well as their own state council meetings. The first meeting of the National Council of Colored People was held November 23, 1853, in New York. At least one council member each from the states of New York, Connecticut, Rhode Island, and Ohio was missing, but because of the great distance the other council members had traveled, the meeting continued. After proceeding with the meeting, one delegate from Ohio appeared and demanded that all prior proceedings be nullified. This caused great distress among the council members and created a somewhat hostile working environment, which contributed to the short life of the council. Despite the bleak beginnings of the national council, the state councils operated much more smoothly and with enthusiasm.

Disagreements Continue
In both the national and state councils, the idea of an African American school was revisited. Frederick Douglass defended the school plan unsuccessfully for two years. The country was experiencing an economic depression, which made it hard to fund the school. There also was still concern over the exclusive nature of an African American school. The idea of a separate African American school brought many emotions to the forefront. Integrationists were wary of accepting such a school plan because of the isolation of the school and its students, yet even they saw benefits in an all African American school. Emigrationists considered the proposal and were much more willing to begin work on construction. Amid much opposition, in October, 1855, the convention elected to discontinue plans for the proposed school. The other committees set up by the first national convention and their ambitious plans to assist African Americans in business pursuits and the creation of a library and museum seemed to have stopped on paper.

The second meeting of the National Council of Colored People was scheduled for May 24, 1854, in Cleveland, but it was postponed in order to accommodate more delegates. Eventually, only a few delegates were able to attend. Among the members attending, a debate developed over the recognition of Ohio at the national level, creating a deadlock. A suggestion was made to dissolve the organization, but after a close vote, the National Council of Colored People continued to operate. Ohio, however, withdrew its participation.

At the meeting of May 8, 1855, nearly all the delegates were from New York, as most others had declined to participate. The issue of an African American school again was discussed and once again defeated. Another issue was discussed for the first time—emigration to Canada. Although most delegates at the convention were willing to remain in the United States, they expressed trepidation on the matter of the United States Constitution and the issue of slavery. The issue of emigration was the last to be discussed before the close of the final meeting of the National Council of Colored People. The state councils continued to operate and pursue social equality for African Americans for a few years longer, with councils in some states surviving longer than others. *Jeri Kurtzleben*

Core Resources

Howard Holman Bell's *A Survey of the Negro Convention Movement, 1830-1861* (New York: Arno Press, 1969) contains substantial information on the Negro Convention Movement, from which the National Council of Colored People was formed. John W. Blassingame and John R. McKivigan edited the multivolume *Frederick Douglass Papers* (Series 1, *Speeches, Debates, and Interviews.* New Haven, Conn.: Yale University Press, 1991): Volume 2, *1847-1854,* includes several references to the industrial college proposed at the 1853 meeting in Rochester, New York; volume 3, *1855-1863,* includes an interview with President Andrew Johnson, in which the intent of the National Convention is discussed; and volume 4, *1864-1880,* contains a speech and several pages of notes from the National Council meeting in May, 1855. Alton Hornsby, Jr., in *Chronology of African-American History* (Detroit, Mich.: Gale Research, 1991), places the National Council of Colored People in the context of relevant information on its foundation. Harry A. Ploski and James Williams are the editors of *The Negro Almanac: A Reference Work on the African American* (Detroit, Mich.: Gale Research, 1989), a beginning source of information on the Negro Convention movement.

See also: Abolition; AME Church; American Anti-Slavery Society; Free African Society; *Liberator, The*; Negro Conventions; Pennsylvania Society for the Abolition of Slavery; Underground Railroad.

National Council of Negro Women

The National Council of Negro Women (NCNW), founded in 1935, seeks to facilitate cooperation among women and act as an advocate for women's issues nationally and internationally. Founded by Mary McLeod Bethune (1875-1955), an African American educator and presidential adviser, the organization is composed of a coalition of thirty-one national organizations and individuals. It has local chapters throughout the United States, the Women's Center for Education and Career Advancement in New York City, and offices in western and southern Africa. The NCNW maintains a clearinghouse in which information that will improve the socioeconomic status of African American women and other women of color is compiled and disseminated. The organization also publishes *Black Woman's Voice*, a periodical, and *Sister's Magazine*, a quarterly. In addition, the council is responsible for an archive for black women's history and the Bethune Museum. One of the primary goals of the council is to assist women in developing

Mary McLeod Bethune, an African American educator and presidential advisor, formed the National Council of Negro Women in 1935.

leadership skills to be used on community, national, and international levels. One of its international projects is to improve social and economic conditions for rural women in Third World countries.　　　*K. Sue Jewell*

See also: African American women; Women of color

National Indian Association

After the Civil War (1861-1865), a series of groups devoted to Indian "reform" arose in the eastern United States. The events of 1876-1878, including General George Custer's defeat in the Battle of the Little Bighorn in 1876, the Nez Perce escape attempt of 1877, and the Bannock War and the tragic Cheyenne escape attempt in 1878, led to the establishment of several influential organizations. Five of these became the core of the Friends of the Indian movement. One was the U.S. government's Board of Indian Commissioners, founded in 1869 and consisting of private citizens who served without pay. Two others, established in 1879, were the Boston Indian Citizenship Commission and the National Indian Association (also known as the Women's National Indian Association), established by a group of Protestant churchwomen in Philadelphia. The Indian Rights Association and the National Indian Defense Association followed in the early 1880's.

Between 1879 and 1886, the National Indian Association established eighty-three branches in cities across the nation. It published a monthly periodical, *The Indian's Friend*, often presented petitions to Congress and the president protesting the mistreatment of Indians, stridently pushed for reform of the Bureau of Indian Affairs, and demanded that the U.S. government follow the provisions of its treaties with the Indians with "scrupulous fidelity." Its other major issues included improving education for Indians (with regard to the number and quality of schools), extending citizenship to all Indians, and dividing Indian lands into private homesteads for each family.

The association participated yearly in the Lake Mohonk Conference of the Friends of the Indian and the annual meeting of the Board of Indian Commissioners. These agencies shared responsibility for helping persuade the government to pass the General Allotment Act (Dawes Severalty Act), enacted in 1887, which subdivided the majority of Indian reservations into individual allotments. This act was ultimately disastrous for Indians, as the National Indian Defense Association had feared. The National Indian Association was successful in increasing the number of schools available to Indians. The association failed to influence the government's honoring of treaties.　　　*Fred S. Rolater*

See also: Allotment system; Education and American Indians; Friends of the Indian; General Allotment Act; Indian Rights Association.

National Indian Youth Council

Ten Native American college students gathered to form the National Indian Youth Council (NIYC) in August, 1961, at Gallup, New Mexico. Two months earlier, these students had met at the National Congress of American Indians (NCAI) conference at the University of Chicago. After hearing the discussions encouraging self-determination and denouncing termination, the students decided to start their own group.

The foundation for the NIYC had been laid in 1953 when Herbert Blatchford (Navajo) initiated the first intertribal student group, the Kiva Club, at the University of New Mexico. Blatchford was also the founding director of the NIYC. At the August meeting, Mel Thom (Paiute) was elected the chairperson; Clyde Warrior (Ponca), president; and Shirley Witt (Mohawk), vice president. The NIYC's founding members came from different tribes and interests, but they had a common bond: a spirit to recover native rights and respect. Differing from the NCAI, the NIYC focused on the voices of the youth and employed strategies that were more aggressive and activist.

During its first decade, NIYC targeted problems with Native American education and discrimination. Members editorialized their opinions through NIYC's first publication, *American Aborigine*, edited by Blatchford. In 1963, the NIYC began publishing its long-running newspaper, *ABC: Americans Before Columbus*. The following year, the NIYC went to Washington State to hold a series of "fish-ins." Members defied state law by fishing in rivers that had been closed to native fishing even though treaty language had reserved for the tribes permanent fishing rights. Other activist groups banded together to assist NIYC's "Washington Project."

With national support, NIYC members stepped into the political arena. Thom encouraged a 1964 Washington, D.C., audience to stand up for self-determination. At a Memphis, Tennessee, poverty conference in 1967, Warrior delivered his passionate speech, "We Are Not Free." When Warrior died the following year, the NIYC initiated the education-based Clyde Warrior Institute in American Indian Studies. A 1967 Carnegie Foundation program researched educational methodology and addressed acculturation. With this growth, the NIYC in 1970 had opened chapters on several college campuses and reservations to serve more than two thousand members.

The NIYC also undertook lawsuits against irresponsible mining companies on reservation lands and instituted native employment and training programs. Other NIYC projects range from conducting voting surveys to creating an all-native film company, Circle Film. To help preserve native sacred lands and to protect native rituals, the group appealed to the United Nations and was granted recognition as an "official and non-governmental organization."

From its headquarters in Albuquerque, New Mexico, the NIYC hosts international native conferences that create strong networks of indigenous views. With its broadened vision, NIYC's nationwide membership had grown to more than forty-seven thousand in 1994.

Tanya M. Backinger

See also: American Indian activism; American Indian Movement.

National Urban League

The National Urban League was founded in 1910 as the National League on Urban Conditions Among Negroes, an organization that helped black migrants coming from the rural South to find work and make transitions to living in northern cities. The league merged in 1911 with the Association for the Protection of Colored Women and the Committee for Improving the Industrial Conditions of Negroes in New York, both groups founded in 1906 to aid urban migrants, and adopted its shorter title. The emphasis of the organization has shifted over the years from serving black workers in northern cities to assisting the rural and urban poor in all regions of the country, and from an educational, service, and investigational association to one involved in political action. A nonmembership organization, it has a centralized structure, with a main headquarters in New York and local units in major cities; the local units have their own boards and budgets and adapt national policies to local needs. The league maintains regional bureaus in Washington, D.C.; Akron, Ohio; St. Louis, Missouri; and Atlanta, Georgia. The national governing board is, according to organization by-laws, interracial, and 25 percent of its members are under the age of thirty.

From 1923 until 1948 the National Urban League published the influential magazine *Opportunity*, which, along with the National Association for the Advancement of Colored People's *Crisis*, also based in New York, was a voice for black intellectuals, writers, and social reformers. From 1910 through the 1930's Depression, the league focused on services to those seeking jobs and housing, and lobbied to end discrimination in federal policies and the labor movement. The league grew in size and influence during World War II, when many

Lester B. Granger was executive director of the National Urban League from 1941 to 1961.

thousands of blacks moved to northern industrial cities to do war-related work. The organization was conservative in its approach until the 1960's, when the severity of the problems of segregated housing, ghetto conditions, and inferior education called for more activist policies.

The league emerged as a major advocate for civil rights under the leadership of Whitney M. Young, Jr., who became its executive director in 1961. Under the influence of the Civil Rights and Black Power movements, Young and the National Urban League pursued active protest politics, including a sponsorship role in the 1963 March on Washington. Young's successors, Vernon E. Jordan, Jr., and John Jacob, established several community-based improvement programs. These include street academies to aid high school dropouts in finishing school; job training and placement services in computer skills, law enforcement, and the construction industry; voter registration drives; a Business Development Program for black businesspersons; and a National Consumer Health Education Program to supply health workers to local neighborhoods.   *Barbara Bair*

See also: Civil rights; Civil Rights movement; Great Migration; National Association for the Advancement of Colored People.

Native American

The term "Native American" is commonly used to refer to the many peoples of North America whose cultures existed on the continent when Europeans first arrived. It does not eliminate the possibility of their foreign origin in an earlier era. The term was coined as a collective name for the native peoples of the Americas that would not carry the obvious falseness and the historically racist overtones of such terms as "American Indian" and "Indian." Yet, as is the case with virtually any collective term suggested, there are problems inherent in the term; for example, literally speaking, anyone of any ethnicity born in the Americas could be considered a "native American."

Beginning in the 1970's, the term Native American lost favor among activist groups and many others concerned with American Indian politics. Nevertheless, the term is still widely used, and some still prefer it to American Indian (although by the 1990's, the latter had become more common). Some American Indians find the offensiveness of all such collective terms to be about the same. All are generalizations that deny the unique, tribal-specific cultural heritage and political legacy of the many discrete nations and bands ("tribes") that inhabited the Americas.   *M. W. Simpson*

See also: Amerind; Indian.

Native American Church

The collection of teachings that became the doctrine of the Native American Church had their beginnings in the 1880's, probably among the Kiowas and Comanches living in Oklahoma. The church emphasizes the brotherhood of all American Indians. Among the main themes of the church's ethical code are mutual aid among members, a strong family, self-reliance, and the avoidance of alcohol.

The Native American Church was chartered as a Christian church in 1918. At that time, American Indians of every tribe were still reeling from the devastating effects of three centuries of contact with European American culture. Indians had been subjected to slaughter, enslavement, forced labor, the destruction of food supplies, the confiscation of land, forced dispersal, catastrophic depopulation, and forced religious conversion. Yet American Indians in the late nineteenth and early twentieth centuries created a monotheistic church with discernible and complex doctrines, ethics, and rituals; a strong sense of morality; a body of symbolically rich origin legends; and an individualistic approach that emphasized profound original spiritual experiences.

The ceremony that was to become central to the Native American Church was first described by anthropologist James Mooney in 1892. Its form was similar to that of present-day meetings. After 1900 the ceremony spread rapidly throughout tribal North America. Opposition to its spread came from traditional tribalists, Christian missionaries, and Indian agencies. Wherever the church entered a tribe, it rejected both significant belief aspects of that tribe and the dominant white culture. In 1918, it was chartered as a legal church. Anthropologists helped write the articles of incorporation and appeared before judicial and legislative bodies in defense of the church, shrewdly aided by insightful Indians who included Christian elements to make the chartering process more amenable to legislatures.

The ingestion of peyote is part of the ritual of the church (the church has sometimes been called the Peyote Church). Peyote produces an altered state of consciousness. To members of the Native American Church, peyote is both a teacher and a healer. The use of peyote is strictly limited to the church's ceremonies, and other use is vigorously opposed. Nevertheless, the use of peyote has at times made the church controversial among Indian leaders and organizations. Jesus is seen as a deified spirit with whom church members can communicate. Today church members find the universalism of Christian ideology acceptable, but it is rare to find Christian symbols in the ceremony. Some songs still appeal to Jesus for health and help. Christian sin, judgment, and redemption are not found in Native American Church doctrine.

By 1947 the Native American Church was widely prevalent among the Indians of the United States and had assumed the proportions of an intertribal religion. In 1960, the church was believed to have about 200,000 members, or half the population of adult Indians. Since U.S. law classifies peyote as a psychotropic drug and prohibits non-Indian participation, non-Indian participation is minimal. The Native American Church continues to exist as an important pan-Indian movement uniting diverse cultures in common goals.

Glenn J. Schiffman

See also: American Indian Religious Freedom Act; Peyote religion.

Native American Church v. Navajo Tribal Council

In 1958, the Navajo Tribal Council, in an effort to limit activities of the Native American Church on its reservation, enacted an ordinance making it illegal to bring peyote onto the Navajo Reservation. Navajo members of the Native American Church filed a suit against the tribe in federal court charging the ordinance violated their First and Fourteenth Amendment rights. They claimed their rights to freedom of religion and to protection against arbitrary and oppressive ordinances were totally disregarded.

In 1959, the United States Court of Appeals heard the case and sided with the Navajo tribe, ruling that tribal councils existed prior to the establishment of the United States and so were not bound to uphold the United States Constitution unless "they have expressly been required to surrender[their sovereign powers] by the superior sovereign, the United States." The decision upheld tribal sovereignty and the right of tribes to manage their own internal affairs without interference. However, the decision also caused many in Congress to perceive a need to lessen tribal authority and extend certain basic constitutional protections to individuals living under tribal governments. *Native American Church v. Navajo Tribal Council* influenced passage of the American Indian Civil Rights Act (1968) by Congress, which, in part, requires tribes to guarantee an individual's freedom of religion when living under tribal governance.

Carole A. Barrett

See also: American Indian Civil Rights Act; Native American Church; Peyote religion; Tribal councils; Tribal sovereignty.

Native American Rights Fund

The Native American Rights Fund (NARF) is a nonprofit, public-interest legal organization that was founded in 1970. It was established to represent tribal clients in litigation in state and federal courts and to strengthen tribal governments. Operations are supported by federal funds as well as by private and corporate contributions. Its attorneys are mostly Native Americans; the group's headquarters is in Boulder, Colorado, with satellite offices in Washington, D.C., and Anchorage, Alaska. One of the organization's primary activities is to handle cases involving "federally recognized tribes" that cannot afford the full financial burden of litigation in U.S. courts. A staff of sixteen attorneys in the early 1990's handled about fifty cases at any given time. NARF also acts as a consultant in the drafting of federal Indian policy.

NARF's objectives include preservation of tribal existence and independence, protection of tribal resources, promotion of human rights such as education and the equitable treatment of Indian prisoners, and development of Indian law to improve tribal legal resources. The Indian Law Support Center and the Carnegie-sponsored

National Indian Law Library are components of NARF, working in conjunction with its Legal Services Corporation. The law library houses a collection of more than six hundred tribal codes.

The Native American Rights Fund has taken on a number of well-known cases involving tribal land and water interests. The group gained national notice and respect for its handling of the 1982 land rights case brought by the Penobscot and Passamaquoddy against the state of Maine. The tribes were awarded $27,000 plus the money to purchase 300,000 acres of land. (An important footnote is that, although the case was regarded as a success story, the money did not go very far for some recipients. In addition, many such cases, even when legally successful, become bogged down by governmental bureaucracy.) NARF has been involved in litigation to strengthen aspects of the 1978 American Indian Religious Freedom Act dealing with the repatriation of ancestral bones and archaeological artifacts. NARF also assists non-federally recognized tribes in attempts to gain official tribal recognition, which may involve the restoration of at least some tribal homelands. It has litigated successfully for the Menominee of Wisconsin and the Siletz of Oregon.

NARF has not been without its critics. Some have argued that, because the organization is not self-sufficient and must rely on federal funding, it cannot truly be an effective advocacy group. From this perspective it may appear to be an extension of the federal system. Another criticism leveled against the group is that it has never attempted to challenge the European American legal paradigm by insisting on complete internal sovereignty for a client; rather, its negotiations seek negotiation, consensus, and settlement.   *M. A. Jaimes*

See also: American Indian Religious Freedom Act; American Indians in the justice system.

Nativism

Significance: Nativism can be defined as negative ethnocentrism, or an intense opposition to an internal minority on the grounds of its alien connections and its apparent threat to the dominant culture. In the United States, periodic upsurges of nativism have resulted in immigration restrictions, attempts to force minority groups to assimilate into Anglo-American culture, and vigilante violence against immigrant groups.

As a nation of immigrants, the United States has always exhibited a certain ambivalence toward immigrants. On one hand, immigrants have been welcomed as a necessary addition to the labor force and as a source of economic growth. On the other hand, they have been feared and resented because of their alien ways and their competition for jobs and political power. Nativists, the most outspoken critics of immigration, feared that the American way of life, and even the republic itself, was in danger from the constant stream of newcomers. They developed an ideology of nativism that comprised three identifiable strains: anti-Catholic nativism; racial nativism; and antiradical nativism. These three strains often overlapped in the various nativist organizations that emerged in the nineteenth and twentieth centuries.

Anti-Catholic Nativism

Anti-Catholic nativism had its roots in the religious views of the earliest English settlers in the American colonies. As products of the Protestant Reformation in Europe, the early colonists viewed the pope as a foreign monarch who exercised dangerous influence through the Roman Catholic Church. The large influx of Irish Catholic immigrants in the early nineteenth century fueled an upsurge of anti-Catholic propaganda, which alleged that Irish Catholics were agents of the pope intent on undermining republican institutions. In the 1830's, inventor Samuel F. B. Morse's tract, *Foreign Conspiracy Against the Liberties of the United States* (1834), which called for the formation of the Anti-Popery Union to resist the papal plot, became required reading in many Protestant Sunday schools. In 1834, an anti-Catholic mob burned the

"WHAT SHALL WE DO WITH OUR BOYS?"

Chinese immigrants became the focus of racial nativism in the 1800's. This cartoon illustrates the perception that cheap Chinese labor took jobs away from white American men.

Ursuline Convent in Charlestown, Massachusetts. Ten years later, riots erupted in Philadelphia when Irish Catholics opposed the use of the Protestant King James version of the Bible in public schools.

The American Protective Association (APA), organized in 1887, was the most visible manifestation of anti-Catholic nativism in the late nineteenth century. Its members swore never to vote for Catholic candidates, employ Catholic workers over Protestants, or join with Catholic strikers. The APA drew strong support from workers in the midwestern and Rocky Mountain states who feared competition from cheap Irish labor. By the late 1890's, however, as Irish and German Catholics became an important part of the electorate, the more extreme anti-Catholic sentiment dissipated. The APA itself disappeared in the 1890's.

Racial Nativism

In the later nineteenth century, a racial strain of nativism, cultivated by the self-professed guardians of Anglo-Saxon culture and apparently supported by scientific research, began to be directed against immigrant groups. Ever since colonial times, white settlers had viewed themselves as culturally and physically different from, and superior to, Native Americans and African Americans. Some intellectuals adapted the biological research of Charles Darwin to argue that certain races would inevitably triumph over others because of their inherent superiority. English and American intellectuals confidently trumpeted the superiority of the Anglo-Saxon "race" and its institutions, and researchers set out to "prove" their cultural assumptions by measuring the cranial volumes of skulls from members of various ethnic groups and devising crude intelligence tests. As a new wave of immigrants from Asia and southern and eastern Europe began to arrive, these newcomers were quickly labeled racially inferior.

Racial nativism reached its zenith in the early twentieth century. Influenced by the European eugenics movement, with its emphasis on breeding the right racial groups, American nativists expressed alarm over the impact of the new immigrants. Madison Grant's widely read *The Passing of the Great Race* (1916) summarized many of the racial nativist arguments. He argued that the superior Nordic "race" was being destroyed by the influx of southern and eastern Europeans, and warned that race mixing would result in an inferior hybrid race and the destruction of Anglo-Saxon civilization. Jewish and Italian immigrants, in particular, were often singled out for criticism in nativist publications because of their alleged racial inferiority.

Antiradical Nativism
Immigrants also came under attack for political reasons in the late nineteenth century. Nativist writers worried that most immigrants came from nondemocratic societies, harbored socialist or anarchist sympathies, and would foment revolution in the United States. The participation of some immigrants in the labor agitation of the period seemed to confirm these fears of alien radicalism. Antiradical nativism intensified following the 1917 Bolshevik Revolution in Russia and the onset of an economic crisis in the United States. Although most immigrants were not socialists, immigrants nevertheless constituted a majority of the membership of the American Socialist Party. During the Red Scare of 1919-1920, when many Americans feared that a communist revolution was imminent, immigrants and radicalism became synonymous in the public mind.

Impact on Public Policy
Nativism had its most significant impact on public policy in the area of immigration restrictions designed to discriminate against Asians and southern and eastern Europeans. In 1882, the Chinese Exclusion Act cut off further immigration by Chinese laborers. During World War I, Congress overrode a presidential veto to enact literacy tests for all immigrants, which discriminated against southern and eastern Europeans who had less access to basic education. In the 1920's, the United States adopted a system of quotas based on national origins for European immigration, imposing a maximum annual limit of 150,000 and allocating most of the slots to northern and western European countries. The national origins quota system formed the basis of immigration law until it was abolished in 1965.   *Richard V. Damms*

Core Resources
The classic historical work on early nineteenth century nativism is Ray Allen Billington's *The Protestant Crusade, 1800-1860: A Study of the Origins of American Nativism* (New York: Macmillan, 1938). For the post-Civil War period, John Higham's *Strangers in the Land: Patterns of American Nativism, 1860-1925* (New Brunswick, N.J.: Rutgers University Press, 1955) remains the standard account, but see also David H. Bennett's *The Party of Fear: From Nativist Movements to the New Right in American History* (Chapel Hill, N.C.: University of North Carolina Press, 1988). For a collection of essays that identifies a resurgence of nativism in the 1980's and 1990's, see *Immigrants Out! The New Nativism and the Anti-Immigrant Impulse in the United*

States, edited by Juan F. Perea (New York: New York University Press, 1996).

See also: Anglo-Saxon; Anti-Catholicism; Chinese Exclusion Act; Ethnocentrism; Immigration Act of 1924; Intelligence testing; Irish Catholic "race"; Nazism; Nordic "race"; Red Scare; Sacco and Vanzetti trial; Social Darwinism and racism; White supremacist groups; Xenophobia, nativism, and eugenics.

Naturalization Act of 1790

Naturalization is the legal process by which a state or country confers its nationality or its citizenship to a person after birth. In most cases, the primary beneficiaries of naturalization are immigrants.

After the American colonies gained their independence from Britain in 1787, each state adopted different rules for conferring U.S. citizenship upon its residents. President George Washington suggested that a uniform naturalization act at the federal level was needed.

Article I, section 8 of the U.S. Constitution empowers Congress to pass uniform laws for naturalization. Congress exercised this power, for the first time, when it passed "An act to establish an uniform Rule of Naturalization" on March 26, 1790. This act granted "all free white persons" with two years of residence the right of citizenship. In addition, the act stated that "the children of citizens of the U.S. that may be born beyond sea, or out of limits of the U.S., shall be considered as natural born citizens."

In effect, the act created two separate classes of people: free and white citizens, able to hold political office and entitled to the rights and privileges of citizenship, and nonwhite persons, ineligible for membership in the U.S. community. The act further reinforced the part of the Constitution that limits membership in Congress to citizens who meet stipulated residence requirements and the presidency to natural-born citizens. The Naturalization Act was repealed five years later. *Stephen Schwartz*

See also: Immigration and emigration.

Navajo-Hopi Land Settlement Act

The Navajo-Hopi Land Settlement Act was enacted by Congress on December 22, 1974, primarily to clarify rights of the Navajo and Hopi tribes in the 1882 "Executive Order Reservation" established by President Chester A. Arthur. This executive order set aside 2,472,095 acres "for the use and occupancy of the Moqui[Hopi] and such other Indians as the Secretary of the Interior may see fit to settle thereon." At the time, both Hopis and Navajos were living in the set-aside area. Disputes increased as the Navajo population in the area expanded.

In 1934 Congress consolidated the boundaries of the Navajo Reservation without altering the 1882 Executive Order Reservation. The Bureau of Indian Affairs then established grazing districts on both reservations. District 6, exclusively for Hopi use, consisted of about 25 percent of the 1882 reservation. The remainder was occupied largely by Navajo stock raisers. Disputes between members of the two tribes continued.

In 1958 Congress authorized a lawsuit to settle conflicting claims to the 1882 reservation. In 1962 a federal court, in *Healing v. Jones*, held that for the area outside District 6, the Hopi and Navajo had "joint, undivided and equal interests." Because the Navajos occupied most of the area, however, they controlled the most surface resources in the Joint Use Area (JUA).

Negotiations between the two tribes concerning management of the JUA were unsuccessful. In the early 1970's the Hopis sought and obtained a court order for livestock reduction in the area. The continuing controversy stimulated congressional interest, and the Navajo-Hopi Land Settlement Act was enacted in 1974.

The act was comprehensive. It directed that a mediator make recommendations to the district court, which would then partition the surface rights of the JUA. In 1977, each tribe received half of the JUA. Money was appropriated for livestock reduction and boundary fencing. The act, and a 1980 amendment, allowed for the transfer of some federal lands to the Navajos to help offset lost JUA land. In 1983 about 370,000 acres of "new lands" along the southern edge of the Navajo Reservation were selected.

The act required the removal of members of one tribe living on lands transferred to the other tribe. This involved a relatively small number of Hopis but thousands of Navajos. An independent commission was created to administer the relocation program, but it was inept, contributing to the hardships of relocatees. The $52,000,000 initial appropriation was inadequate. Congress belatedly responded in the 1980's, amending the act to restructure the commission and authorizing hundreds of millions of additional dollars for relocation.

As a final touch of irony, one section of this legislation, designed to resolve controversy over the 1882 reservation, allowed the tribes the right to sue to settle rights in lands within the 1934 Navajo Reservation. In 1992, a federal district court decided that the Hopis and San Juan Southern Paiutes (who had intervened in the lawsuit) had rights in portions of the Navajo Reservation long used by tribal members. *Eric Henderson*

See also: Navajo Rehabilitation Act; Navajo War; Reservation system of the United States.

Navajo Rehabilitation Act

The Navajo-Hopi Long Range Rehabilitation Act of 1950 (Public Law 81-474) was passed by Congress to construct basic facilities on the Navajo and Hopi reservations. Passed in response to more than twenty years of deteriorating economic conditions on the Navajo Reservation, the act authorized funding for school construction, roads, and other projects.

In the 1930's the federal government had initiated a range-management program on the Navajo and Hopi reservations. Central to the program was reducing the amount of livestock on the range. This devastated the Navajo sheep-based pastoral economy. The full effects of stock reduction were partially obscured during World War II, when thousands of Navajos joined the service or worked in war-related industries. When these people returned home, however, livestock regulations and insufficient resources prevented a renewal of the pastoral economy. Unusually harsh winters added to the distress and drew national attention to the impoverished conditions among the more than sixty thousand Navajos residing in Navajo country.

Reservation schools could accommodate only about 25 percent of the student-age population. All-weather roads were practically nonexistent on the reservations. Inadequate roads contributed to health, education, and economic problems. Infant mortality was high and school enrollments low. After passing minor emergency relief measures, Congress considered a more comprehensive approach.

A 1949 bill to fund improvements on the Navajo and Hopi reservations, reflecting a resurgent congressional interest in limiting tribal sovereignty, also included a provision which extended the jurisdiction of state law over the two reservations. Citing this provision, President Harry S Truman vetoed the bill.

In 1950, the president signed the Navajo Rehabilitation Act, which emerged from Congress without the offending jurisdictional provision. This version also provided expanded opportunities for Hopi participation in projects. The act appropriated $88,570,000. The largest portion, $25 million, was for school construction, followed by $20 million for roads and $19 million for rangelands and irrigation projects. Lesser amounts were appropriated for health and water facilities, industrial development, and other projects. More than $9 million was allocated for relocating and resettling individuals away from the two reservations. There were also provisions for loans and leases. Finally, one provision (ignored for more than thirty years) authorized the Navajo tribe to adopt a tribal constitution.

In 1958, Public Law 85-740 provided an additional $20 million to complete road construction. By 1962, more than 80 percent of the total appropriation had been expended, including nearly all the money targeted for roads and schools.

The major benefit of the act was the substantial improvement in roads and schools on the reservation. All-weather roads have provided greater access to job locations and markets. School attendance increased dramatically through the 1950's and 1960's, as did the overall educational attainment of the population.

Eric Henderson

See also: Education and American Indians; Navajo-Hopi Land Settlement Act; Navajo War; Reservation system of the United States.

Navajo War

Disputed grazing lands near Fort Defiance were a major factor leading to the 1863-1866 Navajo War. The site was favored for rendezvous by Navajo medicine men who collected herbs there. For generations, these lands were also used as pasture for Navajo livestock. Shortly after the establishment of Fort Defiance on September 18, 1851, soldiers who wanted to pasture their horses on these lands shot the Navajo-owned horses. Revenge was swift: Navajos raided army herds to replace their losses.

Through the decade, the raids continued and the army retaliated until, in 1859, army troops attacked and destroyed the home, crops, and livestock of the Navajo clan leader, Manuelito. In 1860, Manuelito—aided by leaders of other clans—assaulted Fort Defiance and nearly captured it, but was driven back. The army pursued the attackers into the Chuska mountains but was demoralized by the hit-and-run tactics of the Navajos. In January of 1861, the Navajos met with army representatives and agreed to work for peace. The uneasy truce was broken when, in September of 1861, a riot broke out over a horse race. Artillery was used to quell the disturbance, killing ten Navajos.

Raids for plunder and revenge increased, and the army responded. On September 6, 1863, Colonel Christopher "Kit" Carson was chosen to lead a campaign of "pacification." In the following months, Carson's scorched-earth offensive burned Navajo corn fields, orchards, and hogans; livestock was confiscated and destroyed. Tribes unfriendly to the Navajos were encouraged to attack and harass them. Navajo tribe members surrendered or were rounded up and relocated to Bosque Redondo (Round Forest) in the barren plains of eastern New Mexico. Some clan leaders and their followers held out as long as possible, but by the end of 1864 about eight thousand half-starving Navajos surrendered and were marched to Bosque Redondo. Some two hundred people died on the grueling three-hundred-mile march known as the Long Walk. Manuelito and twenty-six followers surrendered in September of 1866. When another clan leader, Barboncito, surrendered in November of 1866 with twenty-one followers, the Navajo War of 1863-1866 was over.

Moises Roizen

See also: Long Walk; Navajo-Hopi Land Settlement Act; Navajo Rehabilitation Act.

Kit Carson was a major force in the United States war against the Navajo.

Nazism

> **Significance:** Nazism, and its latter-day incarnation as neo-Nazism, subscribes to notions of white supremacy and the inferiority of other racial and ethnic groups. Born of fear and ignorance, this political philosophy has been responsible for the worst intergroup atrocities of the modern age.

A German political movement that advocated racial nationalism (including anti-Semitism), dictatorial government, and expansion into eastern Europe by means of war, Nazism, a contraction of the term "National Socialism," was a German political movement that emerged in the aftermath of World War I with Adolf Hitler as its leader. From the very start, it espoused ideas that rejected Western values of humanitarianism, rationalism, liberalism, democracy, and socialism in favor of extreme nationalism, racism, and a political system of single-party dictatorship. Nazi policies and practices violated human and civil rights, first in Germany and later in conquered Europe, and resorted to violent power politics in international affairs.

Beginnings

The forerunner of Nazism as a political party was the German Workers' Party, which was organized in Munich early in 1919. Adolf Hitler, a lower-middle-class Austrian by birth and a corporal in the German army during World War I, joined the German Workers' Party later in the year. It soon was renamed the National Socialist German Workers' Party, and Hitler, showing oratorical and organizational talent, became its undisputed leader in 1921.

The main tenets of Nazism were drawn from the party program of 1920, Hitler's speeches and writings (especially his ponderous two-volume *Mein Kampf [My Struggle]*), published in 1925 and 1926, and other Nazi publications. They attacked liberalism and parliamentarianism, including democracy, as inherently weak political systems and branded the early leaders of the Weimar Republic, liberals, socialists, and Jews as "November criminals" of 1918, who had overthrown the imperial government. In place of the failed parliamentary democracy, Nazism offered authoritarian rule rooted in a solid hierarchical system of leaders and followers. At the head would be a führer, or "leader," who, with the support of the Nazi Party, would exercise total control over the society and mobilize it for the achievement of the political and social goals that he postulated.

White Supremacy

Nazism, above all, extolled racial nationalism, which was derived from the nineteenth century racial theories of the Frenchman Joseph-Arthur de Gobineau, the Germanized Englishman Houston Chamberlain, and the German Paul de Lagarde. Proponents of Nazism contended that human races were divided into culture-creating and culture-destroying groups, which were engaged in a Social Darwinian struggle of survival of the fittest. At the top of the culture-creating races stood the Nordic-Aryan-Germanic group, the "master race," which was destined to dominate inferior races. At Hitler's instigation, Nazism singled out the Jews as the greatest threat to the pure Aryans because the Jews, the leading culture-

destroying race, were conspiring to gain domination over the world. In Nazi foreign policy, the idea of the primacy of the Aryan race was combined with a Great German nationalism or imperialism, whose aim it was to create a Great German empire far beyond the borders of the German nation. Such an expansion was to give the German people the *Lebensraum*, or "living space," that it needed to ensure its security and economic independence.

The Nazis did not conceal that, although they would attain power legally, once in office they would destroy the constitutional system. Within one month after Hitler was appointed chancellor early in 1933, he had communists and many socialists confined to quickly established concentration camps and suspended civil rights. Through cajolery, pressure, and terror, he prevailed upon the Reichstag (parliament) to give him dictatorial powers, which he used to eliminate trade unions and all political parties except the Nazi Party. In 1934, he murdered the top leadership of the Storm Troopers, or S.A., and some non-Nazis, when he felt threatened by a rival from within his own ranks. He justified these acts of criminality by declaring: "I was responsible for the fate of the German people and thereby I became the Supreme Judge of the German people."

The Nazi practices of eliminating opponents by sending them to concentration camps or murdering them, persecuting Jews purely on racial grounds, maintaining a police state, and pursuing an aggressive foreign policy left no room for the observance of ethical principles in politics. It is important to realize, however, that liberal democratic governments also generally do not feel bound by ethical constraints if the national interest is at stake. Though idealists among philosophers and scholars argue that, for example, foreign policy must be based on prudence and ethical principle, realists (and they are a majority) maintain that in world politics moral or ethical concerns must be subordinated to national interest. Given the absence of accepted international standards of morality and effective bodies of enforcement when violations occur, each government, being concerned with military security, the integrity of its political life, and the well-being of its citizens, must act on its own to protect its national interests. Implied in this stance, however, is a sense of moderation and responsibility when pursuing the national interest in international relations.

World War II and the Holocaust

The Nazi regime under Hitler's direction defined national interest in the most expansive terms. Hitler once characterized Germany's foreign policy by declaring: "Germany will become a world power or it will not exist at all." In the early years of Nazi dictatorship, he and his associates constantly proclaimed the German Reich's "sincere desire for peace," while unilaterally abrogating the restrictions of the Treaty of Versailles, rearming Germany, and then, in 1938, annexing Austria and the German-speaking Sudetenland of Czechoslovakia. In 1939, Nazi Germany unleashed World War II through aggression against Poland, followed by campaigns into France and other European countries in 1940. One year later, Hitler attacked the Soviet Union, waging a brutal ideological war in the quest for *Lebensraum* in the East.

While worldwide violence was raging as a result of war, the Nazi regime also prepared for the elimination of "racially inferior" populaces and "those of lesser value" in society. The persecution of German Jews culminated in the violence against Jewish property and people of the *Kristallnacht* of 1938. With the outbreak of the war in 1939, a euthanasia program was begun, resulting in the killing by injection or by gassing of almost 100,000 mentally and physically handicapped persons, most of whom were German. Finally, the plan to liquidate all European Jews in Nazi hands—the "final solution"—was implemented by Hitler and some of his immediate associates in 1941. It claimed the lives of almost six million people. In addition, Nazi actions led to the murder of millions of Gypsies, Slavs, homosexuals, and other racial and political "enemies." This unprecedented mechanized genocide was only stopped by the defeat of Nazi Germany and the suicide of Adolf Hitler in 1945.

After the total defeat of Germany and the inglorious death of the führer, Nazism never revived as a significant force. Following the establishment of the Federal Republic of Germany in 1949, its Federal Constitutional Court outlawed the noisy but unimportant Socialist Reich Party in 1952 as a neo-Nazi organization. In the 1960's and 1980's, two right-wing parties were formed: the National Democratic Party and the Republicans. Both have shown some neo-Nazi features but have achieved little influence. More noteworthy have been a number of small neo-Nazi groups formed since the 1970's, whose racist hate propaganda and violence, directed not primarily against Jews but against foreigners, especially Turks, have aroused consternation since the unification of Germany in 1990. These groups cannot, however, be viewed as the forerunners of an organized neo-Nazi movement.

George P. Blum

Core Resources
Useful books on the subject of Nazism include K. D. Bracher's *The German Dictatorship: The Origins, Structure, and Effects of National Socialism*, translated by Jean Steinberg (New York: Praeger, 1970), Alan Bullock's *Hitler: A Study in Tyranny* (rev. ed., New York: Harper & Row, 1962), Gerald Fleming's *Hitler and the Final Solution* (Berkeley: University of California Press, 1984), Adolf Hitler's *Mein Kampf,* translated by Ralph Manheim (Boston: Houghton

Mifflin, 1971), Eberhard Jackel's *Hitler's Weltanschauung: A Blueprint for Power,* translated by Herbert Arnold (Middletown, Conn.: Wesleyan University Press, 1972), and Jackson J. Spielvogel's *Hitler and Nazi Germany: A History* (2d ed., Englewood Cliffs, N.J.: Prentice-Hall, 1992). Also, Anne Marie Donahue has edited *Ethics in Politics and Government* (New York: H. W. Wilson, 1989).

See also: American Nazi Party; Anti-Semitism; Aryan "race"; Ethnic cleansing; Genocide: physical; Holocaust; Holocaust denial; Nativism; Social Darwinism and racism; White supremacist groups; Xenophobia, nativism, and eugenics.

Negro Conventions

Mass conventions were a popular means of protest among African Americans of the nineteenth century. Rooted in constitutional principles of free assembly and petition, these conventions were a product of the group consciousness that emerged among free blacks in northern urban areas following the American Revolution and were a reaction to a burgeoning institutional racism that legitimized slavery and stripped free African Americans of basic civil rights during the postrevolutionary period. The first great national Negro convention, held at Philadelphia in August, 1817, produced resolutions opposing slavery and denouncing a plan proposed by the United States Congress to colonize black Americans in Africa. Although largely symbolic, the convention of 1817 inspired the Negro Convention movement of the 1830's, which was to provide a forum for expressions of militancy and nationalism among the growing population of free northern blacks.

The Negro Convention movement of the 1830's was aided by the emergence of black leaders with national status and varied agendas. Although dominated by antislavery societies, the six national Negro Conventions held between 1830 and 1835 addressed a variety of issues, including the organization of economic boycotts and mass protests, the observance of national days of prayer and fasting, and the establishment of temperance societies and African missionary groups. The conventions exerted a considerable influence upon local black communities, chiefly through the encouragement of verbal agitation; yet the movement was cut short in mid-decade by white abolitionists who, fearing that the black separatism often advocated by convention delegates would damage the antislavery movement, infiltrated the conventions and split their leadership. The Negro Convention movement was briefly revived in the early 1840's, when young black militants in New York and Philadelphia called a convention of black leaders to protest slavery and racial inequality. However, this convention, which failed by one vote to endorse slave insurrection, proved a militant exception to a new spirit of gradualism among black abolitionists. The last notable antebellum Negro Convention, held in Cleveland, Ohio, in 1854, yielded compromise proposals for the repatriation of African Americans that early conventions had so vehemently opposed.

The end of the Civil War and the beginning of Reconstruction sparked a revival of Negro Conventions in the 1870's and 1880's, as southern freedmen and northern agitators sought vehicles to petition the government for civil rights and protection from mob violence. These conventions

The 1876 Colored National Convention in Nashville, Tennessee, pictured here, was one of many political meetings organized by African Americans.

were chiefly local and regional in nature, designed to facilitate political organization and to appeal directly to legislators and state governors. Nevertheless, national conventions continued, the most notable being the National Colored Convention held in Louisville, Kentucky, in 1883, in which the delegates called for an end to economic peonage in the South, equal rights and suffrage for African Americans, and integration of schools and the military.

The Negro Convention movement died out in the 1890's as Jim Crow laws and mob violence swept the South and accommodationism replaced agitation and protest as a political strategy for black leaders. However, the tradition of assembly and militancy brought about by the convention movement survived in the black conferences of the early twentieth century (for example, the Niagara conference of 1909, which spawned the National Association for the Advancement of Colored People), in the mass protest marches of the Civil Rights movement during the 1960's, and in the Million Man and Million Woman Marches of the 1990's. *Michael H. Burchett*

See also: Abolition; Accommodationism; Civil War; Jim Crow laws; National Council of Colored People; Niagara Movement; Reconstruction.

New York City slave revolt

Significance: The New York City slave revolt of 1712 was an abortive uprising that shaped the institution of slavery in New York.

The New York City Slave Revolt of 1712 calls attention to the fact that slavery had become more firmly established in colonial New York than in any other British province north of Chesapeake Bay. Slaves were already an integral part of the labor force when England conquered Dutch New Netherland in 1664. As European immigration lagged, slave labor became increasingly important. Between 1703 and 1723, New York's total population almost doubled, increasing from 20,540 to 40,564, but its black population (slaves and free blacks were always lumped together and listed in the census as Negroes) almost tripled, jumping from 2,253 to 6,171.

Background
As the number of bondsmen increased, so did the anxiety level of white New Yorkers. In 1708, following the grizzly murder of a Long Island planter and his family, four slaves were tried, convicted, and executed "with all the torment possible for a terror to others." Shortly thereafter, the provincial assembly passed An Act for Preventing the Conspiracy of Slaves, which defined the judicial proceedings and made death the penalty for any slave found guilty of murder or attempted murder. Fear of slave conspiracy led whites to look with ambivalence upon Anglican catechist Elias Neau's teaching among New York City blacks and Native Americans.

Small-scale slave owning prevailed in New York. Few white families owned more than a slave or two, so slave husbands, wives, and children might be scattered among several households. Regulations restricting their freedom of movement were bitterly resented by slaves, because they interfered with their domestic life. Such restrictions often were more apparent than real, because slavery in New York City and surrounding villages, where slaves were most heavily concentrated, was tied to a developing urban economy that demanded a flexible, if not free, labor supply. Slaves in New York City and Albany often hired themselves out, splitting the pay with their respective owners, but otherwise lived separately from their masters. The hustle and bustle of the urban economic scene afforded slaves considerable opportunity to meet, socialize, and discuss common grievances, despite the best efforts of whites to keep them under surveillance.

The slave uprising of 1712 apparently began as a conspiracy on March 25, then celebrated as New Year's Day. The ringleaders reportedly were of the Cormantine and Pawpaw peoples, Africans who had not been long in New York; a few Spanish Indian slaves; and at least one free black, a practitioner of African medicine and magic who reportedly supplied special powder to protect the rebels from the white man's weapons. Their motivation, according to both Governor Robert Hunter and Chaplain John Sharpe, was revenge for ill treatment at the hands of their respective masters. Their goal was freedom, which, claimed Hunter and Sharpe, was to be achieved by burning New York City and killing the white people on Manhattan.

The Revolt

During the early morning hours of Sunday, April 6, 1712, about two dozen conspirators, armed with guns, swords, knives, and clubs, gathered in an orchard in the East Ward on the northeast edge of New York City. They set fire to several outbuildings and waited in ambush for the whites who came to put out the blaze, killing nine and wounding seven. Soldiers were dispatched from the fort, but when they arrived, the rebels had dispersed, taking refuge in the woods surrounding the town. The next day, local militiamen systematically searched Manhattan Island for the rebellious blacks. Rather than surrender, six slaves killed themselves, several cutting their own throats.

White New Yorkers were in full panic. "We have about 70 Negro's in Custody," read a dispatch from New York, dated April 14 but published in the *Boston News-Letter* on April 21, but it was "fear'd that most of the Negro's here (who are very numerous) knew of the Late Conspiracy to murder the Christians." Fear of another uprising drove the judicial proceedings. On April 9, a coroner's jury implicated thirty-eight slaves, identifying fourteen of them as murderers. In accordance with the 1708 Conspiracy Act, the coroner's findings were turned over to the Court of Quarter Sessions of the Peace, which convened on April 11. Attorney General May Bickley handled the prosecution, moving the trials on from the Quarter Sessions to the State Supreme Court on June 3.

The Trials

Forty-two slaves and one free black were indicted and tried. Crucial to both the indictments and trials was the testimony of two slaves, Cuffee, who belonged to baker Peter Vantilborough, and Dick, a boy slave owned by Harmanus Burger, a blacksmith. The coroner's jury had found Cuffee and Dick guilty of at least two murders, but Attorney General Bickley apparently promised them immunity, and they became the Crown's prime witnesses. Some whites, including such substantial citizens as former mayor David Provost, coroner Henry Wileman, and lawyers Jacob Regnier and David Jamison, testified for a few of the defendants. However, the general adequacy of defense counsel may well be doubted. Many of the convictions hinged upon the dubious testimony of Cuffee and young Dick, both of whom were manipulated by Attorney General Bickley, described by Governor Hunter as "a busy waspish man." Bickley also demonstrated considerable bias against certain slave defendants, depending upon who owned them. For example, Mars, belonging to Jacob Regnier, a rival attorney with whom Brickley had a private quarrel, was tried twice and acquitted before being found guilty in the third trial and sentenced to be hanged.

Most of the trials were over by early June. Twenty-three slaves were convicted of murder; fifteen slaves were acquitted, along with one free black. Two slaves were found guilty of assault with intent to kill, and two were acquitted of that charge. The twenty-five who were convicted were sentenced to death. Twenty were to be hanged; three were burned alive, one in a slow fire for eight to ten hours until consumed to ashes. Another was broken upon the wheel and left to die, and one was hung in chains and "so to continue without sustenance until death." Eleven were "executed at once," including those burned, broken at the wheel, and chained without food or water. These barbaric executions were defended by Governor Hunter as "the most exemplary that could be possibly thought of."

Yet even Hunter doubted the justice of it all. He postponed the execution of six slaves, including two Spanish American Indians taken during Queen Anne's War (1702-1713) and sold as slaves despite their claim of being free men, a pregnant slave woman, and the much tried and finally convicted Mars. At Hunter's request, the queen pardoned several of them, and perhaps all of those he had reprieved (the record is rather vague), despite the efforts of Bickley in New York and Lord Cornbury, a former governor of New York, in London to obstruct the pardons.

Impact of the Revolt

There were other ramifications of the slave uprising. The provincial government passed laws making it impossible to free slaves without putting up a two-hundred-pound bond and paying the freed slave twenty pounds per year for life. Africans, American Indians, and mulattoes were prohibited from inheriting or otherwise owning property. Finally, due process rights were weakened for slaves accused of murder or conspiracy. In the wake of the revolt, Elias Neau, the preacher and catechist of Trinity Church, found it difficult to continue his school for blacks and Indians. Only two of his many pupils were implicated in the conspiracy, and Chaplain John Sharpe doubted that either was involved in the violence.

After the rebellion, New Yorkers were reluctant to import slaves directly from Africa or to purchase Spanish Indians as slaves. Black slaves from the West Indies were preferred over the other two groups. Yet slavery remained a primary source of labor for both the province and city of New York, slaves constituting about 15 percent of the population. In 1730, other regulations were added to the slave code because "many Mischiefs had been Occasioned by the two great Liberty allowed to Negro and other Slaves." In 1741, white paranoia and slave discontent provoked a so-called slave conspiracy in which 150 slaves and 25 whites were jailed. Of that number, 18 slaves and 4 whites were hanged, 13 blacks burned alive, and 70 were sold and sent to the West Indies.   *Ronald W. Howard*

Core Resources

In Joyce D. Goodfriend's *Before the Melting Pot: Society and Culture in Colonial New York City, 1664-1730* (Princeton, N.J.: Princeton University Press, 1992), chapter 6 provides considerable insight into the life and labors of New York City slaves, both before and after the 1712 revolt. In Michael Kammen's *Colonial New York: A History* (New York: Charles Scribner's Sons, 1975), chapter 11 relates the slave revolts of 1712 and 1741 to larger social and economic problems in colonial New York society. Mary

Lou Lustig's *Robert Hunter, 1666-1734* (Syracuse, N.Y.: Syracuse University Press, 1983) gives a brief but pertinent summary of the slave revolts and the persons most associated with the trials. Edgar J. McManus's *A History of Negro Slavery in New York* (Syracuse, N.Y.: Syracuse University Press, 1966) goes into considerable detail regarding the conditions that contributed to the 1712 uprising. Kenneth Scott's "The Slave Insurrection in New York in 1712," in *The New-York Historical Society Quarterly* (45, January, 1961), describes the revolt and the trials that followed. Peter Woods's "Slave Resistance," in *Encyclopedia of the North American Colonies*, vol. 2 (New York: Charles Scribner's Sons, 1993) relates the 1741 New York revolt to other examples of slave resistance in North America.

See also: Slave codes; Slave rebellions; Slavery: history; Turner's slave insurrection.

Newark race riots

Race relations, already tense in much of the United States in 1967, were especially poor in Newark, New Jersey. In addition to high unemployment, African Americans were angry about a proposal to relocate inner-city residents from their neighborhoods in order to build a medical and dental college. On July 12, 1967, rumors spread through the city that police had beaten an African American during an arrest. Protesters throwing bottles and shouting insults soon surrounded the police station, but the crowd dispersed in the early morning hours. The following night, a full-scale riot erupted, and the governor called out the National Guard. Despite the presence of troops, the rioting continued for several days. Twenty-three people died, and more than fifteen hundred people were injured. Police reported more than sixteen hundred arrests. Damage to buildings and property was estimated at more than ten million dollars. Although the Newark riot evidenced the frustration that many African Americans felt concerning the slow pace of economic and social change in the United States, the violence shocked many white Americans and diminished enthusiasm for continued government efforts in the area of civil rights.

Thomas Clarkin

A police officer begins to search a group of African Americans during riots in Newark, New Jersey, in July, 1967. No one in this group was arrested.

See also: Detroit riots; Kerner Report.

Newberry v. United States

In 1918, Truman H. Newberry, Republican candidate for the U.S. Senate, was tried in Michigan, along with more than one hundred associates, for conspiring to violate the Federal Corrupt Practices Act of 1910. The statute violated had set a limit on campaign financing, and the indictment claimed that Newberry had exceeded this limit in primary and general election expenditures. Newberry and his associates were found guilty in the U.S. District Court for the Western District of Michigan.

The U.S. Supreme Court reversed the conviction and sent the case back to the lower court, finding that the statute on which Newberry's conviction rested had no constitutional authority. The Court argued that prior to the Seventeenth Amendment, the only part of the Constitution empowering Congress to regulate the election process was to be found in Article I, section 4, which pertained only to the time, place, and manner of holding general elections and failed to address such matters as party primaries and conventions, additions to the election process unforeseen by the framers of the Constitution. Consequently, the Court ruled that in the relevant section of the Corrupt Practices Act, Congress had exceeded its authority. The Court also maintained that because the statute antedated the ratification of the Seventeenth Amendment, which extended congressional authority, it was invalid at the time of its enactment. The Court held that a power later acquired could not, *ex proprio*, validate a law that was unconstitutional at the time of its passing. The Court did not question a state's right to regulate primaries and campaign financing, claiming that "the state may suppress whatever evils may be incident to primary or convention."

The *Newberry* ruling imposed an important barrier to the enfranchisement of black Americans in the single-party South. Although the Court would strike down laws expressly prohibiting African Americans from voting in primaries, as late as 1935, in *Grovey v. Townsend*, it upheld legal measures taken in Texas to bar blacks from participating in the state Democratic convention, arguing that such "private" discrimination did not come under constitutional purview. *Grovey* and *Newberry* were finally successfully challenged in *United States v. Classic* (1941), which held that Congress had the authority to regulate both primary and general elections for federal offices.

Three years later a final legal blow to de jure disfranchisement of African Americans was dealt in *Smith v. Allwright* (1944), which held that laws governing all elections—local, state, and federal—could be invalidated if they violated Article I, section 4 of the Constitution. Sponsored by the National Association for the Advancement of Colored People, the plaintiff argued that Texas Democratic Party officials had denied him a primary ballot because of his race. The Supreme Court concurred, noting that state laws regulated both primary and general elections and were therefore responsible for barriers to the ballot box erected on racial grounds.

John W. Fiero

See also: *Grovey v. Townsend*; Jim Crow laws; Poll tax; *Smith v. Allwright*; Voting Rights Act of 1965.

Nez Perce exile

Significance: From June 15 to October 5, 1877, Chief Joseph led his people in retreat for fifteen hundred miles in one of the most remarkable Indian war campaigns of U.S. history.

During the nineteenth century, the Nez Perce tribes occupied various areas of the Northwest, including Washington, Idaho, and Oregon. There were five separate groups, each under the leadership of an autonomous chief. One group occupied Oregon territory in the Imnaha and Wallowa Valleys and was under the leadership of Joseph the Elder, or Old Chief Joseph. In 1855, the governor of the Oregon Territory signed a celebrated treaty with him and numerous other Nez Perce leaders, allowing the tribe ownership of all the land in the Imnaha and Wallowa Valleys. The treaty was ratified by the United States Senate.

The treaty of 1855 proved short-lived, however: The Civil War and the discovery of gold at Orofino, Idaho, in 1860, led to an ever-increasing surge of immigration of white settlers into the valleys and territories claimed by the Nez Perce. Because of increasing tensions between the whites and the natives, in 1863 a new treaty was negotiated. The new terms excluded the Imnaha and Wallowa Valleys and other vast areas of land that had been dedicated to the Indians in 1855. The revised treaty was signed by James Reuben and Chief Lawyer, but Chiefs Old Joseph, White Bird, and Looking Glass refused to ratify it. Thus, the treaty was recognized as having treaty Indians and nontreaty Indians.

The Accession of Chief Joseph
In 1871, Old Chief Joseph died, leaving the leadership of the Wallamwatkins to his son, the new Chief Joseph, or Joseph the Younger. The continuing influx of white immigrants into the Nez Perce lands caused increasing problems between Indians and whites. In 1876, a commission was appointed to investigate complaints, and it was decided that the nontreaty Nez Perces had no standing and that all groups should go onto designated reser-

vations. In 1877, the U.S. Department of the Interior issued instructions to carry out the commission's recommendations. Preparing for the transition, a council of tribal leaders and U.S. government officials was set to meet on May 3, 1877. Chief Joseph and his brother, Alokut, represented the Nez Perce, while General Oliver O. Howard represented the U.S. government. The final understanding was that the nontreaty Indians would be on the designated reservations by June 14, 1877.

On June 15, 1877, word was received at Fort Lapwai, Idaho, that the Wallamwatkins had attacked and killed several settlers around Mount Idaho, Idaho. U.S. Army troops were sent from Fort Lapwai to counterattack. On June 17, troops headed into Whitebird Canyon and engaged in a bitter encounter with the Wallamwatkins. The U.S. Army lost thirty-four troops and numerous horses; the Nez Perce, numbering only seventy warriors, had only four wounded in the battle. On July 1, regular troops and Idaho volunteers under Captain Stephen C. Whipple attacked Looking Glass's village. The troops shot, destroyed property, and looted at random. As a result, Looking Glass joined the war effort with Chief Joseph.

Retreat

By July 13, after numerous skirmishes with General Howard's troops and other soldiers, Chief Joseph led approximately four hundred of his people eastward toward the Lolo Trail in the Bitterroot Mountains. On July 15, Looking Glass urged escape to Montana and proposed joining with the Crow of the plains. Chief Joseph agreed, Looking Glass became supreme war leader, and on July 16, the nontreaty Nez Perces summarily left their homeland.

Chief Joseph and Looking Glass kept track of Howard's position and were able to stall and otherwise frustrate Howard's advance. As a result, the chiefs led the Wallamwatkins through Lolo Trail and into the Missoula area. General Howard subsequently contacted Colonel John Gibbon at Fort Shaw, Montana, and instructed him to take up the pursuit. Gibbon was able to muster 146 men of the Seventh Infantry and 34 civilians.

Chief Joseph and Looking Glass crossed the Continental Divide and encamped their weary followers in the Big Hole Valley, unaware of Colonel Gibbon's pursuit and position. On August 9, Colonel Gibbon's troops made a surprise attack on the Wallamwatkins' camp and engaged in a long and difficult battle. Many Nez Perce lives—mostly of women and children—were lost in the initial confrontation. Chief Joseph and White Bird outflanked Gibbon's troops and led the families to safety, while the warriors under Alokut and Looking Glass split Gibbon's forces. After holding the Army in siege for several days, the warriors eventually broke off the engagement, and the Nez Perce continued their retreat through the Montana territory.

Chief Joseph of the Nez Perce is depicted surrendering to Colonel Nelson A. Miles in October, 1877.

The Bear Paws Battle

By August 27, Chief Joseph had led the Wallamwatkins into Yellowstone Park, with General Howard and his troops in continuing pursuit. By September 6, Chief Joseph and Looking Glass had made their retreat through the northeast corner of Yellowstone Park. Continuing north, Chief Joseph led his people up through the Snowy Mountains and finally into the northern foothills of the Bear Paw Mountains, an easy day's ride from the Canadian border. Unknown to Chief Joseph, Colonel Nelson A. Miles had been notified by General Howard and was in pursuit from Fort Keogh paralleling Chief Joseph's trail from the north. On September 30, Colonel Miles's troops made a surprise attack on the Wallamwatkins' camp. The fighting during the Bear Paws Battle was intense. The army lost fifty-three men and the Nez Perce lost eighteen warriors, including Alokut, Tulhulhutsut, and Poker Joe. On the night of October 4, General Howard rode into Miles's camp and provided the reinforcements that would ensure a final surrender from Chief Joseph. On October 5, General Howard sent terms of surrender to the Nez Perce. A brief skirmish evolved, and Looking Glass was fired on and killed. Colonel Miles assured Chief Joseph that he and his tribe would be allowed to return home to the Northwest in peace. Feeling that he could do so with honor, Chief Joseph offered one of the most famous surrendering speeches ever documented. Turning to the interpreter, Chief Joseph said:

> Tell General Howard I know what is in his heart. What he told me before, I have in my heart. I am tired of fighting. Our chiefs are killed. Looking Glass is dead. Tulhulhutsut is dead. The old men are all dead. It is the young men who say yes or no. He[Alokut] who led on the young men is dead. My people, some of them, have run away to the hills and have no blankets, no food; no one knows where they are—perhaps freezing to death. I want to have time to look for my children and see how many of them I can find. Maybe I shall find them among the dead. Hear me, my chiefs. I am tired; my heart is sick and sad. From where the sun now stands I will fight no more, forever.

Thus ended the Nez Perce War, one of the most remarkable Indian war campaigns of U.S. history.

Exile
Chief Joseph surrendered with 86 men, 148 women and 147 children. The Nez Perces were transported to Fort Keogh for temporary holding. On November 1, despite Colonel Miles's assurances that the tribe would be allowed to return to the Northwest, he was ordered to take his prisoners farther south, to Fort Lincoln, near Bismarck, North Dakota. On November 27, Chief Joseph and his people were moved again (by train) to Fort Leavenworth, Kansas. Kept in unsanitary conditions, plagued by disease and twenty deaths, in July, 1878, Chief Joseph and his people were again moved to the Quapaw Reservation in Kansas territory. By the end of the year, nearly fifty more tribe members had died from disease.

After repeated requests to return to the Northwest, in 1885, eight years after their surrender, the 268 survivors of the nontreaty bands taken into captivity were allowed to return to the Northwest. About half of them were housed at Lapwai, Idaho, and Chief Joseph's Wallowa band was housed at Nespelem on the Colville Reservation in eastern Washington. From the time of his return to the Northwest until his death, September 21, 1904, Chief Joseph attempted in vain to gain permission to return his people to his homeland in the Wallowa Valley in eastern Oregon.   *John L. Farbo*

Core Resources
Sources on the Nez Perce include Norman B. Adkison's *Indian Braves and Battles with More Nez Perce Lore* (Grangeville: Idaho County Free Press, 1967), which chronicles events of the Nez Perce from actual correspondence, journals, and interviews. Adkison's *Nez Perce Indian War*

and Original Stories (Grangeville: Idaho County Free Press, 1966) is a brief chronicle of events of the Nez Perce from actual correspondence, journals, and interviews. Merrill D. Beal's *I Will Fight No More Forever: Chief Joseph and the Nez Perce War* (Seattle: University of Washington Press, 1963) is a detailed history of Chief Joseph and the Nez Perce War. Mick Gidley's *Kopet: A Documentary Narrative of Chief Joseph's Last Years* (Seattle: University of Washington Press, 1981) a brief history that collects various photographs, journals, and correspondence.

See also: Indian Appropriation Act; Indian-white relations: United States.

Niagara Movement

> **Significance:** The Niagara Movement, a progenitor of the National Association for the Advancement of Colored People, was founded on July 11, 1905, and helped to lay the groundwork for the civil rights movement.

In the early years of the twentieth century, two major approaches to achieving African American progress were separated by their differing philosophies: Booker T. Washington was a pragmatist who acknowledged current policies toward blacks and wanted to make the lives of African Americans as easy as possible within that framework. Washington held that "it is important and right that all privileges of law be ours, but it is vastly more important that we be prepared for the exercise of those privileges." He assumed that as African Americans became productive workers who were not troublemakers, they would be seen as valuable assets to U.S. society. Then they would slowly but surely move up the economic and political ladder.

Beginnings
The leaders of what came to be known as the Niagara Movement, by contrast, asserted that Washington's programs would keep African Americans at the bottom of the political, economic, and social ladder. One of the Niagara Movement's major leaders was W. E. B. Du Bois, a professor at Atlanta University at the beginning of the movement. Du Bois maintained that it was important for African Americans to press for the immediate implementation of their civil rights: "We want full manhood suffrage and we want it now. . . . We want the Constitution of the country enforced. . . . We want our children educated. . . . And we shall win!" The leaders of the Niagara Movement were convinced that as long as African Americans were not protected by law, economic and social

advances would never come. They believed that the structures of United States society were developed in such a way that, without the force of law, other advances would never occur. These two different views of how to achieve progress for African Americans not only separated Washington and Du Bois throughout their lives but would remain at the heart of discord over how best to achieve freedom and progress for African Americans in the United States.

The Niagara Movement was formed on July 11, 1905, when twenty-nine radical African American intellectuals, headed by Du Bois, met at Niagara Falls, in Ontario, Canada. (Even though some organizational activities were held in Buffalo, New York, on the other side of the U.S.-Canadian border, most meetings were held in Canada because of the difficulty of finding places in the United States that would accommodate African Americans.) On nearly every issue, the Niagara Movement stood in direct contrast to Washington's approach. In sharp language, in a policy statement entitled the Negro Declaration of Independence, movement leaders placed full responsibility for the race problem on whites, denouncing the inequities of segregation and disfranchisement laws; they maintained that economic progress was not possible in a democratic society without the protection afforded by the ballot; and they insisted, above all, that African Americans could gain their rights only by agitation. Members of the Niagara Movement spoke out against an accommodationist approach at a time when almost all white and African American leaders believed that such policies were critical if blacks were to achieve equality in U.S. society and politics.

About five years after it had been established, the Niagara Movement had approximately four hundred members. Most were Northern, urban, upper-class college graduates. The movement never developed the wide following it wanted. Some assert that the movement did not reach a broad enough spectrum in the African American community, let alone create an appeal to the broader society of which it was part. At first women were excluded from the Niagara Movement, both as members and as a focus of emancipation. Some of the movement's organizers reasoned that fighting for women's rights along with rights for African American males would result in defeat of the movement's policies and goals. Du Bois, however, argued that African American civil rights would not be complete without women as well as men tasting the fruits of freedom. He argued that to obtain male suffrage on the backs of women was immoral and not in keeping with the solidarity that African Americans must maintain in the face of the hostility of the dominant white society. Du Bois's position finally prevailed.

The NAACP

During its existence, the Niagara Movement held conferences in 1906, at Harpers Ferry, West Virginia; in 1907, at Boston, Massachusetts; and in 1908, at Oberlin, Ohio. Civil rights protests in cities across the nation were organized by the Niagara Movement, which gained a reputation for demanding recognition of the equality of all human beings through social protest and demonstrations. In the wake of a race riot in Springfield, Illinois, in 1908, the movement began to dissolve as members turned their attention to a new organization. On February 12, 1909, the ideas on which the Niagara Movement was founded were absorbed into the framework of the National Association for the Advancement of Colored People (NAACP), which not only developed a wider following but also addressed the broader issues of equality and civil rights that the Niagara Movement was not able to address effectively. Important members of the Niagara Movement, such as Du Bois, became instrumental in the NAACP as well. Du Bois, however, decided that even the NAACP was not forceful enough in addressing issues such as lynching, rape, and voting rights. He would end his life in exile in Africa.

Although the Niagara Movement survived only five years—formally disbanding in 1910—it had served as the

W. E. B. Du Bois was behind the formation in 1905 of the Niagara Movement, which sought civil rights for African Americans and became the National Association for the Advancement of Colored People.

foundation upon which later movements were built. It can be seen as both a negative reaction to Washington's accommodationist approach to African American equality and the progenitor of such later groups as the Student Nonviolent Coordinating Committee (SNCC), the Congress of Racial Equality (CORE), and the Black Panthers.

Paul Barton-Kriese

Core Resources

W. Haywood Burns's *The Voices of Negro Protest in America* (New York: Oxford University Press, 1963) discusses twentieth century protest movements, highlighting the NAACP. W. E. B. Du Bois's *The Souls of Black Folk* (1903; reprint, New York: Vintage Books, 1990) is Du Bois's powerful argument that black U.S. citizens will progress only via challenge, struggle, and political protest. Floyd B. McKissick's *Three-fifths of a Man* (New York: Macmillan, 1969) is an account of the racial basis of the Declaration of Independence, the Constitution, and the Emancipation Proclamation, with an examination of how these documents have influenced race relations. Donald G. Nieman's *Promises to Keep: African-Americans and the Constitutional Order, 1776 to the Present* (New York: Oxford University Press, 1991) is a constitutional history of the United States with special reference to charting the impact of the Constitution on U.S. social history. Booker T. Washington's *Up from Slavery* (1901; reprint, New York: Gramercy Books, 1993) describes his idea of the "talented tenth" and how black citizens of the United States will achieve full equality gradually, through hard work and demonstrating their worthiness; a direct contrast to the more aggressive platform of Du Bois.

See also: Atlanta Compromise; Congress of Racial Equality; Nation of Islam; National Association for the Advancement of Colored People; Southern Christian Leadership Conference; Talented Tenth; Universal Negro Improvement Association.

Nisga'a Agreement in Principle

The Nisga'a Agreement in Principle, published in February, 1996, attempted to lead to the "full and final settlement of Nisga'a aboriginal title, rights, and interests." This agreement, dealing with an aboriginal group from the Pacific coast of Canada, covered many areas, including land and reserves, access to the land, fisheries, wildlife, environmental assessment and protection, Nisga'a government, fiscal matters including taxation, and cultural heritage protection.

Under the agreement, the Nisga'a were defined as an aboriginal people under the constitution with all the charter rights, benefits, and obligations of other Canadians; they did not by this agreement acquire any special rights or privileges. The criminal code of Canada continued to govern them, and they continued to pay taxes. In time, the tax-exempt status for Nisga'a citizens was to be eliminated as the Nisga'a began to assume more power for taxation.

The agreement stipulated that the Nisga'a govern themselves in a democratic manner with four village governments and an overall Nisga'a government with its own constitution. This government was empowered to make laws governing cultural, linguistic, social, educational, vocational, environmental, and related matters. In addition, this government, with provincial approval, administered justice through provision of police services and a Nisga'a court with jurisdiction over its own lands. The agreement made the Nisga'a the owners of about nineteen hundred square kilometers of land in the area of the lower Nass River, including the four villages of New Aiyansh, Canyon City, Greenville, and Kincolith. These lands, however, were to remain accessible to the general public for recreation, hunting, and fishing. All existing legal interests on the lands were to be maintained, and the roads in them were to be governed and maintained by the province.

The agreement stipulated that a financial transfer of $190 million, in addition to $11.5 million for the purchase of commercial fishing vessels and licenses, was to be paid over a period of years. The Nisga'a would receive an annual quota of salmon and other fish to be caught and were expected to conserve the stocks. Overall management was shared between the Nisga'a and the federal and provincial governments. The Nisga'a received permission to hunt wildlife subject to existing restrictions and laws of conservation. The Nisga'a were made responsible for overall environmental protection and were required to meet or exceed existing federal and provincial requirements.

Gregory Walters

See also: Aboriginal Canadians; Nunavut Territory; Oka crisis.

Nixon v. Herndon

In 1921, the U.S. Supreme Court ruled in *Newberry v. United States* that Congress lacked authority to regulate primary elections. Southern state legislatures immediately took advantage of this decision to prohibit black participation in state primary elections. "White primaries" were quickly adopted throughout the South. Texas, during the first half of the twentieth century, was part of the Democrat-dominated South. The only competition that mattered was within the Democratic Party, so if blacks were not allowed to participate in the Democratic primary they would effectively be denied any meaningful choice in the electoral process.

In 1924, the Texas legislature passed a law barring blacks from voting in the Democratic primary. L. A. Nixon, a black resident of El Paso, attempted to vote in the primary and was refused by Herndon, an election judge. Nixon and the National Association for the Advancement of Colored People (NAACP) claimed that the Texas law violated the Fourteenth and Fifteenth Amendments. The Supreme Court did not deal with the issue of the Fifteenth Amendment, but a unanimous Court found that the Texas white primary law violated the equal protection clause of the Fourteenth Amendment.

The NAACP won the battle but temporarily lost the war. Texas responded to the Court's decision by engaging in the strategy of "legislate and litigate." By passing a different white primary law after their defeat in *Nixon v. Herndon*, the Texas legislature forced the NAACP to institute another attack on the white primary. When the second law was declared unconstitutional in *Nixon v. Condon* in 1932, Texas came up with a third variation of the white primary. This time, in *Grovey v. Townsend* (1935), the U.S. Supreme Court upheld the Texas white primary, arguing that no state discrimination was present. According to the Court, the Texas Democratic Party, a private voluntary association, decided to exclude blacks from voting in the primary elections. It was not until *Smith v. Allwright* (1944) that a unanimous Supreme Court declared that the Fifteenth Amendment could be used as a shield to protect the right to vote in primary elections.

From the passage of the first white primary law in 1924 until the final abolition of white primaries in the *Smith* case in 1944, blacks were denied the right to vote in Democratic Party primaries, the only election of significance at that time. The white primary cases illustrate one of the dilemmas in using the federal courts—the fact that justice delayed is justice denied.   *Darryl Paulson*

See also: *Grovey v. Townsend*; National Association for the Advancement of Colored People; *Newberry v. United States*; *Smith v. Allwright*.

Nonviolent resistance

> **Significance:** Nonviolence is a central method for expressing political dissent and marshaling the power necessary to bring about political change. In North American race relations, its most visible and effective proponents, including Martin Luther King, Jr., used it to advance the cause of civil rights.

Although the term "nonviolent resistance" is a twentieth century concept based on analysis of the strategies and conditions necessary for successful nonviolent action, its practice is deeply rooted in United States history. Religious groups from Europe such as the Amish and the Society of Friends (Quakers), who practiced a literal understanding of Jesus's teachings forbidding the use of violence, fled to North America to escape persecution. Their continued witness to principles of pacifism has influenced a tradition and philosophy of nonviolent protest. Additionally, the early colonists engaged in nonviolent resistance against British rule. In 1766, Britain passed an import tax, the Stamp Act. American merchants organized a boycott of goods, causing the repeal of the act. This action marked the first organized resistance to British rule and led to the establishment of the First Continental Congress in 1774. The legal basis for nonviolent action was established in the First Amendment to the Constitution, which protects the rights of persons to "freedom of speech," peaceful assembly, and petitioning the government "for a redress of grievances." The United States has a long history of expression of such rights.

Various Applications

In 1845, Henry David Thoreau was jailed for refusing to pay a poll tax in protest of the Mexican-American War. In his essay "Civil Disobedience," Thoreau proclaimed the moral necessity of resistance in the face of immoral government action. Nonviolent protest has accompanied every war in which the United States has engaged, and it was so widespread during the Vietnam War that it became a central reason the United States withdrew from Vietnam in 1974. Nonviolent protest has also been central to various movements seeking to ban and limit nuclear weapons and in war tax resistance movements, in which members refuse to pay taxes to support the military budget. Strategies of nonviolent resistance were also employed by the women's rights movement, which culminated in the right to vote (1920) and in greater social and economic equality for women. The labor movement has used nonviolent tactics in the form of strikes, labor slowdowns, and boycotts to force improvement of working conditions and income. Despite strong, often violent responses by corporate owners, the Wagner Act, passed by Congress in 1935, recognized the legal right of workers to organize and use such methods. César Chávez effectively used consumer boycotts in the 1970's and 1980's to win better conditions for farmworkers. Nonviolent strategies have been used by environmental groups to block construction of nuclear power plants, stop the cutting of forests, or alter policies considered to be ecologically hazardous. They have also been employed since the 1980's by antiabortion groups attempting to close abortion clinics.

Race Relations

The most prolonged, successful use of nonviolent resistance, however, came in the Civil Rights movement led by Martin Luther King, Jr., in the 1950's and 1960's. Drawing on the work of Mahatma (Mohandas) Gandhi, the movement used marches, sit-ins, and boycotts to force an end to legal racial segregation in the South and informal (de facto) segregation in the North. This campaign demonstrated the ambiguity of governmental response to such tactics. Often participants were arrested and convicted under local statutes, only to have such laws ruled invalid by higher courts; this occurred during the Montgomery bus boycott. On the other hand, King and his followers were under constant surveillance by the Federal Bureau of Investigation and were considered threats to political stability by many government officials. The debate has also focused on what constitutes "freedom of expression" and "peaceful assembly." The "plowshares eight," in 1980, protesting nuclear weapons, entered a General Electric plant in Pennsylvania and dented the nose cone of a warhead. They were sentenced to prison on grounds of trespass and destruction of private property.

Demonstrators in Albany, Georgia, in 1962 use nonviolent resistance—a pray-in—in their struggle to achieve integration in the city.

Theory and Strategy

Nonviolent resistance has two distinct traditions. The religious tradition centers on the moral claim that it is always wrong to harm another and that only love of the "enemy" can transform persons and societies. Violence and hatred cannot solve social problems or end social conflict, for each act of violence generates new resentments. This spiral of violence can be ended only if some group absorbs the violence and returns only nonviolence and love. Central to this vision is a commitment to justice that requires adherents to engage injustice actively wherever they find it.

The political tradition focuses on strategies for organizing political and social power to force another, usually a political authority, to change policies. As Gene Sharp, a leading analyst, notes, government requires the consent of its citizens. In nonviolent resistance, dissenters organize forms of power including economic power, labor power, and the power of public opinion in order to undermine consent and force authorities to change policies.

The use of these theories and techniques remains important in stable, democratic societies as a way of resolving conflict, generating social change, and chal-

lenging power structures, especially on behalf of the powerless, whose rights are often ignored. Without the legal sanctions which permit such protest, the only recourse becomes open societal violence and conflict, even to the point of civil war. *Charles L. Kammer*

Core Resources

Broad views of the topic are presented in Peter Ackerman and Christopher Kruegler's *Strategic Nonviolent Conflict: The Dynamics of People Power in the Twentieth Century* (Westport, Conn.: Praeger, 1994); David P. Barash's *Introduction to Peace Studies* (Belmont, Calif.: Wadsworth, 1991); *The Power of the People: Active Nonviolence in the United States* (Philadelphia: New Society, 1987), edited by Robert Conney and Helen Michalowski; and Gene Sharp's *The Politics of Nonviolent Action* (3 vols., Boston: Porter Sargent, 1973). A personal view is contained in Martin Luther King, Jr.'s *A Testament of Hope: The Essential Writings and Speeches of Martin Luther King, Jr.*, edited by James M. Washington (San Francisco: Harper, 1991).

See also: Civil Rights movement; Freedom Riders; Montgomery bus boycott; Southern Christian Leadership Conference; Student Nonviolent Coordinating Committee.

Nordic "race"

This term was one of three pseudo-racial categories employed beginning in the late nineteenth century to classify the population of Europe; the other categories were Alpine and Mediterranean. Nordic people were thought to come from northern Europe, especially Scandinavia. Physically, the Nordic race was characterized as tall, often blond, blue-eyed, and dolichocephalic (having a comparatively long head). Members of the Nordic race were reputed to be superior, naturally individualistic, self-reliant, freedom-loving, and gifted in terms of state organization.

The use of the concept of the Nordic race was popular during the 1920's when "scientific" theories of race were propounded to explain the development of civilization. Significant achievements of humankind were traced to members of the Nordic race. These racist theories were associated with exclusionary immigration and antimiscegenation laws in the United States. Nazi Germany also used this rationale to support its race-cleansing policies.

As Thomas F. Gossett points out in *Race: The History of an Idea in America* (1963), the argument that the important elements of western civilization are due in large measure to the Nordic race is closely related to earlier racist theories of Aryanism and Teutonic origins. According to the latter view, Anglo-Saxons were primarily responsible for the development of democratic institutions, from the town-hall meeting to national systems of representative government.   *Gary A. Cretser*

See also: Anglo-Saxon; Aryan "race"; Race as a concept; "Scientific" racism; Teutonic "race."

North Star, The

> **Significance:** The North Star was the vehicle for the first of Frederick Douglass's newspaper campaigns against slavery and for abolition

When the first issue of *The North Star* appeared on December 3, 1847, critics and readers discovered a newspaper that blended sardonic humor with moral urgency, written in a polished style. Some readers, however, were skeptical of editor Frederick Douglass's sophistication. Fathered by a white man and born to the slave Harriet Bailey in Talbot County, Maryland, Frederick Bailey had worked in bondage as a slave for Thomas Auld, witnessing the horrors of slavery, the brutal beatings, and even murder. In his teens, he had taught himself to read and write from a discarded speller and copybook, and learned public speaking by imitating orations appearing in *The Columbian Orator*, an abolitionist publication. *The Columbian Orator* led to his awareness of the abolitionist movement and influenced his writing style when he later published *The North Star*. Clashing with his master in 1838, Frederick escaped from Baltimore to New York with Anna Murray, a free African American domestic servant. Once married, they settled in New Bedford, Massachusetts, which offered sanctuary. To prevent recapture, Frederick changed his surname to Douglass, in honor of a character in Sir Walter Scott's poem *Lady of the Lake*.

Douglass and Garrison

Douglass became active in local abolitionist gatherings, discovering his gift as a compelling speaker who provided firsthand examples of barbaric slavery. He became a favorite on the lecture circuit during the early 1840's; his autobiography, *Narrative of the Life of Frederick Douglass* (1845), sold more than thirty thousand copies over the next five years. Douglass came under the tutelage of the leading abolitionist of the times, a white man named William Lloyd Garrison. From Garrison's abolitionist newspaper, *The Liberator*, Douglass no doubt learned much about newspaper operations.

As Douglass's fame increased, so did his risk of capture as an escaped slave. In 1845, he sailed for England, then on to Scotland and Ireland, where he passionately lectured on the inhumane treatment of slaves. His newfound friends, moved by his personal plight, arranged to purchase Douglass's freedom for $711.66. Before returning to the United States in 1847, he also received $2,175 to bankroll his own antislavery newspaper.

When Garrison objected to Douglass's projected newspaper, the two close friends became estranged, then bitter enemies. Douglass believed that the white abolitionists thought him a child to be led. African Americans, he insisted, must lead to gain respect. He held that his newspaper could create that leadership and help increase self-respect among African Americans. Douglass knew of the hazards in starting an African American newspaper, because about one hundred such papers already existed in the United States, the first having been started in 1827. He located in Rochester, New York, because of the area's strong antislavery sentiments and because publishing there reduced the competition with *The Liberator* in Boston and the *National Anti-Slavery Standard* in New York City.

On December 3, 1847, the first issue of *The North Star* appeared—a four-page weekly with a subscription cost of two dollars per year, circulation of two to three thousand, and publishing costs of eighty dollars per week at the first print shop owned by an African American. Douglass chose journalist Martin Delaney as coeditor, but the two soon clashed over the issue of "colonization," by which freed slaves would seek a separate homeland in Africa rather than integrate within the United States white society. When a disgusted Delaney left in 1848 to found a colony in the Niger Valley, in Africa, Douglass became sole editor, vigorously espousing the principles of integration, as he did throughout his life.

Advocacy for All

In the first issue of *The North Star*, Douglass urged African Americans to become politically active and pledged that his newspaper would aggressively attack slavery, work to free Southern slaves, and promote African American morality and progress. The lead article recounted the convention of "colored people" of 1847, with its primary objectives of abolishing slavery and elevating free African Americans. In subsequent years, *The North Star* dealt with a plethora of burning issues: injustice, inequality, racism, the avoidance of drink and dissipation, the benefits of integrated school systems, the elimination of segregated hotels and railroads, the folly of war and capital punishment, the worth of laborers, the imperative need for racial unity among African Americans, and the unfair voting practices leveled against African Americans in northern states. *The North Star* came to the defense not only of persecuted African Americans but also of American Indians, the Irish, and other immigrant groups.

From its beginnings, *The North Star* lived up to its masthead: "Right Is Of No Sex—Truth Is Of No Color—God Is The Father Of Us All, and All We Are Brethren." Douglass vigorously supported the women's rights movement, linking enslaved women to the abolition movement itself. At the Seneca Falls Convention in 1848, Douglass was the only one of the thirty-two men attending to speak and vote in favor of Elizabeth Cady Stanton's Declaration of Sentiments, which demanded equality for women. He effectively used *The North Star* to promote Stanton's feminist cause.

Subsequent Papers

Financially, *The North Star* foundered after six months. Douglass mortgaged his house and used his lecture fees to keep the paper going. From time to time, he received financial gifts from Gerrit Smith, a philanthropist, reformer, and wealthy New York landowner. In 1851, the two men agreed to merge the financially troubled *North Star* with Smith's struggling *Liberty Party Paper*. Douglass maintained editorial control over the paper while including political news of the Liberty Party; he broadened his readership to four thousand; and he accepted a comfortable subsidy from Smith. The new effort, *Frederick Douglass' Paper*, appeared in June, 1851, and lasted until 1859. The paper continued Douglass's efforts in regard to abolition, equality, and women's rights. Douglass also dabbled in the Liberty Party campaigns, endorsing Smith and helping him win a seat in Congress. In 1852, Douglass himself became the first African American nominated for vice president on the Equal Rights Party ticket of 1852.

Recurring financial problems forced Douglass to reduce the size and frequency of his paper in 1859. His third effort, *Douglass' Monthly*, circulating in England as well as in the United States, lasted until the middle of the Civil War, 1863. Like the other two papers, *Douglass' Monthly* remained a magnet for African American writers and reformers and framed Douglass's own inimitable style and wit as well. He actively recruited African American soldiers for the war. He viewed Abraham Lincoln as the best hope for his race, pressing for the Emancipation Proclamation that Lincoln delivered in 1863. He proposed land reform, federally financed education, and a national association for African Americans. He believed that interracial marriages would someday eliminate racial hatred.

After the Civil War, Douglass moved to Washington, D.C. There he published the *New National Era*, focusing on the interests of the newly freed African Americans. During that paper's existence (1870-1873), Douglass editorialized on Reconstruction, the rise of mob lynchings in the South, race relations, politics, labor, and education. From 1873 until his death in 1895, Douglass continued to be heard on the lecture circuit and in leading newspapers. A self-made man, rising against great odds from slavery to publisher, race leader, prominent abolitionist, social reformer, and political activist, Douglass is one of the most important African Americans of the nineteenth century and became a powerful symbol in the Civil Rights movement throughout the twentieth century. — *Richard Whitworth*

Core Resources

Frederick Douglass's *The Frederick Douglass Papers*, edited by John W. Blassingame and John R. McKivigan (New Haven, Conn.: Yale University Press, 1979-1992), is a reconstruction of Douglass's thoughts and opinions from fragmentary newspapers, such as *The North Star*, and manuscript sources. Nathan I. Huggins's *Slave and Citizen: The Life of Frederick Douglass* (Boston: Little, Brown, 1980) portrays Douglass as troubled and self-contradictory at times. Waldo E. Martin's *The Mind of Frederick Douglass* (Chapel Hill: University of North Carolina Press, 1984) focuses on Douglass's formative years and the reworking of his views on slavery, inequality, and injustice. William B. Rogers's *"We Are All Together Now": Frederick Douglass, William Lloyd Garrison, and the Prophetic Tradition* (New York: Garland, 1995) juxtaposes the values, beliefs, and actions of Douglass and Garrison. Frederick S. Voss's *Majestic in His Wrath: A Pictorial Life of Frederick Douglass* (Washington, D.C.: Smithsonian Institution Press, 1995) brings together rare photos and commentary to commemorate the centennial of Douglass's death.

See also: Abolition; Emancipation Proclamation; *Liberator, The*; Underground Railroad.

Northwest Ordinance

By the Peace of Paris with Britain (1783), the United States acquired a vast inland empire bounded by the Appalachians, the Mississippi River, the Great Lakes, and the Gulf of Mexico. The task of disposing of this territory fell to the government as it was organized under the Articles of Confederation (1781-1789). Conflicting claims of states, settlers, land companies, and American Indians confused the issue. Lands south of the Ohio River were settled separately from those north of it. The Old Northwest, including the present-day states of Ohio, Indiana, Illinois, Michigan, and Wisconsin, was claimed by Virginia, Connecticut, and Massachusetts. Thomas Jefferson chaired a committee that in 1784 proposed to Congress the creation of a temporary government for the Northwest and the area's eventual division into sovereign states eligible to join the Confederation on terms equal to those enjoyed by the original members. Though the plan was not enacted, it did provide a model for the Northwest Ordinance and facilitated the cession of western lands by Virginia (in 1784), Massachusetts (1784-1785), and Connecticut (1784-1786) to the national government.

If state claims were resolved, those of Native Americans were refused. Under British rule, by the Proclamation of 1763, the entire West had been set aside as Indian Country, starting at the Appalachian Divide. The pressure for white settlement of the region had been a contributing cause of the American Revolution, a lesson the Confederation had learned. As settlers from New England, Pennsylvania, and the South pressed toward the Ohio Country, Indian claims were extinguished. By the Treaty of Fort Stanwix (1784) the Iroquois, exhausted by war, surrendered their claims to western New York and Pennsylvania. The next year, major Ohio tribes relinquished their claims to most of the future state, with the exception of the southwest shores of Lake Erie. Formal concession came within a decade in the Treaty of Fort Greenville (1795), when, for a ten-thousand-dollar annuity, twelve tribes relinquished the southwest portion of the Old Northwest (Ohio and Indiana).

Utilizing Jefferson's plan, the Congress of the Confederation (1787), even as the Constitutional Convention was meeting, established the Northwest Ordinance, by which those lands would be organized as a territory, with a nationally appointed governor, secretary, and judges. It stated that when five thousand free white males resided there, a bicameral legislature was to be created. Eventually three to five states were to be formed (with a minimum of sixty thousand free white inhabitants needed for statehood), each to be admitted to the United States and to be equal in standing to the original states. Freedom of religion, the right to jury trial, public support of education, and the prohibition of slavery were to prevail. While this legislation is traditionally regarded as the greatest achievement of the Confederation Congress, it set a tragic precedent by riding roughshod over the rights of Native Americans.   *C. George Fry*

See also: Treaties and agreements with Indians: United States.

Nunavut Territory

In 1993, the Nunavut Land Claims Agreement was signed with Canada's federal government. It stated that, on April 1, 1999, the Northwest Territories would be divided and the eastern region would become Nunavut Territory. "Nunavut" comes from the Inuit language Inuktitut and means "our land." The Inuit have inhabited these lands for thousands of years, and they made up 80 percent of the population in the late 1990's. The Inuit have long desired a territory of their own, and the agreement gave the Inuit control over more than 350,000 square kilometers of land, mineral rights, and financial aid. This agreement is designed to give the Inuit people control over their own education, health, social services, and many other provincial-type responsibilities.

The government of the territory is to be democratically elected to represent all residents of the territory: about twenty-two thousand people, seventeen thousand of whom are Inuit. The agreement placed the seat of government in Iqualuit and described the territory as containing twenty-eight villages or communities, including Iqualuit, which is located on Baffin Island.

Gregory Walters

See also: Aboriginal Canadians; Nisga'a Agreement in Principle; Oka Crisis.

October crisis

Significance: On October 16, 1970, in response to terrorism and kidnapping in Quebec, the Canadian federal government suspended civil liberties.

The October crisis of 1970 was a tragic period in Quebec's history, marked by kidnapping, murder, and the suspension of civil liberties. It followed a decade of profound change and intellectual turbulence, not simply in the province of Quebec but throughout the world. Decolonization was in vogue, wars of liberation were being fought in several countries, and youth were questioning the values of their parents and the capitalist system. During the 1960's, Quebec society, once rural and religious, had undergone rapid transformation and was well on the way to becoming a modern, secular, progressive society.

The Separatist Movement

Increasingly self-confident and assertive French-speaking Quebecers (Québécois) were no longer willing to accept passively the Anglo-Canadian domination of previous centuries. In addition, they feared for the future of the French language and Québécois culture. This led many to join the ranks of the so-called separatist, or sovereignist, movement, which advocated political sovereignty or even outright independence for Quebec.

While these sovereignists followed a democratic path, others were not so patient. The Front de Libération du Québec (FLQ) was an underground revolutionary movement dedicated to creating a socialist, independent Quebec. Officially founded in 1963, it was composed primarily of French Canadian youth, often college or university students, willing to accept political violence as a means to liberate Quebec and destroy capitalism. They drew intellectual inspiration from the popular left-wing cult figures of this epoch, including Herbert Marcuse, Karl Marx, Mao Zedong, and Ernesto "Che" Guevara. They were also deeply influenced by recent historical events, especially the successful wars of national liberation that had been waged in Algeria and

Cuba. The FLQ perceived itself as part of a worldwide movement fighting for liberation and decolonization, which included such groups as the Weathermen and Black Panthers in the United States, the Palestine Liberation Organization in the Middle East, Roman Catholics in Northern Ireland, and the Viet Cong engaged in bitter conflict with the United States in Vietnam.

The FLQ never had a large membership; it was limited, at any one time, to perhaps fewer than one hundred activists. Nor was it highly organized: There was no mastermind or central committee that operated on a strict hierarchical basis. The FLQ was composed of cells, each one knowing little or nothing about the other, which made it difficult for police to penetrate. Five or ten young zealots would form a cell and then commit acts of violence or publish revolutionary tracts under the FLQ banner.

The FLQ began operations in 1963, planting bombs in post office boxes located in the affluent English-speaking section of Westmount in Montreal. Eventually, other targets were selected, including armories, federal buildings, the provincial Department of Labor building, and the Montreal Stock Exchange, at which a particularly bloody bombing in 1969 injured twenty-five people. FLQ members also robbed banks for funds and stole explosives from construction sites. Occasionally, the police were successful in destroying cells, but there were always new ones to take their place. It was estimated that the FLQ was responsible for some two hundred bombings, seven deaths, dozens wounded, and millions of dollars in property damage between 1963 and 1970. Although their propaganda was crude and unsophisticated, it resonated with many Québécois who could understand the forces that propelled young people to lash out against the injustices of society.

October Violence

This violence, at first directed mainly against property, took a deadly turn in 1970. On October 5, one cell kidnapped the British trade commissioner in Montreal, James Cross. The kidnappers' ransom demands included receiving $500,000 in gold, the release of twenty-three political prisoners, and broadcasting the FLQ manifesto. The federal and provincial authorities allowed the broadcast but rejected the other demands, although they did offer to fly the kidnappers out of the country if they released their hostage. On October 10, another FLQ cell kidnapped Pierre Laporte, the provincial minister of labor and immigration.

The immediate result was confusion and chaos. In Montreal, Mayor Jean Drapeau believed his city was close to panic. Police forces throughout Quebec appeared stymied and incapable of protecting property or individuals. No one knew if this was the work of a few individuals or whether the province was facing the prospect of a large, well-organized left-wing insurrection. Quebec's premier, Robert Bourassa, was inexperienced, only thirty-seven years of age, and in office for only five months. His cabinet was divided as to whether to negotiate with the kidnappers or take a tough line. Police pushed for more legal powers to combat terrorism, while Laporte's friends and wife pressed the cabinet to negotiate.

Responses

The federal government in Ottawa was in no mood for compromise. The Canadian prime minister, Pierre Trudeau, a Quebecer, was pushing authorities in Quebec to take a stiff line, and John Turner, the federal minister of justice, feared an erosion of will on the part of the Quebec government. Gérard Pelletier, the Canadian secretary of state for external affairs, privately was alarmed at what he thought was too much sympathy for the FLQ on the part of many students, intellectuals, and sovereignists within Quebec. Eventually, the Quebec government formally requested that the Canadian Army be sent into the province and that the War Measures Act be invoked. On October 12, the army moved into Quebec in order to guard public buildings and protect government officials, and on October 16, the War Measures Act was proclaimed. Public opinion polls showed that Canadians and Quebecers overwhelmingly approved of these federal actions.

Nevertheless, implementation of the War Measures Act eventually caused much controversy. This act permitted the government to suspend normal civil liberties and empowered authorities to use a variety of weapons—including censorship, arrest, detention, deportation, and control of transportation—to fight a state of apprehended insurrection. Many civil libertarians believed this proclamation was heavy-handed and unnecessary. Even Trudeau, who advocated a tough stance, was not enthusiastic about using this legal tool, but he deferred to the judgment of authorities on the scene in Quebec. More than 465 people were detained, but no charges were filed and most of those arrested were innocent of any criminal wrongdoing. It appears that the authorities considered almost anyone who was a sovereignist or embraced left-wing views to be a potential insurrection-

ist. Civil libertarians later pointed out that when the kidnappers were apprehended, it was due to routine police work and not to the special legal powers granted to the authorities.

On October 18, Laporte was found dead in the trunk of an automobile, having been strangled by his captors the previous day. In early December, the police located the hideout at which Cross was detained. After negotiations, Cross was released unharmed and the kidnappers allowed to fly to Cuba. Later that month, police finally apprehended the men responsible for the kidnapping and death of Laporte. Paul Rose and Francis Simard were found guilty of murder and sentenced to life imprisonment, although neither served more than twelve years before being paroled. In January, 1971, the army withdrew from Quebec, although the state of emergency legislation remained in effect until April 30, 1971.

After these events, the Front de Libération du Québec went into a period of steep decline. The organization had completely alienated public opinion in Quebec, including leftists and sovereignists. Moreover, the increasing popularity of the Parti Québécois, founded in 1968 to fight for sovereignty, was convincing many people that there was a viable alternative to violence and revolution. The memory of the October Crisis remained firmly imprinted upon the Québécois psyche, one of the darkest moments in their modern history.

David C. Lukowitz

Core Resources

Quebec, Canada and the October Crisis (Montreal: Black Rose Books, 1973), edited by Dan Daniels, is a collection of the revolutionary literature of the period, including documents, pamphlets, and poetry. Louis Fournier's *F.L.Q.: The Anatomy of an Underground Movement* (Toronto: NC Press, 1984), translated by Edward Baxter, is a detailed, sympathetic account of the organization, placing it and the October crisis within the context of national and global events. In Gérard Pelletier's *The October Crisis* (Montreal: McClelland and Stewart, 1971), translated by Joyce Marshall, the Canadian secretary of state at the time justifies his agonizing decision to support the use of the War Measures Act. *Power Corrupted: The October Crisis and the Repression of Quebec* (Toronto: New Press, 1971), edited by Abraham Rotstein, collects essays by Anglo-Canadians highly critical of the suppression of civil liberties in Quebec. In Pierre Elliott Trudeau's *Memoirs* (Toronto: McClelland and Stewart, 1993), the Canadian prime minister justifies his actions in a relatively brief section dealing with the events of 1970, but leaves many questions unanswered.

See also: Bloc Québécois; French Canadians; Official Languages Act; Separatist movement in Quebec.

Official Languages Act

> **Significance:** The Official Languages Act, the foundation of Canada's multilanguage policy, encouraged the growth of a multicultural society.

The implementation of the Official Languages Act of 1969 was a crucial element of Prime Minister Pierre Elliott Trudeau's policy of maintaining a united Canada. It also was a major step in developing a policy enabling French, English, and immigrant and aboriginal communities to maintain their ethnicities and languages. To maintain national unity while promoting cultural diversity, Canada assumed that a workable language policy was crucial. Canada was unique, in that it attempted to implement a language policy designed to influence language usage in ways to serve the interests of the Canadian people—a mutable policy developed without establishing linguistic territoriality. The Official Languages Act of 1969 became the foundation to this process.

Origins of the Language Conflict
The language issue in Canada was not new. The conflict between the two major colonizing powers in North America, the French and the English, set the stage for ongoing contention. When the French territory was ceded to the British, the French were allowed to practice their Roman Catholic religion, and the French language continued to assert itself. Since then, a two-language and two-culture policy has been in effect. The Constitutional Act of 1791 divided the colony of Quebec into two units, Upper Canada and Lower Canada, where the majority of the Parliamentarians were francophones. Although challenged in practice, administratively and legislatively, the French language remained vigorous. The Constitution of 1867, from which Canada claims its origins, institutionalized the use of French in the Quebec legislature and in some federal and Quebec courts. The constitution seemed to enable the French language and culture to spread. In addition to the right to use French in Quebec, Francophones were led to believe that as French settlers moved west, they would find adequate guarantees of linguistic rights elsewhere. Also, the French viewed the constitution as an agreement between two "founding people."

The next fifty years proved disastrous for the use of French. In 1890, Manitoba abrogated the use of French (which was not restored until 1985); Ontario abolished French schools in 1912; and limitations were imposed on instruction in French in other provinces. Francophones became increasingly confined to Quebec, with Montreal becoming an anglophone area. It was the high birth rate of the French in Quebec that compensated for the large French emigration from Quebec to the United States and English-speaking immigrants flocking into Montreal. In spite of accommodations to allow French in the courts, military, and other official bodies, it was clear that English was ascending over French and any other language. As a result of the majority rule principle and the decline of French language usage, the two peoples became cut off from each other—the French had to separate themselves or they would, under majority rule, lose to the English and become extinct.

By the 1960's, the language issue required serious attention. The French language was in rapid decline outside Quebec and, although less rapidly, inside the province as well. Within Quebec, the birthrate of the French had declined to one of the lowest in the world. It was becoming apparent that English was not only the language of North America but also the international language. Even Francophones were learning and using English.

The B & B Commission
This situation resulted in civil unrest and a movement to have Quebec separate from Canada. In 1963, Prime Minister Lester Pearson created the Royal Commission on Bilingualism and Biculturalism (the B & B Commission) to examine the relationship between English and French Canada. More specifically, the commission was asked to review and assess Canadian language policy. The primary concern was to promote a federal-provincial response to the crisis in English-French relations. The commission also had to consider the increasing number of Canadians who had no inborn allegiance to either French or English.

In its report, the commission rejected territorial solutions. It found, however, that the use of French had fallen behind English, for example, in public service, to a politically and socially unacceptable level. It urged that a new charter, founded on the concept of "equal partnership," be implemented at both the federal and provincial levels. It was in response to the commission's recommendations that the Official Languages Act of 1969 was created.

The B & B Commission endorsed the value of linguistic diversity as an "inestimable enrichment that Canadians cannot afford to lose. . . . Linguistic variety is unquestionably an advantage and its beneficial effects on the country are priceless." What happened eventually was the establishment of the "official languages," English and French, and the "heritage languages," recognized languages of other ethnic communities. Initially, the issue of heritage languages was not supported, but after pressure from other communities, three types of heritage programs were in place by the 1990's: instruction incorporated into the school curriculum, instruction in the school system but afterhours, and instruction that used school resources but was not part of the school program.

In the meantime, Canadian nationalism was rising, especially against U.S. policies concerning Vietnam. Outside economic and cultural influence on Canada was resented, especially in 1971, when Canada's economic dependency on the United States was made manifest—the United States could not buy enough of Canada's products, and Europe provided no help. In Quebec, the decline of French was becoming a prominent issue. In Montreal, riots promoting Quebec's nationalism became endemic. One particular disturbance was in 1968, when rioting had broken out at the Saint-Jean Baptiste Day parade, and Trudeau coolly faced a bottle-throwing crowd. The maintenance of a united Canada was a central issue for Trudeau. Dismissing the "two nations" vision of Canada, he argued that Canada must be a truly federal state with equality for all provinces, yet also a homeland for both French and English culture. The Official Languages Act became the key to this policy.

The Official Languages Act of 1969 was supported by the opposition as well as the party in power. Based on the findings of the B & B Commission, the act named French and English as the official languages and guaranteed official-language minorities in the country certain basic rights in dealing with the federal government and its various agencies. It was, however, the francophone minority outside Quebec that needed such guarantees. The act also set forth a number of measures to provide the francophone community with the same guarantees outside Quebec that the English enjoyed within Quebec. Parliament's intention was to place French on an equal footing with English as far as the federal government was concerned. The federal government improved its capacity to deal with Canadians in the official language of their choice and to allow public servants to use either language at work, in certain areas. Some provinces, such as Ontario and New Brunswick, provided government services in both languages and tried to implement their own language policies, particularly in regard to minority and second-language education.

As a result of the act, a commissioner of official languages was created and appointed—a linguistics ombudsman to report annually on the progress of implementing various provisions of the act. However, the commissioner had to devote much time to persuading Canadians that the reforms were necessary and just.

The act created a great deal of controversy. Some anglophones complained that the act forced French on them. The act was also criticized for giving French a position it no longer merited, especially in areas where speakers of languages other than English outnumbered francophones. In spite of the controversy, principles of the Official Languages Act were incorporated into the 1982 Canadian Constitution through its Canadian Charter of Rights and Freedoms. The British Parliament renounced any future legislative role in amending the Constitution, and on April 17, 1982, Queen Elizabeth II proclaimed the Constitution effective. Quebec, headed by René Lévesque of the Parti Québécois, did not agree to the Constitution and refused to sign it, charging that it did not go far enough in protecting Quebec's unique place in Canada.

Arthur W. Helweg

Core Resources

Conflict and Language Planning in Quebec (Clevedon, Avon, England: Multilingual Matters, 1984), edited by Richard Y. Bourhis, analyzes the internal policy implications of the language issue for the province of Quebec. Leo Driedger's *The Ethnic Factor: Identity in Diversity* (New York: McGraw-Hill Ryerson, 1989) includes an outstanding chapter on the language issue for Canada. Augie Fleras and Jean Leonard Elliott's *Multiculturalism in Canada: The Challenge to Diversity* (Scarborough, Ont.: Nelson Canada, 1992) contains a good analysis of the language issue within the multicultural policy of Canada. Ronald Wardhaugh's *Language and Nationhood: The Canadian Experience* (Vancouver, B.C.: New Star Books, 1983) is a classic, often-cited work delineating the language issue for Canada.

See also: Bloc Québécois; Francophone; French Canadians; Human Rights Act; Immigration Act of 1976; Multiculturalism Act; Multiculturalism in Canada; October crisis; Separatist movement in Quebec.

Oka crisis

The conflict that erupted in early July, 1990, at Oka in Quebec was the result of long-standing problems both within the Mohawk community in Canada and between that community and various other—mainly governmental—bodies. It was brought on in large measure by disputes regarding the ownership of the relevant lands at Oka that dated back to the early eighteenth century.

The lands at Oka do not fit the usual pattern of disputed territory, and for this reason, a 1975 land claim presented to the federal government was rejected outright. The Mohawk community nonetheless continued to make a claim based on territorial sovereignty, treaty rights, the Royal Proclamation of 1763, unextinguished aboriginal title under common law, and land rights from obligations imposed by order of the King of France in the eighteenth century.

More recent origins of the conflict date back to 1987 and pertain both to internal conflicts in the Mohawk community over issues of governance and legitimacy of leadership in the community and to external conflicts with various governments, chiefly local, about disputed land known as "the Pines." By the late 1980's, the Municipality of Oka had proposed to allow expansion of a local golf course onto the disputed lands and followed the lead of the federal government in refusing to consider a Mohawk land claim against the "the Pines." Mohawk protest ensued in the form of barricades, which the Municipality asked the Sureté du Québec to dispense with in restoring law and order. It was the move on July 11, 1990, by the Sureté that brought about the armed conflict and resulted in the death of a Sureté officer. As the report of the Parliamentary Standing Committee on Aboriginal Affairs stated, "Eventually the controversy over land use in the Pines became symbolic of Mohawk land rights in general. This pattern of escalating conflict continued until the shaky state of peace that managed to hold from 1987 was completely shattered by the events of July 11, 1990."

Those events would unite the previously fractured Mohawk community and would galvanize public opinion in general in favor of a solution to the land claim problem provided violence was not again used. This public support prompted the standing committee, in its fifth report, *The Summer of 1990*, to set forth several recommendations. The committee did not explore all the historical and other details of the conflict but concluded its report with a series of recommendations to resolve aboriginal issues in general and the Mohawk-Oka conflict in particular. Those recommendations included the formation of a royal commission; a review of the National Defense Act, under which Quebec was able to ask and receive from the federal government the use and support of the army in resisting the Mohawk standoff; and a better process for federal land claims and dispute resolution. More specifically, they proposed that there be an independent inquiry into Quebec's handling of native issues and of the Sureté in responding at Oka; the appointment of a mediator to resolve the conflict around land claims; and a process of healing and compensation begun in order to build a better future for all concerned.   *Gregory Walters*

See also: Aboriginal Canadians; *Delgamuukw v. British Columbia*; Indian-white relations: Canada; Nisga'a Agreement in Principle; Nunavut Territory; Royal Commission on Aboriginal Peoples.

Oklahoma Indian Welfare Act

A major reform of U.S. policy toward American Indians resulted in the Indian Reorganization Act (IRA, or Wheeler-Howard Act), enacted by Congress on June 18, 1934. With this act, further allotment of tribal lands to individual Indians was prohibited, purchase of additional lands for Indians by the secretary of the interior was authorized, and a fund (the Revolving Loan Fund for Indians) was established that could be used for tribal enterprises. The IRA allowed and encouraged the tribes or groups to adopt written constitutions allowing for self-government, gave Indians applying for positions in the Bureau of Indian Affairs preference over other applicants, and called for very strict conservation practices on Indian lands. Oklahoma, however, was excluded from the IRA because the IRA was essentially a system of reservation government, and it was deemed inappropriate for Oklahoma because, at the time of statehood, the Five Civilized Tribes had given up their autonomy.

In 1936, the benefits of the IRA were extended to Oklahoma by way of a separate statute, the Oklahoma Indian Welfare Act. This act authorized the secretary of the interior to purchase, at his discretion, good agricultural and grazing land, from within or without reservations, to hold in trust for the tribe, band, group, or individual Indian for whose benefit the land was acquired. Title to all lands was to be taken in the name of the United States and held by the United States. All land was exempt from any and all federal taxes, but the state of Oklahoma could levy and collect a gross production tax upon all oil and gas produced from the land. The secretary of the interior was responsible for overseeing the payment of these taxes to Oklahoma. Any tribe or band in the state of Oklahoma was given the right to organize for its common welfare and could adopt a constitution and bylaws; these had to follow the rules and regulations set forth by the secretary of the interior. Any ten or more Indians, as determined by the official tribe rolls, or Indian descendants of such enrolled members, in convenient proximity to each other, could be chartered as a local cooperative association for the following purposes: credit administration, production, marketing, consumers' protection, or land management. Funds from the Revolving Loan Fund for Indians could be used to provide interest-free loans to these groups.

Lynn M. Mason

See also: Indian Reorganization Act; Indian Territory; Indian-white relations: United States.

Ole Miss desegregation

Significance: The October 1, 1962, enrollment of the first African American student at the University of Mississippi provoked a national controversy.

James Meredith is interviewed on his first day as a student at the University of Mississippi in the fall of 1962.

In January, 1961, James Meredith, a native Mississippian and an Air Force veteran attending Jackson State College, one of Mississippi's all-black colleges, decided to transfer to the University of Mississippi, affectionately called "Ole Miss." His application was rejected because, Ole Miss officials maintained, Jackson State was not an approved Southern Association Secondary School and because Meredith did not furnish letters of recommendation from University of Mississippi alumni. On May 31, 1961, he filed a lawsuit against the university, charging that he had been denied admission because of his race. In its 114-year history, the University of Mississippi had never admitted an African American student.

Meredith's Legal Victory

A federal district court judge dismissed Meredith's suit, but in June, 1962, a U.S. court of appeals ruled that Meredith had been rejected from Ole Miss "solely because he was a Negro," a ruling based on the *Brown v. Board of Education* school desegregation case of 1954. The court ordered the university to admit Meredith, and the ruling was upheld by Justice Hugo L. Black of the United States Supreme Court. On September 13, Mississippi governor Ross Barnett delivered a televised speech and stated, "No school will be integrated in Mississippi while I'm governor." A week later, the board of trustees of Ole Miss appointed Governor Barnett as the university's registrar, and he personally blocked Meredith from registering for courses that same day.

Throughout Meredith's court appeals, the U.S. De-

partment of Justice had been monitoring the case. Attorney General Robert F. Kennedy, the brother of President John F. Kennedy, made more than a dozen phone calls to Governor Barnett, hoping to persuade him to allow Meredith to matriculate and thereby avoid a confrontation between the state of Mississippi and the federal government. The attorney general had provided Meredith with federal marshals to protect him as he attempted to register.

On September 24, the court of appeals that initially had heard Meredith's case again ordered the Board of Higher Education of Mississippi to allow Meredith to register. The following day, Meredith reported to the registrar's office in the university's Lyceum Building, but again Governor Barnett was there to block his registration. During a phone conversation with Attorney General Kennedy that same day, Barnett declared that he would never agree to allow Meredith to attend the University of Mississippi. When Kennedy reminded Barnett that he was openly defying a court order and could be subject to penalty, Barnett told Kennedy that he would rather spend the rest of his life in prison than allow Meredith to enroll. On September 26, Meredith again tried to register for courses, and for the third time, Governor Barnett turned him away. Two days later, the court of appeals warned Barnett that if he continued to block Meredith's admission to Ole Miss, the governor would be found in contempt of court, arrested, and fined ten thousand dollars per day. On Saturday, September 29, Governor Barnett appeared at an Ole Miss football game and proudly announced, "I love Mississippi, I love her people, her customs! And I love and respect her heritage. Ask us what we say, it's to hell with Bobby K!"

That evening, President Kennedy called Governor Barnett and told him that the federal government would continue to back Meredith until Ole Miss admitted him. Under direct pressure from the president, Barnett began to reconsider. Finally, he agreed to allow Meredith to register on Sunday, September 30, when, the governor surmised, few students and news reporters would be milling around the campus. On Sunday evening, Meredith arrived at the Lyceum Building protected by three hundred marshals, armed in riot gear and equipped with tear gas.

As Meredith and his escorts approached the campus, a group of twenty-five hundred students and other agitators attempted to block their passage. The crowd began to shout and throw bricks and bottles at the federal marshals, who retaliated with tear gas. Some of the protesters were armed with guns and began firing random shots. One federal marshal was seriously wounded by a bullet in the throat. Two onlookers, Paul Guihard, a French journalist, and Roy Gunter, a jukebox repairman, were shot and killed by rioters.

Kennedy's National Address

On Sunday evening, while Mississippians rioted on the Ole Miss campus, President Kennedy addressed the nation on television. The Meredith crisis had captured the country's and news media's attention, and the president attempted to show Mississippians and other U.S. citizens that his administration's commitment to civil rights was serious and unwavering. He reminded his audience that "Americans are free . . . to disagree with the law but not to disobey it. For in a government of laws and not of men, no man, however prominent or powerful, and no mob, however unruly or boisterous, is entitled to defy a court of law." He told Mississippians, "The eyes of the nation and all the world are upon you and upon all of us. And the honor of your university—and state—are in the balance."

The situation at the University of Mississippi was deteriorating. The federal marshals, low on tear gas, requested additional help to control the unruly mob. President Kennedy federalized Mississippi National Guardsmen and ordered them to Oxford. At dawn on Monday morning, the first of five thousand troops began arriving at Oxford to restore order. During the evening's rioting, more than one hundred people were injured and about two hundred were arrested, only twenty-four of whom were Ole Miss students.

On Monday morning, October 1, at 8:30 A.M., Meredith again presented himself at the Lyceum Building to register. He was closely guarded by federal marshals, and National Guardsmen continued patrolling the Ole Miss campus and Oxford's streets. Meredith, dressed impeccably in a business suit, registered for classes and began his matriculation at the University of Mississippi. "I am intent on seeing that every citizen has an opportunity of being a first-class citizen," Meredith told a reporter the next day. "I am also intent on seeing that citizens have a right to be something if they work hard enough."

During his tenure at Ole Miss, Meredith was often the target of insults and threats. Federal marshals remained with him during his entire time at the university. On August 18, 1963, Meredith graduated from the University of Mississippi with a bachelor of arts degree in political science. After a year of study in Africa, Meredith enrolled at Columbia University of Law. In 1966, the year before he completed his law degree, Meredith was wounded by a sniper's gunshot during a voter registration march from Tennessee to Mississippi.

Meredith's Impact

As a result of his successful effort to desegregate Ole Miss, Meredith became one of the heroes of the Civil Rights movement. In his "Letter from Birmingham Jail" (1963), Martin Luther King, Jr., states that "One day the South will recognize its real heroes. They will be the James Merediths, courageously and with a majestic sense of purpose facing jeering and hostile mobs and the agonizing loneliness that characterizes the life of the pioneer."

Meredith's victory at the University of Mississippi was a key triumph for the Civil Rights movement during the 1960's. Within two years, the University of Alabama, the University of Georgia, and other Southern colleges and universities that had prevented African Americans from enrolling were also desegregated, as the era of overt segregation in U.S. institutions of higher learning came to an end.

The Meredith case also convincingly demonstrated that the federal government would use its power to end racial segregation in the South. Despite Governor Barnett's defiance, President Kennedy and his attorney general were able to force the state of Mississippi to comply with a federal court order, signaling that the South would be unable to block the subsequent wave of federal legislation designed to void the region's segregation laws.

James Tackach

Core Resources

Russell H. Barrett's *Integration at Ole Miss* (Chicago: Quadrangle Press, 1965) discusses Meredith's attempt to integrate the University of Mississippi. James H. Meredith's *Three Years in Mississippi* (Bloomington: Indiana University Press, 1966) is Meredith's own story of his years at Ole Miss. Arthur M. Schlesinger, Jr.'s *Robert Kennedy and His Times* (Boston: Houghton Mifflin, 1978) details Kennedy's involvement in the Meredith case. Sanford Wexler's *The Civil Rights Movement: An Eyewitness History* (New York: Facts on File, 1993) devotes a chapter to Meredith's integration of Ole Miss.

See also: *Brown v. Board of Education*; Civil Rights movement; Little Rock school desegregation; Montgomery bus boycott; Southern Christian Leadership Conference.

Oliphant v. Suquamish Indian Tribe

On March 6, 1978, the United States Supreme Court in the case of *Oliphant v. Suquamish Indian Tribe* decided that tribes do not have jurisdiction over non-Indians who commit crimes on reservations. In 1978, during a tribal celebration, two non-Indian residents of the Port Madison Reservation of the Suquamish Tribe (Washington) violated tribal laws. Mark Oliphant was arrested for assaulting tribal police officers and resisting arrest, and Dan Belgarde was arrested for hitting a tribal police car in a high-speed chase. The two argued the Suquamish tribe had no criminal jurisdiction over non-Indians, and they took their case to federal court.

The Supreme Court agreed with them and determined that non-Indians, even those residing on a reservation and charged with a crime, are not subject to the jurisdiction of tribal courts. This ruling dealt a major blow to tribal sovereignty and the authority of tribal courts because it determined that tribes lack the power to enforce laws against all who come within its borders. This ruling created serious and important law-and-order problems on reservations. Some tribes have approached the problem by cross-deputization with local and county police or by arranging for non-Indians on the reservation to submit voluntarily to tribal authority.

Carole A. Barrett

See also: Tribal courts; Tribal sovereignty.

One-drop rule

The one-drop rule is a definition of race that says that a person with any known amount of black ancestry is to be legally and socially classified as black. Although there is no "pure" race, some people believe otherwise and want to keep the dominant group racially "pure" and delegate all "impure" people to the subordinate or stigmatized group. The one-drop rule originated in the southern United States before the Civil War (1861-1865) but had not been rigidly conceptualized, and a few black-white mixed-race individuals (who physically appeared white) were accepted as white by the dominant white culture. White attitudes became more rigid at the time of the Civil War, and the one-drop rule became strictly enforced and largely accepted throughout the United States. In 1896, the United States Supreme Court (in *Plessy v. Ferguson*) approved the one-drop rule as a legal definition by defining it as "common knowledge." Although state laws against mixed-race marriages (miscegenation) were declared illegal by the Supreme Court in 1967, the one-drop rule still applies in some states. Socially, some whites support the rule to maintain "white racial purity," and some blacks support it to keep from losing members of their group to the dominant white group. The one-drop rule is unique to the United States.

Abraham D. Lavender

See also: Biracialism; Blackness and whiteness: legal definitions; Hypodescent; Hypogamy; Interracial and interethnic marriage; Miscegenation laws; Multiracial identity; Mulattoes; Passing; *Plessy v. Ferguson*; Race as a concept.

Operation Bootstrap

Operation Bootstrap was a program instituted by the Puerto Rican government in 1947 for the purpose of transforming the island of Puerto Rico—a U.S. territory lacking natural resources whose economy was based largely on the exportation of agricultural products—into a modern urban-industrial economy. This goal was to be accomplished by attracting industrial investment from the U.S. mainland. Incentives offered included freedom from island taxes, cash grants for operational costs, and assistance with site location. In addition, new companies would benefit from the island's federal income tax exemption, and exports to the mainland would be free of tariffs.

This program was part of a comprehensive plan not only to modernize industry but also to improve the health and education of the population, relieve unemployment, elevate living standards, and improve the island's infrastructure. The endeavor was initiated by the Popular Democratic Party (PPD), led by Senator (later Governor) Luis Muñoz Marín, which had gained legislative control of the island government in 1940. In 1942, the government established several industries that manufactured products previously imported. It was hoped that these enterprises would stimulate private-sector economic initiatives. In 1947, as a result of several factors (including limited available capital), these were sold to private island interests and the new policy, Operation Bootstrap, was instituted.

In 1950, legislation established the Economic Development Administration (EDA), known as FOMENTO. This agency established offices in major mainland cities, conducted research, and devised programs to attract new industry. By 1958, five hundred new factories had located on the island, adding tens of thousands of new jobs. From 1940 to 1955, island production increased 120 percent, averaging more than 6 percent annual growth. During this same period, per-capita income increased 300 percent. Accompanying these economic dividends were significant improvements in the life expectancy and literacy of the Puerto Rican population.

The establishment in Puerto Rico of facilities by more than five hundred mainland corporations contributed to the diffusion of U.S. Anglo culture throughout the island. The resulting familiarity with mainland culture and products, in combination with high island unemployment, a booming post-World War II economy on the continent, and inexpensive transportation, resulted in a massive migration from Puerto Rico to the mainland United States, primarily through New York City. The number of persons of island birth residing on the mainland increased from fewer than 70,000 in 1940 to more than 615,000 in 1960.   *Edward V. Mednick*

See also: Latinos in the United States; Puerto Rico.

Operation Wetback

A fact of life for the nation of Mexico is the existence of a highly prosperous colossus to the north, the United States. While there has long been a tendency for Mexican workers to seek to enter the more prosperous United States to work, the government of Mexico took a number of steps in the 1940's and 1950's to provide good jobs to keep workers at home. These steps included the building of irrigation projects and factories. Most of these projects were located in northern Mexico and had the effect of drawing a large number of workers to the border area. Jobs were not available for all who came, and many chose to make the short trip across the border into the United States to find work. The average annual income of workers in the United States was more than ten times that of Mexican workers—a strong enticement for Mexican laborers to emigrate to the United States, legally or illegally, temporarily or on a permanent basis.

Mexican laborers who crossed the border into the United States in the early twentieth century most often found seasonal agricultural jobs. Starting about 1930, however, the Great Depression meant that many now-unemployed U.S. workers were willing to do back-breaking work in the fields for low pay. Accordingly, job opportunities for Mexicans evaporated, and those who did not leave voluntarily often were deported. Then, in 1941, war raised levels of employment in the United States, and as U.S. farmworkers departed to enter the military or to work in war factories, Mexican workers again began to enter the U.S. to do agricultural work. Most of the jobs they found were in California, Arizona, and Texas.

The Bracero Program

The U.S. and Mexican governments worked together to start a formal system called the bracero program. The program involved recruitment of Mexican laborers, the signing of contracts, and the temporary entry of Mexicans into the United States to do farm work or other labor. The Mexican government favored the bracero program primarily because the use of contracts was expected to guarantee that Mexican citizens would be fairly treated and would receive certain minimum levels of pay and benefits. The U.S. government favored this formal system because it wanted to control the numbers of Mexicans coming into the United States and hoped the use of contracts would make it easier to ensure that the workers left when the seasonal work was completed. Labor unions in the United States supported the program because bracero workers could be recruited only after certification that no U.S. citizens were available to do the work.

The bracero program worked with some success from 1942 until its discontinuation in 1964. In some years, however, and in certain localities, the use of illegal, non-bracero workers from Mexico continued. Some U.S. employers found too much red tape in the process of securing bracero laborers, and they also noted that bracero wage levels were much higher than the wages that could be paid to illegal immigrants. Many Mexicans crossed the border illegally, because not nearly enough jobs were available through the bracero program. When the U.S. economy stumbled in 1953 and 1954, many U.S. citizens began to speak out against the

Although the bracero program started in 1941 welcomed Mexican agricultural workers such as these arriving by train in California, the U.S. government deported thousands of Mexicans in June and July, 1954, in a program called Operation Wetback.

presence of illegal aliens. They complained that illegal immigrants were a drain on U.S. charities and government programs. They also claimed that the immigrants took jobs at substandard wages that should go to U.S. citizens at higher wages.

When reporters first asked President Dwight D. Eisenhower and Attorney General Herbert Brownell if they intended to enforce vigorously the immigration laws, both men seemed uninterested in the issue. As popular agitation increased, however, the Eisenhower administration began to develop plans for Operation Wetback. The operation was designed to round up illegal aliens and deport them, while forcing large farming operations to use the limited and controlled bracero labor instead of uncontrolled and illegal alien labor. Operation Wetback was under the overall control of the Immigration and Naturalization Service (INS), directed by Joseph Swing, while day-to-day operations were supervised by an official of the Border Patrol, Harlon B. Carter.

Operation Wetback Begins

Operation Wetback took its name from a slang term first used in the southwestern United States to refer to Mexican immigrants who swam the Rio Grande or otherwise crossed into the U.S. illegally, seeking economic opportunities. The INS and its Border Patrol launched the operation in California on June 10, 1954, relying heavily on favorable press coverage to secure the support and cooperation of the general public. INS officials greatly exaggerated the number of agents they had in the field and the number of illegal aliens who had left or had been deported. Press coverage in California was generally quite favorable to Operation Wetback, praising the professional attitude of Border Patrol and INS agents. On the first day, more than a thousand persons were sent out of California on buses chartered by the INS. For several weeks, the number of daily deportations hovered around two thousand. The deportees were handed over to Mexican authorities at border towns like Nogales in Sonora, and the Mexican government sent them farther south by rail, hoping to prevent any quick reentry into the United States.

By July 15, the main phase of Operation Wetback in California was complete. On that day, Border Patrol agents began their work in Texas. There, they met stiff local opposition from powerful farm interests, who were quite content to hire illegal aliens and pay them only half the prevalent wage earned by U.S. or bracero workers. Agents met a hostile press as well, and in some cases had trouble securing a meal or lodging. Still, the operation resulted in the deportation by bus of tens of thousands of illegal workers from Texas. The INS conducted smaller phases of Operation Wetback in Arizona, Illinois, Missouri, Arkansas, Tennessee, and other states. Most of the illegals picked up nationwide were farmworkers, but some industrial workers were apprehended in cities from San Francisco to Chicago.

During the operation, some complaints were registered about the conduct of Border Patrol officers. The officers sometimes were characterized as harsh and hateful in their actions, and they were regularly accused of harassing U.S. citizens of Mexican ancestry. Some of these complaints seem to have been without foundation, particularly in Texas, where the powerful farm interests opposed the entire operation. On the other hand, there were a number of documented cases of U.S. citizens who had darker skin or Hispanic surnames being apprehended and deported to Mexico. Many of the aliens who were detained were kept in camps behind barbed wire pending their deportation. Some Mexicans and Mexican Americans spent several months hiding in terror, having quit their jobs to prevent their being apprehended at work. Deportees had to pay for their bus passage back to Mexico, to the dismay of human rights activists, who pointed out the unfairness of making someone pay for a trip he was being forced to take. The INS responded that the deportees should agree that paying for a bus trip back to Mexico was preferable to prosecution under the immigration laws and a possible jail sentence.

Stereotypes

Operation Wetback opened the door to stereotypes of Mexicans in the non-Hispanic community: Some press reports implied that the aliens were ignorant, disease-ridden union busters. As for the effectiveness of the operation in meeting its goals, nearly one hundred thousand illegal immigrants were returned to Mexico in the space of about three months. On the other hand, INS claims that more than one million illegal immigrants fled to Mexico on their own rather than face arrest were grossly exaggerated. Moreover, the boost to the bracero program given by Operation Wetback was only temporary; many employers returned to the use of illegal workers before the end of the 1950's. Operation Wetback, while effective in the short term, provided no long-term solutions to the needs of Mexican workers, U.S. employers, or those who clamored for a more restricted U.S. border. *Stephen Cresswell*

Core Resources

Juan Ramon García's *Operation Wetback: The Mass Deportation of Mexican Undocumented Workers in 1954* (Westport, Conn.: Greenwood Press, 1978) thoroughly reviews the background, the deportation program, and the aftermath. Carrol Norquest's *Rio Grande Wetbacks: Migrant Mexican Workers* (Albuquerque: University of New Mexico Press, 1971) discusses Operation Wetback in the larger context of Mexico-United States immigration issues. The U.S. Immigration and Naturalization Service's *Annual Report of the Immigration and Naturalization Service* (Washington, D.C.: Government Printing Office, 1954 and 1955) gives the U.S. government's official explanation of the events known as Operation Wetback.

See also: Bracero program; Illegal aliens; Immigration and emigration; Mexican deportations.

Oppositional culture

Oppositional culture refers to a system of beliefs and practices that challenge the dominant way of life. Also referred to as "cultures of resistance," these systems counter hegemonic and dominating ways of life experienced by subjugated groups. They often include aspects of a traditional culture that have been devalued or partially destroyed. Thus, they serve to enhance the survival of social groupings under the conditions of colonialism, enslavement, and other forms of racial/ethnic oppression. In their study of racial and ethnic groups in the United States ("America's Non-European Cultures: The Myth of the Melting Pot," in *The Inclusive University: Multicultural Perspective in Higher Education*, 1995), sociologists Bonnie Mitchell and Joe Feagin found oppositional culture to be a powerful survival tool for groups blocked from formal avenues of power and influence. They found that these practices temper the negative effects of sociocultural dominance, reaffirm a sense of peoplehood, and distinguish the practicing group from the dominant culture. The development of an oppositional culture can be an important strategy for survival and contestation for subordinated racial/ethnic groups. *M. Bahati Kuumba*

See also: Discrimination: responses to; Resistance, cultures of; Subordinate group.

Oppression mentality

Jews are one of the oldest ethnic groups in the world, tracing their history back to Abraham and Sarah about eighteen centuries before the beginning of the Christian era. Jewish identity involves national, religious, and genetic aspects. A long and diverse history of oppression has accompanied Jewish history. As a people whose small nation was conquered by larger nations and who for much of their history were forced to live in other countries far from their Middle Eastern homeland, Jews have frequently suffered from religious or genetic ("racial") oppression. Jews have struggled to maintain their dis-

tinctive identity within larger societies that were different both culturally and religiously. Often, the dominant group reacted with hostility and even persecution.

In Christian countries especially, Jews have been oppressed not only because of their distinctiveness but also because of the Christian teaching that held Jews responsible for the death of Jesus and the Christian belief that Christianity is the only true religion. Major examples of oppression of Jews in Christian countries include the Crusades in the early Middle Ages, the Spanish Inquisition in the 1400's, the pogroms in Eastern Europe in the few centuries leading up to the twentieth century, and the Holocaust in Nazi Germany in the 1930's and 1940's, in which six million Jews (almost 40 percent of the world's Jewish population at the time) were killed. Islamic countries also have oppressed Jews, although usually not nearly as severely as Christian countries. Some communist countries have oppressed Jews because of the Jewish refusal to give up religious identity. Opposition to contemporary Israel by Arab countries basically has been based on disputes over land, but frequently anti-Semitic stereotypes have been used against Israel. This history of oppression has led to a belief by some Jews that their existence is precarious, and that oppression is eventually to be expected everywhere.

In the United States, Jews frequently suffered from restrictive quotas in college admissions and discrimination in housing, jobs, and other areas until shortly after World War II, when conditions slowly began to improve. Shock at the magnitude of the Holocaust somewhat modified negative attitudes toward Jews. Moreover, the increasing ethnic diversity of the United States has made Jews stand out less as a minority group. U.S. Jews thus face a dilemma. They live in a society where anti-Semitism is widespread but persecution is not.

Nevertheless, the Holocaust, the treatment of Jews in the former Soviet Union, the rise of neo-Nazism in Germany, and other events point out the continuing threat to Jews. Regardless of the reasons for the conflicts between Jews and Arabs, one major reason for American Jews' strong support for Israel is the belief that there must be one safe place in case there is renewed major oppression in the future.

Some American Jews, especially those who are acculturated or assimilated, emphasize the advances Jews have made and deny any possibility of oppression. Other American Jews emphasize the history of oppression, current world events, and fear of history repeating itself. They are labeled paranoid by the acculturated, while they label the acculturated as deniers or naïve. Most American Jews fall between these two extremes. *Abraham D. Lavender*

See also: Anti-Semitism; Holocaust; Jewish stereotypes.

Options for ethnic identity

The United States is not a static society in which ethnic identities remain the same. Some ethnic groups and some people within certain ethnic groups have opted for new ethnic classifications. Some people receive new ethnic labels regardless of whether they want them. There are two reason for this relabeling. First, the United States and similar pluralistic countries such as Canada have increased their populations by accepting immigrants from a vast variety of cultures and nations. As these immigrants succeeded financially, politically, and socially in the receiving country, their cultures were changed or they attempted to change their group or personal cultures. Cultural change meant ethnic identity changes. Second, the mythology regarding the characteristics of a stereotypical American persuaded many immigrants to opt for cultural characteristics that reflected this myth. The myth was largely formed about English-oriented cultural traits or what is colloquially called Anglo culture. Immigrants have perceived that there are advantages to being as American or Anglo as culturally possible. This is called the Anglo-conformity model, which means that people and groups are subtly encouraged to accept these characteristics if they want economic, social, and political success. Two groups from two different racial identifications are examples of these options for ethnic identity.

The massive immigrations of Irish to the United States in the nineteenth century resulted in discrimination against them. However, the Irish had several advantages: They were needed for manual labor; they were Catholic but had a strong sense of separation of church and state; and they formed influential institutions, such as political organizations, that helped make them social powers in the larger society. They were also white. Increasingly, the Irish in the United States married non-Irish, so that by the 1960's, more than half of Irish American men married women from other ethnic groups. By the 1990's, it was difficult for census workers to determine who could be categorized as Irish because so many Irish Americans considered themselves to be fully American and to have the same cultural characteristics as English Americans. They had risen socioeconomically from what had been termed "shanty Irish," to "lace-curtain Irish" seeking social acceptance, to Americans whose original characteristics had been superseded by conforming to Anglo models. They had opted for a differing ethnic identity.

A second example of ethnic options is taken by many Afro-Caribbean immigrants to the United States. Those from English-speaking nations often conform culturally to the American myth of the United States being a land of unusual opportunity if one is educated properly and willing to work diligently. These immigrants may per-

ceive African Americans as rejecting this opportunity and may attempt to distance themselves from black Americans and not want to be perceived as being similar to them. They may even reject the idea of race, claiming that national ethnic characteristics are a person's identity rather than physical traits associated with race. Black Caribbean immigrants interpret this distance to be an advantage to them: They do not always choose to associate with the oppressed history of African Americans, their culture, or their racial self-identification. Instead, they opt to identify as Jamaican Americans or Bahamian Americans or others who share English or Anglo values, and who expect to succeed in the receiving country without being racially stereotyped. Afro-Caribbeans have often achieved a higher social status than African Americans with educational levels and family income levels surpassing those of African Americans in many cities. By distinguishing their ethnicities from the African American ethnicity, they may negotiate better social statuses in a white-dominated society.

William Osborne and Max Orezzoli

See also: Afro-Caribbeans; Anglo-conformity; Biracialism; Censuses, U.S.; Ethnicity and ethnic groups; Euro-American; Irish Americans; Jamaican Americans; Multiracial identity; Multiracial movement; Race vs. ethnicity.

Orangeburg massacre

On Thursday night, February 8, 1968, three African Americans (two male college students and the teenage son of a college employee) were killed by police gunfire on the campus of almost entirely black South Carolina State College in Orangeburg. Twenty-seven other students were injured. Nearly all were shot in the back or side as they attempted to flee an unannounced fusillade of police gunfire. One police officer had been seriously injured by an object thrown at the police, but despite uncorrected false reports in the media, the students were unarmed. African American students had started protesting three nights earlier because the only bowling alley in Orangeburg continued to exclude African Americans despite pleas from local white and black leaders and students.

The Orangeburg massacre was the first incident of U.S. college students being killed by police because of protesting, but the killings received almost no national attention, largely because many white Americans had developed negative attitudes toward black protesters following a series of urban riots in 1967. Twenty-seven months later, the killing of four white students at Kent State University in Ohio during a Vietnam War protest received international publicity. Jack Bass and Jack Nelson's *The Orangeburg Massacre* (1970, revised 1984) is a detailed study of the massacre. A campus monument memorializes Henry Smith, Samuel Hammond, Jr., and Delano Middleton, whose lives were taken "in pursuit of human justice." *Abraham D. Lavender*

See also: Civil Rights movement; Segregation.

Orderly Departure Program

In reaction to the massive flood of boat people leaving Vietnam in the late 1970's, the international community, led by the United Nations High Commissioner for Refugees, established the Orderly Departure Program (ODP) in 1979 to discourage the irregular and dangerous flight of Vietnamese refugees. The United States was one of the first countries to accept Vietnamese for resettlement under this program, which gave preference to those seeking reunification with spouses, children, parents, and siblings already residing in the United States. Those with close ties to the U.S. military or who were former employees of the U.S. government were also accepted for resettlement under the ODP. Many other countries joined the ODP program in subsequent years.

In 1984, the United States extended the ODP qualifications to include Amerasian children (most of whom had Vietnamese mothers and American fathers) and to political prisoners and reeducation camp victims and their families—classes of people who experienced considerable discrimination in Vietnam. Amerasian children faced special hardships because of their mixed racial background. During the 1980's and early 1990's, tens of thousands of Vietnamese availed themselves of the ODP to secure resettlement in the United States and in many other countries, including Canada, Australia, and France. *Robert F. Gorman*

See also: Amerasian Homecoming Act of 1987; Vietnamese Americans; Vietnamese Canadians.

Orientalism

According to Edward Said's 1978 study, Orientalism is a Eurocentric perspective that reflects the domination of the West (the Occident) over the East (the Orient) from the early expansion of capitalism and imperialism to the present. It is a racist construction of Eastern societies as stagnant, militaristic, irrational, and despotic in contrast to Western societies as progressive, civil, rational, and individualistic. By extension, this approach also portrays the peoples of Asia as intrinsically inferior to Europeans. Hence, Orientalism is an ideology that justifies the op-

pression and colonization of Asians in Asia and North America.

Increasingly, Orientalism also refers to an overgeneralized and stereotypical way of thinking about all Asian Americans as physically and culturally identical. This style of thought or misconception is very common among white Americans as well as other non-Asians. Chinese and Vietnamese Americans are often mistaken for Japanese Americans, who may in turn be mistaken for Korean Americans. Non-Asian Americans, because of what they perceive as Asian Americans' indistinguishable non-European appearance, frequently view Asian Americans as "foreigners" regardless of their nativity, generation, nationality, and citizenship status. The misconceived Asian cultural homogeneity breeds cultural insensitivity. Furthermore, the misconception of Asian similitude from time to time results in anti-Asian violence based on "mistaken identities." In 1982, Chinese American Vincent Chin was "mistaken" for a Japanese and murdered; in 1989, Chinese American Ming Hai Loo was murdered by people who thought he was Vietnamese. *Philip Q. Yang*

See also: Asian American stereotypes; Asian Americans; Chin, Vincent, murder; Ethnocentrism; Eurocentrism; Loo, Ming Hai, murder.

"Other" theory

The "other" theory has been advanced by sociologists and cultural critics of racial and ethnic relations, including Winthrop Jordan. In this theory, the "other" represents the totality of difference, the race that is apart from the self and therefore can be exoticized, appropriated, and dominated. Because white people have historically been the dominant group socially, politically, and economically in North America, the other refers to nonwhite people. "Otherness" is a psychological and social construct that assumes various forms. The three most typical expressions of the other theory are seen in fashion, sexual imagining, and projected images of aggression.

On the level of fashion and style, white identification with the other is represented by what scholar Cornel West calls "the Afro-Americanization of white youth": young men who sport dreadlocks, baggy jeans, and backward baseball caps. For young women, the markers of this identification include corn-rowed hair and big gold earrings, though these markers are less distinct in the popular imagination.

Fashion is a benign form of "otherizing," or fetishizing, and may or may not lead to a more sexual imagining of the other, referred to by cultural critic bell hooks as "eating the other." In this instance, the salient experience in the confrontation with the other is the desire for sexual pleasure and domination. Difference is seductive not only because of historical myths about the more primitive, sensual, and sexually uninhibited nature of black people but also because, as some scholars describe it, "the other is coded as having the capacity to be more alive, as holding the secret that will allow those who venture and dare to break with the[incapacity for happiness] and experience sensual and spiritual renewal" (bell hooks, *Black Looks*, Boston: South End Press, 1992). Once otherness and whiteness converge, physically and spiritually, in the white imagination, the abhorrent history of subjugation and exploitation of dark others by white people is magically obviated. Whites can not only experience the other, they can become the other.

In the midst of this racial transcendence, how does the creation of the other in the white imagination lead to racism and racial violence? Encounters with the other invite both a vicarious engagement with primitive desires and a further psychological distancing between the white person and the dark other. When an individual from the dominant group believes that an individual from a minority group is so different from himself or herself that the minority group member's humanity is unrecognizable (a central justification for slavery was that Africans were not human), then fantasies have free rein. For while the other is perceived as having liberating, primitive qualities, the repugnant side of racial mythmaking, fed by images in popular culture of the black male "thug," is the notion of the dark other as more aggressive and violent. Historically, the dominant group has responded to the perceived threat of violence with swift, preemptive violence.   *Chalis Holton*

See also: African American stereotypes; Black "brute" and "buck" stereotypes; Racism: history of the concept.

Out-group

An out-group is a group to which a person does not belong. People differentiate between the groups to which they belong (in-groups) and the groups to which they do not belong (out-groups). Out-group membership can be based on ethnicity, gender, geographic location, class, team membership, or any other feature that people use to differentiate themselves from others.

Out-group categorization affects how people are perceived. For example, people categorized as out-group members are more likely to be viewed according to unfavorable stereotypes. Out-group members also are seen as very similar to one another, a phenomenon called out-group homogeneity. Many people have an in-group bias and more readily perceive negative behaviors in out-group members than in-group members. In-group members often exaggerate differences between themselves and the out-group on traits that the in-group members regard as superior. People in Eastern (collectivist) societies tend to differentiate between in-groups and out-groups more than people in Western (individualistic) societies. One way to reduce prejudice toward out-group members is to recategorize them as in-group members.   *Lyn M. Van Swol*

See also: Ethnocentrism; "Other" theory; Social perception of others; Stereotype.

Ozawa v. United States

Significance: In *Ozawa v. United States*, the U.S. Supreme Court on November 13, 1922, ruled that Japanese aliens did not qualify as "white" and therefore could not be naturalized as citizens.

In the early twentieth century, naturalization was under the effective control of local and state authorities. In California and other Pacific states, fears of the "yellow peril" or "silent invasion" of Asian immigrants were deeply entrenched and politically exploited. In such states, citizenship had been repeatedly denied to both Chinese and more recent Japanese settlers, although there were some rare exceptions. The prevailing belief among the nativist majority was that such settlers should be ineligible for U.S. citizenship.

Background
Partly to test the Alien Land Act—a California law passed in 1913 that barred non-citizens from owning land in that state—Takao Ozawa sought U.S. citizenship in defiance of a 1906 law (U.S. Revised Statute, section 2169) that limited naturalization to "free white persons," "aliens of African nativity," and "persons of African descent." Although born in Japan, Ozawa had been educated in the United States. He was graduated from high school in Berkeley and for three years attended the University of California. He was aware that some Issei (first-generation Japanese immigrants) had been naturalized, even in California. Specifically, Ozawa may have known of Iwao Yoshikawa, the first Japanese immigrant to be naturalized in California. Yoshikawa had arrived in San Francisco from Japan in 1887. A law clerk in his homeland, he had studied U.S. law in his adopted country and served as a court translator. In 1889 he began the naturalization process, which, presumably, was completed

five years later, although there is no extant record of his naturalization. His case was publicized because it broached such issues as mandatory citizenship renunciation and the legality of dual citizenship.

Regardless of Ozawa's knowledge of Yoshikawa, on October 16, 1914, Ozawa applied for U.S. citizenship before the district court for the Territory of Hawaii. He argued that he had resided in the United States and its territory of Hawaii for a total of twenty years, had adopted the culture and language of his host country, had reared his children as Americans in heart and mind, and was, by character and education, wholly qualified for naturalization.

The district court ruled against Ozawa on the grounds that his Japanese ethnicity denied him access to naturalization. Ozawa then took his case to the Ninth Circuit Court of Appeals, which passed it to the U.S. Supreme Court for instruction. In turn, the Supreme Court upheld the laws that in effect declared Ozawa ineligible for citizenship.

Rather than question the justice of the racial restrictions on naturalization, the opinion limited its focus to clarifying the meaning of the term "white persons" and distinguishing between "Caucasian" and "white person," determining that the latter, while a more inclusive term than the former, is not so inclusive as to include persons of Asian extraction. It concluded that "a person of the Japanese race is not a free white person, within the meaning of U.S. Rev. Stat. § 2169[the 1906 law], limiting the provisions of the title on naturalization to aliens being free white persons, and to aliens of African nativity, and to persons of African descent, and therefore such Japanese is not eligible to naturalization as a United States citizen. . . ."

In tracing the history of the naturalization laws, the Court attempted to demonstrate that all statutes preceding the 1906 act contested by Ozawa had the same intent: the selective admission to citizenship based on the interpretation of "white," not as a racial appellation but as a reflection of character. It argued that the words "free white persons" did not indicate persons of a particular race or origin, but rather that they describe "personalities" and "persons fit for citizenship and of the kind admitted to citizenship by the policy of the United States." According to that doctrine, any non-African alien, if desired by Congress, might be deemed "white." Thus, the Court reasoned, "when the long-looked-for Martian immigrants reach this part of the earth, and in due course a man from Mars applies to be naturalized, he may be recognized as white within the meaning of the act of Congress, and admitted to citizenship, although he may not be a Caucasian."

Regardless of this race disclaimer, however, the Court, in reasoning through its arguments, distinguished be-

tween "whites" (all Europeans, for example) and "non-whites" (such as the Chinese) on ethnic grounds pure and simple. The decision throughout sanctioned racial biases that assumed that an individual's character was in some way delimited by his or her racial heritage. For example, at one point it provided a formulaic approach to determining citizenship eligibility for persons of mixed blood, supporting the idea, widely observed, that in order to be construed as white, a person must be "of more than half white blood." Clearly, the decision upheld the seriously flawed assumption that character and racial heritage were inextricably interrelated.

Nativist Sentiment
The Supreme Court's ruling reflected the prevailing nativist bias against Asian immigrants, an attitude that was reflected in both law and policy through the first half of the twentieth century. In fact, no more formidable barriers to citizenship were erected than those facing the Issei (first-generation Japanese), Chinese, and other Asian immigrants. In 1924, an isolationist Congress enacted an immigration act placing numerical restrictions on immigrants allowed into the United States based on national origin. One provision of the Immigration Act of 1924, known as the Johnson Act, excluded immigrants ineligible for naturalization. Its obvious aim—to bar entry of Japanese aliens—quickly led to a deterioration in the diplomatic relations between Japan and the United States.

The plight of Japanese already in the United States also worsened in the anti-Asian climate. In separate rulings, the Supreme Court went so far as to revoke citizenship that had been granted to some Issei. In 1925, it even denied that service in the armed forces made Issei eligible for naturalization, overturning a policy that had previously been in effect. Not only were Issei barred from naturalization; in many states, "alien land laws" prohibited them from owning land and even entering some professions.

That codified prejudice partly accounts for but does not justify the terrible treatment of Japanese Americans during World War II, when 112,000 of them, including 70,000 Nisei (persons of Japanese descent born in the United States), were rounded up and incarcerated in detention centers that bore some grim similarities to the concentration camps of Europe. It was not until the passage of the Immigration and Nationality Act of 1952 that the long-standing racial barriers to naturalization finally came down.   *John W. Fiero*

Core Resources
Thomas J. Curran's *Xenophobia and Immigration, 1820-1930* (Boston: Twayne, 1975) traces the origins of anti-immigrant movements in America, relating the xeno-

phobic tradition to the exclusionist laws and practices of the inclusive period. Bill Hosokawa's *Nisei: The Quiet Americans* (New York: William Morrow, 1969) is a good general study of Japanese Americans and their struggle against legal and social discrimination. David J. O'Brien and Stephen Fugita's *The Japanese American Experience* (Bloomington: Indiana University Press, 1991) is a scholarly study with focus on the legal and social problems confronting Japanese Americans before World War II and their rapid acculturation in its wake. Ronald Takaki's *Strangers from a Different Shore: A History of Asian Americans* (Boston: Little, Brown, 1989) is an excellent and sensitive overview of Asian American history, with extensive notes and photographs.

See also: Alien land laws; Gentlemen's Agreement; Immigration Act of 1917; Immigration Act of 1924; Japanese American Citizens League; Japanese American internment; Nativism; Xenophobia, nativism, and eugenics; Yellow peril campaign.

P

Page law

Significance: The Page law, designed to prohibit Chinese contract workers and prostitutes from entering the United States, eventually excluded Asian women in general.

On February 10, 1875, California congressman Horace F. Page introduced federal legislation designed to prohibit the immigration of Asian female prostitutes into the United States. Officially titled "An Act Supplementary to the Acts in Relation to Immigration," the Page law evolved into a restriction against vast numbers of Chinese immigrants into the country regardless of whether they were prostitutes. Any person convicted of importing Chinese prostitutes was subject to a maximum prison term of five years and a fine of not more than five thousand dollars. An amendment to the law prohibited individuals from engaging in the "coolie trade," or the importation of Chinese contract laborers. Punishment for this type of violation, however, was much less severe and was much more difficult to effect, given the large numbers of Asian male immigrants at the time. As a consequence of this division of penalties, the law was applied in a most gender-specific manner, effectively deterring the immigration of Asian females into the United States. Within seven years following the implementation of the law, the average number of Chinese female immigrants dropped to one-third of its previous level.

Enforcement and Implementation

An elaborate bureaucratic network established to carry out the Page law's gender-specific exclusions was a catalyst for the decline in Chinese immigration rates. American consulate officials supported by American, Chinese, and British commercial, political, and medical services made up the law's implementation structure. Through intelligence gathering, interrogation, and physical examinations of applicants, the consulate hierarchy ferreted out undesirable applicants for emigration and those suspected of engaging in illegal human trafficking.

This investigative activity evolved well beyond the original intent of the law's authors. Any characteristic or activity that could be linked, even in the most remote sense, to prostitution became grounds for denial to emigrate. Most applications to emigrate came from women from the lower economic strata of society; low economic status therefore became a reason for immigration exclusion. The procedure was a complicated one. Many roadblocks were placed in the way of prospective immigrants. Acquiring permission to emigrate took much time and effort. Passing stringent physical examinations performed by biased health care officials was often impossible. Navigating language barriers through official interviews aimed at evaluating personal character often produced an atmosphere of rigid interrogation, bringing subsequent denial of the right to emigrate. Such a complex system aimed at uncovering fraudulent immigrants placed a hardship upon those wishing to leave China.

Because Hong Kong was the main point of departure for Chinese emigrating to the United States, all required examinations were performed there with a hierarchy of American consulate officials determining immigrant eligibility. In a sense, the Page law actually expanded consulate authority beyond any previous level.

Corruption Charges

Such increased power of the consular general in implementing the law provided an opportunity for possible abuses of power. In 1878, the U.S. consul general in Hong Kong, John Mosby, accused his predecessors of corruption and bribery. According to Mosby, David Bailey and H. Sheldon Loring were guilty of embezzlement. Both men were accused of setting up such an intricate system to process immigration application that bribery soon became the natural way to obtain the necessary permission to do so. Mosby went on to charge that Bailey had amassed thousands of dollars of extra income by regularly charging additional examination fees regardless of whether an exam was performed. Mosby also accused Bailey of falsifying test results and encouraging medical personnel to interrogate applicants in order to deny immigration permission to otherwise legal immigrants.

Most of the allegations of corruption surrounded the fact that monies allotted by the federal government for

One effect of the 1875 Page law was the creation of a largely male Chinese American population. This street scene in San Francisco's Chinatown demonstrates this imbalance.

implementation of the Page law were far below the amount Bailey required to run his administration of it. Given this scenario, the U.S. government scrutinized Bailey's conduct. No indictments came from the official investigation, however, and Bailey, who had previously been promoted to vice consul general in Shanghai, remained in that position. Further examination of Bailey's tenure in Hong Kong has suggested that, if anything, he was an overly aggressive official who made emigration of Chinese women to the United States a priority issue of his tenure there rather than an opportunity for profit.

Bailey was replaced in Hong Kong by H. Sheldon Loring. Unlike his predecessor, Loring did not enforce the Page law with as much vigor, allowing a slight yet insignificant increase in the annual numbers of Chinese immigrants. Nevertheless, Loring did enforce the law in an efficient manner, publicly suggesting that any ship owner who engaged in the illegal transport of women would be dealt with to the fullest extent of the law. Even so, Loring was accused of sharing Bailey's enthusiasm for

the unofficial expensive design of the immigration procedure. During Loring's tenure, questions about his character began to surface mostly on account of his past relationships with individuals who engaged in questionable business practices in Asia. By the time that Mosby replaced him, such questions had become more than a nuisance. The new U.S. consul to Hong Kong began to describe his predecessor as a dishonest taker of bribes. Once again, the official dynamics of such charges brought forth an official inquiry from Washington. Like the previous investigation of Bailey, however, this investigation produced no official indictment against Loring. The only blemish concerned an additional fee that Loring had instituted for the procuring of an official landing certificate. As there was precedent for such a fee, Loring, like his predecessor, was exonerated of all charges.

Having decided that his predecessors were indeed corrupt, yet unable to prove it, Mosby pursued enforcement of the Page law with relentless occupation. Keeping a posture that was above accusations of corruption, Mosby personally interviewed each applicant for emigration, oversaw the activities between the consulate and the health examiners, and eliminated the additional charges for the landing permits. In the end, the numbers of Chinese immigrants remained similar to those of Loring and below those of Bailey, with the numbers of Chinese female immigrants continuing to decline. Aside from being free from charges of corruption, Mosby's tenure in office was as authoritative as those of his predecessors.

Regardless of the personalities of the consulate officials in charge of implementing the Page law, the results were the same: The number of Chinese who emigrated to the United States decreased dramatically between the 1875 enactment of the law and the enactment of its successor, the Chinese Exclusion Act of 1882. Furthermore, the law's specific application to Chinese women ensured a large imbalance between numbers of male and female immigrants during the period under consideration. In the long run that imbalance negatively affected Asian American families who had settled in the United States. The barriers that the Page law helped to erect against female Chinese immigrants made a strong nuclear family structure within the Asian American community an immigrant dream rather than a reality.

Thomas J. Edward Walker and Cynthia Gwynne Yaudes

Core Resources

Lucie Cheng and Edna Bonacich's *Labor Immigration Under Capitalism* (Berkeley: University of California Press, 1984) examines the development and intent of political movements among immigrants in the United States before World War II. Philip Foner and Daniel Rosenberg's *Racism, Dissent, and Asian Americans from 1850 to the Present* (Westport, Conn.: Greenwood Press, 1993) traces the political and social segregation of immigrants. George Anthony Peffer's "Forbidden Families: Emigration Experience of Chinese Women Under the Page Law, 1875-1882" (*Journal of American Ethnic History* 6, Fall, 1986) shows the relationship between the Page law and engendered immigration of Chinese during the first seven years of its existence.

See also: Chinese American Citizens Alliance; Chinese Exclusion Act; Chinese Six Companies; Immigration and emigration; Yellow peril campaign.

Pan-Africanism

A broad movement aimed at the political unification of Africa through the destruction of European colonialism, Pan-Africanism includes the political independence and freedom of all peoples of African descent who live in the West Indies, the Americas, and other concentrated areas. Pan-African Congresses provide the forum at which movement members can disseminate ideas. The first Congress was held in London during the summer of 1990. W. E. B. Du Bois, credited as the father of the concept, and George Padmore, a West Indian intellectual, were both prolific advocates and key theoreticians of the Pan-African ideology.

Early post-colonial nation-states' leaders—Kwame Nkrumah (Ghana), Eric Williams (Trinidad/Tobago), Norman Manley (Jamaica), Gamal Abdel Nasser (Egypt), Jomo Kenyatta (Kenya)—were significantly influenced by Pan-Africanist philosophy and espoused and utilized its concepts in forming their own organizations to advance the liberation of peoples of African descent. Marcus Garvey's Back-to-Africa social movement in the 1920's was the largest and best approximation of this movement in the United States. Finally, this movement can also be regarded as the theoretical precursor to the black nationalism movement that swept the United States in the 1960's. *Aubrey W. Bonnett*

See also: Black nationalism; Black Power movement; Universal Negro Improvement Association.

Panethnicity

Panethnicity (or macroethnicity) refers to inclusive group identities formed through the merger of smaller national, regional, or tribal groups. For example, the Hispanic or Latino American panethnicity encompasses such ethnicities as Puerto Rican, Mexican American, and Cuban American. Some major panethnic groups are Hispanic Americans, Euro-Americans, Jewish Americans, Asian Americans, Native Americans, Arab Americans, West Indians, and African Americans (if the term is applied to all peoples of the African diaspora).

For individuals, panethnic affiliations represent one choice among multiple layers of ethnic identity. Depending on the context, a person could present himself or herself as, for example, Afro-American, West Indian, or Jamaican—the more specific identities being especially meaningful within the panethnic group. As a social phenomenon, panethnicity reflects the social construction and variable nature of ethnic identities. Although early discussions of panethnicity emphasized the importance of cultural similarity, recent works have focused upon the role of structural forces. In *Asian-American Panethnicity: Bridging Institutions and Identities* (1992), Yen Le Espiritu observed that the creation of panethnic groups involves both the active building of political coalitions among smaller groups and the imposition of labels by external groups, such as racial categories employed by the U.S. government. Consequently, panethnic identities are constantly undergoing change.

Ashley W. Doane, Jr.

See also: Biracialism; Censuses, U.S.; Ethnicity and ethnic groups; Multiracial identity; Multiracial movement; Options for ethnic identity; Self-identification among Asian Americans; Self-identification among Latinos.

Pan-Indianism

> **Significance:** American Indians have long attempted to balance tribal loyalties and affiliations with the possibilities and benefits afforded by intertribal unity; during the latter half of the twentieth century, pan-Indianism became a hotly contested issue.

Since the 1960's American Indians have become increasingly politicized and reform-minded. This mobilization has occurred along three lines: tribal, pantribal, and pan-Indian. Tribal activity focuses on organizations or actions by and for members of a specific tribe. This type of movement usually concentrates on the protection or expansion of a single tribe's rights or opportunities. Pantribalism occurs when two or more tribal entities unite in pursuit of a mutually beneficial goal. The Council of Energy Resource Tribes (CERT) is an example of such activity. Tribal and pantribal mobilizations are distinct from the pan-Indian movement, which promotes the universality of the Indian experience and emphasizes ethnic identification rather than tribal affiliations. According to Vine Deloria, Jr., a nationally recognized authority on Indian rights, in his work *The Nations Within: The Past and Future of American Indian Sovereignty* (1984), "the tribes are concerned with the substance of Indian life while the ethnics [pan-Indianists] look to the process."

Historical Background

The pan-Indian movement had its inception during the opening decades of the nineteenth century. The first definable pan-Indian action occurred during the War of

This poster urges people to support the American Indian Movement, an organization working for the common good of all American Indians.

1812 at the instigation of the Shawnee chief Tecumseh and his brother, a revivalist religious leader named Tenskwatawa (the Shawnee Prophet). Urging the various tribes at the frontier to put aside their differences and to oppose the encroachment of the U.S. government, Tecumseh proclaimed in 1810, "The only way to stop the evil is for the red men to unite in claiming a common and equal right in the land, as it was at first and should be now—for it was never divided but belonged to all." The pan-Indian activity during the remainder of the nineteenth century focused on a combination of strategies and objectives guided largely by religious inspiration. The most notable of these mobilizations remains the Ghost Dance revivals of the Great Plains fostered by the Paiute spiritual leader Wovoka.

At the beginning of the twentieth century, this movement acquired different direction and form. The focal point shifted from religious revival toward political and civil equity and more formal organization. In 1912, for example, a group of Indians drawn together by common experience founded the Society of American Indians. This group continues its commitment to collective action and its promotion of a variety of pan-Indian and pantribal activities. One such organization was the National Congress of American Indians, founded in 1944 by the Indian employees of the Bureau of Indian Affairs. Its primary purpose remains the lobbying for American Indian causes and rights.

Developments Since World War II

During the last half of the twentieth century, distinctions between pantribal and pan-Indian mobilizations became more pronounced. Government programs and policies aimed at termination of tribal status gave the movements greater impetus. The general atmosphere of protest and reform during the 1960's and early 1970's radicalized the behavior of Indian reformers. An early indicator of the growing schism and changes in tactics was the founding of the National Indian Youth Council in 1961. Frustrated by the "poetic" responses of the older, more established pan-Indian organizations, a group of younger, more radical leaders led by Clyde Warrior, a Ponca, and Mel Thom, a Paiute, formed a new organization. They urged their audiences to come to grips with the continued paternalism of the federal government and its failure to correct dire social and economic conditions confronting Indians everywhere. Their cause, according to Thom, was "a Greater Indian America." This action also foreshadowed the development of the Red Power mobilizations of the 1970's and the constituency within which they would find their base. This movement attracted the interest of urban Indians whose identification was ethnic rather than tribal in nature.

Among the most important and visible organizations of the next generation of organizations was the American Indian Movement (AIM), founded in 1968 in Minneapolis by Dennis Banks, George Mitchell, and Clyde Bellecourt of the Chippewa (Ojibwa), and Russell Means, a Sioux. This group advocated a much broader range of tactics to accomplish their purpose. In addition to legal recourse, they employed protest demonstrations, sit-ins and occupations, and occasional violence to promote their causes. Two of the most memorable of these activities were the occupation of Alcatraz Island in 1969 and the violent stand-off at Wounded Knee in 1973. The founding of the International Indian Treaty Council and the Women of All Red Nations represents institutional outgrowths of the AIM mobilization.

During the 1970's and into the 1980's, this movement has also discovered some limitations, especially with regard to goal setting and continued competition with traditional tribal organizations. The strongest supporters of the pan-Indian mobilization remain urban Indians whose tribal affiliations have eroded. In large and often hostile cities, Indians of various tribes find it easier to identify with one another than with the larger communities that surround them. They acknowledge a common ethnic origin and welcome partnerships across tribal lines. This tendency places them at odds with many tribalists who are more traditional in their approach and perceive this blending as a dilution of their identities. Pan-Indianists have also realized that defining themselves, their ideals, and their objectives in the abstract is much simpler than developing specific plans of action. All but the broadest of their objectives involve groups too specific to be truly considered pan-Indian in nature.

Martha I. Pallante

Core Resources

Pan-Indianism is variously explored in Russel Lawrence Barsh and James Youngblood Henderson's *The Road: Indian Tribes and Political Liberty* (Berkeley: University of California Press, 1980); Vine Deloria, Jr., and Clifford M. Lytle's *The Nations Within: The Past and Future of American Indian Sovereignty* (New York: Pantheon Books, 1984); Hazel W. Hertzberg's *The Search for an American Indian Identity: Modern Pan-Indian Movements* (Syracuse, N.Y.: Syracuse University Press, 1971); and Sharon O'Brien's *American Indian Tribal Governments* (Norman: University of Oklahoma Press, 1989).

See also: American Indian activism; American Indian Movement; Ghost Dance religion; National Congress of American Indians; National Indian Youth Council; Society of American Indians; Tecumseh's Rebellion; Women of All Red Nations; Wounded Knee occupation.

Pasadena City Board of Education v. Spangler

In 1968, several students and their parents filed suit against the Pasadena Unified School District in California, alleging that the district's schools were segregated as a result of official action on the part of the district. In 1970, the federal district court found for these plaintiffs, concluding that the district had engaged in segregation and ordering the district to adopt a plan to cure the racial imbalances in its schools. The federal court's order provided that no school was to have a majority of minority students. The district thereafter presented the court with a plan to eliminate segregation in the Pasadena schools; the court approved the plan, and the district subsequently implemented it.

Approximately four years later, the Pasadena Unified School District asked the district court to modify its original order and eliminate the requirement that no school have a majority of minority students. The district contended that though it had abandoned its racially segregative practices, changing racial demographics had created new racial imbalances in the district's schools. The federal district court refused to modify its original order, however, and the Ninth Circuit Court of Appeals upheld the district court's ruling.

Reviewing this decision, Justice William H. Rehnquist, joined by five other justices, concluded that the district court had abused its authority in refusing to remove the requirement that no district school have a majority of minority students. According to the Court, there had been no showing that changes in the racial mix of the Pasadena schools had been caused by the school district's policies. Since the school district had implemented a racially neutral attendance policy, the federal district court was not entitled to require a continual reshuffling of attendance zones to maintain an optimal racial mix. Justices Thurgood Marshall and William Brennan dissented from this holding, emphasizing the breadth of discretion normally allotted to federal district courts to remedy school segregation once a constitutional violation had been shown.

The majority's decision signaled that the broad discretion with which the Court previously had seemed to have invested federal district courts was not without limits. It had been widely thought that once officially sanctioned or de jure segregation had been shown, a federal court had great latitude in eliminating not only such de jure segregation but also de facto segregation— that is, segregation not necessarily tied to official conduct. The majority's decision in this case, however, signified otherwise.

Timothy L. Hall

See also: *Brown v. Board of Education*; Segregation: de facto and de jure; *Swann v. Charlotte-Mecklenburg Board of Education*.

Passing

Passing is the concealment of one's racial identity or ethnicity to gain access to another racial or ethnic group, usually to obtain social and economic benefits. Passing has been used by African Americans, Asian Americans, and Hispanic Americans as a means of transcending racial stigmatization and marginalization, especially during the period of segregation. Most commonly, individuals of biracial or multiracial descent who had certain characteristics associated with whiteness broke from their minority heritage and lived within the dominant white community. These characteristics included a light skin tone, "European" facial features, and a high level of acculturation to white society. Because the differences in skin tone and facial features are typically less dramatic, Asian Americans and Hispanic Americans generally had an easier time passing for white than did African Americans. Asian Americans and Hispanic Americans who wished to pass as white and have the necessary physical characteristics might only have had to anglicize their names or adopt white surnames. African Americans unable to pass as white often passed as Asian Americans or Native Americans to achieve a slightly higher status in society.

Passing could be temporary or permanent. It was a largely urban phenomenon, since individuals in rural areas were more likely to be recognized and hence were less able to escape their racial identities. The most common form of passing involved a temporary leave from one's racial identity, possibly to enter a white establishment or to hold a job; cases of individuals who permanently left their racial identities to assume lives within white society were probably less common.

There were drawbacks associated with both temporary and permanent acts of passing. For example, those who passed temporarily in order to hold jobs were faced with the constant pressure of operating in two different and antagonistic worlds while keeping their two identities separate. Those who chose to pass for white permanently were generally forced to leave behind their families and friends, and they lived with the constant fear that someone might learn their secret. Because of the secretive nature of the phenomenon, it is impossible to assess with any accuracy the number of individuals who have engaged in passing. It is also difficult to know whether passing has actually decreased in the era of desegregation, though the greater access that racial minorities have to all realms of society has probably removed the immediate impetus behind the act of passing.

The concept of passing is based on ideas of racial purity and the drawing of rigid racial boundaries by which individuals of biracial or multiracial descent are considered part of the minority group. An example of this is the "one-drop rule," which stipulated that any individual with even one drop of black blood was black. The idea of passing thus has meaning only within a society that defines race as mutually exclusive categories. Two important works that deal with the issue of passing are Paul R. Spickard's *Mixed Blood: Intermarriage and Ethnic Identity in Twentieth-Century America* (1989) and Maria P. P. Root's *Racially Mixed People in America* (1992).

Erica Childs

See also: Blackness and whiteness: legal definitions; Miscegenation laws; One-drop rule.

Patriarchal system

"Patriarchy" is defined as institutionalized power relationships that give men power over women. Motherhood, according to feminist poet Adrienne Rich, is also a social institution. In American society, motherhood is characterized by its isolation; it is difficult, tedious, and often frustrating work. The experience of motherhood is a mixture of satisfaction and pleasure plus anger, frustration, and bitterness; it is also a role exclusively reserved for women.

Patriarchal systems, in which men dominate the social institutions of society by creating, developing, and managing those institutions, are maintained when women are designated as the primary child rearers. By ensuring that the weight of the responsibility for child rearing falls on women's shoulders, men win for themselves the right of "paternal neglect" (throwing themselves into their work, which ensures their primary role as economic provider). When women carry the primary responsibility for child rearing, their opportunities for professional success are necessarily limited, and as a result their economic dependence on their husbands is maintained. Alternative arrangements for rearing children and for balancing work and family commitments are not pressing concerns for men; the structural relegation of women to domestic service suits men's interests very well. Simply put, women's responsibility for children in the context of the nuclear family is an important buttress for a male-dominated society. It helps keep women out of the running for economic and political power.

Rochelle L. Dalla

See also: Discrimination: direct institutionalized; Ethnic identities of women; Women and racism; Women of color.

Peltier killings

On June 26, 1975, two agents of the Federal Bureau of Investigation (FBI) were killed in a shootout on the Lakota Indian Reservation in Pine Ridge, South Dakota. Leonard Peltier, a member of the American Indian Movement (AIM), was found guilty of the killings. Peltier declared himself innocent. Peltier appealed his conviction many times. During the appeals, the court found that the government had acted improperly in arresting and trying him. Federal authorities admitted to falsifying affidavits used to extradite Peltier from Canada. Witnesses in the original trial had been coerced, and evidence supporting Peltier's claims was suppressed. In spite of these irregularities, the courts refused to overturn Peltier's conviction. Peltier's case became known throughout the world. Many people believed that, even if he were guilty, he had not been granted a fair trial. Amnesty International declared him a political prisoner, and important religious leaders spoke out on his behalf. A book and three films were made about the case. In 1992, a "Mr. X" confessed to the killings. Peltier's supporters continued to hope that they could win him a new trial.   *Cynthia A. Bily*

See also: American Indian activism; American Indian Movement; Pine Ridge shootout.

Pennsylvania Society for the Abolition of Slavery

> **Significance:** The Pennsylvania Society for the Abolition of Slavery was the first antislavery society in America.

On April 14, 1775, a group of men gathered at the Sun Tavern on Second Street in Philadelphia to establish the first antislavery society in America. After electing John Baldwin their president and adopting a constitution, they named their organization the Society for the Relief of Free Negroes Unlawfully Held in Bondage. Sixteen of the twenty-four founders were members of the Society of Friends, or Quakers. The creation of this antislavery society was instigated when Philadelphia Quakers Israel Pemberton and Thomas Harrison aided Native American Dinah Neville and her children, who were being detained in Philadelphia pending their shipment to the West Indies to be sold as slaves.

Harrison was fined in a Philadelphia court for giving protection to the Neville family. When this incident gained notoriety, members of the Quaker Philadelphia

Meeting mobilized to form the antislavery society. At its first meeting, the antislavery society enlisted legal counsel to help the Nevilles and five other victims illegally held in bondage and to form a standing committee to investigate any conditions of slavery in the Philadelphia area.

The Revolutionary War interrupted regular meetings until 1784. At this time, Quaker abolitionist Anthony Benezet revived the antislavery society as members learned that two African Americans had committed suicide rather than be illegally enslaved. Benezet increased the membership to forty, including Benjamin Franklin, James Pemberton, and Dr. Benjamin Rush. The society renamed itself the Pennsylvania Society for Promoting the Abolition of Slavery, for the Relief of Free Negroes Unlawfully Held in Bondage, and for Improving the Condition of the African Race. Since the majority of the members were Friends, the group developed directly from Quaker religious beliefs and within the Quaker social structure. To explore the founding of the Pennsylvania Society for the Abolition of Slavery, it is critical to trace events and movements within the Society of Friends in seventeenth century colonial Pennsylvania.

Quaker Beginnings
One of the basic principles espoused by Quaker founder George Fox was that all people are created equal. On a visit to the colonies in 1671, Fox spoke at Friends' meetings and encouraged Quaker slaveholders to free their slaves after a specified period of service. In 1676, Quaker William Edmundson, an associate of Fox, published the first antislavery literature in Rhode Island. While Quakers were formulating an antislavery position early in their movement, German Mennonites migrating to America had vowed that they would not own slaves. Several members of the Mennonite community and Dutch Pietists adopted Quakerism and became members of the Friends' Germantown Meeting. These German Quakers, their minister Pastorius, and other Friends of the Germantown Meeting delivered a petition to the Philadelphia Meeting in 1688 demanding that slavery and the slave trade be abolished. The protest addressed to slave owners of the Philadelphia Monthly Meeting challenged these Friends to explain why they had slaves and how such a practice could exist in a colony founded on the principles of liberty and equality.

Representing the radical leadership of Philadelphia Friends, George Keith published a tract entitled *An Exhortation and Caution to Friends Concerning Buying or Keeping of Negroes.* He gave several directives: that Friends should not purchase African slaves except for the express purpose of setting them free, that those already purchased should be set free after a time of reason-

This drawing from an antislavery publication shows a slave being flogged. Antislavery societies such as the Pennsylvania Society for the Abolition of Slavery created and distributed publications demonstrating the horrors of slavery.

able service, and that, while in service, slaves should be given a Christian education and taught how to read.

During the early eighteenth century, the conservative, wealthy membership of the Philadelphia Meeting took a somewhat confusing position on slavery. Their inconsistent policies included a separate meeting for African Americans, a request that Quakers in the West Indies stop shipping slaves to Philadelphia, and disciplinary measures for members of the meeting who were engaged in antislavery activity. Many prominent Quakers, such as James Logan, Jonathan Dickinson, and Isaac Norris, continued to purchase and own slaves.

The customary procedure of resolving issues at Friends' meetings was to achieve a consensus. Thus, the Quaker drift toward an antislavery sentiment gained momentum with the efforts of a few radicals but achieved success only when the majority bowed to the principles of Quaker conscience.

Unpopular radical member Benjamin Lay was unwelcome at the Philadelphia Meeting because of his unorthodox promotion of the antislavery cause. For example, Lay once had kidnapped a Quaker youth in order to illustrate the tragedy of abduction of African children for the slave trade. In 1738, at the Philadelphia Yearly Meeting, he wore a military uniform to emphasize the connection between slavery and war and concealed un-

der his cloak an animal bladder that he had filled with red juice. Delivering an inflamed speech on the evils of slavery, he concluded by saying that slavery took the very lifeblood out of the slave, simultaneously piercing the bladder and splashing the horrified audience with simulated blood.

By the 1730's, the effects of the antislavery movement were evident among Quakers as more Friends provided for the manumission of their slaves in their wills. In addition, the increased immigration of Germans in need of work eliminated the demand for slave labor in the Middle Colonies.

John Woolman

Much of the credit for the success of the antislavery movement among Quakers must be given to New Jersey Quaker John Woolman. Known for his gentle, persuasive approach as a Quaker minister, he began a series of visitations to Quaker slaveholders in New England, the Middle Colonies, and the South in 1743. In 1754, he published *Some Considerations on the Keeping of Negroes*, which proclaimed the evils of slavery and the absolute necessity for Friends to free their slaves. Meetings throughout the colonies and England effectively used his visitations to pressure Quakers to free their slaves. By 1774, Quaker meetings in England, New England, and

Pennsylvania had adopted sanctions to disown any member for buying slaves or for serving as executor of an estate that included slaves. It also required slaveholders to treat their slaves humanely and to emancipate them as soon as possible.

Some have argued that Quakers were willing to emancipate their slaves because slavery was not profitable in Pennsylvania in the absence of labor-intensive agriculture. Others claim that Quaker sensitivity to antislavery was aroused not by their own religious ideals but rather by eighteenth century Enlightenment philosophy, which held that liberty is a natural human right. These may be considered arguments; nevertheless, it was the Quakers who first championed the antislavery cause and who organized the first antislavery group in America.

Spread of the Antislavery Movement

The Pennsylvania Society for the Abolition of Slavery served as a model for other antislavery groups. As early as 1794, other states that had formed antislavery societies were asked to send representatives to Philadelphia for annual meetings. As new associations were formed, Friends constituted a majority of the membership. Statesmen such as Franklin, Rush, Alexander Hamilton, John Jay, and Thomas Paine believed that the institution of slavery contradicted the ideals of the Declaration of Independence and joined in support of the Friends' antislavery campaign. *Emily Teipe*

Core Resources

David Brion Davis's *The Problem of Slavery in the Age of Revolution, 1770-1823* (Ithaca, N.Y.: Cornell University Press, 1975) is an exhaustive study of the slave question immediately before the American Revolution and in the succeeding federal period, which includes the pioneering efforts of the Quakers. *The Quaker Origins of Antislavery* (Norwood, Pa.: Norwood Editions, 1980), edited by J. William Frost, is a history of the Quaker antislavery cause that includes a comprehensive collection of Quaker documents. Sydney V. James's *A People Among Peoples: Quaker Benevolence in Eighteenth Century America* (Cambridge, Mass.: Harvard University Press, 1963) discusses antislavery as an outreach of Quaker religious piety, along with the Quakers' other efforts for the good of the social order. Gary B. Nash's *Quakers and Politics: Pennsylvania 1681-1726* (Princeton, N.J.: Princeton University Press, 1968) places the antislavery cause within the larger framework of troubled politics in colonial Pennsylvania. Jean R. Soderlund's *Quakers and Slavery: A Divided Spirit* (Princeton, N.J.: Princeton University Press, 1985) is a study of the Philadelphia Yearly Meeting and its progression to an antislavery philosophy.

See also: Abolition; Free African Society.

People of color

This term refers to nonwhite, non-Anglo ethnic minorities who historically have been the victims of discrimination by the dominant majority group. The concept is inclusive of all people whose skin color or other physical features are not commonly perceived as white. The term specifically includes African Americans, Asian Americans, American Indians, and Mexican Americans and other Hispanics such as Puerto Ricans and Central and South Americans (even though many Hispanics self-identify as "white"). The term "people of color" is neither politically loaded nor derogatory; in fact, it is both neutral and respectful in referring to the combination of these ethnic and racial groups.

The term is often broken down to "men of color" and "women of color" to refer to groups of men or women, respectively, who are from the ethnic and racial groups noted above. The experiences of both of these groups, although they overlap with the experiences of the general population, are different in several important ways from those of whites as well as from each other. Women of color, for example, often experience the discriminatory consequences of both ethnicity and gender. *Celestino Fernández*

See also: Ethnicity and ethnic groups; Minority and majority groups; Race as a concept; Women of color.

People v. George Hall

In *People v. George Hall* (1854), the California Supreme Court ruled that a Chinese person could not testify against a white person in a California court. The court overturned the murder conviction of a white man by invalidating the testimony of Chinese witnesses for the prosecution based on a state law prohibiting "black or mulatto person(s), or Indian(s)" from giving testimony against whites in court. Writing for the majority, Chief Justice Hugh C. Murray argued that the term "Indian" was meant to include Asians, whom he characterized as a genetically inferior people largely "incapable of progress" and unfit to participate in determining the fate of white Californians. *People v. George Hall* provides a striking example of how white supremacist philosophy dominated the political and social structures of the antebellum United States. In addition, the case demonstrates the pervasiveness of anti-Asian sentiments in the nineteenth century American West and illustrates how state officials in California legalized the classification of Asian Americans as second-class citizens during the nineteenth and early twentieth centuries. The California Supreme Court upheld the *Hall* decision eighteen years later in *People v.*

McGuire (1872), but legislation that overturned state laws restricting the legal testimony of Chinese Americans took effect in January, 1873, nullifying court decisions upholding the restrictive statutes.   *Michael H. Burchett*

See also: Asian American stereotypes; Chinese Americans; Criminal justice system; *Roldan v. Los Angeles County.*

Peyote religion

> **Significance:** Since the late nineteenth century, peyote has played a central part in an American Indian religious movement; peyote is viewed as a spiritual teacher, and its use forms a part of a long, complex ceremony.

To the American Indians who practice peyotism, peyote is considered a spiritual being. This is a concept which defies accurate definition in Western terms. Indians describe peyote iconically and refer to it as "medicine"; it is used as a sacrament. The ritualistic use of peyote in a religious setting to communicate with and be instructed by "spirit" is accepted as a way to "return to the source."

Peyote itself comes from a type of cactus with the scientific name *Lophophora williamsii*, a small, spineless cactus with a rounded top. The parts of the cactus that contain peyote are referred to as "buttons." A peyote button contains more than fifty alkaloids, one of which, mescaline, induces a state of consciousness that its users liken to a healing or religious experience.

Peyote Religion
The religion, often called peyotism or the Peyote Cult, is at the center of a pan-Indian movement. The religion has doctrine, an ethical code, unique rituals, and origin legends. Fire, water, the medicine, the eagle, and a drum are the central symbols. Precise rituals involve long, extensive prayer meetings and require knowledge of many songs with repetitive, chanted musical bridges. The peyote religion, referred to formally as the Native American Church of North America (NAC), is pan-Indian, both geographically and tribally. It appeared suddenly after 1880 and spread rapidly.

The origin of the peyote religion as practiced in North America is unknown. James Slotkin (*The Peyote Religion*, 1956) describes twenty-nine different traditions of origin. The ritual of the modern Native American Church is very different from the pre-Columbian and Mexican Indian use of peyote. Peyote reveals itself to the Indian people as a transformer which is integratable and renewing. After 1880, tribal religious traditions, devastated by the relentless encroachments of European Americans,

opened to the inevitability of profound change. The church origin legends reflect the devastation suffered by the old ways and depict the need for transformation in the Indian psyche.

Origin legends and doctrinal formulations are of secondary importance to Indians, who are more concerned with original religious experiences. If there is doctrine, it can be said that God put humankind on Earth for a purpose, and it is up to humans to learn that purpose directly from God on "the peyote road," the mediation of peyote, prayer, and focus or awareness. People should then fulfill that purpose via a moderate lifestyle, outlined by Slotkin as "care of one's health and welfare, care of family, brotherhood, self-reliance, and by belief in the power of peyote to 'teach one how to live.' "

Church Ritual
Church members describe their religion and ritual as uniquely Indian. Some standards seem to have developed, leading to various forms referred to as Kiowa-Apache, Southern Plains, and Oklahoma Fireplace. A number of elements, however, are consistent at every meeting since James Mooney's description of a peyote ceremony in 1892. At all the fireplaces the door opens east, and the roadman, or church leader, sits opposite the door. The meeting (as the church services are called) opens with the placing of the Chief Peyote on the altar and closes with the Chief's removal. The most common form for the altar is a crescent or "half moon" shape. There are five officers, or roadcrew, who have various formal functions in the ceremony: roadman, drummer, cedarman, fireman, and dawn woman. Each one at some point during the meeting will offer a "prayer smoke"—each will roll tobacco in a corn husk and pray with this smoke communicant.

All movement during the meeting is clockwise. The drum is a water drum made from a six-quart metal pot into which are placed water and four coals from the fire. The vessel is then covered with a hide, usually deerskin, and tied with a long rope which wraps around seven stones pocketed in the hide so that the rope makes a seven-pointed star, seen as the morning star, around the bottom of the vessel. The fireman, aside from keeping a ritually constructed fire going through the night, maintains a poker or burning stick from which all "prayer smokes" are lit. Other ritual paraphernalia invariably found at meetings are a bone whistle, gourd rattles, a beaded staff, sage, feather fans, and corn husks and tobacco used in making the hand-rolled prayer smokes. There are always four stages to each meeting: opening, midnight, morning, and closing ceremonies. Particular songs are sung in conjunction with these stages no matter which tribe or fireplace is holding the ceremony, because these particular songs were given through the origin story. Four foods—meat, berries, corn, and water—are also always a part of the ceremony.

Some details of the four stages vary with each roadman. The reason is that peyote teaches a roadman his way; this is a mark of the church's and the religion's vitality. These variations come from prayer, searching, and the medicine. A roadman's ceremony is called his Fireplace.

Meetings usually last a minimum of twelve hours, and the roadman is in control of all of it and aware of the psychological state of every member of the meeting throughout. The ceremony often has aspects of a long, soul-searching journey through the night for each of the participants. It is understood to be a prayer meeting from beginning to end. Church members come to a sacred area, concentrate on its transcendental center or source, and sit with their peers in community to receive healing and instruction. *Glenn J. Schiffman*

Core Resources

Peyote's religious uses are discussed in Weston LaBarre's *The Peyote Cult* (1938; reprint, Hamden, Conn.: Shoestring Press, 1964); John H. Laney's *On the Symbolism of the Native American Church of North America* (Zurich, Switzerland: C. G. Jung Institute, 1970); Ruth Shonle's "Peyote, the Giver of Visions" (*American Anthropologist* 40, 1932), and James Slotkin's *The Peyote Religion* (Glencoe, Ill.: Free Press, 1956).

See also: Native American Church; Pan-Indianism.

Philadelphia riots

> **Significance:** From May 6 to July 5, 1844, during a period of rising immigration and intercultural friction, nativists rioted against Irish Catholic workers.

Rapid population growth, industrialization, and cultural conflict characterized urban America in the 1840's and helped produce bloody anti-Irish riots in Philadelphia's industrial suburbs of Kensington and Southwark in the summer of 1844. Already the second largest U.S. city in 1840, Philadelphia grew by more than one-third in the 1840's, from twenty-five thousand people to thirty-six thousand. Irish immigrants, hard-pressed by the Great Famine that had decimated the potato crops in their homeland, stimulated this growth and made up 10 percent of Philadelphia's population in 1844. Prior to commuter railroads and automobiles, most people lived near their workplaces and cities were densely populated. Low-income newcomers such as the Irish resided in cheap, substandard housing and symbolized the ill effects of disorderly urban growth to longtime Philadelphians.

Nativist Sentiment

Lacking in job skills and capital, Irish immigrants filled the bottom rungs in the emerging industrial order's occupational ladder. As its population grew, Philadelphia expanded its involvement in large-scale manufacturing. By 1840, half of Philadelphia's sixteen thousand working adults labored in manufacturing, and 89 percent of the workers in Kensington toiled in industrial trades. American-born whites predominated in such well-paying craft occupations as ship carpenter and ironmaker, leaving low-paying jobs requiring less skill, such as weaving, for Irish newcomers. Perceiving immigrants and African Americans as competitors, many white American workers used violence to drive them from trades and neighborhoods.

In the 1830's, Philadelphia, like other major cities, hosted a strong working-class trade union and political movement. At its height, the General Trades Union (GTU) of Philadelphia City and County included more than ten thousand workers representing more than fifty different trades. Collective action in an 1835 general strike for a ten-hour day succeeded in winning shorter hours and wage hikes in numerous workplaces. GTU activists voted against conservative Whigs opposed to strikes and Catholic immigrants. The Panic of 1837 weakened the GTU and undermined the solidarity of its culturally and occupationally diverse constituency.

In the 1840's, native-born Protestant skilled workers fought for a dwindling supply of jobs and received little help from the financially weakened GTU. Evangelical Protestants from all social classes joined moral reform campaigns for temperance and strict observance of the Sabbath. Temperance and Sabbatarianism symbolized American-born white workers' efforts to survive hard times through personal discipline. Workers made up the majority of temperance societies in industrial suburbs such as Kensington and Southwark. Moral reforms often attacked immigrant cultural institutions, such as the Roman Catholic church and Sunday tavern visits. Economic contraction and moral reform eroded the GTU's bonds of working-class solidarity, which might have prevented ethnic conflict in 1844.

The American Republican Party, dedicated to eliminating the influence of Catholic immigrants in public life, best exploited the anxieties of native-born workers. The party flourished briefly in eastern cities in the mid-1840's, drawing support from American-born workers and middle-class professionals such as Philadelphia's Lewis Levin, a struggling lawyer and aspiring politician from South Carolina. In the spring of 1844, American Republicans campaigned against Catholic voters' attempts to protect their children from Protestant instruction in the public schools. Protestant-dominated Philadelphia schools used the King James version of the Bible as a classroom textbook. Objecting that the King James version was not authoritative, Catholics preferred the Douay Bible, which included annotations written by the Vatican. Philadelphia's Catholic bishop, Francis Kenrick, wanted public schools to allow Catholic students to bring their Bibles to class or be exempted from Protestant religious instruction. American Republicans accused Philadelphia Catholics of plotting to remove the Bible from the schools entirely and to have priests take over classrooms.

In April, 1844, American Republicans staged rallies across the city to whip up support for their nativist program. Violence between the Irish and nativists broke out when nativists gathered near Irish neighborhoods. American Republicans scheduled a mass meeting for May 6 in Kensington's third ward, a neighborhood composed mainly of Irish weavers. On May 6, rain drove hundreds of nativists who traveled to the third ward rally to seek cover at the Nanny Goat Market, a covered lot of market stalls. Approximately thirty Irish waited at the market, and one yelled, "Keep the damned natives out of the market house; it don't belong to them. This ground is ours!" Samuel Kramer, editor of the pro-American Republican *Native American* newspaper (named for Anglo-American nativists, not American Indians), tried to finish his speech against the Catholic proposals for the Douay Bible, but Irish hecklers drowned him out. A shoving match escalated into fistfights and gunfire as nativists and Irish battled for control of the market house. Police arrived at dusk and temporarily restored order. Four men died, three of them nativists, and many more were wounded in the fighting.

The next day, nativists massed in Kensington for revenge. The *Native American* ran the headline: "Let Every Man Come Prepared to Defend Himself!" A parade of nativists marched through Kensington under a U.S. flag and a banner declaring, "This is the flag that was trampled underfoot by Irish Papists." Nativist mobs rampaged through Kensington for two more days, burning homes and invading two Catholic churches, where rioters defaced religious objects and looted valuables. Although Sheriff Morton McMichael tried to calm public disorder, police were too few in number to stop the violence. Needing reinforcements, McMichael called on General George Cadwalader, commander of the First Brigade of Pennsylvania state militia, stationed in Philadelphia. On May 10, state troops brought peace to the city and kept it under martial law for a week.

Tension prevailed in June, amid criticism of city officials and militia commanders for failing to prevent violence. American Republicans still had public support,

and Catholics worried about more violence. Catholics feared that nativists would use July 4 patriotic celebrations as a pretext to riot. Parishioners at St. Philip's Church in Southwark, just south of Philadelphia, hoarded weapons inside the church in order to defend it. Hearing of the arms cache, on July 5, Levin led thousands of nativists, including volunteer militia with cannons, to St. Philip's to demand the weapons. Stung by earlier criticism, Cadwalader's militia promptly seized the church and ordered nativists away. When the mob refused to move, Cadwalader opened fire and a pitched battle involving cannon and rifle fire ensued for a day and a half. The militia, helped by city police, prevailed in fighting that left two rioters dead and dozens of state troops and civilians wounded.

Consequences
The American Republican Party campaigned on the riots by attacking reigning politicians as the allies of Irish Catholics and making martyrs of the nativists killed in the riots. In October, Levin and another American Republican won election to the U.S. House of Representatives, and nativists captured several county offices, mostly on the strength of votes from working-class Kensington and Southwark. The American Republicans faded in the late 1840's, but nativists returned in the 1850's under the aegis of the American, or Know-Nothing, Party.

The riots forced Irish Philadelphians to band together as an ethnic group. The most prominent Irish opponent of the mobs was Hugh Clark, a master weaver and ward politician worth more than thirty thousand dollars in 1850. Clark had stridently opposed striking Irish journeymen weavers prior to 1844. Master weavers, some of them Irishmen like Clark, cut journeymen's wages in the wake of the Kensington riot, confident that few non-Irish workers would protest the cuts. Bishop Kenrick urged conciliation and softened his public position on the Bible controversy. American Republican anger at police and militia actions temporarily stalled police reform, but in the 1850's, Philadelphia and other cities established professional police departments to prevent more riots like those of 1844.   *Frank Towers*

Core Resources
The Philadelphia riots are discussed in Susan G. Davis's *Parades and Power: Street Theatre in Nineteenth-Century Philadelphia* (Philadelphia: Temple University Press, 1986); Michael Feldberg's *The Philadelphia Riots of 1844: A Study of Ethnic Conflict* (Westport, Conn.: Greenwood Press, 1975); Dale T. Knobel's *Paddy and the Republic: Ethnicity and Nationality in Antebellum America* (Middletown, Conn.: Wesleyan University Press, 1986); Vincent P. Lannie and Bernard C. Diethorn's "For the Honor and

Glory of God: The Philadelphia Bible Riots of 1844" (*History of Education Quarterly* 8, Spring, 1968); Bruce Laurie's *Working People of Philadelphia, 1800-1850* (Philadelphia: Temple University Press, 1980); David Montgomery's "The Shuttle and the Cross: Weavers and Artisans in the Kensington Riots of 1844" (*Journal of Social History* 5, Summer, 1972); and Sam Bass Warner, Jr.'s *The Private City: Philadelphia in Three Periods of Its Growth* (Philadelphia: University of Pennsylvania Press, 1968).

See also: Anti-Catholicism; Immigration and emigration; Irish Americans; Irish Catholic "race"; Race riots of 1866.

Philippine insurrection

> **Significance:** In the Philippine insurrection of February 4, 1899-July 4, 1902, U.S. and Filipino forces, which had worked together to end Spanish control of the Philippines, found themselves fighting as enemies in a long, brutal struggle for domination of the Philippine Islands.

United States involvement in the Philippines began during the Spanish-American War of 1898. U.S. naval strategists already had a plan for attacking the Spanish fleet at Manila Bay in the event of war with Spain. As relations between the United States and Spain worsened in 1897, Commodore George Dewey, commander of the United States Navy's Asiatic Squadron, was ordered to move his fleet to Hong Kong, with instructions to attack Manila Bay in case of war. War was declared on April 24, 1898. On the morning of May 1, Dewey's fleet steamed into Manila Bay. By noon, his ships had sunk or disabled every Spanish ship.

Washington was slow to react to the victorious news. The quick defeat of the Spanish fleet was unexpected, and President William McKinley had not planned what to do with the Philippines once the war was ended. McKinley considered either taking the entire archipelago, establishing a naval base, or returning the islands to Spain. Complete independence for the islands was never seriously considered. While McKinley contemplated the fate of the Philippines, relations between the U.S. military occupation force at Manila Bay and the Filipino population deteriorated. At first, the Filipinos welcomed Dewey's forces as liberators. The Filipinos soon realized that the Americans intended to control the islands at least until the end of the war, perhaps longer. In early May, McKinley dispatched an expeditionary force, under the command of General Arthur MacArthur, to Manila

Bay. MacArthur arrived just in time to accept the Spanish garrison's surrender at the end of the war, an honor Filipino forces had assumed would be theirs.

Filipino Insurgency
Filipino insurgents had been fighting the Spanish since early 1896. Spanish efforts to destroy the infant revolution had failed; rebel leaders fled to the jungled hills of the islands to hide out and organize bases for guerrilla warfare against the Spanish. In 1897, both sides, weary of the increasingly bloody war, agreed to a cease-fire to discuss peace. The Spanish authorities refused to consider independence, forcing the Filipino insurgents to continue their rebellion. Under the military leadership of Emilio Aguinaldo and the intellectual direction of Apolinario Mabini, rebel leaders established a base of operations at Hong Kong, where they could easily purchase supplies and arms. It was at this time that the Spanish-American War began, bringing an unexpected opportunity for the rebels.

Filipino leaders first believed that the United States would assist them in expelling the Spanish and establishing an independent Philippine state. Aguinaldo accepted anticolonial statements by U.S. consular officers at face value. The Filipinos soon found, however, that Dewey was more cautious, speaking only of military cooperation to defeat Spain and saying nothing of independence. Aguinaldo organized an army of thirty thousand men and won notable victories; nevertheless, the United States held supreme authority, accepting the surrender of Manila Bay and refusing to allow Filipino forces into the city without permission. When the Spanish flag came down, the Stars and Stripes, not the Filipino revolutionary flag, replaced it.

Faced with the realization that the United States was going to annex the islands, Aguinaldo moved to organize a new government. On June 12, 1898, he proclaimed independence for the Philippines. In September, a constituent assembly was convened, and on November 29, a constitution was adopted. The United States largely ignored this move toward independence. The McKinley administration, mainly because of racial prejudice, arbitrarily decided that the Filipinos were not ready for self-government. In addition, there was a fear that an independent Philippines might fall easy prey to an ambitious European power, such as Germany or Great Britain. Therefore, the United States proceeded to obtain full control by a provision for annexation of the Philippines in the peace treaty ending the war with Spain.

Armed Conflict
While the United States Senate debated ratification of the peace treaty, a series of clashes between U.S. and

Filipino forces beginning on February 4, 1899, soon escalated into large-scale fighting. The Philippine insurrection against U.S. rule had begun. The United States, because of its decision to assume responsibility for "civilizing" the Filipinos, was forced to wage a bitter war, which would cost much more money and take many more human lives than the war with Spain.

The Philippine insurrection was, in many ways, a prototype of modern guerrilla warfare. Filipino revolutionary leaders quickly lost the support of conservative Filipinos who accepted U.S. rule. As a result, Aguinaldo and his forces retreated to fight the U.S. troops in the jungles, as they had done earlier against Spanish forces. In early 1899, United States forces moved into central Luzon, where they captured and burned Malolos, the rebel capital. Rebel forces, however, escaped into the hills, where they were supplied by sympathetic villagers until spring rains forced U.S. troops to withdraw.

U.S. commanders finally admitted that Aguinaldo had extensive popular support and that total war was necessary to pacify the islands. Washington responded by sending reinforcements, bringing the number of U.S. troops in the Philippines to seventy-four thousand. As the scale of the fighting rose, vicious tactics and brutality on both sides also increased. Both sides committed atrocities involving soldiers and civilians. U.S. forces systematically burned villages and took hostages in an effort to deny popular assistance to rebel forces. Gradually, the overwhelming strength of the United States

prevailed, as U.S. forces took rebel strongholds in the hills and rural regions. By 1901, 639 U.S. garrisons dotted the islands, breaking Filipino resistance.

The insurrection finally collapsed with Aguinaldo's capture in March, 1901. He was seized by Colonel Frederick Funston and three other U.S. officers pretending to be the prisoners of a group of Filipino defectors, who led the officers directly to Aguinaldo's headquarters in northeastern Luzon. After his capture, Aguinaldo reluctantly took an oath of allegiance to the United States. By July 4, 1901, civil government, under United States auspices, was instituted everywhere in the Philippines, except in southern Mindanao and the Sulu Islands, where Moro tribesmen continued resistance.

On July 4, 1902, the Philippine insurrection was formally declared over. The United States issued a proclamation of general peace and amnesty. As a result of the struggle, the United States suffered forty-two hundred dead and twenty-eight hundred wounded. While close to twenty thousand rebels were killed in the war, another two hundred thousand Filipinos died from disease, famine, and other war-related causes.

William Howard Taft served as the first U.S. governor of the Philippines. Taft continued to be heavily involved in the administration of the islands as secretary of war and president of the United States. It was Taft who coined the phrase "little brown brothers," which referred to his hope that the United States could somehow "Americanize" these native peoples. This phrase remained a strong racial force in U.S. relations with the states in the Pacific and Latin America. The Philippine Islands remained under U.S. jurisdiction until 1934, when Congress passed the Tydings-McDuffie Act, granting independence to the Philippines. World War II delayed complete independence for the islands until 1946.

Theodore A. Wilson, updated by William Allison

U.S. troops guard captured Filipino revolutionaries in the Philippines around 1899. The Filipino rebels lost their bid for independence, and the Philippines did not become independent until 1946.

Core Resources

H. W. Brands's *Bound to Empire: The United States and the Philippines* (New York: Oxford University Press, 1992) emphasizes the interaction of cultural forces in United States-Philippine relations and traces the development of the Philippine independence movement. Stanley Karnov's *In Our Image: America's Empire in the Philippines* (New York: Random House, 1989) argues that the United States was inept and ineffective in dealing with the Philippine Insurrection and its aftermath. Stuart Creighton Miller's *Benevolent Assimilation: The American Conquest of the Philippines, 1899-1903* (New Haven, Conn.: Yale University Press, 1982) is a study of the war in the Philippines and its consequences, including the atrocities committed by the U.S. Army. Bonifacio S. Salamanca's *The Filipino Reaction to American Rule, 1901-1913* (Quezon City, Philippines: New Day Publishers, 1984) is a Filipino historian's harsh criticism of U.S. policy in the Philippines during the insurrection and the following years.

See also: Filipino Americans; Filipino Veterans' movement; Platt Amendment; Tydings-McDuffie Act.

Pine Ridge shootout

In 1973, members and supporters of the American Indian Movement (AIM) occupied the town of Wounded Knee, South Dakota, on the Pine Ridge Reservation. The activists were demonstrating against what they considered to be autocratic and sometimes corrupt practices of the Oglala Sioux tribal political leaders, especially Richard Wilson, the tribal chairman. Wilson, an aggressive opponent of AIM, along with local Bureau of Indian Affairs (BIA) officials, requested federal support in removing the activists. The occupation evolved into a state of siege lasting seventy-one days and leaving two native people dead. AIM leaders were indicted, but the case was dismissed after a federal judge accused the Federal Bureau of Investigation (FBI) of gross misconduct.

Discontent and strong opposition to the Pine Ridge Reservation tribal government and the chairman continued. On June 25, 1975, violence erupted again when a BIA policeman killed a young Oglala man. The following day, in an exchange of gunfire, two FBI agents were slain outside a house about fifteen miles from the town of Pine Ridge. Although the occupants of the house fled, two Oglala men were ultimately apprehended and charged with the murders; they were acquitted. Leonard Peltier, another suspect, was arrested in Canada, extradited to the United States, and sent to prison after a controversial trial in which he was sentenced to two consecutive life terms. After Peltier's imprisonment, Indian rights activists lobbied for his release, and he was considered to be a political prisoner by Amnesty International. Other victims of the 1975 violence included Leonard Crow Dog, an Oglala medicine man and spiritual leader of the movement who was arrested at his home on the neighboring Rosebud Reservation, and AIM supporter Anna Mae Aquash, a Micmac Indian woman, believed by the FBI to be a witness to the killing of the two agents. Aquash was found murdered in 1976. *Lucy Ganje*

See also: Alcatraz Island occupation; American Indian activism; American Indian Movement; Peltier killings; Wounded Knee occupation.

Platt Amendment

> **Significance:** The Platt Amendment of 1903 underscored Cuba's independence from Spain and secured U.S. influence in Cuba for the next three decades.

In 1895, Cuban revolutionaries initiated what was ultimately to become a successful revolt against Spanish colonial domination. The break from Spain was brought about by a variety of factors, the two most critical being the repressive nature of the colonial rule of Spain and a change in U.S. tariff policy as a result of the recessions and depressions in the United States during the 1890's. The Wilson-Gorman Tariff of 1894 imposed a duty on Cuban sugar arriving in the United States, which previously had entered duty-free. With the economy of Cuba reeling from dwindling Cuban-United States trade because of the new tariff, Cuban dissidents, who had been waiting for an opportunity to act, launched a revolution.

Led by José Martí, who had strong ties to the United States, the rebels who called for Cuban independence began a guerrilla war against the Spanish. Even after the death of Martí during the first year of fighting, the ranks of the Cuban rebel forces continued to increase. Spanish authorities responded to the groundswell of domestic support for the rebels by attempting to separate the rebels from their supporters in rural areas. Under a new policy known as reconcentration, more than a quarter-million Cubans were interred in concentration camps guarded by Spanish soldiers. Thousands of Cubans died in the unfit camps, which served as breeding grounds for disease. U.S. sympathy for the Cuban rebels was stimulated by reports of atrocities occurring as a result of the new Spanish policy, and people in the United States began to call for an end to the conflict through reconciliation. The mysterious sinking of the battleship *Maine* in Havana harbor on February 15, 1898, ended all hope of a peaceful resolution to the conflict.

The Spanish-American War
The sinking of the U.S. battleship, which had been ordered to Cuba in an effort to display U.S. concern for events unfolding on the island and to protect U.S. citizens, drew the United States further into the conflict. Naval investigators concluded that a Spanish mine had caused the explosion. U.S. president William McKinley responded to events by demanding that Spain grant

Cuban independence. Finding the Spanish response unsatisfactory, McKinley requested on April 11, 1898, that Congress grant him authorization to stop the war in Cuba by force, if necessary. Following some debate, on April 19 Congress declared that Cuba was and should be independent, demanded an immediate withdrawal of Spain from Cuba, authorized the use of force to accomplish that withdrawal, and vowed not to annex the island. Known as the Teller Amendment, the vow not to annex Cuba was perhaps the most controversial of the issues debated.

Despite the Teller Amendment, the entrance of the United States into the conflict initiated the beginning of an exploitive relationship between the United States and Cuba, which was dictated by the former. As the war drew to an end and Spanish withdrawal began to be realized, the United States downplayed the role of the Cuban rebels in the success of the military campaign. The Treaty of Paris, which halted the conflict, required Spain to surrender all claims to Cuba, but the McKinley administration refused to recognize the former Cuban rebels as a legitimate government or the Cuban people as being capable of self-rule. For two years, the U.S. military performed the functions of government. Although the U.S. military made substantial improvements in the infrastructure of Cuba and generally improved the quality of life on the island, Cubans resented the U.S. occupation. Many Cubans felt that they had traded one colonial master for another.

In 1900, Cubans were allowed to draft a constitution and hold elections. The United States refused to withdraw its troops, however, until provisions were made for the continuation of Cuban-United States relations. Elihu Root, the U.S. secretary of war, proposed such provisions, which ultimately were included in a bill sponsored by Senator Orville H. Platt. Platt, a Republican from Connecticut, attached a rider to the Army Appropriations Bill of 1901 that essentially made Cuba a U.S. protectorate.

The Platt Amendment, as the provisions would come to be known, severely restricted Cuba's ability to make treaties and its right to contract public debt. The United States also declared its right to intervene in Cuban affairs in order to preserve Cuban independence and maintain order. Cuba also was expected to give the United States the right to maintain naval bases and coaling stations on the island. The Cuban government reluctantly appended the provisions of the Platt Amendment to the Cuban constitution. The last U.S. forces finally withdrew from Havana in 1902. The Platt Amendment became a formal part of a U.S.-Cuba treaty on May 22, 1903.

The Platt Amendment formed the basis for United States-Cuban relations for the next sixty years, until Fidel Castro emerged as the leader of Cuba. Forced to submit to the will of the United States, Cuba was soon inundated with U.S. investment. Foreign investors controlled and manipulated Cuban politics and the economy. U.S. troops reoccupied Cuba from 1906 to 1909, under the authority of the Platt Amendment, following an uprising that protested, among other things, U.S. involvement in Cuban affairs.

The Roosevelt Administration
The election of Franklin D. Roosevelt as U.S. president in 1933 initially brought little change in U.S.-Cuban relations, despite his "good neighbor policy," which was based on the belief that no state had the right to intervene in Latin America. Roosevelt was forced to deal with a Cuba in turmoil. President Gerardo "the Butcher" Machado y Morales, who had dominated Cuban politics for a decade, was forced to resign in 1933 because of popular opposition and U.S. pressure. His successor, Ramón Grau San Martín, was no more acceptable to the Roosevelt administration. Viewed as too radical by Roosevelt, the government of Grau was never recognized as legitimate by the U.S. administration.

It was not until Fulgencio Batista y Zaldívar led a coup and installed a government acceptable to the United States that the Roosevelt administration agreed to discuss revoking the Platt Amendment. The second Treaty of Relations, as it came to be known, eliminated the limitations on Cuban sovereignty imposed by the Platt Amendment. The new treaty did allow the United States to retain its naval base at Guantanamo Bay, which could be revoked only by mutual consent of both states.

Despite the formal end of U.S. involvement in Cuba, the new Cuba, which was controlled by Batista, was no less tied to the United States financially or politically. Batista was viewed by many international observers as a puppet for the U.S. government. Cuba attracted more U.S. investment under Batista than ever before. Many Cubans argued that despite the end of the Platt Amendment, Cuba was still a U.S. dependency. It was this sense of frustration over their inability to achieve a true sense of sovereignty that served as a catalyst for Fidel Castro's successful coup in 1959.   *Donald C. Simmons, Jr.*

Core Resources
Lester D. Langley's *The Cuban Policy of the United States* (New York: Wiley, 1968) is an exceptionally detailed account of the United States' Cuban policy. Louis A. Perez, Jr.'s *Cuba: Between Reform and Revolution* (New York: Oxford University Press, 1988) is an in-depth look at Cuba's history of economic and political relationships. Perez's *Cuba Under the Platt Amendment: 1902-1934* (Pittsburgh: University of Pittsburgh Press, 1986) is a well-written account of Cuba during its early years of independence. Hugh Thomas's *Cuba: Or, The Pursuit of*

Freedom (New York: Harper & Row, 1971) is one of the most extensive works written about the country.

See also: Cuban Americans; Cuban Revolution.

Plessy v. Ferguson

> **Significance:** The Supreme Court's 1896 decision in *Plessy v. Ferguson* upheld American apartheid as constitutional if public facilities were "separate but equal."

On July 10, 1890, the Louisiana General Assembly, over the objection of its eighteen African American members, enacted a law which read, in part:

> . . . all railway companies carrying passengers in their coaches in this state shall provide equal but separate accommodations for the white and colored races, by providing two or more passenger coaches for each passenger train, or by dividing the passenger coaches by a partition so as to secure separate accommodations.

The law empowered train officials to assign passengers to cars; passengers insisting on going into a car set aside for the other race were liable to a twenty-five-dollar fine and twenty days' imprisonment. In addition, the company could refuse to carry an obstreperous passenger and, if it were sued for doing so, was immune from damages in state courts. A third section outlined the penalties for noncomplying railroads and provided that "nothing in this act shall be construed as applying to nurses attending children of the other race."

Opposition to the Law

The prominent black community of New Orleans organized to mount a legal attack on the new law. A group calling itself the Citizens' Committee to Test the Constitutionality of the Separate Car Law, led by Louis Martinet and Alexander A. Mary, organized to handle the litigation and enlisted the services of Albion W. Tourgée. Tourgée was to serve as chief counsel and devote his considerable talents to rallying public opposition to the Jim Crow system typified by the Louisiana law. Martinet engaged James Walker to assist in handling the Louisiana phase of the controversy. Before the first test of the Louisiana law (also featuring an African American who could "pass for white") could be settled, the Louisiana Supreme Court decided that the 1890 law could not be applied to interstate travelers since it was an unconstitutional regulation of interstate commerce (*State ex rel. Abbot v. Hicks*, 11 So. 74 in 1892). The *Plessy*

case, then, relitigated the question raised in the 1890 Mississippi railroad case, but as a problem in the constitutional law of civil liberties rather than one of interstate commerce.

The person recruited to test the segregation law was Homer Adolph Plessy, a person of seven-eighths Caucasian and one-eighth African ancestry, in whom "the mixture of colored blood was not discernible." On June 7, 1892, holding a first-class ticket entitling him to travel on the East Louisiana Railway from New Orleans to Covington, Louisiana, Plessy took a seat in the car reserved for whites. The conductor, assisted by a policeman, forcibly removed Plessy and, charging him with violating the segregation law, placed him in the parish jail. The state prosecuted Plessy in the Orleans Parish criminal district court before Judge John H. Ferguson. Plessy's plea that the law was unconstitutional was overruled by Ferguson, who directed the defense to address itself to the questions of fact. Having no defense in the facts, Tourgée and Walker appealed Ferguson's ruling on the law's constitutionality to the Louisiana Supreme Court by asking that court to issue a writ of prohibition which in effect would have directed Ferguson to reverse his ruling on the constitutional question.

On December 19, 1892, Associate Judge Charles E. Fenner of the Louisiana Supreme Court ruled the law constitutional in an opinion which served as a model for that written later by Justice Henry Billings Brown of the U.S. Supreme Court. After a delay of almost four years— a delay that Tourgée encouraged on the grounds that it gave the opponents of segregation needed time—the United States Supreme Court heard the arguments in Plessy's case on April 13, 1896. On May 18, 1896, Justice Brown handed down the majority opinion, supported by six other justices (Justice David Brewer did not participate, and Justice John Marshall Harlan dissented).

Justice Brown first disposed of Tourgée's argument that the segregation law was a "badge of servitude," a vestige of slavery prohibited by the Thirteenth Amendment (1865). Decisions in 1873 (*Slaughterhouse* cases) and 1883 (*Civil Rights* cases), wrote Brown, indicated that it was because the Thirteenth Amendment barred only outright slavery and not laws merely imposing "onerous disabilities and burdens" that the movement for the Fourteenth Amendment was successful.

Brown in his opinion delivered a famous statement on the relationship between law, prejudice, and equality:

> The [plaintiff's] argument also assumes that social prejudice may be overcome by legislation, and that equal rights cannot be secured to the negro except by an enforced commingling of the two races. We cannot accept this proposition. If the two races are to meet on terms of social

equality, it must be the result of natural affinities, a mutual appreciation of each other's merits and a voluntary consent of individuals.

The law in question, however, specifically interfered with the "voluntary consent of individuals."

Effects of the Decision

The Court thus sanctioned Jim Crowism. What comfort blacks derived from the case had to be found in the strong dissenting opinion of Justice Harlan, who once again proved himself to be a staunch champion of a broad interpretation of the Reconstruction amendments. Harlan construed the ban on slavery to cover segregation laws; he insisted on Tourgée's thesis that a railroad was a public highway and that under the Fourteenth Amendment government could make no racial distinctions whether one considered the case under the privileges and immunities, due process, or equal protection clauses of that amendment. Harlan attacked the Court's reliance on pre-Fourteenth Amendment precedents; his most memorable language appeared in connection with his charge that the majority usurped constitutional power by assuming authority to decide on the "reasonableness" of state social legislation:

> The white race deems itself to be the dominant race in this country. And so it is, in prestige, in achievements, in education, in wealth, and in power. So, I doubt not that it will continue to be for all time, if it remains true to its great heritage and holds fast to the principles of constitutional liberty. But in view of the Constitution, in the eye of the law, there is in this country no superior, dominant, ruling class of citizens. There is no caste here. Our Constitution is color-blind, and neither knows nor tolerates classes among citizens. In respect of civil rights, all citizens are equal before the law.

Harlan turned out to be a competent soothsayer:

> The destinies of the two races in this country are indissolubly linked together, and the interests of both require that the common government of all shall not permit the seeds of race hate to be planted under the sanction of law.

It would, however, take the general public and the justices of the Supreme Court decades to adopt Harlan's views and interpretation of the Constitution. *Plessy's* strong sanction of segregation in transportation lasted formally until 1950 *(Henderson v. United States)* and in education until 1954 *(Brown v. Board of Education)*. Antimiscegenation laws were not outlawed until 1967 *(Loving v. Virginia)*.

James J. Bolner, updated by Brian L. Fife

Core Resources

Paul G. Kauper's "Segregation in Public Education: The Decline of *Plessy v. Ferguson*" (*Michigan Law Review* 52, 1954) contends that the Court did not deal definitively with the validity of segregation legislation, relying instead on its view of "reasonableness." Charles A. Lofgren's *The Plessy Case: A Legal-Historical Interpretation* (New York: Oxford University Press, 1987) concludes that *Plessy* did not cause Jim Crow but instead confirmed the American

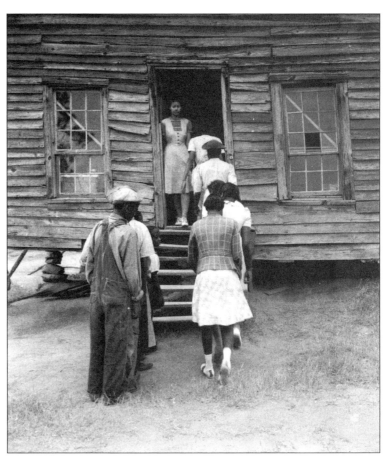

The 1896 decision in *Plessy v. Ferguson* allowed for "separate but equal" facilities. In practice, as this 1939 photo of a school for African Americans shows, segregated schools and other public facilities were rarely equivalent.

racism of its era. John P. Roche's *"Plessy v. Ferguson: Requiescat in Pace?"* (*University of Pennsylvania Law Review* 103, 1954) asserts that the *Plessy* decision reflected the political climate of its time and was a judicial attempt to deal with a social and political problem. C. Vann Woodward's *American Counterpoint: Slavery and Racism in the North-South Dialogue* (Boston: Little, Brown, 1971) discusses the irony of Justice Brown's and Harlan's positions in the light of the origins of the two men.

See also: Black codes; *Brown v. Board of Education*; *Civil Rights* cases; Jim Crow laws; Segregation: de facto and de jure.

Pluralism vs. assimilation

> **Significance:** Pluralism promotes the maintenance of the separate identities of ethnic and other cultural groups, while assimilation stresses the merging of groups into a single, shared culture. The latter generally involves the adaptation by minorities of the culture of the society's dominant group.

The Great Seal of the United States and several American coins carry the Latin motto *E pluribus unum*, or "One composed of many"—a social paradox that lies at the heart of the controversy over pluralism and assimilation.

These two terms represent contrasting views on the question of whether American society should perpetuate its diverse cultural and ethnic patterns or, rather, should blend homogeneously into a single culture with a common set of social practices. Those who favor pluralism want the distinctive features of the multiple social subgroups to flourish; those who favor assimilation think that all subgroups should move toward merger with the United States' traditional culture, which uses the English language and historically has been most heavily influenced by European—particularly British—social patterns. Pluralists fear that assimilation leads to a crushing social conformity, while assimilationists fear that pluralism leads to the social disintegration of the nation.

The terms used in this debate have many variants. Approximate synonyms for pluralism include "multiculturalism" and "cultural pluralism." The term "segregation," though it carries many negative connotations because separateness was once legally enforced on African Americans, also describes extreme pluralism, since absolute pluralism would keep ethnic identities separate and intact. Hardly any theoretical academicians favor this extreme. However, some members of racial and ethnic subgroups fiercely defend their own social patterns and

unique attributes, effectively accepting self-segregation as an ideal. The idea that blacks, for example, comprise a "separate nation" follows the teachings of the Nation of Islam.

Assimilation

Assimilation—also sometimes called "depluralization," "amalgamation," "acculturation," and "Americanization"—is nearly synonymous with what in the 1960's was promoted as social integration. This was a process by which minorities (especially African Americans) could move into the dominant culture and enjoy its socioeconomic advantages. The Civil Rights movement of the 1950's and 1960's, led by leaders such as Martin Luther King, Jr., advocated assimilation as a means to achieve a just society that deemphasized ethnic differences and removed class and racial barriers to progress. Most white liberals and social planners supported social integration. Yet by 1990 the various experiments (and many failures) at making it work—notably compulsory busing as a means of achieving educational assimilation—had created widespread skepticism that social unity could be achieved. Some observers had come to doubt that a single society with common customs was even a worthy goal. Meanwhile, the economic gap between middle-class white Americans and the poorer classes—containing high percentages of black and Hispanic people—had widened.

Through most of the nation's history, Americans have viewed their country as a cultural "melting pot," and a pattern of cultural assimilation has been taken for granted. Second-generation immigrants—often white Europeans—generally drifted away from their cultural heritages, learned English, and moved into the social and economic mainstream. The myth grew that the United States had an amalgamated culture.

Rise of Pluralism

Beginning in the late 1960's and early 1970's, however, vocal minorities launched the "new ethnicity" movement to gain respect for their native cultures and ethnic identities and to question the traditional patterns of assimilation. Hispanic Americans joined in, as that group grew numerically in the Southwest and in many American cities. American Indians found leaders to voice their protests against the cultural majority. The black ethnocentrism of the 1970's had rediscovered the African heritage and promoted black pride. In 1977, Alex Haley's immensely popular book *Roots: An American Saga* (1976) was turned into a television miniseries; the book and series helped give African Americans a sense of collective identity—a shared story of suffering and survival to replace old cultural insecurities and negative images. By the late 1970's, many subgroups of Americans were vocal about expressing their own unique identities as well as their own grievances and political demands.

The traditional American ethos of the melting pot came under fire from feminists, gays, and other groups, including people with disabilities. They claimed that the dominant American culture had discriminated against them and had never let them assimilate; therefore, the way to meet their goals was to emphasize their differences. Increasing attention was paid to the idea that the American melting pot, rather than creating a unique society by melting many cultures into a new, synthesized culture, actually forced other cultures to acculturate to the ways of the dominant culture, which was largely of Anglo descent. The term white Anglo-Saxon Protestant (WASP) became an increasingly pejorative tag. Among the political ramifications of this perception was the fact that the U.S. Congress was increasingly seen as a club of privileged white males who did not represent the American people. President Bill Clinton, after his 1992 election, vowed to make his administration "look like America," thereby acknowledging the popular appeal of social pluralism.

One clear irony of the movement toward pluralism in the late 1980's and 1990's was that, in the 1960's, assimilation had been essentially a liberal movement aimed at social reform. Yet by the early 1990's, the idea seemed conservative and, to many liberals, an outmoded idea. The new liberal position was to accept and respect ethnic and cultural diversity.

Context
Except for American Indians, the United States is a "nation of immigrants," so every American has a "first" culture demanding some degree of recognition. Thus, despite the "melting pot" myth, pluralism was not really new in 1970. African Americans had always been mostly segregated, because of white racist policies as well as immigration patterns, and maintained their own social patterns. Forced onto reservations in the eighteenth and nineteenth centuries, American Indians had also held on to vestiges of their heritages. Neither of these groups had been able to participate in the American dream of upward mobility. American Jews, though often economically successful, had also faced discrimination and traditionally maintained a social separateness. Every large American city had its "Little Italy" or "Chinatown"; ethnic sections and suburbs had always existed, proliferating as new groups of immigrants such as Middle Easterners and Asian Indians settled in the country. Separate religious sects such as the Mennonites and the Amish had also refused assimilation. Though many other Americans paid only lip service to the "hyphenated" part of their self-definitions, a widespread sense of heritage persisted among large numbers of individuals.

The 1990 census showed a mosaic of racial and ethnic

groups in the United States, with African Americans comprising 12 percent of the population; Hispanics, 9 percent; Asian Americans, nearly 3 percent; and American Indians, Eskimos (Inuits), and other native peoples, 0.8 percent. The projection is that by 2050, racial and ethnic subgroups will make up nearly half of the country's population. It appears that "managing" pluralism so as to take full advantage of diverse cultural strengths while avoiding ethnic splintering of the country will be the greatest social challenge of the twenty-first century.

Roy Neil Graves

Core Resources
Ellen K. Coughlin's "Sociologists Examine the Complexities of Racial and Ethnic Identity in America" (*The Chronicle of Higher Education*, March, 1993) discusses the difficulty of defining racial and ethnic groups, noting diversity within traditionally labeled groups. James A. Crispino's *The Assimilation of Ethnic Groups: The Italian Case* (Staten Island, N.Y.: Center for Migration Studies, 1980), a case study of Italians in Bridgeport, Connecticut, indicates continued assimilation during the 1970's, despite the general "ethnic revival" of that decade. Lawrence H. Fuchs's *The American Kaleidoscope: Race, Ethnicity, and the Civic Culture* (Hanover, N.H.: Wesleyan University Press, 1990) traces the historical origins of the American "civic culture" and of the ethnic factions and conflicts within that framework. Wallace E. Lambert and Donald M. Taylor's *Coping with Cultural and Racial Diversity in Urban America* (New York: Praeger, 1990) examines group attitudes, finding general support for pluralism (and opposition to assimilation) among all ethnic groups. Gordon D. Morgan's *America Without Ethnicity* (Port Washington, N.Y.: Kennikat Press, 1981) sketches the rise of cultural pluralism in the United States and argues against the trend, advocating assimilation.

See also: Assimilation: cultural and structural; Assimilation theories; Cultural pluralism; Ethnocentrism; Multiculturalism; Pluralism vs. Particularism.

Pluralism vs. particularism

These terms describe the ways that groups and individuals of differing ethnic, religious, cultural, racial, national, or other characteristics relate to one another and to society at large. Pluralism does not have a single meaning. Generally, it refers to the fact that modern society, at least in the West, is characterized by a diversity of fundamental philosophical, religious, and sociopolitical ideas or beliefs.

The early twentieth century educator and philosopher Horace Kallen originated the concept of cultural pluralism to represent an ideal society where ethnic groups would live in cooperation, harmony, and mutual respect, a democracy of nationalities free to cultivate difference while sharing loyalty to the nation. Kallen's view contrasted with assimilationist positions of his day, which sought to homogenize immigrant groups into a new American nationality.

Pluralism signifies conditions that encourage group diversity and the maintenance of group boundaries. Sociologist Milton Gordon theorized that various groups, each with a psychological sense of its own historical peoplehood, maintain some structural separation from each other in intimate primary group relationships and in certain aspects of institutional life. This separation creates the possibility of maintaining cultural patterns that are different from those of other groups and from the larger society.

In his textbook *Race and Ethnic Relations: American and Global Perspectives* (1985), Martin N. Marger identified several dimensions of pluralism. Cultural pluralism denotes the existence of distinct but coexisting groups within a common economic and political system, each preserving its own tradition and culture but loyal to the national unity. Structural pluralism entails the existence in some degree of segregated ethnic communities within which much of social life occurs for group members. Equalitarian pluralism occurs when groups maintain cultural and structural integrity and autonomy and remain relatively equal in power, participating freely and equally within common political and economic institutions. Inequalitarian pluralism results where groups maintain structural segregation and cultural distinctiveness but are unequal in political and economic power. Finally, in some nations, corporate pluralism arises where structural and cultural differences are protected by the state, and provisions are made to create an ethnically proportionate distribution of political and economic power.

Particularism implies the undivided adherence or devotion to one particular party, system, or interest. Sociologist Talcott Parsons paired particularism with universalism and termed them a pattern variable, a basic pattern of decision making and action for individuals and groups. Particularism, in contradistinction to universalism, depicts an orientation in which the values and criteria used to organize action and to make choices are internal to the person or group, without any reference to values or criteria beyond themselves.

A stance of particularism encourages people to identify only with their own ethno-racial category. Taking pluralism to the extreme, particularistic arguments deny that any common culture is possible or desirable. Extreme forms of particularism result in attitudes of ethnocentrism, cultural superiority, and separatism.

New multicultural models of pluralism emerged in the 1990's, seeking to redress the racial and economic inequalities of American society. Multiculturalists insisted on promoting cultural equality rather than mere mutual respect and tied equality to empowerment and the equalization of power relations. This development sparked intense controversy among scholars and extended the ongoing debate on how a nation embraces human diversity and simultaneously promotes a commitment to a common culture. *Eric M. Levine*

See also: Assimilation theories; Cultural pluralism; Ethnocentrism; Multiculturalism; Pluralism vs. assimilation.

Plyler v. Doe

In May of 1973, the Texas legislature amended its education laws to require that persons who were illegally in the United States and in the state of Texas pay a modest tuition charge for attending the public schools. In passing the amendments, the Texas legislature noted that the federal government denied the benefits of at least eight federal programs, including the food stamp program and Supplemental Security Income (SSI), to illegal aliens. According to the state, the purpose of the amendment was to "prevent undue depletion of its limited revenues available for education, and to preserve the fiscal integrity of the state's school-financing system against an ever-increasing flood of illegal aliens." It further claimed that it did not have the same responsibility to provide free benefits at taxpayer expense to those people illegally within the state as to its own citizens.

A bare majority of five Supreme Court justices disagreed, on the grounds that a policy of charging illegal aliens a modest tuition fee was not a rational means of furthering the state's legitimate fiscal ends.

The majority conceded both that public education is not a fundamental right granted by the Constitution and that illegal aliens cannot be treated as a suspect class since they are in violation of federal law. The Court declined, however, to accept any suggestion that "illegal immigrants impose any significant burden" on the economy and therefore concluded that the policy, which provided free tuition to lawful citizens but declined free benefits to unlawful ones, failed to further a substantial state interest and therefore violated the equal protection clause of the Constitution.

The minority view, expressed by Chief Justice Warren Burger, argued that the legislative policy was clearly related to the legitimate state purposes of preserving the fiscal integrity of the state school system and not placing the burden of educating foreign nationals illegally in the state on its own taxpaying citizens: "It is simply not 'irrational,' " Burger concluded, for a state to determine that "it does not have the same responsibility to provide benefits for persons whose very presence . . . is illegal as it does to provide for persons lawfully present." Noting that Congress itself had denied certain benefits to illegals, the dissent was of the view that "by definition, illegal aliens have no right whatever to be here, and the state may reasonably, and constitutionally, elect not to provide them with governmental service at the expense of those who are lawfully within the state."

This case was cited in an injunction against the implementation of Proposition 187, passed by the California electorate in 1994, which sought to deny certain benefits to illegal aliens in California. *Plyler v. Doe* has been a focal point in the debate over immigration policy and the problems in providing services to illegal immigrants. It should be noted that the Court in this case found only that Texas had failed to put forward sufficient evidence of the state's legitimate purpose in enacting the statute. This left open the possibility that future litigation on this issue may turn on the ability of a state to provide more complete evidence in the record of the state's objective and interest in such policies.   *Robert M. Hardaway*

See also: Illegal aliens; Immigration and emigration; Welfare reform: impact on racial/ethnic relations.

Pogrom

Originally a Russian word meaning "destruction" or "devastation," as an international term, "pogrom" was applied to coordinated mob attacks by Russians against the lives and property of Jews, and to the systematic persecution of Jews living under the Nazis. A pogrom is an expression of religious and racial hatred that is directed toward an easily identified powerless minority and is either approved or condoned by authorities.

In modern Russian history, pogrom-like attacks were initially leveled against the Armenians, Tatars, and the Russian intelligentsia. As it is employed in many languages specifically to describe the pillage, murder, and rape of Russian Jews, however, the term "pogrom" denotes three large-scale waves of devastation between 1881 and 1921. Each of these pogroms surpassed the preceding one in scope and savagery and occurred during periods of severe social and political upheaval in Russia. For example, the first pogroms of the 1880's followed the assassination of Czar Alexander II as a result of false rumors about widespread Jewish involvement in the plot. Mobs from more than two hundred towns, inspired by local leaders acting with official support, took part. Pogroms greatly influenced Russian Jewry and history. In their wake, the Russian government adopted

systematic policies of discrimination, harassment, and persecution of the Jews. The murder of innocent individuals and whole families was commonplace. This led numerous European anti-Semites to conclude that violence was legitimate and thus helped to pave the way for pogroms to be carried out later in Poland and Germany.

Andrew C. Skinner

See also: Anti-Semitism; Ethnic cleansing; Genocide: physical; Holocaust; Nazism.

Police brutality

> **Significance:** Police brutality includes the excessive use of force to compel a citizen to obey police orders or to arrest someone, the excessive use of force to compel an assembly of people to disperse, the physical maltreatment of someone who has already been taken into police custody (often for purposes of extracting a confession), and the use of deadly force against a fleeing suspect unless it is necessary to save the officer's own life or the lives of others.

Because of the stresses inherent in their work, some tendency toward brutality has probably always existed among police officers. In the second half of the twentieth century, however, the changing racial makeup of large cities has made the American public (and that of some other countries) more sensitive to the problem than ever before. Although urban riots triggered by allegations of police brutality made headlines in the 1960's, 1980's, and early 1990's, a less well publicized, peaceful struggle against police brutality has proceeded throughout the United States along several fronts: the push for civilian complaint review boards, civil suits and criminal prosecutions, Supreme Court decisions, and reforms within the police departments themselves.

Police Subculture and Police Brutality
To do their job, police officers must be able to use physical force as a last resort to compel obedience, and they inevitably must be granted a certain amount of leeway, or discretion, as to when such force is to be used. The decision to use force, although it can easily be second-guessed at leisure, often must be made with great speed, and it is often difficult to know exactly how much force is "excessive" in any particular instance. The main protection that police officers believe they possess is the respect and fear that others have of them; if they encounter signs of defiance or disrespect on the part of a citizen, they may feel compelled to arrest the person—and to

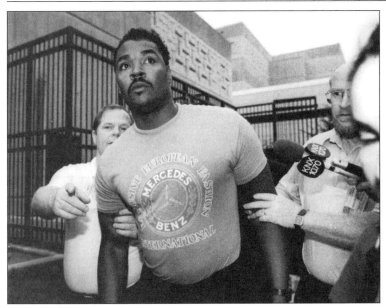

The videotaped beating of Rodney King by four white Los Angeles police officers in 1991 was viewed by many Americans as a clear-cut case of police brutality. In July, 1992, King was arrested for investigation of drunken driving.

use force if the person resists. The possibility of death and maiming at the hands of criminals is, moreover, a hazard of the job. The trust that police officers must place in one another in order to survive sometimes produces an "us versus them" attitude of distrust of citizens. When the public at large demands that police crack down on crime at all costs, police officers are tempted to violate individual rights in order to get results. Moreover, police officers' need to make split-second decisions tempts them to stereotype citizens by age, sex, and race; hence, decisions regarding whom to stop and when to use force may be made, or seem to be made, in a discriminatory manner.

Urban Racial Change and Police Brutality

From 1940 to 1990, the major cities of the northern and western United States, once overwhelmingly white, witnessed dramatic increases in their African American and Hispanic populations. Until the 1970's, however, the ranks of police officers consisted overwhelmingly of non-Hispanic whites. The tendency of big-city police officers, as time went on, to live in predominantly white suburbs further alienated them from many of those they policed, as did the replacement of foot patrols by two-person patrol cars. High unemployment among young urban blacks promoted petty crime and disorderly conduct, thereby making police-citizen confrontations more likely. The high physical identifiability of most African Americans, and the tendency of white Americans

to stereotype them as potential criminals, made police brutality an issue with resonance for middle-class as well as poor blacks. In New York City, Chicago, Denver, and Los Angeles, complaints about police brutality frequently arose among Hispanics as well as blacks.

Although many controversial incidents of police use of force have elicited only peaceful protests, minority group anger over alleged police brutality has sometimes exploded into violence. For example, riots erupted in New York City in July, 1964 (after a police officer killed a black youth); in Los Angeles in 1965; in cities throughout the United States in 1967; in Miami in May, 1980 (after the police officers who had beaten to death a black motorcyclist were acquitted); in Miami again in January, 1989 (after a black motorcyclist was shot to death by a police officer); and in Los Angeles on April 29-May 1, 1992 (after the acquittal of police officers involved in the videotaped beating of black motorist Rodney King).

Police Brutality and Public Assembly

Excessive use of force against people demonstrating publicly for particular causes was a common complaint in the 1960's, a decade of unusual political ferment in the United States; even after that era ended, such incidents sometimes occurred. Examples include the use of police dogs against blacks demanding desegregation in southern cities in the early 1960's, the clubbing of youthful (and mostly white) demonstrators against the Vietnam War in Chicago in August, 1968, and the use, in 1989, of painful restraint devices against predominantly white antiabortion demonstrators in Los Angeles.

Civilian Police Review Boards

Handling citizen complaints about police brutality was the exclusive concern of police department internal affairs units until the late 1950's and early 1960's, when the American Civil Liberties Union joined minority civil rights activists in demanding the establishment of civilian review boards (bodies with at least half their members from outside the police department) to hear such complaints. A civilian review board was instituted in New York City in 1966 but was abolished after a referendum; it was not reestablished until 1993. By 1990, about half of the fifty largest American cities had some form of civilian oversight over the police.

Police officers who opposed civilian review boards feared that such bodies would be dominated by militant antipolice activists; on the other hand, it was also argued that civilian arbiters would accept excuses for brutality that would never pass muster with professional police officers. By the early 1990's, scholarly advocates of civilian review boards, while conceding their imperfections, viewed them as a necessary (although inefficient) way to assure citizens that complaints of brutality would be treated fairly.

Fighting Police Brutality Through the Courts
Even though the beating of Rodney King by members of the Los Angeles Police Department on March 3, 1991, was recorded on videotape, the four officers who had beaten him were acquitted in their first jury trial, before a state court, on April 29, 1992. For a number of reasons, many police officers suspected of acts of brutality are never brought to trial at all. District attorneys, who need willing police cooperation to try cases, are usually reluctant to prosecute police; police officers are usually unwilling to testify against other officers; it is widely understood that jurors often sympathize with police officers; and victims of police brutality are not always entirely blameless individuals. One of the few cases in which a police officer was both prosecuted and convicted of brutality in a state criminal trial was that of New York City patrolman Thomas Ryan, sentenced in 1977 to four years in prison by a Bronx jury for beating Israel Rodriguez to death in 1975. Another was the sentencing of two white Detroit police officers to stiff prison terms in 1993 for the 1992 death of a black man, Malice Green.

Police officers can also be tried on federal criminal charges of having violated the brutality victim's civil rights. In April, 1993, two of the four officers who had beaten Rodney King were convicted of such charges. In *Monroe v. Pape* (1961), the Supreme Court laid the basis for such legal action by holding that the Civil Rights Acts of 1871 (originally passed to protect African Americans in the South) applied to abuses of power by local police officers anywhere in the country. As of the early 1990's, however, federal trials of local police officers were rare. The Department of Justice lacked the personnel to check up on police abuses throughout the country.

Two milestones made civil suits a more effective means of obtaining redress: the Supreme Court decision (unconnected with police brutality) in *Monell v. New York City Department of Social Services* (1978), holding local governments financially liable for the transgressions of their employees, and a 1976 act of Congress permitting judges to award attorneys' fees to a plaintiff if the plaintiff wins the case. In April, 1994, Rodney King was awarded $3.8 million in damages from the city of Los Angeles; other American cities have also paid out considerable sums.

Brutality lawsuits have the best chance of success when the victim has suffered obvious physical harm.

The Supreme Court and Police Brutality
In the decisions *Brown v. Mississippi* (1936) and *Rochin v. California* (1952), the Supreme Court voided criminal convictions based on confessions extracted by torture. Under Chief Justice Earl Warren (whose term lasted from 1953 to 1968), the Supreme Court increasingly imposed on state and local police forces the restrictions of the Bill of Rights, which had been formerly imposed only on federal authorities. In *Mapp v. Ohio* (1961), the Court ordered local police to obey the Fourth Amendment's ban on searches without warrant; in *Miranda v. Arizona* (1966), it ordered the police to inform those in custody of their rights to remain silent and to have legal counsel. The Court provided no guidelines for disciplining erring officers; it only stated that evidence obtained through torture or illegal searches could not be used in a trial.

After Warren's retirement, the Supreme Court no longer led the way in the fight against police brutality. In *Rizzo v. Goode* (1976), the justices, in a 5-4 decision, declined to interfere in the operations of the Philadelphia police department, which had been accused of systematic brutality toward minorities. In *Lyons v. Los Angeles* (1982), the Court refused to outlaw the use of chokeholds by the Los Angeles Police Department. In two cases decided in 1984, the Court allowed certain exceptions to the rules established in *Mapp* and *Miranda*. In 1985, in *Tennessee v. Garner*, the justices decreed that the police should no longer automatically have the right to shoot at a fleeing felony suspect, but this doctrine had already been adopted by many local police departments before the Supreme Court ratified it.

Police Chiefs' Efforts at Reform
In the 1960's, critics of the police accused police chiefs of automatically defending any officer accused of brutality. During the 1970's and 1980's, however, chiefs of police in many American cities took measures to discipline officers guilty of brutality and to reduce the number of incidents in the future. Black and Hispanic police chiefs, becoming more common by the 1980's, made special efforts in this regard. In 1972, New York City police commissioner Patrick V. Murphy instituted strict new rules governing the use of deadly force; in 1985, New York City police commissioner Benjamin Ward punished officers who had used stun guns against suspects in their custody. In 1990, Kansas City police chief Steven Bishop summarily dismissed officers who had severely beaten a suspect involved in a high-speed car chase. Police departments in Oakland, California, and Miami, Florida, aided by social scientists, instituted

programs to teach officers how to defuse potentially violent police-citizen confrontations. Some departments brought back foot patrols to enable officers to get to know people in minority neighborhoods better. Even in Los Angeles, where real reform began only after the 1992 riot and the subsequent retirement of police chief Daryl Gates, widespread public outcry in the early 1980's ended the use of chokeholds.

Minority Recruitment and Police Brutality

Affirmative action has increased the percentage of minority officers in police departments and reduced somewhat the level of prejudice-motivated brutality, but it has not worked miracles. Minority police officers are sometimes guilty of brutality themselves. In 1994, in Detroit, Michigan, and Compton, California, black police officers were accused by Hispanic activists of brutality against Hispanics. The Miami police officer who shot to death a black motorcyclist in 1989 was Hispanic.

Progress in Controlling Brutality

Although considerable progress in decreasing police brutality was made in the 1980's, the Rodney King beating brought home the fact that brutality was still a problem in the 1990's. Three examples of events that engendered protests from 1994 and 1995 illustrate the continued existence of the problem. Protests arose in New York City in April, 1994, after a black man died in police custody; in Paterson, New Jersey, in February, 1995, after police shot a black teenager; and in Cincinnati, Ohio, in April, 1995, after a white police officer was videotaped beating an eighteen-year-old black youth.

In spite of such examples, however, many scholars see a general trend toward stricter regulation of the police use of force. They view the actions and attitudes (and what was described by an investigative commission as the "siege mentality") of the pre-1992 Los Angeles Police Department, for example, as an exception rather than the rule. Although in 1990 civil libertarians in Chicago accused the police of torturing alleged police-killer Andrew Wilson while he was in custody, torture of suspects by the police was almost certainly much less common by the mid-1990's than it had been in 1931, when the federally appointed Wickersham Commission found such "third-degree" tactics to be widespread. Between 1970 and 1984, shooting deaths of fleeing suspects, although not completely eliminated, decreased in number, and the once yawning gap in police shooting deaths between blacks and whites had appreciably narrowed.

Paul D. Mageli

Core Resources

Jerry Bornstein's concise *Police Brutality: A National Debate* (Hillside, N.J.: Enslow, 1993) contains synopses of a wide range of brutality incidents of the 1980's and early 1990's. Chapters 8, 9, and 11 of Samuel Walker's *The Police in America: An Introduction* (2d ed., New York: McGraw-Hill, 1992) connect the brutality problem to the broader issues of police discretion, accountability, and police-minority group relations. *Above the Law: Police and the Excessive Use of Force* (New York: Free Press, 1993), by Jerome H. Skolnick and James J. Fyfe, ably combines grand theory with down-to-earth examples and offers both historical and comparative perspectives (including insights from the British experience). *The New Blue Line: Police Innovation in Six American Cities* (New York: Free Press, 1986), by Jerome H. Skolnick and David H. Bayley, is enlightening on efforts to curb police brutality in Houston, Texas, and Oakland, California. In the chapter on police discretion in *Taming the System: The Control of Discretion in Criminal Justice, 1950-1990* (New York: Oxford University Press, 1993), Samuel Walker provides a brief summary of two decades of effort to regulate the police use of deadly force. *Chief: My Life in the LAPD* (New York: Bantam, 1992), by Daryl Gates, exemplifies the "us versus them" mentality to which police officers are susceptible. Another retired police chief, Anthony V. Bouza, offers a more liberal viewpoint in *The Police Mystique: An Insider's Look at Cops, Crime, and the Criminal Justice System* (New York: Plenum Press, 1990).

See also: King, Rodney, case; Los Angeles riots of 1992; Miami riots of 1980; Race riots of the twentieth century; Watts riot.

Polish Americans

> **Significance:** Because of their large numbers and tendency to settle in culturally diverse areas, Polish Americans have figured prominently in interethnic relations. As they moved through the assimilation process, Polish Americans have been both victimized by prejudice and accused of discriminating against other ethnic and racial groups.

Polish Americans are generally defined as those whose heritage was connected to the Polish language, culture, and Roman Catholicism. Polish Americans who arrived between 1608 and 1800 came for personal reasons, and those emigrating from 1800 to 1860 came to escape foreign control over their homeland. The third and largest wave, of 2.5 million immigrants between 1870 and 1924, sought to escape the economic hardships of their homeland. After World War II, a fourth wave of Poles came to the United States as displaced persons or political refugees fleeing the communist government.

Polish Americans parade down the streets of New York City, celebrating their heritage on Polaski Day.

whether Poles could ever adapt to American society. Established Americans also mistrusted Poles because of their support of labor unions and their use of alcoholic beverages, which were contrary to Protestant ideals of individualism and sobriety.

Relations between Polish Americans and earlier immigrants were often strained. Poles resented the English, Welsh, Scottish, and Irish immigrants who constituted the skilled laborers and bosses in the mines, mills, and factories. The Poles reacted against Irish American control of the Roman Catholic hierarchy by forming their own ethnic national parishes. This desire for a separate Polish Catholic identity became so strong that a schism with Roman Catholicism occurred when the Reverend Francis Hodur founded the Polish National Church in 1904.

Although this group of Poles faced circumstances similar to those faced by other immigrants from southern and eastern Europe, relations between these groups were not always the best. Poles held stereotypical views of and harbored resentments against other Slavs, and many had come to the United States with a tradition of anti-Semitism. When Poles and Lithuanians shared churches, the result was less than harmonious, and splits were usually the result. Although direct confrontations with Italians were not common, each group often accepted the prevalent stereotypes about the other.

However, Polish American businesspeople often had solid working relationships with people of various ethnic backgrounds. Many young Polish immigrant women served as domestics in the homes of Euro-Americans or Jewish Americans and built a warm relationship with their employers. Despite the remnants of Old World anti-Semitism, Polish laborers and Jewish shopkeepers developed respectful and trusting business dealings. Poles cooperated with other immigrants from eastern and southern Europe to form labor unions. Their success in this venue played an important role in the establishment of unions as a powerful force in the United States.

Assimilation and Intergroup Relations
By the 1920's, the passage of time and restrictive immigration laws hastened the assimilation process. Although Polish Americans were becoming more Americanized,

Intergroup Relations
The relatively small number of Poles arriving during the first two immigration periods meant that intergroup relations were rather limited. The settlers who arrived from 1608 to 1800 did not establish communities, and relations with others in the United States were almost exclusively on an individual basis. However, Polish Americans who served during the American Revolution were regarded positively, and the political refugees, who made up the bulk of the next wave, gained the respect of Americans for their dedication to independence, nationalism, and liberalism. The large group of Poles arriving during the 1870-1924 wave interacted as a group with established American society, with earlier immigrants, and with other eastern and southern European immigrants.

Because most Polish immigrants came to the United States to work as unskilled laborers in urban-industrial areas, established Americans viewed them as essential but not necessarily welcome additions. The vast differences in language and customs and the formation of distinct ethnic communities caused many people to question new social structures were being established, altering intergroup relations. During the latter part of the twentieth century, Polish American intergroup relations involved the relations of the more elderly urban blue-collar workers, the white-collar professionals, and the new associations of refugees from Poland.

Many urban blue-collar workers came of age during the Great Depression and World War II. They endured a life of sacrifice and want but were able to gain social and economic mobility in the postwar boom years. However, by the 1970's, economic decline had hit the major employers of many Polish Americans, and an increasing number of African Americans and Hispanics had moved into traditionally Polish neighborhoods. Although most Polish Americans had adequate financial resources to sustain them into retirement, the combination of their weakened economic situation and the loss of their ethnic communities often resulted in resentment toward the newer residents. Although violent conflict was rare, tensions were high between urban Polish Americans and their new neighbors, the African Americans and Hispanics. Polish white-collar professionals, who often married non-Poles, tended to identify less with the ethnic group and more with the concerns of their socioeconomic class. At times, this caused them to become estranged from the older Polish Americans. The refugees from communism, relatively small in number, tended to affiliate with their socioeconomic and employment peers.

Despite the differences in class and status, Polish Americans still face a certain degree of discrimination. Stereotypes that depict Polish Americans as lacking intelligence have been especially hurtful. Polish American acceptance of such humor has, perhaps, contributed to this prejudice. Although Polish Americans increasingly identify with middle-class values, some of these traditional patterns of intergroup dynamics persist.

Paul J. Zbiek

Core Resources

Early works on Polish Americans, such as Emily Greene Balch's *Our Slavic Fellow Citizens* (New York: Charities Publication Committee, 1910. Reprint. New York: Arno Press, 1969) and William I. Thomas and Florian Znaniecki's *The Polish Peasant in Europe and America* (Boston: Richard G. Badger, 1918. Reprint. Urbana: University of Illinois Press, 1996), reflect Progressive era ideals or are somewhat subjective. By mid-century, an increasing number of academic studies focused on Poles in specific regions of the United States, such as Victor R. Greene's *The Slavic Community on Strike: Immigrant Labor in Pennsylvania Anthracite* (Notre Dame, Ind.: University of Notre Dame Press, 1968). Overviews of the Polish American ethnic experience include Helena Z. Lopata's *Polish Americans: Status Competition in an Ethnic Community*

(Englewood Cliffs, N.J.: Prentice-Hall, 1976) and John J. Bukowiczyk's *Polish Americans and Their History: Community, Culture, and Politics* (Pittsburgh, Pa.: University of Pittsburgh Press, 1996). For a good statistical analysis, see *Immigrant Destinations*, by Caroline Golab (Philadelphia: Temple University Press, 1977).

See also: European immigration to the United States: 1790-1892; European immigration to the United States: 1892-1943; Jokes and humor; Stereotype.

Political correctness

> **Significance:** The political correctness movement sought to eliminate racially and negatively charged terms and usage from the English language. This effort to foster sensitivity has been criticized as excessive and too controlling.

Political correctness, or PC, although reputed to be a form of censorship, can justly claim that it has made a positive contribution to improving race relations. It is an ideology based on the principle that in a truly democratic, egalitarian, and multicultural society, there must be a sympathetic understanding of the needs and rights of all people, without regard for race, sex, nationality, age, physical condition, or even sexual orientation. Fundamental to PC is the belief that racially and other negatively charged words must be purged from discourse, including both blatantly offensive terms and those that have been interpreted as carrying subtler or hidden slurs. The movement has thus helped sensitize people to the fact that language and certain types of seemingly innocent behavior can mask, among other things, racial stereotyping and bias. For example, a "flesh-colored" bandage is colored so that it matches the skin tones of whites, not African Americans or Asian Americans. Calling someone an "Indian giver" perpetuates a usage based on an old stereotype of Native Americans.

Although the term "political correctness" was coined in 1975 by the president of the National Organization for Women, Karen DeCrow, it was not widely used until the late 1980's, when opponents employed the term in critical attacks on the ideology's adherents and their aims. Detractors argued that the movement to divest the English language of derogatory terms and grammatical usage had gone to irrational lengths—finding, for example, racial and gender insults in perfectly innocent expressions. The term thus carries the implication of an excessive, witch-hunting effort to control both language and thought, and it has become the object of condemnation that has at times seemed justified.

PC and the Disadvantaged

Whatever its excesses, PC has promoted a multicultural sensitivity working in tandem with the civil and human rights movements. It is not, of course, limited strictly to language or racial concerns. For example, the visuals in media programming have also been scrutinized for offensive, stereotypical images that carry negative messages about various groups, including African Americans, women, the elderly, gays, religious minorities, and the handicapped. Politically, PC has been identified with the Left, largely because it has advocated changes that undermine the status quo; therefore, from a conservative perspective, it is seen as an insidious tool of political liberals, particularly dangerous because of its influence on schools and their curricula.

PC and Education

Although many advocates of curriculum revision in public schools argue that there is really no such thing as political correctness, since the early 1980's a continuing effort has been made to select books and develop lesson plans and courses that reflect a new multicultural awareness and tolerance for others who do not have a stake in the heterosexual male, Euro-American heritage that has dominated traditional schoolbooks and much course content in the humanities. Opponents of these changes have used political correctness as a tarring brush, claiming that proposed revisions have been politically motivated by special-interest groups less interested in learning than in advancing their own interests and political agendas. In higher education, critics complain, history is being badly distorted and the literary canon attacked, not by consideration of merit but by the political ends of underrepresented writers, including African Americans. According to detractors, the revamping of the canon has forced the exclusion of deserving works simply because they were written by "dead white males." Thus it is that academia remains the principal battleground for PC advocates and those who support a return to "the three R's" (the fundamentals: reading, writing, and arithmetic).

Political Incorrectness

In the 1990's, it became fashionable to be politically *incorrect*, not by using offensive language but by mocking the flagrant extremes to which adherents of PC have sometimes gone in efforts to rid language of hurtful words and phrases. No educated, rational person would promote the use of racially offensive or demeaning words in public debate or discourse. However, some PC advocates have made the ideology susceptible to ridicule through their extreme efforts to make language agreeable to all. They have tried to replace simple and direct words with neutral but colorless words, awkward circumlocutions, and ridiculous neologisms, whereby, for example, short people become "the vertically challenged" and the unemployed become "the involuntarily idled." Some, in their excesses, have made the job of the parodist easy, as in the efforts of radical feminists to expunge the word "man" from the English language, replacing, for example, "manhole" with "femhole." Such substitutions are easy to mock and attack as examples of reverse discrimination. They give fuel to those who believe that the true agenda of PC is to replace the dominant cultural values of the United States and Canada with those of minority and special-interest groups without regard to truth or fact. The harshest critics claim that the movement is a new sort of tyranny imposed from the political Left and warn that reactions to it could result, not in improving, but in deteriorating racial and ethnic relations.

The Need for PC

Political correctness remains a theoretical lodestone for improving the lot of society's disadvantaged. It accepts as a fundamental concept what linguists and social psychologists have argued for years—that language does more than simply reflect social values; it both facilitates and empowers the biases of those who shape and control it. Its advocates must be cautious, however. Little is gained if one sort of intolerance is replaced by another, if, for example, one group is demonized in an effort to facilitate the political agenda of another.   *John W. Fiero*

Core Resources

Henry Beard and Christopher Cerf's *The Official Politically Correct Dictionary and Handbook* (New York: Villard Books, 1993) offers an engaging spoof of PC. Richard Berstein's *Dictatorship of Virtue: Multiculturalism and the Battle for America's Future* (New York: A. A. Knopf, 1994) relates PC to multiculturalism and race relations in the United States. Dinesh D'Souza's *Illiberal Education: The Politics of Race and Sex on Campus* (New York: Free Press, 1991) traces the impact of PC on higher education and its burgeoning influence on society. Nat Hentoff's *Free Speech for Me—but Not for Thee* (New York: HarperCollins, 1992), as its subtitle suggests, examines the ways in which "the American Left and Right relentlessly censor each other." George Orwell's *Nineteen Eighty-Four* (New York: Harcourt, Brace, 1949), a dystopian novel, reveals how government manipulates language to control thought.

See also: Epithet transfer; Epithets and pejorative language; Hate speech; Prejudice: reduction; "Reverse" racism; Stereotype.

Racial and Ethnic Relations in America

Categorized List of Entries

Jury selection
Mainstreaming
Majority and minority
Meritocracy myth
Migrant superordination
Multiculturalism
Multiracial identity
Multiracial movement
Nativism
Nonviolent resistance
Oppositional culture
"Other" theory
Out-group
Panethnicity
Passing
Patriarchal system
People of color
Police brutality
Political correctness
Politics of hate
Positive ethnocentrism
Poverty and race
Power elite
Psychological theories of intergroup
    relations
Psychology of racism
Racial hierarchy
Resistance, cultures of
Sabotage
Self-determination movements
Sell-out
Sexual fears and racism
Social Darwinism and racism
Social mobility and race
Social perception of others
Social rearticulation
Socialization and reference groups
Stereotype
Stereotyping and the self-fulfilling
    prophecy
Subordinate group
Symbolic racism
Tokenism

Tolerance
Transnationalism and ethnonationalism
Triple oppression

Theories of racial/ethnic relations
Assimilation: cultural and structural
Assimilation theories
Attitude-receptional assimilation
Authoritarian personality theory
Behavior-receptional assimilation
Caste model
Civic assimilation
Class theories of racial/ethnic relations
Colonial model of racism
Competition theory and human ecology
Conformity theories
Conquest and annexation
Conservatives and racial/ethnic
    relations
Contact and adaptation patterns
Contact hypothesis
Cress theory
Cultural pluralism
Ethnogenesis theory
Frustration-aggression theory
Identification assimilation
Indigenous superordination
Internal colonialism
Marital assimilation
Marxist models
Melting pot theory
Moynihan Report
Multiculturalism
Pluralism vs. assimilation
Pluralism vs. particularism
Progressive inclusion theory of
    assimilation
Race relations cycle
Racial/ethnic relations: theoretical
    overview
Segmented assimilation theory
Separatism
Social stratification theories

Somatic norm theory
Split labor market theory
Structural assimilation
Syncretism
Transnationalism and ethnonationalism
Underclass theories
Urban underclass and the rural poor

Treaties and agreements
Alaska Native Brotherhood and Alaska
    Native Claims Settlement
Gadsden Purchase
Gentlemen's Agreement
Guadalupe Hidalgo, Treaty of
Trail of Broken Treaties
Treaties and agreements with Indians:
    Canada
Treaties and agreements with Indians:
    United States

Women
African American women
American Indian women
Asian American women
Colored Women's League
Ethnic identities of women
French Canadian women
Gendered racism
Immigrant women
Jewish women
Latinas
Million Woman March
National Association of Colored
    Women
National Black Women's Political
    Leadership Caucus
National Council of Negro Women
Triple oppression
War Brides Act
"Welfare queen" stereotype
Women and racism
Women of All Red Nations
Women of color